D0561009

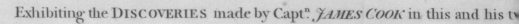

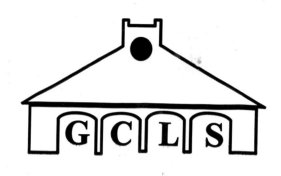

Gloucester County
Library System

CHART:

ceeding VOYAGES; with the TRACKS of the SHIPS under his Command.

Engraved for Cook's Voyage. O

CHART:

eeceeding VOYAGES ; with the TRACKS of the SHIPS under his Command .

Engrav'd for Cook's Voyage .

CAPTAIN COOK

CAPTAIN COOK

MASTER OF THE SEAS

FRANK McLYNN

YALE UNIVERSITY PRESS
NEW HAVEN AND LONDON

Published with assistance from the Annie Burr Lewis Fund

For information about this and other Yale University Press publications, please contact:
U.S. Office: sales.press@yale.edu   www.yalebooks.com
Europe Office: sales@yaleup.co.uk   www.yalebooks.co.uk

Set in Fournier MT by IDSUK (DataConnection) Ltd
Printed in the United States of America

Library of Congress Cataloging-in-Publication Data

McLynn, Frank.
Captain Cook/Frank McLynn.
    p. cm.
ISBN 978–0–300–11421–8 (cl:alk. paper)
  1. Cook, James, 1728–1779. 2. Explorers—Great Britain—Biography. 3. Voyages around the world—History—18th century. 4. Oceania—Discovery and exploration. I. Title.
  G420.C65M35 2011
  910.92—dc22

                                                                            2010036481

A catalogue record for this book is available from the British Library.

10 9 8 7 6 5 4 3 2 1

For Daniel and Ellen

Contents

Illustrations

ILLUSTRATIONS

MAPS

1 Cook's First Voyage, 1768–71. xvi
2 Cook's Second Voyage, 1772–75. xvii
3 Cook's Third Voyage, 1776–80. xviii
4 Cook's North Pacific Voyage, 1778. xix

ENDPAPERS

A General Chart: Exhibiting the Discoveries made by Captain James Cook in this and his two preceeding Voyages; with Tracks of the Ships under his Command, 1785. Historic Maps Collection (HMC01.40). Department of Rare Books and Special Collections. Princeton University Library.

Charting Cook

Cook was a supremely gifted surveyor and star navigator. His discoveries, and the accurate cartographic depiction of them, were of incomparable benefit to his contemporaries. A selection of those maps and charts accompanies the following chapters.

Chapter 1
Coal first called Cook to the seas. The young merchant mariner cut his teeth in the collier trade from Newcastle to London and mastered the Baltic timber route. Detail from *A new and accurate map of Europe* . . . by Emanuel Bowen, 1747. David Rumsey Map Collection, www.davidrumsey.com.

Chapter 2
As master of the *Pembroke* Cook wintered in Halifax during the Seven Years War, compiling charts of the coast of Nova Scotia and evolving new pioneering methods of surveying. *A draught of the harbour of Hallifax and the adjacent coast in Nova Scotia: survey'd by order of Commodore Spry, by James Cook*, 1766. National Library of Australia (RM430).

Chapter 3
In 1765 Cook surveyed the coast of Newfoundland, including Fortune Bay, aboard the *Grenville*. His maps, which the Admiralty permitted to be published under his own name, were of great political and commercial value. *Part of the south coast of Newfoundland* . . . 1766. © National Maritime Museum, Greenwich, London.

Chapter 4
The presumed existence of the great Southern Continent lured many men to explore the South Pacific, and was one reason among others that the Admiralty dispatched Cook on his first voyage. *Carte des Terres Australes* by Phillippe Buache, from Guillaume de L'Isle's *Cartes et tables de la géographie physique ou naturelle* . . ., 1757. Historic Maps Collection, Princeton University Library.

Chapter 5
Cook's survey and chart of Tahiti in 1769 (published in 1773) was a masterwork, productively combining inland navigation, triangulation and marine methods. *Chart of the Island Otaheite* . . ., 1773. © National Maritime Museum, Greenwich, London.

Chapter 6
The Tahitian Tupaia deftly piloted the *Endeavour* through the myriad islands of Polynesia. Cook and his crew had to be just as wary of the social structures of the Society Islands. *A Chart representing the Isles of the South Sea ... collected from the accounts of Tupaya*, from Johann Reinhold Forster's *Observations Made during a Voyage Round the World ...*, 1778. © The British Library Board (984.e.1).

Chapter 7
To prove that New Zealand was an island, and not the famed *Terra Australis Incognita*, Cook doggedly circuited and surveyed it, even in raging storms. *Chart of New Zealand, explored in 1769 and 1770 by Lieut. J. Cook, Commander of His Majesty's Bark Endeavour*, 1772. © National Maritime Museum, Greenwich, London.

Chapter 8
Existing maps of the Dutch East Indies were unclear – sometimes deliberately so, in order to hinder competitors. The *Endeavour*'s voyage homeward, nearing the end of Cook's first expedition, took longer than the maps suggested. *A Map of the East-Indies and the Adjacent Countries; with the Settlements, Factories and Territories, explaining what belongs to England, Spain, France, Holland, Denmark, Portugal &c ...* by Herman Moll, published London, 1719.

Chapter 9
Dusky Bay provided a blissful berth for the men of the *Resolution*, who had braved four months on hellish Antarctic waters during Cook's second voyage. *Sketch of Dusky Bay in New Zealand; 1773*, by James Cook, 1777. © National Maritime Museum, Greenwich, London.

Chapter 10
A chart of the Southern Hemisphere; shewing the tracks of some of the most distinguished navigators accompanied the publication of Cook's 1777 account, *A voyage towards the South Pole, and round the World*, and detailed many of the latitudes and longitudes of the islands of the South Pacific measured by Cook. David Rumsey Map Collection, www.davidrumsey.com.

Chapter 11
Previous explorers had described the New Hebrides (Vanuatu), but Cook meticulously mapped the entire island group – one of his most superb achievements of surveying and cartography. *Chart of discoveries made in the South Pacific Ocean in his majesty's ship Resolution under the command of Captain Cook, 1774* by James Cook, 1777. © National Maritime Museum, Greenwich, London.

Chapter 12
Cook's exploration on his second voyage of the deep southern Antarctic Ocean was beset with difficulties and dangers. The penultimate island before the pack ice was Georgia, which Cook named after his king, christening many of its inlets and features with the

names of his sometime truculent crew. From *A voyage towards the South Pole, and round the world* by James Cook, 1777, no IV.

Chapter 13
Disillusioned with its inhabitants and delayed by contrary winds, Cook did not endeavour to circumnavigate Van Diemen's Land (Tasmania) – and therefore assumed it was joined to the mainland. *Chart of Van Diemens Land* by James Cook, copied by Henry Roberts, 1784. National Library of Australia (Map T 332).

Chapter 14
The Cook of the third voyage was altered from the explorer of old. Misjudging the seasonal winds when trying to reach Tahiti, he found harbour in the Friendly Islands, but his sojourn at Tongatapu was much longer than necessary, and beset by thievery. *Sketch of Tongataboo Harbour, 1777. The writing engraved by Mw. Smith*, by William Bligh, published 1785. David Rumsey Map Collection, www.davidrumsey.com.

Chapter 15
The unsuccessful attempt to find the famed Northwest Passage proved the wild inaccuracy of the existing charts of the Bering Strait and Alaskan and Siberian coastlines, which Cook did much to rectify for posterity. Thomas Conder's chart of 1784–86 shows Cook's sea-tracks (dated August and September 1778) alongside those of Charles Clerke (July 1779) who took command of the *Resolution* and the *Discovery* following Cook's death. *Chart of Norton Sound . . .*, 1784–84. National Library of Australia (Map RM 550/11).

Chapter 16
Cook returned to the Sandwich Islands in November 1778 but, for unknown reasons, did not make landfall until January. The map – the original of which is attributed to William Bligh, Shipmaster aboard the *Resolution* – shows how for weeks the *Resolution* strangely zigzagged around the north coast of Hawaii. Was Cook punishing his crew, protecting the natives, or had he lost his reason? *Chart of the Sandwich Islands* by Thomas Conder, 1784–86. National Library of Australia (Map RM 550/19).

Chapter 17
Neither crew nor natives relished the prospect of returning to Kealakekua Bay to repair storm damage to the *Resolution*. It was on these shores that Cook died. Detail from chart by William Bligh, 1779. Geographicus Rare Antique Maps, www.geographicus.com.

Chapter 18
A General Chart: Exhibiting the Discoveries Made by Captn. James Cook in this and his two preceeding Voyages, with the Tracks of the Ships under his Command. The greatest explorer of the age traversed every degree of longitude and remapped the known world with a staggering degree of accuracy. From the atlas volume of Cook's *A Voyage to the Pacific Ocean . . .*, 1784. Rare Books Division, Princeton University Library.

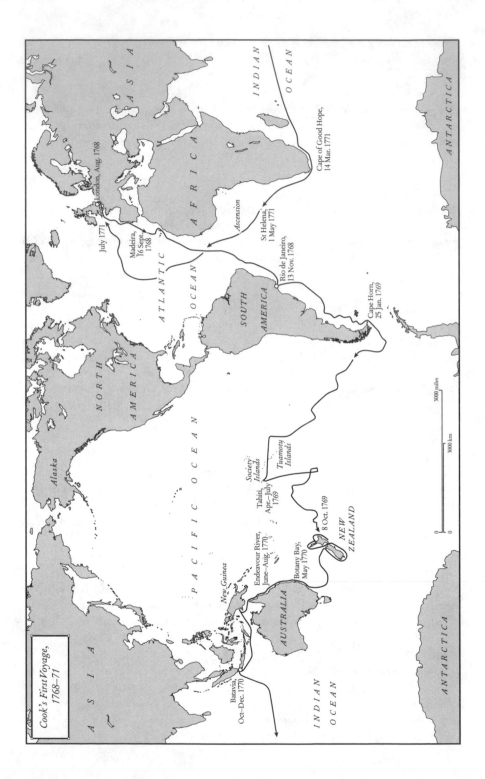

Cook's First Voyage, 1768–71

ASIA

ASIA

AFRICA

INDIAN OCEAN

ANTARCTICA

London, Aug. 1768

July 1771

Madeira, Y 6 Sept. 1768

Ascension

St Helena, 1 May 1771

Cape of Good Hope, 14 Mar. 1771

ATLANTIC OCEAN

NORTH AMERICA

Alaska

SOUTH AMERICA

Rio de Janeiro, 13 Nov. 1768

Cape Horn, 25 Jan. 1769

PACIFIC OCEAN

Society Islands

Tahiti, Apr.–July 1769

Tuamotu Islands

8 Oct. 1769

NEW ZEALAND

Endeavour River, June–Aug. 1770

Botany Bay, May 1770

New Guinea

AUSTRALIA

Batavia, Oct.–Dec. 1770

INDIAN OCEAN

ANTARCTICA

3000 miles

3000 km

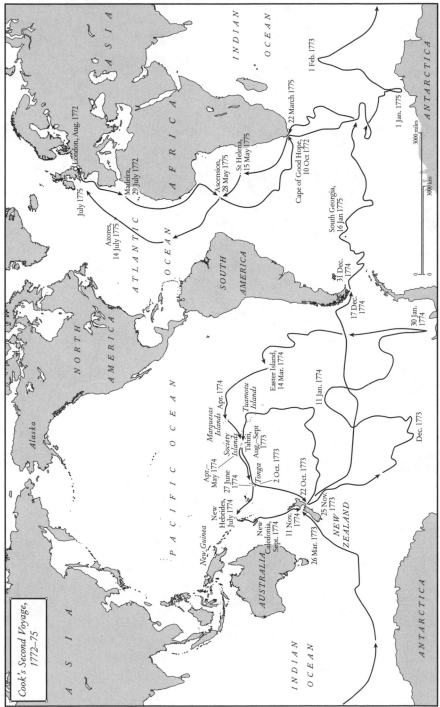

Cook's Second Voyage, 1772–75

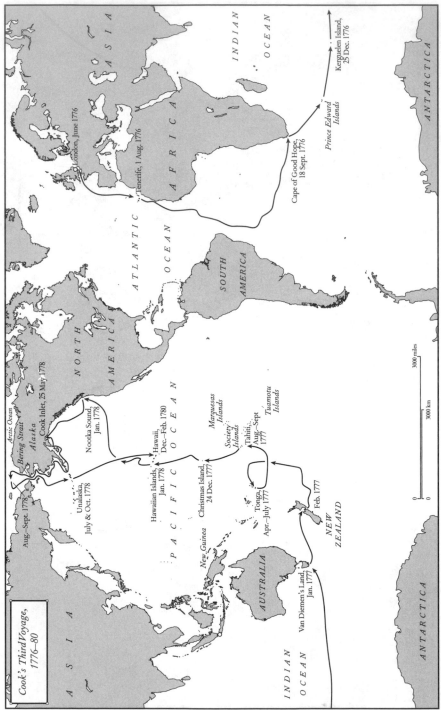

Cook's Third Voyage,
1776–80

ASIA

ASIA

AFRICA

INDIAN
OCEAN

London, June 1776

Tenerife, 1 Aug. 1776

ATLANTIC
OCEAN

NORTH
AMERICA

SOUTH
AMERICA

Cape of Good Hope,
18 Sept. 1776

Prince Edward
Islands

Kerguelen Island,
25 Dec. 1776

ANTARCTICA

Arctic Ocean

Bering Strait

Aug.–Sept. 1778

Alaska

Cook Inlet, 25 May 1778

Nootka Sound,
Jan. 1778

Unalaska,
July & Oct. 1778

PACIFIC
OCEAN

Hawaii,
Dec.–Feb. 1780

Hawaiian Islands,
Jan. 1778

Christmas Island,
24 Dec. 1777

Marquesas
Islands

Society
Islands

Tahiti,
Aug.–Sept.
1777

Tuamotu
Islands

Tonga,
Apr.–July 1777

New Guinea

AUSTRALIA

NEW
ZEALAND

Feb. 1777

Van Diemen's Land,
Jan. 1777

INDIAN
OCEAN

ANTARCTICA

0   3000 km
0   3000 miles

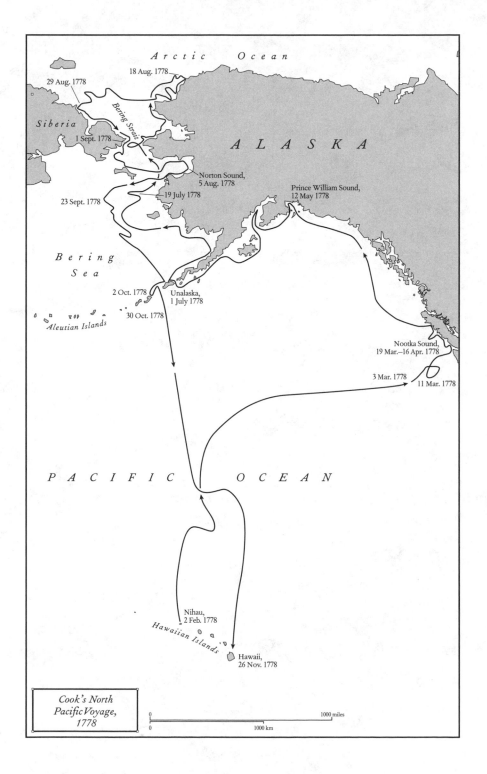

Arctic Ocean

18 Aug. 1778

29 Aug. 1778

Bering Strait

Siberia

1 Sept. 1778

ALASKA

Norton Sound,
5 Aug. 1778

23 Sept. 1778

19 July 1778

Prince William Sound,
12 May 1778

Bering
Sea

2 Oct. 1778

Unalaska,
1 July 1778

30 Oct. 1778

Aleutian Islands

Nootka Sound,
19 Mar.–16 Apr. 1778

3 Mar. 1778

11 Mar. 1778

PACIFIC OCEAN

Nihau,
2 Feb. 1778

Hawaiian Islands

Hawaii,
26 Nov. 1778

Cook's North
Pacific Voyage,
1778

0   1000 miles

0   1000 km

CHAPTER ONE

A Yorkshire Apprenticeship

EXPLORATION is an activity that calls for extraordinary talents, among them physical courage of an incredible kind and an ability to 'bracket' the reality of the physical world in pursuit of impossible dreams. All explorers, we may confidently assert, are psychological oddities, and the jury is out on whether true psychic pathology is involved, or merely a heightened form of normal sensibilities. If we except polar exploration, which in so many ways is a thing in itself and an exception even to the general proposition we can advance the impulse 'to boldly go', there are really just two types of exploration, that by land and that by sea. The most impressive feats of discovery on land were carried out by European explorers in Africa – for such as Orellana in South America, Mackenzie in North America and Sturt in Australia are not really in the class of the celebrated African quintet of Livingstone, Burton, Stanley, Speke and Baker. An examination of this quintet also throws up other fascinating propositions: that the great explorers are either upper-class misfits and semi-mystics (Burton, Baker, Speke) or those who have surmounted a background of acute poverty and deprivation (Livingstone, Stanley).[1] A similar division between high-born naval aristocrats and low-born adventurers is discernible in the case of magnificent voyages into the unknown in defiance of the mighty oceans. James Cook, the finest maritime explorer in the history of the world, was born into indigence, the son of a farm labourer. It is a relevant observation that Henry Morton Stanley, greatest of all land-based explorers, was also a product of penury and hardship, with his early years spent in a Welsh workhouse. In both men the early years and the subsequent trial of surviving the snobbery of their 'betters' left a legacy of subterranean rage, more easily visible from an early age with Stanley, but in Cook's case slowly germinating with ultimately fatal results.

James Cook was born in the village of Marton-in-Cleveland, in the north-east corner of the North Riding of Yorkshire. His father, also called James, was a Scotsman, from the village of Ednam in Roxburghshire in the border country. James Cook senior was the only son of John Cook and Jean Duncan, who had married the year before the boy's birth in 1694. James senior experienced the same obscure years of struggle his son would face until the age of 20, possibly working as a shepherd or millhand. In some way lost to us in the mists of history the economy of Roxburghshire was badly affected by the aftermath of the failed Jacobite rising of 1715.[2] Without talents, qualifications or obvious skills, James senior set out to seek his fortune south of the border, and began eking out a precarious living as a day labourer. Family legend states that when he left the bosom of his family his mother pronounced the words 'God give you grace', but the deity must have misheard her, for instead of the divine chrism He provided him with a young woman named Grace Pace, a native of Stainton-in-Cleveland in the North Riding.[3] The couple married on 10 October 1725 (James was 31 and Grace 23) and settled first in the village of Moreton in the parish of Ormesby. Here, in January 1727, a son, John, was born to them. Later that year the family moved to Marton, another village just one mile away to the west. They lived in what was known in the North Riding as a 'biggin', not dissimilar to the bothies James senior would have known in Scotland. In this two-roomed clay-built thatched cottage, full of smoke from the open fire, where farm animals wandered in and out at will, a second son was born on 27 October 1728 and given the name James. The first sensory impression of the new arrival was doubtless the primitive carpeting of sacking and meadowsweet laid down by the parents to keep down the damp and the smell. James and Grace produced six other children, most of them victims of the eighteenth century's cruel way with infant mortality. The firstborn John survived until his twenties, but four other children died young. Mary, born in 1732, died before her fifth birthday, and Jane, born in 1738, expired in her fifth year. Another Mary, born in 1740, lasted just ten months, while a third son, William, born in 1745, clocked up just three years of age before likewise being carried off. The only true adult survivors apart from the future explorer were his sisters Margaret and Christiana, of whose lives little is known. Christiana married a man with the surname Cocker and at once faded from the historical record. A little more is known about Margaret, who married a fisherman named James Fleck and moved to Redcar. In 1776, when Cook was already rich and famous, Fleck was indicted for smuggling and appealed for help to his celebrated brother-in-law. Convinced of Fleck's guilt, Cook did nothing to help him.[4]

To survive at all James Cook junior had to be an exceptionally tough and wiry baby, and all later evidence regarding Cook as a physical specimen bears out the obvious inference. Life was hard and food scarce, so that the child would quickly have become an omnivore. In the days of his fame he would astonish fellow officers by the coarseness of his palate, as he would devour anything – penguin, walrus, albatross, kangaroo, monkey and even dog; as long as it was meat, Cook would invariably describe it as 'most excellent food'. As a young boy he was one of the wretched of the earth, and detailed historical records are not kept of those born in humble and obscure circumstances. But there are three obvious pointers to the lad's young life: his heredity, his life chances and his physical environment. Much nonsense has been written about his parentage, with the Scots father standing in for patience, intelligence and industry and the mother supposedly representing Yorkshire independence and self-reliance.[5] It is not denied that every individual is to an extraordinary extent the product of his or her parents, but such reductive determinism cannot be pushed very far before it lurches into absurdity.[6] As for life chances, these must realistically be counted close to zero. In an age of limited social mobility and opportunity, the odds were heavily in favour of Cook living out his life like his father and his grandfather before him. The life of a journeyman labourer was severely circumscribed, both financially and geographically. It is unlikely that James Cook senior strayed much beyond the radius of surrounding villages until he moved to Redcar later in life (he would die there, aged 85). The physical environment of the North Riding was also unprepossessing: the monotony of moors, hills and farmland was broken only by a sprinkling of farms and labourers' cottages. In this rural backwater the young James spent his first eight uneventful years. By this time he was already a veteran of sowing seeds, digging ditches, hedging and back-breaking labour in general. His education was rudimentary, though he could read and write by the age of eight, having been taught his alphabet by a Mrs Walker, wife of the farmer of Marton Grange, in exchange for running errands and helping with household chores. Writing in particular was a difficult art to master, for in those days children had to be taught from scratch, as it were, how to hold a pen; unlike today's children, they had not used crayons or pencils from an early age.[7]

In 1736 James Cook senior was promoted to be a 'hind', a kind of overseer or farm manager at the village of Great Ayton, five miles from Marton. His prudent stewardship places him perfectly within the paradigm of the sober, thrifty pre-Industrial Revolution worker later recalled with dubious nostalgia.[8] Cook senior's benefactor was a rich farmer named Thomas Skottowe, of Airyholme farm, who presumably negotiated his release from the Walkers' employment. The increase in family income doubtless lifted young Cook's spirits, but possibly they were also lifted because he was aware of having moved to a superior village. Ayton, much larger than Marton, was close to the market town of Stokesley and was itself a place of some local importance, since it boasted a watermill, a tannery, a brick-kiln and a brewery, and provided work for weavers as well as farm labourers.[9] It was set on the edge of the Cleveland hills and dominated by Roseberry Topping, the highest summit in the North Riding. It was at Great Ayton that the first puzzle in young Cook's life is recorded.[10] The village school, being fee-paying, was beyond the reach of the Cook family, yet Thomas Skottowe is said to have discerned promise in young James Cook and paid the fees so that he could attend. Since similar largesse was not provided for Cook's elder brother John or indeed for any of the rest of the Cook family, the inevitable suspicion has arisen that Skottowe must have had an ulterior motive. Two things are clear: young James Cook was more talented than his siblings, and he received a better education. Was Skottowe perhaps the young boy's real father?[11] It is indeed a wise man who knows his own father and cast-iron certainty is rarely possible in such matters, but there is no compelling circumstantial evidence that would blacken Grace Pace with the taint of infidelity. The prima facie evidence makes the suggestion seem highly unlikely. Skottowe was a true gentleman farmer, an established member of the gentry rather than a yeoman farmer. Dalliance with the wife of a farm labourer would be plausible only in the case of a woman's exceptional beauty, and local oral tradition would certainly have recorded this aspect of Grace if it had been the case.

At the village academy known as Postgate school Cook was taught elementary English and mathematics, drilled in the catechism, and nudged by the pedagogue to improve his skills in basic literacy. Although it was rumoured that the schoolmaster, William Rowland, was a mere part-timer who 'moonlighted' as a weaver, he seems to have done a good job of improving on Mrs Walker's inchoate efforts, for he not only turned the boy into an efficient reader but taught him a workmanlike copperplate handwriting. No formal records of young James's schooling were kept, but local tradition says that, though no future academic or intellectual, he showed distinct promise in mathematics, perhaps already foreshadowing the skilful navigator of later years. Other oral testimony stresses that the boy was very much a loner and was habitually left out of the typically boyish excursions of his peers. It was not so much that he was unpopular, rather that he was already exhibiting signs of the 'control' syndrome that would afflict him in later life: he insisted on doing things his way, and was obstinate, inflexible and even somewhat unpleasant. Yet it is significant that there are no stories of bullying – an outcome one might expect. There was something ruthless and determined about the boy that made his fellows back off and regard him with cold respect, viewing him as someone not to be trifled with. If ever he was engaged as part of a group discussion, on the best place to go bird's nesting, say, Cook was always adamant that he knew the best spot, and his very vehemence usually resulted in his arriving at the supposed rendezvous alone.[12] Yet the precise mixture in his life of schooling, schoolboy adventures and hard work in the fields – which we can infer was his lot between the ages of eight and sixteen – is lost to the historical record. It was 1745 when the young James Cook emerged into clear light. Because of the detail in the anecdote we can pin down the precise date (November 1745) of the next inconsequential story related about his youth. Always a devotee of hill-climbing, Cook particularly liked to scale Roseberry Topping, and he had an established route to the top where there was a spring and he could take a long drink of fresh water before clambering down again. On this occasion he decided to abandon the tried and tested route and went in search of a more adventurous descent. On his way down he saw a jackdaw flying into a cleft in a rock, and made the correct deduction that there was a nest there.[13] An avid bird's-nester, the boy scooped up the eggs, put them in his cap, and held the cap between his teeth while making a tentative and vertiginous descent. Suddenly he lost his footing and in panic grasped at a plant, which began to come away at the roots. Unable to find a secure purchase and thus effectively marooned, Cook began crying for help. Fortunately for him sentries had been posted on all the summits of the Cleveland hills to give warning if Bonnie Prince Charlie's rebel army from Scotland decided to make for London by a north-easterly route after crossing the border.[14] The Roseberry Topping sentinel heard the plaintive cries and soon organised a rescue party.

1745 was also the year Cook became a shop assistant in the fishing port of Staithes, fifteen miles from Great Ayton. Staithes was one of the numerous villages and towns south of the Tees – Redcar, Saltburn, Brotton, Sandsend, Whitby, Robin Hood's Bay, Ravenscar, Hayburn Wyke – that depended entirely on fishing. Cook was already in a different world from the farming communities inland which had hitherto been his sole experience of human life, and it was almost as if he had been steadily inching towards his destiny. One would give a lot to have a record of his thoughts and feelings on first sighting the sea. But for eighteen months he was resolutely land-based. His employer was William Sanderson, a grocer and haberdasher, who had been impressed by Skottowe's tales of the mathematical prowess of his protégé and agreed to take him on trial as a trainee shopkeeper; there were no formal indentures as this was not an apprenticeship in the true sense. Sanderson's emporium was on the seafront and was a 'double shop', with two front doors leading, respec-tively, to the grocery and the drapery. Sanderson and his family lived above the shop, and Cook took his meals with them, but he was in no sense 'one of the family', since he made a primitive 'den' under the shop counter and slept there with his handful of possessions. Dutiful and hard-working, Cook swept out the shop, opened it in the morning, closed it at night, served behind the counter and kept accounts. Yet it was clear very early on that his heart was not in his trade, and that he had already heard the call of the sea. The entire town of Staithes was permeated with talk of fishing and the oceans, and after-hours yarning with the sailors led the 17-year-old to experience vicariously the thrills of venturing outside the bay into the open sea. Many people are put off by their first encounter with this cruel and malevolent mistress but Cook, always endowed with superlative physical courage, brushed aside the Jeremiahs who stressed the dangers of the North Sea. His determination to forge a maritime career must have hardened over eighteen months of 'fumbling in a greasy till' (Yeats's phrase), but the story usually told of his 'career crisis' is probably apocryphal. The tale goes that Cook one day received as payment a shilling piece minted around 1720 at the time of the South Sea Bubble, bearing the legend of the great South Seas. Besotted by this talisman, he replaced it in the counter drawer with an ordinary shilling piece of his own.[15] Sanderson spotted that the striking coin was missing and accused Cook of stealing it. The misunderstanding was cleared up but, at least on Cook's side, left a sour taste, so he gave in his notice. Sanderson evidently forgave the 'theft', for when Cook said that it was his ambition to go to sea the shopkeeper said he would help him. However, many doubt that the incident ever happened and Cook's great biographer John Beaglehole dismisses the anecdote as 'a trivial affair blown up to dramatic proportions by more than one romancer'.[16]

Local tradition is adamant that Sanderson was instrumental in introducing Cook to his next employer, a wealthy Quaker shipowner named John Walker of Whitby, who discerned promise in the lad. This time there was a formal apprenticeship and Cook signed a three-year indenture as a 'servant', hoping to learn the craft of a merchant seaman. The indenture was a standard 'boiler-plate' contract for the merchant navy, but it has an odd ring to modern ears. The contract with Walker committed Cook 'not to play at dice, cards, bowls or any other unlawful games . . . (nor) haunt taverns or playhouses . . . commit fornication nor contract matrimony'. In return Walker agreed to provide lodging, food and drink, laundry, and instruction and training in 'the trade, mystery and occupation of a mariner'.[17] For the first six of his nine years in the merchant navy Cook lived with Walker and his family in a large house in Haggersgate on the west bank of the river Esk. (Even though Beaglehole long ago established that Walker did not move to his well-known house in Grape Lane until 1752, successive writers on Cook insist on peddling the myth that that was where the young man did his navigational studies of an evening.)[18] There need be no serious doubt about the studiousness, which especially recommended him to John Walker and his brother and partner Henry. Indeed the Walkers' housekeeper Mary Proud turned young Cook into something of a 'teacher's pet' by providing him with a special table and extra candles to aid his studies.[19] Without question Cook absorbed some of the heavy Quaker ethos at Haggersgate, but the extent of the influence of the ideology of the Friends is problematical. The role and status of the great Quaker families – the Walkers, Chapmans, Taylors, Saunders, etc. – in the Whitby shipping industry can hardly be overstated, though they were living on borrowed time, for Quaker austerity proved unable to hold the line against the eighteenth century's ever increasing hedonism, consumerism and permissiveness.[20] Nonetheless, during Cook's apprenticeship the Friends were still 'hegemonic' in Whitby. Cook certainly imbibed a work ethic from them and the conviction that work should be regarded as good in itself. Other salient influences can be traced in his modesty, plainness, taciturnity, hatred of idleness and gossip, disbelief in a transcendent god, and general humourlessness. As someone who always disliked arguments and confrontation, he learned from the Quakers the skill of arbitration by observing their pacific method of settling disputes.[21] On the other hand, by 'flashing forward' to Cook's later career we can see that there were limits to the legacy of Quakerism. He made a point of addressing people by their titles, as the Friends did not on the grounds of egalitarianism. And he quickly learned the art of flattery and sycophancy to his social superiors – necessary for an ambitious man but alien to Quaker principles. Nor he was a pacifist. Although physical force was never his first port of call, he believed in it as the ultimate deterrent and, as he grew older, came to believe in it more and more.

Cook's sojourn in Whitby and the apprenticeship with John Walker marked the definitive point where he turned away from the land towards the sea that would ultimately make him famous. Did he, then, derive anything from his early years as a farmer and landsman? Certain influences are detectable. The early death of so many of his siblings hardened him to mortality and helped to make him unafraid of the terrors of the deep. His liking for hill-climbing never left him, and shades of Roseberry Topping can be found in the many scarps, hills and eminences he would climb on his voyages. As a farm boy he took an interest in seeds, livestock and agriculture not discerned in other naval officers; in the Pacific he kept detailed journal entries about which 'improving' seedlings and domesticated animals he had left in the islands. But the inference is that his childhood left him cold and detached about North Yorkshire. It has been pointed out that he never named newly discovered geographical features after any place he had known in his childhood and youth, though he was quite prepared to name them after sailors on his ships as well as 'Admiralty bureucrats and second-rate aristocrats'.[22] Once in Whitby, his gaze was always towards the sea, and the very shape and contours of the town almost compelled such concentration. At Whitby the Esk left the somnolent wooded valleys and plunged into the North Sea through beetling cliffs. Two stone piers jutted out into the sea, protecting the harbour from the many storms it had to sustain – so frequent that the Whitby lifeboat was already famous for the number of shipwrecked mariners it had saved from a watery death. Known to history as early as the year 664 for the synod at which Bishop Wilfrid successfully introduced Roman church practices in place of the Ionian rituals and modalities hitherto typical of British Christianity, Whitby in the mid-eighteenth century was a thriving port with a population of 5,000, important enough to spark Daniel Defoe's interest when he passed through on a noteworthy tour through all England.[23] The mouth of the Esk was virtually a gateway to adventure and danger and Whitby would produce many celebrated sons, not just the Arctic explorer Luke Foxe and the whaling captains Scoresby, father and son, but also the guerrilla leader Thomas 'Bumfoot' Brown, two years Cook's junior, who would live among Indians in North America and lead a band of mounted loyalists in Georgia against the 'sons of liberty' and the Continental Army in the American War of Independence.[24]

Naturally Cook's apprenticeship did not involve merely navigational mathematics at his desk and midnight lucubration. He had to master the art of handling sailing ships, at which he soon proved a natural. The first thing was to learn the nature and function of every sail: the main topsail and main topsail yard, the mizzenmast, mizzen topgallant and mizzen topsail, the spanker, foremast, foresail, fore topsail, fore topgallant, main top gallant and main topgallant yard. He was taught to reef – to reduce the extent of a sail by taking in or rolling up a part of it and securing it. Words like jib, bend, reef point, hawser, cable, crossjack, jib, fluke, stream anchor, gaff, yard slings, staysail haulyards, gasket, shears and cordage had to become second nature, so that one could almost sleepwalk through one's orders when afloat. He had to learn to tack – to work to windward by changing course alternately from starboard to port tack; to veer – to put a vessel on to the other tack by turning the stern into the wind; to bring to – to stop a ship by bringing her head to the wind; to ply – to beat up against the wind and to bring the ship to windward by putting it about frequently; and to warp – to move a vessel from one mooring in a harbour to another.[25] Hardest of all, he had to go aloft, working perhaps 100 feet above the deck, furling and unfurling sails in all weathers. The climb up the ratlines (rope ladders) was bad enough in fair weather but to accomplish this and then cling on to the rigging in storms, high seas, at night and with ice coating every rope pushed even the toughest man to the limits of his endurance. The old cliché 'firm but fair' was often applied to John Walker, but he would tolerate no slackers, and without question life was tough for the apprentice mariners. On shore they had to learn about life in the riotous and violent atmosphere of Whitby's tavern, while at night, in Walker's attic, they huddled together in dormitory conditions, sometimes ten apprentices bedding down together. Cook took comfort from the thought that the seafaring life was a passport to a wider world and better things. Perhaps he already knew that the famous navigator William Dampier had had a similar upbringing to his. But he certainly knew that for an ambitious man born into poverty in the eighteenth century, the sea was perhaps the *only* escape route.[26]

Cook's apprenticeship must be set in a historical, sociological and even geographical context. John Walker was an owner of colliers, and Cook's training was directed towards the seaborne coal trade, an industry of paramount importance in mid-eighteenth-century Engand. In 1700–1830 between a quarter and a third of the country's consumption of coal was conveyed to customers by coastal navigation. Already by 1700 some 600 ships were carrying coal from Newcastle to London, stimulated by the demand for iron, new industries and an expanding navy.[27] Coal arrived in London either by canal or by ship from the east coast. (The west coast coal trade was unimportant, with ships travelling no more than sixty miles.) In Lancashire, Somerset, the East and West Midlands, inland Scotland and South Wales road transport was paramount. Although river and canal navigation were important in some parts of the country, in the north-east their importance was negligible, but collier owners kept a wary eye on their rivals in barges and vehemently opposed any extension of canals that would make inroads on the London–Newcastle seaborne trade.[28] Almost all ports on the English east and south coasts were supplied from the coalfields of the north-east, where the utmost ingenuity was exercised to get the mineral from the pits to the Tyneside ports.[29] Newcastle, Sunderland and Blyth accounted for over 80 per cent of the coastal shipping, and Newcastle alone shipped out over 60 per cent of the coal from the north-east – between 685,000 and 742,000 tons annually during Cook's period in the merchant marine. Whitby, with twenty colliers operating out of the port, had a small but significant share of this trade. In Cook's time London took about 60 per cent of the coal of the north-east but almost every port on the east and south coasts as far west as Exeter received cargoes from Tyneside and Whitby.[30] Apart from London, other significant destinations for seaborne coal were Hull, King's Lynn, Yarmouth, Wells-next-the-Sea, Rochester, Sandwich and Southampton; and it is a fair inference that in nine years Cook visited all of these places at least once.

John Walker was a shrewd businessman who never speculated recklessly but diversified his investments into land and securities. In the coal trade itself he spread the risks by issuing shares in the colliers, with the ship's master always retaining the Grand Bill of Sale which made him de facto manager of the ship. Apart from losses through shipwreck, the owners of coalships had to beware both the profiteering of middlemen and the rapacity and price-fixing agreements of London lightermen.[31] Even so, in normal years profits were high, with returns of at least 12 per cent and often nearer 20 per cent; recent studies have shown that profit levels were higher than previously thought, largely because of the high degree of vertical integration in the coal trade, but also because of exiguous manning levels.[32] Crews of colliers tended to be small, no more than seven or eight men and boys; a typical watch would be a two-man affair, or rather one callow youth and one experienced sailor. The 600 colliers in service in 1703 employed just 4,500 men.[33] A master of diversification, Walker built his colliers in such a way that they were not specialised coal-carriers but could take general cargo if ever the coal trade was slack. A shrewd owner knew that fluctuations in demand for coal in London could lead to heavy losses for them, so had the timber trade of the Baltic as an 'ace in the hole'. Case studies bear out the general proposition that ships rarely left Newcastle or Whitby without a full cargo. One ship, the *Molly and Jenny*, built in 1752, made thirteen voyages out of Newcastle in its first year at sea (1752–53), six of them to London with coal, the others to Hamburg, Amsterdam, Norway and the Baltic.[34] Henry Taylor, who was born in 1737 and finished his indentures in 1756, is the great source if one wants to work out by inference what Cook's life as a merchant seaman was like. Taylor recorded that a typical collier would load coals for Scandinavia, then proceed through the Baltic to load timber for Hull. The voyage to Riga would normally take a month, 'often under reefed courses, long nights and cold weather'.[35]

Sociologically, the North Sea coal trade was a proving ground for the very best seamen, and produced its fair share of characters. One of them was the same Henry Taylor, who after long years in colliers converted to Methodism, but not before undergoing some singular adventures. He recalled that on one trip to Riga the captain, master and mate were all habitually drunk during the month's outward voyage and again on the way back – no wonder there were so many shipwrecks, he remarked ruefully – and that he and the other ordinary seamen had to work out how to steer the ship and set a true course.[36] Another larger-than-life figure was William Hutchinson (b. 1716), a jack of all trades: mariner, shipowner, trader, boatbuilder, inventor and hydrographer.[37] As Thomas Jefferson later remarked, England's top sailors were always those who had learned their trade carrying coal from Newcastle to London.[38] This was because the ability to manage and manoeuvre a cat-built Whitby collier – the so-called 'cat' – was the ultimate test of seamanship. The 'cat' was a squat and ugly ship, built for strength and endurance rather than speed, with a narrow stern, blunt prow, and a deep 'waist' (that is, broad-bottomed). Between 300 and 400 tons, it could carry 400–600 tons of cargo, and was so designed that, although coal was the primary cargo, other freight, such as lumber, could easily be substituted. It required careful and skilled handling, not just in storms and high seas but in the narrow entrances of small river harbours, around bars and sandbanks and in shifting tides. He who could master a 'cat' would find manoeuvring a man-o'-war simple by comparison.[39]

The other reason the collier trade was such a proving ground for young mariners was the violence of the North Sea. The east coast of England from the Humber to the Thames was the worst of all English coasts for outlying dangers. Even today sailors treat it with a wary respect because of its treacherous tides, tidal streams, sandbanks, sand-spits, sunken rocks and rocky shelves; two hundred and fifty years ago such dangers were all the more minatory as there were no lighthouses, buoys or other markers, or even any adequate charts. Worst of all were the frequent storms and high seas. The most dreaded of all maritime phenomena, the 100-foot oceanic wave, is encountered as often off the coast of Norway as in the Agulhas current off the coast of South Africa (where the Indian and Atlantic oceans collide). The pioneer ocean navigator Pytheas of Massilia, a Greek who flourished around the time of Alexander the Great and who made a famous circumnavigation of the British Isles, reported a 100-foot wave in the Pentland Firth and was habitually derided for credulity until unimpeachable scientific data in 1995 established the truth of the phemonenon he had observed.[40] Even without its ultimate weapon the North Sea is still a fearful place, notorious for its high and unpredictable winds. Four storms along the Dutch and German coasts in the thirteenth century killed at least 100,000 people each, and one of them is believed to have accounted for the death of 400,000 souls. Storms on 11 November 1099, 18 November 1421 and in 1446 are estimated to have carried off 100,000 people each in England and the Netherlands combined.[41] The All Saints' Day flood of 1–6 November 1570 is thought to have killed another 400,000. Famously, the Spanish Armada of 1588 was hit by a five-day running storm off the east coast of Scotland, which generated huge seas and tore the heart out of Philip II's 'invincible' fleet.[42]

Things were no better in the eighteenth century. A hurricane in the English Channel on 26–27 November 1703, with wind speeds of 170 kilometres per hour, sank every ship in the Channel with the loss of 8–10,000 lives. Other severe storms with heavy fatalities occurred in 1634, 1671, 1682, 1686, 1694 and 1717. Colliers were particularly vulnerable when heavy laden and caught by a sudden gale before they could retreat to the shelter of an east coast harbour or the lee of a headland. Sometimes the sea was so dangerous that no ships could sail at all, as in 1782 when all colliers were harbour-bound with adverse winds for six weeks and coal miners had to be put on short time.[43] Obviously it is difficult to generalise or quantify the risks. In really bad years the impact of the weather could be utterly disastrous, as in 1800 when 69 out of 71 ships carrying coal from Newcastle to London were wrecked, or in 1824 when a hundred colliers were overwhelmed in an October gale. Statistics compiled for the years 1701–10 reveal that 71 colliers were lost at sea in this period, 46 of them in the terrible North Sea hurricane of November 1703.[44] Taylor, our best source for the collier trade, tells of being caught in a terrible storm off Yarmouth in 1770,[45] and also divulges awesome statistics that confirm the general picture regarding the winds off the east coast. Only six of fifteen 'cats' that set out from South Shields in the winter of 1767 survived the ferocious storms, and in October 1789 calamitous seas destroyed 23 of 42 colliers at sea, with the loss of 300 seamen.[46] Of course, as Taylor pointed out, the drunken incompetence of some ships' captains, such as his skipper on the run from Riga above, did not help matters. The best Taylor could do was to issue general guidance for mariners. All masters and mates *must* keep a conscientious watch, particularly at night; a good roadstead is better than a bad harbour in a gale; always strike the topmast but not the foreyard in a storm; a ship will ride better in high seas with a very long scope of cable and one anchor than with less length and two anchors.[47]

It is a notable feature of Cook the mariner that he always remained unfazed by storms and other sea states that terrified even veterans of the ocean. As a very late starter in the merchant navy – he was nearly 18 when he signed the indentures with Walker – he caught up fast and was soon recognised as the most promising of the intake of the late 1740s in Whitby. Whereas the least prepossessing apprentices were given routine tasks such as sweeping the deck or scrubbing out the boats, Cook made it a point of honour to be first up the rigging, to carry out a close reef, to hold a luff, to haul off when faced by a hazard, to use the handspike when heaving on the windlass and in general to perform those tasks memorably described by Taylor as 'To haul out the weather earing when the topsails were to reef, to ship the first handspike and to cat the anchor.'[48] There was a multiplicity of tasks to perform: handling the headsails, clearing away the anchors to let go, and catting and fishing them when unmooring. Once aloft he would have begun by serving a mini-apprenticeship at the relatively unskilled work, hauling on sheets, halliards and braces. From this he would have graduated to 'top' work, hauling and loosing the most complex sails and, finally, as an upper yardman, working on the highest sails: the topgallants and royal yards. This required exceptional stamina and was young man's work, but Cook was physically well capable of anything that was asked of him. By his late teens he was over six feet tall, with a gaunt, rawboned look, with high cheekbones, deep-set brown eyes, a long, straight nose and thin lips. But life aboard was not all physicality. He was also mastering the arts of navigation, reading the barometer correctly, calculating latitude by noonday fixes and making running surveys of the coastline. Cook had to be an un-Hogarthian apprentice, for Walker would not tolerate slackers. Taylor, his near contemporary, paid him the ultimate compliment by describing him as a 'natural': 'he was a striking instance of the power of emulation, united with sobriety and an ardent application; his example is worthy of the imitation of every seaman'.[49]

Cook's first ship was the *Freelove*, a square-rigged three-masted vessel, 106 feet long and 341 tons. It was a new ship, built at Great Yarmouth in 1746, and boasted a larger than usual complement: master, mate, carpenter, cook, five seamen and ten apprentices, all from Whitby and with ages ranging from 15 to 19 (so Cook was one of the oldest). Although Walker himself sailed as master on two voyages to London in 1747, the usual skipper was John Jefferson, aged 32, and his mate Robert Watson, 27, who worked peculiarly well in tandem. Cook's earliest voyages were on the run to London. His first trip took nearly two months, whereas the fastest Newcastle–London round trip in the eighteenth century took a month; in theory a ship could complete nine round-trips a year at this rate, but this presumed permanently favourable weather, and in fact a 'cat' working steadily on the run over a twelve-month period would average more like four trips.[50] Walker's practice was to get the apprentices to sail the ship on their own as far as possible, with the master as overall director. Evidently Cook impressed Jefferson for, when Walker launched another new ship and assigned Jefferson to command her, Cook was one of six apprentices he took with him. The new vessel was the *Three Brothers*, at 600 tons nearly twice as large as the *Freelove*, and young Cook took part in her rigging and fitting out.[51] Cook served in the *Three Brothers* continuously from 14 June 1748 to 8 December 1749. At first he continued on the Newcastle–London coal run, but then the ship was switched to a new route, having been chartered by the government as a troop transport, specialising in conveying cavalry from Flanders (at the end of the War of the Spanish Succession) to Dublin and Liverpool. After completing his apprenticeship, Cook signed on as an ordinary seaman for the first time on 20 April 1750, this time on the *Mary* of Whitby, owned and commanded by relatives of John Walker. On the *Mary* he got to know the Baltic timber route, and was continuously engaged on this for eight months until 5 October 1750, when he was discharged at London.[52] This, then, was the year when he mastered the wrinkles of the Baltic, not only Stockholm, Malmö, Danzig (Gdansk) and Königsberg, but also the tricky Danish waters of the Skagerrak and Kattegat.

After a brief spell on a Sunderland vessel, whose name does not survive, Cook returned to the *Three Brothers* during 1751–52, all the time studying for his mate's examination. This involved a more advanced study of navigation – the use of instruments such as the quadrant, ring-dial, cross-staff, backstaff, azimuth compass and nocturnal dipping-needle – plus a smattering of astronomy and geometry. The key to practical seamanship was supposedly mastery of the three Ls: latitude, lead and lookout. Lookout is self-explanatory, and casting the lead was the time-honoured way of ascertaining depth of water or, in shallow water, the nature of the sea bottom – the only way one could avoid navigating blind in thick fog.[53] Fixing latitude was still very much a matter of taking noonday sightings of the sun. Cook demonstrated that he could combine study with hands-on seamanship by giving a good practical account of himself while studying, much to the satisfaction of his captains. The new master of the *Three Brothers* was Robert Watson, who had been the mate on Cook's first voyage. Evidently the two struck up a notable rapport, for when Watson transferred as skipper at the end of 1752 to another Walker ship, the *Friendship*, Cook, newly qualified, went with him as mate. He could now regard himself as a true master of the North Sea, which meant perfection in negotiating tideways and difficult narrow channels.[54] For two and a half years Cook was mate on this vessel, under three different masters: first Watson, then John Swainston, and finally Richard Ellerton, who remained a friend. There was no reason on paper why Cook should have expected accelerated promotion, for there were hundreds of mates in the north-eastern coal trades, all seeking the few openings as master. But Walker was an accomplished talent-spotter and had already seen Cook's great potential. After less than three years as mate and just nine years after he had begun his naval apprenticeship, Cook was offered the post of master of the *Friendship*. It must have seemed like a dream come true. But to fairly general stupefaction Cook turned down Walker's generous offer and announced his intention of abandoning the merchant marine. He intended to join the Royal Navy as an able seaman.[55]

Cook's decision has puzzled biographers and historians ever since, and has appeared as, at the very least, a mighty risky gamble. It is often considered an eccentric resolution, and some have speculated that Cook must have been convinced of his lucky star, for it was scarcely rational to expect that in the Royal Navy he would encounter patrons to match Skottowe and Walker.[56] Was he, then, tired of Whitby and bedazzled by the London he had glimpsed on shore leave from the 'cats'? Was he simply bored with life on a collier, or finding the coastal trade dull? Had he always intended to join the Royal Navy, was he actuated by simple, naïve patriotism in time of imminent war, or did he simply consider that 'naval service, whatever its drawbacks, offered a lively mind more variety and more excitement'?[57] Certainly some of the motivations ascribed to him fail to convince. It has been said that he foresaw the coming of war between Britain and France – imminent in 1755 and already raging in North America – and feared that he would be swept up by a press gang.[58] But this is absurd: as the master of a collier he was exempt from pressing. Others claim that the coming of war would have made his life as master of a collier intolerable, and it is true that from 1757 French privateers swarmed off the Yorkshire coast, disrupting both the coal trade and the inshore fisheries.[59] Still others argue from sociological data and bring the nascent whaling industry of Whitby into the equation. From the early 1750s Whitby was diversifying into whaling; in 1753 its merchants formed a Whale Fishing Company and to jump-start the new industry brought in Dutch specialists. By 1770 Whitby was the major whaling port in England.[60] Is it possible that Cook spotted this trend and (wrongly) concluded that the colliery trade was about to go into a decline? On the other hand, if a mere lust for adventure was his motive, whaling offered the prospect of sailing the seven seas in search of the Leviathan. A taste for adventure cannot explain the decision to join the Royal Navy, since Cook could easily have transferred from being master of a collier to a similar position with the East India Company in the Indian Ocean or with the many enterprises focused on the Atlantic.

It is much more likely that, in switching from the merchant marine to His Majesty's fighting ships, Cook was evincing signs of a cold, calculating, long-haul ambition. The circumstantial evidence of a chess player's mind is there, for Cook's most famous biographer, John Beaglehole, stressed the apparent disadvantages of the Royal Navy vis-à-vis the coal trade:

> Its physical conditions were worse; its pay was worse; its food was worse, its discipline was harsh, its record of sickness was appalling. To the chance of being drowned could be added the chance of being flogged, hanged or being shot, though it is true that deaths in battle were infinitely fewer than deaths from disease. The enemy might kill in tens, scurvy and typhus killed in tens of hundreds.[61]

But against this litany can be set contrary arguments. Not all scholars agree that conditions of service in the merchant navy were superior; some say the wages and food were better, the medical treatment was superior and that, certainly in wartime, life at sea was easier in the Royal Navy. There are other considerations. To a man obsessed with control, as Cook always was, the slack discipline in the merchant service could well have been a trial. The issue of wages has been confused, for some have looked only at the enlistment bounty

of £2 or the able seaman's wages of 24 shillings a month, ignoring compensation payments and pensions.[62] Yet overwhelmingly, two issues seem salient
and cardinal. Wartime in the Royal Navy opened up the lucrative possibilities
of prize money from the capture of enemy ships. As a historian of the
Georgian navy has commented: 'Simply to reach warrant rank was, socially
and financially, to "break even" by the change, for the low pay in the Navy was
counterbalanced by prize money, half-pay and widow's pensions. To reach
commissioned rank was to open new worlds of honour and profit.'[63] More
generally, the Navy was the sole meritocratic avenue of advancement in the
eighteenth century. The most successful merchant navy master would never
be considered a gentleman. Moreover, real talent and ability, skill in navigation
and surveying and excellent seamanship could not be discounted, for otherwise ships would be sunk or the enemy would be victorious. Meritocracy
was further rewarded because naval patronage was controlled by senior
officers who had themselves been admirals, not simply men of money, weight
and influence in society generally.[64] Since the Royal Navy was the one route
whereby a man of talent could rise to the top without money or the advantage
of an aristocratic background, it makes sense that an ambitious man should opt
for it. That Cook was secretly ambitious, perhaps even chillingly so, cannot
reasonably be doubted. It is the one area where we see most clearly the limits
of Quaker influence on him. A restless soul with thoughts of climbing the
greasy pole and dreams of exploring new worlds could not be constrained by
a creed that taught inner peace and acceptance. John Walker was sad to see his
protégé go and gave him glowing references, but in more than one sense he
had been harbouring a cuckoo in his Whitby nest.

     In summary, we are justified in concluding that Cook by this stage
had almost totally jettisoned his Quaker background and influence. Later
testimony points to a ruthless pragmatism, informed by Enlightenment scepticism. He was probably a deist, sharing deism's disbelief in many aspects of
Christianity. Totally without superstition, and thus already a rare bird among
seamen, he never spoke of religion, would tolerate no priests or ministers
on his ships and seldom observed the Sabbath.[65] Most significantly, he cannot
have taken Quakerism and pacifism seriously or he could not have joined the
Royal Navy, itself almost a metaphor for brutality, violence and aggression.
Nor could a genuine Quaker have tolerated the libertinism of his future
patrons and protectors in the Navy, in particular the lustful Lord Sandwich.[66]
Cook was certainly a power-worshipper and, as such, he could not fail to be
impressed by the Navy's 'hegemonic' status in Georgian Britain. Taking 60
per cent of National Expenditure, the Navy was considered both a superb
fighting force and a model of administration. It was divided into four main

sections: the Admiralty Board which decided on blue-water policy overseas and the disposition of fighting ships; the Navy Board, responsible for building and purchasing and then maintaining its vessels; the Ordnance Board, responsible for gunnery, arms and ammunition; and the Board of Sick and Hurt, to do something for the tens of thousands of disease-ridden sailors in peacetime and the wounded in wartime.[67] The discipline and efficiency of the Royal Navy appealed mightily to Cook's deep character (the corruption of its contractors was another matter). The Navy admired, respected and appreciated pure technicians of the nautical arts, whatever their personal characteristics, and this made it the right kind of organisation for Cook. Lacking in the charm or social graces that might have advanced him in another sphere, stern and unsmiling, Cook was in many ways an odd fish, apparently lacking a powerful sex drive (as later evidence suggests) and so unlikely to be sidetracked by fleshly pursuits. Tall, handsome, slightly built, with a dark brown complexion, with a large head, nose, forehead and brown eyes, probably speaking with a Yorkshire accent, he often seemed in a world of his own and later, when a commander, would often sit at table with his officers without saying a word.[68] We are back with the oldest wisdom of all: great explorers are seldom outstanding human beings.

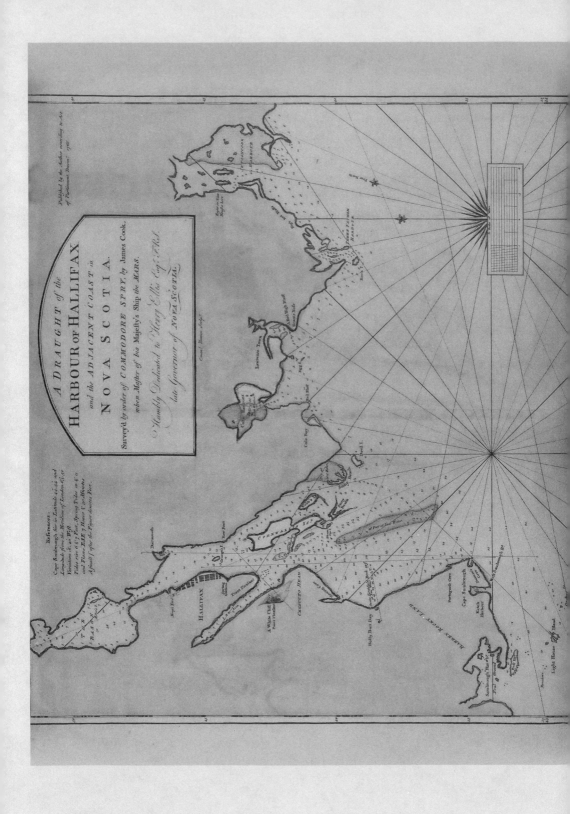

A DRAUGHT of the
HARBOUR of HALLIFAX
and the ADJACENT COAST in
NOVA SCOTIA.

Survey'd by order of COMMODORE SPRY, by James Cook,
when Master of his Majesty's Ship the MARS.

Humbly Dedicated to Henry Ellis Esq.r F.R.S.
late Governour of NOVA SCOTIA.

Published by the Author according to Act
of Parliament December 1766

Carol. Douwes Sculp.

References.
Cape Sambrough lies in Latitude 44.34 and
Longitude from the Meridian of London 63.32
Variation 10.30 West.
Tides rise 6¼ Feet, Spring Tides 10.4¼
and Flows E.N.E 7 Hours ¾ at. Minutes
A full ¼ after the Figure denotes Feet.

CHAPTER TWO

The Seven Years War

COOK formally joined the Navy at Wapping on 7 June 1755 and was assigned to the *Eagle*, Captain Joseph Hamar, a 60-gun ship moored at Spithead. There has been fanciful speculation that the recruiting officer must have been delighted at such a catch volunteering as a mere seaman, but it is more likely that the signing of Cook was all in a day's work. To Cook the hierarchy in the Royal Navy was something new, for on His Majesty's ships executive decisions were shared between the captain and the master. Within a remarkably short time – almost exactly a month – Hamar had spotted his latest recruit as 'one to note' and promoted him to master's mate, the master being Thomas Bissett.[1] The *Eagle* itself was in poor shape, having emerged from Portsmouth docks in a state of semi-repair two months before Cook joined her. It took three months to make her seaworthy, in which time her sailing orders were changed from the interdiction of French commerce with the French West Indies to a supporting role in Admiral Hawke's blockade of the Brittany coast, operating mainly between the Scilly islands and Ireland.[2] Although war had not yet been formally declared between Britain and France, a state of war existed between the two nations. It would take more than a year before the struggle for mastery in the Americas was subsumed in the wider European conflict known to history as the Seven Years War. Perhaps Captain Hamar was impressed by Cook simply because he could delegate so much responsibility to him. The inference that Hamar was a fainéant, lethargic and lacklustre skipper is strengthened by his actions once at sea. First he mistook a Dutch merchantman for a French warship. Then, when gales and squalls battered his ship, he decided to run for home. The last straw was a 'monstrous great sea' off the Head of Kinsale in Ireland. The Nelson touch was distinctly lacking in Hamar and the beginning of September found him back in safe anchorage at Plymouth, ostensibly because the mainmast was sprung between decks.[3] But the shipyard repairers found nothing wrong with the *Eagle* after two weeks of exhaustive investigations. The Admiralty testily ordered Hamar to put to sea at once, but the reluctant captain found a fresh reason for delay, this time pleading the necessity to put the vessel into dock to have its bottom tallowed. This was too much for the Lords of the Admiralty, who abruptly dismissed Hamar from his command.[4]

The new captain, Hugh Palliser, was to be a key figure in Cook's career and featured as the third of his great patrons, after Skottowe and Walker. It would transpire that Cook's gamble had paid off, that his luck had held and that he had yet again found a powerful protector. Palliser, five years Cook's senior, had already been at sea for twenty years, having gone to sea aged 12, despite being the son of an army captain and of gentry stock in the West Riding. He passed all his examinations and became a lieutenant aged 18 – according to Admiralty regulations, three years before any man should receive a commission.[5] A veteran of the War of the Austrian Succession, he had been in action at the battle of Toulon in 1744 (when Cook was still tending sheep) and gained his first command in 1746, when Cook began his apprenticeship with Walker. Since then he had clocked up service off the Coromandel coast in India, in the West Indies, on patrol off the English coast and in transatlantic convoy duties. His career illustrated how far behind the high-flyers Cook was at this stage. Palliser seems to have noticed Cook's talent right from the start, and perhaps the common Yorkshire background was also an element in the solidarity he always showed with his younger subordinate.[6] Capable and energetic, Palliser displayed none of Hamar's timidity. Once out at sea on 8 October, with orders to cruise the western approaches as part of a general blockading force under Admiral Temple West and the ill-fated vice-admiral John Byng, Palliser ran into the storms, gales and monstrous seas that had knocked the sand out of Hamar. Dispirited by the wind and waves, the sailors nonetheless rallied to Palliser with gusto, motivated by the mouth-watering prospect of prize money. Administered by a Navy agent, prize money, rated according to the value of the enemy ship captured, was divided into eight parts, of which the capturing vessel's captain was given three-eighths, the commander-in-chief one eighth, the officers one-eighth, the warrant officers one one eighth, and a quarter to the men. This meant that an officer could collect well over £1,000 while even an ordinary seaman could hope for £100 – a vast amount given general wage levels at the time. The greatest prize ever taken was in 1762 when the Spanish treasure ship *Hermione* was intercepted out of Peru, and the lowliest seamen received the staggering sum of £485 each.[7]

Leaving Plymouth on 8 October, the *Eagle* was for five weeks mostly on her own. Ploughing through hard gales and white squalls, she chased any sail that appeared on the horizon, but most of these proved to be neutral merchantmen: Spanish, Swedish, Dutch, German. She managed to haul in a few minnows in the shape of French fishing boats returning from the Newfoundland Banks, but significant quarry eluded her. On the one occasion she came close to a major capture, a sister ship, the *Monmouth*, nipped in to scoop the prize. The weather continued to be atrocious, and in early November Palliser lost his main topgallant mast in a severe squall. On 13 November he joined West and Byng in the Bay of Biscay and helped them to bring down major prey in the form of the 74-gun *Esperance*, which sank after a long-running fight with West's squadron; the encounter, in a heavy gale, was something of a foretaste of the battle of Quiberon four years later. With his ships badly battered both by the gales and French guns, Byng ordered a return to Plymouth for a major overhaul and refit. The *Eagle* was thus out of action from 21 November to 13 March 1756. The crewing situation on board was now chaotic, and Palliser wrote to the Admiralty to complain of inadequate manning; that is, the undermanning that would result once he had stripped from his ship the supernumeraries, invalids and other sick or incapacitated men who had been dumped on him during the short cruise of October–November.[8]

Cook meanwhile continued to find favour with his new patron. On 22 January 1756 he was promoted to boatswain, responsible for ropes, sails, cables, anchors and flags as well as boats, and thus securing a pay rise from £3 16s. to £4 a month. But Palliser continued to employ him also as master's mate, so the promotion may have been more apparent than real as Cook was now in effect doing two jobs. Perhaps as a consequence in February we find Cook in sick bay with an unspecified illness.[9] On 13 March the *Eagle* put to sea again. She arrived off Cape Barfleur on the Cherbourg peninsula on the 19th and joined two other ships in surveillance of the port of Cherbourg. The weather was once more bad and there was little to assuage the boredom of routine patrol except a few picayune encounters with French smugglers. For two weeks in April Cook was given temporary command of one of the *Eagle*'s cutters, which moved in close to the Brittany coast at Morlaix.[10] When Palliser was suddenly ordered to return to Plymouth, Cook had to find passage on the commodore's ship *Falmouth* in order to regain his own ship. But once more he was assigned independent cutter duty, this time accompanying Admiral Edward Boscawen from Plymouth to Ushant aboard the 60-gun *St Alban's*. It was 3 May before he rejoined the *Eagle*, which was now definitively part of Boscawen's armada attempting to bottle up the French fleet in Brest – for war had been formally declared in May. And now at last the *Eagle* finally secured a prize, albeit a minor one – a vessel from the West Indies carrying tea and coffee. Cook was sent back to Plymouth with the prize and then had to take it round the coast to London. He was back in Plymouth on 1 July to find the *Eagle* refitting but Palliser in despair at the swathe that illness had scythed through his crew, with 27 already dead and another 130 in hospital, most of them seriously ill.[11]

Palliser now applied to the Admiralty for warm clothes for all pressed men and an extra ration of food; surprisingly, his request was granted.[12] The next to fall sick was Palliser himself, so that for a very brief interval Cook served under a new captain, Charles Proby. But Palliser was soon back on the bridge, and in early August the *Eagle* was ready to sail again, after extensive repairs.[13] What followed was *opéra bouffe*. A Swedish merchantman had reported seeing a squadron of nine 90-gun French warships off the Isle of Wight. The *Eagle* was one of those ordered by Rear Admiral Harrison to investigate, intercept and interdict. When no signs whatever of such an armada were found, it was suspected that the Swede might be a French agent who had deliberately planted disinformation. In retaliation, the British kept him at Portsmouth for several months, looking into 'irregularities' in his ship's papers.[14] The *Eagle* was then detached to assist in Boscawen's blockade off Ushant, but her long cruise in the Atlantic was tedious and uneventful. By the time she headed back to Plymouth in mid-November disease once more stalked the ship; morale was low, and the exiguous prize money doled out for the the *Eagle*'s petty captures scarcely improved matters.[15]

By the end of 1756 the *Eagle* had brought her crew up to full strength (around 420 men) and set out again on her tedious blockading duties. Only five days out she was caught by a ferocious gale off the Isle of Wight which ripped away most of her sails. Back into Spithead she went for another month in the doldrums, until on 30 January she sailed again with Vice-Admiral West's squadron, this time to the Bay of Biscay. Another uneventful period ended on 15 April with shore leave in England. On 25 May 1757 the *Eagle* put to sea again in company with the 60-gun *Medway*, and this time saw some stirring action. Palliser, evidently a better seaman than the *Medway*'s captain Proby, managed to engage the 50-gun French man-o'-war the *Duc d'Aquitaine* out of Lisbon while Proby's incorrect sailing instructions left his ship out of the picture. After an hour's fierce pounding, the French vessel was disabled in the main and mizzen masts, and struck. Here at last was a major prize.[16] This was Cook's first experience of naval combat, and a grim business it proved, with twelve of the *Eagle*'s crew dead and eighty wounded, while the French suffered casualties of fifty dead and thirty wounded. Cook was rewarded by promotion to master, and thus escaped the violently tempest-tossed Atlantic crossing to which Palliser and the *Eagle* were next assigned. When Palliser and his leaking ship limped back to England in late September, having been reduced to jury masts and with a crew decimated by disease, he was perhaps not in the best state of mind to receive a well-meaning but politically naïve intervention by John Walker and William

Osbaldeston, MP for Whitby, petitioning for a commission for James Cook. With as much patience as he could muster, Palliser wrote back to say that preferment was beyond his ability to confer; he stressed that naval regulations could be waived only if one of the great and good of Georgian England entered the lists on behalf of a protégé, and neither Osbaldeston nor Palliser himself fell into that category. According to the regulations, Cook would have to serve as a mate for at least six years before he could be considered for a commission, so he was at least four years shy of the target.[17]

Even though Walker's ham-fisted efforts on his behalf had failed, Cook himself was in good spirits. Shortly after returning from the capture of the *Duc d'Aquitaine*, he passed his examinations (held at Trinity House, Deptford) and qualified as a ship's master. Theoretically, Cook had now reached the farthest point a meritocrat could go in the Navy without capital, and even so most masters usually owned shares in their ships.[18] He was the chief professional on board, though not of course the highest ranking one. His sphere was the navigation of the ship, its general management and its stores, and he had overall responsibility for masts, yards, sails and rigging, whose day-to-day details devolved to the boatswain. It was he who kept the ship's log. He was also supposed to be the brains behind pilotage and harbour work, responsible for taking soundings and bearings and, crucially, making new charts and correcting the existing ones. Ubiquitous and omnipresent, the master represented the heart of the ship and the captain its head. There was almost a sense in which the master was outside the normal ranking in the hierarchy, for he alone wore no uniform. The captain was in charge of strategic and tactical decisions and was ultimately answerable to the Admiralty for the conduct of the ship, but shrewd captains usually took care to heed the advice of their masters and not override their prerogatives or question their expertise. A good master was a prized asset, but his very excellence could work against him, for the Admiralty did not tend to waste precious talent by promoting such a person. Masters, like boatswains, pursers, gunners, carpenters and cooks, were sometimes given the misnomer 'standing officers', which in theory meant that they were tied to a given ship in perpetuity or unless it was lost. In fact such men were often promoted from small ships to large ones, and even exchanged duties with each other, swapping with those who wanted to go to sea, and vice versa. In sum, the master was the most senior of the warrant (non-commissioned) officers and in some respects, including pay, his status equalled that of a lieutenant.[19]

Reluctantly Palliser had to discharge Cook from the *Eagle*. At the beginning of July 1757 he was assigned the position of master on a 24-gun frigate, the *Solebay*, captain Robert Craig. The *Solebay*'s duties were to patrol the east coast of Scotland to prevent smuggling or raids by French privateers. Cook travelled overland via Yorkshire and visited his parents and John Walker before joining his ship at its base in Leith on the Firth of Forth on 30 July. Sailing two days later, Cook got his one and only look at Scotland on a voyage to the Shetlands, calling at Stoneham (Kincardineshire), Buchan Ness (Aberdeenshire), Copinsay and Fair Isle in the Orkneys before anchoring in Lerwick harbour.[20] The inconsequential foray into the North Sea ended with the *Solebay* back in the home port of Leith by the end of August. Cook does not appear to have been aboard for much more than another week or so before he was transferred to the *Pembroke* where he superseded his old friend Bissett, whose mate he had been on the *Eagle*.[21] The *Pembroke* was a state-of-the-art 64-gun warship, 1,250 tons, captain Simcoe, and the appointment to be her master was considered prestigious. Cook joined his new ship in Portsmouth, where it had been fitting out after a cruise to Lisbon,[22] and was soon again in familiar waters, down the Channel and south into the Bay of Biscay and on to Cape Finisterre, once more in pursuit of an enemy who never appeared. On 9 February 1758 the *Pembroke* was back in Plymouth, but this time the Admiralty had great and ambitious designs for the ship: she was to take part in Prime Minister William Pitt's attempt to destroy the French in North America.

Pitt's master strategy was to use the well-funded National Debt as the financial basis for making large subsidies to Prussia and its German allies in Europe, while concentrating on the global struggle against France in India and the Americas. Until the end of 1757 the war in North America had overwhelmingly gone France's way. Their talented general Louis-Joseph Marquis de Montcalm had won a string of victories over the British, including the particular humiliations at Monongahela in 1755 and Fort William Henry in 1757.[23] Now Pitt aimed to reverse the trend, and he began by sacking the British commander-in-chief in North America, Lord Loudoun, and replacing him with General James Abercromby. Pitt always had the Napoleonic gift of luck, and by the beginning of 1758 a unique conjuncture of events favoured his designs. On at least half a dozen different indices the pendulum in North America was about to swing decisively. The deep, overarching factor that would secure British triumph in less than three years was sea power. With its decisive command of the seas, the Royal Navy could slowly begin to throttle the French colony in Canada; New France, as it was called. The interception of ships bearing supplies and reinforcements from France was part of a slow but sure process of remorseless attrition that would eventually consign French Canada to its fate.[24] At the same time Pitt reversed Loudoun's self-defeating policy of trying to make the anglophone North American colonists pay for British military endeavours. Instead he decided to subsidise them and pay bounties to native recruits. The upshot was that when he implemented his massive multi-front campaign against

New France he could pit at least 14,000 redcoats and up to 25,000 colonial irreg-
ulars against French forces that were numerically far inferior. Montcalm
commanded at most 6,800 French regulars plus 2,700 marines; in addition there
was a raw militia of dubious military worth, maybe 16,000 strong, composed of
all able-bodied males between 15 and 60.[25]

Before 1758 the French had been able to compensate for the disparity in
numbers by calling on their Indian allies, espcially the Abenaki and Micmacs,
to redress the balance. But in early 1758 the tribes were hit by a devastating
smallpox epidemic that took them out of the picture. Meanwhile New France
was suffering dire shortages of food and supplies, exacerbated by the failure of
two consecutive harvests, in 1756 and 1757. French Canada was on starvation
rations over the winter of 1757–58, even as the corrupt intendant François
Bigot, who was supposed to guarantee the food supply, made a private fortune
for himself through a series of scams and defalcations.[26] Montcalm and the
governor of New France, Pierre Rigaud, Marquis de Vaudreuil, loathed each
other, so that there were divided counsels at the top about how to deal with the
British threat. Moreover, France itself was paralysed by financial chaos and
political indecision. Inflation was rampant: France spent two million livres a
year on Canada in 1754 but by 1757 the costs had escalated to 12 million. In
Canada itself inflation meant that merchants and farmers started hoarding,
while Bigot's unwise attempt to force his business community to accept worth-
less paper money simply meant that all specie arriving on ships from France
was likewise squirrelled away against the day when financial stability would
return.[27] In the political sphere Louis XV had no ministers of any ability on
his council until the very end of 1758, when the Duc de Choiseul became
Foreign Minister. At the very moment Pitt had decided to hold the ring in
Europe and concentrate on the struggle in the colonies, France moved in the
opposite direction. Its grand strategy of 1758 – in so far as anything deserving
that title can be discerned – stressed the European theatre: victory in Germany
and the preparation of an armada to invade England became the priority, and
New France was neglected.[28]

Against this dispiriting picture of waning French power, with factionalism,
corruption and economic chaos rampant, Pitt had the advantages of naval hegemony, clean and uninterrupted supply lines and a united command. Although
Pitt himself liked to take credit for the grand strategy of 1758 in the Americas,
the true military mind behind it was Field Marshal Ligonier. He it was who
suggested the offensive in North America and he too who appointed (over
the strenuous opposition of George II), four talented generals to serve under
Abercromby. The campaign would be three-pronged. Abercromby, supported
by George Augustus, Viscount Howe, would advance overland against Canada

via Lake Champlain, aiming at Fort Carillon. John Forbes, the second of the
quartet, would attempt to capture Fort Duquesne and Fort Frontenac at the
forks of the Ohio river.[29] The other two of Ligonier's 'four musketeers', Jeffrey
Amherst and James Wolfe, were given the task of taking the fortress of
Louisbourg so that there would be no French garrison in the British rear when
they advanced up the St Lawrence river to attack Quebec. Loudoun's view had
been that Louisbourg was unimportant and could be bypassed by an expedition
bound for Quebec, but neither Pitt nor Ligonier accepted such optimistic
thinking. A crucial part of the strategy was that major detachments of the the
Royal Navy would cross the Atlantic and remain on station off the American
coast to give Wolfe and Amherst all necessary back-up. The man given
command of the naval contingent was Admiral Edward Boscawen, a hero
because of his achievements in the War of the Austrian Succession (1740–48).
Called 'Wry Neck Dick' from his habit of cocking his head to one side
(allegedly the result of a war wound), Boscawen already had credentials in
combined operations, having covered the siege of Pondicherry in India in 1748
with warships.[30]

Boscawen's armada comprised eight ships of the line and several smaller
vessels. It was with Boscawen's fleet that Cook sailed in the *Pembroke*, one of
the eight warships, from Plymouth on 22 February 1758. To be more precise,
the *Pembroke* seems to have joined an expedition that was already at sea, for
Boscawen and most of his ships left St Helen's on the Isle of Wight on the
19th.[31] The ships soon ran into storms and high seas, and the less robust
members of the assault force surely quaked in their military boots, for this
seemed an ominous rerun of the disaster of the year before. In 1757 Loudoun
had attempted to besiege Louisbourg but was forced to call off the attempt. At
the end of September the British fleet that had been playing a key role in
combined operations was caught by a frightful hurricane about thirty miles off
Louisbourg which 'in another day, if it had continued, would have destroyed
them all'.[32] It was this encounter with the elements that had left the *Eagle*
looking like a ghost ship. This time the storms did not quite reach hurricane
force, but they were enough to alarm all normal souls. Wolfe, aboard the
Princess Amelia, later recalled that 'From Christopher Columbus's time to our
days there perhaps has never been a more extraordinary voyage.'[33] Cook, by
contrast, treated even the most severe storms with insouciance, noting the wind
force with clinical detachment, almost as if he was already convinced of his
ability to deal with the very worst the oceans could throw at him. It seems that
the convoy shifted track several times to avoid the battering from gales, for an
itinerary from England to Newfoundland via Tenerife and Bermuda makes no
sense otherwise. It was 9 May before the weary *Pembroke* reached Halifax, the

port the British had built up as a counterweight to Louisbourg. Twenty-six men had died on the passage, and many others were hospitalised as soon as the ship anchored in the port; additionally there were five desertions.[34]

Halifax, on the Nova Scotian coast, was about two days' sail (that is, in good weather) from Louisbourg, which was on the south-eastern corner of Cape Breton island, and commanded the approaches from Newfoundland to the St Lawrence. An important town, port and fortress, it was the centre of the French fishing industry in the New World and possessed a kidney-shaped harbour capacious enough to contain a large fleet. The British had captured it in 1745, and the French had made a major attempt to retake it in 1746. Where military effort failed, diplomacy succeeded and, at the end of the War of the Austrian Succession in 1748, France regained the town in exchange for giving up Madras in India. Determined not to let Louisbourg fall into British hands again, the French then tried to turn it into an impregnable fortress, and it certainly looked impressive to the casual observer, yet the appearance belied the reality. There were formidable gun emplacements in the fortress, shore batteries and eleven warships in the harbour. But the imposing-looking walls had been weakened by damp in the mortar, and the landward fortifications were poorly sited. On the other hand, these weaknesses could be exploited only by an invader prepared to launch a daring amphibious assault.[35] At first the very elements seemed tilted against a British success. During the crossing the storms had scattered the fleet and when Boscawen and Wolfe arrived in Halifax in early May there was no sign of Amherst. They were already a month behind schedule in the very tightly plotted military scenario for 1758. They therefore laid plans in accordance with the contingency instructions from Pitt in case Amherst was lost or delayed. They were just about to clear for Louisbourg when Amherst finally arrived on 28 May. As a point of principle, he changed the plan Wolfe had elaborated for the capture of Louisbourg, insisting that they land at Gabarus Bay under the enemy's big guns, rather than make a ten-mile march there overland.[36] But even the short trip from Halifax to Louisbourg was dangerous, with the fleet once more being dispersed by a gale (on 30 May).

Finally, with 157 transports and warships, and 13,000 troops, Amherst and Wolfe came in sight of their objective. Their overall aim was to land, secure a beachhead, then gradually spread out to envelop the harbour and steadily advance on the fortress itself, which they would reduce to rubble with big guns. The French governor, Augustin de Boschenry de Drucour, watched the enemy's approach with apprehension, well aware of the intrinsic weakness of his position and grimly conscious that he was outnumbered: he had a garrison of 3,500 troops and could summon perhaps that number again from the warships in the harbour.[37] The British were ready to launch their amphibious assault by 3 June but, with a 15-foot surf running, dared not attack. On the 4th Amherst decided that his original plan of attacking in three waves was too ambitious; there would be just one landing, led by Wolfe, and spearheaded by 3,000 of his crack troops.[38] But high winds, a heavy swell and fog delayed the attack for another four days. Only on 8 June were weather conditions suitable. The French still remained confident that the narrowness of the beach and the continuing surf would turn any assault into disaster. The landing was touch and go but ultimately successful. The vainglorious Wolfe, who later claimed the credit for everything, at one moment signalled retreat – only to have the order ignored by some intrepid Highlanders.[39] Once they had secured a beachhead the British were already two-thirds of the way to success. The next task was the destruction of the French warships, which was achieved by non-stop cannon-ades and mainly completed by 21 July. Sailors from Boscawen's fleet, concealed by a thick fog, entered the harbour in boats. The circle was closing, but the real *coup de grâce* for the French was the non-stop twelve-hour bombardment of the town on 25 July, during which 1,000 rounds of shot and shell rained down on the beleaguered citadel.[40] Next day Ducour hoisted a flag of truce and asked for terms. The six-week siege had turned out triumphantly for Amherst, but its conduct was marred by systematic atrocities and the deliberate massacring of all Indians in revenge for the defeat at Fort William Henry the year before. Both Amherst and Wolfe were hard, ruthless men, habitually addicted to war crimes and even genocide. In contrast to Montcalm's chivalrous instincts at Fort William Henry, Amherst denied Ducour all honours and insisted as part of the surrender terms that all French combatants be sent to England as prisoners of war; meanwhile the civilian population was to be deported to France.[41]

Cook made no comment on this departure from the norms of civilised warfare, but then he was always very careful never to make critical comments about his superiors and 'betters'. In any case he did not see much of the siege of Louisbourg for, when Boscawen departed on 28 May, the *Pembroke* remained in Halifax, waiting for her quota of sick to be released from hospital so that the vessel once more had a credible crew. The ship cleared from Halifax on 7 June but was then (one is tempted to say inevitably) delayed by storms and gales, and so did not reach Louisbourg until the 12th. The *Pembroke* had not been long at anchor in Louisbourg before she and others had to cut their cables and run for the open sea to avoid being overwhelmed by a severe gale; they were then at sea for a further two days.[42] Cook finally got into action just before the French surrender. The 21st of July was a black day for the French, for three of their warships, the *Célèbre*, *Entreprenant* and *Capricieux* were destroyed by British gunnery. With the frigate *Aréthuse* having made a daring escape from the harbour on 15 July, bearing the grim tidings of Louisbourg's likely fate to

France, that left just two warships on which Ducour could pin his slender hopes: the *Bienfaisant* and *Prudent*.[43] Boscawen decided that these two, of 64 and 74 guns, respectively, should be 'taken out' by boarding parties attacking in boats. A night-time assault on the evening of 25 July by two divisions of 300 men each, in fifty boats with muffled oars and hooded lanterns, was amazingly successful. The assailants achieved complete surprise in overrunning the *Prudent* and, although the crew of the *Bienfaisant* made more of a fight of it, the ultimate result was the same. Whether by accident or design the *Prudent* was set on fire and gutted.[44] The loss of the final two warships, allied to the twelve-hour bombardment of the fortress, gave Ducour no choice but surrender. Boscawen, Amherst and Wolfe congratulated themselves on a signal example of inter-service cooperation. Not only had the amphibious operation at Gabarus Bay on 8 June been a total success, but Amherst's request to Boscawen to destroy the enemy warships had been clinically and efficiently carried out.[45]

The day after the French surrender was a significant one in Cook's life. He went ashore at Kennington Cove, the precise location on Gabarus Bay where Wolfe had made his landing seven weeks previously. Soon his attention was caught by a man who seemed to be carrying out mathematical observations with the use of a square table and tripod, making notes all the while. Cook engaged the man in conversation and the latter introduced himself as Samuel Holland, a military surveyor. A Dutchman, born in the same year as Cook, he had served in the Army of the United Provinces before being commissioned as a lieutenant in the British Army in 1755. He went to North America with Loudoun in 1756 and had served with distinction in some of the nasty skirmishes in the Hudson River/Lake Champlain corridor, where he had surveyed Fort Carillon (Ticonderoga).[46] Evidently a man of some real verve and charm, he was even on friendly terms with the notoriously vain and prickly James Wolfe, to whose staff he was then attached. He and Cook took an immediate liking to each other, for Holland soon recognised a serious professional rather than one of the aristocratic fops in which the upper echelons of the British armed services then abounded. He explained that his plane table enabled him to make accurate surveys. He would sight over the top at distinguishing marks on the horizon and then make careful notes of his observations. This allowed the creation of an accurate diagram in which all physical features could be placed in relation to each other. Cook was at first fascinated, then besotted: he had found another obsession to add to his mastery of navigation and hydrography. Over the next weeks the friendship and professional collaboration with Holland ripened and deepened, and was enhanced when Cook reported his 'Eureka!' moment to Captain Simcoe.[47] The captain expressed an interest in Holland and invited him to dine on the

Pembroke. Soon the trio of Cook, Holland and Simcoe were like the three musketeers, all for one and one for all. One of the advantages of the long, stormy traverse of the Atlantic was that Cook had created another fan in Simcoe, who thus joined the long line of Cook promoters which now included Skottowe, Walker, Palliser and Captain Richard Ellerton (of the 'cat' *Friendship*).[48]

Despite the triumph of Louisbourg, Pitt's grand design of 1758 was thrown off balance by Montcalm's defeat of Abercromby at Ticonderoga in July – a signal disaster made worse by the death of the popular Lord Howe. Compensation in the shape of the capture of Fort Frontenac, taken by the ingenious Colonel John Bradstreet, and of Fort Duquesne, taken by General Forbes, came too late in the year for Amherst to feel confident of pressing on with the assault on Quebec.[49] The late arrival at Halifax, the six-week siege of Louisbourg and the major setback at Ticonderoga combined to produce a situation where it was too late in the year to proceed with the would-be *pièce de résistance* of the campaign. Amherst sailed for Boston at the end of August to rally Abercromby's defeated army and make the city his base for the winter. Meanwhile the deeply unpleasant Wolfe (for two hundred and fifty years now the subject of unaccountable British imperial hero worship), revealed himself in his true colours. First, he sailed for the Gaspé Bay in the Gulf of St Lawrence and began a campaign of devastation aimed at destroying the French fishing industry. Wolfe had already proved in Scotland after the '45 that he was by any standards a war criminal, and now he undertook a vindictive programme of vicious brutality.[50] Secondly, in correspondence with Amherst and Pitt, he meanly and despicably traduced the Royal Navy, and especially Sir Charles Hardy, for an allegedly lacklustre performance at Louisbourg, even though it was the Navy that had eliminated the French warships, and would prove the key to Wolfe's ultimate apotheosis as the conqueror of Quebec. Thirdly, although supposed to winter over in Halifax, Wolfe unilaterally decided that this did not suit him, so he fabricated a pretext to enable him to return to England, despite the furious reprimand of the Secretary of War Lord Barrington.[51] Pitt and his circle had, however, created a Frankenstein's monster. Having built Wolfe up in the press as a great, glorious hero, they could hardly now portray him as an insubordinate glory-hunter without undermining their own credibility. Accordingly, Wolfe got away with what he did. He embarked with Boscawen's fleet on 1 October and spent the winter of 1758–59 in England.

It was Cook's fate at this juncture to have his career embroiled with that of Wolfe, and not just in the mutual relations with Samuel Holland. When Wolfe went on his savage war against the French fisheries in the St Lawrence with his three battalions of redcoats, Sir Charles Hardy escorted him with a squadron that included the *Pembroke*. So Cook was forced to endure what Beaglehole has called, with considerable understatement, 'inglorious service'.[52] The *Pembroke* managed to take a few small prizes, and uplifted cargoes of bread, butter and wine, thus further impoverishing the wretched French fishermen, but the real significance for Cook of the Bay of Gaspé interlude was the harmonious bonding of the trio of Simcoe, Holland and Cook and the invaluable surveying and charting work they did on the upper reaches of the St Lawrence. The charts of Chaleur and Gaspé Bay that they produced were of inestimable importance to Admiral Durell in 1759.[53] The 'three musketeers' also discovered that existing maps of Newfoundland and the Gulf of St Lawrence were woefully imprecise in latitude and longitude. Together they pored over relevant tomes: Charles Leadbetter's *Complete System of Astronomy* (1728) and his *Young Mathematician's Companion* (1739), and presumably many others whose titles escape the ken of history.[54] With their minds thus occupied, they doubtless ignored or blotted out Wolfe's daily atrocities. After making the French a farewell present by gutting a sloop and a schooner, Hardy's seven warships returned to Louisbourg, where the main fleet lay at anchor from 2 October to 14 November. Under Admiral Durell the ships then endured five storm-tossed days making the difficult passage to Halifax. Boscawen (legitimately) and Wolfe (illegitimately) returned to England while Amherst stayed in America. It was the mournful fate of the *Pembroke* to remain in Halifax for the winter.

Halifax in 1758 was an unprepossessing place, perched on a peninsula 4.5 miles wide and two miles long. Founded in 1749 with 2,500 settlers as a counterweight to French Louisbourg, in ten years the town had already attracted immigrants from Scotland, Ireland, Germany and New England. Its main landmark, Citadel Hill, looked down on a dirty, muddy town of log stockades and plank buildings. It was a dark, dank locality, suffused with fog and damp, where the only landscape to gaze out on was rocky scrubland. The streets were rutted tracks, arranged in parallel to the harbour, and the buildings no more than rude huts where the useful trades of a seaport were carried on: ship repairing, dry-docking (for the town acquired a naval dockyard in 1758), carpentry, sailmaking, storekeeping, tending licensed premises and prostitution. The one thing Halifax did have was an excellent harbour, with deep water that never froze over.[55] Here the *Pembroke*'s crew were set to work, cleaning, repairing and careening the ship, mending sails and strengthening masts. Inevitably, the boredom of such an existence, with long winter nights given over to drunkenness and brothels, brought in its train a plethora of disciplinary offences. As master, Cook had responsibility for punishment, and his log records the dreary catalogue of offences: fires, started accidentally while the men were lying in a drunken stupor, causing damage to valuable fabrics; disobedience, insubordination and insolence to officers; drunken neglect of duty; stabbings; purloining ship's stores and wine for sale on the black market or barter for other desirables.[56]

Since the issue of Cook's role as a disciplinarian often surfaces in discussions of his career and personality, it will be as well to place crime and punishment on his ships in a wider context. All sailors on board His Majesty's ships were bound by the Articles of War, which were more draconian in theory than in practice, and in this respect rather like the general 'Bloody Code' of eighteenth-century English society, though even the theoretical provisions of the Articles were not as severe as those in the code of domestic land-based law. There were eight offences that were theoretically capital, but in practice only murder and buggery attracted the death penalty. The Royal Navy's attitude to crime and indiscipline was Janus-faced. On the one hand, it was not generally perceived as a major problem, if only because the ruling elite had total confidence in the order and stability of their political system and the rightness of its inegalitarian hierarchy. In any case, very high levels of violence were tolerated in the everyday life of the eighteenth century. Moreover, on land there was an anti-Navy ethos (just as there was also an anti-Army one) which encouraged the prosecution of ship's officers by ordinary seamen. Because of the subtext of hostility from civilian courts, the Admiralty did its best to keep cases beyond their reach.[57] On the other hand, when its credibility and legitimacy were challenged, either explicitly or implicitly, the reaction of the Navy could be ferocious. Common punishments were floggings (sometimes 'around the fleet') or 'running the gauntlet': running between rows of determined chastisers armed with knotted ropes that raised weals and gashes on the body. Twelve lashes justified the time-consuming spectacle of a flogging, and a dozen strokes of the 'cat' was usually accepted as the right level of punishment for drunkenness or mutiny. Of course, captains who were harsher disciplinarians often awarded twenty-four or more lashes but did not record the floggings in their log books.[58] Apart from murder and buggery, the crimes most severely punished were those that seemed to threaten the comfort, safety or *esprit de corps* of the ship. This was why, paradoxically, theft was often treated more harshly than desertion or mutiny. A single court on the same ship on the same day sentenced a deserter to 200 lashes, a mutineer to 300 and a thief to 500; there were cases of crews complaining that a thief had received the lenient punishment of 'only' 400 lashes. Appeals against floggings were inevitably self-defeating. One sailor who refused a routine flogging and appealed was given 600 lashes by a court-martial. Another who knocked down a midshipman and refused twelve lashes was then given 200 by a court-martial on appeal. It was one of the paradoxes of crime and punishment in the Navy that it was often preferable to be sentenced to death than to a flogging.[59] Only one-fifth of those found guilty of desertion in 1755–62 were actually sentenced to death, and only a quarter of those (that is, one-twentieth of those found guilty) were executed, almost always for aggravated offences, such as murder while absent without official leave. It followed that it was in some ways better to gamble with a death sentence, with a high chance of pardon, than to be flogged, for the latter sentence was certain to be carried out.[60]

Sodomy was regarded with a peculiar horror in the eighteenth century, both as an 'unchristian' act not fit to be mentioned in polite company and as an activity detrimental to hierarchy and social order. Life afloat without women inevitably raised sexual frustration to extraordinary heights and, equally inevitably, this deprivation was often 'solved' by homosexual behaviour. But it was a dangerous activity, for it was almost impossible to conceal at sea, and buggery was one crime which was highly likely to incur the death penalty.[61] Cook was in general relaxed about promiscuous heterosexuality, as he demonstrated later in the Pacific.[62] But on homosexuality he shared the prejudices and dislikes of wider society. When one of the crew of the *Pembroke* attempted sodomy with a messmate, Cook had him flogged where some masters or captains would have opted for capital punishment *in terrorem*.[63] Some critics of Cook, however, claim that both he and Vancouver, also an explorer and officer in the Royal Navy, were more draconian than more legendary floggers such as Lieutenant William Bligh of the *Bounty*. This rests largely on Cook's record during his last great Pacific voyage, of which we shall say much more later. The first two South Seas voyages do not show him to be a notable disciplinarian. On the *Endeavour* voyage twenty-one of the eighty-five crew were punished, five of them twice, with a maximum chastisement of 24 lashes and a total over three years of 342 strokes of the cat. On the second voyage (1772–75), just nineteen men were punished, with one sentence of 24 lashes, two of 18, sixteen of 12 and six of 6, making a total of just 288 lashes in three years.[64]

Yet the winter of 1758–59 was not all boredom suffered and punishment meted out by the master. These were the halcyon days when Cook, Holland and Simcoe pored over maps and charts of the Gulf of St Lawrence and of the great river itself. The legend that Cook in person personally surveyed the St Lawrence river that winter and made an accurate chart of its entire length is pure fantasy – for one thing the river was iced over – but he did collate every scrap of infomation in chart form available. The data assembled during these midnight lucubrations would be of inestimable value when the Navy conveyed Wolfe's army to Quebec in 1759.[65] Cook was fascinated by the prospect of being able to record by triangulation every cove, indentation, reef and set of rocks on a coastline and to integrate this with a general relief map. He was well equipped for the task, having a good mathematical background and having improved his knowledge of plain and spherical trigonometry during the second part of 1758 under Simcoe's aegis. Holland added an extra dimension to his skills. He taught Cook all the secrets of his tripod-based table and the telescope mounted on it. By marking headlands and other relief features on drawing paper pinned down on the table and surrounding the telescope, and using an appropriate scale, the observer first collated the angles of observation and then by trigonometry calculated the distances between the different geographical features.[66] For Cook this opened up the vista of a really accurate survey of coastlines. He already had the expertise necessary to make accurate hydrographic soundings and to estimate bearings at sea. By marrying Holland's skills with his own, he glimpsed the possibility of coastal surveys accurate far beyond anything yet achieved in Admiralty charts. Further refinements were later added, including the use of sextants, theodolites and a measuring rod known as a Gunter's Chain. Cook was already well on his way to becoming a master surveyor as well as a master navigator.[67] Already we can discern one skein in Cook's nautical genius: he was, so to speak, a Renaissance Man of the oceans. Polymath and versatile all-rounder of the seven seas, he crossed over barriers most sailors never crossed. For example, mariners were usually either deepwater or coastal specialists, but Cook was both. As his great admirer John Beaglehole has written: 'He who had grounded in the Esk could ground in the Endeavour River . . . The man who mastered the Barrier Reef was the man who made the great oceanic sweeps of the second voyage; the man who charted New Zealand was the man who went down to Latitude 71 South.'[68]

The Halifax winter gradually released its icy grip. It should be remembered that these waters are cold even in summer: in June 1755, off Cape Breton Island, Boscawen noted that he and all his men had chilblains from the cold. Not surprisingly, many men marooned in these latitudes in the winter of 1758–59 died of frostbite, for winter work even in the harbour was dangerous and much of it impossible, since the running ropes froze in the blocks and the sails were stiff with ice and snow, 'like sheets of iron'. The men complained that they could not expose their hands long enough to the cold to do their duty aloft, so that the topsails could not be handled.[69] Admiral Durell was accused of inactivity, laziness and lack of enterprise in not attempting to move into the St Lawrence before the main fleet returned from Britain, but much of the criticism came from Wolfe, a man woefully ignorant of the reality of the sea and seafaring, and even of the elements, though he complained loudly enough when he himself was the victim of seasickness.[70] Harsh even by normal standards, the winter of 1759 saw sailors in nearby Louisbourg amusing themselves by jumping from ice floe to ice floe in the harbour. Almost the only

beneficiaries of the cruel weather were the French, who were able to run the
supposed blockade by the Royal Navy at Halifax and Louisbourg in their fast
navires de flute, stripped of all guns, carrying only supplies and thus able to
bring to Montcalm and the defenders at Quebec not just food supplies and
ammunition but the unwelcome news that the British were preparing a massive
effort to take Quebec.[71]

Massive the enterprise certainly was. In addition to Durell's squadron of ten
ships of the line and four frigates already at Halifax, Pitt assigned a further fourteen warships, six frigates, three bomb-vessels and three fireships to accompany
a further 12,000 redcoats, to be commanded by Wolfe. The plan for 1759 was that
Amherst would complete the conquest of the French wilderness strongholds in
Canada and, if successful, would proceed to Montreal and then Quebec to assist
Wolfe, who would meanwhile approach up the St Lawrence with an independent
command. Wolfe's promotion was surprising, given his previous insubordination and some eccentric behaviour while home on leave during 1758–59, but he
retained the confidence of Ligonier, whom Pitt did not wish to override. Even
Ligonier, though, drew the line when Wolfe asked to be assigned to duties and
insisted he had to return to the New World in the spring of 1759. This, as it
turned out, was to be Britain's *annus mirabilis*, when she decisively defeated
France in India, the West Indies, Germany and North America as well as scoring
two knockout naval victories over her ancient enemy.[72] Naturally, none of the
contemporary participants could have envisaged such an outcome. Boscawen,
the steadying influence of 1758, was assigned to duties in the Mediterranean, and
would win the memorable victory of Lagos in July. Commanding the fleet this
time was Vice-Admiral Charles Saunders, hand-picked as the least prima-
donnaish of old salts and therefore unlikely to inflame Wolfe. A highly versatile
individual, Saunders had been round the world with Admiral Anson on his epic
circumnavigation, was a permanent protégé of Anson's and with his help
climbed the ladder eventually to become First Lord of the Admiralty. He was
also MP for Hedon in Yorkshire, had his portrait painted by Sir Joshua Reynolds
and was himself a talented artist who produced a famous painting on the death of
Montcalm. He was one of those men who was good enough to rest content on his
merits and did not need to prove anything. Even the acidulous Horace Walpole,
who rarely had a good word for anyone, claimed that 'No man said less or
deserved more.'[73]

On 17 February Wolfe and Saunders sailed from Portsmouth and endured
another rough passage across the Atlantic, with the ocean again at its winter
worst. After two months of pitching and rolling, the intrepid Saunders found
himself confronted on 21 April by a sea of ice. For a week he tried to get
through this, failed, then changed tack from Louisbourg to Halifax, where he

anchored on 30 April. With his dislike of the Navy, Wolfe immediately found fault with Durell for not having already started up the St Lawrence. The verdict of historians since, and the Admiralty then, was against Wolfe, for Durell had been promoted to rear admiral of the Blue while at Louisbourg and further promoted to rear admiral of the Red in February 1759.[74] Goaded and chivvied by Saunders, Durell finally cleared from Halifax on 5 May as part of an advance reconnoitring party, of which the newly furbished *Pembroke* was part. Their initial task was to provide a credible chart and sailing directions from Louisbourg as far as Bic, the first part of the 400-mile estuary of the St Lawrence. Cook had already been through the Cabot Strait and the Gulf of St Lawrence as far as Gaspé; beyond that were 200 miles of deep water and secure sailing to the small islands of Bic and Barnaby.[75] At first the thirteen ship convoy sailed through what seemed like schools of loose ice – the first time Cook had observed the phenomenon. Personal tragedy struck Cook almost at once for, off Anticosti Island on 16 May, his great friend Captain Simcoe, who had been ill with pneumonia, died and was committed to the deep after a 20-gun salute. Cook recorded the great loss in the log with an almost stoic resignation.[76] The new captain, John Wheelock, transferred from the *Squirrel*, was a shadowy figure who made no impact on Cook.[77]

The French had long regarded the St Lawrence as their first line of defence. Moreover, they had learned valuable lessons from the two abortive British attempts on Quebec, in 1690 and 1711, the second of which was essentially defeated by the river itself. Montcalm had laid first-rate contingency plans to deal with any British riverine invasion, and these included the placing of batteries at Gaspé, the Ile-aux-Coudres, Cape Tourmente, the Ile d'Orléans and, Pointe-Lévy (Point Levis) as well as blocking the narrow channel known as the Traverse by sinking ten blockships in it. Because of financial shortages, lack of manpower and the long-running dispute with Vaudreuil, however, none of these eminently sensible measures was adopted. Montcalm was reduced to having his weapon of last resort deployed as the very first one, for he intended to use fireships against any British men-o'-war who got through to the confined spaces below Quebec.[78] This meant that Durell had a trouble-free passage up to Barnaby island, where he anchored on 20 May. Now he demonstrated how fatuous Wolfe's criticism of him for being idle and over-cautious was by exceeding his orders and pressing on upriver. He left a few ships at Bic for liaison and held on for the Ile-aux-Coudres with the majority, including the *Pembroke*. Whereas up to Bic the only real shipping hazard was the coastline and the few islands with shoals, beyond Barnaby Island the St Lawrence was notoriously intricate. The north shore was a maze of shoals and rocks where the Sanguenay River fed into the mainstream, and then came a labyrinth of islets, reefs, shoals and bars, all tricked out with tides, eccentric currents, eddies and stretches of rapids which had to be carefully bypassed. Two-thirds of the way to Quebec from Bic came the Ile-aux-Coudres, with a narrow channel separating it from the north shore and the broad stretch of the St Lawrence to its south. Capturing three supply ships en route, Durell learned to his consternation that Montcalm had not only been able to send an envoy to France in late 1758 to request reinforcements and new orders but that the man sent, the future Pacific explorer Louis-Antoine de Bougainville, had actually been to Versailles, received orders and made good his return though, sadly for Montcalm, without accompanying troops.[79] In a spirit of pique Durell gulled a number of French river pilots, enticing them aboard by flying false (French) colours.

At the Ile-aux-Coudres Durell landed some troops but found it unoccupied. Emboldened by this, he sent his ships even farther south-west towards Quebec, as far as the Ile d'Orléans, also close to the north shore, overlooked by the high, forested Cap Tourmente where Montcalm had wanted to site a battery. The captured French pilots were pressed into service and given to understand that any navigational errors arising from their advice would be regarded as sabotage and punished accordingly. The passage from the Ile-aux-Coudres to the Ile d'Orléans was also supremely perilous, being a maze of islets.[80] Thinking a landing on the Ile d'Orléans, which was within sight of Beauport and the Montmorency river would surely be contested, Durell sent as escorts for his troop transports four men-o'-war including the *Pembroke* and *Squirrel*. When this island also turned out to be deserted, the French having pulled back to their defensive inner perimeter in the environs of Quebec, Durell ordered the advance party into a stretch of water known as the Traverse. Whereas hitherto there had been narrow passages between the major islands and the north shore but a broad span of the St Lawrence to the south, at the Ile d'Orléans the river narrowed alarmingly into the south channel at the foot of the island. Even to reach the south channel from Cap Tourmente, one had to make a diagonal crossing over the Traverse, notoriously treacherous and difficult to navigate, full of shifting tides and unpredictable currents.[81] The French had never brought large vessels this far up the river, and no adequate charts existed; local pilots knew the way through with the aid of buoys and markers but, in the one sensible defensive measure Montcalm had been able to implement, these had all been removed. All of Cook's skill and expertise gained on the North Sea coast were now required. On 8 June he and the other three masters commenced a *via dolorosa* by water, proceeding with agonising slowness, sounding and marking the passage. For two days the wearisome chore continued, but Cook and his colleagues were so successful that they found not just the old route used by the French pilots but a secondary one as well. They then withdrew to inform Durell; Cook in his usual laconic matter recorded a great triumph in his log in his customary throwaway style.[82]

Once Cook and his fellow masters had made straight the ways, the task of Durell and Saunders was relatively straightforward. Wolfe, Saunders and the main fleet left Louisbourg on 4 June and made slow but steady progress up the Gulf of St Lawrence and into the estuary. The Navy's lead division passed through the Traverse safely on 25 June, with the ship's boats acting as buoys.[83] To Montcalm's consternation the British had penetrated his first line of defence as if they were swatting away a fly. Naturally, as always, success has a hundred parents, and the heroic efforts of Cook and his comrades were soon being depreciated. The master of the transport ship *Goodwill* boasted that he had not needed Cook's reconnaisance or the boats acting as markers and declared: 'Damn me if there are not a thousand places in the Thames more hazardous than this.'[84] By the 27th all the ships were safely through, and the whole fleet anchored in the Quebec basin between the tip of the Ile d'Orléans and Point Levis. But the odds turned suddenly in favour of the apprehensive French the following day, for a terrible storm destroyed many of the boats and drove many of the transports ashore. Taking advantage of the confusion, Montcalm launched his fireships against the enemy fleet, but the French ignited them prematurely, allowing the British to evade them or tow them clear.[85] Wolfe then seized the initiative. His troops captured Pointe-Lévy on 29 June, and landed east of the Montmorency Falls on 9 July. He then commenced the first of his many controversial acts of brutality during the siege by the remorseless shelling of Quebec, regardless of the presence of civilians. What Cook really thought of Wolfe we will never know, but doubtless their mutual friend Samuel Holland encouraged a positive opinion. Holland was by this time so deeply in Wolfe's counsels that the general took him as his aide on a reconnaissance of the south bank of the St Lawrence.[86]

Cook and the *Pembroke* spent most of July inactive; the ship was anchored off Point Levis. But suddenly, on the night of 18 July, there was a brief upsurge of naval fighting. The trigger was Wolfe's habitual impatience with the Navy. Like Napoleon later, Wolfe knew nothing whatever about seas, rivers and seamanship. Almost criminally ignorant of the problems of pushing upriver beyond Quebec – principally that strong ebb tides ran for eight hours a day and that there was a contrary wind from the west – he attributed all delays by the fleet to timidity, defeatism or incompetence. Finally the Navy achieved the near-impossible and thus made Wolfe's ultimate success possible – but then predictably were written out of the victory script. The French had long been convinced that it was impossible for large ships to pass through the narrows under Quebec's guns and into the upper St Lawrence, but on the evening of the 18th the frigate *Diana*, with six other vessels, made the attempt. While her comrades got through, the *Diana* ran aground and the *Richmond* was sent to her aid. As often happens, a small engagement soon escalated into a larger one and the *Richmond* in turn was in trouble, under attack from French cutters. The much more formidable *Pembroke* made short work of these intruders with her big guns.[87] Meanwhile Wolfe was getting nowhere with his multi-point probing skirmishing and shelling. At the end of the month he shifted his attention from the upper river and decided on an attack on the French position at Beauport near the Montmorency Falls. Cook in person advised Wolfe that the two redoubts on the extreme right of the Beauport shore could be seized, since a 'cat' could get close enough to provide covering fire of a withering type.[88] Two of them were to be run aground at high tide with commandos, a hundred yards from the first redoubt; the disembarked troops would then capture the first objective. Once again 'mission creep' manifested itself. The initial commando attack failed, then more and more troops were committed to the assault. Even so, the assault was a disastrous failure: the British sustained 440 casualties against sixty French dead and wounded. There were several blunders, which enabled the various players to blame-shift with gusto after the event. Cook's calculations were far too optimistic, and the cats grounded too far out, so that the firepower covering the landing was inadequate. On the other hand Wolfe changed his plans and landed at low water, far too close to the French entrenchments.[89]

The *Pembroke*, after its dramatic nocturnal excursion on 18–19 July, continued to ride at anchor at Port Levis and would remain there until 19 September. But its master was out and about on various energetic pursuits and on one of these came close to capture. He was out on the river near the Ile d'Orléans when a party of Montcalm's Indians (tribe unmentioned) tried to cut him off from the shore. He made the shore just ahead of his pursuers, who were then driven off by Wolfe's men on the island.[90] Yet if Cook had had a narrow escape, Wolfe's fortunes were even sunnier. For a while it looked as though 1759 was going to be ultimately as unsuccessful as 1758. Although Montcalm and his men were short of food, if they could just hold out until the end of September, ice and the threat of being trapped in Canada for the winter would force Wolfe's mighty armada to set its sails for home. Wolfe's chances seemed very slender, even though he was buoyed up in the days immediately after the Beauport/Montmorency disaster by the welcome news that Amherst had scored a series of victories: at Ticonderoga, Crown Point and Niagara.[91] With the Iroquois now decisively on the British side, the battle for the interior seemed won; only Quebec and Montreal continued defiant. Yet Wolfe left his decisive move until the last possible moment. During August he seemed to have no master idea except the brutal scorched-earth devastation he practised in the environs of Quebec. Suddenly, however, he pulled his masterstroke of landing on the north shore in darkness at the Anse au Foulon, clambering up by a secret path to the Heights of Abraham and then defeating Montcalm outside Quebec (12–13 September). The death of both commanders in battle seemed to place them for a while beyond criticism. Whether the landing at Anse au Foulon really was Wolfe's own idea, as he claimed (Samuel Holland backed him up, though this is what one expects from a friend) or whether the track leading up to the Heights of Abraham was really divulged to him by Robert Stobo, is a matter that lies outside the purview of a biography of James Cook.[92]

Cook was involved in this decisive denouement in two ways. The attack via the Anse au Foulon required very precise knowledge of the onset of the ebb current on the night of 12–13 September and the position of the moon. Since Cook was the man who probably knew more about the St Lawrence tidal patterns than anyone else in the fleet, we can be reasonably certain that Wolfe consulted him.[93] Moreover, Cook was involved in the elaborate feint carried out that night at Beauport, scene of Wolfe's previous failure, when the British attempted to convince the French that their commander was coming back for a second attempt. On the 11th Admiral Saunders ordered his men to place buoys off Beauport, pretending to mark obstacles for the assault craft to avoid. On the 12th he surpassed this with a very ostentatious *coup de théâtre*. Every last rowing boat in the fleet was assembled for a showy flotilla seen to be making its way across the river to the Montmorency Falls, together with the clangorous clamour of matelots seemingly aping the methods of beaters on a tiger-shoot.[94] Montcalm took the bait and concentrated his forces at Montmorency. Only in the small hours of the morning did a signal come from Quebec to announce the 'incredible' news that Wolfe was even then debouching on to the Plains of Abraham. However, Wolfe's victory was not the blazing triumph it has sometimes been said to have been. He died before the second part of his plan could be implented, which involved trapping Montcalm's remaining troops at Montmorency; these escaped to fight another day. Yet Wolfe in his death won immortal fame and in this prefigured by twenty years the fate of the master of the *Pembroke* who had so valuably advised him.

Quebec did not surrender immediately. Indeed, once again the Navy can be seen as the key actor for it was only when Admiral Saunders brought his best seven battleships into the Basin and prepared to blow the lower town apart with devastating broadsides that the city's commandant, Chevalier de Ramezay, decided he had had enough.[95] The perfectly natural joy Cook felt at the fall of Quebec may have been tempered by sentimental regret when, five days later, at Saunders's command, he was transferred as master to the

Northumberland, a 70-gun man-o'-war with a crew of 500.[96] Although the new ship's captain was Alexander Lord Colville, a second appointment as captain was made in the shape of one William Adams, another shadowy figure in the Cook biography.[97] It has been speculated that Saunders intended to have Colville promoted to commodore and that he was therefore 'phasing in' a new commander. Although he had a new ship, in many ways Cook had to languish as before, for once again he was to spend a long winter in Halifax, essentially five more months of boredom, study and punishing refractory sailors; at least conditions in Nova Scotia were better than those faced by the luckless British garrison in Quebec. Saunders, with most of the fleet, returned to England, where he later noted Cook's outstanding charts and drew them to the attention of the Admiralty.[98] Left behind in Halifax were five ships of the line, three frigates and some sloops. Though he did not know it, Cook had seen the last of battles with a European enemy. Although there would be shots fired in anger in the future, never again would the *Northumberland*'s talented master have to face a broadside from the big guns of France, the ancient foe of England. From now on the real enemy would always be the cruel, implacable ocean.

CHAPTER THREE

Charting Newfoundland

A FTER the high drama of 1759, Cook's life entered a limbo. His career from 1760 to 1762 was one of tedium and inactivity. He continued his surveying and navigational studies, but it cannot have been the same without the two comrades who had made the winter of 1758–59 so enjoyable. Simcoe was dead and Holland was elsewhere. Reputedly one of those who attended Wolfe in his death throes on the Heights of Abraham, Holland remained in Quebec working as a military engineer while Cook was stationed at Halifax. In April 1760 Holland was promoted to chief engineer and then spent two years surveying parts of upper Canada before being sent back to England with his reports and surveys.[1] Cook was not back in the environs of Quebec until June 1760. Although Commodore Colville on the *Northumberland* set out two weeks earlier than Durell the year before (on 22 April) he fared even worse with the elements. Stuck fast in the ice just two days out of Halifax, he was still battling with fields of ice on 12 May.[2] He and his fleet arrived just in time to save the Quebec garrison from humiliation. Brigadier James Murray, who assumed the command on Wolfe's death, foolishly allowed himself to be tempted into battle by the Chevalier de Lévis, the new French commander in Canada. Some claim that the second battle of Quebec was more significant than the first, and even, therefore, that 1760 was a more significant year than 1759.[3] Murray lost badly, had to retreat and then found himself besieged by Lévis in Quebec. The approach of Colville's armada forced Lévis to withdraw and soon he was under pressure from Amherst, who planned a three-pronged attack to finish off the colony of New France. He himself would lead 12,000 men from Albany to Oswego, then down the St Lawrence to Montreal; a second army under General Haviland would advance along the Champlain corridor from Crown Point; finally Murray, reinforced by Colville, would ascend the St Lawrence by ship. Short of food, men and materiel, with no hope of reinforcement from France and abandoned by their Indian allies, the French were in an impossible position. It did not take Vaudreuil long to persuade

Lévis that resistance was hopeless. Montreal surrendered in September. The long war in North America was over.[4]

There was another change of captain on the *Northumberland* in September, when Adams was transferred to the *Diana* and Nathaniel Bateman was appointed in his stead. Whereas there had been no significant relationship with Adams, with Bateman Cook achieved close rapport and would later name an Australian landmark after him.[5] Three weeks after the changeover, on 10 October, the *Northumberland* weighed anchor and returned to Halifax (reached a fortnight later) for the winter. Thereafter the ship left her moorings only once before August 1762 when she was careened and overhauled. Cook's log is a tedious narrative of punishments and floggings for minor infractions of discipline, usually being absent without official leave. But Saunders's high praise for the St Lawrence survey back in London must have been noticed, for in January 1761 he was awarded an *ex gratia* payment of £50 for his surveying work, over and above his usual master's salary of six guineas a month.[6] By this time Cook and all those who longed for action must have been chafing at the news from around the globe. Although France's role in the Seven Years War after 1759 was almost entirely European, Spain entered the war in 1761 and there was great British naval derring-do at Havana and Manila in the Philippines. Cook and Colville meanwhile had to attend to routine matters such as scurvy among the sailors. The commodore lobbied the Admiralty for better victuals, but the evidence on naval health in Halifax is puzzling, as the diet seems to have been better than average in the Royal Navy.[7] Perplexed by this, Cook began his eccentric investigations into scurvy, which would lead him to the ultimate bizarre conclusion that warm clothing was the key. Yet mainly in these two years he worked on a meticulous survey of the coast of Nova Scotia, providing minute detail on landmarks such as Cape Sambro, Chebucto Bay, Bell Rock, Easteron Banks, Point Sandwich, Cornwallis Island and George's Island as well as a virtual inch-by-inch description of Halifax harbour itself.[8]

After nearly two years of inactivity, dramatic news came in of developments in Newfoundland – an island with which Cook's fate would be inextricably linked for the next half-dozen years. Although France had surrendered all its possessions on the eastern American mainland, the country wanted to retain its fishing rights on the Grand Banks, south-east of Newfoundland. The French Foreign Minister, the Duc de Choiseul, declared that the Newfoundland fisheries were more valuable to France than either Canada or Louisiana, and with this in mind sent four warships under Admiral de Ternay to seize St John's (on board one of the ships was the future French explorer of the Pacific, La Pérouse). Choiseul's aim was to retain St John's as a bargaining counter at the peace talks due to open shortly in Paris; meanwhile French troops could devastate the British fisheries as revenge for France's likely expulsion from the lucrative fishing grounds on the Grand Banks.[9] Ternay avoided the Royal Navy blockade at Brest, landed 600 troops and captured St John's without difficulty on 27 June. HMS *Syren*, captain Charles Douglas, heard of the attack and alerted the Navy. Lord Colville at Halifax sent word to Amherst, who decided that all available forces for a counter-offensive should rendezvous at Placentia, on the western coast of the Avalon peninsula in Newfoundland. He chose this rendezvous as it was the destination of Captain Thomas Graves, the new governor of Newfoundland, known to be on HMS *Antelope* accompanying a British fishing fleet across the Atlantic. The *Northumberland* with Colville and Cook, and the *Gosport*, captain Jervis, set out from Halifax for Nova Scotia on 10 August 1762 and passed St Pierre and Miquelon before putting in at Placentia three days later.[10] Here they were joined by Graves and the *Antelope* and Douglas in the *Syren*. Leaving instructions for all troops and transports to follow with all speed, Colville and Graves left Placentia on the 22nd and sailed down the west coast of the Avalon peninsula, heading for St John's on the east coast. They cruised off St John's for two weeks, based at Bay Bulls, hoping to scare off or intercept any French reinforcements being sent to Ternay.[11] Here, on 12 September, Amherst's brother William arrived from Massachusetts in the *King George,* along with transports bearing 1,300 troops. When the troops began landing the following day at Tor Bay, nine miles north of St John's, Ternay realised the game was up, and re-embarked with his four ships, leaving the troops to shift for themselves. Evading the blockaders in a thick fog, they made good their escape; a gale made pursuit impossible. Ternay's luck continued to hold: he could not re-enter Brest because of the blockade but came safely to anchor in the allied port of La Coruna in Spain. Colville, who had fancied himself receiving the French admiral's sword in surrender, was indignant at the 'shameful flight' but was left to fume while the army commander Joseph Louis Bernard de Cléren d'Haussonville accepted William Amherst's terms on 19 September.[12]

The *Northumberland* entered St John's in triumph and here on the 20th Cook was able to greet an old friend. Captain Palliser had been sent from England with a squadron to help deal with the French incursion and now arrived, just too late for the action.[13] It cannot have harmed Cook's career that no fewer than three of his admirers – Colville, Graves and Palliser – sat in conclave in Newfoundland. Perhaps it was their combined patronage that opened the door to fresh surveying opportunities. Already in Placentia he had surveyed the harbour and drawn another of his impressive charts. Now in St John's he was given an extra fillip, for he was ordered to cooperate with the

Army's resident surveying maven. With Amherst's force, there arrived another European-born surveyor of genius, in some ways a second Samuel Holland, though older and more crossgrained. J. F. W. DesBarres was a 41-year-old military engineer who had been born in Switzerland and then trained at the Royal Military Academy in Woolwich.[14] A remarkable individual who would live to 102 and later become lieutenant-governor of Cape Breton Island and later still governor of Prince Edward Island, DesBarres had personality defects that made his army career a slow, halting affair; he did not reach the rank of full colonel until the age of 77. He was one of those unfortunate men, intemperate and impetuous, who get people's back up and, having crossed very many senior officers, he was still only a lieutenant. Obviously a difficult character, who always knew best, saw things in black and white, had strong opinions and always had to have things done his way, DesBarres made a tiresome colleague.[15] Cook was used to the easy charm and affability of Holland and must have found his enforced collaboration with DesBarres difficult at first. Two things mitigated Cook's plight. Cook, whatever his thoughts and emotions, was outwardly a very self-effacing man, the model of professional objectivity. And, despite his failings, DesBarres had real talent as an engineer and surveyor. Experts differ as to whether Holland or Desbarres was the greater surveyor, but both had rare skills which enabled Cook to hone his own abilities. Together they worked on a masterly survey of Carbonera Island and Harbour Grace, important fishery settlements.[16] Cook discovered that deep-draught ships could safely enter and lie at anchor in both places. Colville was deeply impressed and drew the Admiralty's attention to Cook's research.[17]

On 7 October the *Northumberland* sailed for home. This time the Atlantic was merciful, the winds were favourable and the ship reached Spithead in nineteen days. Colville was promoted to rear admiral of the *White*. With little more to do in the western hemisphere now that Canada was totally pacified and Havana had fallen, the expectation was that the *Northumberland* would once more be deployed on the blockade of Brest, Lorient and Rochefort. Suddenly, on 3 December came news that a truce had been agreed and that hostilities were at an end, pending the signing of a definitive treaty. In any case Cook had already been transferred from the *Northumberland*. He made his last entry in the ship's log on 11 November, recording squally weather; he was not to know that this was his last time in a front-line man-o'-war.[18] He then drew his pay of £291 19s. 3d. (about £25,000 in today's money), which in terms of wages and salaries in the eighteenth century made him a rich man in consumer terms, if not in accumulated capital.[19] It was presumably already in the collective mind of the Admiralty that this man's special gifts should be harnessed, and that he should be employed henceforth as a surveyor rather than a journeyman master.

If there was any doubts about this, the expansive missive sent to the Admiralty secretary at the end of the year by the newly promoted Rear Admiral Colville must have settled them. One sentence was especially striking: 'On this occasion, I beg leave to inform their Lordships, that from my experience of Mr Cook's genius and capacity, I think him well qualified for the work he has performed, and for greater undertakings of the same kind.'[20] Cook's seven-year gamble had paid off. Switching from the mercantile service to the Royal Navy now looked like an act of Solomonic wisdom. The factor which Cook's later critics had discounted was that the captains Cook worked with, and especially those of the calibre of Palliser and Colville, were the Admiralty lords of tomorrow. When the time came for an unparalleled exploit of high adventure they would have personal knowledge of Cook's talents.[21]

Once ashore Cook, with his usual decisive energy, decided to get married and did so. We cannot follow all the thoughts and emotions that led up to this step; Cook's private life is as much a blank on the biographer's map as was Hawaii on maps of the Pacific at the time. One can speculate, of course, albeit fruitlessly. Was the boredom of the long winter nights in Halifax the trigger? Or did Cook, as a conventionally minded son of the eighteenth century, simply assume that this was one of life's tasks that he should now perform, especially as he had the necessary funds to be a credible suitor? The idea of falling in love or *coup de foudre* seems alien to Cook's personality as we can perceive it. Sex never seems to have been an important factor in Cook's life, as his later behaviour in the Pacific clearly demonstrated. Indeed the obsession with surveying, navigation and exploration seems almost a textbook demonstration of the Freudian notion of sublimation. Limited as he is to the facts, the historian must simply record that within six weeks of stepping ashore from the *Northumberland,* Cook had a wife. She was the 21-year-old Elizabeth Batts, of the parish of Barking in Essex. Whether he knew her before, or for how long, must also remain a mystery.[22] An only child, she was the daughter of John Batts, a taverner and boarding-house keeper, who died when she was three, so the marriage was sober and sensible rather than spectacular. 'Respectability' seems mainly to have been guaranteed by Elizabeth's mother, Mary, whose brothers were a shipping agent and a watchmaker. Whatever the precise details of Elizabeth's background and Cook's motives for marrying her, all accounts agree that she was level-headed, commonsensical, capable, a no-nonsense character of strength and resilience.[23] On 21 December 1762, Cook and his fiancée walked together over the meadows to St Margaret's, Barking, where they were married by special licence. They then crossed the river to lodgings in Cook's parish. The idea of a honeymoon was unknown in the eighteenth century, but we do know that when Cook next sailed out Elizabeth was pregnant.[24]

In order to elucidate the next phase of Cook's life, it is necessary to divert briefly into the history of Newfoundland. There was hard bargaining by the French before they signed the relevant articles of the 1763 Treaty of Paris (ending the Seven Years War) over the status of the lucrative fisheries there. We have already seen Choiseul's concern for this outpost of France's economic empire. By the Treaty of Utrecht in 1713 the British enjoyed overall sovereignty in Newfoundland, yet France retained fishing rights on the coast between Cape Bonavista and Pointe Riche (the so-called 'French shore') but shifted the hub of its fishing industry to Louisbourg on Cape Breton.[25] Meanwhile a burgeoning British fishery, initially dominated by Devonian fishermen backed by West Country merchants, throve on the southern shore of the island from St John's to Trepassey. Just as there were two kinds of mariners, offshore and deep-sea, so fishermen divided into those specialising in inland fisheries and those who trawled in the Grand Banks. But this neat dualism soon splintered as Newfoundland society became more heterogeneous.[26] Slim pickings after 1715 led the Devonshire domination of the Banks to tail off. On the one hand, the fishing fleets increasingly brought in workers from Ireland – and this would later lead to large-scale Irish emigration to Newfoundland. By the 1750s Scots, many refugees from the disaster of the Jacobite rising of 1745, started to flood in also.[27] On the other, the boundary between bank and inland fisheries became blurred at the edges as bye-boat fishermen came to dominate the inshore catches. Non-resident, renting everything they needed, with consequent lower overheads and higher productivity, the bye-boat men also began to branch out into the Bank fishery. As if that was not enough, Americans from the mainland started to get in on the act in the late 1740s. This worried the authorities on two counts: the American immigrants were largely people escaping their debts in Massachusetts and the other colonies; and American encroachment threatened the long-term future of London's domination of Newfoundland, which it also valued as a nursery for seamen.[28] All this was taking place while the pattern of exports was itself becoming multifaceted. As the century wore on, Italy and the West Indies joined Spain and Portugal as the principal export markets for the fish; in wartime the Spanish trade was embargoed but large catches of cod were still landed by smugglers in the Iberian peninsula.[29] If to this already turbid brew is added the still important French factor, one can readily see why Newfoundland loomed large in the Admiralty's mind in the early 1760s.

When the Treaty of Paris was finalised, the French hung on in Newfoundland by their fingertips, retaining the islands of St Pierre and Miquelon and also the right to dry their catch in their traditional domains, from Point Riche to Cape Bonavista. The presence of the French, the terrible weather around Newfoundland, with its fog, ice and frequent storms and the danger of the coast itself all demanded that the Admiralty at last undertake a credible survey of the island and provide up-to-date charts for this hub of the Atlantic cod fishing industry, which was perceived as a vital part of the expanding British Empire. When Thomas Graves was reappointed governor of Newfoundland (his first tour was in 1762), he knew just the man for the work: he had not only seen Cook's St Lawrence charts but was an eyewitness to his sterling work at Placentia and St John's in 1762. For Graves it was a matter of urgency that Cook go back with him to the great cod-fishing island and undertake this important work.[30] His appointment, still with the rank of master, was to be a king's surveyor, which meant that in terms of the day-to-day running of the ship he would count as a supernumerary. He was to be paid the generous sum of 10 shillings a day – exactly what a Royal Navy captain in a fourth-rate warship received. The Admiralty was planning a grand slam in Canada. They already had DesBarres at work in Nova Scotia, Holland was earmarked for the province of Quebec (where he took up his duties in 1764), while the third member of the great surveying troika, James Cook, would be assigned to Newfoundland.[31] But it took an unconscionable time before all the necessary paperwork was completed and Cook's demands for specialised equipment were met; naturally, when money was to be voted, the delays were even longer. Apart from theodolites and drawing instruments – all expensive items – Cook wished to employ at least one draughtsman, preferably an experienced member of the Ordnance Office sited at the Tower of London. The fact that a new Admiralty secretary was appointed at this precise moment (Philip Stephens replaced John Clevland) simply compounded the delays. Graves's correspondence with his superiors became more and more testy.[32]

The dead weight of bureaucracy was finally lifted, but only after further nitpicking and changes to orders that infuriated the already exasperated Graves.[33] Graves was authorised to purchase two 60-ton vessels once in Newfoundland: one for Cook's survey and the other for anti-smuggling duties. On 19 April 1763 he was also ordered to take on board as supernumeraries Cook and a draughtsman named William Test, seconded from the Tower. For reasons that are not at all clear – one suspects he did not relish the Atlantic voyage and found excuses not to join Graves – Test did not appear at Plymouth for the embarkation and his place was taken at the last moment by another draughtsman, Edward Smart.[34] At long last Graves's ship, the *Antelope*, cleared for Newfoundland. Graves's detailed instructions informed him that the survey of Newfoundland was both to ensure safe and knowledgeable access to the St Lawrence via the Strait of Belle Isle and Anticosti Island

and to monitor French fishing activity within the permitted limits, to make sure it did not exceed those limits and that the French did not indulge in any illicit or contraband activities. In Article 9 of his instructions, which seems almost to hint at Admiralty paranoia, Graves was informed that the governor was expected to visit as many parts of the coast as he could, 'in order to check his captain's reports against his own observations'.[35] Cook and Graves had many discussions as they crossed the Atlantic. Cook told his superior that he intended to use both land-based surveys and 'running surveys' conducted from the sea, triangulating with the theodolite on land and backing this with masthead and sextant observations when afloat. Having learned so much from Holland and DesBarres, Cook approached his work like a true mathematician. He had the skill to combine the 'desk-work' of drawing and compiling charts; and he had mastered the use of instruments that would enable him to do fieldwork. The land-based theodolite observations would enable him to correct the errors arising from a purely maritime 'running survey' which were threefold: the fact that some land features seen from sea masked others that could be seen only on land; the inability to determine soundings and submarine features precisely; and the difficulty of fixing the ship's track and position with pinpoint accuracy.[36]

The *Antelope* made landfall at Cape Race on the extreme south-east of Newfoundland in early June 1763 and anchored in Trepassey harbour. Ahead of Cook loomed the prospect of charting 6,000 miles of coastline, for the Newfoundland coast is even more indented and extensive than Ireland's. Graves had the *Antelope* and five smaller vessels under his command. Cook was assigned to the 25-gun *Tweed*, captain Charles Douglas.[37] His task was to survey the islands of St Pierre and Miquelon, the islands having been returned to France according to the Treaty of Paris. The idea was that the islands could be surveyed before the official handover ceremony took place, but the French jumped the gun, so that when Cook and Douglas arrived there, they found a French ship, the *Licorne*, at anchor and a French governor, M. d'Anjac, already claiming sovereigny. Choiseul's concern for French fishing rights was evinced in the party of settlers he had already sent out to the islands to displace the uprooted Britons: 150 fishermen and traders with their families.[38] Graves sent orders that not an inch of territory should be ceded until the survey had been completed, even though his orders from the Admiralty specified a handover date not later than 10 June.[39] The indignant d'Anjac sent him a blistering letter, but Graves was well schooled in the traditional British arts of stalling and prevarication; the apoplectic Frenchman was held at bay until Cook had completed his work. The transfer of power on St Pierre finally took place on 4 July, over three weeks late, and that on Miquelon at the end of July.[40]

Once the survey was complete, Douglas landed Cook at Ferryland, a small harbour on the east coast of the Avalon peninsula, whence Cook made his way overland to St John's. Graves decided to reward Cook for his brilliant work on St Pierre and Miquelon by giving him his own ship, the 68-ton schooner *Sally*, which was promptly renamed the *Grenville*, after the new Prime Minister. For the first time ever Cook was truly the skipper on his own vessel. He took the *Grenville* on a short cruise to the extreme northern tip of Newfoundland and along the Labrador coast before doubling back to St John's at the end of September to await further orders from Graves.[41] The governor's orders were that he should go back to England in the *Tweed* for a well-earned winter's rest, as he told the Admiralty:

As Mr Cook, whose pains and attentions are beyond my description, can go no farther in surveying this year, I send him home on the *Tweed* in prefer-ence to keeping him on board, that he may have the more time to finish the different surveys already taken to be laid before their Lordships – and to copy the different sketches of the coasts and harbours taken by the ships on the several stations by which their Lordships will perceive how extremely erroneous the present drafts are, and how dangerous to ships that sail by them – and how generally beneficial to navigation the work now in hand will be when finished. Indeed I have no doubt in a year or two more of seeing a perfect good chart of Newfoundland and an exact survey of most of the good harbours in which there is not perhaps a part of the world that more abounds.[42]

Cook was already becoming, from the Admiralty's point of view, 'one to note'. Not many masters (maybe not any) had his spread of knowledge and expertise. Not only was he a superlative surveyor and chart-maker but he was an effortlessly talented seaman, for whom skippering the *Grenville* was child's play. Moreover, and what was rare in highly talented individuals, he could take direction and work as a team player. Simcoe, Palliser, Colville and Graves had all said the same thing: here was the consummate Royal Navy professional, the ultimate duty-bound navigator.

The return trip to England once more showed the North Atlantic at its most vile, and pointed up the perennial moral that in these seas a navigator's life was always on a razor's edge. The crossing took a month, and not until 29 November did the *Tweed* anchor at Spithead. From there Cook sped to London to gaze upon his first child, James, born on 13 October.[43] Now that he was a family man, he took the logical next step, which was to buy a house, and the location chosen was Mile End Old Town in Stepney. Although 7,

Assembly Row, his new address, was on the main Mile End Road – a stage-coach route to Essex – and the stench from a nearby gin distillery was undesirable, the house had a garden, access to meadows and was a highly respectable, if not yet affluent, domicile, a definite step up from the lodgings in Shadwell. Over the winter Cook worked hard on his sketches and maps of St Pierre and Miquelon. In March 1764 he wrote a warm and effusive, though not sycophantic, letter to Graves on his return from Newfoundland.[44] It had been decided that Cook's old patron Hugh Palliser was to be the next governor and commodore of the St John's flotilla. In his letter to Graves Cook referred to Palliser as 'a gentleman I have long been acquainted with' – which was perhaps a somewhat arch allusion to a man Cook had been corresponding with assiduously over the winter, ever since the transfer of command had been announced by the Admiralty. There was, for example, a long and detailed screed about existing maps of Newfoundland which Cook wrote to Palliser just eight days before the letter to Graves – for Palliser was determined to have this talent at his side when he went out as governor.[45] Cook was learning to be something of a diplomat and politician. He did not want the still influential Graves to have any feeling that his protégé might, so to speak, be transferring his flag to the rising star of Palliser. Cook wanted all his patrons to push and lobby in the same direction, not fall out among themselves or be consumed by petty jealousies that might catch him in the crossfire.

Elizabeth was pregnant with her second child when Cook sailed for Newfoundland in the *Lark*, captain Samuel Thompson, on 7 May. Cook was in generally good spirits, for Palliser had intervened with the Admiralty to ensure that Cook would not just continue as the king's surveyor on the *Grenville* but would also be her permanent master. The considerable extra administration the command would entail was, Palliser ensured his superiors, well worth the paltry three shillings a day extra they would have to pay him. The Lords of the Admiralty agreed, extra men were found for the *Grenville*, to be shipped out with Cook in the *Lark*, and his new pay scale was set. He was now, in official language, 'Master of a Sixth Rate' – which Palliser obviously intended as the wedge that would eventually secure his protégé a regular commission.[46] Cook arrived in St John's on 14 June and, immediately transferring to the schooner *Grenville*, read the Articles of War to his crew and began moving stores from the *Lark*. The rest of June was spent 'sea victualling' (with particular emphasis on bread and beef) and the routine preparations for a long summer cruise: overhauling deficient rigging, rigging masts, making fore-shrouds, caulking the ship's sides, filling up the bulkheads, repairing decks, taking in ballast and then getting the schooner hove down on both the port and starboard sides. Cook was a precisian in all these matters; his crew would doubtless have said he was a martinet. His carpenters were held firmly to their tasks of caulking decks and repairing boats and anchors while the seamen were meticulously put through their paces, with special emphasis on reefing the running rigging – the ropes and chains used to work or set the sails and yards. Finally, on 4 July, the *Grenville* weighed anchor and stood away to the north.[47]

The 1764 survey was designed to cover the Newfoundland shore of the Strait of Belle Isle from Quirpon to Point Riche. It was smooth sailing in the early days of the voyage, first north-west across the face of Notre Dame Bay, past Funk Island, to the west of Fogo Island and then off Cape St John. Soon the *Grenville* was passing areas that Cook had surveyed the year before and it was not long before Bell Island and Groais Island (the Grey Islands) were also left astern. By 11 July they were at Quirpon Island, the northern tip of the northern peninsula, and also the entrance to the Strait of Belle Isle, as barren and mountainous a locale as any in Newfoundland. Cook made his first base in Noddy Bay, an inlet on the nothernmost part of the peninsula, and began fixing his survey flags. His journal notes in great detail the multiplicity of places surveyed and the suitability of the various bays as fishing harbours. It must be emphasised that Cook was genuinely blazing a trail here, for none of this area had ever been charted or surveyed. On 23 July he made a second base of operations at Pistolet Bay and by the end of the month had painstakingly worked round to what would later be known as Cook's Harbour, all the time impeded in his operations by intermittent fog. On 4 August the *Grenville* headed towards the Strait of Belle-Isle, but, still exposed to the open Atlantic, immediately ran into the perennial hazard of sailing in Newfoundland waters: violent storms.[48] Cook and his men had a hard time of it. Always inclined to downplay the terrors of the sea, even Cook expressed surprise at the massive seas, the ferocity of the gale and the hard white squalls. Since Cook is a master of understatement, perhaps we can bring in as a witness the seaman Aaron Thomas who was caught in a storm off Newfoundland in 1794:

> The sea this day may with truth be said to run mountains high, the long tremendous swells, formed into mountains, broke over the *Boston*'s gangway, while the gunwhale on the larboard side lay under water. Some vessels of our convoy not half a mile from us buried some minutes from our sight . . . I have often wondered that artists do not exercise their talents in picturing a Captain's cabin after a gale of wind. I can only account for it by supposing that few men of abilities make long voyages at sea. Quadrants, chairs, compasses, tables, quoins, guns, tackle, port, maps, pistols, tomahawks, lanthorns, windows and quarter galleries – split, cracked, stoved, rended, dashed and broke all to pieces, would form a good subject for a humorous limner.[49]

Next day the *Grenville* found itself off the island of Belle Isle itself but as the ship recovered from its terrible battering by the storm, Cook himself sustained a bad accident. A large powder horn blew up in his right hand, shattering it horribly and wounding a bystander. As there was no surgeon on board, Cook had to return to Noddy Bay to find one, leaving his master William Parker to continue the survey; fortunately, Parker proved to be a man of great ability, who would in time become an admiral. At Noddy Bay a French surgeon tended the wound. The hand healed, but left an an unsightly gash between the thumb and forefinger and a great scar as far as the wrist which, ironically, would in later years serve as an important identifying feature. While Parker was busy surveying Griquet Bay, the restless Cook tried to convalesce and spent a good deal of time in the company of yet another of Palliser's protégés, this time a Moravian missionary named Jens Haven.[50] The Moravians were originally followers of Jan Huss, who was burned at the stake for heresy in 1415. Forming themselves into the Moravian Brethren in 1457, Huss's disciples claimed to be the first Protestants, having rebelled against Rome a good seventy years before Martin Luther. Persecuted during the Thirty Years War, the Moravians enjoyed a spectacular revival in the eighteenth century and reconstituted themselves in 1722. Gaining a foothold in England, they sent out missionaries to Africa and the Far East, but especially to the Americas, all the way from the Caribbean to the Arctic.[51] From 1750 they worked from independently administered provinces. In 1752–71 they made a determined effort to become the dominant religion in Labrador, and in this process Johann Christian Erhardt and Jens Haven were the principal figures. Erhardt overreached himself in his missionary zeal and was murdered by the Inuit in 1752, but Haven seems to have been at once more cautious and more persevering. Eventually he would receive a land grant from George III and found a settlement at Nain on the Labrador coast (1770), though without ever managing to set up a permanent station among the Inuit. At this stage he was near the beginning of his missionary endeavours, but Palliser thought the Moravians might be useful in ending the perennial warfare between Europeans and the Inuit which made southern Labrador and the Strait of Belle Isle dangerous and often hostile territory for the British.[52] Haven, aged 40 in 1764, impressed Cook with his resolution. Cook knew that he was a potentially important player in Palliser's Newfoundland schemes, for the governor had confided to him that the aboriginal peoples, both Indian and Eskimo, were actually more of a problem for him than the French, ostensibly the Number One enemy. Palliser particularly disliked the Inuits' migratory instincts, which regularly brought them down from the far north to spend the summer in Newfoundland.[53]

The *Grenville* remained in Noddy harbour until 25 August. Cook tried at once to keep the men busy and to find a remedy for scurvy by getting them to collect leaves and branches of spruce trees from which an extract was boiled down and added to ale to provide 'spruce beer'. Cook's experiments with spruce beer would lead to trouble in the future and probably did so here, for sailors objected to worthy *bien pensant* captains messing with their grog. Although no causal link is implied, the log entries about spruce beer are followed immediately afterwards by the report of a major outbreak of indiscipline. Three men were implicated: 14-year-old Peter Flower, usually a docile Cook loyalist, Henry Jefferies and Andrew Shepherd. All three were confined on deck on charges of mutiny and drunkenness while Cook investigated further. He quickly concluded that Shepherd had been the ringleader and evil genius and sentenced him to run the gauntlet, lashed to a wooden grating.[54] From 26 August Cook was fully recovered from his injury and directing operations with all his old elan. After a quick stop in Pistolet Bay, by the end of the month he was off the north-west coast of Newfoundland in the Strait of Belle Isle, surveying Green Island while contending with a heavy swell. September was boisterous, with a very heavy gale on the 11th, but Cook persevered and got as far as Ferolle Point by the end of the month. As the weather continued to deteriorate, he decided the season's work would have to be concluded. The *Grenville* rounded the northern tip of Newfoundland once more and retraced its passage past the Grey Islands and Fogo Islands, all the time beating up against a very heavy swell from the south-east. The ship came to anchor in St John's harbour on 14 October. The stress of a stormy summer's surveying was too much for some of the crew who disobeyed Cook's orders about shore leave, stole a boat and toured the fleshpots anyway. Once again there was a trio of culprits. James McKenzie, Christopher Hearon and John Young all received twelve lashes; curiously, Cook wrote 'mutiny' on the charge sheet against the first two but 'theft' against Young's name.[55]

The *Grenville* commenced the Atlantic crossing on 1 November, but there was to be no respite from 1764's constant storms, so that it was a tempest-tossed crew that gratefully glimpsed the Cornwall coast on 3 December. But the gales continued in the Channel, so that it was 9 December before they reached Dover, another three days before they put in to Woolwich and 20 December before the vessel was finally berthed at Deptford dockyard.[56] Over the winter repairs were carried out to the ship's bottom, which Cook alleged was worm-eaten and, with the permission of the Admiralty, he had the rig altered from the fore and aft of a schooner to the square rig of a brig; the more the ship was made to resemble a brig and the less a schooner, the better, in Cook's professional opinion. Palliser meanwhile wrote from Newfoundland to urge strongly that the *Grenville*'s complement should be raised to twenty, to avoid having to borrow men from other ships (which increased the propensity to desertion) and that, as an independent vessel, she should be armed with six swivel guns and twelve muskets. All this was agreed.[57] Cook's winter settled into the usual routine of domesticity with Elizabeth and the newest addition to the family – a second son, Nathaniel, born just days before Cook arrived home – alternating with writing up the Newfoundland survey. The refit and revictualling of the *Grenville* was completed by mid-April 1765, and on the 22nd he sailed from Deptford. His log enables us to track his route with meticulous accuracy: Greenwich, Woolwich, Gravesend, Nore, Margate, on the Downs (off Deal), Dungeness, Beachy Head, the Isle of Wight, Portland Bill and Plymouth. He finally cleared for the open Atlantic on 4 May, passing Lizard Point, Wolf Rock and the Scilly Islands. Cape Race was sighted on 31 May.[58]

It will already be clear that Cook's surveys always had an ulterior political, military and strategic purpose, and the point was emphasised at the start of the 1765 season when Palliser ordered him not to resume where he left off in the Strait of Belle-Isle but to proceed instead to the south coast. It seems that Palliser had two worries this year. One was apprehension of a French revival on the islands of St Pierre and Miquelon. The other was fear that the French might forge a military alliance with the powerful Micmac Indian tribe. Palliser, concerned about a possible Micmac concentration in southern-central Newfoundland, ordered the warships under his command to prevent members of the tribe from travelling by sea.[59] Cook had already alerted him to the strategic reality that Placentia Bay, Fortune Bay and the Bay d'Espoir all terminated and converged close together, so that a permanent settlement of Micmacs there could control most of the important harbours of southern Newfoundland. Palliser's policy, therefore, was twofold: to clear the Micmacs out of south and central parts of the island into the west, and to prevent any contact with the French. In contrast to his predecessor – for Graves was mainly concerned with illegal *trade* between the Micmacs at Codroy and the French on the islands – Palliser fretted about the security situation and conjured a scenario whereby a French–Indian alliance on Newfoundland might replicate the situation on the Canadian mainland during the Seven Years War.[60] In fact his fears were chimerical. The French authorities themselves did not want the Micmacs to visit their islands and Choiseul had expressly ordered the governor of St Pierre and Miquelon not to permit this.[61] Yet whatever the unreality of Palliser's imaginings, they were the reason why Cook did not resume his survey at Ferolle Point.

On 2 June Cook anchored in Great St Lawrence harbour on the south coast of the Burin peninsula and immediately began his survey. His crew was a happier one than the year before, possibly because of the full complement Palliser had obtained and possibly because they knew it was idle to test Cook's resolve after the punishments he had meted out in 1764. It was not insignificant, either, that the most notorious troublemakers no longer shipped with him and that four of the 1764 crew were returnees (not counting Cook and Parker and excluding the reformed character Peter Flower). This time around Cook used four local pilots, one for the Great St Lawrence area, one for Connaigre and Hermitage bays, one for the Bay d'Espoir and one for Fortune Bay. The survey proceeded rapidly as the Burin peninsula was about one mile long and there was no time to waste. By 16 June the Great St Lawrence area had been charted, so the *Grenville* moved west along the coast, adding Lawn Bay and Lawn Island to the growing inventory of detailed maps and drawings. By 5 July the vessel was rounding the southern tip of the Burin peninsula, with the French islands of St Pierre and Miquelon (first visited by Cook in 1763) about twelve miles to the west. On 10 July the *Grenville* was off Grand Bank Head, and two days later, at Garnish, Cook took on board two starving and emaciated Britons who had been lost in the wilderness for a month after trying to get from Burin to St Lawrence. Calamity nearly overtook Cook himself a week later when the ship ran ashore on a rock while turning into Fortune Bay. It was found necessary to shear her up with her own yards and lighten her of water and ballast before floating her off on a midnight tide. The rest of July was spent in a thorough survey of Fortune Bay and Belle Bay. By 17 August Cook had worked systematically round to Harbour Breton, which he used as a base for exploring the narrow inlets of the Bay d'Espoir. Hermitage Bay, reached on 11 September, marked his farthest west that year.[62]

On 10 October Cook turned for home and four days later was again passing St Pierre and Miquelon. The weather had been relatively kind to him this year, but two days out from St John's the Atlantic reminded him of its true nature with a two-day storm; even Cook noted the 'hard gales and excessive squalls'. Since Palliser and the squadron were to accompany him back to England this time, Cook was forced to tarry two weeks in St John's, and the delay could have cost him dear by pitching him into the most dangerous Atlantic storms. The very worst was avoided, but the flotilla had a hard time of the crossing, as the dates suggest: the squadron left for home on 5 November but the *Grenville* was not moored in Deptford until 17 December. As so often, the Channel proved troublesome, for England was first sighted on 28 November; additionally, Cook put in to Portsmouth to make a report.[63] He had reason to feel pleased with the year's work. The worst of the giant waves and dense fog banks of Newfoundland had not assailed them, and they had made spectacular progress given the difficulty of the terrain. The coastline he had charted could almost have been devised by a demented demiurge, for it was a twisting mass of bays, inlets, harbours, capes, headlands, islands, shoals and rocks; it was certainly wise of Cook to use local pilotage. On the other hand, the very anfractuous nature of the coast had enabled Cook to spend a large portion of the time out of the *Grenville*, either on shore or in the cutter. There had been no disciplinary problems and Cook was especially pleased with the work of his carpenters and his devoted mate William Parker. Palliser, as usual, was delighted with his protégé's work – so delighted in fact that he wrote to the Admiralty suggesting that Cook be allowed to publish maps of Newfoundland under his own name. Cook and Palliser were very much in favour with their Lordships, who readily agreed to the proposal.[64]

Since Palliser had stressed that Cook's surveys of the Burin peninsula, Fortune Bay and the Bay d'Espoir had been of inestimable value in the promotion of the Newfoundland fisheries, the Admiralty lords also found no difficulty in granting Cook his miscellaneous requests, such as the demand for a tent in which he could shelter at night and in bad weather; for he now tended to spend long stretches of time ashore, in the cutter or otherwise away from his ship.[65] The winter passed in the usual alternating pattern of hydrography and domesticity and on 20 April 1766 the *Grenville* left Deptford, was on the Downs on the 28th and off Beachy Head on the 30th. On 29 May the lookout sighted Cape Race through a screen of icebergs, and on 1 June Cook anchored in Bonne Bay (Kilback Cove), an inlet on Newfoundland's south coast, ready to begin where he had left off the previous autumn. A week later he had worked his way west as far as Richards Harbour, once again usually absent from the *Grenville* while Parker managed the ship. Morale was by now high on board the vessel, as evinced by the nine returnees from 1765 among the crew of twenty. Cook had made the point that he would brook no nonsense and would flog and punish as necessary, but he was both fair and predictable, and the men respected him for it. By 2 July he was at the mouth of the Grey river and spent much of the month exploring the Ramea islands, about twelve miles south-east of Burgeo.[66] Buffeted by very strong gales and squalls, Cook anchored on the west side of Bear Island near the entrance to Bear Bay and made an inland journey. On 24 July, after manoeuvring in thick fog, he made his base at Grundy's Cove, where the modern town of Burgeo stands. For two weeks he continued his surveying in a fuliginous atmosphere of almost continual fog but then, on 5 August, the mists suddenly cleared, allowing him to make a detailed observation of a solar eclipse (on the appropriately named Eclipse Island, one of the tiny Burgeo islands).[67] This was not the rare total eclipse of the sun but the more common 'annular' eclipse when the sun and moon are exactly in line but the apparent size of the moon is smaller than the sun; since the sun appears as a very bright ring or annulus surrounding the outline of the moon, the annular is second in the hierarchy of eclipses, behind the total variety but ahead of the 'partial' type when the sun and moon are not exactly in line. Using a variety of instruments, including a brass telescopic quadrant, Cook used the eclipse to fix his longitude exactly by comparing his readings with another set taken at Oxford. It was this exploit that brought him to the attention of the Royal Society, which published his findings in its *Philosophical Transactions* of 1767.[68]

The solar eclipse was the high point of the 1766 survey, but Cook did not allow himself to become complacent because of this one achievement. Slowly but surely he worked his way west. The 16th of August found him off Grand Brut, the base for another fortnight of meticulous reconnaissance. By 10 September he reached his farthest west at Port aux Basques, after which he worked his way north-west to Cape Ray and the Codroy complex of river, roadstead and island before finishing the season at Cape Anguille on the south-western side of the island. Now it was time to return to St John's but first he had to spend a fortnight in La Poile Bay, which he had bypassed in his eagerness to press ever west, and which he now reconnoitred thoroughly. After spending the middle two weeks of October there, taking on wood and water in the teeth of snow, frost, sleet, gales and hard squalls, Cook made the four-day run to Cape St Mary's and three days later anchored in the narrows of St John's harbour.[69] After conferring with Palliser, Cook cleared for England on 5 November and, with almost continual westerlies, sighted England a fortnight later. He was at Deptford on 30 November, having once again obtained the Admiralty's permission to berth his vessel there 'for greater safety'.[70] Once again family life alternated with chart-making, and for the third time Cook had the pleasure of seeing the first credible map of yet another part of the Newfoundland coast published. Vaulting ambition was obviously now an element in the Cook psyche, for he took it upon himself to communicate with the physician Dr John Bevis, an influential member of the Royal Society with astronomical interests. Bevis in turn contacted an even more talented astronomer and mathematician named George Witchell, who immediately saw the value of Cook's findings, more especially as they chimed with observations of the eclipse taken at Oxford and London. Having mastered the art of triangulation in surveying, Cook was thus able to 'triangulate' his own astronomical findings. More to the point, he had demonstrated to a wider audience that he was not just a brilliant navigator and cartographer but now had impressive credentials in astronomy.[71]

Cook was not present when his paper on the eclipse was finally read to the Royal Society, for the *Grenville* left Deptford on its annual pilgrimage to the wild waters of Newfoundland on 20 April. Once again there were changes, to the ships's rigging and decks, to the personnnel (this time there were just five returnees in a crew of nineteen), and to the equipment. In 1766 Cook had requested a tent but this time, in line with his widening ambitions, he petitioned for a reflecting telescope which would enable him, he alleged, to fix the longitudes of the 300-mile wide Newfoundland with more precision. It is indicative of Cook's rising status at the Admiralty that this was granted him without demur.[72] Another change was, however, far less welcome. Cook's *fidus Achates*, William Parker, finally got his just reward by being promoted to lieutenant and assigned command of the *Niger*. His replacement was Michael Lane, another joint protégé of Graves and Palliser, a young man of talent and marked mathematical ability and an alumnus of the new mathematical school of navigation at Christ's Hospital founded in 1763. Palliser had nurtured him as a possible future master surveyor and now produced him as the solution to the *Grenville*'s problem, to the great satisfaction of Cook himself.[73] Yet the 1767 voyage seemed at first ill-starred. The *Grenville*, still moored with the hawser, was in collision with a Sunderland collier, *The Three Sisters*, which smashed into the Royal Navy vessel in the Thames and carried away its bowsprit cap and jib boom. The symbolism seemed almost too neat: Cook's past in the Tyneside coal trade catching up with his present triumphant rise in the Navy. Even more suspicious is the alleged circumstance whereby an angry Cook was on the point of tearing into the master of the collier only to discover that the man was an old chum from the Ayton days. The best authorities dismiss this circumstantial detail as no more than a good story.[74]

Sober history must be content to recall that the *Grenville* did finally stand away on 8 April and was off Lizard Point on the 16th. The crossing occupied 17 April–8 May. Since this was two weeks earlier than in previous seasons, the voyagers encountered many more icebergs on the approach to Newfoundland; the Labrador current brought down a plethora from the icy wastes of Greenland, Baffin Island and the Davis Strait. The seas were rough, and the *Grenville* experienced great difficulty rounding the French islands of Miquelon and St Pierre. Cook arrived off Cape Ray on 14 May and a day later was at his 1766 finishing point at Cape Anguille.[75] In 1764 he had come down the Strait of Belle-Isle as far as Ferolle Point and it was now his task to complete the survey of the west coast by joining up the farthest south of 1764 (Ferolle Point) with the farthest north of 1766 (Cape Anguille). In some ways too this was the easiest part of the survey so far, since the south-west and western parts of the island were the best known; Basque fishermen from northern Spain and southern France had been visiting them for more than a century. Beginning his survey with gusto, Cook soon pushed into St George's Bay, where he found a large colony of Micmacs, Palliser's bugbear, looking for new fisheries. The Micmacs were evidently none too pleased at this incursion by their old enemies the British and reminded Cook querulously how they had been expelled by his political masters from their original hunting grounds in Nova Scotia and Cape Breton purely because they were Catholic and pro-French.[76] Cook brushed aside their lamentations and continued with his hydrography. Soon he was as far advanced as Cape St George and the Port au Port peninsula. Even though fog interrupted the survey, by hard driving on 20 June he got as far as the Bay of Islands on the 21st – a large inlet on the west coast of Newfoundland with several islands at its mouth. Inside the bay was a cove called York harbour where Cook anchored. His initial survey completed, on 24 June Cook cleared for points north but was soon driven back into the Bay of Islands by a ferocious gale. Making a virtue of necessity, he completed a more thorough survey of its inlet and rivers.[77]

Not until 9 July did conditions allow Cook to start exploring north of the Bay of Islands. A day later he was at Bonne Bay and completed the survey of the bay and its environs in five days. Moving with great speed and unprecedented energy, he was at Cow Head on 25 July and just south of Pointe Riche three days later. Feeling more relaxed now that he was within reach of his target, Cook made an exhaustive reconnaissance of Keppel Island and Hawke's Bay to the south of it. On 19 August he was at St John Bay, just south of Ferolle Point. Having reached his farthest south in 1764 and sounded the coast between Pointe Riche and Point Ferolle, Cook even allowed himself the luxury of a cruise to the other side of Belle-Isle Strait where he surveyed the mountains just inside present-day Quebec province, near the Labrador border. Even by his own exacting standards the 1767 survey had been an outstanding triumph. After returning to the Bay of Islands for some dotting of 'i's and crossing of 't's on his already exhaustive charts, Cook cleared for Cape Anguille but was once again forced back into the bay by hard gales. Even when he did get to sea, it took him a week in mountainous seas to achieve the relatively short run to the cape. Another ten days took him to St John's where, after a nine-day layover for refurbishment, it was once again time for the Atlantic crossing.[78] This time the sea flattered to deceive. The voyage across the ocean was remarkably speedy and the Isle of Wight was sighted on 8 November. Confident of an uneventful sail to the Thames, Cook took on the pilot at Deal, but this seemed to be the signal for the elements to punish him for his complacency. A tremendous storm struck the ship and the *Grenville* ran aground off the Nore lighthouse. Because of the severity of the gale, the crew was taken off by cutter. Two days later, when the storm had blown itself out, it proved possible to float the vessel off in high water. The ship was anchored at Sheerness until a competent river pilot was found to guide her to the usual berth at Deptford.[79]

There was more excitement in the Cook household, for in his absence Elizabeth had given birth to Cook's first daughter, also called Elizabeth. As always, details of Cook's private life and emotions are exiguous, not to say non-existent. In the usual sketchy way we can trace his public career in the winter of 1767–68, for this was once again the old routine of producing charts for publication (his fourth) and petitioning the Admiralty for further resources. He had lost a man to disease in Port au Port, and this rankled with him; the next time he shipped out he wanted a competent surgeon on board. Once again the Admiralty granted his request.[80] Meanwhile Palliser hired him in a private capacity to do technical drawings and blueprints of his landed estates.[81] But most of Cook's energy went on the preparation of his fifth chart for publication. There were now four superb surveys of the Newfoundland coast available to interested parties: the first, a chart of the Straits of Belle-Isle with the adjacent coasts of Newfoundland and Labrador; the second, the islands of Miquelon and St Pierre and part of the south coast of Newfoundland; the third, a larger study of the southern coast but incorporating some of the detail in the second chart; and fourth, a superb distillation of all that Cook had explored and measured on the west coast in 1767.[82] Arranged on a scale of one inch to a mile, they were state-of-the-art works, complete with sailing directions and elaborate symbols denoting soundings, rocks, harbours, high- and low-water marks and a wealth of other details necessary for navigation and fishery. Yet the Admiralty's attitude to these masterworks was astonishingly cavalier. Although they placed no obstacle in the way of Cook's publishing the data, essentially they lost interest in his work once it had been completed. Having borne the considerable expenses of an annual survey of Newfoundland, they put the results 'in a cupboard'[83] and forgot about them. This was the English cult of the amateur at its apogee. The Admiralty did not even have a hydrographic department until 1795, in contrast to the French Ministry of Marine which had had one since 1720.[84] Although he did not yet know it, Cook's work in Newfoundland was over. His achievement was enormous, though overshadowed by his later Pacific career. But for the fame he acquired in the South Seas, Cook would surely be known as a key personality in the early history of Canada. It should be remembered that the years 1763–75 saw the British fishery in Newfoundland at its height, with a volume catch that never fell below 500,000 quintals a year and in two of those years exceeded 700,000 quintals.[85] By the late 1760s 20,–30,000 men were engaged in the Newfoundland fishery. Cook's work coincided with the best ever years and he deserves to be remembered as a key enabler in this process. When he came to Newfoundland in 1762 most of the island was known only in vague outline. After five years of his surveys it was as well mapped as parts of England, and all the harbours suitable for fishermen were intimately known.[86] Even without the Pacific, Cook would have been a great historical figure.

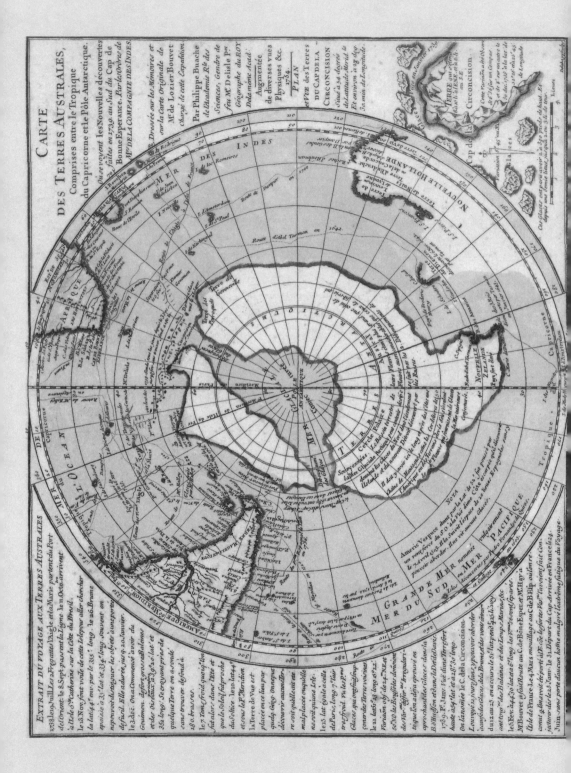

CARTE
DES TERRES AUSTRALES,
Comprises entre le Tropique
du Capricorne et le Pôle Antarctique.

où se voyent les Nouvelles découvertes
faites en 1739. au Sud du Cap de
Bonne Esperance. Par l'ordre de
Mr. DE LA COMPAGNIE DES INDES.

Dressée sur les Mémoires et
sur la Carte Originale de
Mr. de Lozier Bouvet
Chargé de cette Expédition.

Par Philippe Buache
de l'Académie R^{le} des
Sciences, Gendre de
feu Mr. Delisle P^r
Géographe du ROY
De la même Acad.

Augmenté
de diverses vues
Physiques &c.
1754.

PLAN
de Vue des Terres
DU CAP DE LA
CIRCONCISION

Situé à 54. degré
de latitude Merid. le
Et environ à 27. deg.
3a min. de Longitude.

TERRE qui a été
découverte le 1er IENS. et à la
SE.

Cap de la Circoncision.

EXTRAIT DU VOYAGE AUX TERRES AUSTRALES
1738. les 19 Juill. Les 2 Fregates l'Aigle et la Marie partent du Port
de l'Orient. le 8 Sept. passent la Ligne. le 11 Octo. arrivant
à l'Isle Ste Catherine sur la Côte du Bresil.
le 18. Nov. font voile de cette Isle pour aller chercher
la latit. d'env. par le 35.° long. le 26. Brume
épaisse à 35.° lat. et 33.4° long. trouvent en
ne pouvoit attaquer les objets il ne pouvoit
aborder. Elle a duré, jusq. 20 Janvier.
le 3 déc. On a Commencé à voir du
Goudmon, défaire grosses Baleines
et des Oiseaux à 43,5° lat. et
35. long. Se voyant près de la
quelque Terre en a conste
à nous trouver défendu à
18 o. brasses.

le 7 Tomb. Froid que si l'on
fût à la v. dans l'Eau et
que le Soleil fut proche
du solstice. Vers la lat. 44.°
se trou la P. Meridien
la Terre de Vue est
placée en ce lieu par
quelq. Geogr. On ne peut
toujefo. en a déja éprouvé
jusque la déja épreuve et dans la
approchant des glaces dans la
B. Nauffion et dans la Desle Batist.
1739. P. Janv. Vue d'une Terre fort
haute à 54. lat. et a 28.° 30' long.
On la nomme le C. de la Circoncision.
Le voyage le n'ay fait s'y pouvoir aborder
lenifieda des glaces, de la Brume, de les vents ....
du 12. au 25. on a couru les S.^r e. ont paru fac. O.
entr'eux ..... les Baleines et des Loups de Mar ....
le 8 Fev. à 44.30' de lat. à 62 long. le 18. avoient ....
M. Bouvet a fait Route au C. de Bône Esper. ou M. Hay a
l'Isle de France. le 24 Mars mouillage au Cap de B. Esp. mise .....
comt. à bout ret. du report d'H.B.O.E. de porte. Fa.^t lauren. fait. con ...
le d'être décès le 5 Janv. le 31. Départ du Cap arrivée en France le 24.
Juin .... que n'ont pu aucun homme malgré l'extreme fatigue du Voyage.

NOTA
Americ. Vespuce dans ..... la Lat. 52.° fait p ....
en renforce du S.O. de la fuit l'Oure Côte ....
le 7 Avril 1503. à la Sud'Espace de 20 lieue .....
pouvoir aborder. Il ne vit aucune glace ....

GRANDE MER ou
MER DU SUD nommée
PACIFIQUE

CHAPTER FOUR

The Challenge of the Pacific

COOK'S ascent from being a well-regarded professional, still only a warrant officer for all his surveying achievements, to the status of world-famous explorer was extremely rapid and is an amazing story in its own right, the product of layer on layer of multi-causality. Cook's mind, essentially critical, analytical and practical, would acquire an extra dimension that was creative and aesthetic. The fusion of his energies, in the realms of planning, administration and foresight, would undergo a qualitative transmogrification. From being a superb naval technician, he would embrace new disciplines – anthropology, languages and botany – and the enforced self-education this produced would make him intellectually curious and autodidactic. It could hardly be said of the pre-1768 Cook that he was an educated man, but once released from his Newfoundland yoke into new worlds he added to his other accomplishments by becoming almost scholarly. As Beaglehole has remarked: 'He departed from England (in 1768) a good sailor, a first-rate marine surveyor, an able mathematician; and returned a great commander, a great discoverer and a man with a greatly heightened sense of the scope of human thought.'[1] All this came about because he had the indispensable Napoleonic attribute of luck: he simply happened to be in the right place at the right time. Until April 1768 Cook had no idea he was not to return to Newfoundland and had made all his plans on the assumption that he would. His sense of family may have been strengthening, for events were closing the door on the past. His mother Grace died at 63 while he was in Newfoundland, and five of Cook's siblings had also passed away. His father had gone to live with the surviving daughter Margaret in Redcar, where she was the wife of James Fleck, and Cook's wife was pregnant for a fourth time. Sadly, Cook would never see his third son, Joseph, born in September 1768 and dead within a month.[2] The cult of the amateur at the Admiralty has already been mentioned, but the Navy was afflicted with yet another paralysing aspect of the British political culture: dedication to excessive secrecy. Palliser and others had known for months that Cook was being considered for the command of an expedition to the Pacific, but no hint of this was ever dropped. Until the very last moment Cook was simply waiting for his orders to re-embark on the *Grenville*.[3] Suddenly he learned that he was to be employed elsewhere and that Michael Lane would be the new commander of the *Grenville*. Such is the pathological desire of the English establishment to cover its tracks that even today we cannot be certain exactly when the decision to appoint Cook was made. All we can say for sure is that he was chosen by the Admiralty some time between 5 and 12 April.[4]

The decision to send James Cook on a voyage of exploration to the South Pacific is a perfect example of an 'overdetermined' historical event, where immediate triggers meld with deeper-seated motives. The immediate precipitant was the desire by the Royal Society to make an accurate observation of the transit of the planet Venus, but behind this were strategic, political and even economic considerations: Enlightenment frustration at human ignorance about large areas of the globe; the desire to build on the humiliation of France during the Seven Years War by giving the Bourbons yet another poke in the eye; the hope that the presumed and expected discovery of a great southern continent would yield an El Dorado, or at the very least a lucrative outlet for trade and investment. Yet it would be wrong to deny the role of prime mover to the Royal Society. Even at the scientific level we can see the multi-causal mixture of motives, for their transit of Venus enterprise was, as has been well said, 'A collaboration of civilian science under royal patronage with royal finance, joined with private enterprise funded from a country rent roll and executed under Admiralty management.'[5] Founded in 1660, the Society had not yet lived up to the hopes of its founding fathers. The eighteenth century was experiencing a revolution in scientific thought and witnessing an explosion in new discoveries. Yet so far it was the French who had been in the vanguard. It was Diderot and d'Alembert who launched the project of an *Encyclopédie* (eventually published in seventeen volumes) that would be a synopsis of existing knowledge. And it was French explorers who had shown how to build on Newton's cosmological theories. Charles Marie de La Condamine in Peru in 1735–43 and Pierre Louis Moreau de Maupertuis in Lapland in 1736 had made the astronomical observations that confirmed the hunches of Kepler, Newton and Leibniz.[6] The French Enlightenment had spawned distinguished offshoots, of which the Scottish brand is probably the most famous. Mathematical physics, chemistry, botany, zoology, physiology, astronomy and geography all sustained quantum jumps both in the collection of data and in the sophistication of their theoretical models. A list of distinguished scientists in the eighteenth century is in danger of becoming a litany, but it is important to be clear that the best-known names – Newton, Priestley,

Cavendish, Franklin, Watt, Linnaeus, Lamarck, Laplace, Lavoisier – are merely the tip of the iceberg.[7] Most importantly, the century saw a fusion of empiricism and rationalism, which is why Kant is probably *the* key figure in the entire history of philosophy.[8]

Cook was about to be caught up in the maelstrom of intellectual history, to be swept along by profound currents whose existence he can scarcely have suspected before 1768. Astronomy had already swum into his ken, most notably with the solar eclipse of 1766, but the Royal Society's project for the observation of the transit of Venus would open up a wider universe for him. For the first time he would be encouraged to think beyond the narrow 'thing-in-itself' worlds of surveying, hydrography and trigonometry to their cosmological implications. Eighteenth-century science aimed at an overarching system of knowledge and at placing the earth within a context of planetary knowledge. In this respect the expected transit of Venus in 1769 was a key event. During a transit Venus can be seen from earth as a small black disc moving across the face of the sun – a process lasting six hours or more. Transits occur every 243 years, with pairs of transits eight years apart separated by long gaps of 121.5 years and 105.5 years. For example, there were transits in 1761 and 1769, again in December 1874 and December 1882, followed by the pair on 8 June 2004 and (to be followed) 6 June 2012, and then there will be another long gap until 2117 and 2125.[9] The importance of such phenomena in allowing mankind to measure the distance from the earth to the sun was recognised as early as the time of Johannes Kepler, and Jeremiah Horrocks did important pioneering work in 1639 only to be 'called away on urgent business'[10] at the crucial moment so that he did not observe the start of the transit. In fact there is a phenomenon known as the 'black drop effect' (or 'teardrop effect') which makes it impossible to time the precise moment when the transit begins and ends. Exactly what causes the 'black drop effect' is still disputed, with some opting for the 'atmosphere' of Venus, while others, more plausibly, point to an optical effect caused by the smearing of Venus's image by turbulence in the earth's atmosphere. The observations made by scientists in 1761 – from Siberia, Norway, Newfoundland, Madagascar and the Cape of Good Hope – all produced unsatisfactory results, but the reason for this was not understood. One student of the subject has lamented that Horrocks in 1639 did not observe the 'teardrop effect': 'Had he done so, he might have saved the eighteenth century astronomical community a good deal of frustration.'[11]

Cook might have missed some of the esoteric nuances of transitology, but he understood clearly enough the principle of parallax, the angle or semi-angle of inclination between two sightlines to a star, depending on the different orbital positions of the earth during the year. It was the old conundrum of the difference in the apparent position of an object caused by a change in the position of the observer. In trigonometry, if one knows the distance between two positions, the angle contained between two straight lines drawn to the object from two different points of view will then give you the object's distance. The transit of Venus, in a word, gave scientists a unique opportunity to calculate the distance of the sun from the earth, and the results obtained in 1769 – with the sun at a distance of 143 million kilometres – were just 2 per cent below the currently accepted figure of 149.6 million kilometres.[12] The great astronomer Edmond Halley, addressing the Royal Society in 1716, urged on its members the importance to science of the transits of the 1760s he would not live to see. His work was carried forward by Joseph-Nicolas Delisle, but there were many who felt that the Royal Society's effort in 1761 was below par and compared unfavourably with the French commitment. In 1765 Thomas Hornsby, professor of astronomy at Oxford, reminded the Royal Society of its coming duty in 1769 but the Society's response was lacklustre.[13] In June 1766 the Council of the Society passed a general resolution to send observers to the four corners of the globe, but the only concrete proposal was to send the Jesuit savant Father Boscovich, of Padua University, to California. Very late in the day, in November 1767, the Royal Society finally set up a Transit Committee, which did at least decide on the locations where they wished to send observers: Norway's North Cape, the Hudson Bay and the South Pacific. It was decided to apply to the Admiralty for a ship for the Pacific venture and to approach the king for the necessary funding, which was beyond the resources of the Society. The president of the Society, the Earl of Morton, opened negotiations with the Navy, but at this stage did not go beyond suggesting that Royal Navy officers worldwide should make their own observations. George III responded well and made a generous grant of £4,000, but the Society did not think through the implications of its approach to the Admiralty, which would have dramatic repercussions.[14]

The seven-man Transit Committee seems to have been dominated by the 'big four': Morton, the president, Nevil Maskelyne, the Astronomer-Royal, Dr John Bevis, the man with whom Cook had corresponded about the eclipse of the sun in 1766, and its resident naval expert Captain John Campbell, RN, a first-class sailor with experience in the coal trade and a distinguished scientist and inventor in his own right. The initial idea was that Captain Campbell would command the ship the Committee hoped to get from the Admiralty and that then a number of qualified observers be appointed. But things started to go adrift almost immediately. The first four would-be observers interviewed – Messrs Dymond, Dunn, Green and Wales – all wanted extravagant annual fees and lavish expenses before they served. Then Captain Campbell dropped his bombshell by announcing that he was not interested in the command in the South Pacific. The reasons remain obscure, but it is likely he could see no clear career advantage in the offer or that he was not being offered enough money.[15] This was the context in which Dr Maskelyne put forward the name of Alexander Dalrymple, a 30-year-old Scot with impressive credentials. As a young man he had been employed by the East India Company and turned himself into an expert in Indonesia and the Philippines, criss-crossing the islands of the East Indies, while also acquiring an encyclopaedic knowledge of the early Spanish exploration of the Pacific.[16] Under the pretext of a master plan to revive British trade in this area of Dutch hegemony, Dalrymple was really aiming to become Britain's premier explorer of the Pacific. He was haunted by dreams of the great unknown Southern Continent, of which he hoped to be the discoverer. His ambition was vaulting and Promethean, aided by an undoubted talent for politics and lobbying. On his return to England from Manila, Dalrymple tried to enlist both Lord Shelburne, secretary of state for the Southern Department, and other political heavyweights. He induced the great economist Adam Smith to lobby for him, and won over Nevil Maskelyne at the Royal Society.[17] For a while Dalrymple carried all before him. Although a man of many faults – he was quarrelsome, contentious, cock-sure, arrogant and a know-all – he compensated with charm, enthusiasm and, most of all, energy, that quality that will always defeat mere talent. At this stage nobody queried his self-assigned abilities as sailor and navigator (which seem to have been nugatory), his ability to manage men (ditto) or indeed his general commitment to science, astronomy and the transit of Venus project, which was likewise negligible. Dalrymple was an assiduous attender at Royal Society dinners and this masked the fact – obvious in restrospect – that he cared little for science but was a glory-hunter who aspired to be remembered as England's greatest explorer.[18] He dazzled his listeners with brilliant descriptions of the attributes of the great Southern Continent, of whose existence he was dogmatically certain. Although Dalrymple was certainly no nonentity – he later influenced Francis Beaufort to devise his famous wind scale[19] – he was not the universal genius he imagined himself to be.

Nonetheless, at first his appointment seemed certain to be nodded through. Dalrymple made it clear that he had no interest in any kind of partnership or 'dyarchy' with a Royal Navy officer; he had to be chief, leader, captain and supremo in all aspects of the expedition. To the obvious objection that the Royal Navy was likely to resent having one of its ships and its officers commanded by a man with no naval rank, Dalrymple cited the precedents of William Dampier and, especially, Sir Edmond Halley; at the least, he thought he could simply be given a brevet rank to smooth ruffled feathers. But it was a grave mistake to bring up Halley's experiences as a civilian in command of a naval vessel on a scientific voyage, as Halley had been on the *Paramour* in 1698–1700 (to study the variations of the compass). The memory of that disastrous experiment, with disaffection and near-mutiny among his contemptuous officers, was deeply etched on the collective memory of the Admiralty.[20] And so, on 3 April 1768 the Earl of Morton had to report to his colleagues on the Transit Committee that their proposal of Dalrymple as commander had been humiliatingly rebuffed; the words used were that such an appointment would be 'totally repugnant to the rules of the Navy'.[21] Moreover, the First Lord of the Admiralty, the fire-eating Sir Edward Hawke, hero of Quiberon Bay in 1759, asserted with vehemence that he would rather have his right arm cut off than sign up to a repeat of Halley on the *Paramour*.[22] Their Lordships may also have realised by this time that, Dalrymple's braggadocio notwithstanding, his longest ocean passage hitherto had been a mere nineteen days, and this was the experience with which he proposed to face the vast Pacific. Dalrymple was given the bad news and accepted it stoically, at least on the surface. He tried to save face by saying that the Navy had been prepared to endorse him but with the appearance of a divided military/civilian command and that he turned this down. In fact the Navy made no such offer. Dalrymple, ever the master politician, obfuscated the circumstances of his humiliation by conflating and confusing talks he had had with the Society with the very different negotiations the Society carried out with the Admiralty. Yet it was a bitter blow to his ambitions. When Cook was given the command, he became a marked man and an eternal enemy in Dalrymple's eyes, though Cook almost certainly never met him and knew little or nothing about him.[23]

By 12 April Cook had been offered, and had accepted, command of the vessel to be sent to the South Pacific to observe the transit of Venus. After a period of leave, on 25 May he finally received a Royal Navy commission as Lieutenant James Cook.[24] Meanwhile, on 5 May, he attended a meeting of the Royal Society and accepted their terms regarding fees, whatever they turned out to be. Perhaps there was an element of putting the Navy upstart in his place, for though Captain Campbell introduced Cook cordially as the Admiralty's appointee, the Committee made no provision for an emolument, while pointedly awarding Charles Green, the astronomer, as their first observer. Green was granted 200 guineas for the term of his observations and 100 guineas a year if the voyage lasted longer than a year; he had originally asked for a flat £300 a year – which meant that the Society would end up £600 to the good for his services. Cook was nominated as second observer, and both observers were granted a victualling allowance of £120 a year.[25] Two weeks later the Society announced that Cook had been granted a single payment of

£100 as their second observer. Thereafter the Royal Society was increasingly marginalised in preparations for the voyage, which became overwhelmingly a Navy affair, though it did successfully petition to have its wealthy patron Joseph Banks sail alongside the commander.[26] Cook had been very lucky, since both the original choice of commander, Captain Campbell, and the strongest contender thereafter, Dalrymple, had fallen by the wayside. In retrospect, Cook's appointment seems incredible, as he had none of the obvious credentials. Of the Navy's two previous Pacific circumnavigators, Samuel Wallis was a post captain of eight years' seniority while John Byron was a commodore and aristocratic scion, with all the right elite connections. There were plenty of ambitious men with more obvious qualifications than Cook who might have expected to have been offered such a prestigious appointment. As Beaglehole rightly comments: 'As this ship was to be sent into the Pacific, a considerable voyage, was it not a little strange to select for her command a mere master, whose most previous command had been a sixty-ton schooner or brig, with a crew of twenty?'[27] Only two explanations seem plausible. One is that the Admiralty originally conceived the voyage as a narrowly focused scientific endeavour, for which an expert surveyor with a background in astronomy and solar eclipses seemed appropriate, and it was only after Cook's appointment that a wider voyage of exploration was decided on. The other is that historians have underrated the intensity of the lobbying on Cook's behalf by an all but unbeatable duo: Palliser and Sir Philip Stephens, the Admiralty secretary, who were able to work on Lord Hawke's disgust at the Royal Society and Dalrymple.[28]

In more senses than one Cook was now venturing into the unknown. It takes an effort of the imagination to appreciate the vast ignorance of the Pacific that obtained in the 1760s, almost exactly two hundred and fifty years after Europeans first dared the winds and waves of that inaptly named ocean. During the sixteenth century the Pacific was almost entirely a Spanish lake, the domain of reckless conquistadores and stern viceroys supposedly controlled by a rigid bureaucracy at Madrid and Seville. No sooner were the Spaniards ensconced in the New World than they were eyeing the 'routes to China' in the ocean beyond. Even before Mexico was conquered, advance parties were making their way towards Cape Horn down the eastern coast of South America. First across the Pacific Ocean was Ferdinand Magellan in 1520–21.[29] His epoch-making voyage has rightly been described as a bizarre combination of luck and miscalculation. After dealing ruthlessly with mutiny on his first winter out, he reached the southern tip of South America and threaded through the straits that later bore his name. He was lucky in that he met no storms and arrived in the Pacific in the southern summer, allowing him to cross the ocean when the north-east trade winds were at their most favourable. But he miscalculated badly by underestimating, as did all his contemporaries, the sheer vastness of the Pacific and then by opting for an eccentric track across it. This meant that he spent ninety-nine days (28 November 1520–6 March 1521) at sea without making landfall, and by sheer chance missed all the archipelagoes. For the first twenty days in the Pacific he sailed north to escape cold seas, then altered course to the west. He sighted small, uninhabited islands on 24 January and 4 February but was unable to land. At the equator he altered course again, heading north-west; had he continued on a westerly course he would have hit the Gilbert Islands in Micronesia.[30] Having provisioned for a maximum eighty-day voyage, by the time he reached Guam his men were drinking putrid water and subsisting on worm-eaten biscuit that stank of rat's urine. After finally making landfall in Guam he sailed on to the Philippines, where he became embroiled in local politics and warfare and was killed at Cebu in April 1521.[31] In 1522 one ship out of the five that originally sailed from Spain reached the home port via the Cape of Good Hope with a face-saving cargo of cloves.

Magellan's voyage had several consequences. It disposed of any lingering vestiges of the Ptolemaic view of the world (that is, that land and not oceans occupied the major part of the earth) and revealed the almost unimaginable vastness of the Pacific – actually 64 million square miles or one-third of the planet's surface. Together with the accelerated Spanish conquest of what later became known as Latin America, it provided the springboard for Spanish expansion into the Pacific, enabling Spain to turn it into a wholly Iberian zone of influence. When the Spanish completed the conquest of the Philippines in the 1560s, they had bases on either side of the ocean. Manila was designed to be the centre to which the spices of the Moluccas, the silks of China and the bullion of Japan would be brought for transhipment to the New World. But after 1526 and the voyage of García Jofre de Loaisa, the route through the Straits of Magellan was no longer used; Mexico and Peru became the principal jump-off points for Spanish voyages across the Pacific. Alvaro de Saavedra blazed an oceanic trail from New Spain (Mexico) in 1527–28 and arrived in the Philippines in time to tip the scales in Loaisa's struggles with the Portuguese.[32] Meanwhile Hernando de Grijalva made the first crossing from Peru to the East Indies in 1537, though his voyage was a disaster. He made the mistake of trying to return to Peru in the low altitudes of the South Pacific where currents and winds made this impossible. Frustrated by this and by Grijalva's refusal to make for the Moluccas and thus trespass on Portuguese territory, his crew mutinied and killed him. Sailing on westwards close to the equator and losing men daily through sickness, the mutineers were finally shipwrecked on the coast of New Guinea.[33] At the mercy of the Papuans, only three mutineers survived, to be picked up two years later by the Portuguese navigator Antonio Galvao. In all the early voyages westward across the Pacific, every single ship (except Mendaña's in 1567) passed through the Tuamotu archipelago, the gateway to Polynesia, but each ship seems to have encountered a different island in the group and no attempt was made to collate the findings of the different explorers.[34]

By far the most important venture attempted in early Pacific navigation was that of Andrés de Urdaneta, a protégé of Loaisa, in 1564. Thought by some moderns to be more missionary than mariner, Urdaneta nonethless proved a better guide to the Pacific than his more experienced pilots and had a clearer idea of the width of the ocean than they did. Moreover, he was an original thinker who experimented with a master idea: that the South Equatorial Current and the south-east trades would carry a ship quickly to Manila from the west coast of the Americas but that if the vessel 'turned round' very fast, it could then exploit the westerlies and the California Current for the homeward voyage and complete the round trip in a single summer season. His journey triumphantly vindicated his theory. After making landfall at Manila he attempted a return route by heading north-east almost as far as latitude 40. There he was turned south by the winds, reached the California coast and fetched Acapulco by running south alongside Baja California. His was one of the great oceanic exploits, for he had covered 20,000 kilometres (12,500 miles) in 130 days between June and October.[35] But because Urdaneta 'blazed trail' around 30N, that route was the one ever afterwards followed by the annual galleon Spain sent from Manila to Acapulco with the cargoes of the East. Sailing close to 40N, subsequent navigators often found the North Pacific stormy and experimented by making the crossing father south, between 32 and 37N. The snag here was that at these latitudes the westerlies were less reliable, so mariners had to balance the 'swings' of a more prolonged voyage farther south with the 'roundabouts' of a stormier but faster route farther north. Yet none of these later problems could be blamed on Urdaneta. His charts and itinerary were regarded as virtually sacrosanct by the unimaginative Spanish authorities, who ever afterwards sent out the annual galleon from Callao in Peru into the South Pacific, ready for a return trip to Acapulco via the North Pacific. As has been well said about the sixteenth-century Spanish voyages, 'on all counts the intellectual discoverer is Urdaneta'.[36]

Because Spanish interest in the Pacific overwhelmingly centred on the trade of the Manila galleon, the very success of the galleon acted as a 'fetter' on the exploration of their 'lake' by the conquistadores. Between the time of

Magellan and that of Cook there were as many as 450 crossings of the Pacific, but most of them were by the Manila galleon.[37] Only three Spanish voyages bucked this somnolent trend and they were stimulated by three convergent legends: Inca belief in wealthy islands far away in the western sea; Chilean myths that King Solomon's Mines were located in the Pacific; and the general European conviction that there 'must be' a great undiscovered continent somewhere in the South Pacific. It was in pursuit of this collective will-o'-the-wisp that the governor of Peru sent out the adventurer Álvaro de Mendaña de Neyra in 1567. Mendaña's de Neyra quest was complicated by the ambition of his collaborators, for his second in command, Pedro Sarmiento de Gamboa, was the chief promoter of the Inca legend while his pilot Hernando Gallego dreamed of a new El Dorado in New Guinea.[38] The expedition left Callao with two ships in November 1567 but by mid-January, with no land sighted and water short, Mendaña's nerve cracked and he effectively handed over command to the ambitious Gallego. On 7 February the ships sighted a group of islands, which they optimistically named after King Solomon. Two days later Mendaña landed at Santa Isabel and took possession of the Solomons in the name of the king of Spain, but as always the conquistador mentality soon engendered hostilities with the locals. Mendaña thought it safer to transfer to the neighbouring island of Guadalcanal, but the pattern of mutual incomprehension and warfare with the locals continued. After a show of strength in which he razed several villages Mendaña left Guadalcanal and finally made his base on the most easterly of the large Solomon islands, San Cristóbal.[39] But Mendaña's attempts to found a settlement were predictably unsuccessful. Finally, in September 1768, following massive pressure from his crew, he agreed to return to New Spain. The two ships headed across the equator into the North Pacific, seeking Urdaneta's return route but were caught in a terrible hurricane off Wake Island, as a result of which the two vessels were separated. Following Urdaneta's recommended route close to 40N, Mendaña made landfall on the coast of California on 19 December 1568. It was September 1569, nearly two years after he had set out, that he finally returned to Callao.[40]

It was a quarter of a century later before Mendaña was able to resume his exploration of the Pacific. In Spain from 1569 to 1577, on his return to Peru, he found himself out of favour with the new viceroy, who was more concerned with the threat from Drake, Hawkins and other English marauders and had no resources to spare for voyages into the South Sea. Finally, with the ending of the English threat and the appointment of a new viceroy, Mendaña's hour came round once more. In April 1595 a new expedition with 378 settlers aboard two galleons plus supporting vessels left from Callao (then calling at Paita in Peru), intending to colonise the 'Isles of Wisdom' (Solomons), that had been visited by Mendaña in 1568. The colonists were directed by the chief pilot Pedro Fernández de Quirós, one of the most talented Pacific navigators ever, but the canker in the rose was the presence of Mendaña's arrogant and turbulent wife, Doña Isabel Barreto, and her three murderous brothers.[41] The expedition launched into the open Pacific on 16 June and at first made good progress. On 26 July they made landfall at the Marquesas, thus becoming the first Europeans to visit this island group. Contact between conquistadores and 'primitive' people invariably ended in violence, and here was no exception. By the time the Spanish left after an unhappy two-week sojourn, 200 Marquesans had been killed. Pressing on through the Cook and Ellice islands, with food and water running short, on 8 September the adventurers landed at Santa Cruz. The usual cycle of misunderstanding, violence and murder began again; this time Quirós was convinced that the Spanish soldiers deliberately sabotaged peaceful relations so they would not have to stay and found a colony.[42] With one galleon wrecked and his ideals shattered, Mendaña died on 18 October. Command of the expedition now passed to Doña Isabel and her brothers. The decision to abandon the colony was taken and on 18 November the depleted expedition put to sea once more. Isabel kept the best food and livestock for herself while sailors died of starvation; her brothers specialised in killing all dissenters. The failed colonists should by all indices of probability have perished on the open sea, but the superlative navigational skills of Quirós brought them to Guam by the New Year of 1596 and then, after surmounting almost insuperable difficulties, to Manila on 11 February. Only 100 of those who sailed from Paita had survived. [43]

Later that year Quirós returned to Acapulco and thence to Peru. In 1600 he went to Spain to lobby the king (and also to Rome to gain support from the Pope) for another expedition. In 1603 he received royal authorisaton for the voyage. By this time Quirós was convinced that Santa Cruz and other islands were the outlying stretches of a great southern continent, and he saw it as his divine mission to convert the benighted heathens there to Catholicism.[44] In two galleons equipped with water condensers he left Callao on 21 December full of confidence and at first headed south-west to latitude 26S. Despite Quirós's brilliance he always underestimated the vastness of the Pacific and the reliability of its wind system. After a month at sea with no sign of land, he lost confidence in his own judgement and turned north-west, heading for a region where he knew there were islands.[45] The ships passed through the northern islands of the Tuamotu archipelago and reached Caroline Island, which Quirós mistook for Mendaña's San Bernardo (discovered on the 1567–68 voyage). On 2 March they came to Rakahanga in the Cook Islands and were entranced by the beauties both of Nature and the locals who, however, proved to be hostile. A near-mutiny on 25 March, when his subordinates pointed out that they had already sailed for 94 days (as against the 64 from Callao to Santa Cruz in 1595), without reaching their goal, led Quirós once more to doubt his own judgement. Melodramatically abandoning his fleet to the guidance of God, on 3 May he found himself on an island he called La Australia del Espiritu Santo (the largest island in the New Hebrides) and convinced himself that this was the Southern Continent.[46] The 'New Jerusalem' he founded, however, lasted less than a month before persistent hostility from the natives led to its abandonment. Quirós seems to have suffered a nervous breakdown as a result and announced that the expedition would leave for fresh lands. Departure was planned for 8 June, but the four days of 8–11 June are still shrouded in mystery. Some say Quirós's galleon was swept out to sea, others that there was a mutiny, but the upshot was that after 11 June the two galleons went their separate ways. [47] Quirós, only occasionally showing sparks of his former navigational greatness, rallied sufficiently to guide his ship north to the tried and tested track of the Manila galleon. After reaching latitude 38N the voyagers swung east and eventually reached Acapulco on 23 November 1606. Quirós spent the rest of his life in bitterness, vainly lobbying in Europe for a third expedition. The separated galleon, meanwhile, under Luis Vaez de Torres, reached New Guinea, thoroughly explored its south coast and even reached the northernmost point of Australia at Cape York.[48] Torres finally arrived in Manila in May 1607.

The death of Quirós ended the heroic age of Spanish exploration of the Pacific. Since Sir Francis Drake, the first single famous individual to make the circumnavigation of the globe (1577–80) (Magellan had been killed in the Philippines), it might have been expected that the British would take up the mantle. But Drake's foray into the South Seas was a buccaneering expedition, pure and simple. Actuated purely by loot, plunder and treasure, like all the Elizabethan 'sea dogs' (not to mention their cynical, money-minded mistress), Drake and his ilk lacked the motivation, commitment, staying power and vision for pure exploration.[49] Gradually the Dutch took over as the leading 'pathfinders' in the ocean, making voyages south from Java to achieve the first European landings in Australia. Increasingly what actuated Europeans in the South Seas was loot; explorers were either monopolists and freebooters, those operating under the aegis of the Dutch East India Company, and precarious, independent operators, sometimes not much more than pirates.[50] The great figure in this era of Dutch expansion was Abel Janszoon Tasman, whose voyage of 1642–43 from Mauritius took him as far as Van Diemen's Land (Tasmania). From there he proceeded east to New Zealand and explored both islands, eliciting a hostile response from the Maoris, who reacted to all interlopers in this way, proving conclusively that violence in the Pacific was not merely the prerogative of Spanish adventurers. Heading north, Tasman discovered Tonga and Fiji before returning to Batavia in the Dutch East Indies. On a further voyage in 1644 he sailed to New Guinea and then along Australia's northern shores, but on neither of his cruises did he encounter Australia's long eastern shore.[51] Tasman was the most enlightened of the Dutch explorers in his attitude to the Pacific islanders. The other big names of the seventeenth century, Isaac Le Maire and Willem Schouten (and Jacob Roggeveen in the early eighteenth) were notorious for their violent methods. Beaglehole speaks of 'Schouten and Le Maire and Roggeveen, whose progress was punctuated by the roar of cannon at most of the islands'.[52] In a way it is unfair to bracket Roggeveen with the other two, for he was a Pacific explorer of genuine talent and originality. His voyage of 1721–22 from Holland to Batavia added Easter Island to the map. He also explored the northern Tuamotus and was the first European to discover Samoa.[53]

In the light of Cook's career it is surprising that the British were so slow off the mark when it came to the penetration of the South Seas. The Spanish were able to hang on to their 'lake' and feel secure in the passage of the Manila galleon only because other nations failed to follow through on pioneering expeditions. Nonetheless, Spanish America did not have things all its own way and certainly did not enjoy a monopoly. In the years 1578–1643 there were eight hostile British and Dutch voyages, two of which (those of Le Maire and Tasman) were genuine ventures of exploration. Between 1644 and 1680 there were several attempts by non-Spaniards at peaceful trading on the Pacific coast of South America plus Henry Morgan's famous sack of Panama in 1672. Then from 1680 to 1740 there were just two trading expeditions and Roggeveen's great journey. If anything, the French seemed to be taking up the challenge of the Great South Sea, for there were at least sixteen friendly voyages from France to the coasts of Chile and Peru, some of which went on to cross the Pacific to China and elsewhere.[54] The sole English irruption had consequences more in the field of literature than geopolitics. William Dampier, a buccaneer who specialised in pillaging the Pacific coast of South America and the trade of the East Indies, made forays into other areas. In 1688 he reached the western shores of Australia, and his subsequent account of this journey *New Voyages*, published in 1697, became a bestseller. On the back of this fame Dampier was given command of a proper naval expedition with the aim of exploring the eastern coast of Australia, but he abandoned this project, confining himself to the discovery of the three islands of New Britain east of New Guinea.[55] Although as an explorer Dampier added little to the pioneering efforts of Tasman, he was a publicist of genius, and his accounts of the South

Sea influenced Defoe's *Robinson Crusoe* and Swift's *Gulliver's Travels*; both Lilliput and Brobdingnag are allegedly located in the Pacific.[56] Yet still there was no sustained interest by the British government in real, flesh-and-blood navigation as opposed to utopian fantasy. When the War of the Austrian Succession broke out, Admiral George Anson was sent out to raid the Pacific coast of Spanish America. Anson lost all but one of his ships and most of his men, but he was able to present his incursion as a triumph because he captured a Manila galleon, laden with treasure, off the Philippines and, after refitting at Canton, completed a circumnavigation of the globe.[57]

Although not a voyage of exploration, Anson's circumnavigation was in many ways a key event for (unlike the voyages of Tasman, Dampier and Roggeveen) it represented a direct challenge by an imperial power to Spain in its 'lake', a declaration of intent by the Royal Navy that henceforth it would roam the seven seas without let or hindrance. Spain had been saved from inter-lopers hitherto mainly because it would take a convergence of new technolo-gies, new attitudes and surplus capital before the risks of deep ocean navigation were really acceptable.[58] The period of almost continual warfare between Britain and France from the 1740s to 1763 delayed the inevitable. But with the global triumph of Britain in the Seven Years War exploration of the Pacific began seriously. It is significant that, until the 1760s, Dampier's discovery of New Britain had been the sole example of purposeful exploration (Roggeveen's exploits were achieved *en passant*, as it were) since Tasman, apart from the voyages of the Russian Vitus Bering in the extreme northerly latitudes of the Pacific and the Sea of Okhotsk.[59] The explosion of activity in the ocean in the 1760s can be seen as an outward displacement of the global rivalry between France and Britain, with Cook and Bougainville playing the transmogrified roles of Wolfe and Montcalm. The passage in British minds from the South Seas as a locus for fantasy and parallel universes to the Pacific as a solid, knowable geographical entity, is to some extent bound up in the gradual change of nomenclature from 'South Sea' to 'Pacific'.[60] Before Cook the boundary between fantasy and reality was fluid. As the German explorer Alexander von Humboldt put it: 'The Pacific no longer appeared as it had done to Magellan, a desert waste; it was now animated by islands which, however, for want of exact astronomical observations, appeared to have no fixed position but floated from place to place over the charts.'[61] Swift's floating island of Laputa had a real satirical point.

The 'Pacific craze' of the 1760s may be said to have begun with the circum-navigation of the earth by Commodore John Byron in 1764–66. The under-lying motive for the Admiralty's sending him out was strategic, and his instructions laid out a threefold objective. First, he was to clear up the mystery of whether there was an island, reported by the buccaneer Ambrose Cowley in 1684 in the South Atlantic off the mainland coast and dubbed by him Pepys Island. Secondly, he was to survey and report on the Falkland Islands; and, thirdly, he was to search for the Northwest Passage.[62] He sailed in June 1764 in the *Dolphin* together with a second ship the *Tamar*, captain Patrick Mouat. He put in at Patagonia and thence made for the Falklands, which he soon concluded were one and the same as 'Pepys Island'. He then rounded the Horn and on 9 April 1765 entered the Pacific. After a stop at Más Afuera Island, he launched into the vast open spaces of the eastern Pacific and in June sighted the most northerly isles in the Tuamotu archipelago; landfall at one of them produced the predictable bloodshed with the locals. Byron then swung north-west, passed through the Tokelaus and the easterly Gilberts and reached the Marshall Islands.[63] There he blatantly ignored Admiralty instructions to explore the coast of California, which would have meant turning east in the well-known track of the Manila galleon. Instead he swung west to the Marianas, stopped at Tinian for nine weeks, passed between Taiwan and the Phillipines into the South China Sea and ran down the coast of Southeast Asia to arrive at Batavia, whence he returned home via the Cape of Good Hope, arriving in England in May 1766. His circumnavigation was the fastest on record to date, but he had achieved this 'blue riband' by, in essence, recognising no superior but himself. Byron, arrogant and self-serving, was one of those people who see difficulties everywhere and habitually turn a drama into a crisis; most emphatically not the stuff of which true explorers are made. The Admiralty instructions, it is true, gave him a free hand in 'emergencies', but Byron chose to construe the entire trip as an emergency. As a voyage of Pacific discovery his was singularly useless.[64]

A month later Captain Samuel Wallis was commissioned to take the *Dolphin* to the Pacific once more, but Wallis proved just as incapable of following orders as Byron had been. The Admiralty instructions clearly stressed that restating the British claim to the Falklands was one of two prime objectives, the other being the quest for the Great Southern Continent or Terra Australis Incognita.[65] He too was given a second ship, the unweatherly *Swallow*, captain Philip Carteret. They left Plymouth in August 1766 and were off Patagonia by December. The two vessels encountered a nightmare of storms and gales at Cape Horn and took *seventeen* weeks to round it, even when using the Straits of Magellan. When Carteret justifiably complained to Wallis that he should never have been ordered to sea in the 'coffin ship' *Swallow*, Wallis chose to interpret this as 'whingeing'. In April 1767 the *Dolphin* lost sight of her sister ship; the consensus view is that Wallis deliberately left the *Swallow* to get rid of Carteret. Again, like Byron, making no attempt to fulfil his instructions, he did not turn south in search of the fabled continent but sailed north and then west at latitude 20S. In early June he was threading through the Tuamotus, but the six islands he passed were small and uninhabited. Finally, a red-letter day for Pacific exploration, on 18 June he became the first European to discover Tahiti.[66] Finding the locals hostile, he was stuck for some days on an isolated coral atoll but on 23 June landed in Matavai Bay. This would become the established port of call for European adventurers during the age of discovery, though it is not the best anchorage in Tahiti; that honour belongs to the harbour at Papeete. Again Wallis had to endure a period of mainly dismal relations with the locals – stones were thrown and muskets discharged (some accounts say significant numbers of Tahitians were killed) – but he was no 'hawk' and contented himself with trading in hogs, fowl and fruit. Wallis's landfall generated the first example of the frenzied coupling between European sailors and young Polynesian women that would characterise, and disfigure, relations between the two cultures.[67] Wallis, evidently a man more interested in love than war, enjoyed a heavy flirtation, and probably more than that, with a local 'queen' named Oborea (properly Purea). Playing Aeneas to this island's Dido, he suddenly left her, brokenhearted, on 26 July. Once again he made no attempt to go south but headed west through the gap between the Samoan and Tongan groups. Then, pleading the necessity to repair a battered ship, he followed a virtually identical track to Byron's, via the Marshalls, Marianas and Tinian, into the South China Sea and to Batavia. Returning via the Cape of Good Hope, he was on the Downs within sight of home on 20 May 1768.

Meanwhile Carteret, apparently abandoned to a watery death off Cape Pilar on 15 April 1767, went on to an astounding achievement of his own. He finally cleared the Straits of Magellan and, after three weeks of terrible storms, reached Juan Fernández Island. He pressed on to Más Afuera in the teeth of more gales and high water, and then on 17 June deduced from the great swell coming from the south that there was no great continent in that direction. He turned west, reached farther south than any circumnavigator before Cook, discovered Pitcairn Island on 2 July, then cruised through the southern edges of the Tuamotus. The *Swallow* was by now in an almost terminal state, her sails splitting and her crew prostrated by scurvy. Improvising as he went, Carteret turned north to pick up the trade winds at Latitude 16S, then turned west and eventually made landfall at Quirós's old haunt, Santa Cruz. Here he lost four men in a brutal affray with the locals, then unknowingly sailed straight through the Solomons to Dampier's New Britain, where he was again attacked by the indigenous peoples. He then threaded a course through New Britain and New Ireland (discovering St George's Channel that separates them), east of New Guinea, then looped north and south to Mindanao and the Celebes before landing at the Dutch settlement at Bonthain (Makassar), where he was held under virtual ship arrest for five months by the suspicious Dutch.[68] At last, in May 1768, he was released and proceeded to Batavia where the *Swallow* was repaired and given a full refit. Crossing the Indian Ocean to the Cape of Good Hope, he spent a further six weeks there. He departed in January 1769 and arrived at Spithead on 20 May. The man who had been despised by his superior for a less than positive attitude had proved he was a far abler and more intrepid navigator. As Beaglehole has remarked: 'This voyage was one of the greatest achievements of the human spirit in the history of the Pacific.'[69]

The French had finally decided to stake a claim to the Great South Sea. They had, so to speak, put down a marker as early as 1715 with the capture of Mauritius and the establishment of the Ile de France, meant both to consolidate their position in India and to act as a launch pad for ventures into the Pacific. But in France, as in Britain, the real 'Pacific craze' occurred in the years immediately following the Seven Years War. In response to Byron, Wallis and Carteret, Choiseul sent out Louis-Antoine de Bougainville from France in 1767 on a circumnavigation completed in 1768, Jean François Marie de Surville from India in 1769 and Yves-Joseph de Kerguelen-Trémarec from the Ile de France in 1771.[70] Bougainville, a distinguished mathematician and adventurer, who had served in Canada under Montcalm and his successors in 1759–60, was influenced by the ideas of both Maupertuis and Charles de Brosses, who propagandised assiduously for French exploration in the Pacific throughout the 1750s, arguing (correctly) that if France postponed her efforts in this direction until the end of the Seven Years War, it would be too late.[71] For de Brosses and Bougainville the enemy was, of course, the British, towards whom Bougainville evinced particular bitterness when he returned home to Francein 1760 as a prisoner of war. But after the Treaty of Paris in 1763 the French wasted at least three years trying to estabish a colony in the Falklands and in California. In both cases the Spanish pre-empted them, and France grudgingly acceded to the demands of her old ally. But that was not the end of the Pacific dream. The French continued to think that there would be spices and precious metals in the South Pacific, which made the prize worth striving for. There was also the possibility of colonising an island off the China coast from where the Compagnie des Indes could dominate European trade with China. Such was the complex of motives behind Bougainville's circumnavigation of 1767–68.[72]

Choiseul used Bougainville as his principal negotiator with the Spanish on the Falklands issue. It was after a mission to Madrid that Bougainville finally set out on his global venture. He was instructed to make a detailed settlement with Spain's envoys 'on the ground' in the Falklands, then to head into the Pacific to search for new lands to colonise, to open up a new route to China and to seek out unknown plants which could be taken to the Ile de France. He left France in November 1766 in the *Boudeuse*, after making arrangements to meet the sister ship the *Etoile*, which was not ready to sail, in Rio later. The detailed negotiations for the handover to Spain in the Falklands took far longer than expected. The *Boudeuse* then headed back to Rio for the rendezvous with the *Etoile*. But a year had already passed, and November 1767 was spent sailing from Rio past Montevideo towards Cape Horn. Bougainville was now under pressure to make a rapid voyage across the Pacific, since his ships had only been provisioned for two years.[73] He entered the Pacific via Cape Pilar in the Straits of Magellan on 26 January 1768. The passage across the ocean that followed was brisk, businesslike and disappointingly inconsequential. Where Cook was always a meritocrat and innovator, Bougainville was a much more typical *ancien régime* navigator. He was the supreme commander of the expedition, but Captain Duclos-Guyot on the *Boudeuse* and Chesnard de la Giraudais on the *Etoile* were the true sailors. Surprisingly for a mathematician, Bougainville had little interest in surveying or cartography and rarely made contact with the cartographer on the *Etoile*.[74] He was also incurious about the islands of Polynesia in a way that Cook would never have been. Once at the Tuamotus, he sighted Nukutavake, Pinaki, Vairaatea and Vahitahi, but made no attempt to land. Finally on 2 April he saw the famous peak of Tahiti and on the 6th anchored at Hitiaa Bay on the north-eastern side of the island in what was to prove a very difficult anchorage.

Although Bougainville named Tahiti the 'New Cythera' and his descriptions gave rise to the eighteenth-century craze for the 'noble savage', it could not be said that his sojourn in the island paradise was a happy one. While his crew reeled incredulously from one lubricious encounter after another with the local young women, bad weather daily assailed his ships. A great swell chafed the cables against the coral bottom; Bougainville lost six anchors in nine days and came close to losing his ships as well. Although they were impressed by the easy trading manners of the Tahitians, the French were less impressed by the endemic kleptomania and did not tarry long. When they left on 15 April they took the local chief Ereti's brother Ahutoru back to France with them. Once again Bougainville displayed his lack of the real explorer's elan by sailing through the Samoan group without investigation. His next significant sighting was the New Hebrides (the Espiritu Santo of Quirós in 1606), where he made landfall and stayed for five days without being able to provision adequately. Heading due east he came up against the impenetrable obstacle of the Great Barrier Reef, which forced him sharply north without sighting the unknown east coast of Australia.[75] He then passed through the gap between the Solomons and New Britain, making brief stops at the western end of Baye Choiseul (Solomons) and Port Praslin (New Ireland) before cruising along the northern coast of New Guinea. In September 1768 he arrived at Buru in the Maluku islands (Indonesia), whence the two ships cleared for the Ile de France. Once there, the *Etoile* remained for extensive repairs while the *Boudeuse* pressed on alone for home, reaching France in March 1769. Bougainville had achieved none of his official aims, and it could be fairly said that the results of his voyage were above all literary. But as a navigator he was not without merit. He had consistently put the welfare and safety of his crew ahead of exploration, and convinced himself that the talk by the *Philosophes* of a great southern continent was nonsense.[76]

Although Cook departed for the Pacific before Carteret and Bougainville had returned, it is unlikely that the latter's scepticism about Terra Australis Incognita would have swayed him, for Cook remained at this stage (and until 1775) remarkably credulous about the likely existence of such a fabled land. Perhaps as a self-made man and autodidact he had an excessive reverence for the products of the academy and for French thought in particular.[77] In retrospect, the 'certainty' with which the Southern Continent's existence was asserted is an astonishing and lamentable demonstration of the power of pure a priori speculation. Both Dalrymple in Britain and Charles de Brosses in France were adamant that there 'must be' such a land, if only because there had to be a counterpart to the Asian land mass in the northern hemisphere to keep the rotating globe in equilibrium.[78] Moreover, they claimed empirical proof for their continent on the grounds that on New Year's Day 1739 the navigator Bouvet de Lozier had found its northern tip, which he called Cape Circumcision. They were even prepared to attribute features to it on a probabilistic basis. It was supposed to be located in latitude 40S and to extend 4,596 geographical miles (or 5,223 statute miles) from about the longitude of Turkey to that of China. Dalrymple even 'knew' that the continent had a population of more than 50 million, offering undreamed of markets for British commerce; by contrast the two million in North America were picayune.[79] His certainty was unshaken by the contrary indications – that all four of the circumnavigations of the 1760s had produced no sign of any southern continent. The early voyages in the Pacific, if studied by Cook – and it is uncertain how much he did study them, apart from the voyagings of Quirós – would, however, have produced far more relevant and useful data. Essentially the Pacific was a reasonably predictable ocean as regards winds and currents. The extremities of the ocean, between 30 and 55N and south of 25S were dominated by fairly reliable westerlies, though they were stormy and turbulent. Other reliable winds were the north-east trades, blowing between about 15 and 25N, and the south-east trades from the equator to 20S. In the eastern Pacific the South Equatorial Current provided the classic galleon route from Peru to the Philippines, while in the western ocean the Japan, North Pacific and California currents likewise provided the classic way back from Manila to Acapulco. Still unknown at this juncture was the true nature of the Equatorial Countercurrent running west–east from the Philippines to Central America. In general there was a wealth of solid geographical and meteorological data available to the would-be explorer of the South Seas. Critics of Cook, perhaps unfairly, say that in 1768 he paid less attention to this solid empirical evidence and far more to the myth of the Southern Continent that suffused his imagination.[80]

Yet in April and May 1768 Cook had more mundane matters on his mind, for he was preparing his ship for sea. The choice of ship had been made before he was appointed to the captaincy, despite the certainty with which some writers insist that Cook 'must have' had a major hand in her selection.[81] Casting around for a suitable ship, the Admiralty at first fastened on a sloop named the *Tryal* but then disovered she could not be prepared for sea before June. Next they opted for an elderly 24-gun frigate, the *Rose*, but it was found that she did not have the storage capacity for a three-year voyage. They then turned to consideration of an east-coast collier or 'cat' and drew up a shortlist of three, finally opting for the *Earl of Pembroke*, a four-year-old Whitby collier, which the Admiralty bought for £2,800. Despite the earlier haste for a spring sailing, it was decided that the ship should go into dock for 'sheathing and filling', which essentially meant that an extra 'skin' was added to the vessel, of thinner boards outside her planks. To give protection against ship-worm (*Teredo navalis*), the sheathing was filled with nails with large flat heads.[82] The one snag about sheathing and filling, as the *Dolphin* had shown, was that copper sheathing corroded and was difficult to repair except in England; for this reason that particular experiment was not repeated on Cook's ship. Finally, on 5 April, the vessel was registered on the Royal Navy lists and renamed as HM bark *Endeavour*.[83] It was to be equipped with six four-pound carriage guns and eight swivel guns. At 369 tons, she was 106 feet long with the tallest of the three masts reaching 127 feet in height, 29 feet broad with a draught of 14 feet. Her flat bottom and very shallow keel made her 'tender'; in other words, she tended to roll exceptionally, even in calm weather.[84] This was not the *Endeavour*'s only problem. In mid-April it was discovered that most of her masts and yards were defective. The Admiralty issued orders that all other work at Deptford was to be laid aside until the ship was properly seaworthy, but there were further delays from another quarter. The spring and summer of

1768 was a time of great turmoil in England, with simultaneous strikes and riots by sailors, coal heavers, watermen, coopers, hatters, glass-grinders, sawyers, tailors and weavers, to say nothing of agitation from John Wilkes and his radical supporters.[85] Consequently, it was not until 18 May that *Endeavour* emerged from dry dock.

Besides the ship itself, there was the crewing and supplying for a three-year voyage to attend to. Providing an exact computation of every soul aboard an eighteenth-century ship is never easy, as many lists contain seamen only; others divide into officers and men; and still others take no account of super-numeraries or civilian passengers. Nevertheless, the best estimate is that there were 106 people aboard the *Endeavour* when she cleared for the South Pacific.[86] Of these, fifty-five were sailors (including the boatswain, two boatswain's mates, the gunner and his mate and the carpenter), twelve were marines, fourteen were officers, while 'gentlemen', eight servants, and other supernumeraries made up the total. Among the 'miscellaneous' personnel were three midshipmen, a clerk, an armourer, a sailmaker and two quarter-masters. Second in command to Cook was the 29-year-old Zachary Hicks; a man of no great abilities, he has been described as 'perhaps born to be a lieu-tenant'.[87] Much more impressive was the third lieutenant (Cook was the first and Hicks the second), a 38-year-old American named John Gore, a man with natural leadership qualities as well as a crack shot and talented hunter. He was a veteran of circumnavigation, having been round the world twice in the *Dolphin*, once under Byron and once with Wallis. The master, 22-year-old Robert Molyneux, was another *Dolphin* veteran, as was the 19-year-old mate Richard Pickersgill, and the master's mate Francis Wilkinson. Yet another *Dolphin* man was the deputy master's mate Charles Clerke, at 27 generally considered a lightweight and playboy, with a reputation for whoring and heavy drinking. Clerke, however, would prove his mettle over the years with Cook and was valued by him for his sunny temperament; a gifted raconteur and joker, he could lift the spirits of the men with a well-timed anecdote or jape. At this stage in his career, Cook was definitely considered a man with a good sense of humour.[88] Another bibulous character was William Brougham Monkhouse, the surgeon; also aboard was his younger brother Jonathan, a midshipman, a person of real talent and ingenuity. Only five men from the Newfoundland survey ship *Grenville* opted to go with Cook to the Pacific. Thomas Hardman, Isaac Smith and William Howson were able seamen and John Charlton had been his servant. Perhaps the most surprising volunteer was the selfsame Peter Flower, now aged 18, whom Cook had disciplined four years previously.[89] Almost the entire ship's complement except for Cook himself was aged under 30. One notable exception was the ancient sailmaker

John Ravenhill, of indeterminate age but certainly over 50; later testimony was adamant that he was permanently drunk throughout the voyage.[90]

Even when the ship's complement stood at eighty-odd in August, there was pressure on living space, but this became acute when the Admiralty and the Royal Society between them decided that the *Endeavour* would carry a credible quota of scientists and artists. Decks had to be subdivided to accommodate the new entrants, and this was in addition to the space cleared for four more swivel guns and a load of extra provisions. The two designated artists were Sydney Parkinson and Alexander Buchan. Cook's maiden Pacific voyage was already garnering firsts. Apart from the marginal discoveries of Dampier and Bering it was the first serious attempt since Tasman to unlock the secrets of the Pacific. It was the first to combine the older buccaneering spirit with the new ethos of the Enlightenment. And now, it transpired, it would be the first Pacific voyage (with the exception of Bougainville's) to carry official scientists and artists.[91] By far the most important of the scientists foisted on Cook by the Royal Society was the 25-year-old Joseph Banks, a naturalist and botanist who would become one of the great names in eighteenth-century natural history.[92] From an immensely wealthy Lincolnshire family, Banks had evinced an independent turn of mind by eschewing the study of classics at Oxford in favour of botany. He had then made a voyage to Newfoundland and Labrador (1766) to collect rare plant specimens.[93] To have a rich aristocrat imposed on him like this might have led to shipboard tensions with an ordinary Royal Navy captain, but Cook and Banks appeared to take to each other immediately and to form a close rapport which, in exploration terms, has been likened to the partnership between Meriwether Lewis and William Clark, the first white men to traverse North America east–west.[94] The common background in Newfoundland was surely a great help. Even without the personal entente, it is unlikely that Cook would have been anything but diplomatic with Banks, for by contributing £10,000 (the equivalent of about three quarters of a million pounds today) to the expedition, the wealthy oligarch immediately placed the *Endeavour* voyage beyond money worries. If Cook had ever felt resentment that the Royal Society had awarded its astronomical expert Charles Green a fee of 200 guineas, in contrast to his own emolument of just 100 guineas, the wealth of Banks made all such considerations appear negligible. Aside from the money, Banks brought valuable personnel on board. His Swedish friend Dr Daniel Carl Solander was the star pupil of Carl Linnaeus, the greatest botanist of the age.[95] Another valuable addition to the party was the 38-year-old Herman Sporing, surgeon, watchmaker and botanist. As one of Linnaeus's correspondents later remarked, the *Endeavour* voyage was the best seagoing scientific expedition ever mounted.[96]

Altogether Banks's party of scientists and artists required eight servants to tend them. Banks and his two scientific colleagues used the services of two valets brought from his country estate in Lincolnshire and two black retainers hired in London. With scarcely room on board to swing the proverbial cat, Cook added to his potential problems by loading on live animals and plentiful provisions. Among the *Endeavour*'s menagerie were two greyhounds, three cats to keep down the rat population, seventeen sheep, four pigs, twenty-four hens and chickens, and a now famous goat that had already been round the world with Wallis. On paper the rations given the seamen – one pound of biscuit and a gallon of beer a day, four pounds of salt beef per week, two pounds of salt pork, three pints of cereal grains, six ounces of butter and twelve ounces of cheese a week – were generous and amounted to 4,500 calories a day. But the main diet of ship's biscuit (hard tack), salt beef and salt pork was both monotonous and foul. Particular discontent was caused by the biscuit, which was infested with insects; on inspection Banks identified five different kinds of pest.[97] Mondays, Wednesdays and Fridays were especially unpopular, for these days were meatless and the men had to eat pease pudding and onions. The Admiralty had provided Cook with a year's supply of sauerkraut as an antiscorbutic, but this was an unpopular item in the diet, frequently refused. Although it is often asserted that Cook prevented scurvy on his ships, perhaps it is more accurate to say that he merely avoided it.[98] Banks himself was aware of the aetiology and dangers of scurvy and had correctly laid in a supply of citrus fruit to provide Vitamin C, but at this stage in his travels Cook naïvely thought that the prevention of scurvy had most to do with personal hygiene and the wearing of warm clothing. This was despite the fact that the correct solution to the scurvy problem had already been published by Dr James Lind. It is curious that neither the Admiralty nor Cook himself paid particular attention to his discoveries, especially since Sir Hugh Palliser, Cook's patron, was a great believer in Lind's methods.[99]

In order to spend years at sea and thoroughly explore the Pacific, the early eighteenth-century mariner had an even more serious problem to solve than scurvy. Although latitude could be established by observing with a quadrant or astrolabe the inclination of the sun at noon or the stars, estimation of longitude was still mainly attempted by the crude method of log and line: essentially, calculating how long a length of rope took to uncoil from a ship into the sea. Nonetheless, technological progress had accelerated in the century immediately before the *Endeavour* voyage. Telescopes, verniers, micrometers and logarithms – valuable aids in determining latitude – were all inventions of the seventeenth century. Moreover, the 1756 surveys of the French Académie

Royale des Sciences in Quito and Lapland confirmed Newton's deduction of polar flattening of the globe and established the mean length of a minute of arc on the meridian as 6,080 feet, which had important implications for dead reckoning by log and line.[100] A major technical breakthrough was John Hadley's quadrant of 1731, allowing altitudes to be taken without any disturbance caused by the ship's motion. In 1760 Captain John Campbell developed this quadrant into a sextant, whereby angles could be read over an arc of 120 instead of the quadrant's 90.[101] Meanwhile Dr Gavin Knight had devised a complicated azimuth compass – Cook actually thought it too complex – which gradually established itself as a standard fixture for the credible navigator.[102] In theory, the sextant could also be used to determine longitude, using the lunar distance method. A seaman could tell the time by measuring the distance between the moon and selected stars. He could then compare the time observed at his location with tables that showed the same time for the same lunar distance at a standard meridian, of which the most obvious were the Paris Observatory or its British equivalent at Greenwich. But the thirst for accurate determination of longitude was to produce the eighteenth century's most famous scientific battle of the giants: a David and Goliath contest in England between the Astronomer-Royal and the scientific establishment on the one hand and a humble watchmaker on the other.[103]

The problem about longitude at sea can be simply stated. Since the earth rotates through 360 degrees in twenty-four hours, one hour corresponds to 15 degrees of longitude. The problem was that no clock had ever been devised that was capable of running consistently at sea, since clocks were vulnerable to the ship's motion; moreover, the pendulum swing depended on the gravity constant, which varied with latitude. Following a series of severe naval disasters and shipwrecks resulting from inaccurate estimates of longitude, the Admiralty petitioned the government for urgent action. A Board of Longitude was set up in 1714, which announced a series of escalating prizes for precision chronometers; for example, one invented that was accurate to within half a degree – two minutes of time or thirty nautical miles – would command a reward of £20,000.[104] While ingenious inventors pursued the chronometrical path, astronomers put their money on the lunar observation method. Since the moon completes a circuit of 360 degrees in 27.3 days, in one hour it will move half a degree. Using a sextant, the navigator proceeds to measure the 'lunar distance': the angle between the moon and another celestial body. He then consults a prepared table of lunar distances and the times at which they will occur – assuming such an almanac exists. Having determined local time by sextant observation, the lunar distance is then correlated with conditions obtaining at Greenwich Mean Time and the longitude calculated accordingly.[105] Nevil Maskelyne, the Astronomer-Royal in a masterpiece of research in 1766 published *The Nautical Almanac*, a completely updated lunar method, which contained complete and accurate tables of the moon's angular distance from the sun and certain fixed stars; the book also provided figures for every three hours at different longitudes in the year 1767.[106] Even so, the lunar method was unconscionably time-consuming. The necessary computations and calculations originally took four hours and although this was whittled down in time to thirty minutes, the factor of cost took a hand. Lunar calculation required the most sophisticated sextants, and eventually it became less expensive simply to buy three chronometers which could be checked against each other, rather than pay for a highly priced sextant. For a while, though, the lunar method reigned supreme.[107]

Yet even as the scientists congratulated themselves on an easy victory of the professionals over the amateurs, they were overtaken by events. John Harrison set himself the task of producing a mechanical timepiece that would give the correct time at London while a ship was at sea, making it proof against the yawing, pitching and rolling of the vessel which invariably knocked existing clocks out of time. The chronometer also had to be proof against the effects of differential climate, humidity, corrosion, friction and variations in gravity. Harrison's work evinced a lifetime of dedication. Altogether he built five chronometers, two of which were tested at sea.[108] By 1728 he had invented two necessary components of his nautical gizmo: a pendulum of combined brass and steel, in which the different rates of shrinkage and expansion of the two metals cancelled each other out; and the so-called 'grasshopper recoil escapement' which eliminated friction. By 1735 he had dispensed with the pendulum and replaced it with two mutually correcting balances. This was the H1 chronometer, which should at least have won one of the Board of Longitude's minor prizes. But Harrison was always bedevilled by jealousy, from rival watchmakers and more seriously from Maskelyne himself and the powerful lobby of professional astronomers. The sole problem with Harrison's spring-driven chronometers was that the early pedestal-mounted models were too heavy and cumbersome to be practicable on board ship.[109] Finally, in 1759 he produced his masterpiece, the famous H4, a convenient timepiece in watch form. It was thoroughly tested by his son on a voyage to the West Indies in 1761 and proved accurate to within one and a quarter minutes of longitude or five seconds of time. Even after five months at sea and a stormy passage home from Jamaica, it was still only one minute and 54½ seconds out (28½ minutes of longitude or 18 statute miles). Sadly, the Board of Longitude tried to welsh on the deal, and the well-merited reward money was paid over only in 1775, after Harrison's death.[110] By 1770 the

Harrison chronometer was standard issue but, because of pedantic nitpicking connected with the attempted non-payment of the reward money, the Admiralty did not issue H4 to Cook; he did, however, take it with him on his second and third voyages. This was why the *Endeavour*, in its purely Pacific rovings (as opposed to the Australasian ones) did not venture far from the tried and tested transoceanic tracks. Nevertheless, when the *Endeavour* finally stood away from the British Isles in August 1768, it carried with it the fruits of up-to-date scientific knowledge, both in the form of Banks and his comrades and in terms of sextants and astronomical tables. The voyage began propitiously, a perfect synergy of buccaneering spirit, Royal Navy discipline, royal patronage, cooperation between Admiralty and the Royal Society, government finance and private enterprise (Banks's money).[111] Cook could hardly have complained about the back-up for his expedition. Everything now depended on his seamanship.

Cook set off from Deptford for Plymouth on 7 August 1768, having made all the last-minute additions to his cre0w, including that of the American midshipman James Magra (or Matra), who later wrote an unauthorised account of the voyage.[112] Presumably the farewells from Elizabeth were fond and tearful but, as always with Cook's private life, we know nothing, except that she had presumably influenced her husband to find a berth for her cousin Isaac Smith, the draughtsman. We know more about Banks, for the young Swiss aristocrat Horace-Bénédict de Saussure, who left an invaluable memoir of London in the late 1760s, was with him on Friday 15 August 1768, when he received an express summons from Cook telling him to come down to Plymouth (where Cook had now arrived) with all speed. Banks, supposedly in love with a wealthy beauty named Harriet Blosset, drank heavily that night to conceal his emotions, whatever they were.[113] Saussure reported:

> Saw for the first time Miss Harriet Blosset, with Mr Banks, her betrothed. Returned on foot from the opera with them and supped together. The eldest daughter, tall, decided, agreeable, a great musician, splendid voice, fond of society, polished. The second, Miss Harriet, desperately in love with Mr Banks, from who she was to part next day – hitherto a prudent coquette, but now only intent on pleasing her lover, and resolved to spend in the country all the time he is away . . . As Banks cannot speak a word of French, I could not judge of his abilities . . . I supped there with him and Dr Solander, who is also starting with him for Isle St George [*sic*]. Miss Blosset, not knowing that he was to start next day, was quite gay.[114]

Although Cook always deferred to Banks socially, and had even given up the Great Cabin to him, and although the philandering young botanist and would-be Renaissance man enjoyed an income of £6,000 a year from his Lincolnshire estates, when his captain summoned him, even he had to go. Next morning he was on the coach for Plymouth. Was it perhaps typical of the *de haut en bas* attitude of Solander that he pleaded last-minute arrangements and set off later?

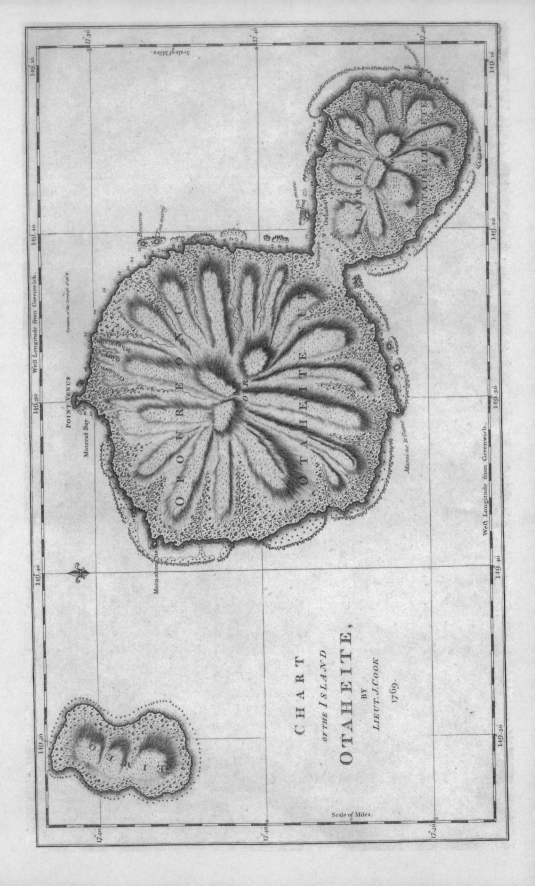

CHART
OF THE ISLAND
OTAHEITE,
BY
LIEUT. J. COOK
1769.

Scale of Miles.

CHAPTER FIVE

First Contacts with Tahiti

Before departing on his great adventure, Cook made financial arrangements for his wife and arranged to have a cousin named Frances Wardale, from Yorkshire, to live with her during his absence. He made over to Elizabeth his final pay as master of the *Grenville* and the fees he received for selling his Newfoundland charts and the publication rights thereof to the publisher Thomas Jefferys.[1] He could not tarry to see the birth of his next child, although Elizabeth was near full term – perhaps just as well, for the infant, Joseph, born on 5 September, died before he was a month old. On 30 July Cook 1768 received his instructions from the Admiralty, in two parts. The first part instructed him to go to Plymouth, pay his crew two months' wages in advance, and then to proceed to Madeira to buy stocks of wine for the voyage. There followed detailed advice on the trip to Tahiti and the procedures for observing the transit of Venus. Only when all the scientific work on the transit was complete was he to open the second, most secret, part of the instructions, which laid on him the task of searching for the Great Southern Continent and, if unsuccessful in that endeavour, he was to make a detailed survey of the land of New Zealand reported by Tasman. He was to find out all he could about the indigenous peoples, investigate the soil and tropical products and bring back mineral and plant specimens.[2] There was now nothing to detain Cook. After bidding farewell to Elizabeth and his children on 6 August, he took the *Endeavour* on a leisurely passage to Plymouth, where he paid his sailors and summoned Banks and his party from London. It was 18 August before the last of his party arrived, in the form of Solander. Meanwhile, as already related, Cook received orders for the last-minute addition of ten sailors and the party of marines which further cramped and shoehorned the ship's complement into tiny living spaces. Finally, on 19 August, Cook assembled the ship's company and, as protocol required, recited the thirty-six clauses of the Articles of War; among the stipulations was a requirement for the holding of divine service, even though the *Endeavour*'s captain was not a practising Christian.[3]

Ready to sail by the 20th, the *Endeavour* was not able to put to sea until the afternoon of 26 September because of adverse winds with driving rain. The ship's progress was always painfully slow – no more than 7–8 knots in ideal conditions and much slower even in a light wind. Nevertheless, for the first twenty-four hours Banks and the other scientists were delighted to see large numbers of dolphins breaching and gambolling within sight of land. But as the sea condition escalated from smooth to moderate, Banks went down with severe seasickness, and soon he was confined to his cabin, from which he did not emerge for the next four days.[4] Once into the Bay of Biscay the ship encountered the hard westerly gales for which that stretch of water is notorious: 50-foot waves have been reliably reported there. The gale carried off the boatswain's small dinghy and – from Cook's point of view much more seriously – it swept overboard some four dozen poultry. Banks reported that the artist Sydney Parkinson could not set pencil to paper because of the violent pitching and rolling of the ship. Not until 2 September did the weather moderate. Cook took sightings and found himself off the northernmost shores of Spain, running down towards Cape Finisterre. According to the astronomer Green, Cook was hopeless at estimating longitude by the lunar method and had to be schooled in the technique.[5] If so, he made rapid progress and had mastered the essentials by the time they came to Rio. It may be that in the early stages of the voyage Cook was preoccupied with issues of discipline and making sure the *Endeavour* functioned as a harmonious vessel. The lower deck always liked to keep to itself and expected the quarterdeck to do likewise. Unlike Lieutenant William Bligh on a notorious later voyage, Cook was well aware of this social dimension and realised that 'slum-dwellers resent do-gooders'.[6] Also, in the first few days of the voyage Cook was genuinely concerned about cuisine and the standard of food. He had originally been assigned a lame man as cook, for the Admiralty liked to employ those who had been injured on naval service in 'civilian' capacities to avoid the expense of a pension or welfare payments. When Cook protested that the man was of no use in the galley, the Admiralty substituted John Thompson, but the new 'chef' proved to have no right arm. Cook again protested, but this time the Admiralty dug in and refused to replace him. Fortunately for Cook and the rest of the *Endeavour*'s complement, Thompson proved to be fully competent, at least given the general low standard of Navy cooks.[7]

Cook was, in Royal Navy terms, what might be called a moderate conservative. In other words, as a captain he insisted on a high level of discipline and efficiency, but he was no martinet and did not go looking for trouble. He knew the likely sources of trouble from below decks: food, shore leave, grog, women. He was well aware that the ordinary seamen loathed getting wet in their hammocks when rain or spray leaked through the decks above; this, and the omnipresence of rats, was often held to be a major cause of desertion. He knew how tough conditions were aboard, with the latrines or 'heads' mere holed planks extending from the bow, from which it was not unknown for seamen to fall and drown in the deep, especially in bad weather. All this he took into consideration when gauging the temper of his men, but he was never a 'bleeding heart' humanitarian, and it is probably true that he was more worried about the loss of precious chickens in the gale in the Bay of Biscay than about the death of an expendable crewman.[8] Yet in some respects he was shrewd and enlightened. The usual system at sea was that everyone kept two watches, and the men were divided into larboard and starboard rotas. Each watch lasted four hours, except for the two-hour dogwatches between 4 and 8 p.m. The quartermaster of the watch kept a half-hour sandglass; when it turned, he rang the ship's bell. At eight bells the watch changed, which meant that no one got more than four hours' sleep at any stretch and even then could be roused if a genuine emergency arose. Lack of sleep was a constant hardship for those on watch at sea.[9] After taking advice from Wallis the circumnavigator, Cook decided to put his men on eight-hour watches, thus ensuring better rest and a potentially uninterrupted slumber.

Cook knew that in the Pacific he and his crew might face sea conditions even more extreme than any they had experienced hitherto. For this reason he insisted on a high standard of expertise aloft. Going aloft meant grasping the vertical shrouds which had ratlines strung horizontally to create a lattice up the mast. The climbing, breathless seamen would reach the underside of a platform called the fighting top. To reach it they had to grab hold of cables called futtocks and do a short but nerve-racking climb while dangling backwards at a 45-degree angle. They then had to clutch the bar at the rim of the platform and hoist themselves up on to the fighting top.[10] It was already much colder than on deck but the climbing sailors were still only halfway up the mast. Next it was necessary to 'step' on to the yard, which meant tiptoeing sideways along a narrow, drooping foot line beneath the yard, which ran perpendicularly from the mast; this was the yardarm where criminals were hanged. Bending over the yard, taking care not to get caught in the cobwebs of lines – claws, bunts, reefs – the sailor then had to reach down to untie the knots around the sails, taking care not to look down at the sea. It was not unknown for men to drop exhausted from the yards, though this happened more rarely in the Royal Navy than in the merchant marine.[11] But the least favourite task of all was reefing the topgallants. In order to furl these, the sailors had to climb up to the crosstrees: three narrow strips of wood perched beneath the top yard. Reefing a sail was much more cumbersome and tiring than letting it down, since when one raised a sail, it was necessary to tie it to the yard – looping a rope under the sail, cinching it tight, then throwing the spare line over one shoulder before edging along the yard to tie up another clot of sail, at an elevation of 100 feet from the deck. When it is considered that height has a fivefold effect on a ship's roll, and all this work had to be done while the vessel pitched and rolled, work aloft represented men literally at the end of their tether.[12]

Every Royal Navy ship was its own mini-universe, a floating self-contained world. Hierarchy was strictly observed. Those with His Majesty's commission had a clear status, but there was a twilight area of what one might call 'half officers' occupied by the master, the most senior of the non-commissioned officers, the master's mates and the midshipmen, in theory no more than ratings except that a warrant officer could be court-martialled for striking them.[13] These 'half officers' were in time expected to take the king's commission. At sea petty officers and seamen divided into watches and each watch into a number of 'parts of the ship'. The least experienced joined the afterguard on the quarterdeck. Here, under the eye of the commissioned officers, they did the unskilled work: hauling on sheets, halliard and braces. The cleverest and most skilled seamen worked aloft as topmen. The upper yardmen, the youngest of the topmen, worked on the topgallants and royal yards, the highest of all, whose sails and gear were lightest. Older seamen joined the forecastle-men under the boatswain, handling headsails, clearing away the anchors to let go and catting and fishing them when unmooring. The marines, under the direct charge of their own officer, were expected to help with the pulling and hauling in normal circumstances, but could not be ordered aloft.[14] It was obvious that without strict discipline, hierarchy and deference any ship faced potential disaster in difficult or stormy conditions for, lacking steam power, eighteenth-century mariners were entirely at the mercy of wind and waves. No one knew this better than Cook, so it was a worry for him when, no farther forward on the voyage than Madeira, he ran into problems with his crew. First, two seamen refused to eat their beef allowance and had to be punished with a dozen lashes apiece. This was Cook showing at an early stage that he could be tough and was not to be trifled with. Then the anchor slipped in the night owing to the carelessness of the matelot who was supposed to make it fast. Even worse, one of the men sent to retrieve the anchor was drowned.[15]

In general the five-day stay at Madeira (13–18 September) does not seem to have been a happy one. Evidently there was some minor trouble with the Portuguese authorities, which was later exaggerated into the false and absurd story that Cook had lent the *Endeavour* to an attempt by a Royal Navy frigate to bombard the fort of Loo on the island.[16] Cook was actually much too busy laying in provisions and the supplies of wine the Admiralty had authorised him to take on at Madeira. He ordered that twenty pounds of onions were to be issued to each man – another anti-scurvy measure – and later increased the quota to thirty pounds; this was also a way of reinforcing the message about diet he had already sent by ordering the flogging of the two recalcitrant seamen. He also took on board a further 270 pounds of fresh beef, a live bullock weighing 613 pounds and a quantity of poultry to replace those lost in the Bay of Biscay gale. A further 10 tons of fresh water was loaded aboard. The most astonishing statistic concerns the alcohol taken on at Madeira. Apart from 1,200 gallons of beer, a further 1,600 gallons of spirits (brandy, rum, arrack) and 3,032 gallons of wine were purchased from the Portuguese.[17] The men's daily ration was a gallon of beer or a pint of rum, served twice daily with water as 'grog'. Some of the more alcoholic souls mixed beer with rum or brandy to make the lethal concoction known as 'flip'. Cook took a tolerant attitude to drink provided drunkenness did not get out of hand, and recorded in a matter-of-fact way that his crew was semi-drunk throughout the entire voyage.[18] At midnight on 18 September the *Endeavour* stood away for the Canaries and fetched Tenerife on the 24th. While Cook had laboured methodically on Madeira, Banks and his entourage had enjoyed themselves, housed as they were in a convent while they went out each day to collect botanical specimens and then entertained liberally in the evening by the British consul.[19]

There followed five or six weeks of delightful weather, with calm seas as the ship was wafted along by the north-east trades.[20] Numbers of flying fish flopped aboard to add to the crew's protein intake, and much fun was had catching sharks with rod and line; unfortunately Banks's scientific instincts failed him at this point, for he neglected to name the species.[21] Since the *Endeavour* was at the time passing near Boa Vista in the Cape Verde islands, and this is a favourite haunt of the oceanic white-tip, the shark responsible for more human fatalities in history than any other, it would be more than interesting to know if a specimen of *Carcharinus longimanus* was among the pelagic predators hooked by the matelots. On 25 October the ship reached the equator, still making 40–50 nautical miles a day, and the traditional Crossing the Line ceremonies were held.[22] Anyone who could not provide documentary evidence that he had crossed the line before was plunged deeply into the sea in a cage lowered by block and tackle; the only way to 'compound' or avoid the ritual was to forgo four days' grog. Banks noted with amusement that many of the sailors preferred to be ducked rather than lose four days' allowance of alcohol; the 'gentlemen', himself and Cook included, elected to pay the customary fine in rum rather than lose face in the roistering rough-and-tumble. Banks's description of the ritual makes it sound like a grim ordeal, which some of the less fit of the twenty-five men thus baptised only just survived.[23] Two days later Cook estimated the ship's position to be some sixty miles from the curious keyhole-shaped island of Fernando de Noronha which confronts most modern navigators on the run from Rio north-east across the Atlantic. On 8 November the mainland of South America was sighted; the ship's company hailed a Portuguese fishing boat and bought enough fresh fish to satisfy over a hundred ravening stomachs.[24] On 13 November the *Endeavour* came to anchor in the spectacular harbour of Rio de Janeiro. The original suggestion from the Admiralty was that he should make his first long stopover at Port Egmont in the Falklands, but Cook reasoned that the Falklands could provide him with water only, whereas at Rio he could purchase food and live-stock as well, to say nothing of careening and cleaning his ship.

Since the Portuguese were supposed to feel warmly towards their ancient and traditional ally, the reception Cook received was a severe shock.[25] The elderly viceroy of Brazil, Dom Antonio Rolim de Moura, Conde de Azumbuja, responded with the utmost coldness to his visitors and made it plain in a dozen different ways that they were not welcome. He conveyed to Cook by an inter-mediary his conviction that the *Endeavour*'s real purpose was not a genuine voyage of discovery but espionage on the Portuguese empire in the Americas. He scoffed at the idea that its aim was to observe the transit of Venus, ignorantly remarking that all the necessary sightings could be done perfectly well in Europe. Moreover, he effectively embargoed the *Endeavour* by decreeing that only Cook could leave the ship, and that even he had to be accompanied every-where by an armed guard. Portuguese soldiers also had to accompany all boats plying to and from the ship, and Cook was obliged to employ an 'agent' (on commission, naturally) when buying provisions.[26] Cook protested vociferously that these requirements were an insult to the British flag and thus to the royal personage of King George. So far from being moved by this, Azumbuja arrested some of Cook's men who had tried to evade the regulations and wrote to Cook that if he did not like the arrangements in Rio he was welcome to leave at any time. Cook's blood was up, and he wrote again in the strongest possible language to protest about his reception. The viceroy witheringly declared that he doubted the *Endeavour* really was a Royal Navy ship, let alone one engaged in a voyage of exploration; his interpretation was now that the English were smugglers and their ship a privateer. Cook was in a state of barely suppressed fury, which he managed to project by punishing a seaman, John Thurman, who was foolish enough to choose this moment to refuse to assist the sailmaster in repairing the sails; he received twelve lashes.[27]

We are entitled to ask why Cook experienced such an extraordinary recep-tion. Some say that he had no gift for diplomacy and alienated a curmudgeonly viceroy by talking about the honour of England, and that, as a mere lieutenant, he did not treat the Portuguese grandee with enough deference. Others claim that the problem was more deep-seated, that Azumbuja was merely obeying orders from the Portuguese chief minister, the Marquis de Pombal, who distrusted the English. Rio had been attacked twice during the eighteenth century and sacked in 1711, and Pombal himself had been coldly received in London on an official mission in 1764 – in striking contrast to the fuss made of him in Paris and Madrid.[28] Not only did Pombal think that the trade privileges enjoyed by the British in Latin America benefited no one but the British, but he also promoted the popular line that all so-called explorers and geographers were really spies; the great Alexander von Humboldt would receive a dose of this medicine in 1800. Most incredibly of all, given the fanatical anti-Catholicism of eighteenth-century England, Pombal believed that England was a secret ally of his deadly enemy the Jesuits.[29] Whatever the true reasons for Azumbuja's behaviour, the result was that the month spent in Rio (13 November–7 December) was not a happy one. Cook's mood continued grim, and there were further punishments. Robert Anderson was given twelve lashes for attempted desertion, and the marine William Judge was flogged for insolence to the officer of the watch. Cook's contempt for the viceroy was obvious and he privately accused him of being involved in every conceivable money-making scam. As final proof of this, when Cook asked the viceroy for a pilot to negotiate the exit from Rio harbour, Azumbuja sent one with a note requiring immediate payment for a mandatory large boat (costing ten shillings a day) as well as a pilot's fee of £7 4s. – which Cook doubted the pilot would ever see.[30] The viceroy's orders were in any case being flouted as Banks and his party took to stealing ashore at night under cover of darkness and prowling the waterfront stews.

The *Endeavour* cleared from Rio on 8 December. Sailing out of the bay Cook suffered a personal loss when able seaman Peter Flower, who had been with him since the early days of the Newfoundland survey, fell overboard and was drowned. Now there were 2,000 miles to sail to the Le Maire Strait, Cook's preferred approach to Cape Horn. Banks had been aware of Cook's difficulties with the viceroy and sympathised, but his main interest in Brazil had been the pursuit of the local women, who he claimed were experts in the lubricious arts.[31] Never a great sailor, he suffered grievously as the *Endeavour* ran into increasingly bad weather on the run to Buenos Aires and points south. For two weeks he had to endure a very heavy swell and occasional white squalls and was astonished that the sailors seemed unfazed. Christmas Day 1768 was celebrated in traditional fashion. Banks noted: 'All hands got abominably drunk so that at night there was scarcely a sober man in the ship – wind, thank God, very moderate or God knows what would have become of us.'[32] From 27 December until 6 January the seas were continually high and tempestuous, with gales and thunderstorms and Banks was hardly able to sleep because of the ship's violent pitching and rolling. The swells were so enormous that the fore-topgallant mast was lost; it sometimes seemed as though the sails were permanently reefed; frequently Cook had to heave to in monstrous seas, with bunks smashing on the sides and tops of cabins all night long. Biting cold now came into the picture, and on 6 January 1769 Cook issued the cold-weather fearnoughts (heavy felted jackets and trousers) not so much out of compassion for the crew but for fear of scurvy.[33] The strong gales and heavy squalls continued, but on 11 January the lookout sighted Tierra del Fuego. Cook's intention now was to make for Cape Horn via Le Maire Strait – the passage between Staten Island and the south-eastern tip of Tierra del Fuego – but he was driven back three times at the western entrance by the tremendous power of the tide race (the current flowed west to east) before he succeeded.

Cook then manoeuvred the *Endeavour* into a bay (the Bay of Success) but even with this protection from the ocean the heavy swell made the ship roll so much that it was not possible to stand up without holding on to something for support.[34] On 15 January Cook sent out a landing party through heavy showers of rain and snow. The idea was that the working element of the party would gather wood and water while the gentlemen botanised. Meanwhile Cook would sail up and down the local coast looking for a way through the adverse currents of Le Maire Strait. Cook duly made a meticulous survey of the bay and his currents, often working in blinding snow showers. The landing party made contact with about forty Fuegians who had gathered on the shore and seemed friendly. They were much taken with trade beads but showed a strong inclination to theft.[35] Banks and his fellow scientists were among the first ashore and were due back aboard on the evening of the 17th. When they did not return, Cook grew anxious. What happened was that the scientists, almost academic clichés in their absent-mindedness, became distracted by their researches and did not begin the return journey to the ship until too late. They then trekked through a snowstorm in the gathering gloom until they found a suitable camping place. Then tragedy struck. Their two black servants had refused to walk another step in the snowstorm, even though they were just a quarter of a mile from the hastily improvised communal fire. By an error a large supply of brandy was left behind with them. When the servants began drinking wildly and irresponsibly, the solitary sailor left to supervise them staggered forward through the snow to the main camp to alert Banks. It was decided not to send out a rescue party until first light. When the rescuers set out at dawn, they soon came on the servants, stone dead. Hopelessly drunk, they had lain down in the snow and succumbed to hypothermia.[36]

Back on board after a narrower escape from death by exposure than he appears to have been aware of, the sanguine Banks probably soon wished he was back in the terrestrial snowdrifts. Further expeditions ashore were impossible, as Cook explained: 'All the middle and latter part of this day (18 January) it blew very strong from the south-south-west and south west, attended by snow, hail and rain, and brought such a sea into the bay, which ran surf to such a height that no boat could land. The same stormy weather and surf continued all night.' Next day found the *Endeavour* rolling 'prodigiously' in the swell, even though she was in a sheltered bay.[37] It was 21 January before Cook could recommence the voyage. In a masterpiece of careful navigation, still beset by squalls, snow and hail, though to a lesser extent than before, he inched his way down to Cape Horn which he formally 'rounded' on 26–27 January. Later seamen who battled with the Horn were aghast that he set studding sails in such seas. But this was just one of the many ways in which Cook showed his confidence and disregard for the sailing instructions recommended by Admiral Anson. Cook made it plain that he considered the passage through Le Maire Strait and round the Horn preferable to the route through the Straits of Magellan, even though Anson had encountered the most terrible storms on the Le Maire route.[38] Cook's experience, indeed, made this route the preferred itinerary for all Pacific-bound vessels until the completion of the Panama Canal in 1914. (Cook himself returned to Cape Horn only once, when sailing eastwards at the end of his second great voyage of 1772–75.) He considered his feat of 'doubling' complete when he had clocked up 1,500 miles since sighting Tierra del Fuego and was at the same latitude (50S) on the Pacific side. It had taken thirty-three days to achieve the passage through Tierra del Fuego and round the Horn – a much better performance than that of Byron or Wallis and, though Cook was lucky with the weather – as a navigator he was always lucky – he was not boasting idly when he commented: 'I can now venture to assert that the longitudes of few places in the world are better ascertained than of Strait Le Maire and Cape Horn, being determined by several observations of the Sun and Moon, made both by myself and Mr Green the astronomer.'[39]

Once into the Pacific Cook set the *Endeavour* on a north-westerly track. The weather was surprisingly variable. For most of the next two months there was a heavy swell from the south-south-west, which Cook (correctly) construed to mean there could be no great land mass in that direction. Sometimes there were pleasant breezes and sometimes there was persistent fog, which reminded Banks of his time in Newfoundland.[40] More usually, though, there were gales and squalls. Banks's entry for 10 February read: 'During all last night the ship has pitched very much so that there has been no sleeping for landsmen.' During 16–17 February very high seas were running as a strong gale tore into the *Endeavour* from the south-south-west. A huge sea carried away the ship's driver boom on the 16th, and on the 17th the main topsail split. By the 23rd it was no longer possible to see the horizon and as the ship corkscrewed (pitched and rolled simultaneously) the waves broke over the quarterdeck; a mere thirteen miles' progress was logged in the entire twenty-four-hour period.[41] But whenever there were favourable winds, Cook ordered the studding sails set and ate up the miles: 130, 132, 140 knots were the figures recorded on those days when it was calm enough for Banks to descend into the sea in a small boat and slaughter a few more seabirds – his favourite pastime. By 3 March Banks made a diary entry noteworthy for his amazing naïvety about the inaptly named Pacific Ocean: 'Rather squally this morning and had been so all night – it did not however blow up to a gale though the ship had a good deal of motion. Indeed, I begin to hope that we are now so near the peaceful part of the Pacific Ocean that we may almost cease to fear any more gales.'[42] This time Banks's ignorance proved blissful. From about 10 March the winds turned easterly, the sea became calmer and seabirds were sighted. Westerlies in the third week of March pushed the vessel across the tropic of Capricorn, but there was still no sight of land. Cook resisted the obvious temptation to try to find Pitcairn Island, which he knew about and which according to his calculations was the nearest land. 'I did not think myself at liberty to spend time in searching for what I was not sure to find' was his pithy comment.[43]

As the *Endeavour* neared the Tuamotu archipelago – that vast congeries of islands stretching north-west by west between latitudes 19 and 15S – the tranquillity of the ship was disturbed by another serious incident below decks. A young marine named William Greenslade, in circumstances that are far from clear, was entrusted with the care of a large sealskin which was to be cut up by the matelots to make tobacco pouches. Since Greenslade had been expressly forbidden a share of the sealskin by a kangaroo tribunal of the able seamen, one can only conclude that they entrusted it to him to tempt him to take the very action he did take. In short, he cut a piece from the sealskin to make his own pouch. When the 'theft' was discovered, Greenslade was vociferously denounced and then sent to Coventry. The sergeant of marines thought it proper to bring the persecution to Cook's attention but, again in a sequence of events that is far from clear, Greenslade either threw himself overboard in despair or, more likely, was made away with by his malign comrades while visiting the 'heads'. Since it was so easy for an accident to happen in this location, the suspicion of murder had to remain just that, but the atmosphere on board was badly soured.[44] Suicide seemed all the more unlikely, since two days before the 'man overboard' cry (26 March), the first signs of land were detected, leading Cook to surmise that he was close to the islands discovered by Quirós in 1606. The first atoll actually sighted (on 4 April) was a tiny sliver of land surrounding a lagoon, which Cook named Lagoon Island. Soon the *Endeavour* was threading her way through a succession of islets and rocky outcrops, including Bougainville's Ile des Lanciers (Akiaki) and La Harpe (Hao) until on 10 April Cook was definitely able to identify the islands charted by Wallis and called by him Osnabrück (Mehetia) and King George's (Tahiti). A few Polynesians came out to the ship in canoes, bearing coconuts and tokens of friendship, but declined to go on board. Under a clear sky and gentle breezes the *Endeavour* came to anchor at Matavai Bay in Tahiti on Thursday 13 April. The passage from Plymouth to Tahiti had been a remarkable feat of seamanship, especially since this was Cook's first open-ocean voyage. He had been lucky, but knew how to build on his good fortune; Cook perfectly exemplified Mark Twain's later saw that the harder he worked, the luckier he got. He had already been farther west in the high latitudes of the Pacific than any previous voyager. He was ahead of schedule in terms of observing the transit of Venus, and had lost just four men in eight months, none of them to sickness.[45]

The first thing that struck the European travellers was the awesome beauty of Tahiti. The peaks of the seven thousand-feet-high mountains towered above lush green vegetation that ended just short of the summits. Striated by deep valleys and swift, rushing rivers, the land fell away sharply to the shore-line for much of the island, but in the north there were extensive sandy beaches. A barrier reef surrounded the island, about half a mile to two miles offshore, forever booming and thundering as the great Pacific rollers beat on it. Numerous breaks in the reef provided entrances and exits for canoes but the only obvious harbourage for oceangoing ships was at the northern point of Matavai Bay. Affording almost complete protection from contrary winds and high seas, the bay itself was a jewel, its black volcanic sands fringed by the myriad sentinels of coconut trees. The views in all directions were spectacular and the only thing preventing the northern shore of Tahiti from seeming to be an earthly paradise was the plague of black flies that infested the beach; Cook and his men used mosquito nets to ward them off, the dreaded anopheles mosquito itself being unknown in Polynesia.[46] Cook's remarks on natural beauty tend to be brief, curt and pragmatic. The burdens of leadership led him to concentrate on the expected cultural clash with the Polynesians, about which he had received some hints from previous navigators. He drew up a list of rules which he exhorted his men to learn by heart, warning that any infraction would court serious punishment. There were five main clauses. The first commanded that all men should deal peacefully and in a friendly way with the 'Indians' (as Cook and his men at first called them); the second that all trade would be conducted through a single British overlord, yet to be named, and that not even senior officers could evade this monopoly; the third warned that anyone losing weapons or tools ashore would have the full cost of a replacement deducted from his pay; the fourth imposed the same penalty for any theft or embezzlement; and the fifth forbade the exchange of iron for any reason except as directed by the appointed market supremo.[47]

Throughout the voyage Cook had quizzed Charles Clerke, John Gore, Francis Haite and the eight other veterans of the *Grenville* and *Dolphin* expeditions both about their previous experience of Tahiti and the *Endeavour*'s likely reception there. Their reports and suggestions underlay Cook's five rules. All the veterans told Cook that Tahitians had a positive mania for iron and that the natural posture of the people towards strangers was hostility. Wallis had had to deal with initial aggression by the islanders by firing a nine-pounder over their heads, and Gore had wounded a man when Tahitians tried to intercept the cutter on its return to the ship; when the canoes again attacked, two Tahitians were shot dead.[48] The throng of locals in their huge canoes had created another problem, for when the *Dolphin* initially tried to anchor in Matavai Bay, the ship could not read the signals from her small boats because of the press of indigenous craft. With difficulty Wallis got to sea and then made another approach prior to anchoring; he then set a strong guard over the vessel. Brazenly, a multitude of islanders in war canoes, maybe 4,000 strong, again tried to attack the *Dolphin*, trying to distract the seamen with the sight of curvaceous young women dancing provocatively on the beach. Caught in a crossfire of rocks and slingshots, the Europeans opened fired with everything they had: muskets, deck guns with small shot, cannons with round and grapeshot. They sank many canoes, killing and wounding scores of warriors, then bombarded the shoreline, killing many more dozens of onlookers.[49] Next day the Tahitians had seemed both chastened and frightened, so Wallis sent his marines to take possession of the island in the name of King George. Thenceforth the Europeans were no longer seriously threatened. Thinking the powerful strangers must be emissaries sent by the god Oro – whose cult was then sweeping the Society Islands – the islanders began to bring groaning baskets of food as peace offerings. Clerke and Gore confessed that they found the local government and religion a mystery, and were astonished at the pervasive worship of sharks.[50]

The other notable phenomenon reported by the *Dolphin* veterans was the easy and permissive sexuality on the islands, with Tahiti a lubricious cornucopia. Women made themselves available for sexual congress with the sailors, seemingly with the connivance of their menfolk, and even girls as young as 10 and 11 were plying their trade. The serpent in this apparent carnal paradise was that the Tahitians demanded payment in iron for their free and easy prostitution. The seamen, heedless of everything but immediate gratification, removed nails and iron from the ship in vast quantities, putting the vessel seriously at risk. Wallis's carpenter reported that every wooden cleat in the ship had been exhausted and the hammock nails stolen. When the officers tried to discover who was responsible for the most barefaced thefts, the seamen closed ranks and refused to identify the culprits. When a man was caught red-handed and sentenced to the traditional punishment of running the gauntlet, his comrades used the whips so lightly that the chastisement became an open farce.[51] Perhaps even more seriously, the ship's surgeon was browbeaten to say that men were not suffering from venereal disease when it was quite obvious that they were. The spread of sexually transmitted afflictions turned into an epidemic, even during the *Dolphin*'s relatively brief stay.[52] The Tahitians, noticing the horrible engorged suppurations and other manifestations of the disease, thought that they were being visited with a plague, because of the malevolence of the Europeans or the anger of the gods, resulting from the breach of *tapus* (taboos) by the Europeans.[53] Wallis concluded that discipline was breaking down irretrievably and decided to leave the island as soon as possible, remaining longer than he originally intended only to observe a solar eclipse. The islanders saw them making observations, concluded that the gods were angry, and that their agents, the white men, were therefore attacking the sun.[54] All in all, the contacts between Tahiti and Wallis and the *Dolphin* had scarcely been happy. Pondering all this, Cook knew he had a major problem on his hands. He was seriously concerned both about the likely loss of iron and the spread of venereal disease but also knew that no ship's captain, however mighty, could trump human nature. From the viewpoint of personal morality he took a complaisant view of promiscuous sex, though he never indulged in the luxury himself. Some have concluded that his Quaker roots ran deep and prevented him from taking a casual and permissive attitude to sex personally, though this is unlikely, for in other areas the Quaker ethos was no more than skin deep. Others have speculated that, like the explorer H. M. Stanley, Cook had a low sex drive but, as with his marriage, the evidence about Cook's private life is far too tenuous for such a conclusion. The most likely explanation for his abstinence was his sense of duty, the need to lead by example, and the sense that a ship's captain had to exist as a being apart and distinct from his men and even his officers.[55]

The first real contacts with the Tahitians took place on 14 April, though the day before (the day of arrival) Cook had received an enthusiastic welcome, with the locals offering apples, breadfruit and fish for trade; pigs, however, were only available for trade with iron and this Cook was not yet prepared to allow. Some of those who had been with Wallis on the *Dolphin* identified a man called Owhaw as a likely guide and interpreter, so on the 13th Cook went ashore briefly in company with Banks, Solander and an armed party; Sydney Parkinson, who accompanied them, was stunned by the island's beauty.[56] The *Dolphin* veterans claimed that no one they met that day was of any consequence, but next day Cook was visited on his ship by a Tahitian of higher rank. The next month would see a gradual escalation of social contacts, with Cook and his men meeting more and more important local dignitaries and gradually feeling their way into a most complex culture and society. The first breakthrough came on 14 April, with Cook being offered a splendid meal by a local minor chief. They dined plentifully off coconuts, plantains and breadfruit, but declined the raw fish offered.[57] Banks showed, as he was to show more than once during the stay on the island, that he was no diplomat. Yet the combination of his forceful character and his womanising propensities evidently struck a chord with the Polynesians. The wife of their host showed an obvious interest in him but she was old and ugly so he snubbed her and instead beckoned to a pretty girl in the audience. It was fortunate that the host's wife did not take this as an insult and, though put out, continued to serve Banks at table. Banks soon had occasion to show another side of his character. Suddenly Solander and Monkhouse announced that their pockets had been picked as they sat at table, and that they were now missing an opera glass and a snuffbox. The embarrassed host tried to buy Banks off with bales of cloth but he insisted on return of the stolen items and struck the butt end of his fore-lock musket on the ground. This energetic display of authority caused a momentary panic. The flustered host departed while Banks continued sitting with his wife on one side and the new girlfriend on the other. About an hour and a half later the flustered chieftain returned with the missing items.[58]

Having obtained permission from the locals to build a fort and observatory, Cook spent 15 April looking for a suitable spot for his astronomical observations. He dubbed the promontory on Matavai Bay 'Point Venus' and began to build a station known as 'Fort Venus'.[59] He marked out the extent of his 'fortress', drew a line in the sand and explained to the Tahitians that no one was to cross it except Owhaw and any specially designated chiefs. While this work went on, Cook decided to take an armed party into the woods, despite the anxiety this seemed to cause Owhaw. Almost immediately the undiplomatic Banks was again to the fore. He fired his gun at some ducks and killed three of them with a lucky shot, which caused consternation. All at once the sound of gunfire was heard from the fort. When Cook and his party rushed back they found that one of the locals had demonstrated the famed Polynesian expertise in thievery by filching a musket from the party left behind to guard the 'fort'. The midshipman in charge of the guard detail, Jonathan Monkhouse, ordered his sentries to open fire, and the thief fell dead. It now became apparent why Owhaw had been so flustered when Cook went into the woods. He suspected such an assault might be made and so had tried to dissuade the white men from leaving the beach.[60] The death of the thief made a deep impression on the Tahitians. The next day was ominously silent, with no sign either of Owhaw or the locals. An apprehensive Cook warped the *Endeavour* nearer to the shore and moored her in such a way as to command the north-east of the bay (where the fort was being built) with her guns. But if he was expecting death, it came from a different quarter. On the 17th the painter Alexander Buchan died of complications arising from epilepsy and was buried at sea. This meant that the entire burden of painting expedition scenes now fell on Sydney Parkinson. At least the fears about the locals were assuaged, for later that day what Cook at first took to be a couple of local sub-chiefs arrived with propitiatory gifts and made it clear they wanted the shooting incident forgotten. Much relieved, Cook spent the night with Green observing an eclipse of one of Jupiter's satellites. The object was to determined their exact longitude, but thick cloud cover prevented this.[61]

It now turned out that the 'sub-chiefs' of the day before who had arrived with plantain branches as the symbol of peace were important players in Tahitian politics. Facetiously referred to by Banks as Hercules and Lycurgus, the two men were, respectively, Tuteha and Tepau. The latter was the son of a great chief or *arii* and the former was one of the most significant figures in island affairs. Later Cook would learn something of the extreme complexity of Tahitian society, but the salient fact was that Tahiti was dominated by three great chiefs or *arii nui*, one of whom was Tu (also known as Otoo). Tu, a timid and not very bright young man, would later achieve great things, but at this stage he was dominated by Tuteha who, though not an *arii nui* himself, had enough political sway to overshadow and patronise Tu – to the point where Cook thought Tu was Tuteha's son. Tuteha himself was the uncle of Tu's father Teu.[62] Tuteha's advent at Matavai Bay stabilised the situation. While he made it plain that the white men were on his island on sufferance – Cook could not even cut down a tree without his permission – he was well disposed to the aliens and built up a particular rapport with Banks, who seemed to have the knack of hitting the right note with Polynesians. Recognising this, Cook designated Banks as the monopolist trader in charge of commerce with the locals (he had Solander as his assistant), and Banks's acumen ensured a good supply of basics (breadfruit and coconuts; the much-desired pigs appeared only occasionally as personal gifts from Tuteha). Meanwhile he pressed on with the construction of the fort, which, by the beginning of May, was complete. There was a ravelin and trench at each end, with four-pounders facing the landward side and six swivel guns in embrasures of primitive palisades on the seaward side.[63] The only violence witnessed during this period was punishment meted out by Cook to the ship's butcher, who had assaulted one of the Tahitian women. Cook ordered a public flogging. The curious Tahitians crowded round to witness the chastisement, but after the very first stroke recognised the extent of the brutality routinely practised in the Royal Navy and begged Cook to halt the proceedings. Cook, feeling his own prestige and credibility to be at stake, refused. Cook was evidently in a baleful mood at the end of April for reasons that remain obscure but probably he was concerned about the near-epidemic of sexual intercourse between his sailors and the local women. Robert Molyneux, the master, claimed to have intervened with him at this time to save a man from a flogging who did no more than lightheartedly suggest that the crew should mutiny if ordered to sea again and away from their 'sweethearts'.[64]

Molyneux was also the prime mover in establishing another important contact, with Purea (aka Oberea). Banks was a great favourite with the Tahitian women and, on entering his tent on 28 April, Molyneux noticed that among the throng of females paying him court was one he recognised from the Wallis voyage: then, he claimed, she had been a 'queen'.[65] Although the Europeans consistently misinterpreted Polynesian society by calling their important personages kings and queens, Molyneux's identification was not entirely erroneous. Power in Tahiti was shared between three powerful clans, located respectively in the north, south and south-east of the island, but kinship and the uneasy mixture of secular and divine complicated the picture. Simplifying the situation, we can say that in the early 1760s Purea was one of the dominant figures in island politics. She was the daughter of the chief of Faaa, an important district in the north-west; Tepau, an elder child, was her brother. Purea made a great marriage to Amo, the high chief of the Papara district in the south-west; because Paea bordered on Papara, the chief there, Tuteha, was linked to Amo's family by marriage.[66] From the union of Amo and Purea was born Teri'irere (in 1762). Even aristocratic Tahitian children often fell victim to the endemic custom of infanticide, but Purea was a doting and overprotective mother who prepared her son for his future role as *arii nui* with elaborate rituals which excited jealousy and alienated her female relatives. Amo's niece (Teri'irere's first cousin) conceived a bitter hatred for Purea and set about to ensure her undoing. She spotted that the way to cause trouble was via the custom of *rahui*, which essentially meant restricting consumption and saving produce for a great festival in the future.[67]

Among the the elaborate rules for the fast of *rahui* was one which said that if during the fast a chief of equal rank visited another, the *rahui* had to be broken and the accumulated bounty given to the visitor. Usage dictated that tactful people never visited during *rahui,* but the niece and sister-in-law of Purea engineered a visit by the family and tried to call on her, enlisting the support of the high priest of Papara for the purpose. Purea, however, spotted the dodge and refused to receive the visitors. When sufficient produce was amassed, she went ahead with the great feasts in Teri'irere's honour. By now the niece had managed to whip up the whole island into a ferment of seething jealousy; the festival was interrupted, and the most powerful man on the island, Chief Vehiatua of Tautira (in the south-east) joined Purea's enemies. In December 1768, six months before Cook's arrival, two armies converged on Papara from east and west. In a great battle the men of Papara were defeated (Cook later found their bones bleaching on the beach).[68] Purea, Amo and the young Teri'irere fled across the mountains to the north while Vehiatua carried back the jawbones of the defeated to his homeland. The real victor in the conflict was Tuteha, who by joining Vehiatua effectively became the second most powerful man in Tahiti; he carried off the prized red-feather girdle or *maro-ura* (roughly the symbol of supreme power) to his stronghold in Paea. Yet in accordance with the esoteric rules of Tahitian culture, Teri'irere was still recognised as an *arii nui*; it was made clear that the war had been a personal one waged against Purea and not a dynastic struggle. Amo and Purea were forced to bow the head to Tuteha and concede the dignity of the *maro-ura* to his protégé Tu. Vehiatua agreed to this arrangement, though both he and other chiefs remained secretly vexed at Tuteha's sudden ascendancy. It turned out that Tuteha had successfully intrigued against Purea only to make himself, long-term, even more powerful enemies. Unknowingly, by dealing with Tuteha as a de facto ruler of Tahiti, Cook had stepped into the maelstrom of island politics.[69]

All of this explains why Purea, previously perceived by Wallis as a 'queen', had come down in the world and was now a 'spear carrier' in a drama directed by Tuteha. Accounts differ as to how old she was: Cook implausibly says 40, but the probability is that she was in her late twenties. From the fact that Banks, a compulsive philanderer, was attracted to her, we may infer that she was still a good-looking woman. Once identified as a person of distinction, she was invited aboard the *Endeavour* and given a doll as a present. At this Tuteha went into a jealous rage, which Cook tried to assuage by also giving him a doll, but Tuteha took the doll and threw it away contemptuously.[70] Cook, with remarkable naïvety, interpreted this as 'childish jealousy' but the reality was that Tuteha was enraged for political reasons. He had reduced Purea to a subsidiary position in island politics but she now seemed to be bidding fair to make a revival with the unconscious assistance of the powerful foreigners. Banks, without knowing the facts, had keener antennae for Tahitian realities and intuited that Purea was worth cultivating. Next day he called on Purea and found her in bed with a young 'toyboy'.[71] Polynesians found nothing odd about such casual sexual encounters; more surprisingly, perhaps, neither did Banks. He soon discovered the secret of gaining access to high-class Tahitian women. Hitherto all liaisons had been between seamen and women of the lowest class. Purea now told him that he could enjoy the favours of any of her 'ladies in waiting' who took his fancy, but that first he would have to bed her, as a mark of respect and de facto initiation ceremony. Banks duly obliged but Purea confessed herself disappointed by the white man's equipment and performance. Banks later related that 'she dismissed him with evident contempt, informing him that he was not to be compared with her own men and requesting that for the future he would devote his attention to the girls of his suite'.[72] This suited Banks perfectly, and the suspicion arises that he might have underperformed to avoid becoming one of Purea's regular consorts. He got his own back by describing the 'queen' later as an undesirable old crone. Soon he was engaged in a passionate affair with one of her maids named Tiatia.[73] Whether Cook knew about the affair is uncertain, but it hardly helped his campaign to cut down on sexual licence among his men. Cook always trod warily around rich and powerful young gentlemen at this stage and would scarcely have intervened even if he had known what was going on. His diary entry of 9 May, recording Purea's visit to the *Endeavour* in the company of her retinue, makes no mention of Banks. Besides, he valued Banks both as a scientist and for his all-round competence. Purea was also a source of the much sought after pork, for which she drove a hard bargain, insisting on a hatchet in exchange for a hog.[74]

By this time Cook's fortress on the shore was ready for the observation of Venus and made an imposing sight. Some thought it looked like a small garrison with its cannon and swivel guns and the forty-five armed men guarding the precious astronomical instruments. There was also a forge, a bakery, workshops for the sailmaker and cooper and tents for the accommodation of the officers and gentlemen – the whole surrounded by high walls and a ditch. Such was the ingenuity of the Tahitians, however, that they managed to penetrate the lines, unpack a wooden crate and make off with a heavy quadrant. This was a serious loss, for without it Cook's scientists could not observe the Transit.[75] Banks now came into his own. Utilising his singular contacts with the locals – he was by far the most popular of the white men – he set out with Green on a gruelling seven-mile hike to the place where 'Lycurgus' (Tepau) told him he would find the precious quadrant. On tracking down the thieves, they found that other stuff had been stolen from the fortress as well, inclusing a horse-pistol. There was some tough talking, and Banks had to threaten the theives by brandishing his pistol before the quadrant was returned intact.[76] Unfortunately Cook had shown a tendency to overreact and this would eventually darken his relations with Polynesians. He ordered all the canoes in Matavai Bay seized and all chiefs held hostage pending the return of the quadrant. To Cook's great mortification Banks and Green returned in triumph to find none other than Tuteha himself in captivity in the fort and in evident fear for his life. If Cook had had any inkling of the dynamic in Tahitian politics, he would not have offered such an insult to the second most important man on the island. Embarrassed, Cook released him with apologies and then spent a lot of time appeasing and calming down the agitated Tahitians.

Next day the affronted Tuteha sent his servant to demand reparation and Cook had the wit to send back suitable gifts – an axe, a shirt and a broadcloth gown rather like a South American poncho. Although not realising Tuteha's importance, he knew that he could not observe the transit of Venus if he was at daggers drawn with the locals. Accordingly he spent much of May appearing as the 'hail fellow well met', going to local celebrations and to wrestling matches aranged in his honour by Tuteha, and giving presents of axes made out of scrap iron.[77]

By mid-May good relations had been re-established between the Europeans and their hosts; large supplies of coconuts and breadfruit were delivered daily to the ship, though it always took tough haggling to get the Tahitians to part with their precious pigs. Protein was available in the form of fish, snipe, duck, teal and rat, though pork was gold dust on the hoof in Polynesian society. Meat was offered to the sailors in the form of baked dog, but at first they were revolted by the idea and preferred to eat stewed rat. In the end many came round to the idea of canine flesh. Banks especially relished this but Parkinson thought it had the taste of coarse beef.[78] Yet if food was plentiful, Tahitian thievery continued to be a trial, and the Europeans continued to marvel at the locals' ingenuity, which would have put the footpads and petty criminals of London to shame. Every single one of the officers and gentlemen from the *Endeavour* reported losses, some of them displaying mind-boggling artifice. Banks, retiring for the night with Tiatia in Purea's tent, found all his clothes missing the next morning.[79] But even elaborate precautions failed. Cook, knowing of the Tahitians' light fingers, made a point of putting his stockings under his pillow before going to sleep at night, so that anyone trying to steal them would surely wake him. Next morning he had slept soundly but the stockings were gone.[80] Perhaps tiring of being sitting ducks, Cook and the senior members of his party set off on a landward tour of the island in the third week of May, returning to the fort on the 29th in time for the transit. As a result of his reconnoitring and mindful of the disappointingly wet and cloudy weather, Cook decided to send ancillary parties out to different parts of Tahiti as a fail-safe in case the main observations from the fort did not produce the desired results. Lieutenant Gore, Dr Monkhouse and Herman Sporing were sent to the offshore island of Moorea with Banks, while Lieutenant Hicks, Charles Clerke, Richard Pickersgill, and others went to the eastern rim of the island also to take readings. Cook, Greene, Solander and Molyneux made up the four observers at 'Point Venus' (the fort).[81]

For the rest of the *Endeavour*'s complement May mainly meant caulking and repairing the bowsprit and fore rigging, and finding opportunities to steal away for sexual intercourse with the local women. Although an unbeliever, probably a deist, by this stage in his life, Cook was nevertheless compelled by the Articles of War to hold regular Christian service. The minimal significance of this in the daily life of the crew on Tahiti can perhaps be conveyed by an ironical juxtaposition in Cook's diary. On 14 May, 'divine service' was held at the fort, in the presence of uncomprehending and unimpressed Tahitian chiefs. 'Such were our Matins,' Cook writes. 'Our Indians thought fit to perform vespers of a different kind.' A youth had sexual intercourse in public with a 12-year-old girl, while women, including Purea, watched and shouted out instructions to the girl 'which, young as she was, she did not seem to stand much in need of'.[82] So much for pagan 'insults' to the Almighty. As a man of the Enlightenment, Cook felt the pull of science rather than religion and became fretful and neurotic in his desire not to disappoint his patron Lord Morton. The great day came at last, and Saturday 3 June dawned clear and cloudless. Meticulously Cook and his party checked and rechecked their instruments. In the boiling temperature of 119°F – the hottest they had experienced so far – they watched as the penumbra of Venus blurred its outline at the precise moment the disc crossed the sun. For six hours they watched the small black spot of the transit but it was soon apparent that they had missed the exact moment of the start and would miss the exact moment of the end. Anxiously Cook awaited the findings of the other parties. When he collated the figures from the different sightings, they did not match. Resignedly, Cook and his scientists agreed on a compromise set of results. The Venus sightings had been a flop, just as in 1762, but no blame should attach to the *Endeavour* party, since the same difficulties were experienced at the later sightings of 1874 and 1882. Because Venus was mantled by the 'dusky shade' that prevented true observation, science eventually concluded that the distance between the sun and the earth would have to be worked out by other means.[83]

It might have been expected that, with the transit of Venus over, Cook would have set sail immediately. Several factors, however, prevented such an early departure. In the first place, Cook wanted to make a proper survey and chart of Tahiti, which meant sailing round the island. Then he wanted to have the *Endeavour* in superb condition before he ventured into more uncertain southern latitudes; that meant careening the ship, covering the keel with pitch and brimstone, caulking and repainting the vessel, varnishing the spars, meticulously inspecting the rigging and restoring the cables, to say nothing of laying in a three-month supply of food and water. All of this took time, especially as the men were in two bases, some in the fort, others in the ship.[84] But above all Cook was concerned about the uncertain temper of his crew, for in the immediate aftermath of the Venus observations he was assailed on two flanks. Indiscipline and insubordination increased among his men at the very time that thievery by the Tahitians reached epidemic levels. Dalliance with the local women was a positive mania with the seamen, but they required payment and the Tahitians were brilliant at spotting the truly valuable goods possessed by their visitors. When 120 pounds of nails were found to be missing from the stores. Cook realised he had a serious problem which would not only distort the entire Tahiti market but jeopardise all his future trading endeavours. A trap was set. On 4 June Archibald Wolfe was found with a large quantity of nails in his pockets. Since this represented more than he could possibly trade himself, it was obvious he had collaborators. When he refused to divulge their names, Cook ordered a punishment twice as heavy as usual. Wolfe was given twenty-four lashes.[85] A week later it was the turn of two more seamen, John Thurman and James Nicholson, who were similarly punished. On 19 June James Tunley received twelve lashes for stealing rum from the quarterdeck cask. On the 23rd a Portuguese sailor deserted. Cook saw that stern measures were called for, since the below-decks scuttlebutt indicated that the men were considering mutiny if forced to leave their South Seas fleshpots. Cook offered the Tahitians a much-treasured hatchet to anyone who would bring the runaway back. The offer did the trick, and soon the Portuguese was hauled before Cook. He concocted the implausible story that he had been taken prisoner. Cook knew the truth, that he had absconded to live with his Tahitian 'wife', but decided not to punish him; a flogging for a sexual peccadillo might unleash the very mutiny he was trying to avoid.[86]

It did not help in this general tourbillion of sexuality that the gentlemen themselves set a poor example. The heterosexually omnivorous Banks exchanged 'high words' with Monkhouse over a dusky beauty before the quarrel was patched up.[87] With this unsatisfactory state of affairs in his own ranks, Cook faced a perfect storm of Tahitian thieving. There was a particularly audacious theft of an iron coal-rake from the fort on 14 June; by this time the Tahitians had perfected the art of throwing fishing lines over the walls from the outside and hooking objects within. Although Cook had laid down strict standing orders that thieves were not to be fired on, something in him snapped when the coal-rake was stolen. Again demonstrating his tendency towards overkill, Cook ordered every canoe in Matavai Bay seized with the threat that they would be burned if the stolen items were not returned.[88] This was both risky and injudicious. Risky because, as Cook himself admitted, 'not that I ever intend to put this (the burning) into effect'. This meant he was gambling that the locals would not call his bluff. Injudicious, because, as Banks pointed out, it meant punishing the innocent along with the guilty; this was not just a blunt and crude instrument of punishment, but would destroy Cook's reputation for fairness and justice. Moreover, it was easy for him, with his excellent contacts, to discover who the real culprits were.[89] Cook's matelots grumbled that he was harsh with them and would flog and flay for the most trifling offence, but was indulgent and dovelike with the Tahitians. Cook's general views on crime and punishment are interesting, given the draconian 'Bloody Code' of eighteenth-century England where one could be hanged for stealing an apple. Cook did not think theft merited death: 'That thieves are hanged in England, I thought no reason why they should be shot in Obaheite.'[90] There was, after all, no equivalent of the Bloody Code in Tahiti, and it would have been monstrous cultural arrogance to try to introduce it. Generally a humane and compassionate man, unless his passions got the better of him, Cook explained why shooting at thieves on Tahiti was a bad idea. In the first place it would give carte blanche to his trigger-happy sentries, brutal men who believed in shooting first and asking questions later. Besides, opening fire was an all-or-nothing affair. Firing warning shots or using powder only would cause no physical harm and have no deterrent effect. But firing with shot was likely to be fatal and would mean war with the locals.[91] Lacking a middle path, Cook at first opted for the equally unsatisfactory seizure of canoes.

On 26 June Cook finally set out with Banks, an armed party and local guides to make the circuit of the island. Moving eastwards, they spent the nights in sheltered coves and bays, initially on the Taravao peninsula, later in creeks when steep cliffs towered above them and there was no beach. Roughly speaking, on the tour round the island the landscape changed from beach to cliff to woodland. The guides were nervous when they reached the territory of the mighty Vehiatua and told Cook they were now in 'enemy country'; they were only partially reassured when Cook's guards primed their weapons.[92] Cook made contact with the great man and met him in Vaitepiha Bay where he sat on the shore in state with his daughter; 'a thin old man with very white hair and beard', he was remarkably affable and friendly with the visitors.[93] Cook was soon impelled to speed up his project when it turned out that there were food shortages in this part of the island and the voyagers had not brought enough provisions with them. Apart from his detailed surveying, Cook's circumnavigation in the pinnace was uneventful, notable only for the many temples or *marae* (pagodas or pyramids of red coral stone and basalt) they saw, including the lavish ones on the southern coast built by Purea for her son which had triggered the outburst of island warfare six months before Cook arrived.[94] In the district of Vaiuru in the south there was an attempt to steal Cook's cloak and a temporary alarm when his men thought the pinnace had been stolen overnight: it had merely drifted from its moorings. Still, it was an anxious moment, since all their powder and ammunition was on board, and at first they thought the 'theft' was the prelude to an attack.[95] After a total circuit of six days and five nights, the party returned to Matavai Bay. Cook had achieved another masterpiece of surveying and charting. Time and conditions did not allow him to be as meticulous as he had been in Newfoundland, with shore landings being particularly problematical. Both on this occasion and when he was charting on the *Endeavour*, his maps were drawn by a continuous running survey from the ship, with compass bearings and sextant angles taken on shore features and a good deal of masthead sketching.[96] On the *Endeavour* voyage Cook carried out most of the surveys in person, though on his later journeys he tended to delegate to his officers. He liked to hug a coastline, noting the course and distance travelled, taking sightings of the features on the land from different locations and plotting the positions of these features by compass and quadrant cross-bearings. If there was enough time, he would land and fix the coordinates of the features charted. Cook was a natural at running surveys because these required skill in inland navigation – the exact craft Cook had mastered during his early training in coastal waters. In sum, it can be said that Cook combined the land surveying techniques of triangulation with existing marine methods and then raised them to a new level by his own acumen.[97]

Cook spent a further week in Matavai Bay, vainly trying to buy more produce. Although Banks's skills as a merchant and negotiator here were superb, Cook was short of food; it was not that the locals did not want to trade but that the island itself could barely feed itself. The ships' carpenters were ordered to dismantle the stockade at Point Venus so that the *Endeavour* could be laden with the wood; even at this juncture there was thievery, with the locals attempting to steal part of the gate. Banks, who had made up with Monkhouse, went with him on a private expedition, then, concluding that his botanical researches were complete, branched into anthropology.[98] On 5 July he watched a 12-year-old girl being tattooed on the buttocks (on Tahiti tattoos were a universal fetish) and described the ceremony as follows:

> The instrument used upon this occasion had thirty teeth and every stroke, of which at least 100 were made in a minute, drew an ichor or serum a little tinged with blood. The girl bore it with most stoical resolution for about a quarter of an hour but the pain of so many hundred punctures as she had received in that time then became intolerable: she first complained in murmurs, then wept, and at last burst into loud lamentations, earnestly imploring the operator to desist. He was, however, inexorable, and when she began to struggle, she was held down by two women, who sometimes soothed and sometimes chid her and now and then, when she was most unruly, gave her a smart blow.

The operation lasted more than an hour.[99]

Cook was now ready to leave but before he could weigh anchor there was another crisis, again involving desertion for reasons of sexual dalliance. The shock of departure and the trauma of leaving their sweethearts led two of the marines, Clement Webb and Samuel Gibson, to desert. Cook at first let it be known that he would grant them an extra day's furlough and that they would not be punished provided they returned then, but when there was no sign of them after twenty-four hours, he took a number of chiefs hostage against the marines' return. Cook then sent two of his men with a party of Tahitians to fetch the runaways, but they did not come back, later claiming they had been seized and held as counter-hostage. The chiefs, still in captivity, were pressurised to send a higher-level delegation together with an armed party from the *Endeavour* to stress to those sheltering the absconders that if they were not returned the hostage chiefs would be killed. This did the trick, and the luckless lovelorns were finally brought in at seven o'clock on the morning of 11 July, minus their weapons, which took several more hours to recover.[100]

Cook was furious with Webb and Gibson, not least because their actions had jeopardised the relations with the Tahitians he had spent three careful months building up. At the same time he could not connive in their desertion, for this would be an 'open sesame' to his matelots to jump ship at the next island paradise. Nonetheless, he spent a day visiting Tuteha, Tepau, Purea and all other offended parties, apologising, bringing lavish presents and generally making soothing noises.[101] Yet it was clear that, with the food shortages on the island worsening, the locals now wanted their visitors gone. As the ship began to clear from Matavai Bay there was a sudden last-minute addition to the complement. Tupaia, Purea's high priest and adviser, had long wanted to voyage to England with Banks. He was an interesting character, aged about 45, and had at one time lived in a curious (to Europeans but not to Polynesians) *ménage à trois* with Amo and Purea. His desire to travel with the *Endeavour* was primarily a function of island politics. Purea wanted to make sure that Tu's interests were promoted and those of Tuteha and Vehiatua were blunted, and to this end Tupaia was ostensibly prepared to travel to the far side of the globe.[102] Cook did not want to take anyone from Polynesia unless he could guarantee their return, but Banks proved a powerful advocate for the priest. He knew Tupaia well as a highly intelligent man with massive local knowledge and a deep understanding of wind, waves and currents in Polynesia, which he derived from his family of famous local seamen. When Banks, with his influence and huge fortune, wanted something, even Cook had to pay heed. Banks seems to have decided to take Tupaia with him on a whim, remarking patronisingly that if other men could keep pet lions and tigers, he should be allowed to have a Polynesian as a 'curiosity'.[103] The upshot was that Tupaia embarked along with his 13-year-old servant Taiata. More dispassionate observers of this strange outcome say that Tupaia had his own pressing reasons to want to leave Tahiti. He could not desert Purea but had read the runes of

Tahitian politics correctly and realised that she was a spent force; if Vehiatua moved against her again, this time he might decide to eliminate all her supporters and underlings.[104] On Thursday 13 July the *Endeavour* slipped out of Matavai Bay. Avoiding the obvious and nearby landfalls of Moorea and Tetiaroa, Cook stood away westwards for Huahine, one hundred miles from Tahiti. Tupaia watched the novel sight of Webb and Gibson getting their two dozen lashes each.

At Huahine Tupaia proved himself to be an exceptionally skilful pilot, insisting on exact reports of the depth *Endeavour* was drawing in the harbour.[105] His expertise in island customs also paid off when he had the shrewdness to go through a lengthy propitiation ceremony at Huahine so that the local gods would not be angry at the coming of strangers. Tupaia's presence reassured the Huahine Polynesians about the peaceful intentions of Cook and his party, and the local chief, Ori, struck up an immediate friendship with Cook. Not as preoccupied with thievery as the Tahitian Polynesians, they were even more interested in inveigling the powerful newcomers into their island wars, but Cook had the good sense to decline this invitation. He continued his leisurely cruise among the Society Islands, with the aim of settling the men after the three months of hedonism on Tahiti and (he hoped) to enabling them to recover from venereal disease. Next Cook visited Raiatea, twenty miles west but was detained there when the weather suddenly turned bad; this accounts for the bizarre track he followed around Raiatea from 20 July to 9 August.[106] Fresh south-easterly gales prevented him from landing on Bora Bora and also kept him hove to off the western coasts of Tahaa and Raiatea for two days. It was 2 August before he could land on Raiatea to take on water, stones for ballast and to repair a leak in the powder room. Banks and Solander used the time to explore the interior.[107] While he was on Raiatea Cook was visited by the chief of Bora Bora who seemed to him boorish and stupid and not at all in the same class as the genial Ori. Banks continued his investigations. He was dismayed to find that infanticide seemed to be universal in the Pacific islands. It was the prerogative of every male to order all children born to his wives, concubines or mistresses to be strangled at birth if he did not relish the prospect of bringing them up.[108] Banks had his own absurd prejudices and preconceptions, however. Convinced that a great southern continent existed, he was impatient for Cook to implement the second part of his orders, and to swing into more southerly latitudes to find it. His leave-taking of the Society Islands was typical Banks: 'We again launched out into the ocean in search of what chance and Tupaia might direct us to.'[109]

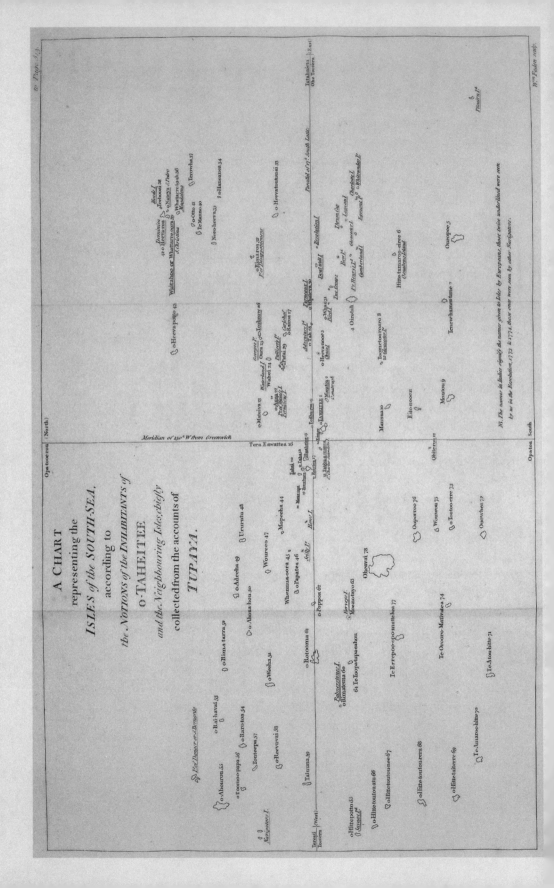

CHAPTER SIX

The Isle of Cythera

SINCE Cook was to visit Tahiti four times on his three voyages and spent long periods of time there, his knowledge of, and insight into, the social structure of the Society Islands warrants further investigation. Cook and his fellow explorers were keen observers and, at the level of phenomena, there was not much that escaped their attention during the three-month sojourn on Tahiti. There was, at the most obvious level, the sheer physical beauty of the island to which all responded enthusiastically, most notably Parkinson both in his journal and in his paintings.[1] Cook himself wrote 8,000 words on Tahiti's mountains, harbours and produce, dilating on the variety of fish, the bread-fruit, coconuts, bananas, plantains, sweet potatoes, yams, sugar cane, pineapples and edible nuts, and ending with remarks on housing, tattooing, clothes, music and dancing. Cook entered in his journals minute details of the island's geography, its economy, the physical appearance of the Polynesians, their housing, tools, boats and even their religion and theology.[2] It has been pointed out that his attitude to Tahitians was engaged and excited, in strong contrast to his dismissive view of the Fuegians.[3] On the other hand, the deeper structures and deeper meanings of the culture largely passed Cook by. He was never at his best with what one might term socio-economic data and in this category we might include his remarks on the island's population. His estimate for the entire Society Islands is 200,000 – a figure usually thought impossibly high, though Cook has some modern scholarly supporters.[4] Moreover, there was no real interest in where the Tahitians had originally come from or the longevity of their culture. Modern scholarship tends to give the following answer: from Asia, especially the Taiwan area, with the first settlements on Tahiti occurring around 950 BC.[5]

Cook's more thoughtful comrades, and especially Dr Johann Forster and his son George and other observers on the second voyage, were far more interested in the religion and politics of the Society Islands and filled in some of the gaps, though again their insights tend to focus on phenomena rather than deep structure. It was not surprising that they found Tahitian religion enigmatic, as the older pantheistic or polytheistic creeds were rapidly being subsumed in the cult of Oro: a limited polytheism with four main gods. Since Cook was so exercised about theft, it might have come as a revelation to him that the Tahitians actually had a god of theft, Hiro, the son of Oro.[6] Intrigued by the many nuanced and seemingly contradictory religious manifestations, the Europeans tried to make sense of it all by reference to belief-systems they already knew or understood. James Magra (Matra) thought that in some respects the Tahitians were more sophisticated in their religion, since they believed in a remote deity unconcerned with this world – rather like the deism of many European intellectuals – not one you could pray to or ask to intercede in the here and now.[7] On Cook's second voyage the botanist Anders Sparrman would compare Tahitian religion, with its incantations, rituals, red feathers and other exotic symbols, to the gaudy paraphernalia of Catholicism, while his shipmate John Marra covered his bets by invoking not only Catholicism but also Druidism, Hinduism and Zoroastrianism.[8] The rituals that Tupaia performed to protect the *Endeavour* were as involved as many of the ceremonies in the sacred office of the Christian Church, Catholicism especially, which fed easily into the widespread eighteenth-century prejudice against 'popish idolatry'.[9] It never seemed to occur to the visitors that Tahitian religion might be unique, *sui generis*, a one-off, as indecipherable as Etruscan and irreducible to European modalities. The same problem plagued the travellers when they tried to explain Tahitian politics. Using a savagery–barbarism–civilisation model or, even, in the more intellectual observers, a type of proto-Marxian trinity of slavery, feudalism and capitalism, they usually 'placed' Tahiti as 'barbaric-feudal'.[10] Observers on Cook's later voyages also tied themselves in knots over Tahitian politics. Joseph Gilbert thought the extreme factionalism on the island could be likened to the warring states of Germany, whereas Lieutenant James Burney considered that the correct analogy was Poland, notoriously torn apart in the eighteenth century.[11]

Where Cook, Banks and the others went wrong was in imagining that the social organisation of all societies must resemble that of eighteenth-century Europe and therefore that there must somewhere be a supreme ruler or 'king'. In fact Tahitian society was of fiendish complexity, combining as it did aspects of medieval feudalism, Weberian patrimonialism, the Indian caste system and the kinship nexus of the Scottish clans. Tahiti exhibited the usual pattern of an hereditary ruling class, a middle class and a large class of toilers, but there were many nuances and many exceptions to the overall pattern. On some Polynesian islands, unlike in Melanesia, there were rigid pyramids of lower and higher chiefs culminating in a paramount chief who might control the entire island.

Tahiti was not like that, for power was distributed both vertically and horizon-tally (that is, territorially). At the apex of the system were the great chiefs or *arii nui* (sometimes called *arii rahi*) and below them the clan chiefs (*arii nii* or *ariki*), whose relationship to their superiors was rather like that of a chief exec-utive to the chairman of a modern corporation. These were the major landowners, who extracted a surplus from the sweating masses. There was then a middle class of small landowners, the *raatira*, typically craftsmen, boat-builders, tattoo artists and other small-scale entrepreneurs. The lower class were the *manahune* – essentially serfs, though some were allowed to own small-holdings, provided these were well inland and far from the sea.[12]

This apparently simple system masked myriad 'contradictions'. In the first place the eight main clans of Tahiti did not necessarily automatically generate authentic *arii nui*. Although the clans were supposed to be autonomous and equal, the reality was that three septs tended to dominate island politics, those of Papara in the south, Vaiari in the south-east and Punaavia in the west, although in Cook's time Tuteha had put together a loose northern alliance extending from Purionu in the north-west to Hitiaa on the eastern side of Tahiti-Nui. Even if in 1769 Tuteha was probably the Number Two player in Tahitian politics, he did not have the right, as the three major clans did, to wear the traditional red feather girdles. His power came from his manipulation of the youthful Tu, formerly (before his mother's indiscretions) heir apparent in Papara. The alliance of Tuteha and the displaced Tu proved conclusively that political power did not necessarily follow rigidly from the status of being *arii nui*.[13] Vehiatua, chief of the Teva clan and overlord of Papara, was the most important person on the island and he possessed both symbolic and actual power; the other two *arii nui* lagged behind Tuteha in this respect. Nonetheless, *arii nui* had impressive privileges and prerogatives. They were absolute rulers who commanded absolute obedience, were addressed by special titles and had their person, clothing and possessions protected by *tapu* (taboo) They were considered sacred, as were their houses, canoes and the very ground on which they stood. Their bodies, and especially their heads, were *tapu*, and to touch them was sacrilegious. In the presence of the chief men had to strip off their clothes to the waist and women to below the shoul-ders and they had to do likewise when passing the chief's house or anything else of his that was *tapu*. The *arii nui* could not travel by foot, had to be carried everywhere and could enter only certain houses hallowed for the purpose; all land trodden on by him automatically became sacred. All who infringed the chiefs' *tapus* were thought certain to die of leprosy. *Arii nui* also had their own private retinue – a priest, a war chief, and orator, a personal aide, etc. – their own pyramid or *marae*, and the right to sit on other *marae* belonging to their kin. They had a private hill for political asemblies, a personal rod and spear, a *fare-oa* or portable house or cabin for journeys by land and sea, and they had the right to issue decrees restricting the use of products of the soil, the sea or industry. The *arii* themselves were governed by elaborate rituals, including a ban on marriage with other classes unless the girl was a virgin and had been 'sanctified'. The newly weds were then secluded and fed at public expense until the birth of their first child. The firstborn son, the *matahiapo*, was an object of special veneration; he was at once recognised as the head of the tribe and his father relegated to the status of regent.[14]

The core of the power and influence wielded by the *arii nui* was supposed to be *mana*; roughly, charisma in both the sacred and secular senses. This embraced psychic power, divine right and totemic principles supposedly guaranteeing the chief's authority and his ability as a a thaumaturge. Part of the meaning of *mana* was that a chief, because of his divine origin, was in closer touch with the spirits. It was thought that a chief's possessions, such as his canoes, also had *mana*.[15] The *arii nui* could demand taxes and compulsory labour service, but in return had to provide welfare and security. Failure to do this could lead to the chief's being deposed, in which case he was held to have lost his *mana* while still retaining his ritual functions by divine and indefeasible right. Feasts were of great importance, as they reinforced a chief's prestige, functioned as social cement and acted as a safety valve by redistributing wealth. There was also the complex Polynesian custom of exchanging gifts, the basic idea being that this would reinforce notions of cooperation, reciprocity and mutuality. However, more cynical observers alleged that in Tahiti redistribution via gift exchange never went beyond a clique of retainers near the top. Europeans were rarely able to understand *mana*, but *tapu* was more familiar to them, since unfriendly chiefs would often embargo trade or even contact with their visitors by using this device.[16] Cook and the other explorers did have a reasonable understanding of *tapu* and its functionality. For example, the *arii nui* had to be carried everywhere, because if they walked and turned the soil into something sacrosanct the ground could not be tilled and the people would starve. Yet the Europeans failed to identify the many ways in which *tapu* and *mana* engendered other phenomena, such as cannibalism. The pre-European Pacific witnessed endemic warfare, not primarily for economic reasons but for *mana*. The aftermath of such battles was celebrated by cannibalism which Polynesians indulged in for three main reasons: to increase their intake of protein; for ritual reasons, such as at the funeral of chiefs; but mostly to gain more power or *mana*.[17]

Below the *arii nui* in the hierarchy came the *arii rii* or *ariki*, the 'little lords', again few in number. The *raatira* or middle class presented fewer problems of interpretation and they later proved much more susceptible to the appeal of Christianity than the *arii nui*, so the *raatira* were always a subject of abiding interest to European travellers (and later anthropologists).[18] Some observers correlate the entire class system in Tahiti with successive waves of invaders. According to this model, the lowest class or *manahune* were the aboriginal inhabitants who were displaced by later arrivals who in turn were conquered by the very latest arrivals, who then became the *arii nui*.[19] Yet the term *raatira* covers a very wide spectrum of individuals; some were in danger of sinking down into the *manahune* while others had intermarried with the *ariki* to form almost a new class, sometimes referred to as the *eietoai*. Even in the *manahune* there were nuances because some were allowed to own small tracts of land provided they were far inland and away from the sea, while certain *manahune* families were regarded as genuine 'untouchables'.[20] These, the so-called *titi* or *taata ino* (literally 'the low folk' or 'the evil folk') were earmarked as human sacrifices on special occasions designated by the high chiefs and would have their skulls dashed out by stone clubs on the *marae*. To make matters even more complex, there was a group of hereditary retainers of the *arii* known as the *teuteu* who, while not called *manahune*, were indistinguishable from them in socio-economic terms.[21]

It is not surprising that all these nuances were completely beyond Cook and his companions, given that they spent just three months on Tahiti. Cook's attitude to Polynesians was always pragmatic: who has the power, who can give us what we want, how do we stop thievery? A deeper understanding of the culture would have enabled him to understand some of the motives behind the pervasive, perennial and vexatious thievery. Although it was intensely irritating to the visitors that many of the thefts were of objects essential to them (like the quadrant) but useless to the pilferers, they discounted the likely motive of 'compensation' for food taken by the visitors in a context of shortage – which of course they were too proud to admit to Cook.[22] Moreover, on some islands (whether on Tahiti is uncertain) there was a tradition that whatever came to the island was the islanders' property.[23] In many ways the Europeans' superior weaponry merely aggravated the problem as a demand for supplies backed by firepower could easily be construed as highway robbery. More sophisticated European satirists later made the point that it was philosophically impossible to distinguish the theft of a quadrant from Cook's 'taking possession' of an island in the name of the king.[24]

As if the social structure of Tahiti was not complex enough, a further cross-grained layering was provided by the secret society of the *arioi*. The *arioi* seemed to Cook and Banks no more than sex-obsessed strolling players, but they were right at the heart of Tahitian mores and folkways. The reason they

were so difficult to fathom was that they combined features usually found sepa-
rately in Western culture. Partly a freemasonry, partly a showbusiness organisation something like the Order of the Water Rats, partly a Polynesian version
of the Eleusinian mysteries, they often swam into Cook's ken because they
performed on public and festive occasions, staging shows with a very strong
sexual content, which were meant to point forward to the lubricious delights of
Paradise.[25] The *arioi* were very much to the fore on these occasions, since the
greater the feast, the greater the prestige of the chief staging it. In
the privacy of their *marae* they practised rites whose content is unknown, since
the temples were *tapu* to Europeans. Aside from their organic role in Tahiti, the
arioi were important on at least five counts. By ramming home the idea of *tapu*
to the bemused visitors, they gave the Europeans the basic idea, so that very
soon ships' captains and commanders were imposing their own artificial taboos.
Secondly, the *arioi* were open to both sexes and thus provided women with an
important role in a highly patriarchal society. Thirdly, they functioned as the
guardians of tradition – important in a society with no writing. Fourthly, they
acted as a social safety net since the *arioi* were allowed to poke fun at the *ariki*,
which in normal circumstances no one was allowed to do. Fifthly, they
provided almost the only means for social advancement through meritocracy.
They mirrored the structure of Tahitian society by having eight grades,
through which a member could be promoted, though the highest degrees in the
arioi could usually be attained only by members of the highest social classes.[26]
To be accepted into the *arioi* one had to prove one's chutzpah by gatecrashing
their meetings in a trance-like state and in such a way that the members
believed one was possessed by the god Oro. The *arioi* then decided whether or
not to accept the newcomer as a member, basing their decision on criteria such
as physical beauty, knowledge of religious texts, skill in recitation, dance, or
pantomime. Each grade had a special tattoo, so that one promoted to a higher
grade had to be re-tattooed. The *arioi* practised free love and remained child-
less so practised universal infanticide. When at the age of 35 or so men or
women decided they wanted children, they simply resigned from the *arioi*. But
since membership was almost the only means of social mobility, this decision
was not taken lightly. The privileges of membership also explained why about
one-fifth of the population was *arioi*.[27]

Overwhelmingly the aspect of Tahiti that most impressed the visitors, both
about the *arioi* and about the island in general, was what appeared to be the
unbridled sexuality of Polynesia. Undoubtedly in relation to both the
Europeans exaggerated their experiences, because the public performances of
the *arioi* emphasised this aspect of life and because the local women seemed so
eager to consort with the crew of the *Endeavour*. One could argue that the only

difference between Georgian England, which genuinely was a permissive society, and Tahiti was that in the latter place there was no hypocrisy or repression deriving from Christianity. Some have argued that the alleged sexual promiscuity of Polynesia was massively over-hyped and that the visitors saw only those women eager for sexual congress or, more accurately, sexual commerce.[28] There is no evidence that upper-class Tahitian females were 'easy' and indeed we can readily infer the opposite, since the entire social structure and the privileges of the aristocracy depended on keeping a lid on Eros. One of the reasons, despite some superficial resemblances, why Tahiti in the eighteenth century cannot be categorised under the rubric of 'feudalism' is not just that land ownership was completely different (property rights were communal and customary with the clan leader the only real owner), but also because kinship, not vassalage or fiefdom, was the real key to social structure.[29] Tahitians worried about the 'purity' of their kin and loathed the idea of miscegenation. Besides, the upper classes had a general dislike of children which by an obvious association led to fastidiousness about sex. There were two obvious reasons for the prevalence of infanticide and the corresponding cult of childlessness among the *arioi*. One was that unbridled sexuality would lead to high levels of interbreeding between the *arii* and the lower classes. The other was that since reputation and prestige was passed down in the male line, an aristocrat stood to lose his high standing if a son was born. It is a justifiable conclusion that the behaviour of Tahitian women with the sailors was no more typical of Tahiti than the behaviour of London whores was of London society, and indeed probably a good deal less. Far more stable societies than eighteenth-century Tahiti have been thrown off balance by visiting fleets and the subsequent behaviour of prostitutes.[30]

Cook took a very relaxed view of sexual intercourse between his sailors and Polynesian women, provided it did not impede their duties and provided it did not further the spread of venereal disease.[31] Certainly he worried about the possible impact of syphilis and gonorrhoea and was at pains to try to discover how a disease, thought to be entirely European in nature, could have reached the South Sea islands. Early on the voyage he had had the ship's physician inspect the men and he reported only one sailor suffering from gonorrhoea. Nonetheless, sexually transmitted disease made its appearance on the *Endeavour* in May, and soon between one-third and a half of the ship was affected. At first Cook thought the *Endeavour* itself might have brought it, or possibly the *Dolphin*, then his suspicions shifted to the Spanish, until finally he decided that Bougainville was the culprit.[32] It is thought that many of the cases Cook identified as venereal disease were in fact yaws, which has the curious quality of providing immunity to syphilis. Yaws produces ulcerated and crusted skin lesions and there were many cases of this but, ominously, there also appeared a virulent disease associated with loss of hair and nails, definitely a symptom of gonorrhoea. From the vantage point of two and a half centuries and with modern drugs, Cook's anxiety about venereal disease might appear overdone and even neurotic, but the entire subject was a major concern in the eighteenth century and a frequent topic of discussion in the press.[33] It is one of the ironies of Cook's career that he, who was so fastidious and painstaking on this subject, should in later *bien pensant* criticism have been held responsible for spreading venereal disease around the Pacific. Even in Enlightenment Europe the allegedly free and open sexuality of Polynesia was a cause for concern and ambivalence, with commentators caught between an obvious immediate attraction to an Eden of unbridled sensuality and a deep fear that importing such notions into Europe would be like King Aeolus releasing the winds and might herald the end of civilisation. Even though Rousseau did not introduce the notion of the 'noble savage' or even the phrase (it is usually wrongly thought that he did), he and Bougainville were somehow conflated to conjure a bogeyman, vaguely linked to the 'New Cythera' or sexual utopia. When Cook's account of the *Endeavour* voyage was added to Bougainville's, this may have triggered Diderot's savage attack on the attractions of primitive society in his *Supplement to the Voyages of Bougainville*.[34]

The final irony of the *Endeavour* voyage was that, except in narrow circles, Cook's great discoveries and his conquest of the ocean were ignored in favour of the absorbing question of sexuality. Then, as now, all a mass audience wanted to read about was sex. In some circles Cook's strictures on unbridled sexuality and the spread of disease were regarded as the ingenuous musings of a meritocratic farm boy who knew nothing of real life, and perhaps it is significant that he could get no real support from his officers on this issue, and still less from hedonists such as Banks. The only man to write in favour of Cook's views was Parkinson, who stated forthrightly that fornication was always 'moral turpitude' no matter what the latitude and longitude in which it took place.[35] However, the 'gentlemen' roundly asserted that Parkinson himself was a hypocrite. Solander reported that on one occasion when he took home a new conquest (not Tiatia) 'the first thing he saw was Shyboots Parkinson in bed with the girl's sister'.[36] Cook's isolation on the sexual issue has two interesting sidelines. On the one hand his patron Lord Sandwich was a notable rake and libertine. He was a member of the 'Monks of Medmenham', sometimes known as the Hell-Fire Club and, though we can confidently dismiss the canard that Sandwich and his fellow cabalists such as John Wilkes and Benjamin Franklin conducted black masses, they certainly presided over orgies.[37] Sandwich would therefore have reacted with amused contempt to his protégé's views regarding sexual intercourse and his preferred sexual abstinence. The other point is that Cook allowed the sexual issue to fuel his already strong dislike of France and the French. He would often criticise Bougainville for his amateurishness as a navigator and the inaccuracy of his charts. Beyond that, he held him responsible for the popularisation of the Pacific islands as a 'New Cythera' – in his view the most baneful legacy of European contact with Polynesia.[38] On this issue Cook seems guilty of 'shoot the messenger' syndrome, for Bougainville did not invent the sexually permissive South Pacific; he merely reported it. The law of unintended consequences is a many-tentacled beast, and one of its tendrils saw the at root anti-permissive Cook unwittingly responsible for the spread of an image of the Pacific that is vibrant even today.

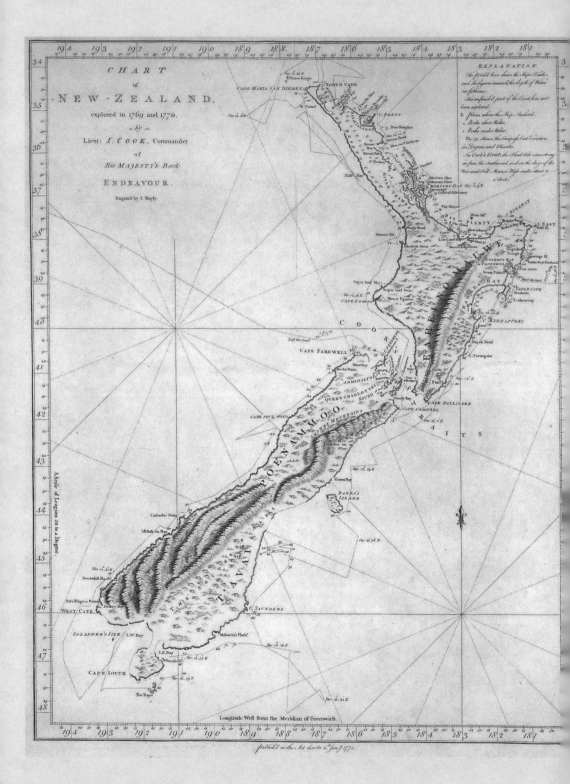

CHAPTER SEVEN

Peril in Australasia

FOR the first two days on the open ocean Banks, unused to the giant swells after three months on Tahiti, was violently seasick. On 14 August the *Endeavour* sighted Hiti-roa or Rurutu – which Tupaia had accurately predicted. This was a high, dark-green coral island which provided no anchorage for a ship. Cook launched the pinnace with Banks, Gore and Tupaia aboard, to see if the inhabitants could provide them with further information, but the locals were hostile and tried to seize the boat, so Cook gave up, made a circuit of the island and then set a course for the south.[1] The increasingly assertive Tupaia protested loudly that they should be going west but Cook had his instructions to fulfil. There was some excitement on 16 August when a line of cloud was mistaken for land, causing a morning's diversion before the mirage was discovered, though Cook himself was always sceptical. As the *Endeavour* headed due south towards latitude 40S, the weather got colder and the sea rougher, with a persistent heavy swell from the south-west. The hogs and fowls Cook had taken from Tahiti were used to eating only Tahitian vegetables, refused the animal feed served to them and soon sickened and died.[2] Tropical seabirds and sharks were seen less and less but whales and albatrosses (also pintadoes and shearwaters) more and more. On 25 August the gentlemen celebrated the anniversary of their sailing from England with a cask of porter and some Cheshire cheese. Evidently some of the crew decided to ape their 'betters', for on 28 August a seaman named John Reading died of alcoholic overindulgence. At first nobody could understand where he had got the drink from, but a captain's court of inquiry established that the boatswain had fed him three half-pints of rum, in contempt for his fondness for liquor.[3] Two days later they saw a bright comet in the sky; the 1769 comet was also observed in London and Paris.[4]

As the ship pressed on relentlessly due south, the gales became harder and escalated into full storms. On 31 August Banks noted: 'Blows very fresh with a heavy sea. The ship was very troublesome all last night and is not less so today.' This was a prelude to a month of almost continual gales, squalls and storms. Cook noted in his log on 1 September that they had a long heavy swell from the south-west plus 'very strong gales and heavy squalls with rain . . . a great sea from the westward'. On the 3rd he loosed the reef out of the main sail, set the topsails double reefed and before noon had all the reefs out. Large numbers of the crew were prostrated with seasickness as the vessel was buffeted by 50-foot waves and shaken like a rag doll by the ocean, with intense cold gnawing away all the time. The very high seas and storms continued non-stop until the 8th.[5] The artist Sydney Parkinson gave his own version of the ordeal: 'On the 1st of September we had hard piercing gales and squalls from the west and north-west with violent storms and hail and rain. The sea ran mountain-high, and tossed the ship upon the waves; she rolled so much that we could get no rest or scarcely lie in bed, and almost every movable on board was thrown down and rolled about from place to place. In brief, a person who has not been in a storm at sea cannot form an adequate idea of the situation we were in.'[6] The cruel Pacific played with its pawns, often moderating to a deceptive calmness so smooth that Banks was able to go out in a boat and shoot birds, but always returning to gale force with renewed fury. It even seemed to taunt the voyagers by presenting a fog bank on 10 September, which they at first mistook for land. In the fourth week of September Solander fell ill and Banks, tending his sick friend, began to grow anxious about the shrinking inventory of meat and fruit. Banks himself kept his sanity and equilibrium in these testing times by blasting away at anything that moved in the sky. On 2 October he was out shooting in the boat again and this time brought down an albatross with a wing span of 10'8'' – a Wandering Albatross, the very largest kind. Banks the scientist had no time for sailors' superstitions about these birds.[7]

Throughout the dreadful month of September 1769 Cook crept ever closer to latitude 40. When he reached the desired latitude and there was still a heavy swell from the south, Cook concluded there was no land in that direction and turned north. The result was almost miraculous: storms decreased to gales and soon the gales to occasional squalls, with hail and drizzle. By the first week of October they were in reasonable weather. Cook distributed malt to any of his crew that looked as though he had scurvy and began to see hopeful signs of land; even the squalls were of the kind usually associated with a nearby land-fall. At 2 p.m. on the 6th a boy at the masthead, Nicholas Young, shouted 'Land ho!', earning himself a gallon of rum for the privilege.[8] This was no mirage, no fog or cloud bank, though it took another twenty-four hours for the high mountains to be clearly visible. Banks, cocooned in his a priori theories, was convinced that this was the Great Southern Continent, but Cook knew better; for one thing, his estimated latitude and longitude were close to Tasman's. The *Endeavour* had in fact fetched the eastern coast of New Zealand, on the North Island, which it is unlikely that any vessel had approached from the open sea for more than six centuries.[9] The native inhabitants, the Maoris, had migrated from Polynesia in waves in AD 800–1000. They were lucky to find a ready source of protein in the moa, a flightless bird which, unable to escape its human predators, was fated to become as extinct as the dodo of Mauritius. Moas were probably extinct on the North Island by 1500 but clung on in the more challenging environment of the South Island until the late seventeenth century. Cook was not to know that New Zealand was a far more violent society than Polynesia proper, and had been so since the fourteenth century. It was a culture of warfare triggered not by pressure on the land but by a warrior ethos driven by an elite bent on exploitation in all forms, whether raiding the land of others to gain an economic surplus or the simple joy of conquest and sending the defeated into exile.[10] Cook knew nothing of this, but he did know that to prove his theory that the new land was not the Great Southern Continent he would have to explore it fully.

Cook anchored in what he later dubbed Poverty Bay and a party went ashore on 8 October in the pinnace and the yawl. They spied some locals on the shore and set off for what they hoped was friendly contact. Cook was in the yawl with Banks and Solander and there was an armed party in the pinnace. To their alarm, as they neared land, they saw four warriors with lances rushing to attack the pinnace which was commanded by the coxwain. He fired warning shots over their heads but, when the Maoris took no notice, he ordered his men to use deadly force. One of the warriors dropped dead and was hauled away by his fellows. Cook ordered a retreat to the ship for a rethink.[11] Next morning he sent out three boats packed with armed men and marines and again took Banks and Solander with him, this time hoping to use Tupaia to parley with the locals. Fifty Maoris were sitting calmly on the beach on the opposite bank of a river and at first they seemed peaceful, but when Tupaia addressed them in his Tahitian dialect (which they understood perfectly) they sprang up brandishing their weapons and told the interlopers to be gone. Tupaia persisted and made them understand that all the visitors wanted was food and water in exchange for iron. The Maoris invited them to cross the river to trade, but Cook insisted that first they should lay down their weapons. Eventually one of the Maoris broke the deadlock by stripping off and swimming across the stream; thirty of his fellows then joined him in the water but, ominously, they brought their lances with them. Tupaia warned Cook that the oncomers were not friendly, which seemed to be confirmed when in the first white–Polynesian contact the leading Maori snatched away

Mr Green's hanger, the short, curved sword he had at his waist. Banks, always a hawk in such situations, explained that the man should not be allowed to get away with it, but the seizure seemed to be the signal for a general advance from the other bank. Banks wounded the thief with a shot and Monkhouse finished him off with another, but by this time Cook was anxious that they would be outnumbered and overwhelmed. He ordered the marines to open fire, and three more warriors fell wounded, after which the others retreated across the river.[12] Cook now decided to row round the bay and, while prevented by heavy surf from making a second landing, he intercepted a fishing boat coming in from the ocean. Once again there was violence. Tupaia called to the boat to stop, it did not, shots were fired, three more Maoris were killed and another three taken prisoner on board the *Endeavour*.[13]

The three prisoners on board thoroughly enjoyed themselves and, Cook, noted, 'seemed much less concerned at what had happened than I was myself'.[14] But all who had witnessed the day's events were deeply depressed. As Banks commented: 'Thus ended the most disagreeable day my life has yet seen – black be the mark for it and heaven send that such may never return to embitter future reflection.'[15] Cook realised that the incident at Poverty Bay would scarcely redound to his credit and at first wrote in his journal self-accusingly:

> I can by no means justify my conduct in attacking and killing the people in this boat who had given me no just provocation and was [*sic*] wholly igno-rant of my design, and had I had the least thought of their making any resistance I would not so much as have looked at them, but when we was [*sic*] once alongside of them we must either have stood to be knocked on the head or else retire and let them gone off [*sic*] in triumph, and this last they would of course have attributed to their own bravery and our timorousness.[16]

Later he rewrote his journal, changed the emphasis, excluded the self-blame and stressed that he had European prestige and credibiity to uphold, adding that only those who had never been in such a ticklish situation would censure him. Censure him they have, for Poverty Bay has become a second battle-ground, for those eager to portray Cook as an especially vociferous agent of imperialism. Particular discrimination and nuance is needed in this case, for the two separate encounters cannot be meaningfully conflated, even if they are causally connected. The shouting match across the river and subsequent violence can at least partly be laid at the door of Maori martial culture. On the other hand, Cook's actions in intercepting the boat show the 'overkill' (in more senses than one) which was one of his besetting mindsets; the tendency to overreact was there from the very beginning. The first killings could conceivably be palliated as justifiable homicide; the second could not.[17]

Next day Cook landed again, partly to release their three captives, who seemed extremely unwilling to leave. The activities of Cook's wood-cutting party were cut short when some two hundred warriors suddenly appeared on the opposite bank of the river. Tupaia arranged a brief gift-exchange cere-mony, but Cook decided to break off contact early, before the Maoris' mood could sour again. Next morning at 6. a.m. the ship left the now definitely named Poverty Bay. Cook intended to sail south (along the south-eastern shore of North Island) for a week, making running surveys and investigating future prospects. By 15 October he found himself becalmed in a large bay, where he was again approached by the aboriginals. They claimed they wanted only to trade, but one of them at once stole some red cloth while others grabbed Tupaia's servant boy and carried him off towards the shore. The outraged crew opened fire; three more Maoris were killed and the terrified servant boy was rescued, half drowned and exhausted. Cook called the nearby white cliffs Cape Kidnappers (close to modern Napier) and the bay itself Hawke Bay, after the famous victor of Quiberon Bay in 1759 (now First Lord of the Admiralty).[18] By the 17th he had once again reached latitude 40 and, at Cape Turnagain, named for obvious reasons, he put the ship about and headed north. Sailing at first farther out to sea, he passed the Mahia peninsula and put in again at Anaura Bay. Here the locals were much friendlier and a brisk trade began, Cook's men buying up sweet potatoes, scurvy grass and wild celery. He then learned that the food and water he sought were even more plentifully available in nearby Uawa (Tolaga) Bay. Here he made his base for five days, trading cloth, beads and nails for fish, sweet potatoes and other vegetables.[19] The district chiefs were even invited aboard the *Endeavour*, and this was prob-ably the occasion when Tupaia cut loose, brazenly telling the Maoris that this was his ship and all the white men on it his slaves, with the result that they regarded him as a demigod.[20] Cook knew nothing of this – it emerged only later from Maori oral tradition – but he was already thoroughly exasperated with Tupaia, who acted as if he was captain of the ship and gave himself too many imperial airs and graces. As Cook wrote later: 'He was . . . proud and obstinate, which often made his situation on board both disagreeable to himself and those about him.'[21]

After a reluctant departure from this idyll, Cook began to round the East Cape on 30 October and soon found an anchorage in an inlet at the north of the Bay of Plenty for a planned observation of a transit of Mercury. Predictably enough, the inlet received the name Mercury Bay. Once again they found the locals friendly, trade easy, wood, water and vegetables abundant and plenty of fauna and flora to absorb the scientists. The North Island of New Zealand had more land below 300 metres than all Polynesia, Fiji and New Caledonia put together. But even though the climate was warmer in the period 1000–1600 than thereafter, the tropical Polynesian staples such as bananas, coconuts and breadfruit could not be grown. Yam and taro had a slender footing, but the predominant crop was sweet potato. Cook liked to use this, with wild celery and oatmeal grass, as the basis for a soup which was served with oatmeal for breakfast as an antiscorbutic. He accordingly made an eleven-day stopover there.[22] His sojourn was marred only by another shooting incident when, on the very day of the observation of the transit, Gore shot a Maori for the alleged theft of a cloth. Cook, who had been absent with Hicks overseeing the astronomical observations, was furious with Gore. 'I must own,' he wrote, 'that this did not meet with my approbation because I thought the punishment a little too severe for the crime, and we had now been long enough acquainted with these people to know how to chastise faults like this without taking their lives.'[23] The incident was a classic example of cross-cultural failure to communicate, because according to Maori customs barter need not be completed at once; it was permissible to take something and then pay for it a week or two later. It was fortunate that the Maoris took a lenient view of this shooting. Oral tradition relates that they contemplated massive retaliation but eventually concluded that the thief had been in the wrong as much as Gore, for not taking into account the cultural prejudices of the other party.[24] That an all-out conflict with the Maori would have gone hard for Cook and his men became apparent when he took a trip up a mangrove river and saw a spectacular example of the Polynesians' moated, stockaded and ramparted *pa* or hill fort. There were many of these on the North Island – maybe one every 5–10 miles – eloquent testimony to the violent society New Zealand had been for four hundred years.[25]

Cook's contacts with the Maori in October–November 1769 marked him down as a force of evil in Maori oral culture. When entering the Bay of Plenty he had again ordered his men to open fire when the Maoris tried to steal lines hanging over the ship's side. Nettled by the constant close pursuit by canoes, he had given the order to open fire on 4 November when a spear was thrown.[26] Finally there was the fatality on 9 November. The tradition handed down into the nineteenth century was that the ship itself was a supernatural monster or a giant bird with sails as wings or even a floating island, that the white men were *tupua* (goblins or demons), that they had sticks that spoke with lightning and killed, but that some of the goblins were kind and had introduced new foods to the grateful Maori, some of which can be tentatively identified as pork or salt beef, and some of which may more definitely be pinned down as a new kind of potato.[27] Yet his place in legend was hardly Cook's pressing priority in mid-November 1769. Before leaving Mercury Bay he indulged in another of those curious quasi-imperialistic gestures by 'taking possession' of the land in the name of King George III. He next sailed round the Coromandel peninsula into Hauraki Gulf, anchored there on 19 November, explored a river which he dubbed the 'Thames' then turned up the north-east coast in a strong gale towards the Bay of Islands.[28] Banks recorded foul weather all the way up there, monotonously noting the names of landmarks – Waikawau Bay, Mount Mangatiwhiri, Mahungarare Island, Cape Colville, the islands of Ponui, Waiheke, Rakino, Rangitoto, Bream Bay, Waipu river, the Cavalli Islands – like the worst hack scientist and as if he were doing the running survey himself.[29] The truth was that Banks hated being at sea and was only really happy when he had firm ground under his feet and something to explore.

Cook anchored the *Endeavour* in the lee of one of the first islands in the plethora that made up the Bay of Islands, that stunningly beautiful assemblage of hills, valleys, forests, islets and anchorages. Yet the fertility and fruitfulness of the location made it one of the most densely populated, and soon there was the familiar problem of thronging, jostling, importunate canoes, which led Cook to move the ship farther out in case an attack was intended. The 30th of November was another black day in Maori–European relations. A series of petty thefts made Cook sound a warning with his big guns, but the trouble escalated when Banks and Solander tried to land and were surrounded by some 300 warriors, some of whom broke into a war dance while the others tried to seize the boat. This time it was Hicks on the bridge who took action: he swung the ship round and fired another volley from cannon which, according to Cook, made the assailants 'as meek as lambs', though other reports speak of shots continuing to be fired on the beach and Cook doing his best to avoid adding to the roster of native fatalities.[30] It was noticeable on his voyages that Cook often displaced his anger and frustration relating to indigenous aggression on to his own men and so it turned out here. Matthew Cox, Henry Stevens and Emmanuel Parmyra were given a dozen lashes each for assorted charges of leaving their posts and stealing from the Maoris. Cox was then placed in the brig on the *Endeavour* for swearing up and down that he had done nothing wrong and was being punished unjustly. Ever thereafter he retained a rankling sense of injustice and on his return to England tried to bring a judicial action against his captain. Cook dealt with his contumacy by giving him another half-dozen lashes and releasing him from the brig.[31] The rest of the time in the Bay of Islands was uneventful. Cook managed to lay in a vast store of fresh fish from trade with the locals, not just mackerel, mullet and sea-bream but more exotic 'delicacies' such as shark and stingray.

After a week in the Bay of Islands Cook put to sea again on 5 December, heading for the most northerly point of North Island. December 1769, though, proved something of a replay of September, with ferocious gales blowing for much of the time. He reached the North Cape on 10 December, explored Karikari Bay and Cape Karikari in the most capricious weather, with the sea alternating with alarming suddenness from deceptive smoothness to furious storms of wind and rain, all the time surveying, albeit in the most difficult conditions. The really alarming gales began on 13 December, with wind speeds so severe that the *Endeavour* was driven off the coast; as Cook logged it: 'No land in sight for the first time since we have been upon this coast.'[32] Unable to make significant progress and thrown this way and that, Cook found himself back at North Cape on 19 December, still beset by strong gales and a heavy swell from the west. Almost incredibly, there was another European navigator in these waters at this very time. The French captain Jean François Marie de Surville had sailed from Pondicherry in India in June 1769 and became snarled up in the Solomon Islands. He then headed south, hoping to follow in Tasman's footsteps, reached 35S then changed course to the east and sighted North Island on 12 December. Surville and Cook came within an ace of sighting each other, and probably would have done but for the gale of the 13th. The same winds which blew Cook out of sight of land were kinder to Surville. On 16 December the latter rounded North Cape (Cook was then fifty miles to the north), and anchored his ship *St Jean Baptiste* in the very Doubtless Bay which Cook had passed on the 9th. Surville's crew was in a dreadful state, with sixty men dead and most of the rest stricken with scurvy.[33] The great storm of 27 December which would nearly engulf Cook smashed over him as he lay at anchor, destroying anchors, cables and a dinghy. Refusing to believe that the storm could carry away his dinghy, Surville accused the locals of theft, inevitably got involved in a running fight with them, and eventually had to put to sea virtually crewless to avoid massacre. Amazingly, after all these vicissitudes he reached Peru, but was then drowned in heavy seas while attempting to land. Thus did one of history's would-be famous meetings fail to materialise. Beaglehole remarks: 'A good seaman, he was an adventurer rather than an explorer. One has difficulty in picturing the scene had he and Cook met.'[34]

The stormy weather continued but, as in the year before, eased off on Christmas Day as if in deference to a bibulous crew. Off the Three Kings Island (previously seen by Tasman) that day, Banks recorded the scene: 'Our goose pie was eat [sic] with great approbation and in the evening all hands were as drunk as our forefathers used to be on the like occasion.'[35] But on the evening of the 26th a gale began, increased to storm force, and at last became a hurricane. The horrified Banks wrote: 'All our people said that they never before were in so hard a summer's gale.' Even Cook was alarmed. On the 28th he steered east for land under the foresail and mainsail, but was soon forced to take the latter in. He recorded in his journals:

> It began to blow very hard and increased in such a manner that by eight o'clock it was a mere [*sic*] hurricane attended with rain and the sea run prodigious high. At this time we had the ship hauled up to the foresail and brought her to with her head to the north-west under a reefed mainsail, but this was scarce done before the main tack gave way and we were glad to take in the main sail and lay under the mizzen staysail and balanced mizzen, after which we reefed the foresail and reefed both it and the mainsail.[36]

By the end of the year, with the *Endeavour* off Cape Maria Van Diemen, Cook was seriously concerned about the continuing storm and their consequent inability to make way: 'It will hardly be credited that in the midst of summer and in Latitude 35 such a gale of wind as we have had could have happened, which for its strength and continuance was such as I was hardly ever in before. Fortunately at this time we were at a good distance from land, otherwise it might have proved fatal to us.'[37] Consultation with officers and veterans with decades of service on the seven seas revealed a universal consensus that no one had ever seen a storm like it. The wave heights were prodigious, not surprisingly, as these are determined by a threefold causation, all present in this case: Force 12 wind speeds, a storm lasting a week or more, and an uninterrupted oceanic fetch. They were witnessing the Pacific at its most cruel and fearsome.

Gales, high seas and a colossal swell from the south-west did not abate until 8 January. All the time Cook continued with his running survey, high seas, rain, clouds, thunder and lightning notwithstanding. On 10 January the *Endeavour* was off Hokianga harbour and the mouths of the rivers at False Hokianga and Whangape. Once the weather cleared, they could see Mount Taranaki, which Cook named Mount Egmont, after one of his sponsors. Finally, on 15 January Cook put into Queen Charlotte Sound on the extreme north of South Island – another beautiful spot, which was to become his favourite location in New Zealand – and found a snug anchorage in Ship's Cove. Here Cook and his men stayed for three weeks, enjoying fine weather and gentle breezes. Banks was happy again, able to explore at will and delighting in the welcome sounds of birdsong. He was particularly intrigued by the New Zealand version of the nightingale – the nocturnal bellbird which the Maoris called *korimako*, which began its melody at 1 a.m. and continued until sunrise.[38] The Maoris in this area, darker in complexion and evidently poorer than those on the eastern side of the island, were more friendly, albeit always volatile and liable to loose off a volley of stones if the visitors displeased them. Cook found them more commonsensical than their eastern brethren, if only because they were quite willing to trade fish, especially mackerel, for nails. Both he and Banks were alarmed to find clear and unmistakable evidence of cannibalism, although it was the practice of sodomy that most intrigued Banks; although a voracious heterosexual, he was hardly a pansexualist.[39] Probing further into cannibalism, Cook learned that the Maori ate only the bodies of enemies killed in battle and consumed only the brains. Cook's two weeks in Queen Charlotte Sound were well paced: alternating ship repair and loading of food, water and wood with rest and recreation for the crew, while he and the officers carried out local exploration and surveying. Taking just one sailor as a companion, he climbed to the top of Kaitapeha ridge, 1,200 feet high (now called Cook's Lookout).[40] Convinced that he could verify (and in some cases falsify) Tasman's findings, he developed a positive relish for steep hill ascents, making the next one with Banks and Solander. From 22 January to the end of the month Cook was rarely still, exploring inlets, islands, bays and coves. On the last day of the month he crowned his final hill ascent by taking possession of Queen Charlotte Sound in the name of King George and drinking a bottle of wine to celebrate.[41]

Once at sea on 1 February Cook sailed through the strait separating North and South Island, passed Cape Palliser, and then methodically worked north for forty miles to Cape Turnagain, thus completing the circuit of North Island and assuring himself that there was no great southern continent in that direction. It was now time to explore South Island. On 14 February he passed Cape Campbell in the opposite direction (having passed it when going north on the 8th), still receiving trading visits from the Maori canoes that had dogged them all the way through the Cook Strait. Making his way down the eastern coast of South Island, Cook honoured his fellow traveller by naming two of the features they passed Banks Island and the Banks peninsula.[42] The final week of February saw the bad weather returning. On the 23rd Cook logged the gradual appearance of a large, hollow swell and by the time he reached Cape Saunders (named after another admiral) two days later the winds were chaotic and unpredictable, with rain and mist making it difficult to see land. The ten days from 23 February saw the Pacific at its most capricious, alternating between lulling calms and sudden violent gales from the south, with a head sea that carried away small spars and split sails. Cook hugged the coast with something like desperation, not wishing to lose sight of it lest his survey be incomplete but in so doing taking obvious risks. He lost a lot of ground when he tacked, to make sure the land was continuous after losing sight of it in a squall. He was fighting yet another patch of heavy weather, this time lasting from 23 February to 14 March. The waves were pyramidal and confused, there was a large hollow sea from the south-west, and the constant gales would sometimes morph into violent squalls. Cook described the conditions:

> The wind wiffling all round the compass, sometimes blowing a fresh gale and at times almost calm. At 5 o'clock [on 25 February] it fixed at west-south-west and soon blew so hard as to put us past our topsails and to split the foresail all to pieces . . . at 1 a.m. the wind moderating, set the topsails one reef out, but soon after daylight the gale increased to a storm with heavy squalls attended by rain; this brought us again under our courses, and the main topsail being split we unbent it and brought another to the yard.[43]

Banks's gloomy journal entries have the same story to tell: '25 February. Wind boxing the compass. 26 February. Still blew hard with some squalls. 27 February. No standing upon legs without assistance of hands as yet. 1 March. Weather sufficiently troublesome. 3 March. Swell almost as high as ever which gave great spirits to the "no continent" party.'[44]

Cook spied Stewart Island through the murk, but in such conditions it looked like part of the mainland. He reached latitude 48 before turning north when a heavy south-west swell convinced him there was no land in that quarter – but not before narrowly escaping some dangerous rocks in latitude 47° 26′ S. By 3 March he was back at Cape Saunders, with whales and seals gambolling around the ship. Banks still longed for evidence of a great southern continent, but the sailors wished with all their hearts that they could prove this new territory an island so that they could be done with the adventure and go home.[45] But when the *Endeavour* rounded the point of Solander Island Banks finally conceded that his hopes were vain. Painfully Cook began to coax the *Endeavour* up the western coast of South Island, marking off the landmarks – Chalky Island, Doubtful Harbour, Banza Island, Big Bay, Open Bay Island, Jackson's Bay – which brought him very close to Tasman's landfall in New Zealand on 13 December 1642.[46] Banks kept urging Cook to land but this was impossible because of the huge surf and swells, unless they could find landlocked bays or inlets – also impossible in the hostile weather. Besides, as Cook noted, 'it certainly would have been highly imprudent of me to have put into a place where we could not have got out but with a wind that we have lately found does not blow but one day in a month'.[47] It was the old problem of the landsman's inability to understand seafaring and its constraints; Banks was no more talented in this way than was Napoleon later. The voyagers sighted the Southern Alps and the glaciers and at last, on 24 March, were at the most northerly point of the west coast, off Cape Farewell. There followed three days of bad weather and difficult tacking until finally, on 27 March, they came into safe anchorage at Queen Charlotte Sound. The epic circumnavigation was complete.[48]

The *Endeavour* spent three days in Queen Charlotte Sound. The main thing Cook had to decide was the itinerary for the journey home. He himself was minded to return via Cape Horn but his officers, having tasted some of the worst the Pacific had to offer, were in no mood for running eastabout in the stormy latitudes of the roaring forties. They expressed their doubts as to whether the already battered *Endeavour* was up to the task and had similar views when Cook then proposed taking the ship across the Indian Ocean and round the Cape of Good Hope. Cook saw the force of the argument and, always versatile, said that in that case they would try to chart the eastern coast of New Holland (Australia) and then go north to find the lands explored by Quirós nearly two centuries before. He hoped thereby to clear up at least two riddles: was New Guinea part of Australia or was it separated by a strait? and were the lands found by Quirós at the north of Australia and thus part of a great continent? As for the fabled Great Southern Continent, after exploring three-quarters of its putative locations Cook remained sceptical but agnostic: 'Of what may lie further to the southward than 40S I can give no opinion.'[49] Already he had done enough to enter the pantheon of the great navigators of the ages, and his circumnavigation of New Zealand and his surveys there – 2,400 miles of coastline charted in six and a half months often in high seas and tumultuous storms – was a magnificent achievement, all the more so as subsequent voyagers found his charts stunningly and almost supernaturally accurate. The only thing he could be faulted for was not spotting that Stewart Island *was* an island, but then he was surveying it in intermittent visibility.[50] The carping and the ungenerous occasionally tried to belittle his achievements – as when Matthew Flinders pointed out that Cook had missed certain geographical features between Port Jackson and Ram Head – but Flinders neglected to say that *any* shipbound explorer would have missed them, as one needed to reconnoitre by boat to make sense of the complex geography.[51] Against this, too, can be set the major achievement of settling the dimensions of Cook Strait between North and South Islands. As usual, Cook and Banks observed what they saw with care and insight. They both noted that the Maori were more warlike than other Polynesians, more thickly tattooed, and prone to treating their women much more severely.[52] Cook particularly admired their war canoes, which reminded him of New England whaleboats, and was especially shrewd in spotting that Polynesia must have been settled from Asia, not America. *Pace* Thor Heyerdahl, scholarly opinion overwhelmingly supports Cook in this conjecture.[53]

Banks was jubilant at the 400 new plants he had been able to collect from his eight landings (six on the North Island and the two visits to Queen Charlotte Sound). But he faced with dismay a voyage across the notoriously stormy Tasman Sea to Australia. Yet at first Fate was with him and the ocean was astonishingly gentle. On 9 April, ten days out from Queen Charlotte Sound, he noted: 'The sea both yesterday and today was as smooth as a millpond.'[54] His luck held until the middle of the month. Cook, who had had little to do for a fortnight except order the marine John Bowles twelve lashes for insolence to an officer, finally had to ascend the bridge two days out from the Australian coast when huge seas began to batter the *Endeavour*. Banks noted on the 17th: 'During last night and this morning the weather was more variable with continual squalls and wind shifting all round the compass.'[55] It was the scenario famously described to Odysseus, whereby the traveller's greatest danger comes at the end of a journey. The Tasman Sea finally lived up to its reputation; as Beaglehole puts it, it 'shook itself, as it were, and considered its true character'.[56] Cook was driven farther to the north than he had intended, to 38N. The night of 17–18 April was fraught, with the ship running under foresail and mizzen and soundings being taken every two hours. The atrocious weather continued all next day (18 April) and into the dark hours. On instinct, and possibly taking his cue from the myriad seabirds seen the day before, Cook brought the ship to. At 6 a.m. Hicks clearly saw land, about 15 to 20 miles off, extending from north-east to west. Cook aimed for the easternmost point of land, meanwhile dubbing the southernmost spit Point Hicks (today's Cape Everard) and calling the whole New South Wales. Almost on cue the wind abated and the sea subsided.[57] Now well north of Van Diemen's Land as pinpointed by Tasman, Cook decided that the remaining issue of the Tasman voyages – whether Van Diemen's was an island or part of New Holland – would have to be cleared up by a subsequent expedition. At Cape Howe he turned north and began a running survey, keeping clear of the heavy surf and the water's edge, heading out to open sea at night and returning to the coastline in the morning. Bateman Bay, Mount Budaway and Pigeon House all found their way into the log. It was eight days before he attempted to land, but the first attempt, on 27 April, was a failure because of the heavy surf running. Only the following morning was a bay discovered, to become famous in history as Botany Bay. There Cook anchored the *Endeavour*.[58]

A party of aborigines had gathered on the shore to watch the approach of the yawl. Cook in capricious mood had decided that his wife's young cousin, Isaac Smith, should be the first to set foot on land. Otherwise the landing party contained the usual suspects: himself, Tupaia, Banks and Solander and an armed squad. As the yawl came in to land, the aborigines decamped, except for two men who yelled defiance at the forty invaders and brandished their primitive spears.[59] Tupaia called out a friendly greeting but the response was angry, so Cook ordered a warning shot to be fired, which had no effect. He then decided to open up with small shot, which did finally clear the beach. After beaching the boat the landing party found a small village and saw an old woman with a group of children shivering behind a shield. Cook immediately noticed that the Australian aboriginals were darker in complexion and more primitive than the Maoris and, having been mightily impressed by the Maori war canoes, found the Australian equivalent almost ludicrously deficient. He gave the children some beads but, finding no water, decided to return to the ship. Next morning Cook and his comrades made another landing, saw no humans, but found that their 'generous' gifts, the beads, had been left behind. This time, however, they did find a plentiful source of fresh water as well as shellfish which the locals had been cooking on smouldering fires. With such a good source of water, fish and wood to hand, Cook stayed for a few days; he named the bay Botany Bay because of Banks's enthusiasm for finding new plant specimens.[60] They saw many signs of the aborigines and even tried to tempt them to make friendly contact by going unarmed into the woods, but all in vain. On the rare occasion when Tupaia was able to exchange words with the locals, they did not understand him; indicating that 'New Holland' was well outside the cultural and linguistic ambit of Polynesia. The visitors also saw their first marsupial, though the descriptions make it sound more like a wallaroo or wallaby than a kangaroo properly so called. Lorikeets and cockatoos also abounded. Very heartening was the local food supply; not only were the tidal inlets full of shellfish but Gore soon proved himself a mighty marine hunter and brought in two stingrays, weighing 600 pounds together and described as good eating.[61] The ship's company was in good spirits when the *Endeavour* left Botany Bay on 6 May.

Cook's eloquent descriptions of Botany Bay as an Eden were instrumental in persuading the authorities in London to send the 'first fleet' of settlers and convicts there in 1788, but its inadequacies soon became apparent and the colony was switched to nearby Port Jackson (Sydney harbour). Cook's critics have seized on this and other examples to accuse him of always following the line of least resistance in his choice of anchorages, and thus always missing the best harbours. In Tahiti he missed Papeete because Matavai Bay was easy, comfortable, beautiful and had plentiful supplies; moreover he never experienced the dangerous westerlies and north-westerlies that drove Bligh farther west and led him to Papeete. In New Zealand it was the same story. Waitemata, off the Hauraki Gulf and the site of modern Auckland, was hidden behind a screen of islands and not discovered until 1820, while in the

Cook Strait in February 1770 he was too far offshore to notice the entrance to Port Nicholson, the harbour of Wellington. In Australia he used the unsatisfactory Botany Bay while a few miles to the north lay the most spectacular anchorage on the eastern coast of Australia; he also missed Jervis Bay and Newcastle harbour.[62] Yet we should remember that Cook's primary concern was always charting and exploration, not finding the optimum anchorage; his approach to stopovers was pragmatic and functional, and he also had deadlines to meet. At the mercy of the winds, Cook simply could not afford the time for intricate investigations that did not bear on his main purpose. His log for May shows the most nuanced concern for the winds, as they altered from northerlies to south-easterlies. With generally fair weather he made full sail during the day but took in the studding sails at night. There were some delightfully moonlit nights with a generally tranquil sea (though the twitchy Banks was able to record a heavy squall on 10 May and Cook recorded another on the 15th, forcing the topsails to be reefed), and the *Endeavour* made remarkably good progress throughout the month.[63]

Banks was impressed by the water spouts he saw from the deck and the two venomous sea snakes that swam past the vessel. Cook occasionally put in to the land, and spent much of 23 May ashore at Bustard Island (so called because of the profusion of bustards). Ominously, in light of later developments, Cook found a channel full of shoals which led to a mangrove lagoon, where Banks was able to note large ants in a giant nest, overgrown stinging caterpillars and other tropical delights, though he recovered his composure by shooting at ducks and pelicans.[64] Yet 23 May was a black day in Cook's calendar for suddenly he was faced with a very grave case of indiscipline that roused him to fury. It says something for Cook's talents at man-management – for the lash was by no means the ultimate deterrent in the Royal Navy – that he had so far kept the lid on a hundred men cooped up in a ninety-seven-foot-long vessel, with no room to swing a cat – except, of course, the cat-o'nine-tails itself. It has already been remarked that his crew was half-drunk at least half the time; the grog ration was generous and was certainly supplemented by theft and smuggling. Off the coast of Australia, after two years at sea, something snapped in one of the men below decks. Richard Orton, Cook's clerk, went to bed drunk and, while he was asleep, someone cut the clothes from off his back; not content with that, the malefactor then cut off part of both his ears.[65] Cook ordered an immediate inquiry, and the obvious suspect was an American midshipman named James Magra, who was known for cutting off people's clothes while they slept and had been heard to issue threats against Orton; the most dire was that, but for laws against murder, he would surely have murdered Orton by now. Cook interrogated Magra closely but could find no conclusive evidence of his guilt. Nevertheless he dismissed him from the quarterdeck and suspended him from duty. Cook commented: 'he being one of those gentlemen, frequently found on board King's Ships, that can very well be spared, or to speak more plainly, a good for nothing. Besides, it was necessary in me to show my immediate resentment against the person on whom the suspicion fell lest they should not have stopped there.'[66]

This was indeed a curious affair, and Cook's gnomic remarks deepen the mystery. After noting that Orton was not a man without faults, Cook went on:

> Some reasons might however be given why this misfortune came upon him in which he himself was in some measure to blame, but as this is only conjecture and would tend to fix it upon some people in this ship whom I would fain believe would hardly be guilty of such an action, I shall say nothing about it unless I shall hereafter discover the offenders, which I shall take every method in my power to do, for I look upon such proceedings as highly dangerous in such voyages as this and the greatest insult that could be offered to my authority in this ship, as I have always been ready to hear and redress every complaint that have [sic] been made against any person in the ship.[67]

From these Delphic and sibylline utterances, certain things seem reasonably clear. Cook suspected that the motive for the assault was sexual, that Orton was the object of homosexual jealousy, and that the perpetrator might have 'set up' Magra, using the dodge of cutting off clothes to frame the American as it was well known that that was one of his tricks. Also intriguing is Cook's use of the plural 'offenders', almost as if he had a pretty good idea who the real criminals were (more than one) and that they occupied an alarmingly high place in the ship's hierarchy. What is quite evident is the suppressed anger; Cook took the incident as an implicit personal insult, and this rankled. He made good his threat that he would not let the matter rest. Once in Batavia and back in 'civilisation', he offered a cash reward plus fifteen gallons of alcoholic spirit to anyone who would reveal the guilty party. At once Patrick Saunders, another midshipman, deserted and was never seen again.[68] But did Saunders act alone in the assault on Orton, or was he perhaps a minor player in the drama, who agreed for a consideration to go on the run, so that Cook would let the affair drop for the real villain not to be exposed? The truth will never be known. What *is* evident is that Cook saw himself as a fount of justice, and that the assault was not just a challenge to his authority as captain and his credibility as a leader of men, but in some sense impugned his claim to be a 'tough but fair' man. Here was a brutal, thuggish crew, ill requiting the efforts of a humane captain. Cook's self-image and *amour propre* were wounded by the atrocity, as much as Orton's ears. There was an almost paranoid chippiness about his journal entries on the incident, almost as though he felt the Admiralty would be bound to blame him and might even conclude that the event might never have occurred if a real gentleman and not a meritocratic labourer's son had been at the helm.

The *Endeavour* continued its steady run north, past Curtis Island and Keppel Bay, between Great Keppel and North Keppel Islands to the cape at the northern end of Townshend Island; all this area was later minutely explored by Matthew Flinders.[69] The beginning of June found the ship making steady progress past Cape Repulsion, Repulse Bay, Cape Upstart, Halifax Bay and Fitzroy Island to Cape Grafton. But now came the great crisis of the entire *Endeavour* voyage, or rather two interconnected crises, from which Cook would escape only through fortitude, persistence, impeccable seamanship and a great deal of luck. He began to notice islands all around him and grew concerned about the number of shoals in his path. He had the ship's boats lowered and they then proceeded ahead of the *Endeavour*, taking soundings and trying to find a passage through the labyrinth of shallows, sandbanks and rogue tides. Men constantly swung the lead (certainly not the proverbial light task in these circumstances) to gauge the depth, which rose and fell alarmingly, one moment seven fathoms, the next second down to three fathoms. Again and again a boat would signal 'shoal water', forcing Cook to anchor at night in the lee of one of the islands. There was a two-day stopover at Thirsty Sound (so called because they could find no fresh water there), making repairs while the rain fizzed around them and plagues of mosquitoes moved in to attack after dusk.[70] He blessed his good fortune that his ship was a 'cat', light, manoeuvrable, with strong timbers and a broad bottom. But as the succession of shoals began to seem limitless, even a consummate seaman such as Cook must have feared that sooner or later his luck would run out. The strain on the nerves of his crew was palpable. Somehow, miraculously, they navigated the maze of shoals while Cook compiled charts of an accuracy that would astonish later generations of mariners. As the weather improved, he threaded a course past Whitsunday Island, Cape Upstart, Magnetic Island, Rockingham Bay, Palm Island, and Cape Grafton. At Mission Bay (east of modern Cairns) Cook hoped to find water but there was none to be had, so he pressed on. Weighing anchor under a golden moon with fair winds and good visibility, they contrasted the midnight beauty with the deadly peril they were in.[71]

Cook was not to know that his troubles had barely begun, for north of Cape Grafton began the Great Barrier Reef, today hailed as one of the wonders of the world but in the eighteenth and nineteenth centuries a graveyard for shipping. Sixteen hundred miles long, extending over an area of 133,000 square miles, this tangle of more than 2,900 reefs and 900 islands represented the world's biggest single structure made by tiny organisms (coral polyps). It is home to 215 species of birds, as well as a multitude of turtles, stingrays, sharks and saltwater crocodiles so ferocious that they often preyed on the sharks; to round off this 'paradise' there were seventeen diferent species of sea snakes.[72] What might have fascinated Banks was a source of transcendental terror to Cook the seaman. The reef lies off the north-eastern Australian coast, not parallel to it but at an altering angle, farthest from the coast at its southernmost point at latitude 22. Yet at the southern end the passage lay through a narrow funnel between shore and reef. The night of 10 June was passed nail-bitingly, but at least it was a moonlit night, the sea was calm and all the obstacles were visible. Around 9 p.m. the reading on the plumb line dipped from 14–21 fathoms to eight. An anxious Cook ordered all hands on deck but suddenly the *Endeavour* again emerged into deep water.[73] Thinking the crisis was over, Banks and the other gentlemen retired for the night. They had just passed Pickersgill Reef. Suddenly, just before 11 p.m. the readings lurched alarmingly from 21 fathoms to 17. Before the men could take another sounding, there was a sickening thud: the ship struck and stuck fast. They were marooned on a jagged coral reef at high tide, lying in just 3–4 feet of water, about twenty miles from the shore; with the turn of the tide they would be helpless for another twelve hours or more.[74] Cook ordered the anchors put out and the boats lowered: the idea was that they would try to wrench the ship off the coral by dropping anchors from the boats and winding them up with capstan and windlass. It was impossible to haul her off the rocks with boats and ropes, and all the time a fearful creaking and groaning was heard as the ship's keel scraped on the coral beneath.

The 11th of June 1770 would live for ever in the memory of the *Endeavour*'s crew. In an effort to budge the vessel they lightened her by throwing overboard everything heavy – the six half-ton guns and their carriages, huge 56-pound 'pigs' of iron and stone ballast, casks of wine, firewood, 50 tons of stores and much more. There was no panic and Banks was deeply impressed by the men's morale: 'The seamen worked with surprising alacrity, no grumbling or growling was to be heard throughout the ship, no not even an oath.'[75] Just as there are no atheists in foxholes, so there are no whingers in a life-and-death maritime emergency. There was no doubting the gravity of their situation. Banks and the scientists laid in emergency provisions for a voyage in the longboat, but with little hope that they could reach land; even if they did, with all guns and ammunition jettisoned, they would be helpless prey for the aborigines.[76] Nonetheless, even with all this lightening, the ship would not budge. When high tide came round again, there was a determined effort to heave her off with cables and block and tackle, but in vain. The only advantage the beleaguered mariners had was that the weather was calm. Suddenly the *Endeavour* heeled to starboard and began to take on water. A torrent gushed in through a new hole and the pumps proved useless. There was total silence as the men looked death in the face; by 5. p.m. the water was rising and the exhausted men were fighting a rearguard action for their lives. All hands were commanded to the three pumps (there was a fourth but it failed to work) – including Banks and the scientists – sweating and labouring profusely in fifteen-minute shifts.[77] By 9 p.m. on 11 June the leak was gaining markedly on the pumps and destruction seemed certain and imminent. With a hole that size in her keel, even if she could be floated into deep water she might capsize and go to the bottom in minutes as the water flooded through her gashed bottom. But the risk had to be taken. A huge concerted effort was made with capstan, windlass, cables and anchor lines. At last, at around 10 p.m., twenty-three hours after she had struck, the *Endeavour* floated free. Cook ordered the anchors brought in and the fore-topmast set. The bower and the stream anchor were lost, but the ship had enough sail to limp to the land, twenty miles away. What prevented the feared capsize was the brilliant technique known as 'fothering' whereby a sail sewn with tufts of wool and oakum and spread with sheep's dung was used as a patch over the leak, with the force of the water holding it in position. It is a mistake to say that Cook knew nothing of fothering – he was far too good for such ignorance and it was in any case standard naval practice – but he had no personal experience of the technique. This was where Jonathan Monkhouse came into his own: he was virtually a technical expert, having specialised in fothering in ships off the Virginia coast. Cook allowed himself the dry comment that Monkhouse had executed the technique 'very much to my satisfaction'.[78] One immediate consequence was that the leak which had previously gained on all three pumps was now contained by just one. This was just as well as the first possible anchorage that was investigated – Weary Bay, Cook called it – had no water; they had therefore to spend the night two miles offshore, at anchor among shoals. Next morning the pinnace found a good haven, just in time, for the weather was turning squally and they had to enter a deep river mouth with the elements against them. Even so, it took Cook another two days to manoeuvre the ship through the narrow gaps between shoals and bars, twice running aground before mooring beside a steep bank. It was 16 June before the *Endeavour* lay safely at anchor and by now it was blowing a full gale.[79]

They were now in the Endeavour river, where they would remain until the beginning of August. It was only when the crew examined the ship's bottom that they realised how lucky they had been. The reef had shorn away much of the keel and sheathing, and the ship's planks were torn away as neatly as if someone had been working on them with a tool. Amazingly, a large piece of coral had snapped off and stuck in the gash it had made – and this alone probably prevented the *Endeavour* from sinking. Relieved of the worst anxiety, Cook reflected on the narrow scrape and how well his men had borne themselves. He decided to restore Magra to his duties, ostensibly because he could not make any charges against him stick, but probably as a thanksgiving offering to the gods and because of Cook's temperamental aversion to feeding an idle pair of hands.[80] Now he set all hands to work. For nearly two months the crew worked on extensive repairs, surrounded by estuarine mangrove swamps where salt-water crocodiles lurked and with the wind howling almost constantly. The men had to unload the ship, float it ashore with the tide, then raise it on its side so that the carpenters and caulkers could patch the bottom. With no women to distract them, and poisonous snakes, crocodiles and sharks as a constant hazard, they were in no mood to desert or wander far from the camaraderie of their fellow workers. Banks and Solander went out on their usual botanical and zoological field trips, observing kangaroos, dingoes and other fauna.[81] Tupaia was ill with serious symptoms of scurvy that had first manifested themselves before they reached the Barrier Reef. He felt very sorry for himself and rationalised this with some savagely acidulous observations on the aborigines, which influenced Banks's attitudes. Banks seemed unable to see through Tupaia as Cook could. The navigator-priest was essentially a snob obsessed with hierarchy and social status, and this tended to merge into a curious racism. He despised the Maoris as a degenerate sept of Polynesians, but thought the aborigines an even lower form of life and barely human. Some observers suspected that Tupaia felt he had lost caste by being unable to interpret the aborigines' tongue as he had done with the Maoris.[82]

Food supplies proved reasonably plentiful in the countryside around the Endeavour river though there were no game animals on land except the kangaroo, which was generally considered not good eating. Wild plantains, taro and palm cabbage provided the staples, topped up with shellfish and, increasingly, stingrays and turtles being caught by the more intrepid hunters from the yawl. As in Tahiti, the issue of food caused tension with the locals. Early contacts with the aborigines on 10 July seemed to promise friendly rela-tions, but on 19 July a more exigent party visited Cook and demanded that he give them one of the turtles the white men had caught; the aborigines prized these as a great delicacy but found them hard to catch. Since turtle was a prime source of protein for his men, Cook refused. The locals were offered a biscuit to taste, but their leader angrily threw it overboard. The aborigines then tried to seize the turtle anyway, but were restrained. They stormed off in fury and soon found an ample means of revenge. Banks and others had tents pitched on the shore, but the aboriginals started a bush fire by setting the grass alight. They managed to burn down an improvised laundry but, luckily for Cook, the powder kegs he had had on the shore earlier to dry were now back on the *Endeavour*.[83] Had the angry confrontation with the aborigines happened two days earlier, Cook would have been left seriously short of firepower. As it was, the incident led to yet another salvo being fired over the heads of indigenous peoples. The pattern was becoming depressingly familiar.[84] Meanwhile Cook, sometimes accompanied by Banks, made several ascents of nearby hills, one 1,000 feet high, and gazed out to sea in the hope that they would see some way to get out of the 'insane labyrinth' of reefs and shoals that lay ahead of them. He also sent out Molyneux in a small boat to navigate through the tangle of sandbars and obstructions, but his reports were gloomy, suggesting there was no way through for at least twenty miles. Finally, on 20 July, after all repairs had been completed and the crew had laid in goodly supplies of shellfish, shark, stingray and turtle, the ship put out from the Endeavour river, only to be forced back there by contrary winds.[85]

It was another frustrating two weeks before, on 4 August, the *Endeavour* finally set sail. Still in the maze of reefs, for six days Cook made barely any progress. The obvious route was north but that was barred by shoals and sand-banks. Cook tried an easterly track, then swung north, then east again, taking constant soundings and narrowly dodging shoals. These are seas in which few vessels have dared to venture to this very day. To make matters worse, there were strong gales and murky weather. Molyneux urged him to turn back, but Cook argued that, even if the winds made it possible, there was still no escape that way and that, sooner or later, they would have to follow the very track they were now on. Everyone was highly anxious, for even with a three-month food supply, they might face starvation if they were to wander for ever between the winds. And would the hastily patched up ship be able to endure the conditions in which they now sailed?[86] Every time Cook thought he had found a path to the open sea, more breakers and reefs would be sighted from the masthead. He put to shore on various occasions to climb hills and try to see a way out of the labyrinth with the naked eye. He climbed the headlands at Cape Flattery, at Point Lookout and Lizard Island. Almost despairing at a reef which seemed to stretch endlessly from north-west to south-east, Cook thought he saw a glimmer of hope in the fact that the sea broke over the reef to the east at a great height, as if that was the reef's outer rampart. Molyneux was sent out again and returned with word that there was a narrow and dangerous passage to the open sea. After conferring with his officers, Cook set a course somewhere between the Howick and Lizard islands. After another display of careful and meticulous seamanship, the *Endeavour* came at last into clear blue water and seemed free from the maze of reefs where she had been trapped since 26 May. On 14 August there was no land at all to be seen.[87] Cook could now have made a clear run east into the Pacific Ocean but, determined to prove that Australia and New Guinea were not connected and fearful of overshooting the passage between them, he set a course for the north-west. For the moment his chief concern was whether the *Endeavour* was truly seaworthy, and his journal reflects his anxiety:

> Yet the very waves, which by their swell convinced us that we had no rocks or shoals to fear, convinced us also that we could not safely put the same confidence in our vessel as before she had struck; for the blows she received from them so widened her leaks that she admitted no less than nine inches of water in an hour, which, considering the state of our pumps and the navigation that was still before us, would have been a subject of more serious consideration to people whose danger had not lately been so much more imminent.[88]

Yet the decision to explore the putative strait between New Guinea and Australia was nearly Cook's undoing. At noon on the 15th land again appeared and shortly afterwards huge breakers between it and the ship, rolling from one end of the horizon to the other. High winds and mountainous waves from the sea now drove the ship remorselessly towards the reef heralded by the foaming breakers. In such conditions Cook was helpless: he could neither anchor nor heave to. He tried to delay the inevitable by putting the longboat and yawl into the sea ahead to get the ship's head round and delay its progress. The crew spent a sleepless night listening to the roaring of the surf increasing in volume, and at daybreak they saw the maelstrom towards which they were being pitched, not a mile distant.[89] The giant rollers would pick up the *Endeavour* and smash her against the reef, which they knew from their wanderings since May would be a wall rising steeply from the ocean floor; the ship would be smashed to pieces like matchwood and death would be instant. Cook in his usual phlegmatic way did not dramatise the danger, but he knew he was looking down the barrel of a musket: 'A wall of rock rising almost perpendicular from the unfathomable ocean. All the dangers we had escaped were little in comparison of being thrown upon this reef where the ship must be dashed to pieces in a moment.'[90] By 6 p.m. the pounding surf brought the *Endeavour* to within forty yards of the reef: 'between us and destruction was only a dismal valley the breadth of one wave.' Death seemed certain. Suddenly a freak puff of wind blew them away from the reef for a few minutes; the heartened men took to the boats and desperately tried to tow the ship through the surf, but in vain. Another rogue gust carried the ship within reach of a narrow break in the reef through which an ebb tide gushed. Cook failed to get the *Endeavour* through this gap but the outrush, like a millstream, carried them about two hundred yards from the real danger. Soon Cook spotted another slim passage in the reef. When the tide shifted he used it to flood in through the gap, the *Endeavour* surging in like a toy boat in a weir. The exhausted crew immediately found themselves in a new environment; from the raging ocean they were now in calm (if shoal-strewn) waters enclosed by the reef. They had endured eighteen hours of hell. Cook dubbed the gap through which they had passed Providential Channel and remarked with a full sense of irony: 'It is but a few days ago that I rejoiced at having got without the Reef, but that joy was nothing when compared to what I now felt at being safe at an anchor within it, such is the vicissitude attending this kind of service and must always attend an unknown navigation when one steers wholly in the dark without any manner of guide whatever.'[91]

The 17th of August was spent feasting on 240 pounds of giant cockles which a foraging expedition brought back from the reef. The *Endeavour* lay at anchor for a day while the pinnace was repaired.[92] Now Cook had to decide what to do next. He considered returning outside the reef to the open sea through Providential Channel, but that would have meant waiting indefinitely for the right wind; moreover, he knew he would have to stand far away to the east thereafter and thus would not be able to solve his self-assigned New Guinea 'riddle'. So he decided to head north-west, once more through the agonies of the Barrier Reef labyrinth, keeping the coast in sight. There followed four more days of painstaking progress through the shoals, always with the boats ahead scouting the passage and always anchoring at night. Matthew Flinders would later say that only a man with nerves of steel could 'thread the needle' like this, that lesser men would perish or despair.[93] Yet this was Cook's second progress along the via dolorosa. Islets and keys were now added to shoals and sandbanks as possible dangers, but Cook recorded that the more one had to endure the unendurable, in a curious way the less the frustration and the more the insouciance. At daylight on 21 August to his stupefaction Cook could see no danger ahead at all and crowded on sail for the most northerly point of land. This proved to be another maze of islands, but by noon he was through and had reached Cape York.[94] Cook took possession of the whole of 'New South Wales' in the name of King George and by 23 August, having turned west, he had dropped the coast of Australia astern. Now he was running through the Endeavour Strait, at first between Woody

Island and Possession Island, later south of Cape Cornwall and thence north-west to Booby Island. There was a landing at Booby Island – so called because it abounded in the birds called boobies, a brace of which Banks predictably shot while collecting plant specimens. Soon Cook was able to prove conclusively that Australia and New Guinea were two separate land masses.[95] There was a final joust with shoals in the Torres Strait, before they made landfall on New Guinea on 28 August. Cook made a formulaic landing with Banks and Solander, a 'thing-in-itself' just to say he had set foot on New Guinea (its exploration was no part of his brief), but an encounter with hostile Melanesians with poison darts did not encourage him to tarry. He set a course for Batavia, where he intended to lay up the *Endeavour* for extensive repairs.[96]

The *Endeavour* was now in charted waters so that, technically speaking, her cruise was no longer a voyage of exploration. Yet the trauma Cook had undergone on 16 August remained a vivid scar. In his journal for 17 August he revealed something of the tension he had lived under. He complained bitterly that a navigator was bound to be damned if he did and damned if he didn't. The explorer facing supreme peril will inevitably be accused either of timorousness or temerity. If he had left the north-eastern coast of Australia unexplored and not sailed through the Endeavour and Torres straits, his critics might say he had not carried out his orders because he was cowardly and afraid. On the other hand, by acting as he had done, he could incur the charge of recklessness, of endangering ship and crew for vaulting ambition.[97] Defending himself in advance against the indictment of being rash and foolhardy in venturing among the treacherous shoals of the Barrier Reef, he argued that the minute calculation of risks was the only way important geographical questions could be cleared up.

> The danger of navigating unknown parts of this ocean was now greatly increased by having a crazy ship, and being short of provisions and every other necessary. Yet the distinction of a first discoverer made us cheerfully encounter every danger and submit to every inconvenience; and we chose rather to incur the censure of imprudence and temerity, which the idle and voluptuous so liberally bestow upon unsuccessful fortitude and perseverance, than leave a country which we had discovered unexplored, and given colour to a charge of timidity and irresolution.[98]

He refers to 'aspersions' which he is confident cannot be levelled against him, then, perhaps realising he has said too much, signs off with: 'It is time I should have done with this subject which at best is but disagreeable and which I was led into on reflecting on our late danger.'[99]

Why Cook thought he had to apologise for his actions is a puzzle. Perhaps he did not yet realise the scale of his achievement in having mastered the Great Barrier Reef. His successors would soon realise it. HMS *Pandora*, sent out to track down the *Bounty* mutineers, would come to grief here in 1791, the first of many wrecks in the labyrinth.[100] Cook seemed to discount his own stupendous achievements between April and the end of August when he surveyed the entire east coast of Australia in little more than four months, seven weeks of which were spent in harbour repairing the ship or waiting to get to sea on a favourable wind. As has been rightly said, to follow Cook through the rocks, shoals, coral banks, keys and islands of the Great Barrier Reef 'is oneself to undergo a spiritual depression'.[101] Cook proved that he was determined, patient, tenacious and obstinate, but that he combined these qualitities with flair and brilliance as a seaman – a quickness of reflex, intelligence of response and dexterity of technique that went far beyond brute willpower. As always, Cook was superficially modest about his achievements, admitting only to 'no small satisfaction' when he finally got to the open sea at Cape York.[102] So what is the deep import of his 17 August journal entry? There is a strong whiff here of protesting too much, and the journal entry is an important clue to Cook's deep character. It is significant that he claims that being the *first* to discover something makes up for danger that would otherwise be insupportable. Moreover, we see a perennial dualism in the Cook personality on display. On the one hand, as he showed in his reaction to theft in Polynesia, he was prone to anger and overreaction. On the other, he was wont to indulge in quasi-paranoid reflections, anticipating possible criticisms of his behaviour. In this effusion there is at the very least an element of doubt and self-pity. He reveals himself as unhappy, brittle and in mortal fear of being judged and found deficient. It is almost as if he were saying that his ambition would not support the fate of the many one-trip navigators who had been weighed in the balance of public opinion and had been found wanting. Ever conscious of his lowly origins, Cook knew that most elites and most 'establishments' are merciless to those who are not 'one of us', and that he could expect no support arising from class solidarity. He was constantly aware that 'big brother' Admiralty was watching. His lot was to be judged *entirely* on results. As one Cook-watcher has shrewdly remarked: 'At these and other moments, Cook's extraordinary drive and self-reliance can seem corrosive: the marks of a compulsively driven loner, obsessed with control and prone to gnawing fears of persecution.'[103]

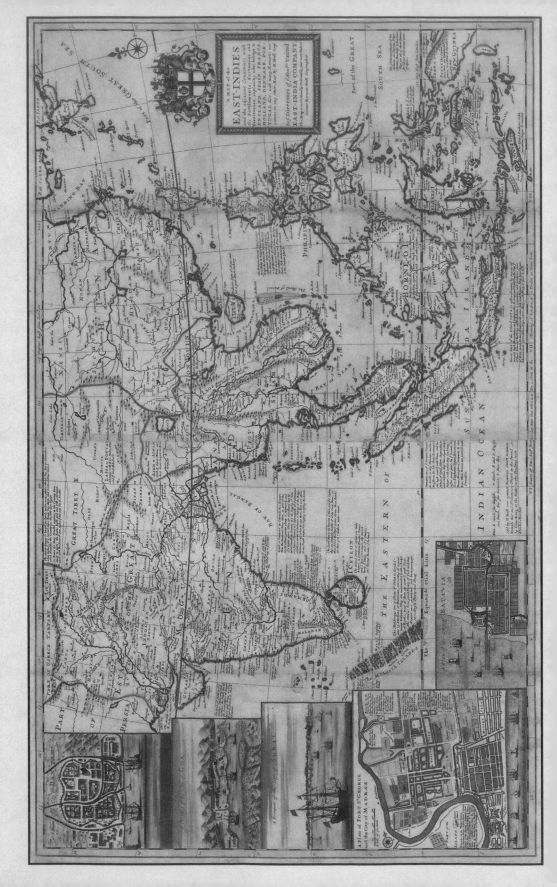

CHAPTER EIGHT

Homeward Bound

THE waters through which the *Endeavour* now sailed had been extensively charted by Dutch navigators, but the United Provinces, fearful that their imperial possessions could be seized by more powerful maritime nations (they particularly had Britain in mind), tended to publish imprecise and obfuscatory charts of the coastline of the Dutch East Indies. The uncertainty about location, plus contrary winds, meant that the ship took much longer to reach Batavia than Cook had expected. The crew amused themselves by landing two sharks, off which they dined heartily on the night of the 11th. Cook fetched the coast of Timor on 13 September 1770 when what the lookout identified as a cloud bank turned into a mountain range. The ship's company was startled to see the coastline lit up by hundreds of fires, indicating a populousness they had not encountered since Tahiti. Lights of a different kind illuminated the sky on 15 September when they saw what Banks called 'a phenomenon like the Aurora Borealis' (actually the Aurora Australis).[1] After four days of cruising along the coast of Timor, they came to the island of Savu, though because of the misleading Dutch charts, they did not immediately recognise it as such. Here were herds of cattle with mounted cowboys tending them, rich flocks of sheep, men on horseback and houses of a kind they had not seen since leaving Rio de Janeiro eighteen months before. Hopeful of taking on food and water, Cook sent Gore ashore in the pinnace. He was received in a 'civilised' way by Indonesians, clearly used to Europeans, who told them there was good anchorage and a cornucopia of supplies on the other side of the island. It seemed that Savu was divided into five principalities, each one ruled by a 'rajah' who in turn answered to his Dutch overlords.[2] Gore reported back to Cook, who sent him on a mission to the island's rajah, warning him, however, to be careful, for he already feared Savu might be another Rio in more senses than one, and his reception by the Dutch like that by the Portuguese in 1768.

Gore set off on his embassy while Cook moved the *Endeavour* round to the suggested anchorage. Gore was given an escort of thirty tatterdemalion

soldiers bearing the Dutch colours and introduced to the rajah, who turned
out to be a grossly obese individual of about 35. Through his Portuguese
interpreter Gore explained what he wanted. The rajah appeared friendly but
said he could do nothing without the permission of the Dutch governor or
factor. Cook accordingly invited this governor and the rajah aboard
Endeavour for a bibulous dinner. All seemed sweetness and light, but when
Cook and Banks landed next morning on a return visit to pick up the water
and buffaloes promised, they found nothing. Instead the governor (a German
named Johan Christoph Lange) claimed he had just received new orders from
his superior in Concordia, ordaining strict limits on the goods he was allowed
to trade with foreigners.[3] It soon became obvious that Lange was applying
pressure behind the scenes on the rajah not to sell anything to the visitors
except at exorbitant prices from which he himself would expect a rake-off.
Sydney Parkinson scarcely helped matters by inquiring in the disinterested
spirit of science whether there were spices on the island. Lange immediately
took this as evidence that the British planned to break in on the cherished
Dutch monopoly on the spices of the East Indies. By paying over the odds,
Cook managed to buy a 'disappointing' quantity of buffaloes, sheep and hogs,
a large quantity of chickens and vats of diluted palm wine. The locals had
obviously unloaded all their inferior animals on to the British and then charged
a fortune for doing so; a single spavined buffalo cost five guineas. The rajah
was at first quite happy for trade to be done in kind or barter, but Lange
suspected he would not make the profits he wanted that way and insisted that
all transactions be in cash; naturally, he claimed he was merely obeying the
orders of 'superiors'.[4] Cook was furious about the profiteering and even
Banks, a multimillionaire usually insouciant about money, raised an eyebrow.
The final tally loaded on to the ship was six sheep, three hogs, five buffaloes,
300 fowl and some limes and coconuts. The visitors also bought a large
number of eggs, half of which were later found to be rotten. The only advantage gained from this dispiriting stay in Savu was that by plying Lange with
drink they opened the garrulous Teuton's tongue and learned a vast amount
about Dutch government and economy in the East Indies.[5]

   The journey from Savu to Batavia lasted from 22 September to 8 October.
The track of the *Endeavour* now lay along the southern coast of Java. Cook
made a brief landfall at the eastern end of Java to check both the ship's
seaworthiness and his calculations of longitude. Banks reports thunder and
lightning with heavy rain all that night, but a sense of security was engendered
by the lights of myriad fishing boats bobbing all around them. From a Dutch
East Indiaman they heard their first news of the world. Philip Carteret had
called at Batavia two years ago in the *Swallow*, which meant at least that he had

survived the Pacific; the Russians were besieging Constantinople; there had been riots in London following the Wilkesite agitations; and there was serious trouble in North America, where the colonists were refusing to pay taxes and more British troops had been sent.[6] Cook made good progress along the coast of Java except on the last day, when the weather turned squally, the main topsail was badly split, and Cook reported that his sails were in such poor condition that they could hardly bear a puff of wind. He had been anxious that his dead reckoning might fail him and that he would shoot past the Sunda Strait, but on 3 October he made the northward turning into the strait which would wind round to the northern coast of Java and thence to Batavia. After reaching Bantam Point, the most north-easterly point of the strait, he then had to endure four painful and frustrating days, battling strong currents and another farrago of islands, reefs and shoals which made him think he was back on the Barrier Reef.[7] It was 7 October before he was off the Batavia roads and another two days before he finally came to anchor, with the dome of the great church of the town clearly visible. The Dutch sent out a boat to inquire who the newcomers were. Cook, in best 'name, rank and number' mode, replied that his ship was English, her name *Endeavour* and they were homeward bound. Banks noted that the Dutch officers 'were almost as spectres, no good omen of the healthiness of the country we were arrived at; our people, however . . . truly might be called rosy and plump, for we had not a sick man among us, [and they] jeered and flouted much at their brother seamen's faces.'[8] With this utterance Banks managed to combine hubris and foresight.

Once landed, Cook at once sought permission from the Dutch governor-general to carry out repairs to the *Endeavour*. He was granted everything he asked for, but then suffered the embarrassment of having to go back to ask the governor's council for a loan (with a note of hand to the Admiralty as security) to finance the work. There were the usual bureaucratic delays, but finally on 18 October he moved the ship from its anchorage to the dry dock on Kuyper's Island. There was a further shock when Cook discovered that his men could not do the necessary work, as the Dutch claimed a monopoly on all dry dock repairs and could consequently name their own price. Further haggling meant that the technicians at the yard on Kuyper's Island did not actually start work until 6 November. The Dutch had driven a hard bargain but in the circumstances Cook had no options. The *Endeavour* was leaking twelve inches of water an hour; her main and false keels were badly damaged; her sails in shreds and tatters; she was still punctured from the Barrier Reef; and her pumps were in dire need of repair. Cook sent the bad news of this to the Admiralty on a Dutch ship, together with sealed dispatches dated 23 October, giving an interim report of his voyage and discoveries.[9] When the

Dutch inspected the *Endeavour*, they found that Cook's chief carpenter, Mr John Satterley, had not exaggerated. All the damage he had diagnosed was confirmed; additionally a good deal of sheathing had been lost and on the larboard side near the keel two six-foot planks were just one-eighth of an inch away from having been eaten through by worms. The Dutch told Cook it was a miracle that the ship had stayed afloat after the Barrier Reef. Satterley for his part was deeply impressed with their expertise – they were particularly skilled at careening – so the long wait before they started work proved worth it in the end. After nine days of intensive labour Cook was able to move his ship back from the Onrust yard to the haven at Kuyper. He then had his men make up for lost time, getting stores and water on board, rigging the ship and mending and repairing the sails. Much of this work was done while the men were continually lashed with storms and rain with the advent of the westerly monsoon.[10]

Banks and Solander had rented a house in the centre of town and invited Tupaia and his servant Taiata to live with them. Tupaia had still not recovered completely from the scurvy that had afflicted him ever since the Endeavour river, but he took to sightseeing with gusto and was bowled over by the sights and sounds of European civilisation – something beyond his wildest imaginings. By Polynesian standards Batavia was a phenomenon, for it was the greatest European commercial outpost in Asia. There were 20,000 people inside the city walls and another 100,000 in the suburbs and greater Batavia.[11] The Dutch had been the dominant power in the East Indies since the early seventeenth century, and Batavia was the visible symbol of the power of the Dutch East India Company (Vereenigde Oostindische Companie) in the Indian Ocean. The Company used Batavia as its great entrepôt, to which all the produce of Asia had to be taken for transhipment (the Company's rivals more sensibly shipped it direct to Europe) but by 1771 the city's glory days were behind it.[12] The town, or city as it really was, was cosmopolitan in every sense, for the Portuguese also had an important foothold here (Portuguese, rather than Dutch or Malay, was the lingua franca) while 20,000 of the 120,000 population were Chinese.[13] The Dutch, pining for their homeland, had tried to create a new Holland by building a model conurbation, complete with the kind of town houses one could see in Amsterdam, and canals, warehouses and large public buildings that reminded them of Rotterdam or The Hague. In relative decline in the late eighteenth century, Batavia was notorious for the high levels of corruption and peculation by company officials, the low wages paid to local workers and, worst of all, for being a death trap for Europeans; 50,000 people a year were said to succumb to malaria, typhoid fever and cholera. The main culprits were the beloved canals: not only were they cut across the city breeding grounds for the anopheles mosquito, but raw sewage and garbage was tipped into them without let or hindrance; to top it all, the many ships arriving from all parts of the world brought in new bacteria and viruses.[14]

What happened was predictable. The personnel on the *Endeavour* began to succumb to one or other of the three great tropical diseases. The first to die was the surgeon Bill Monkhouse, on 5 November. Banks and Solander both fell gravely ill; Solander was able to drag himself to Monkhouse's funeral but Banks was too sick. Soon death came even closer to Banks's door, for his two Tahitian protégés were the next to go. Parkinson described their melancholy exit:

> When Taiata was seized with the fatal disorder, as if certain of his approaching dissolution, he frequently ... said '*Tyau mate oee*' or 'My friends, I am dying.' He took any medicines that were offered him, but Tupaia, who was ill at the same time and survived but a few days, refused everything of that kind, and gave himself up to grief, regretting to the highest degree that he had left his own country. When he heard of Taiata's death he was quite inconsolable, crying out [his name] frequently.[15]

There were mixed feelings about Tupaia's death. Cook was thoroughly disillusioned with him and reported that 'Tupaia was by no means beloved of the *Endeavour*'s crew, being looked upon as proud and austere, extorting homage, which the sailors who thought themselves degraded by an Indian were unwilling to pay.'[16] Taiata, by contrast, 'was the darling of the ship's company'.[16] 'Proud' was a particularly pejorative epithet in Cook's vocabulary, given his Quaker upbringing. It is quite obvious that Tupaia was intellectually arrogant, abrasive and tactless, and that he considered himself a cut above the white men and even the real commander of the ship; indeed he told the Maoris as much. He was incapable of deference: in his own mind he knew it all and had nothing to learn from Europeans and their science. He even declared on one occasion that, as an *arioi*, he far outclassed the king of England in status.[17] His champions on board the *Endeavour* were Banks (naturally, as he had insisted on his accompanying the ship), Charles Green and Sydney Parkinson, who admired his talents as an artist – a talent which has been belatedly recognised by scholars, previously convinced that Tupaia's drawings were mere copies of originals by Parkinson.[18]

Soon disease cut a swathe through the *Endeavour*'s complement. Cook himself fell ill, but refused to take the malady seriously. Solander for a while hovered close to death. Next, Green's servant John Reynolds died, and three able seamen. Soon every man on the ship was ill except for an old man, John

Ravenhill, a sailmaker who was permanently drunk and seems unknowingly to have used alcohol as a febrifuge. Cook came to be glad that the Dutch had insisted on doing the repairs to the ship, for his own crew would have been unable to manage this.[19] By the time the work started he had only twenty officers and men fit for duty, and by mid-November this number was down to twelve. To make up the gaps in the ship's company, Cook recruited fresh hands, mainly British, who were hanging around the stews of Batavia. One of them nearly precipitated an international incident. An Irishman calling himself John Marra and allegedly from County Cork volunteered for the *Endeavour*, but the Dutch claimed he was really a Dane from Elsinore called Jan Marre who had deserted from one of their ships. They asked for him to be given up, but Cook refused. Not wishing to provoke the Royal Navy to retaliate by seizing him from the *Endeavour* – which they could easily have done – the Dutch let the matter rest, though in their letters to the directors of the Company in Holland they complained bitterly that Cook had behaved boorishly and discourteously; even worse, he proved himself ungrateful after all they had done to get the *Endeavour* seaworthy.[20] It is not too far-fetched to see Cook here gaining transmogrified revenge for his treatment by the governor of Rio two years earlier. On the occasion of the escape from the reef on 16 August, Cook had originally thanked God for his deliverance, then, taking a more secular line, had scored the words out. In a somewhat similar vein, Banks seemed to ascribe his deliverance from malaria to a benign force that had taken cognisance of his implicit pantheism. Many years later, Banks boasted that he had eaten all forms of life at one time or another, then corrected himself:

> I never have eaten Monkey, although when at Batavia Captain Cook, Dr Solander and myself had determined to make the experiment, but on the morning of our intended feast I happened to cross the yard of the house in which we resided and observed half a dozen of those poor little devils with their arms tied upon cross sticks laying [*sic*] on their backs preparatory to their being killed. Now as I love all sorts of animals, I walked up to them and in consequence of their plaintive chattering and piteous looks could not resist cutting the strings by which they were bound and they immediately scampered off so that we lost our Monkey dinner.[21]

The *Endeavour* finally cleared from Batavia on 26 December, with seven men of her complement already dead from disease. She made slow progress, for the Sunda Strait again delayed her with rainy, squally weather. The physical condition of the crew was giving concern, so Cook put in at Panaitan Island (then called Prince's Island) at the southern entrance to the strait, in search of fresh food for the sick and more wood and water. A week's stopover here provided turtles, hogs, poultry and fruit as well as limes to put in the water butts, since Solander reported seeing mosquitoes breeding there, meaning that they were carrying death with them.[22] It was 16 January 1771 before Cook was ready to turn the prow into the open spaces of the Indian Ocean. Then came disaster. The brackish water they had taken on at Panaitan caused an outbreak of dysentery, which for malaria-stricken men was the last straw. Banks took to his bed again, almost paralysed by 'the bloody flux', but after a long illness he survived. He was one of the lucky ones. The real death toll began on 24 January with the loss of John Truslove, corporal of marines. Next to go was Hermann Sporing, Banks's assistant.[23] Even Ravenhill, the heroic drinker, succumbed this time around. Charles Green died too, but perhaps the most lamented loss was that of Sydney Parkinson, on 26 January. The month ended with the loss of John Thompson the cook, and three able seamen. In the second week of February there were five more deaths, including that of Jonathan Monkhouse, the hero of the fothering patch-up on the Barrier Reef. In the third week died John Satterley the carpenter, whose skills had enabled them to leave the Endeavour river; also another seaman and a marine. In the fourth week, four more seamen died. The strain of trying to survive, manning a ship, and making allowances for the ailing, was too much for some of the crew. On 21 February Cook recorded in his journal that he had given twelve lashes to Thomas Rossiter, drummer in the marines, for beating up the sick and then assaulting the officer of the watch.[24] Altogether (including another five who died later on the way home), Cook lost 23 men on the homeward journey. Although he wrote sympathetic words about the departed at the time that they died, he was later to conclude that such deaths were largely the men's own fault for not taking adequate health precautions. This is another aspect of the ruthlessness in Cook's character, though in fairness such 'displacement' is said to be a common phenomenon, an obvious defence mechanism, when the comrades of adventurers, mountaineers, war correspondents, etc. come to grief.[25]

With such losses through death, and the rest of the crew sick and weakened, it is perhaps not surprising that the *Endeavour* nearly foundered on the coast of Natal, though some scholars blame Cook's faulty dead reckoning. On the evening of 4 March the lookouts falsely called 'land-ho', so that maybe next morning when he heard the same cry Cook concluded it was a case of 'wolf'. In fact it was almost a repetition of the near-disaster on 16 August 1770. It turned out that the *Endeavour* was racing towards land, no more than six miles away, in high seas and with a strong south-easterly wind at her stern. With great difficulty Cook 'wore' the ship and stood away to the east, but not before they had spent four nerve-wracking hours battling with the adverse elements.[26] Cook was now in one of the most dangerous stretches of ocean in the world, where the Indian and Atlantic oceans collide and the action of the swift Agulhas current against contrary winds can pile up waves one hundred feet from trough to crest. Fortunately for his peace of mind, Cook knew nothing of the supreme danger of Cape Agulhas. He rounded the capes, sighted the Cape of Good Hope on 13 March, and came to anchor under Table Mountain the next day. The Dutch governor of Cape Town proved accommodating and the 29 seriously ill crew members were found lodgings ashore.[27] Cook stayed at the Cape for a month for rest and recuperation. The dauntless Banks recovered, and spent a lot of time ministering to the stricken Solander. Needless to say, when he was not collecting specimens, Banks was eyeing up the local women: 'In general they are handsome with clear skins and high complexions, and when married (no reflection on my countrywomen) are the best housekeepers imaginable and great child-bearers. Had I been inclined for a wife I think this is the place of all others I have seen where I could have best suited myself.'[28] Cook's thoughts were elsewhere and he returned to the self-pitying mode of 17 August the year before. It now occurred to him that he himself might be held responsible for the loss of life on the *Endeavour* and hence began to shift blame: on to Batavia, on to the Dutch and even, as noted, on to the victims themselves. Once again this is the paranoid Cook protesting too much.[29]

Cook weighed anchor again on 14 April. It seems to have been a peculiarity of his that, having left a major port, he would immediately wonder if he had completed every last task and thus put again to land to double-check. This is a motif that can be traced through his voyages, and so he had no sooner cleared from Cape Town than he anchored off Robben Island at the mouth of the bay and sent men ashore in a boat; on this occasion he was baulked, as Robben Island was already used as a convict labour camp, and the Dutch would allow no one to land. Once out into the ocean, Cook had more deaths on his hands. On 15 April Robert Molyneux died, the very able master; Richard Pickersgill was promoted in his place. With favourable winds, the ship reached St Helena in a fortnight. Here Cook found the 50-gun *Portland* and the sloop *Swallow* escorting twelve Indiamen back to England, and decided to accompany them. After a four-day stay (1–4 May), allowing Banks to botanise, the convoy reached Ascension Island on 10 May.[30] Banks was now taking the good weather for granted, and so deeply resented the irruption of storms and gales. As he commented on 30 May after one such 'blow': 'A heavy sea so that the ship pitched and tumbled very disagreably [*sic*] to us whom a continuance of fine weather has made almost unfit for a gale.'[31] It may have been these storms that broke up the convoy, or maybe the *Portland* was making way too fast for Cook, with his doubts about the *Endeavour*'s seaworthiness. At any rate, on 23 May the convoy disappeared ahead of them; curiously, it made the home port only three days before Cook. Two days later Lieutenant Zachary Hicks joined the roster of the fallen, and was replaced by Gore.[32] By the time the ship reached the Azores, there were frequent sightings of other vessels, mainly whalers. Yet Cook was in something of a race against time, for the ship's sails were splitting and the new carpenter reported the main topmast sprung in the cap. There were daily sightings of ships now and from one of them, on 7 July, Cook learned that none of the dispatches he had sent on to the Admiralty had arrived. Finally, on 10 July, Lizard point was sighted by the boy, Nicholas Young, who had first seen New Zealand. On 12 July the *Endeavour* came to safe haven at Deal, having completed an epic three-year circumnavigation.[33]

Cook punctiliously wrote to the Admiralty on the very day of his arrival, pursuant to the exact terms of his original remit which read, in that half-pompous, half-minatory way so typical of the eighteenth-century Navy: 'Upon your arrival in England you are immediately to repair to this Office in order to lay before us a full account of your proceedings in the whole course of your voyage.' Cook at once informed his superiors of the death of Hicks and the promotion of Charles Clerke, and advised them that he would be with them in person at the earliest possible moment.[34] He took it for granted that, even if the dispatches he had sent from Batavia with the Dutch had not arrived, those carried by the *Portland* surely must have. There followed for Cook an anxious limbo period, when he hovered, uncertain in his own mind, between the reality of what he had achieved and the lurking suspicion that he might be blamed or censured for some of his actions over the previous three years. Objectively, there could be no questioning what he had achieved. As an exploit of seamanship, the *Endeavour* voyage was in a class of its own. As an epic of exploration, what he had accomplished had already put him among the all-time greats. As a feat of surveying and charting, his work was peerless, with the map of New Zealand he had produced being an astonishing masterpiece. As Beaglehole points out, he had matured immensely, developing from a narrow technician of sailing ships into a more rounded and intellectually curious individual, interested in languages, culture, anthropology, and even botany. 'He departed from England a good sailor, a first-rate marine surveyor, an able mathematician; he returned a great commander, a great discoverer and a man with a greatly heightened sense of the scope of human thought.'[35] Cook himself, with his usual understatement summed up his circumnavigation more succinctly: 'I presume that this voyage will be found as complete as any before made.'[36]

The only area in which Cook could be faulted was in his approach to scurvy, where, curiously, he soon acquired the unjustified reputation of being the conqueror of the disease. In so far as the proposition is true, this was only because he took a scattergun approach to its prevention. His main 'remedies' had been sauerkraut and carrot marmalade, allied to hygiene and avoidance of the cold through warm and dry clothes. He was not unique among ship's captains in his concern with scurvy (Wallis had been another one), yet he was the first to make dietary considerations an integral part of his overall system, which was why he tried to avoid the monotony of shipboard cuisine by making so many island stopovers. But neither he nor his surgeons knew why they had really avoided scurvy, even though the evidence was before their eyes, for Banks had cured himself by using lemon juice. Cook himself expressly declared that he had no great confidence in fresh lemons and oranges as anti-scorbutics, and it was simply his good fortune that during his time in the South Seas he acquired large stocks of fruit and vegetables because the more desirable foodstuffs such as meat were not available in large quantities. Cook's most severe critics say that he actually set the battle against scurvy back and that his views and those of his surgeons would cause the death of thousands of seamen during the War of American Independence.[37] Cook himself thought the likely criticism would be based on four grounds: that he had miscalculated and made errors on the Barrier Reef; that his punishment regime was wrong; that the losses sustained on the *Endeavour* from sickness and disease were unacceptable; and that he had been guilty of 'overkill' and excessive violence against the indigenous peoples he had encountered. Certainly the death toll on the ship was high, for 38 of the original 94 members of the ship's company had died, plus another eight who had joined in the course of the voyage. As for punishment, twenty-one men had been punished (six of them twice) with a total of 354 lashes.[38] The Admiralty, however, took the line that the flogging regime was about what might be expected on a three-year voyage, and actually below average, which said something for Cook's authority as captain. The Board showed its contempt for Matthew Cox's attempt to sue Cook for unjustifiable bruality by burying his lawsuit in its own version of a Jarndyce case, and Cook was very early assured he need have no worries on that score.[39] As for the mortality from disease, the Sea Lords knew all about Batavia and its fearsome reputation as a deathtrap.

That left Cook's treatment of the Polynesians and Australasian natives, and here Cook was more vulnerable. On his departure in 1768 he had received instructions and advice from the Earl of Morton, president of the Royal Society, which were unhelpfully *bien pensant* and unrealistic: 'To exercise the utmost patience and forbearance with respect to the natives of the several lands where the ship may touch . . . Therefore should they in a hostile manner oppose a landing, and kill some men in the attempt, even this would hardly justify firing

among them, 'til every other gentle method had been tried.'[40] There is something in this of the liberal fallacy of using Gandhi's methods against the Nazis,
and Cook rightly ignored the advice, not just on the grounds that it was
armchair moralising by someone who had never been in the front line, but on
the more cogent and immediate grounds that he was not prepared to be
knocked on the head or have his men so treated just to satisfy the foibles of an
aristocrat in a London club. The real problem for Cook was that he had, so to
speak, an enemy within the gates, for the influential Banks shared Morton's
liberal views and obviously thought that Cook had overreacted at times. When
the midshipman Jonathan Monkhouse opened fire on the Tahitians (see p. 106),
Parkinson reported that his men 'obeyed with the greatest glee imaginable, as
if they had been shooting at ducks ... What a pity, that such brutality should
be exercised by civilized people upon unarmed ignorant Indians! When
Mr Banks heard of the affair, he was highly displeased, saying, "If we quar-
relled with those Indians, we would not agree with angels." '[41] Although it was
true that Banks's pacific methods were often efficacious, and that he was by far
the most popular, sympathetic and effective of all the men on the *Endeavour*, he
was not quite the paragon he imagined himself to be. On the tour round Tahiti
in the pinnace he had caused great offence to the locals by desecrating a temple
through sheer carelessness.[42] Cook might have been more worried if he had
realised that Banks always entertained ambivalent feelings about him, despite
the superficial cordiality. As a gentleman and oligarch, Banks did not enjoy
taking orders from a mere career ship's captain. Cook's refusal to make landfall
on the west coast of South Island, New Zealand – not simply justifiable but the
only sane decision in the circumstances – always rankled with Banks. In 1803,
twenty-four years after Cook's death, the wound was still fresh and Banks
declared: 'Had Cook paid the same attention (as Flinders) to the Naturalists,
we should have done more at that time. However, the bias of the public mind
had not so decidedly marked Natural History for a favourite pursuit as it now
has. Cook might have met with reproof for sacrificing a day's fair wind to the
accommodation of the Naturalists.'[43]

On 13 July Cook left his ship on the Downs and set off in a post-chaise for
London, accompanied by Banks and Solander. While they dropped off at New
Burlington Street, Piccadilly, for a round of the London clubs, Cook made his
way to the Admiralty. He was received affably, but there seemed little enthusiasm at the top: he learned that the Lords Commissioners of the Admiralty
would not be interviewing him immediately.[44] It was probably still with some
foreboding that he sped to his house in Mile End. There he received bad news.
His fourth child Joseph, whom he had never seen, had died soon after his birth
while the four-year-old Elizabeth had also died, just three months previously.

James junior, aged eight and Nathaniel, nearly seven, seemed to be doing well. Cook settled down to a mass of paperwork, writing further reports to the Admiralty, to the Victualling Board and the Royal Society, plus technical reports on compasses, scurvy, Pacific tides and astronomical observations, to say nothing of personal correspondence. Among this was the melancholy duty of informing George Monkhouse that both his sons had died and that their personal effects had been valued at £229.[45] At the end of the month he received word that the *Endeavour*'s company had been paid off and dispersed and that the ship itself was at Woolwich dock, where she was to be resheathed ready for her future task of carrying stores to the Falkland islands. Her days of Pacific roving were over. She was retired from the Navy in 1775, became a collier again, and ended by being scuttled by the British in Rhode Island harbour in 1778.[46] It was also the end of an era for other sentimental attachments. The famous goat, which had now been round the world twice, had been retired to calm pastures and admitted as a 'pensioner' at Greenwich Hospital, where she had died on 28 March.[47] There was a curious prelude to the goat's demise. Dr Samuel Johnson met Banks in February and decided to compose two lines of Latin to be written on her collar. The cod-Virgil 'distich' read:

Perpetui, ambita bis terra, praemia lactis
Haec habet, altrici Capra secunda Jovis.

('Now that the globe has been twice circled, this goat, second only to Jove's nurse, is thus rewarded for her never-failing milk'.)[48]

While Cook toiled away in Mile End, attention was focused on Banks and Solander, who hogged the limelight shamelessly. On the one hand they had a certain justification, as the purpose of the voyage had been scientific discovery; otherwise it would have been rather mindless glory-hunting. On the other hand, but for Cook's superlative skills as a seaman, both men would have been at the bottom of the ocean, and now they were being lionised as though they had been on a two-man expedition. The *London Evening Post* led the way with the announcement that Banks and Solander had arrived back in England; Cook and the rest of the crew of the *Endeavour* were relegated to the role of spear-carriers.[49] Ten days later the *Post* went into overdrive: Banks and Solander, it now reported, had discovered a southern continent near 'the Spice Islands', Solander had mastered the Polynesian tongue, and they had brought back wondrous botanical specimens from the forty islands at which they had touched, on a voyage so perilous that seventy of the crew had been lost.[50] Only the part about the specimens was true, for more than 3,000 plants, rocks and artefacts had been brought back, together with 955 drawings by the ill-fated Parkinson, about a quarter of them in colour. The aristocracy and the scientific world turned out in force to see the olio of curiosities Banks had brought back, while press coverage became more and more enthusiastic, claiming that the illustrious duo had made 'more curious discoveries in the way of astronomy and natural history than . . . have been presented to the learned world for these fifty years past'.[51] The two of them were the first to be presented to King George, who inspected Parkinson's sketches with great interest and suggested that all the plants should at once be taken to the Royal Gardens at Kew. By the end of August Banks and Solander were firm favourites in royal circles: 'they have the honour of frequently waiting for His Majesty at Richmond, who examines their collection of drawings and plants and views of different places'.[52] Still just 28, Banks received the kind of treatment that in a later age would be meted out only to movie and rock stars. Both Joshua Reynolds and Benjamin West painted him, with the latter portrait featuring Banks (absurdly) in a Maori cloak.

Cook's hour had not yet come but it was approaching. While all the Banks brouhaha went on, he kept his head down and wrote patiently to the Admiralty with a list of recommended promotions. He recommended Pickersgill, the master, for a lieutenant's commission, Frank Wilkinson and Richard Oron Clerk, who wanted a spell ashore, for positions in the Customs House, Richard Hutchins, the boatswain's mate, for promotion to boatswain, and John Edgcumbe, sergeant of marines, for adancement in that service; Cook also entered the names of two youths, too young for preferment, as ones to note. The legend that he recommended himself for promotion to post captain is a mere canard, for he knew perfectly well that no such vacancies existed at the time.[53] Cook himself was interviewed by the Lords of the Admiralty on 1 August but Lord Sandwich, the First Sea Lord seemed noncommittal, remarking only that he approved the voyage and saying nothing of Cook's direction of it. It seems that he was humouring his close friend and protégé Banks – a man of very similar tastes in sexual matters, for whom Sandwich had made early introductions to top-class whores and whom he enrolled in the Monks of Medmenham (the Hell-Fire Club).[54] Banks arrived at the Mile End house with a letter from the Secretary to the Admiralty the very next day. Cook opened it to read the following: 'I have the pleasure to acquaint you that their Lordships extemely well approve of the whole of your proceedings and that they have great satisfaction in the account you have given them of the good behaviour of your officers and men and of the cheerfulness and alertness with which they went through the fatigues and dangers of their late voyage.'[55] Cook was promoted to commander, and all the other promotions he asked for were confirmed. He wrote at once to Banks, sensing that his influence with Sandwich must have played a part: 'The reputation I may have acquired on this account by which I shall receive promotion calls to mind the very great assistance I received therein from you which will ever be remembered with most grateful acknowledgements.'[56]

On 14 August he had an hour-long interview with King George, who expressed his pleasure. In Cook's mind this now gave him the freedom to write to his friends and associates more freely; until he had received this final accolade he still felt inhibited. To his old mentor John Walker of Whitby he was a mixture of the official modest Cook and the private ambitious and self-confident man, as is well summed up in one single sentence: 'I however have made no great discoveries yet I have explored more of the Great South Sea than all that have gone before me.'[57] A month later he wrote to Walker to say that a second voyage of two ships to the Pacific was being talked of, which he hoped to command. Meanwhile he was given command of the *Scorpion* sloop, a converted fireship earmarked to take part in a survey of the English coast; this was a mere 'holding' operation to keep him in full employment and on full pay until the Admiralty made a final decision about a second expedition.[58] A change of attitude in the media is discernible by the end of August, once it was realised how strongly the Navy favoured Cook. For the first time the voyage of the *Endeavour* began to be characterised as 'Cook's discoveries', as if the capital's journalists were beginning to read the runes.[59] Banks meanwhile was telling anyone who cared to listen that he was certain to command the next Pacific expedition, which would consist of six vessels, including warships. The Admiralty held its counsel, adopting a 'wait and see' policy. The Sea Lords had not been deceived by the public relations campaign directed by Banks's supporters in July and August; they knew who the real author of the successful *Endeavour* voyage was; besides, they were very much opposed to a civilian commanding their ships. Only the powerful patronage of Sandwich kept Banks in the ring. His selling point was that he still believed in a great southern continent, the fabled Terra Australis Incognita, whereas Cook did not, and so Cook was running up against a general will to believe while Banks was humouring it.[60] Even so, if Banks were to have any chance, he needed to keep a clean sheet and attract no scandal in the second half of 1771. Banks's actual behaviour, however, smacks most of all of Greek tragedy, of hamartia, a fatal flaw, and of hubris and nemesis.

Superficially, Banks in the autumn of 1771 was still on a winning streak, with Oxford University conferring an honorary doctorate on him in November, though the last time the press mentioned him without also mentioning Cook was in late August.[61] Yet he was increasingly being perceived in wider circles as a moneyed ingrate, an egotist with no real commitment to scientific knowledge, a sexual profligate and a man with no talent for human relations. His treatment of his fiancée Harriet Blosset was much commented on. Banks left London in 1768, having made a clear commitment to marry Blosset on his return. The experiences in Tahiti built on the lubricious delights to which Sandwich had introduced him in the Hell-Fire Club, and convinced him that a life of sexual indulgence was the only way forward for a red-blooded male. It followed that a respectable marriage to Harriet Blosset formed no part of that agenda. On his return he wrote to Blosset, formulaically mentioning that he still loved her but claiming that he was now too 'volatile' for marriage. She decided to travel to London to confront him. Banks hated confrontation, so he backed down and promised to go ahead and marry her. Sensing his obvious reluctance, Harriet gave him fourteen days to think it over. In that fortnight he wrote to her to say he could not proceed; the luckless young woman was paid off with £5,000 to prevent a damaging breach of promise suit.[62] Meanwhile Banks had become embroiled with Parkinson's brother Stanfield, who belied his Quaker faith by being ruthless and unscrupulous, as well as illiterate. He began by questioning Banks's honesty in settling his brother's affairs. Banks made over all his valuable paintings to him, but then Stanfield got wind of a journal kept by Parkinson which he sensed could be a money-spinner. Banks airily waved Stanfield's concerns away, remarking that when his treasure trove was finally unpacked, the journal might turn up. An altercation arose which became bitter and vituperative, with Stanfield accusing Banks of deliberately holding out on him. He got the well-known Quaker physician Dr John Fothergill[63] to act as go-between, and his intervention ended with Banks agreeing to pay £500 to buy the journal. The cunning Stanfield then 'borrowed' his brother's journal, on Fothergill's pledge to Banks that the papers would not be misused. Stanfield hired a ghost-writer to prepare the journal for publication, hoping to publish it before the official volume that was being prepared by Dr John Hawkesworth. Fothergill was appalled and disgusted that his word to Banks had been broken by a fellow Quaker. In the end Stanfield was prevented from pipping Hawkesworth to the post only by a legal injunction; when his volume finally appeared in 1773 it contained violent denunciations of both Fothergill and Banks in the preface. Stanfield himself gained little profit from his Machiavellian enterprises as he died three years later.[64]

In September Banks met Dr Charles Burney, father of the more famous Fanny and himself a notable musician and musical critic, who suggested Hawkesworth as a suitable person to write up Cook's account of the voyage; Hawkesworth was paid £6,000, but when his volume appeared, it was heavily criticised for inaccuracies and cultural misunderstanding.[65] It was a sign of the values of aristocratic London that a talented hack, a disciple of Dr Johnson but one who had been dismissed from the master's inner circle for his presumption, should have been paid more for *writing* about the voyage – and bowdlerising Cook's observations into the bargain – than Byron, Wallis, Carteret and Cook put together had been paid for facing the perils of the Pacific. Yet the Burney connection proved interesting. Later, through Banks, Cook met Dr Charles, who successfully lobbied for his 21-year-old son James (who had been in the Navy since the age of 10) to accompany Cook on the second expedition.[66] Cook was soon drawn into the Burney circle. In February 1773 Burney discussed Bougainville's voyage with him, and showed him his copy of *Voyage autour du monde*. Burney asked how Cook's track across the Pacific differed from Bougainville's, and his daughter describes the sequel: 'Captain Cook instantly took a pencil from his pocket-book, and said he would trace the route; which he did in so clear and scientific a manner, that I would not take fifty pounds for the book. The pencil marks having been fixed by skinned milk, will always be visible.'[67] While Cook was making friends, Banks was losing them, including some of the most important figures of the day. The great Swedish botanist Linnaeus, delighted that his star pupil Solander had done so well, wrote to Banks to congratulate him immediately on his arrival in London, and his letter was particularly eulogistic. But by October Linnaeus was fuming and angry, since neither Banks nor Solander had bothered to reply to him. Desperate to see Banks's thesaurus of specimens and fearful that he was doomed to play Moses to Solander's Joshua and view the promised land only from afar, Linnaeus was reduced to asking his faithful English correspondent, John Ellis the natural historian, if he would be allowed to see just a few of the plants Banks had brought back.[68]

All of Banks's personal deficiencies must have been at the back of the communal mind of the Admiralty when the Board came to its final decision to back a second expedition. On 25 September the Admiralty instructed the Navy Board to purchase two suitable vessels of about 400 tons each for service in Pacific waters.[69] Naturally, Cook's advice was sought. His view was that the prerequisite was a ship that could stay at sea for a long time, which meant one big enough to carry large quantities of stores and provisions without drawing a great deal of water; yet she should not be so large that she could not be beached and careened. Once again that meant 'cats', or vessels in the coal trade.[70] He earmarked three colliers, and in November the Navy Board chose two: the *Marquis of Granby* and the *Marquis of Rockingham*, both built at Whitby. The first was 426 tons (larger than the *Endeavour* by 100 tons) and the second 340 tons).[71] On 27 November the Admiralty ordered these two fitted out as sloops and renamed the *Drake* and the *Raleigh*. Cook was appointed commander of the former. The two ships were to be sheathed and filled at Deptford dock, ready to sail in March 1772. The appointment was a sign of Cook's high stature in Admiralty eyes; he already had the long-standing support of Hugh Palliser, now Comptroller of the Navy Board and Sir John Williams, Surveyor of the Navy; these were, after all, men who admired professional expertise of the kind Cook possessed so abundantly. But the increasing entente with the all-powerful Earl of Sandwich was more surprising, for Sandwich was usually on friendly terms only with his social equals: men such as Banks. Cook used his contacts to good effect. He liked to call in person at the appropriate office, explain what he wanted, write the formal letter of request on the spot, and thus get the swiftest possible answer. Every single significant request was granted: extra wheat, extra sauerkraut, extra oatmeal, sugar, lemons, oranges, patent medicines.[72]

By December Cook felt that preparations were sufficiently well advanced that he could ask for three weeks' leave to transact family business in Yorkshire. Permission was readily granted, so Cook set off with his wife Elizabeth, who had never before met any of the extended Cook family. The journey by stage coach to York in winter, on rutted and muddy roads, was almost more of a trial than some of his oceanic journeys and took three days. At Great Ayton Cook struck up a firm friendship with Commodore William Wilson, who in 1758 had discovered the Pitt passage to China between the Moluccas and New Guinea. On New Year's Eve Cook travelled from Ayton over to Whitby to meet his old mentor John Walker. The shipowner had told his household to act deferentially towards a man who was now famous, but Mary Proud, the housekeeper who had given him extra candles while he was Walker's apprentice studying mathematics, was overcome with emotion and treated him like a long-lost son. Now a very old woman, she embraced him warmly: 'O honey James, how glad I is to see thee!' were her reported words of welcome.[73] Cook had originally intended to travel on to Hull to meet Captain Hammond, the shipbuilder responsible for the two ships Cook had chosen for the second voyage. But his wife had found the jolting journey north a particular trial, and did not relish an even longer homeward trip. Cook therefore made his way to York on 4 January to pick up the London stage. In his absence the *Drake* and *Raleigh* had undergone yet another change of names. It was a question of politics at the highest levels. Britain was anxious at this juncture not to offend Spain, for a quarrel over the Falkland Islands had only just been patched up with Madrid. *Drake* and *Raleigh*, the names of Elizabeth I's most notorious sea-dogs, might seem to have been calculated to insult the Spanish, already aggrieved at the extensive British incursions into the Pacific, their 'lake'. The Secretary of State William Henry Zuylestein, 1st Earl of

Rochford raised the point delicately with Sandwich – he could not command him – and Sandwich took the hint. The two ships were thus given the names with which they would become famous: the *Resolution* and the *Adventure*.

On his return to London, Cook wrote to Sandwich, giving his views on what the objects of this second expedition should be. He pointed out that the outstanding issue of the Great Southern Continent could be solved only if ships penetrated much farther south than latitude 40 and that this, though still highly perilous, could be attempted only in summer, which of course meant that the expedition should not be leaving Cape Town before October. His confidence in being able to cruise at these latitudes was enhanced by the news that he would be taking along the fourth chronometer by the great John Harrison (H4). This chronometer looked like a very large flat watch, and a duplicate had been made by the master craftsman Larcum Kendall of the firm of John Arnold. The Astronomer-Royal Nevil Maskelyne had recommended H4 most strongly, and three more precision instruments from John Arnold's that he had tested were to accompany Cook.[74] Meanwhile Banks was still proceeding as if *he* would command the expedition. As Beaglehole remarks in a notably witty passage:

> From the moment it was known that he was to go on a second voyage communications descended upon him as if he were another department of state – in English, French, Latin, from London and the counties, France, Holland, Germany, Switzerland, making suggestions on every conceivable matter, asking for anything from the command of a ship to the essential parts of a whale; asking, the great majority of them, to go too. For some of them ruin, even suicide, is the alternative; they 'pant' to go with Banks. It is not merely civilians, a little unhinged, who seek his patronage; seamen in the Royal Navy ... write to him rather than adopt a less dramatic mode of volunteering. They acknowledged his fame; they prophesied his immortality.[75]

There was a momentary shadow over Banks's ambitions when he discovered that Alexander Dalrymple, the would-be Cook of the *Endeavour* voyage, had resurfaced, and was being backed by the Royal Society in a proposal for an expedition to New Zealand. Dalrymple enlisted the powerful support of Benjamin Franklin and secured other influential backers; the Royal Society may have been feeling piqued that they were the prime movers in the first expedition but that now the Admiralty had stolen their thunder. However, it was felt in many quarters that the Royal Society's proposal was divisive and carried an implicit criticism both of Banks and Sandwich. More crucially, no

1 The earliest known portrait of James Cook, dated 1759.

2 The well-known late eighteenth-century folk song 'The Ploughboy' by William Shield (1748–1829), detailing how a 'flaxen-headed ploughboy' rises to wealth and fame, could almost have been written about Cook, who began life as a farm labourer and became the most famous explorer of his age. This is a reconstruction drawing of the humble cottage in Marton where Cook was born on 27 October, 1728.

3 Cook relished scaling Roseberry Topping as a youth living in Great Ayton. An avid hill-climber, he would go on to mount many more exotic scarps and knolls on his voyages.

4 Cook's father built this house at Great Ayton in 1755; by 1788 it was already being commemorated for its connections to the great explorer, though Cook himself never lived there. The cottage was presented to the Victoria State Government in 1934 and now stands in Fitzroy Gardens, Melbourne, Australia.

5 Cook's apprenticeship with John Walker in the thriving port of Whitby set the young man on a new course towards the oceans. The booming collier trade, shipping coal from Newcastle to London on the treacherous North Sea, was a proving ground for many young mariners like Cook. He was recognised above his peers for his application and natural talents aboard the colliers, one of which can be seen here leaving Whitby Harbour.

6 The Seven Years War, sometimes called the 'Second Hundred Years War', was a gruelling, slugging affair on land and sea, in which the Royal Navy always had the upper hand against the under-financed French Ministry of Marine. Louisbourg, the capital of Cape Breton Island (now part of Nova Scotia) and named for Louis XV, was one of the most important commercial and military centres in 'New France' and its capture by the British in 1758 signalled the beginning of the end for the French in Canada.

7 A man after Cook's heart, a surveyor and hydrographer of very high talent, Samuel Holland (1728–1801) collaborated with Cook in 1758–59 in the charting of the St Lawrence River and the Gulf of St Lawrence. After the Seven Years War he was appointed Surveyor-General of Quebec and later became the first Surveyor-General of British North America.

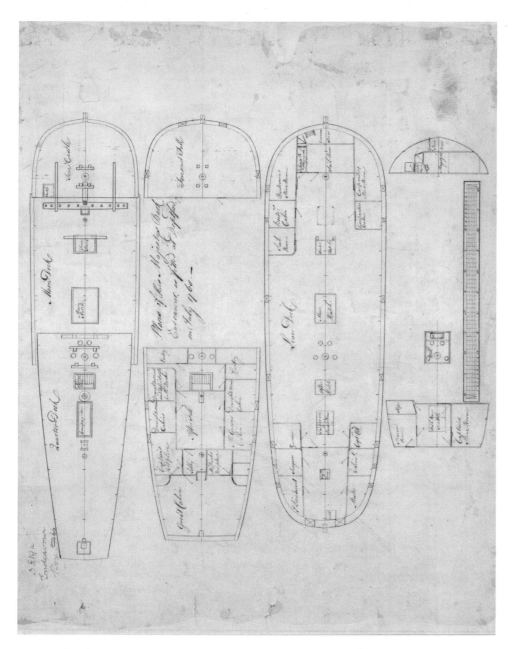

8 Given that the *Endeavour* was only 106′ long and 29′ broad, with 106 souls aboard, that gave each person just a foot in length to work in. There was barely room to swing the proverbial cat – though Cook often enough swung the nine-tailed variety. Even more bizarrely, there were three actual cats aboard in addition to the human complement, to say nothing of two dogs, seventeen sheep, twenty-four chickens, four pigs and a goat.

9 Immensely wealthy, Sir Joseph Banks (1743–1820) was a talented botanist and naturalist as well as a prima donna and compulsive womaniser. He was also the founder of the African Association, an organisation to promote the exploration of Africa, and the presiding genius of the Royal Botanical Gardens, Kew. Promoter of the voyages of Vancouver and the ill-fated *Bounty* voyage of Captain Bligh, he also recommended the founding of a colony at Botany Bay, where the convict-bearing First Fleet arrived in 1788.

10 Tahiti has always been a byword for beauty, with 7,000′ peaks towering above lush vegetation that ends just short of the summits. The island contains dramatic cliffs, sandy beaches, deep valleys and rushing rivers, making it also the *locus classicus* of a Pacific paradise.

HKF | Courses | Winds | Remarks on Wednesday 12th Apr 1769 –

Calm & Cloudy, hot sultry weather

Light airs next to a Calm with small rain

King Georges Island Extending from N WbW to S W Dist from the nearest shore 6 or 7 Leagues

Calm

Lightning all round the Compass

Extreams of the Island from SSW to WbN

Several of the Natives of the Island came off to us in their Canoes and brought with them Cocoa Nutts and a Fruit very much like a large Apple but did not eat not half so well, for these we gave them Beads &c

Extreams of the Island from ... South to WbN ... from the nearest land Dist ...

HKF | Courses | Winds | Remarks &c on Thursday 13 Apr

Cloudy and squally with Showers of rain

The N E Point of Port Royal Bay WbN & Clarkes point S 29 E Distance of Shore 2 or 3 Leagues

Sounded got ground at 40 fathm 2 Remarkable Peaks SbW

Sounded 45 fathom Rocky ground with Coarse brown sand

Do 12, 18, 22 the 2 Peaks SbW Do aft off shore 3 Miles, observed the Tide to set from the WNW –

Brought too main topsail to the Mast

Made sail for the Bay, at 6 hoisted out the Pinnace and sent her a head to lay on the Shoal that is at the entrance of the Bay – at 7 Anchored in the Bay in 13 fathom with the Best bower a great Number of the Natives in their Canoes came off to the Ship bringing with them a few Cocoa Nutts and other fruits and these they sum'd & set a great Vally upon hoisted out the Boat and landed with a party of Men under arms, Mr Banks and the other Gentlemen in Company – Unbent the Stays'l and all the small sails

11 The *Endeavour* journal, in Cook's own hand, records his first encounter with the Polynesians in Tahiti on Wednesday 12 April 1769: 'Several of the Natives of the Island came off to us in their Canoes and broath with them Cocoa Nuts and a Fruit very much like a large Apple but did not eat not half so Well, for these We gave them Beads…'

12 Matavai Bay in Tahiti became the established port of call for European adventurers in the age of discovery. More crucially for Cook, it was the chosen spot to anchor the *Endeavour* and construct Fort Venus, which can be discerned in the background.

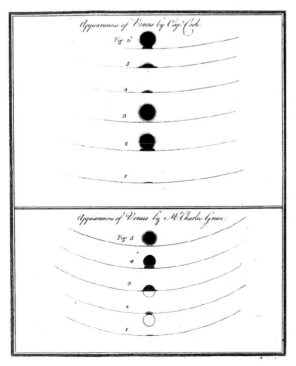

13 Cook's drawings of the transit of Venus. The planet is typically seen from earth as a black disc moving across the sun – a process that lasts six hours or more.

14 The Maoris practised a pure and ferocious warrior culture and built formidable *pa* or hillforts that were a severe test of British military ingenuity in the grim colonial wars of the 1860s. The Maoris did not fight for food or precious resources so much as for martial prestige, the joy of conquest and the acquisition of slaves. Hostile to strangers, they massacred one of Cook's parties on the second expedition, producing the greatest mortality from armed conflict in Cook's entire career.

15 Tupaia inveigled Cook into allowing him to leave Tahiti with the *Endeavour* in July 1769. His utility as a go-between in New Zealand was counteracted by his 'proud and obstinate' nature, which infuriated Cook. Tupaia's drawing (attributed to the Artist of the Chief Mourner) depicts Banks bartering with a Maori, but contact between Europeans and locals was often fraught and laced with violence and misunderstandings.

16 The morning after. The *Endeavour* was beached and careened on the eponymous river shortly after one of Cook's closest ever brushes with death, when his ship was holed and ran aground on the Great Barrier Reef in June–July 1770.

17 and 18 These cartoons, published in 1772, mock Joseph Banks and Daniel Solander for (respectively) their fly-catching and 'simpling' (or sampling) proclivities. A macaroni was a fop or dandy who dressed and spoke in an epicene manner; macaronis typically feigned androgyny or bisexuality. On tour with Dr Johnson in Scotland in 1773 James Boswell taxed his portly friend with being a 'macaroni' on the grounds that he was a poor horseman.

19 The great scientific genius John Harrison produced five chronometers. This is master-craftsman Larcum Kendall's duplicate of Harrison's H4, made in 1769 for the firm of John Arnold. Cook had no chronometer on the *Endeavour* trip but took Kendall's watch with him on his second and third voyages, thus allowing him to chart his longitude with precision.

20 Tobias Furneaux, captain of the *Adventure* on the second voyage, had two strikes against him in Cook's eyes. He ran a far from tight ship and, at the first real pretext, he took his ship home rather than face the terrors of the Antarctic Ocean.

21 The *Resolution*, Cook's ship on the second and third voyages, has rightly been described by biographer John Beaglehole as one of the greatest vessels in history. Cook called it 'the ship of my choice ... the fittest for service of any I have seen'. The *Resolution* was the first ship to cross the Antarctic Circle and did so three times in 1773–75. In 1778–79 she added to this feat by crossing the Arctic Circle twice.

22 Prickly, humorous, egotistical, pedantic, absurdly overpaid, the Forsters were a stone in Cook's shoe during the second voyage. Johann Reinhold, Forster *pere*, Banks's replacement as botanist, has been described as a typical Teutonic Herr Doktor Professor; he probably made the voyage purely for the £4 fee. His son, George, who gradually learned humanity, was a talented artist, linguist and scientist.

millionaires at the Banks level were found to back the project, which soon languished through lack of funds.[76]

Banks set about assembling a posse of scientists and savants for his great southern journey, reminiscent of the party later gathered by Napoleon for his invasion of Egypt in 1798. He signed up fifteen eminent academics in all, of whom the most notable was Dr James Lind, who was even voted a Parliamentary grant of £4,000 to further the important scientific discoveries he was thought likely to make, most of them in mineralogy at the South Pole, since Banks the fantasist assured him he could get him there.[77] Even more incredibly, Banks had invited Dr Johnson along. Johnson, always down to earth, saw the large element of fantasy in Banks's make-up and declined, ostensibly on the grounds that Banks and Solander were too narrowly interested in botanical research, and that the other savants also had narrow interests so that there would be no worthwhile general intellectual conversation afloat.[78] Banks had now set himself on a collision course with Cook. When he first saw the *Resolution* he was dismayed because, though much bigger than the *Endeavour*, she was not nearly large enough for the floating academy he had in mind – a laboratory-cum-artist's-studio-cum-library. By this time Banks had effectively painted himself into a corner. By his loud-mouthed vociferations all over Europe he had given hostages to fortune and his credibility was at stake. This was to be the great Joseph Banks spectacular, and what he wanted he had to have. He expected Cook to be a mere executive officer, a ship's master or pilot rather than a real commander. Cook, on the other hand, was assuring the Admiralty that the *Resolution* was perfect the way she was.[79] Here was a classic case of the irresistible force against the immovable object. Cook was the irresistible force because he had such extensive knowledge of seamanship and the Pacific, and was backed by Palliser and all the top professionals on the Navy Board. Banks was the immovable object because eighteenth-century England was very far from a meritocracy. It was a system of patronage and influence, and Banks had the ear of his friend Sandwich. Banks insisted that the ship would have to be modified to provide adequate space for his fifteen scientists and savants, their servants and their equipment. The Navy Board refused. Banks went over their head to Sandwich, who overruled them; it seems he may also have been concerned for the reputation of the Royal Navy if it got into a slanging match with Banks, currently the darling of international opinion. Cook was forced to bite his tongue and go along with the 'modifications' to *Resolution*, which he was convinced would make her unseaworthy.[80]

Throughout March and April 1772 the absurd refurbishments took place. *Resolution* acquired a broader 'waist', an additional upper deck and a raised poop or roundhouse to accommodate Cook, who had been thrown out of the traditional 'Great Cabin' by the usurping cuckoo Banks, who took it all as his natural right and still complained about the tiny size of the accommodation. All the extra space was filled by the Banks party and their impedimenta. There was even to be a separate cabin for a mistress Banks intended to take with him to while away the oceanic hours, doubtless to be dumped once he reached Polynesia. A host of visitors came to see the renovations, including the French ambassador, Sandwich and his mistress Martha Ray, David Garrick the actor, John Zoffany the painter and many other celebrities or, to put it in Cook's caustic words, 'many of all ranks . . . ladies as well as gentlemen, for scarce a day passed on which [the *Resolution*] was not crowded with strangers who came on board for no other purpose but to see the ship in which Mr Banks was to sail around the world'.[81] Finally the ship was so overbuilt and overloaded that her draught was 17 feet and it was obvious to any seaman that she was liable to capsize. There was little excuse for Banks's abysmal ignorance on this score, for he was no benighted landlubber but a man who had sailed round the world in all weather conditions. But he was neither the first nor the last individual who, in his pride and arrogance, thought he could disregard the laws of physics. The moment of truth came on 10 May when the ship had its first sea trials. The pilot with great difficulty got her as far as the Nore by the 14th but then abandoned the hopeless task; the ship was absurdly top-heavy and would capsize in the first moderate gale. Charles Clerke, appointed a lieutenant to the *Resolution*, did not mince his words to Banks: 'By God, I'll go to sea in a grog tub if desired or in the *Resolution* as soon as you please; but must say I think her by far the most unsafe ship I ever saw or heard of.'[82]

Sandwich and Banks were now in a state of consternation. Cook, in 'I told you so' mode, advised the Admiralty Secretary that the modifications would have to be dismantled to make the vessel seaworthy again. A hectic day involving a virtual essay-writing contest between the Navy Board and the Admiralty ended with Sandwich admitting defeat. The *Resolution* was taken to Sheerness and the painstakingly constructed roundhouse, upper deck, larger masts and bigger guns cut away and jettisoned. Banks stormed down to Sheerness, saw what was being done and virtually ran amok. 'He swore and stamped upon the wharf like a madman, and immediately ordered his servants and all his things out of the ship.'[83] It was Banks as he had never been seen in public before, but his comrades on the *Endeavour* could have told a tale or two. This had been his reaction in Rio de Janeiro in 1768 when forbidden to land. Writing to William Perrin, his friend and correspondent, Banks said: 'you have heard of Tartarus in hell, you have heard of the Frenchman laying [*sic*] swaddled in linen between two of his mistresses both naked using every possible means to excite desire. But you have never heard of a tantalized wretch who has borne his situation with less patience than I have done mine. I have cursed, swore, raved, stamped and wrote memorials to no purpose in the world, they only laugh at me!'[84] Banks was in a frothing frenzy now and, instead of keeping quiet about his frustations, sent an intemperate screed to Sandwich. After asking – demanding – that Sandwich make over the 44-gun ship of the line *Launceston* as compensation so that he could go on a separate expedition, he blamed the Navy Board for incompetent renovation work, complained of lack of consultation and generally implied that Sandwich had let him down. In a bitter sideswipe at Cook, he remarked acidly that there were many commanders in the Navy eager to show that success depended on qualities of endurance and perseverance, whatever ship was assigned to them. He also alleged that Cook always provided cramped accommodation for his crews and was at it again, implying a poor relationship between master and mariners on the *Endeavour*. Cook was now in his sights simply because he had warned that Banks's 'improvements' would lead the *Resolution* to go crank, and he had been proved right. Finally, Banks threatened to appeal to public opinion about the whole affair.[85]

Now thoroughly alienated from Banks, Sandwich composed a blistering reply for use in case Banks made good his threat. At the last moment Banks drew back from the brink, but his supporters did not. One letter to the press ran as follows: 'From what I can see, Mr Banks, Dr Solander, Dr Lind and Mr Zoffany are likely to be excluded from a voyage which, from their sharing it, did honour to the nation; and in all probability, the noblest expedition ever fitted out will dwindle to nothing, and disgrace this country.' Another argued that the cancellation of the Banks expedition 'is a memorable instance of how little it is in the power of Majesty to perform, when the servants of the Crown are determined to oppose the sovereign's will'.[86] The most slithery insinuation was that Cook had set Banks up, that he had deliberately designed alterations that would make the sloop unseaworthy simply to make Banks a laughing stock.[87] Yet Banks had gone too far and lost the support of his one true 'ace in the hole', Sandwich. Palliser and the other senior personnel had no time for Banks's nonsense and remained adamant that Cook would command their expedition. Banks flailed around a little longer in desperation. He tried to recruit the help of the East India Company for a rival circumnavigation, failed, and then contented himself with chartering a ship, complete with officers and men, for a botanical trip to Iceland. His one and only coup was to seduce John Gore from Cook's entourage, but Gore had long been nursing a grudge against Cook after being reprimanded for his actions at Poverty Bay in New Zealand.[88] In any case, as he later admitted, he felt that having survived three circumnavigations, with Byron, Wallis and Cook, he had pushed his luck with the Pacific Ocean as far as it would go.

During all these prima donna tantrums by Banks, Cook had remained calm, reasonable and dispassionate. He granted Banks his great talents and pointed out that both he and his officers had gone out of their way to defer to Banks on all matters save navigation during the three years on *Endeavour* so he could not understand what his complaint was. Banks's plans for a new Pacific expedition were quixotic and chimerical, and Banks himself lacked the experience and expertise to be the true ship's commander that he wanted to be. Cook's remarks, on the surface a model of restraint, were in fact deeply excoriating: 'To many it will no doubt appear strange that Mr Banks should attempt to overrule the opinions of the two great Boards who have the sole management of the whole Navy of Great Britain and likewise the opinions of the principal sea officers concerned in the expedition.'[89] Nevertheless the entire cause célèbre left scars. It took Banks a long time to forgive Sandwich and even longer to make his peace with Cook, but he never came to terms with Palliser, whom he identified as the real enemy working for his downfall. After assuring himself that Banks (mercifully) would not be on the ship, Cook set to work to rationalise the equipment and manning of the *Resolution* and *Adventure*. The officers for the ships had been decided in November 1771 and their commissions and warrants then signed.[90] The *Resolution* boasted a crew of 204 plus twenty-two marines and forty gentlemen, naturalists and other experts. The *Adventure* had a crew of 134, thirteen marines and other experts. Second in command to Cook on the nearly new (fourteen months old) *Resolution* was Robert Palliser Cooper, first lieutenant, a kinsman of Banks's bête noire, the Comptroller, who had served on Cook's old watch in Newfoundland. Solid, unexceptionable, unexciting, Cooper would feature as the type of quiet professional whose very competence was attested to by the fact that he barely receives a mention in the next three years. A horse of a very different colour was the second lieutenant Charles Clerke, a bibulous raconteur and wit, interesting, mature, original, very human, the ideal guest at a dinner party.[91] Clerke was one of only three officers (the others being Edgcumbe and Pickersgill) who had sailed with Cook on the *Endeavour*. Banks tried very hard to detach him from Cook and recruit him for his Iceland trip, with lavish financial promises, but Clerke replied that he had 'stood too far on this tack to think of putting about with any kind of credit'.[92] That sounds like four-square integrity, but Clerke always had his reservations about Cook and was prepared to criticise him to Banks, as in the following:

Captain Cook never explained his system of stowage to any of us; we were all very desirous of knowing, for it must have been a new plan entirely . . . he kept whatever scheme he had quite a secret, for Cooper asked my opinion, and repeatedly declared he could form no idea how it was possible to bring it about . . . They're going to stow this major part of the cables in the hold to make way for people even now. I asked Gilbert [the master] if such was the present case, what the devil should we have done if we had all gone. 'Oh, by God, that was impossible,' was his answer.[93]

Richard Pickersgill, the third lieutenant, was a talented amateur astronomer and maker of charts, though his critics said that he, like Clerke, was over-fond of the bottle. A complex, tormented man, romantic and gloomy by temperament, incapable of Clerke's levity or wit, Pickersgill may have been the first clear example of the Peter Principle.[94]

Joseph Gilbert, the master, was, at 40, rather old for his line of work but he had solid credentials in surveying, having also served in the Newfoundland–Labrador theatre, and was a highly skilled draughtsman. Whereas on the *Endeavour* voyage Cook had done most of the surveying and chart-making himself, on the second expedition he deputed much of this work to Gilbert, showing the enormous trust he placed in him. All the officers on the *Resolution* were well known to him, but those on the *Adventure* were appointed more on past form than because of Cook's acquaintance. Tobias Furneaux, the commander, a 37-year-old Devonian, selected himself in the Admiralty's eyes because he had been acting commander on the *Dolphin* when both Wallis and his first lieutenant fell ill. A good seaman, though a trifle slack on discipline, he was a natural follower, a technician rather than an explorer, a natural executive officer rather than a true captain. Not particularly gifted with brains, imagination or initiative, Furneaux was a by-the-book Navy man.[95] His first lieutenant Joseph Shank effectively jumped ship at Cape Town, allegedly suffering from gout. That gave the second lieutenant Arthur Kempe an instant promotion. Kempe, who had sailed the Pacific with Byron, even more than Furneaux exemplified the 'being there' principle. Initially in Cooper's shadow as they climbed the greasy pole, he eventually out-topped him and ended as an admiral. James Burney, promoted at the Cape to second lieutenant and switched from the *Resolution* to her sister ship, was easily the most interesting of the *Adventure*'s officers, intelligent, articulate, professional, with scholarly interests, multi-talented, in every way a worthy member of the scintillating Burney family. The maverick in the *Adventure*'s company was James Scott, lieutenant of marines, some of whose actions and outbursts sound like those of a psychopath.[96] Not surprisingly, less is known about the *Adventure*'s company than the *Resolution*'s. Among the midshipmen who made the voyage was John Elliott, who left a valuable memoir, and the future explorer George Vancouver, then aged 15. Elliott said it was considered 'quite a great feather, in a young man's cap, to go with

Captain Cook', and his father had pulled strings to get him his berth, hopping from Palliser to Cooper and finally to Cook, who agreed to take him.[97]

After Banks's departure, there were few scientists left, much to Cook's joy, though those who remained were to prove trial enough. William Wales, the astronomer on the *Resolution*, had observed the transit of Venus for the Royal Society in Hudson's Bay in 1769, while his counterpart on the *Adventure*, William Bayly, had observed it at the North Cape. Elliott liked this pair and praised them for their down-to-earth approach, contrasting them with Banks (whom he disliked as a snob), at whom he jeered for his proposal to take his mistress with him on a South Seas voyage.[98] The object of almost universal detestation was Banks's replacement as botanist, Dr Johann Reinhold Forster, who was accompanied by his son George, at 17 already a talented artist, a skilled linguist and an accomplished scientist. Dogmatic, suspicious, self-satisfied, Forster the elder (and his son) have been well summed up as 'standard Teutonic Herr Doktor Professors'.[99] This is perhaps unfair to George, who was a definite improvement on his father and at times could be charming, genial and even almost humorous. Their defenders claim that their overbearing attitude was the prickliness of professional scientists trying to establish themselves in a culture riven by the cult of the amateur, where seriousness was instantly subject to ridicule. The Forsters were also described as 'in part inheritors of a German moralising pietistic tradition, in part men of the Enlightenment, in part avant-garde Romanticists. They ministered both to the scientific demands of the Enlightenment and to the emotional demands of the Age of Feeling.'[100] Why such men should have come on a perilous sea voyage is a mystery, perhaps explicable solely in terms of the fee of £4,000 that Dr Forster was offered. Deeply unpopular – on several occasions the sailors threatened that they would throw him overboard – Forster the elder would suffer the indignity of being ejected from Cook's cabin, threatened with arrest by Clerke, and punched to the floor by the master's mate. Cook must have thought he was ill-starred; he had got rid of one prima donna in Banks only to be landed with one who was even more insufferable. Nonetheless, Forster's undoubted talents have won him many posthumous admirers.[101]

One of the reasons Cook had so few officers who had served on the *Endeavour* was that he had expressly forbidden all officers, no matter how highly placed, from bringing servants with them. There would be no passengers of any kind on the second voyage, and Cook warned the midshipmen that, for the first year at least, they would have to perform the same duties as the ordinary seamen, including going aloft. In compensation he promised that he would teach them how to make accurate astronomical and chronometrical observations, so that they would return as skilled veterans. He experienced the utmost difficulty in getting sailors for his venture, mainly for two reasons. He had the reputation of being an 'unlucky' captain, for of the 94 men who had set out on the *Endeavour* only 41 survived – a mortality rate of over 60 per cent, well above average.[102] Of these 41, only 13 able seamen and one marine volunteered. Most of the rest had to be pressed or commandeered and, not surprisingly, when they heard where Cook was bound, they deserted in large numbers. Forty-eight men ran away from the *Resolution* before she even left England (as against eighteen in the same circumstances on the *Endeavour*). When he made his first landfall, at Madeira, Cook had to hire local boatmen as police, to prevent more of his men from absconding. Those that remained were mainly savage, brutal, drunken and licentious characters, though by and large they did what was asked of them. John Elliott thought them, in a double cliché, both rough diamonds and the salt of the earth.[103] One of Cook's few success stories from the first voyage was Samuel Gibson, who had deserted at Tahiti but was now a devoted Cook follower and admirer and had been promoted to corporal; he would later turn out to have marked talent as a Polynesian linguist.

Finally, all was ready for the great southern adventure. The two ships were supposed to have left in March but, because of the Banks fiasco, it was 21 June 1772 before Cook bade farewell to Elizabeth, who had just given birth to another son, George. As he weighed anchor to run round to Plymouth, he had on board thirty gallons of antiscorbutic carrot marmalade, 20,000 pounds of sauerkraut, 19 tons of beer, 1,400 gallons of spirits and 642 gallons of wine. As a morale booster Cook promised the officers generous bonuses at the end of the cruise and disbursed all back pay plus two months' wages in advance to the ordinary sailors. This proved to be not so wise, as the men went on a drunken rampage and nearly wrecked the *Resolution* on the rocks at the entrance to Plymouth harbour.[104] It was hardly a promising omen.

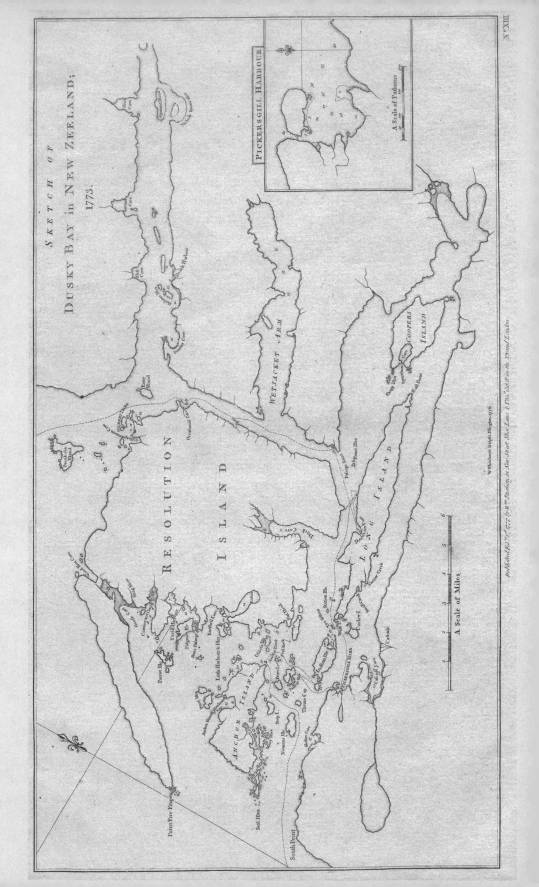

SKETCH OF

DUSKY BAY in NEW ZEELAND;
1773.

PICKERSGILL HARBOUR

A Scale of Fathoms

RESOLUTION ISLAND

WET JACKET ARM

LONG ISLAND

COOPERS ISLAND

ANCHOR ISLAND

Point Five Fingers

South Point

Seal Isles

A Scale of Miles

Publish'd Feb.y 1st 1777 by W.m Strahan, in New Street, Shoe Lane, & Tho.s Cadell in the Strand London.

W.Whitchurch Sculp.t, Islington 1776.

CHAPTER NINE

Antarctica

'I should prefer this voyage to any in the world if my ill stars had destined me a sailor,' was Fanny Burney's comment as she waved her 21-year-old brother goodbye.[1] The ambivalence was no doubt prompted by the gale force winds already blowing as the *Resolution* and *Adventure* headed down the Channel towards Cape Finisterre. Johann Forster was already proving a second Banks in one respect: he was immediately laid low with seasickness, which he tried to remedy by the unusual method of drinking mulled red wine. Once in Spanish waters the two ships were challenged by coastguards, who demanded to know their business, much to the fury of the splenetic Forster who blustered that such interrogation was 'humiliating to the masters of the sea'. Cook, however, knew it was elementary Iberian *amour propre* and replied civilly. The Spaniards were deeply impressed by the name of Cook and wished the travellers Godspeed.[2] There was a brief stop at Madeira between 29 July and 2 August to take on fresh meat, water and wine, but Cook was anxious to get to sea again; the farther away from England he sailed, the less attractive were the prospects of desertion. Cook was already delighted with his ship. The stiff 'blow' they had in the Bay of Biscay showed the *Resolution* to very good advantage, particularly when compared with the *Adventure*; the flagship had not had to take in its topsails, but Tobias Furneaux's vessel could not carry hers.[3] One readily understands Beaglehole's paean to the *Resolution*: 'One of the great, one of the superb ships of history. Of all the ships of the past, could she by magic be recreated and made immortal, one would gaze on her with something like reverence.'[4] But Cook was not so pleased with the crew. As they sailed away from Madeira, the first flogging of the voyage was carried out. John Marra, who had attempted to desert at Deptford, was punished with twelve lashes for insolence. This was very much the Cook method: impress upon your men very early that there will be no nonsense and offer them convincing proof of toughness. Cowed by this display of exemplary discipline, the matelots made no protest when Cook ordered the ship thoroughly cleaned and fumigated below deck with charcoal fires; sea water was also pumped through the bilges and a regular hygiene and laundry regime instituted.

Before they left Madeira there was high comedy. A botanist with the name of Burnett came forward and was disappointed to find that Banks was not on board. Burnett told a story about having been instructed by Banks to rendezvous with him here. It soon transpired that the 'botanist' was in fact a woman dressed as a man. This was not an inspirational story about a heroine determined to transcend the perceived limits of her gender, but a barefaced wheeze by Banks to smuggle a mistress aboard. Piqued by comments from Sandwich and others about the inadvisability of taking a woman aboard at Deptford, Banks had hit on the idea of sending his girlfriend ahead to Madeira and smuggling her on to the ship under the pretence of picking up a fellow botanist. It shows something of the suppressed irritation Cook felt for Banks that he sent this story back to Banks's arch-enemy Palliser.[5] Fortified by Madeira's supplies of oranges, walnuts and onions, the men were in generally good spirits as the two ships proceeded to Porto Praya in St Jago, one of the most southerly of the Cape Verde islands, where even more plentiful food-stuffs were available: pigs, goats, fruit and even a bullock. The governor of the island was unfriendly but did not try to stop the strangers landing. The sailors thronged the market and for some reason a craze for buying pet monkeys sprang up. Dozens were brought on board but proved dirty and lousy. Tired of seeing the simian urchins running squealing around the ship, Cook ordered them thrown overboard. Elliott defiantly hung on to his pet for a month but one day it crept into the quarters of the master's mate, John Whitehouse, and threw ink over him. Whitehouse drew his pistol and blasted the monkey out of the window. Ever afterwards Elliott hated him and set him down as 'Jesuitical, sensible but an insinuating litigious mischief making fellow'.[6] The animal kingdom seemed to hit back a few days later when a carpenter's mate fell over-board and was taken by the sharks that followed the ship; the Cape Verde islands are a favourite haunt of the oceanic white-tip.[7]

The two ships continued southward in reasonable weather. Cook experi-mented by launching a boat to test the currents and take the temperature of the water, using a submersible thermometer.[8] On 8 September the vessels crossed the line, which occasioned the usual outburst of horseplay on the *Resolution*. Men were lathered with a noisome mixture of tar and mud, then 'shaved' with rusty iron hoops and hosed down with ice-cold water. About fifty of them were ducked from the yardarm. The only way to avoid these rites of passage was to pay a forfeit to Neptune of a gallon of rum, quaffed by the rest of the crew with avidity.[9] It is curious and interesting that Furneaux, generally considered to have a much lighter touch than Cook as a disciplinarian, did not allow ducking on the *Adventure* as he considered it too dangerous; for the same reason he would not allow Bayly to make the experiments in his boat that Wales made on the *Resolution*. Furneaux's instincts may have been sounder on this occasion; it is easier to release the genie from the bottle than stopper him up again, as Cook discovered when, two days after the ceremony at the equator, he had to flog two men for insolence.[10] Cook further alienated the men by giving them experimental beer instead of grog; finding it disgusting, they cried out that they would rather have water and, when Cook persisted, tried to turn his experiment into farce by drinking the entire barrel of 'beer' dry so that it could not be served to them on a daily basis. On 14 September Furneaux came on board the *Resolution* to dine. He and Cook had a lot to discuss. Amazingly, in light of the desertion rate, Furneaux had found a stowaway on his ship but, more seriously, two of the *Adventure*'s crew had died of a fever, which Furneaux ascribed to their having bathed in contaminated water at St Jago.[11] It is likely that Cook suspected that Furneaux had not been carrying out his anti-scurvy regime meticulously, and this was hinted at by Clerke, who wrote: 'Our people all in perfect health and spirits, owing I believe in great measure to the strict attention of Captain Cook to their cleanliness and every other article that respects their welfare.' Cook and Furneaux also discussed how difficult it was for the two vessels to keep together, even in fine weather. By this time Cook had revised his opinion of the *Adventure* which, in terms of its 'stiffness' or metacentric height and its general weatherliness, now seemed to have the edge on the *Resolution*.[12]

The two ships passed close to Ascension Island on 16 September but did not sight it. Instead they observed the familiar galaxy of near-land birds: boobies, gannets, men-o'-war; to these were added shearwaters, albatrosses and pintadoes as they pressed farther south. Where Banks had blazed away at these birds on the first voyage, this time the crews favoured the method of catching seabirds by baiting a hook, throwing it into the sea and then hauling in the unwary flyers.[13] As September slipped into October, the weather turned squally; as on the *Endeavour* voyage, Cook approached Cape Town through storm-tossed seas, this time with the waves lit up by myriad phosphorescent insects. On 30 October Table Mountain was sighted, with no further fatalities or illnesses having occurred, except for Lieutenant Shank on the *Adventure*, who was so stricken with gout that he left the expedition at the Cape and found passage back to England.[14] The men were in good spirits, and their morale soared when two Dutch East Indiaships put in to Cape Town two days later, having lost nearly two hundred men to scurvy; Captain Cook might have his eccentricities, it was concluded, but he knew what he was doing when it came to health and welfare. In another effortless display of masterly seamanship Cook had taken just seventy-seven days to reach the Cape.[15] The three-week stay in South Africa provided a pleasant interlude. The Dutch governor Baron Joachim Ammena van Plettenberg was under orders from The Hague to provide Cook with every assistance. Wales and Bayly took their instruments ashore and conducted further experiments and observations. Parkinson's successor as ship's artist, William Hodges, painted Cape Town and its harbour. Although not as talented as Parkinson or Banks's protégé John Zoffany, Hodges was a master of landscape painting and experimented with the new light and colour encountered in the Pacific; moreover, because he was such an accurate, naturalistic painter, he particularly appealed to Cook, the draughtsman-precisian.[16] Cook himself was busy with correspondence: to Banks, whom he thanked for a gift of pickled fish, stating he hoped Banks would not hold him personally to blame for the fiasco in Deptford ('some cross circumstances which ... created, I have reason to think, a coolness betwixt you and I [sic]'); and to Walker, tapping the Quaker past and hoping that the 'divine protection' (which we have no reason to think Cook believed in) would help him when he headed south into unknown seas.[17]

The busy Forsters, ranging the countryside in search of plants and insects, chanced upon a Swedish botanist named Anders Sparrman, a student of Linnaeus's, and persuaded him to join the expedition; Cook was dubious about taking on this extra passenger, but in the end acquiesced.[18] His mind was elsewhere, pondering the news the Dutch had given him about three distinct French voyages of exploration. The first was of long standing. In 1739 Jean-Baptiste Charles Bouvet de Lozier spied land on New Year's Day, which he named Cape Circumcision, said to be in latitude 54S, 11E. All the circumstantial evidence Bouvet de Lozier adduced – ice, seaweed, seals, penguins – suggested that he had discovered the tip of a great continent. Needless to say, the gung-ho enthusiasts for Terra Australis Incognita, such as John Callander and Alexander Dalrymple, annexed his report as clinching evidence for their theory; Callander's compendious account of the South Seas, published while Cook was already heading for the Pacific on his first voyage and melding material from de Brosses with an ingenious variety of other sources, took Bouvet de Lozier's tentative suggestions as fact, even though his chief pilot thought (correctly) that the cape they had sighted was merely part of a small island.[19] The latitude Bouvet de Lozier had given for its sighting was correct, though its longitude was significantly out (it is actually at 3'24E). Bouvet Island, as it came to be known, is just five miles long by four wide and over 90 per cent glacier, 'a few square kilometres of ice-capped lava ... the only scrap of land which is literally a thousand miles from anywhere'.[20]

The second French voyage was that of Marion du Fresne, who had passed through Cape Town on his way to deliver back to Tahiti the first ever Polynesian taken to Europe, the Ahutoru of Louis Antoine de Bougainville's expedition; Ahutoru illustrated the high mortality rate for Polynesians taken out of their hemisphere to Europe by dying of smallpox. More interesting were the reports, less than a year old, from the navigator Yves-Joseph de Kerguelen-Trémarec, who discovered the Kerguelen group of islands in the Indian Ocean in February 1772 at 49S 69E and claimed that they too were an outlying part of the Great Southern Continent.[21] The thinking at the time was that the Great Southern Continent might stretch all the way round the world; the only land corresponding to eighteenth-century fantasy, Antarctica, actually does, but the Callanders, De Brosses and Dalrymples did not have in mind a continent of snow and ice. Since Cook's twofold instructions from the Admiralty were to explore and chart the entire South Pacific and to search for the Southern Continent, it is not surprising that Cook felt he was on the right track.

Cook's second voyage can be conceived as a five-act drama, of which the prelude was the reasonably trouble-free run from London to Cape Town. Act One, a four-month venture into the stormy southern oceans of Antarctica, began when Cook hoisted sail from the Cape on 22 November 1772. He was going into uncharted waters and had no real idea of the conditions he would encounter. With an intuitive sense, as expressed to Walker, that the voyage would be dangerous, even so he cannot have been prepared for the gigantic seas and immense waves that lay ahead; this was, after all, the Antarctic Ocean where Shackleton ran into a 100-foot wave in May 1916.[22] The elements immediately took over and buffeted him almost continually for more than a hundred days. Cook's journal entries tell their own story: '24 November. Large swell from southward. 26 November. Large swell from eastward. 30 November. Very hard gales with rain and hail. Sea running very high. 2 December. Sea running very high. Sea broke with great violence over the ship.'[23] Forster's narrative switched, from recording the flocks of fulmars, shearwaters, pintadoes and albatrosses that accompanied the *Resolution*, to alarm when all hands were summoned to the pumps.[24] Finally, from 30 November to 6 December the ocean threw everything it had at Cook, testing him to the limit with a violent, snarling storm. Cook had already issued the cold-weather fearnought jackets and trousers to the crew, but they were of little use in the freezing cold of these latitudes, and ten men went down sick with violent colds. To get temporary relief from the wind and waves Cook sometimes hove to, but often the ocean would reach such a pitch of frenzy that not even Cook dared do this. Even when the wind abated from Force 11 to 10, the sea still ran very high, and there was a danger that the ship would founder because the men were too exhausted to manoeuvre her. Cook issued extra rations of food and grog, and in this storm-tossed nightmare the crew ate well, if only because the terrible conditions caused high mortality among the sheep, hogs and poultry.[25]

On 10 December the first iceberg was spotted, so huge that at first it was mistaken for land; it was twice as high as the masthead. Next day there was a veritable archipelago of bergs; Cook needed to thread a careful passage through and ordered the *Adventure* to come in under his stern. These walls of ice formed a temporary respite from the raging maelstrom on the open ocean – so violent that waves regularly broke over the top of 60-foot bergs.[26] The men took to keeping a daily tally of the icebergs while Forster noted the new species of birds that perched on them, especially the penguins and snowy petrels. At latitude 54 the ships' progress was halted by the pack ice, so Cook bore away to the south-east, skirting the rim of the ice, with Forster now most interested in the dozens of whales all around them. On 14 December Cook turned south by south-west, thinking there was clear water in that direction, but soon was in danger of being trapped by the ice so turned north. It was difficult making way through the fog and snow, with the sails and rigging stiff with icicles, yet even in such conditions Cook did not neglect the aims of science. He launched the jolly boat to test the current while William Wales tested the conducting rod that had been pioneered by Benjamin Franklin.[27] Often, though, such observations were impracticable as the fog made it impossible to see from one end of the ship to the other. And always there was snow and ice. On the night of 15–16 December four inches of snow fell and the thermometer resistered five degrees below freezing. On the 17th Cook tried to go south again but once more was stopped by heavy pack ice; still pods of whales played around the ship.[28] He was not to know – as nobody in the 1770s knew anything about the Antarctic – that the pack ice was about to break up and he might well have had three months of clear water ahead of him. By the 18th the ships had sailed ninety miles eastwards along the edge of the ice. Faced with the difficult choice between steering among icebergs in fog or risking going among the pack ice and getting frozen in – two of his men had served in the Greenland trade and spoke of being stuck fast in the ice for nine months – Cook made the wise decision to take his chance among the bergs.[29]

By Christmas Day 1772 the two ships had got down to latitude 57S, passing through several narrow fields of loose ice: usually ice that had not melted the year before had refrozen and was now small and dirty. Cook could not understand why, when he headed north or west, he encountered ice so thick that he had to stand away south to avoid it but then found easier conditions going *south*, which on paper was preposterous. It took the era of whaling in the nineteenth century to clear up this conundrum. Working on the 'tongue of ice' theory, whaling captains discovered that one could push through loose ice between longitude 10W and 30E and then reach clear water at Latitude 60S. As Beaglehole remarks with dry irony: 'If Cook had not been so anxious to look for Cape Circumcision, he might well, at this time, have gone south and sighted, or perhaps even reached, the Antarctic continent.'[30] On Christmas Day Cook was in the lee of a 100-foot iceberg, with dozens of seabirds all around, blue petrels, snowy petrels, giant petrels, Antarctic petrels and the ubiquitous albatross. While he sent out the jolly boat to see if it was possible to get fresh water from a berg – they could not – the men turned riotous. Cook noted cryptically in his journal: 'People were inclinable to celebrate Christmas Day in their own way'; in other words, they were all roaring drunk.[31] Fearful that a sudden gale might catch a drunken crew at its mercy, Cook hove to while the inebriate sailors staged chaotic boxing matches.[32] Cook himself was in pensive mood, reflecting that, but for the length of day, one could immediately imagine oneself at latitude 58 North, not South. On 27 December, with an unwontedly calm sea, he decided to run west as far as the putative meridian of Cape Circumcision. Two days later there was comedy of a kind when Cook again sent his men to try to get fresh water from the bergs, only for them to be driven off by an aggressive school of at least ninety penguins. Pickersgill reported: 'They seemed to perform their evolutions so well that they only wanted the use of arms to cut a figure on Wimbledon common.'[33] The reaction of the crew was predictable: they blasted away at the contumacious birds. It was not just indigenous peoples who felt the lash of European frustration and impatience.

By New Year's Eve the sea was making up again, and it was dangerous to cruise among the ice. The year 1773 opened with a strong gale blowing from the south-east, accompanied by snow and sleet showers. Cook noted on 3 January that he had just had only his second sighting of the moon since leaving Cape Town – an indication of how bad the weather had been. On that date, too, he reached the supposed position of Cape Circumcision (latitude 59S, longitude 11E) and found nothing. Cook was angry when he realised he had been on a wild-goose chase because of the fatuity of the French, battling tempests in search of imaginary lands. 'In short, I am of opinion that what M. Bouvet took for land and named Cape Circumcision was nothing but mountains of ice surrounded by field ice.'[34] He was also beginning to wonder if the received opinion of the late eighteenth century was correct: that icebergs can be formed only from fresh water and that therefore their appearance denotes land.[35] He decided to turn east, run along the line of latitude 60S and see if he would have better luck locating the island group recently discovered by Kerguelen; in fact there was no chance of this for Cook put its longitude at 57–58E whereas in fact the archipelago lay much farther to the east, at 68–70E. It was still bitterly cold, with the snow and ice on the rigging giving the *Resolution* the appearance of a ghost ship or ghastly white spectre. Yet Cook took comfort from the surprisingly high morale of the men, who were enduring well in their fearnoughts, fortified by an extra glass of brandy each morning. This was just as well, for they at once ran into strong gales and a large sea from the north-west. Cook steered to the south, hoping for better weather and passed dozens more icebergs, about which he was now becoming blasé. To his great delight, the men finally mastered the art of melting ice from the bergs. With 15 tons of fresh water and the problem solved, Cook felt confident and set a course south by south-east. The snag now was that the ships were carrying so much water that in a heavy swell, which they were in almost constantly, the vessels themselves were unsteady.[36]

On 17 January, shortly before noon, he crossed the Antarctic Circle, the first man in history known to have done so (latitude 66'36, longitude 39'35E). Soon afterwards the ships encountered another ice field, so Cook stood away to the north-east. He was always and every day the great navigator, noting the strength of the current and adjusting his dead reckoning calculations accordingly, testing the currents and sea temperatures, cross-checking his dead reckoning with meticulous calculations of longitude and latitude. He also tried to estimate the likelihood of land from bird life, but was not helped much by the fact that the white, blue, giant and Antarctic petrels still accompanied them (as well as albatrosses, one of which George Foster shot), though the pintadoes were no longer seen.[37] Once away from the ice, Cook predictably again had high seas to deal with. A huge swell rolled in from the north-east, became a gale and then on 20 January escalated to a full storm, to the point where Cook had to reef topsails and strike top-yards. Fortunately, the full fury abated twenty-four hours later so that he was able to reset the topsails and top-yards, though there was still a formidable swell running, together with showers of snow and sleet that made the deck like an ice rink. The bad weather continued, with a remorseless high northerly sea. On 26 January there was a return to storm force winds, with the sea from the north-east running 'prodigious high'; the foresail, main topsail and the fore and mizzen topsails all had to be reefed. Everything was confusion, with the very high sea now veering round to the north-west, the barometer giving freak readings, icebergs disappearing for a day and then suddenly reappearing. The gales continued until the end of the month when there was a very brief lull.[38] Furneaux sent word from the *Adventure* that he had seen a large mass of seaweed and diving petrels, which seemed to him to suggest the proximity of land. Cook was sceptical, rightly so because of the continual high seas from all directions. With huge waves rearing around them, pyramidal and confused, Cook was pushed to the limit, uncertain which way to steer, as giant seas battered him from all directions: north, north-east, north-west and west. These were conditions even he had never experienced before. What was a navigator to do when there were very high seas from the west and north-west even though the gale itself was blowing from the north?[39]

Exhausted and not a little apprehensive, Cook salved his feelings by railing at the incompetence of French navigators and their inaccurate sightings, bearings and locations. Yet Cook had direct experience of at least part of the reason for the inaccuracy, since the continuing heavy swell made it difficult to take proper bearings as the sloop pitched and rolled in the high seas.[40] On 8 February thick fog was added to the elemental minestrone. Cook ordered the *Adventure* to come under his stern, but suddenly she was gone, lost in the mists. For twenty-four hours he tacked to and fro, firing guns but hearing no answering signal. Cook then made for the first agreed rendezvous in the ocean, in accordance with the contingency plans he and Furneaux had agreed. On 10 February there was a further day-long bid for reunion, with more guns being fired and fires lit. But there was no sign of the *Adventure*. Cook concluded there was no further point in looking for her, and that they would meet up at the ultimate rendezvous in New Zealand.[41] There was something unconvincing about the business of *Adventure*'s sudden disappearance, and the suspicion arises that Furneaux, presumably out of his depth in the appallingly confused seas that had flummoxed even Cook, snapped. He knew Cook's perseverance, which could amount to monomania when he had the bit between his teeth. Of course nothing conclusive can be proved, but he may have decided he had had enough of his demanding superior and feared they might all be lost if he continued with his quest for the Southern Continent.[42] Cook, indeed, showing scant regard for human psychology, actually responded to the loss of his sister ship by turning *south*, to universal dismay, in yet another attempt to find the Southern Continent. The ship's company were appalled and wanted to follow Furneaux to New Zealand. To head out of these waters certainly answered common sense, for the heavy swell and very high seas from the west continued, together with sleet and snow. Cook's attempts to infer possible land from the seabirds had now come to nothing, for the penguins had disappeared but the previously absent pintadoes had returned.[43] Bird life seemed as confused as the seas themselves. The disappearance of the *Adventure* also badly affected morale. Forster admitted he was scared now that there was no back-up in case of emergency.[44] With the crew the discontent took more tangible forms. Five men were sentenced to the cat, two receiving a dozen lashes and three more six lashes apiece, all for theft.[45] Someone less of a martinet might have eased his normal regime while the ship was in such terrible seas, but Cook insisted that his anti-scurvy regulations be followed to the letter and stopped the grog of any men he found with dirty hands; given that in stormy seas extra liquor was served, to be deprived of it was a bitter punishment indeed.[46]

On 17 February Cook and his shipmates saw the aurora australis. With the swell continuing from the west, Cook took the opportunity to heave to under a 200-foot iceberg, to get at least temporary respite from the non-stop pounding of the waves. On the 22nd there was a dangerous moment when Cook launched boats to collect water from a huge iceberg, 400 feet high and half a mile in circumference. As they approached, the berg suddenly turned turtle sending a huge wave whooshing over the boats and powerful enough to rock the *Resolution*.[47] This was another instance of the eighteenth century's woeful ignorance of the Antarctic. Modern studies show that icebergs with such dimensions are highly unstable and should be avoided at all costs. They were certainly in the realm of gigantic bergs by now, and counted eighty of them both on the 22nd and 23rd. Nights passed among so many giants were necessarily uneasy, with storms and swells from the east increasing the danger of collision. Even so, the real danger came not from the massive bergs but the breakaway 'calves'. Cook, while appreciating the danger from these ice monsters, was fascinated by their beauty and often spoke of his 'pretty poison' ambivalence and their austere presence, which only the most talented painter could do justice to. In the end even he admitted that they were simply too dangerous for him to proceed south of the Antarctic Circle again, as he had originally intended.[48] The difficulty of seeing the ice floes at night, especially during the dark nights of the advanced season, would make further progress south madness. Reluctantly Cook stood north, moving in a waltz-like way rather than heading straight, as though he could not bear to tear himself away from Antarctic waters. And still the fascination with bird life went on: a different species of penguin had now put in an appearance, shearwaters and albatrosses were still present, but the white and Antarctic petrels had vanished.[49]

The high swell from the south-east turned into a full-blown storm on 27 February, and this tempest was a nasty one. Forced to strike top-yards and reef topsails, the sailors still found it hard to control the *Resolution*, as the wind kept gusting and shearing from different directions. The storm moderated to a gale on the 28th and they noticed that the ferocity of the storm had cleared the ocean of all icebergs. The toll on the animals Cook had hoped to introduced into New Zealand continued, as he noted in his journal: 'We have a breeding sow on board which yesterday morning farrowed nine pigs, every one of which was killed by the cold before four o'clock in the afternoon, notwithstanding all the care we could take of them.'[50] As the ship gradually made northing, the temperature rose, but their problems were not over since the swell from the north-west collided with another from the south and south-east, again piling up huge, conical, confused waves with breaking crests. The ship pitched and rolled excessively until eventually the north-western swell asserted dominance over its rival. Icebergs were still seen but far fewer than in the more southerly latitudes, and then on 3–4 March they saw the sun for the longest continuous period since leaving the Cape, allowing them to take proper bearings. That the sea state continued violent is shown by this eloquent testimony from Cook: 'This island [sc. iceberg] could not be less than one hundred feet high and yet such was the impetus, force and height of the waves which were broke against it that the water was thrown a considerable height above it.'[51] Morale was plummeting again, so Cook ordered his men to smarten themselves up by taking needle and thread and mending all their clothes; once again, any found with dirty hands had their grog stopped. On 8 March the voyagers experienced a very mild day but it was the proverbial calm before the storm for next day another massive Force 12 onslaught broke over them. By the 11th the tempest had moderated to the point where they could have the reefs and studding sails set and take sightings. What was so wearying was that there was never any significant let-up. As soon as one massive swell subsided, another would take its place. The weather was still very cold, with the men complaining of chilblains and the decks and rigging still covered with icicles.[52]

There was a heavy squall on 15 March and the swell continued. A fine day on the 16th was followed with tedious predictability by yet another gale on the 18th. By now Cook's calculations put him about 800 miles from land, and he anticipated a landfall either in Australia or Van Diemen's Land; in fact the nearest land was Macquarie Island. The sailors construed the appearance of yet another breed of penguins, a seal and some rockweed as likely harbingers of land and were irrationally buoyed up when one of them harpooned a dolphin; yet again the crew showed its talent for harming innocent creatures or rubbing up docile natives the wrong way. The last days at sea were marked by even more strong gales, lasting from 22 to 25 March, with a heavy swell from the west-southwest running all the time.[53] At last on the morning of the 25th came the yearned-for cry of 'land ho' as the masthead lookout spotted what turned out to be New Zealand. At noon Cook put into Dusky Bay on South Island, a landfall on the *Endeavour* voyage, described as 'one of the most remote and wildly magnificent spots in New Zealand'.[54] He had a few errors in his calculations, but the crux of the matter was that he sailed 11,000 miles for 122 days, out of sight of land the whole time, in high seas and storms most of the time, with only intermittent sightings of the sea and moon, yet had managed to bring the *Resolution* to safe haven in a bay he had but briefly glimpsed at dusk three years earlier. The dangers were objectively high, but his successors would at least know what they had to deal with; Cook had literally ventured into the unknown. It was a truly stunning feat of navigation and it is safe to say that no one else in the world would have had the skill, seamanship, tenacity, perseverance and utter fearlessness to bring it off. Beaglehole sums it all up well:

> To complete four months in high latitudes in a small ship would in itself be an achievement; to navigate without accident in one of the stormiest oceans in the world, hampered by fog and constantly among icebergs, was a very remarkable achievement of seamanship indeed. The whole voyage was great, but no one who has had much experience in Antarctic waters will deny that these four months were by far the worst part of it, and by implication the greatest in accomplishment.[55]

Yet such was Cook's modesty – or was it his continuing paranoia? – that he felt the need to justify his decision to go for rest and recreation in New Zealand: 'If the reader of this journal desires to know my reason for taking this resolution I desire he will only consider that after cruising four months in these high latitudes it must be natural for me to wish to enjoy some short repose in a harbour where I can procure some refreshment for my people of which they begin to stand in need. To this point too great attention could not be paid as the voyage is but in its infancy.'[56]

Cook moved to another anchorage on the 26th, then, still not satisfied, finally found what he wanted on the south-east of the bay on the 27th after Pickersgill had reconnoitred it for him. Dusky Bay has always drawn all the superlatives though, curiously, William Hodges's painting on the entrance to the bay makes it look as forbidding as something from an Edgar Allan Poe story. The product of glaciers, the bay's coastline rises up sharply to beetling cliffs and is indented by multiple fjords. From the high-water mark to the snowline, thick forests cling to the slopes; the islets dotting the deep-water bay are similarly forested.[57] The following is Sparrman's description:

Little waterfalls and brooks, peeping forth here and there from the mountains towards the sunlight, crystal clear and shining silver, could hardly fail to make a most lovely effect . . . Enormous mast-trees raised their cedar-like tops proudly and majestically high above the other tall trees in the valleys; the flight of sea birds and pelicans along the shores, and various chirpings and pleasant songs of the land-birds in the nearby dells, enlivened the whole scene. What a splendid contrast to storms, ice and the occasional scream of a penguin in a boundless Antarctic sea![58]

The astronomers were similarly euphoric. Once a site had been cleared at 'Astronomer's Point', William Wales set up a portable observatory and installed a barometer, thermometer and other instruments. Young George Forster thought that taming an acre of wilderness in a few days, which the locals could not have cleared in three months, was the clearest possible demonstration of the superiority of European civilisation over Polynesian barbarism.[59] His father was much more disgruntled and dyspeptic. The local flowers had already bloomed and died, making it impossible for George to apply his beloved Linnaean taxonomy to the local flora. He worked out his frustration by shooting huge numbers of local birds, which he stuffed and mounted in his cabin. Yet that elicited a typical complaint from Johann, who was already angry that Cook had so demeaned his status on the voyage in the Southern Ocean as to have cattle and goats, brought below to survive the storms, huddled in the hallway outside his cabin. There they urinated and excreted freely, causing an unspeakable foetor in Herr Professor's quarters. Now the cabin, not yet recovered from the pent-up stench, was stuffed to bursting with specimens; surely, Johann reasoned, dedication to science should be rewarded with a bigger stateroom.[60] Forster senior, in short, was what would be called in the modern idiom a 'whinger'. Cook could barely tolerate him; he had all Banks's irritating quirks without his money and social status, while the men had no sympathy at all for a man who was being paid £4,000 for the voyage – more even than Cook himself.

Cook was keen to establish friendly contact with the Maoris but, although clear signs of human habitation were seen, the locals were at first shy of contact. One canoe came close to the ship and the occupants gazed at the white men for half an hour before making off. Cook mentally shrugged and sent his men out hunting. Their bags were impressive – ducks, seals, fowls to supplement the plentiful fish. Then from 3 to 6 April there was an intermission, as teeming, pelting rain forced the explorers to hunker down. Finally, on the 6th, when the rains had ceased, Cook made meaningful contact with the locals, whom modern anthropology has identified as a migratory group of hunter-gatherers known as Ngāti Māmoe.[61] That evening while out in his boat he met a man and two women, who did not draw away at his approach. He proved adept at diplomacy, making all the right gestures and throwing gifts out of the boat to encourage the nervous natives. Both Forster and Elliott, who were with Cook that night, were deeply impressed by the captain's skill at conciliating the apprehensive trio.[62] Cook came to regret his facility, for the younger of the two women, once launched on incomprehensible talk, could not be halted. Cook commented that her 'volubility of tongue exceeded anything I have ever met'. One of the sailors was more scathing: 'women did not want tongue in any part of the world'.[63] Next day Cook visited his new friends in their hut; he brought gifts but found them uninterested in anything but hatchets and spike nails, which they sought with avidity. Heavy rain on 10–11 April again interrupted the tentative entente, but on the 12th a much larger party of Maoris visited the ship, not without trepidation. The visit was a curious one. Bemused by the different uniforms, the Maoris seemed unable to grasp that all on board were male and took some of the seamen for women. Cook recorded that one young woman showed an extraordinary fondness for a particular seaman until she discovered his sex, after which she shrank away in revulsion. Cook's reaction was phlegmatic: 'Whether it was that she before took him for one of her own sex or that the man, in order to discover himself, had taken some liberties with her which she thus resented, I know not.'[64]

Cook had the ship completely overhauled and was ready to put to sea by 29 April, but contrary winds delayed him until 11 May. Storms were blowing in from the Tasman Sea, so the officers and scientists went on shooting and exploring trips. On one of these, Pickersgill, exploring an inlet, was trapped in the open for thirty-six hours in a violent thunderstorm. Johann Forster, never the most dauntless soul, was thrown into consternation by the unique mixture of snow, hail, thunder and lightning, and in 'we're all doomed' mood expressed the opinion that to venture out into the ocean was to invite certain catastrophe.[65] Cook fell ill, probably with rheumatic fever, with violent pains in the groin and foot, caused, it was thought, by sitting too long in wet clothes. Always one to play things down, Cook referred to his malady as 'a cold', but it was bad enough to stop him going on any of the reconnaissance or exploring missions. He spent the time writing up a detailed account of Dusky Bay, which he considered one of his best harbours yet.[66] Finally, on the 11th, Cook got out of the bay and began making his way slowly up the west coast of South Island in a 'prodigious swell from the south-west which broke with great violence on all shores which were exposed to it',[67] hoping to fetch Queen Charlotte Sound and find the *Adventure* at the rendezvous there. The seas continued high all the way up to Cape Farewell. On 17 May, as the *Resolution* was heading for Cook Strait, with the wind boxing the compass, half a dozen waterspouts suddenly appeared. These were the dangerous tornadic waterspouts, essentially tornadoes on water though less destructive than the land-based variety. They could have done considerable damage to the ship, especially its mast and sails, so that when one came within fifty yards of them, the sailors were naturally in a state of consternation. The correct response is to put the ship at right angles to the spout, but everything happened too fast for evasive action. Fortunately the spout sheered off at the last moment and slithered off jerkily to the north-east.[68] Next morning, when they arrived at the entrance to Queen Charlotte Sound, the *Resolution* fired a salvo. To universal joy they heard the answering boom of the *Adventure*'s cannons.

When Furneaux came on board the *Resolution* to make his report, Cook learned much of interest, not all of it pleasing and little of it particularly redounding to the credit of the *Adventure*'s captain. After the separation on 8 February, Furneaux reasoned that if the official purpose of the expedition was the search for the Great Southern Continent, his best bet was to follow a track midway between the one taken by Tasman in 1642 and the one he knew Cook intended to follow; that would at least preclude the fluke possibility of there being land in the middle. At the beginning of March, at longitude 106E, he turned north towards Van Diemen's Land and sighted the south-west coast of Tasmania. A year earlier, the French explorer Marc-Joseph Marion du Fresne had been there and had run into a hostile reception.[69] Furneaux anchored off Bruny Island and took on wood and water; after four days he left, having done very little work as botanist, scientist and naturalist; for all that, the few rare specimens he did collect secured him a place in botanical history.[70] Furneaux knew that he should really circumnavigate Tasmania and follow the strait between it and the Australian mainland to Cook's 1770 landfalls,[71] but squally weather, islands and breakers, which would have been a challenge to Cook, were merely a deterrent to him. He was no explorer: he believed in fleeing danger and taking the line of least resistance. The fact that he decided to clear for New Zealand without further ado is in itself circumstantial evidence for the suspicious disappearance in the fog on 8 February. Furneaux wanted to go into winter quarters as soon as possible, and his men were with him on this. After the usual stormy passage across the Tasman Sea he reached Ship Cove on 7 April and celebrated by issuing an extra ration of brandy.[72] There had been frequent contact with the Maoris in the six weeks since then, but their behaviour had been capricious and Furneaux, fearing an attack, ordered six carriage guns set up on deck. Whether the Maoris had really had aggressive intent, thoughts of Mars soon turned to those of Venus and a roaring trade in prostitution developed, with the Maori women offering themselves in return for nails. The news that this desirable item was for sale sucked in more and more Maori canoes, all of them offering women for trade. The peaceful intercourse came to an end on 24 April when war canoes made an attempt on Bayly's improvised observatory (he had acted exactly the same way as Wales in Dusky Bay) and later tried to intercept the jolly boat. Furneaux brought the *Adventure* in closer to shore so that the shore encampment was within range of his guns. There matters had rested until Cook's arrival.[73]

Thus far Cook had heard a narrative denoting a competent but not very enterprising seaman, and what seemed to be an over-liberal and overindulgent commander. As the account was amplified by Furneaux and others, Cook's attitude to his second in command darkened. Furneaux seemed to have run the exact opposite of a tight ship. Lieutenant Scott, commanding the marines on *Adventure*, was a prickly martinet who objected even to his captain 'giving him laws'. On 16 February, while still in the Antarctic Ocean, Scott acted so insolently in the officers' mess that Furneaux took him by the shoulders and threw him out of the Great Cabin. The word throughout the ship was that Scott was deranged, could not take a joke, construed everything as an affront to his 'honour', and generally lived up to the stereotype of the mad Scotsman.[74] There was obviously a strained atmosphere on the *Adventure*, for a few days later a midshipman on watch at the forecastle came running aft in a state of terror, claiming that he had just seen his father's ghost.[75] Then, as if the storms in the Tasman Sea had not given Furneaux enough to deal with, there was a major fracas halfway across on the journey to New Zealand. Bayly was in bed asleep at midnight when First Lieutenant Kempe, Second Lieutenant Burney, Mr Andrews the surgeon, and a midshipman by the name of Hawksey came hammering at his door. All hopelessly drunk and in need of further fuel, they demanded that Bayly give them the brandy he kept in his cabin. When he refused indignantly, they got hold of hammers and chisels and tried to rip the hinges off his door. The incident was about to turn violent, with Bayly nearly apoplectic, when an angry Furneaux appeared and ordered the drunks to their bed.[76] On some ships this incident would have been considered a court-martial offence, but how could Furneaux condemn the offenders when he would have had to drag his senior officers to the bar? It all spelled a serious lack of discipline and leadership, which Cook was not slow to note. But possibly the thing that angered him most was that whereas the *Resolution* was scurvy-free, there were several bad cases on the *Adventure* – which meant that Furneaux had not been following Cook's regime of diet and cleanliness. Cook had to speak firmly to Furneaux about this and tell him to do better. He stopped short of reprimanding him; it was a fixed principle with Cook that one never made a written criticism about a subordinate officer if the document were to be seen by the Admiralty.[77]

It was clear to Cook that Furneaux had unwittingly encouraged a Lotus-land syndrome since arriving in New Zealand and that the hedonistic and scrimshanking *Adventure* crew were settling down complacently to a winter of sex and somnolence. He decided to crack the whip and told Furneaux firmly he must prepare to put to sea at the earliest opportunity. This might have seemed an imperious and even eccentric decision, since orthodox naval captains always rested in the winter season, but Cook justified the decision to Furneaux and the world on the grounds that he could not possibly carry out the multitudinous orders of the Admiralty in three years if he had to keep taking winter breaks.[78] This was plausible, and in any case there was nothing Furneaux could do about it. Cook minuted that his second in command 'readily agreed' to his ideas. Short of staging a mutiny, Furneaux had no choice. There was much grumbling among the *Adventure*'s crew – the seamen on the *Resolution* had presumably been broken by Cook's iron will by now – but Cook had a secondary motive for his unpopular decision. He loathed the sexuality and coupling between seamen and Maori women he saw all around him, and knew the only way he could stop this was by getting out to sea. 'To our shame as civilized Christians,' he wrote, 'we debauch their morals already too prone to vice and introduce among them wants and perhaps diseases which they never before knew and which serves only to disturb that happy tranquillity they and their forefathers had enjoyed. If anyone denies the truth of this assertion let him tell me what the Natives of the whole extent of America have gained by the commerce they had with Europeans.'[79] Beaglehole thinks this effusion untypical of Cook and suspects the influence of Forster and Sparrman.[80] The inference seems justified, for Sparrman noted:

> Captain Cook states that on his first visit in the *Endeavour* he had reason to consider the New Zealand women more chaste than those in other South Sea Islands, and that whatever favours a few of them might have granted to the people in the ship, it was generally done in a private manner, and the [Maori] men did not seem to interest themselves much in it, but that on the second visit the [Maori] men were the chief promoters of a shameful traffic. Undoubtedly the most surprising point about all this is there should have been some members of a civilised nation who were not revolted by the embraces of cannibal women, which one would have thought disgusting enough without the painting, smearing, filth and vermin.[81]

Cook distracted himself from such gloomy thoughts by schemes for 'improvement'. He planted vegetable gardens, coaxed the locals to tend them, and sowed wheat, peas, carrots, parsnips and strawberries. On 20 May he landed the only ram and ewe that had survived the nightmare journey from the Cape, but two days later they were dead, having eaten a poisonous plant. 'Thus my hopes of stocking this country with a breed of sheep were blasted in a moment,' he noted. A fortnight later he put ashore a male and female goat, while Furneaux landed a boar and two breeding sows. Cook had been told that the Maoris would not kill these animals since they were afraid of them, but he had no confidence in this folk wisdom and took a more functional view: 'As the natives knew nothing of their being left behind, it may be some time before they are discovered.'[82] There were signs that domestic animals and the Maoris were not natural soulmates. Cook continued to encourage friendly contacts with the locals and one of the shipboard visits was from a man named Te Wahanga who proved to be, to use R. L. Stevenson's words, 'a crop for the drink'. The Maoris knew nothing of alcohol, not even the kava of the Pacific islands, but once started Te Wahanga made up for lost time. Johann Forster gave him a glass of Madeira which he liked so much that Forster followed with two glasses of Muscatel, which soon had his Maori guest reeling around drunk. A few days later Te Wahanga returned with his small son Koa, to whom Cook gave a present of a white shirt. The boy was delighted and paraded round the deck in triumph, but the ostentation upset Old Will, the ship's billy goat, with consequences described by Cook: 'This freedom used by him [Koa] offended Old Will the ram goat, who gave him a butt with his horns and knocked him backwards on the deck. Will would have repeated his blow had not some of the people come to the boy's assistance.'[83] To the Maoris the goat was an exotic animal, while they took for granted the fauna that so amazed and intrigued the Europeans: not just the kangaroo Furneaux's men had seen in Tasmania, but the sea lion – a new mammal for the seamen which they fired at and chased for an hour but could not catch. Ironically, the only significant long-term change in the animal world as a result of the European advent was that hundreds of rats came ashore from Cook's ships and devastated the local bird population – yet another regrettable unintended consequence of Cook's voyages of discovery.[84]

Cook's secret irritation with Furneaux was exacerbated by an incident which may appear trivial but which to Cook loomed large. Bayly had been involved in the drunken contretemps in the middle of the Tasman Sea and now he produced findings which suggested that Cook's charts located New Zealand 1'20 too far to the east. Even worse, Bayly's figures were borne out by Wales's observations at Dusky Bay. With his tendency to overreact, Cook worried away at the implicit criticism of his abilities and demonstrated the 'short fuse' cross-grained character his associates were increasingly beginning to notice.[85] Cook found his alleged error 'astounding' and kept coming back to the subject in his journal, unable to decide whether his figures were errors and if Wales and Bayly could be relied on. 'Errors as great as this will frequently be found in such observations as these,' he begins in exculpation before having second thoughts. 'Errors I call them though in reality they may be none but only differences which cannot be avoided.' Then he changed tack entirely and oscillated between the suspicion that Wales and Bayly were unreliable and the cavalier assertion that it did not matter much anyway. 'I cannot think the error so great as these two astronomers have made it but supposing it is it will not much effect [*sic*] either geography or navigation but for the benefit of both I thought proper to mention it though few I believe will look upon it as [a] capital error.'[86] Here we surely see the unconscious Cook at work. 'Capital error' has resonances of the capital punishment of the Bloody Code, as if Cook in the inmost recesses of his mind virtually regarded his own mistake as a hanging offence. He protested too much, for he was only out by 40 minutes, not $1'20''$; Bayly was out by 40 minutes, having put New Zealand too far west, and even Wales was 30 minutes out.[87] Yet at some level the whole affair increased Cook's distaste for Furneaux and the *Adventure*, and it may well have been a factor, along with those previously mentioned, in his decision to nail Furneaux down with explicit written orders complete with meticulous contingency plans so that he could no longer exercise discretion. It is a fair inference that Furneaux found this patronising, but really he had only himself to blame.[88]

As the *Adventure* and *Resolution* sailed east into the Pacific from New Zealand, Cook pondered the conundrum of the Maoris and how everything about them seemed opaque, contradictory and ambiguous. There was first the confusion arising from the alleged readiness of the New Zealand aboriginals to sell their children, which later proved to be a mere canard.[89] Then there was the issue of prostitution and casual intercourse with the sailors, which presented a picture of sexuality unlike the situation on the first voyage. This, Cook thought, was deplorable, and it had got to the point where no man could ever be near a woman without the presumption that sexual congress was intended. On one occasion Hodges wanted to paint a young woman, but when she appeared in the saloon she disrobed and lay down on the floor; she appeared discomfited and astonished when Hodges made her sit in a chair so that he could do her portrait.[90] Every proposition asserted about the Maoris seemed refutable by an equal and opposite proposition. Elliott, for example, swore up and down that he had seen unmistakable proof of cannibalism.[91] Wales, by contrast, in dogmatic scientist mood, said he had not seen a scintilla of such evidence. He was prepared to accept that the nomads of Dusky Bay might not practise it, but how could there be an absence of traces in Queen Charlotte Sound when that was the very place where the crew of the *Endeavour* had found 'unimpeachable' evidence in 1769?[92] Then there was the Maoris' alleged bellicosity. On this trip Cook had seen no signs of it and had had frequent friendly contacts with large bodies of Maoris, sometimes entertaining ninety at a time. Yet previous experience indicated extreme volatility and unpredictability. There was Furneaux's experience in Queen Charlotte Sound in April and, more shockingly, the now well known story of the du Fresne expedition. On his way back to Tahiti to deliver Ahutoru to his homeland, Marc-Joseph Marion du Fresne had anchored in the Bay of Islands after an unwelcoming reception in Tasmania. Unfortunately the French sailors broke a local *tapu* by fishing in Manawaora Bay. The Maoris retaliated by a surprise attack: on 12 July 1772 they killed du Fresne and twenty of his men and then ate them. The French struck back by burning down a village and killing 250 Maori, then hurriedly decamping.[93]

Most bizarre was the Maori attitude to Tupaia, whose bones now lay mouldering in a Batavian lime pit. On the *Endeavour* voyage Tupaia had attracted large crowds of Maori listeners as he expounded the history and legends of Polynesia, with particular reference to the creation myths. He had also told them that the *Endeavour* was his floating palace and the white men his servants. The Maori came to regard him as a demigod. When Furneaux arrived in New Zealand almost the first question put to him was where Tupaia was. When told he was dead, they assumed the Europeans must have killed him – which, of course, in an indirect sense they had. The Forsters later reported that a funeral chant was performed in his memory.[94] Cook found that Tupaia's fame had spread through both islands and raised a query: 'It may be asked, that if these people had never seen the *Endeavour* or any of its crew, how they became acquainted with the name of Tupaia or to have in their possession such articles as they could only have got from that ship. To this it may be answered that the name of Tupaia was at that time so popular among them that it would be no wonder if at this time it is known over the great part of New Zealand; the name of Tupaia may be as familiar to those who never saw him as to those who did.'[95] George Forster offered an explanation: 'So much had [Tupaia's] superior knowledge, and his ability to converse in their language, rendered him valuable and beloved even among a nation in a state of barbarism. Perhaps with the capacity which Providence had allotted to him, and which had been cultivated no farther than the simplicity of his education would permit, he was more adapted to raise the New Zealanders to a state of civilization similar to that of his own islands, than ourselves, to whom the want of the intermediate links, which connect their narrow views to our extended sphere of knowledge, must prove an obstacle in such an undertaking.'[96] Tupaia indeed continued to be a legend in New Zealand and was still remembered in Tolaga Bay as late as the 1830s when white traders conversed with the locals.[97] None of this can have been welcome news to Cook, with his low opinion of Tupaia. It remained to be seen whether Purea's high priest and adviser still retained a high reputation in the islands of his birth.

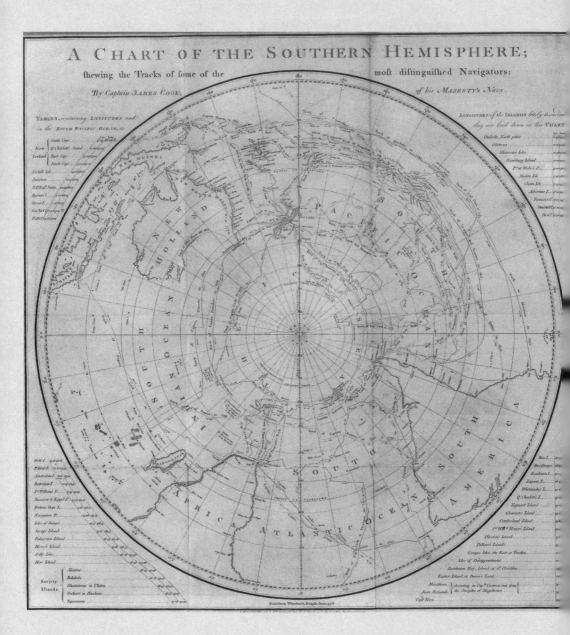

A CHART OF THE SOUTHERN HEMISPHERE;

shewing the Tracks of some of the   most distinguished Navigators:

By Captain JAMES COOK,   of his MAJESTY's Navy.

Guilielmus Whitchurch, Sculpsit. Anno 1776.

CHAPTER TEN

Tongans and Maoris

THE second act of the five-act drama began depressingly. Once again the villain was the weather. The sea state alternated between fresh gales and hard gales, high seas running almost permanently, and both *Resolution* and *Adventure* taking a battering, with split topsails and continual reefing and double-reefing and striking of yards. A heavy swell came in relentlessly from the south and south-west. At first Cook sailed south, to about 45S or the latitude of the southern tip of South Island. Then he decided go down to 47S. Next he turned north-east and reached the 40th degree of latitude at longitude 133′30″W before turning sharply north. Essentially, then, he sailed a more southerly, unknown, part of the Pacific then bisected his routes to and from Tahiti in 1769. Every day the ocean seemed to present fresh hazards, and the hollow seas caused by the swell threw up unexpected dangers: 'A sudden jerk of the tiller carried the man at the wheel clear over it. Luckily the officer of the watch caught it, and replaced him, and put a man on the lee side to assist him. They had been there scarce ten minutes before another jerk carried the man on the weather side over again. The tiller stayed not a moment a-weather, but returned with such velocity as brought the man on the lee side over to windward.'[1] The domestic beasts suffered grievously. On 9 July a goat fell overboard; Cook put about at once and lowered a boat; the goat was rescued but died soon afterwards from the effects of the ducking. It was almost as if the animal world caught the sense of being in a chaotic world and responded accordingly. On 2 August Clerke noted: 'This morning a bitch littered on board when a young New Zealand whelp fell to and had devoured the best part of one of the pups . . . before he was detected – and then 'twas with many hard thumps that he was prevailed upon to spare the rest.'[2] At last, in August, Cook found calmer seas and for one day was even able to set his studding sails. He crossed Carteret's 1767 track on 1 August and tried in vain to find Pitcairn Island. Everything he saw and intuited told him that the Great Southern Continent was a myth but, perfectionist that he was, he wanted his refutation of that mythical land to be based on facts, not conjecture.

Meanwhile things had not been going well on the *Adventure*. Once again scurvy was cutting a swathe through its company. Here is something of a mystery. Cook had given Furneaux as strong a talking-to in New Zealand as any commanding officer could, short of issuing an official reprimand, and Furneaux had promised to mend his ways and rigorously implement Cook's anti-scurvy regime. So what had gone wrong? Once again a suspicion of Machiavellianism in Furneaux arises. Was he to some extent encouraging scurvy among his crew by simply ignoring Cook's advice once the two ships were at sea? He knew that in those circumstances Cook would have no choice but to seek an early landfall. There is very strong circumstantial evidence that Furneaux did not relish his commander's quest for Terra Australis, which he saw as a search for cloud cuckoo land, and that he particularly disliked day after day of gales, storms and high seas. Since leaving Cape Town he had entered many sour and implicitly critical remarks in his log, of which that on 23 November 1772 is the most despairing: 'tossed at the mercy of the waves for near three weeks without one moderate day . . . the sea making a continual breach over us'.[3] Furneaux was the type of seaman who could endure the tribulations of the ocean for a definite purpose, but found Cook's Magian rovings a particular trial. The *Adventure*'s cook died of scurvy on 23 July, though Cook knew nothing of this until a tiny gap in the weather on the 29th allowed him to send a boat to the sister ship. He then learned of twenty men prostrated with the disease. What was Furneaux doing? he wondered, and he must have wondered out loud, for Furneaux heard of his commander's anger and sent a reassuring message on the next fine day (6 August) to say that things were much improved and the 'flux' gone.[4] Whether he was lying and trying to placate an irate Cook, or whether there had been a temporary blip in the ravages of the disease, by 10 August he was forced to admit that a third of his crew were scurvy cases. So depleted was the *Adventure*'s company that Cook had to transfer some of his seamen from the *Resolution* so that the ship could be worked at all.[5] But things were very serious now and Cook could not just go on cruising. He decided to make for Tahiti, to give the stricken men a chance to recover.

From the environs of Pitcairn the track to Tahiti lay due west through the Tuamotu archipelago, a notorious hazard for shipping.[6] Dangerous coral reefs, tricky shoals and islets, treacherous currents and high surf were there in abundance, and as he ticked off the landmarks – Tauere, Tekokota, Marutea, Anna, Tuamotu – Cook found his seamanship tested to the limit. He knew he was clear of danger only when the large swell came in again from the south. Soon he picked up the landmark of Osnaburg (Mehetia), the gateway to the Society Islands. The ships passed the eastern edge of Tahiti on 15 August and at dusk that evening the familiar outline of the Tahitian mountains was clearly visible. With the shore distant about thirty miles, Cook retired at midnight, having left definite instructions for the course to be steered. When he awoke at dawn, he found that the ship was on the wrong course and heading for the reef; obviously there had been gross incompetence, possibly sleeping on duty, by the officer at the watch. Angrily Cook gave orders to haul away to the north, but by now it was dead calm, and the natural motion of the sea was carrying the ships closer to the shore.[7] The crisis continued for most of the day. Outside the reef it was too deep to anchor, but the opening in the reef to a safe haven was too narrow for them to pass. Cook tried one of his newfangled warping machines which the Admiralty had sworn by, but it proved useless. On top of the danger from the reef there was a grave risk of collision with the *Adventure*. Finally Furneaux's anchors held, by which time the two ships were almost touching; the *Resolution* was in less than three fathoms and at every fall of a wave her bottom stuck. When the bower anchor also proved useless, Cook had it cut away, and sent out a kedge to tow him, using coasting anchors. Sweating and pulling with prodigious effort, the seamen prevailed with sheer muscle power, helped both by the slackening of the current and the arrival of a soft breeze from the land. It was 7 p.m. before the boats towed the *Resolution* to safety. Cook sent them back to help the *Adventure* but Furneaux had now got her under sail, leaving behind three anchors, a cable and two hawsers. It had been twelve hours of non-stop nightmare, and the appalled Sparrman saw a new side to Cook. The normally mild-mannered captain had sworn like a foul-mouthed old salt during the long struggle to save the ship. At the end of the ordeal Cook was covered in sweat and completely exhausted. Sparrman visited him in his cabin to bring him a large quantity of Swedish brandy, which Cook quaffed with gusto.[8] A hearty meal restored him to his usual spirits, though the company still had to spend a rainy and squally night offshore before they could anchor next morning in Vaitepiha Bay.

It had been another close call, almost as hellish an experience as the two jousts with death on the Great Barrier Reef two years earlier but at least, here in the Tautira district of Tahiti, Cook could get his sick men ashore and fed with fresh food, especially fruit. The only man to die, ironically, was the marine Isaac Taylor, from the *Resolution*, whose illness (consumption) had nothing to do with scurvy; he was buried at sea. The stricken men on the *Adventure* soon made a full recovery. Cook sent out boats to try to recover the lost anchors: they found the *Resolution*'s but the *Adventure*'s were gone for ever. Still, things could have been worse and they could easily have been castaways, victims of shipwreck. Yet if Tahiti in this sense represented security, it did not take Cook long to be reminded of why he had such ambivalent feelings about the island paradise. Simply put, Tahiti offered two menaces: pilfering and women.[9] The voyagers had scarcely come to rest in Vaitepiha Bay before the thefts began. The Tahitians had come out to welcome the ships even before they reached land, and while Cook and his men were fighting for their lives off the reef, dozens of canoes plied alongside offering plantains and other produce for sale. Reviewing the recent near-disaster Cook concluded that women might have been at the bottom of it, that the delinquent officer concerned might have left his post to make love to one of the first dusky lovelies who climbed aboard in the small hours. Certainly after daybreak one of his officers was caught in flagrante. He was just 'boarding' a girl in his cabin when the 'all hands on deck' alarm was sounded as the tide swept the ships towards the coral. Rushing aloft, he did his duty, only to find on returning to the cabin that evening that his would-be paramour had stolen his bed sheets.[10] Once the ships were in the bay, the locals tried to swarm aboard but were lashed away from the sides. When Cook and his men went ashore they were disappointed to find that they had once again arrived in a season of dearth and all trade in hogs and fowl with the visitors had been banned by the local chief. He turned out to be the son of the old man Vehiatua, whom Cook had met on his tour of the island in 1769 and who had recently died. At first Vehiatua the younger was reluctant to meet the Europeans, for reasons Cook could not fathom, but contact was eventually made. Vehiatua seemed friendly, and he liked to stroll arm in arm with Cook along the beach, thus conferring on the European the status of *arii nui*; Cook, however, thought the affability a mask and suspected that his host was really shifty and unreliable. Unable to winkle further pigs out of him, when he departed Cook left Pickersgill behind to see if he could cajole some from the people; he succeeded, and rewarded himself with a night of love in the harem of Chief Reti, the man Bougainville had befriended.[11]

The sojourn at Vaitepiha Bay was marked by frequent thefts, which in the end, inevitably, led to shots being fired. Cook welcomed a local chieftain and his sons on board for a meal, but was then outraged to find that one of the sons had attempted to steal a silver knife and a pewter spoon from the Great Cabin. Indignantly the sailors threw the young man overboard, but he swam to a canoe and then laughed and pulled faces at them. Cook was now angry at this flagrant ingratitude and fired a musket ball at the reprobate. Alarmed, he dived into the water, but when he surfaced Cook fired another shot at him. The young man and his accomplices then paddled off at speed in a double canoe; Cook ordered out a boat to chase them, but when the boat got close to shore it was met with a fusillade of stones. Matters were rapidly escalating. Cook then got into his own boat with a posse of armed men and rowed for the shore, to the accompanying whistle of a four-pounder being fired overhead at the locals.[12] Fortunately the crowd on the shore dispersed, but they left behind the canoes, which Cook seized. Many observers felt that Cook had overreacted; after all, in the end nothing was stolen, and the would-be thief was guilty of no more than cheek and schoolboy impertinence. One of the sailors later wrote: 'Is it not very natural, when a people see a company of strangers come among them, and without ceremony cut down their trees, gather their fruit and seize their animals, that such a people should use as little ceremony with the strangers, as the strangers do with them; if so, against whom is the criminality to be charged, the Christian or the savage?'[13] Next morning a deputation of locals came to the *Resolution* to ask for the return of the double canoes. Faced with a threat of a total trade ban if he did not comply, Cook acquiesced. Relations then improved dramatically. The Tahitians were intrigued by their visitors – most of them had never seen a European before – and were bemused by their white skins and powerful weapons, to say nothing of the 'magic' of Hodges's sketches. Young George Forster, an able mimic as well as a superlative linguist, had the locals convulsed with laughter by the way he could imitate their accents and clichés to perfection. Cook, as always, remained mildly irritated by the Forsters; doubtless he reflected that they could sightsee and botanise while he had to exercise the daily burden of command. But he certainly agreed with them that Vaitepiha Bay was an idyllic spot – for George Forster the most beautiful place he had seen so far.[14]

After a week Cook told Vehiatua the younger that it was time to go, that since there was such a dearth of meat he would proceed to Matavai Bay. Hearing of the proposed visit to enemy territory, Vehiatua frowned and seemed most displeased until Cook placated him by ordering a Scots sailor to play the bagpipes. The skirl of the pibroch enchanted Vehiatua, who took further pleasure from an examination of Cook's watch. On a sentimental level he was sorry to see his guests go, though glad enough at an instrumental one, since they depleted his food supplies. Even more sorry to leave were the Forsters who seemed to think that they had, in a sense, come home. While George praised the lush and fertile scenery, Johann compared the locality to the Elysian Fields of the *Aeneid*. Johann in fact had something of a Virgil fetish and had been known to console himself with favourite passages even as the monster storms of the Antarctic howled outside.[15] Leaving Pickersgill to complete his hog-buying mission and then catch up as fast as he could, Cook sailed for Matavai Bay on 25 August. He had expected to be greeted by Tu but, though he later learned that Tu had been on the beach when the European vessels first came in sight, he was not there when they landed. His followers, however, were in droves, and they gave an enthusiastic welcome to the

strangers and even more to those who were not strangers.[16] Among these were
Samuel Gibson, in 1769 a lovesick marine who had tried to desert from the
Endeavour and Pickersgill, now on his third consecutive visit to Tahiti. The
Tahitians asked after Banks, Solander and Tupaia, but showed no interest at all
in Ahutoru. A minor chieftain had been delegated to lay out a welcome mat,
and when Cook came ashore and asked where Tu was, the chieftain replied
that he was too afraid to greet him. This may have been genuine, for it will be
remembered that in 1769 Tuteha, then the real power in the land, had kept Tu
under wraps and not allowed him to meet Cook; doubtless he had also kept the
youth in check by fearsome tales of the white man. The first night was spent
by the sailors in a veritable orgy with the local women, but once again it was
noticeable that only women of the lower class offered themselves; as in 1769,
girls from the aristocracy and middle class held aloof from sexual encounters.[17] Cook always held aloof from casual coupling, vainly trying to set an
example to his men so that venereal disease would not spread, but given
human nature, this was like the legendary papal bull against the comet. The
low-class island women despised Cook as an impotent old man, but they gave
their favours lustily to men such as Pickersgill and Clerke.[18] We are not told
whether Gibson renewed his tryst with his local lovely, but we are told that he
was in the thick of the mass lovemaking.

If a week is a long time in politics, in Tahitian politics four years could seem
like an eternity. By the time he had been in Matavai Bay no more than a couple
of days, Cook had pieced together the story of a great civil war that had
occurred in Tahiti since he had last been there. It now became clear why young
Vehiatua had been reluctant to meet the Europeans. Three years of inter-island
warfare had altered the political landscape significantly. In 1770 Vehiatua the
elder had launched an attack on Tuteha, who was betrayed when Purea and
Amo went over to Vehiatua. There was a dreadful battle at sea, where rival
fleets clashed at close quarters and warriors boarded each other's boats, for all
the world like a mini-Lepanto. The loss of life was terrific and the sea was said
to have run red with blood, with sharks cruising the incarnadine ocean in the
latter stages to pick off the wounded. The battle continued on the beach, but
eventually Vehiatua won a great victory; a mountain of skulls was set up near
Taunoa, thereby demonstrating that the Mongols had no monopoly on this
particular form of barbarism.[19] But Tuteha was not among the slaughtered, and
Vehiatua could not rest until he had finished off his deadly rival. Tuteha meanwhile was preparing a bold counter-stroke of revenge. In March 1773 he and
Tu led a large host against Tahiti-iti; in the ensuing battle Tuteha was killed. It
was said that Tuteha and Vehiatua had confronted each other in single combat,
but this should be taken with a pinch of salt; in heroic oral traditions heroes and

leaders always fight face to face, yet Vehiatua's age alone argues against this scenario. At all events Tuteha was killed and his army vanquished, along with Banks's friend Tepau. The bodies of the notable defeated were disembowelled and hung in breadfruit trees.[20] Once again Tu survived and fled into the mountains. Vehiatua marched to Porionnu and Matavai and laid waste the country. Tu, reduced to a paper tiger, some months later concluded a humiliating treaty with Vehiatua whereby he was shorn of all real power yet confirmed as *arii rahi* of Tahiti-nui. This enabled all the other high chiefs or *arii* on the island to patronise Tu. But when Cook returned, young Vehiatua feared that he might feel constrained by a code of honour – he had been Tuteha's friend despite their many differences – to ally himself with Tu and use his firepower to help him mount a campaign of revenge. Cook wisely kept away from direct involvement in island politics, although he and his successors always supported Tu against his rivals; Cook discreetly, Bligh ten years later, blatantly and overtly.[21] Playing the long game and confident of British support against the other *arii*, Tu gradually became the dominant power on the island, and in 1815 his son completed the conquest of the whole of Tahiti.[22]

To complicate matters even further, the Spanish had finally bestirred themselves and tried to reassert ownership of their 'lake'. Their reaction to the Pacific craze of the 1760s was to reclaim their ancient 'rights' and, in a last flicker of activity, to try to relive the glory days of Mendaña and Quirós. They became the second set of Europeans to land on Easter Island in 1770 and in November 1772 Domingo de Bocnechea landed in Tahiti in the *Aguila* out of Callao, with plenipotentiary powers granted by the viceroy of Peru – perhaps fortunately for him, during an interval in the bloody civil war. On what evidence one knows not, but he decided that it would not be worthwhile for other European nations to occupy Tahiti or to have any significant presence there. He therefore returned to Spain with the advice that a permanent Catholic mission should be established in the Society Islands and that the ploy adopted by the Spanish in the Far East in the sixteenth century should be utilised: conversions to Catholicism would open the way to trade and eventual political domination. Boenechea also indulged in what was now becoming something of a favourite European pastime: removing Polynesians to the culture shock of life in Europe. He was on the island from 8 November to 20 December 1772 and took away four Tahitians; by the time he returned in November 1774, Cook had been and gone twice.[23]

Cook at first suspected that it was Tuteha's bad influence that had prevented Tu from coming to meet him, but the more he pondered it, the more he thought there were two other possibilities. Tu might have thought Cook had been 'made over' by Vehiatua on Tahiti-iti and was no longer his family's friend. Or he might have connected his arrival with the recent advent of the Spanish and imagined that there was a general coalition of the *haoles* to conquer Tahiti. At any rate, Cook decided that the only way to break the impasse was to visit Tu himself. On 26 August he, Furneaux, the Forsters, and a large party set out for Tu's village. When they arrived they were received hospitably by the chief himself, whom Cook described as about 30 (looking older than this age), six feet tall and handsome.[24] Cook presented him with gifts and Tu promised them some hogs, while stressing that this was a season of dearth. Yet when Cook suggested a visit aboard the *Resolution*, Tu turned pale and declined, saying he was afraid of the ship's big guns. He was eventually mollified when Cook unleashed his bagpiper on him: Tu was just as beguiled as Vehiatua had been. In the end Cook persuaded him to make the trip to the ship on the following day, and in the meantime his party inspected Port Venus where, amazingly, all the buildings and tents were just as they had left them in 1769.

On the 27th Tu sent them a hog, some fish and fruit, and then appeared reluctantly for his onboard visit, after which Cook took him back in the boat. Tu took with him Johann Forster's spaniel, which he had seen and immediately coveted. Some of the onlookers suspected he had marked the dog down for his night's dinner, since Tahitians regarded dog as a delicacy. Forster seems to have handed his pet over without any sentimental regrets and indeed recorded his opinion that the European distaste for eating cats and dogs was mere cultural prejudice.[25] At Tu's village Cook and his party met Tuteha's mother, who tearfully told him of her son's death. Cook showed his esteem by giving her an axe, but then had to give Tu something even more lavish lest he felt upstaged; fortunately it had always been Cook's intention to introduce goats to Tahiti, so the present to Tu was a brace of these.[26] Tu was displeased by Cook's concern for the old lady; he seemed to be displacing on to her the pent-up resentment he had felt by being isolated, marginalised and patronised by Tuteha. Although the visit counted as a social success, it had not solved Cook's pressing food problems, so on the 28th he sent Pickersgill out on a wide sweep of the main island to buy hogs. Tu paid another visit and brought another hog, but made a point of going aboard the *Adventure* in preference to the *Resolution*, presumably trying to pay Cook back for his loss of 'face' because the captain had consoled Tuteha's mother. Cook retaliated by trying to make him realise what he had missed: he gave Tuteha's sister, who did board the *Resolution*, a sumptuous dress. The game of tit for tat continued when they all returned to Tu's village to attend a dance, and Cook staged another lachrymose encounter with Tuteha's mother.[27] On the 29th there was yet another visit to the village, when there was a more extended programme of dances and theatrical shows, and Cook presented Tu with a sword. Despite his decision to support him against the other *arii nui* of Tahiti, Cook had no very high opinion of Tu. He found him excessively timorous, and indeed Tu owned to the fault: he was scared of guns, scared of swords, scared of Europeans, scared of his own gods.[28]

The evening's festivities ended abruptly when, about 10 p.m., there were alarums and cries of murder. It turned out that some of Cook's sailors, used to the free and easy ways of the lower-class women, had been too free in their overtures to some of the high-born ladies. Cook was obliged to arrest his own men and clap them in irons. Next morning he had them flogged,[29] but this did not appease Tu, who was again sullen and reluctant to see Cook; when he did so he complained bitterly about the tumult caused by the sailors' rowdy behaviour. Cook pacified him by giving him three sheep – animals which the Tahitians regarded with nervous curiosity, being particularly unnerved by their bleating, and which Cook knew Tu wanted, as he had a genuine thirst for the acquisition of Europe's domestic beasts. Not to be outdone, Tu then presented his visitors with three hogs. The undertow of antipathy for Cook was still there, however, in his explicit statement that only one was for Cook, the others were for Furneaux and Johann Forster.[30] Pickersgill meanwhile had returned from Potatu, chief of Attahoura, whom Cook had known in 1769, with four hogs. He had also called at Papara and saw Purea, now living in straitened circumstances. Knowing very well that events not sentiment drove the Europeans, Purea immediately said: 'I haven't got any hogs.' She explained to Pickersgill that her son Tu had ostracised her because she and Amo had supported Vehiatua in the civil war; now even Amo had left her and had taken a new wife. Pickersgill, finding her very fat and indolent, was sorry for her. Against the pleadings of his people, Potatu insisted on going back with Pickersgill to meet his 'old friend' Cook.[31] He arrived just in time to witness the departure of the ships, which in itself was not without controversial incident. Poreo, a young man from the middling classes, along with his friends, devised a scam to get an axe and a spike-nail from the visitors. Poreo volunteered to sail with Pickersgill in exchange for these items, was taken on board but then had his friends intercept the *Resolution* in their canoe to say that Tu demanded that the youth be given back; had Cook consented, the Tahitians would then have been ahead with one axe and a nail on the deal. But Cook called their bluff and sailed on, bearing a tearful Poreo.[32]

Cook now set a course for the leeward island of Huahine. Cook sailed in correctly on the southern channel to Fare harbour but the *Adventure*, which both in itself and in its personnel seemed accident prone (the men flogged by Cook after the incident at Tu's village were from the *Adventure*), somehow took the northern channel and ended up grounded on the reef. Fortunately, this was a temporary grounding, not to be compared to the *Endeavour*'s trauma on the Barrier Reef; Cook had prepared contingency plans for just such an eventuality and had his boats tow the sister ship to its correct berth.[33] Not yet fully provisioned, Cook again sent out Pickersgill on a foraging expedition to the south side of the island, while he, Furneaux and Forster went to meet Ori, their host in 1769, who greeted them emotionally. Food shortages here seemed nothing like as bad as on Tahiti itself; no sooner had they exchanged gifts and Ori handed over four hogs than Pickersgill arrived back with fourteen more.[34] Cook surmised that the dearth on Tahiti had a twofold cause: the recent civil war, and the increasing numbers of foreign ships now calling at the main island. Yet even in Huahine all was not sweetness and light. Ori's people seem to have resented the chief's generosity, for next morning Cook was confronted by a troublemaking minor chief who brandished a club in each hand; Cook simply grabbed them and broke them. The chief seems to have been one of a rival faction led by an *arii* named Te Rii Taria, who thought Ori's reception of Cook was a mistake.[35] Meanwhile Anders Sparrman was set on, robbed, and stripped of all his clothes except his trousers. Cook complained bitterly to Ori, who wept publicly with mortification. He then ordered all the goods taken from Sparrman to be returned and to make sure it happened he offered himself as surety for his people's good behaviour, willingly going on board the *Resolution* as a hostage. Cook, now with all the food he needed, was furious, for the apprehension of the thieves meant delay and he intended to sail the next day. When no word of the thieves came in, Ori insisted on staying on board. In the end, after dining him lavishly, Cook took him back to his village. His people were so overjoyed that the white men had not harmed him that they brought large quantities of food to the ship. In the end there was almost more produce than Cook knew what to deal with: three entire boats full of hogs, fowl and fruit. Most of the stolen items were returned, including Sparrman's hanger and coat and even some oddments stolen from other officers that had not yet been missed.[36]

Although not all of Sparrman's clothes had been returned, when he bade farewell to Ori in an emotional scene on 7 September, Cook thought it better not to mention the matter, lest Ori felt humiliated and the atmosphere was ruined. Just as they were casting off, Ori came on board to say that he had finally caught the thieves and would Cook like to watch their punishment. Cook explained that his ships were already under way with fair winds, so he could not stop. Ori stayed on board until the *Resolution* was out on the open sea, then clambered down into his canoe and departed.[37] Huahine had proved a veritable cornucopia, for Cook's expedition was now carrying 300 hogs as well as the chickens and fruit. Once again the only cloud on the horizon came from Furneaux. He had decided to take on board the *Adventure* a young man named Omai, whom Cook thought useless at every level: he was of low birth and did not even possess the limited knowledge of the islands that Poreo had.[38] Shaking off such negative thoughts, Cook set a course for Raiatea and sailed up the west coast to Haamanino harbour at night, the dangerous passage made easier by the lights of fishermen on the reef. Next morning, 8 September, with contrary winds blowing right out of the harbour, Cook proved his seamanship by a display of extraordinary versatility. He 'borrowed', tacked and warped, taking all day to make safe anchorage; all Furneaux had to do was to observe and follow suit.[39] The local *arii nui*, Reo or Oreo, though not quite the favourite Ori was, ranked quite highly in Cook's affections and over the ensuing days he tried his best to live up to this estimate. Once again there was a lavish exchange of gifts: copious quantities of hogs were exchanged for beads and nails, and hundreds of fowl changed hands. As on the other islands, the seamen particularly prized the acquisition of roosters as these could be trained to become fighting cocks and tournaments staged to while away the hours before the mast.[40] There were dances and theatrical shows as well, even more elaborate than any they had seen before, for Raiatea was the headquarters of the *arioi* cult. Once again Pickersgill was dispatched on a foraging expedition. This seems bizarre when one thinks of the quantity of hogs already acquired, but to keep the animals alive until the time came to slaughter them large amounts of feed had to be amassed.[41]

Once again the complexities of island politics impinged on Cook. While the main island of Tahiti had been beset by civil war, Ori on Huahine had been involved in a vicious conflict with the men of Bora Bora. Cook never liked to take an overt part in these byzantine struggles but had been tempted to make an exception for his great friend Ori. By no means a fool, Ori realised that unleashing the white men might backfire on him; they were deeply unpopular with the rival faction on Huahine who were furious that Ori had not chastised Forster and others for shooting sacred birds during their visit and, in a protracted struggle with Bora Bora, the Huahine faction might form a fifth column and destroy him from within. Ori therefore assured Cook that he had made a lasting peace with Bora Bora. Now on Raiatea Cook heard a rather different story. While Uru, the high chief of the island, still retained his titular position, Puni, the *arii nui* of Bora Bora was the real power in the land and Oreo was his creature and also the regent of Raiatea. It turned out that Omai was a more serious character than Cook had imagined. His motive in joining the *Adventure* was to go to England so that he could bring back a cache of firearms with which he could defeat the Bora Borans; though picked up on Huahine he was actually a native of Raiatea.[42] Omai was made of sterner stuff than Poreo, whom Cook had originally rated more highly. Poreo's response to all this complexity was to fall in love with a local girl and announce to Cook that he

would not be continuing on the voyage. Almost on cue there arose another
Polynesian to take his place. A young man named Hitihiti, a relative of Puni,
came forward and said he wanted to go to England. Cook liked the fact that the
volunteer was an oligarch, and although George Forster tried to warn him of
the terrors of the Antarctic that lay ahead, Hitihiti was not to be dissuaded.[43]
Since he was a Bora Boran, the sailors liked the idea too because, always awed
by brute strength, they had been mightily impressed by the Bora Bora warriors
they had met on the island. The midshipmen on the *Adventure* – imagining them
a South Sea equivalent of the knights of the Round Table despite their heavy
tattoos – dubbed them the 'knights of Bora Bora'; they then decided that, to save
face, they themselves would have to be the 'knights of Tahiti' and accordingly
had themselves tattooed. As part of their new macho code, the knights of Tahiti
took to roasting and eating dog, claiming to prefer it to pork.[44]

Given the underlying powder keg, relations between the visitors and Oreo
and his people were surprisingly cordial. Or they were until Johann Forster
took a hand. Although they had been warned on Huahine that shooting certain
birds was contrary to *tapu*, and Ori had been hard put to paper over the dissen-
sions that arose from the foreigners' blatant disregard of their customs, the
Forsters took the arrogant line that their superior civilisation entitled them to
do as they pleased. Always blasting away at anything that flew, on one hunting
trip they bagged three kingfishers and a grey heron. When they brought back
these trophies, Oreo's 14-year-old daughter wept bitterly to see the sacred
birds dead. Oreo warned the Forsters that he would not tolerate a repetition of
the incident, and Cook added a reprimand. Yet the Forsters thought they owed
obedience only to higher laws than those promulgated by a mere sea-captain.
Johann, already fuming at Cook's dove-like approach to the Sparrman incident on Huahine, argued that leniency was always construed by primitive
people as weakness and that 'violent robbery is an act of violence which ought
not to remain unpunished' as it set a precedent.[45] The Forsters went on a
botanical expedition in the north of Raiatea; an altercation arose with one of
the locals over a routine transaction; and Johann Forster, perhaps still fuming
over Cook's leniency, shot the man in the back. His 'excuse', that his son's life
was in danger, hardly squared with the fact that the man was running away.
On his return to the *Resolution* Johann told Cook what had happened, almost
as if he was reading him an object lesson in the correct way to handle the
natives.[46] That evening at the Great Cabin, in the presence of Furneaux and
his senior officers, Cook publicly reprimanded Forster for his action, The
Herr Professor grew indignant, replied that people had to defend themselves
since their captain showed no interest in doing so, and repeated the refrain that
had made him an object of universal detestation on the *Resolution*: 'I will tell

the King.' Always on a short fuse, Cook reacted indignantly to this threat, the temperature rose, and violent words were exchanged. Cook threw Forster out of the cabin, but not before the German had challenged him to a duel. If the words had come from one of his officers, they would have constituted mutiny. Cook showed his contempt for Forster by entering in his journal that night: 'Nothing happened worthy of note.'[47]

Forster then asked to be allowed to accompany Pickersgill on a foraging expedition to the island of Taha'a due north of Raiatea. There he demon-strated that he had learned nothing from the recent bruising encounters on Raiatea and in the Great Cabin by seeming almost to go out of his way to stir up trouble. They met the local chief Ta, and at first all was fine, but things went wrong when Ta invited them to his large house to sleep for the night. A trigger-happy sentry mistook a guttering candle for an attempt at robbery, raised the alarm and, in the dark, Ta was beaten and mishandled under the mistaken impression that he was the thief. Ta expected compensation for this insult but Pickersgill, egged on by Sparrman and Forster, waved the affair aside as a fleabite. Ta decided to get his compensation anyway and set his expert pickpockets to work. They stole nothing more than knick-knacks, but Forster exhorted Pickersgill to take a hard line. The Europeans then took Ta hostage and ransacked his village, seizing goods 'to the value of' those stolen, but actually worth far more, since several hogs and bales of cloth were expro-priated by the marauders. Not surprisingly after this high-handedness, a hostile crowd began to gather. Pickersgill ordered his men to fire over the people's heads; they did so and caused panic. But Pickersgill, abetted by Forster, would not be satisfied until every last trivial item was returned.[48] The Europeans departed, leaving behind the blackest of reputations. Both Forster and Pickersgill had cavalierly broken Cook's rules of engagement with indige-nous peoples, Pickersgill through stupidity and weakness, Forster with malice aforethought and thoughts of revenge. Back in Raiatea Forster's jibes about softness had gone home in some quarters, for when a local was caught stealing shirts from the *Resolution*, Cook's officers lobbied him to apply the 'Furneaux punishment' for such an offence – long since instituted on the *Adventure* – which was two dozen lashes. Not wishing to alienate his aides to side with the Forster camp, Cook agreed.[49] The result was a boycott of the ships by local canoes. Cook went to find Oreo, who in sombre mood lamented that Cook's men had killed some of his people. His version of events was apparently a farrago concocted from the Forster shooting in the back, the events on Taha'a, news of which had been conveyed across the channel at lightning speed, and some fighting between local braves and men from the *Adventure*; it was always the *Adventure*.[50] Cook tried to patch things up by inviting Oreo to dinner and

laying on a noble spread; the chief showed an impressive ability to down large
bumpers of Madeira without any apparent effect.[51] Using Furneaux as a go-
between Cook then met Forster in the Great Cabin and the two men shook
hands. Cook knew his pacific policies were correct, but when even his senior
officers backed hotheads like Forster, what could he do?

Cook was glad to clear from Raiatea on 17 September, now anxious to get
away before the combination of Forster, his officers and his drunken crew engineered a total breakdown in relations with the Polynesians. Fortunately the ships
left the Society Islands before the pleasant memories could be erased. All who
left memoirs of the past month praised its paradisiacal qualities, the grandeur of
the scenery, the plentiful pork, chicken and bananas, the beautiful women and
the general affability of the men.[52] Cook was among the enthusiasts, though he
would modify his views when he learned from Omai about the less savoury side
of life in Tahiti, such as human sacrifice and cannibalism. He continued to worry
about venereal disease, though he was powerless to do anything about it, and
deplored the casual promiscuity of his men, which led to a downgrading
and devaluing of women in general so that ladies and princesses could no longer
be distinguished from whores and strumpets. He reverted to a familiar theme,
adumbrating on the *Endeavour* voyage that one could no more infer the
general character of Tahitian women from a Matavai Bay harlot than one could
extrapolate from the behaviour of women of easy virtue on the docksides of
Plymouth, Portsmouth or Wapping in England.[53] Certainly the attitude of the
men to casual sex was becoming almost insouciant; what they had greeted with
surprised delight in 1769 was by now virtually taken for granted as a natural
right. The astronomer Wales agreed with Cook, but the younger officers,
Pickersgill especially, were themselves avid for native girlfriends and virtually
encouraged sexual promiscuity among their men. Although this was a disappointing aspect of life in the Society Islands, Cook took comfort from the
qualities of honour and integrity he found among the chiefly classes. John Marra
noted that Tahitians placed great value on friendship and would be faithful to a
friend in the most testing circumstances.[54] Cook explained that this was why Ori
had consented to go aboard the *Resolution* and act as a personal surety when all
his people urged him not to: 'Friendship is sacred with these people. Ori and I
were professed friends in all the forms customary among them and he had no
idea that this could be broke [*sic*] by the act of any other person ... his words
were to this effect; "Cook and I are friends, I have done nothing to forfeit his
friendship so why should I not go with him?" '[55]

On the more general aspects of Tahiti, Cook had little to add to what he had
said in his account of the *Endeavour* voyage. There is no evidence that he
understood the deeper currents of Tahitian society any better, but why should

he have? He was, after all, a navigator and surveyor, not an anthropologist. The only thing clearly in evidence on the second voyage was a pronounced distaste for Bougainville, for his charts, his minimal achievements as a navigator, for introducing venereal disease, and for promoting, even if unwittingly, the absurd idea of the 'noble savage'. There was nothing noble about the Polynesians' almost pathological propensity to stealing, and the more contact they had with Europeans, the worse they would become. Such, at any rate, was Cook's view.[56] It is perhaps more surprising to find that the Forsters, supposedly the inheritors of Banks's scientific mantle, had no very cogent ideas about the Society Islands and their entire oeuvre was shot through with ambivalence.[57] Their record was patchy: as botanists they were far less dedicated than Banks and did far less work – their excuse was that, as the first in the field, Banks had already scooped the pool – though they did catalogue 75 new genera and 220 new species. Having done a lot of work on ice theory in the Antarctic, Johann turned to the study of atolls in the tropics.[58] The Forsters tacked between a hard-headed realism about the undoubted horrors of Tahiti and a countervailing tug back, if not quite, to the 'noble savage', to the desirability of the primitive. By no means immune to the spell of the South Seas islands, they were genuinely shocked by the inequality, corruption and low standards of sexual morality; for Johann the *locus classicus* of this was when Chief Potatu offered his wife to Cook in exchange for a bunch of red feathers.[59]

George moreover had something of a visceral horror of Tahitians, whom he compared to monkeys and orang-utans.[60] Johann also dissented from the famous theory embraced by Aristotle and Montesquieu, according to which civilisation is a function of a temperate climate. Against this he argued that the tropics provided an economic surplus in the form of plentiful food and ready-made shelter, thus freeing thinking men for creative endeavours.[61] Interestingly, father and son diverged on the future of Tahiti. Johann was convinced that European culture would rapidly civilise them,[62] while George was more pessimistic: he could not see that Tahitians would ever abandon their taste for sexual licence and he thought that this, added to the lust for European luxuries, would lead to an increased population, the breakdown of patriarchy, class conflict, and eventually revolution. 'If the knowledge of a few individuals can only be acquired at such a price to happiness,' he concluded, 'it were better that the South Sea had still remained unknown to Europe and its restless inhabitants.'[63] A final difference may be noted. George hoped that intercourse (in all senses) would come to an end before the Pacific islands were corrupted by foreign luxuries. His father, however, thought this would not happen, simply because the Pacific had little to offer Europeans – no spices, tea, precious metals or other desiderata – while visiting Europeans would never provide the

Polynesians with enough iron to lead them to forget how to make their own stone tools.[64] It is interesting to see that while George Forster explicitly rejected the eighteenth-century orthodoxy concerning the four stages of civilisation – hunting, pastoralism, agriculture and commerce – he implicitly accepted a nineteenth-century typology of savagery, barbarism and civilisation.

Instead of making for New Zealand by the shortest possible route, a track by now well traced by previous navigators, Cook decided to angle slightly to the south-west to get into the latitude of the 'Amsterdam Island' reported by Tasman in 1643.[65] The isles of Tonga stretch 175 miles from north to south, and on 1 October he reached the southernmost island of the Tonga group, Eua, a bright green coral atoll surrounded by dangerous reefs and islets, where sheer cliffs ran down to the ocean. The Tonga islands were not unknown – they had been visited by Tasman, Schouten, Le Maire and Wallis – but no one had tried to chart them with any method. Despite Cook's orders against females on the ship,[66] at Eua the native women swarmed over the sides and were soon engaged in the usual energetic coupling with the crew. Cook spent two days on Eua, then sailed over the short strait to Tongatapu to the north-west. Since his men had gobbled up the fruit and vegetables at an alarming rate on the run from the Society Islands, he issued strict orders that nothing but eatables should be bought or traded. Contact with the locals was difficult, as the dialect spoken by the ships' Tahitians was not understood and the local language was impenetrable on such a short stay. There was the usual course of events on any Pacific island: a fulsome welcome, thefts, misunderstandings, shots fired, marines set to guard the boats.[67] On Tongatapu Wales was mugged and had his shoes and stockings stolen. Luckily Cook had struck up a rapport with a local chief called Otago, who from the journal accounts seems to have followed the great mariner around like a lapdog. Cook appealed to Otago, and the stolen effects were returned.[68] Everyone rhapsodised about the rare beauty of Eua and Tongatapu, their luxuriant greens mingling with the yellow of the hibiscus; Cook thought the islands resembled a very superior country park in England. He found Tongatapu a walker's paradise and enjoyed traipsing around with Otago while the Forsters botanised and Hodges sketched and painted.[69] By 5 October Cook had obtained all the food he needed, relaxed the trading ban and allowed his men to barter for whatever they wanted. For reasons the journals do not make clear, on this island the sailors were in a buying frenzy (the modern idiom would be 'shopaholics'), but their passion for snapping up curios and knick-knacks soon excited the contempt of the locals. They started offering sticks and stones as currency; 'One waggish boy took a piece of human excrement on the end of a stick and held it out to everyone he met with.'[70] The Tongans proved just as light-fingered as the

Tahitians, and there were many barefaced thefts, including one from the master's cabin. On this occasion the thief tried to paddle away in his canoe, was fired on, so dived down under the water to escape, not resurfacing for a full three minutes and by then out of range; he was finally captured by a sailor with a boathook.[71]

Cook was introduced to the high chief of the island, whom he referred to as the 'king' (as he always did with chiefs). The man sat on his throne, poker-faced and silent, grunting as Cook's gifts were laid in front of him. Cook thought the chief moronic, but the truth was that stony-faced gravity was expected from him in his role as 'sacred child' – just one aspect of the highly intricate chiefly system of the Tongan islands. In the northern islands was a *Tu'i Tonga* or supreme ruler, and all the chiefs Cook met in the south were essentially rival warlords. Walter Bagehot, the famous analyst of the British constitution, would have recognised in Tongan society both a 'dignified' and 'efficient' side.[72] Wales, who had been censorious about the casual couplings on Tahiti, was bowled over by the beauty of the Tongan women; Cook concurred, finding them the 'merriest creatures' he had yet encountered among Polynesian females.[73] Only one thing impaired the isles of Tonga as a Pacific paradise: the scarcity of drinking water. The wells and ponds were polluted by seawater which seeped in through the coral, and even in those waterholes where salinity did not make the liquid undrinkable, the water was brackish. Cook was there-fore compelled to do what the locals did: use coconuts as the staple drink. Loading these aboard accounted for much of the seamen's labour over the four days. Sexuality was again to the fore. Cook himself was offered a very pretty young woman, whose charms even he acknowledged, but it was a core element of his personal morality, as well as part of the deliberately cultivated mystique of his leadership, that he never consorted with Polynesian women.[74] Needless to say his crew had no such scruples, and dozens of women regularly swam out to the two ships. As George Forster put it, '[they] once more offered to our eyes a scene worthy of Cyrian temples'.[75] By now Cook was eager to be gone. His men had loaded on board 150 hogs, 300 chickens and large amounts of bananas and coconuts, which meant that there should be no shortages on the run to New Zealand. Cook at this stage in his career had very sensitive antennae for the volatile mood of Polynesians, and a spate of petty assaults (on Sparrman and George Forster, seemingly perennial targets in the Pacific), and daring thefts, convinced him that to stay any longer was to risk the inevitable armed confrontation.[76]

As the ships left Tongatapu Johann Forster quoted Virgil in his journal. The rather odd association of ideas may have been prompted by the fact that Polynesian thieves seemed especially drawn to European books, doubtless thinking them to have the qualities of Prospero's volumes. Fielding's *Tom Jones* and Pope's translation of the *Iliad* had been among the tomes stolen on this voyage, along with sundry copies of the *Daily Assistant* and the *Nautical Almanack*, to say nothing of armfuls of logbooks.[77] The two ships made good progress west in generally fine weather, though a shift in wind direction on 17 October caused the *Adventure* to struggle, whereupon Cook on the *Resolution* shortened sail so that she could keep up. That night there was compensation of a kind when the ships sailed through a school of luminous jellyfish, which made the ocean seem as though the stars had fallen into it from the sky.[78] New Zealand was sighted on the 21st, in the environs of Table Cape. Cook had the curious notion that people on the North Island were more civilised than those on South Island, so decided to make them the recipients of domestic animals and seeds. He turned south and put in at Cape Kidnappers, and soon fell in with a Maori chief he thought had the necessary credibility. He made him a gift of two boars, two cockerels and four hens, plus seeds of wheat, beans, cabbage, turnips, onions, carrots, parsnips and yams, explaining that with proper cultivation the Maori could feed themselves on his gifts alone, so that strenuous hunting expeditions need only be for extras. Although neither Omai nor Hitihiti possessed Tupaia's linguistic gifts and seemed unable to make contact using the local dialect, Sergeant Gibson was now a proficient Polynesian linguist and did the necessary translation. The Maori chief promised not to kill the domestic animals for food; the gift was gratefully received and survived in Maori oral tradition.[79]

The ships put to sea again and reached Cape Turnagain by 23 October, but already the sea was making up and a hard gale building. It began as one of those confusing gales typical of the New Zealand spring in the region of the Cook Strait, when the wind and waves rise alarmingly, then fall, then spring up again at the same volume, with the wind boxing the compass, almost as though the ocean's intention is to tantalise and torture the mariner. The *Resolution*'s fore-topgallant mast was destroyed; topsails were reefed and re-reefed, and sails were split and torn in the heavy squalls. After two days of this, the Pacific prepared its *pièce de résistance*, and the gales escalated to a severe storm, as Cook relates:

[it] came on with such fury as to oblige us to take in all our poles with the utmost expedition and to lay-to under our bare poles with our heads to the south-west . . . the sea rose in proportion to the wind so that we not only had a furious gale but a mountainous sea also to encounter, thus after beating two days against very strong gales and arriving within sight of our post we had the mortification to be drove [*sic*] off the land by a furious storm.[80]

George Forster used the occasion to berate his bêtes noires, the seamen who so despised him: 'To complete this catalogue of horrors we heard the voices of sailors, from time to time louder than the blustering winds or raging ocean itself uttering horrible volleys of curses and oaths. Without any provocation to serve as an excuse, they execrated every limb in varied terms, piercing and complicated beyond the power of description. Inured to danger from their infancy, they were insensible to its threats, and not a single reflection bridled their blasphemous tongues.'[81] When the storm struck the ships were only about twenty-five miles from Cape Palliser, but it took the *Resolution* until 1 November to reach it. The *Adventure* drifted away to leeward, but Cook found her again even in the impossible conditions. In the small hours of a dark early morning on the 30th October, however, he lost contact with Furneaux again and never regained it. There was no chance of going to look for the *Adventure*, for Cook reported the wind blowing with greater fury than ever on the 31st, 'so much so that we were obliged to lie to under the mizzen staysail'.[82]

November came in with the *Resolution* still beset by gales off Cape Campbell. Cook had hoped to get to Queen Charlotte Sound by 2 November but the winds were against him. He spent the night plying, but their tacking left them adrift of their starting point since they lost more on the ebb than they gained on the flood. To the east of Cape Terawhiti was an inlet into a bay. Cook had almost managed to put in there when the wind changed from a north-westerly to a north-easterly, stranding him in the entrance of the bay. Some surly Maoris approached in canoes; Cook gave them poultry as a gift but they seemed uninterested. Hoping to meet the *Adventure* at the rendezvous in Queen Charlotte Sound, Cook saw no point in battling the winds to get into the bay and turned away out to sea, but by so doing missing the finest harbour in New Zealand on which the city of Wellington now stands.[83] On 3 November the *Resolution* entered the sound but there was no sign of the *Adventure*. Soon Maori canoes were coming to meet them but Cook discouraged fraternisation, wanting his men to concentrate on caulking the decks, making new sails, repairing stove-in barrels or finding the wherewithal to make new ones. To his intense irritation and disappointment, he learned that the people on shore had killed all the pigs and goats he had left with them, thus destroying Cook's hopes of filling the land with useful animals and destroying the Maoris' chances of breeding future herds; it was the primitive instinct for instant gratification with a vengeance.[84] Of more immediate concern to Cook was the whereabouts of the *Adventure*. He toyed with the idea that she might still be in the Cook Strait and on 15 November (together with the Forsters) he climbed a high hill in East Bay to look for any sign of her. Meanwhile he pressed on with the programme of repairing and overhauling as fast as he could, not helped by teeming rain on the 6 December which halted all work. The men worked well, sustained throughout the day by the thought of the nightly revels to come, for there was a thriving trade in Maori women, in which Hitihiti joined with alacrity, even though he affected to despise the Maoris as inferiors. On 12 December Cook examined the stores and found to his dismay that a lot of the bread and biscuits were mouldy; in compensation the Maoris brought them huge supplies of fish.[85]

Yet already the Maoris themselves were causing him concern. He and his men found unmistakable signs of cannibalism in the vicinity. Cook, who had been pilloried in some quarters in England after the *Endeavour* voyage for a 'credulous' belief in this, took a pragmatic 'I told you so' approach. George Forster, an early cultural relativist, queried whether anthropophagy was any worse than the Bloody Code in England or the wartime atrocities common in contemporary Europe. Sparrman supported him by saying that cannibalism was not an absolute taboo even in the 'civilised' world, for in times of famine and dearth the practice was not unknown in Europe. Wales, previously scep- tical, was now won over by the unimpeachable evidence of skulls and jawbones he saw and hypothesised that the Maoris were cannibalistic epicures with a taste for human flesh. Hitihiti told his comrades, though it is not clear they believed him, that cannibalism had a ritual purpose concerned with increasing power or *mana*.[86] Cook found the Maori the most bellicose of the peoples he encountered and laid down standing orders for dealing with them. Some of them were chimerical and openly flouted, such as the ban on indi- vidual trade for sex or the veto on barter with iron (Cook said this was to be the sole prerogative of the captain and only ever engaged in to purchase food). Some were sensible such as the prescription that boats should never be let out of sight of the ship, that there should always be a great gun loaded with grape ready for instant use, and that landing parties should never scatter or disperse. Repeatedly he emphasised that Europeans had to be tough with indigenous peoples, and must demonstrate their technological superiority and devastating firepower.[87] It was a fixed policy of Cook's that no European should ever get involved in any test of skill or individual combat where there was a chance that a native could emerge superior to a Briton.[88] The problem with the Cook credo, sensible enough as it was on paper, was that it assumed rationality on the part of the indigenous peoples, and it overrated the superiority afforded by firearms which often misfired or missed their targets and thus lessened their credibility in Polynesian eyes.

The Cook credo also assumed rationality and sensible behaviour by his own men, which turned out to be a sad misreading of human nature. The appetite for sex, particularly, led the seamen to pilfer from the local peoples;

the thieving epidemic in the Pacific in the 1770s was certainly not all one-way. The sailors habitually acted stupidly or arrogantly, or overplayed their hand, alienating their hosts, and Cook could not be everywhere to supervise them. Contemptuously aggressive, the below-decks cabals believed in shooting first and asking questions later. The seamen and marines often opened, fire in the face of purely imaginary threats, offended against local customs, and unwittingly breached *tapus*.[89] The Polynesians for their part never understood their visitors, and familiarity with them and their weapons gradually bred contempt. In their desire to have the Europeans as allies against rival clans and families, they tolerated rapine and plunder as long as it was at the expense of their enemies. To the seamen this seemed a green light to do as they liked in any context but here they collided with Polynesian culture and temperament, for the young braves were proud, fiery, quick-tempered and perhaps even over-ready to take offence and see insults where none were intended. Since neither side spoke the other's language with any fluency, and there was simply not enough time even for Cook's savants to master the nuances of local culture, relations between the explorers and the locals were almost a classic of that old cliché: failure to communicate.[90] Cook therefore balanced his tough line with the indigenous peoples with an equally tough one with his own men. As he wrote: 'It has ever been a maxim with me to punish the least crimes any of my people have committed against these uncivilized nations, their robbing us with impunity is by no means a sufficient reason why we should treat them in the same manner.'[91] In accordance with his doctrine he sentenced the seaman R. Lee to twelve lashes on 22 November for stealing a hatchet.

As Cook prepared to leave New Zealand on 25 November he was in a sour mood. He despaired of the local idiocy about domesticated animals and feared that the latest batch of pigs and poultry he had left behind would simply be eaten once his back was turned. The fiasco of his 'improvement' policies among the Maoris seemed to be symbolised when, just before he left, one of the rams on whom he counted for stud possibilities dashed into the sea and was drowned.[92] Even more irritating was the non-appearance of Furneaux and the *Adventure*, but Cook could not spend any more time looking for the sister ship or his summer cruise to the Antarctic would be jeopardised. He left a message in a bottle for Furneaux dated 24 November 1773, placing it under a tree with the words 'Look Underneath' carved on it. The letter mentioned that he intended to be at Easter Island the following March, but was otherwise vague about his plans. Since no further contingency plans had been agreed between them, Cook assumed Furneaux would now head homewards via Cape Horn or the Cape of Good Hope.[93] No one has ever satisfactorily explained why it took Furneaux a month to arrive at the rendezvous in Queen Charlotte Sound. He himself cited hard gales, but the *Adventure* put into Solago Bay shortly after becoming separated from the *Resolution* and showed no particular haste to get out again.[94] Furneaux knew of Cook's plans for a second foray into the Antarctic and guessed that he would sail south before the end of November, since he had headed south on 23 November the year before. His arrival at Queen Charlotte Sound on 30 November was just a mite convenient and does nothing to silence those cynics who postulate that Furneaux deliberately arrived late for the rendezvous, knowing that Cook would have departed. Furneaux by his own admission had no desire to face the giant waves and mountainous seas of the Antarctic Ocean, under the close eye of an unforgiving commander who had already called him to account on several occasions; better by far to make his way home, having fulfilled the letter if not the spirit of his instructions.[95]

Yet by anchoring in Queen Charlotte Sound just after Cook had left it, Furneaux unwittingly reaped the whirlwind his commander had sown. Cook had sensed that the Maoris were reaching the end of their tolerance, and there had in fact been many unsavoury incidents, some involving the irrepressible Clerke and his misplaced sense of humour, which had not been reported to him.[96] From the very first days of his arrival Furneaux seems to have run into a tsunami of thievery and pilfering, which the Maoris probably regarded as 'payback time' for the depredations and indignities visited on them by Cook's men. On 9 December the entire shore encampment was kept awake all night by a nervous sentry blasting away at thieves – who had been tempted to try their luck in the first place because the indisciplined sentry left his post to look for tobacco. On 12 December there was a violent confrontation between a party containing Burney, Omai and the master's mate Jack Rowe and a Maori war party. On 14 December there was another blatant nocturnal theft at the shore camp.[97] Finally waking up to the belligerent mood of the Maoris, Furneaux prepared to depart. In an evil hour he sent a foraging party under Rowe to a nearby bay they called Grass Cove to collect wild greens. Commanded by Rowe, the ten men in the party began to eat a dinner of bread and fish after completing their chore. In an act of consummate folly, the men had only three muskets between them; the rest of their weapons were in the boat two hundred yards away, guarded by a single marine. A party of Maoris approached, snatched at the food, were beaten away, and a general quarrel was precipitated. The sailors fired the muskets and shot two Maoris dead, but the others fell on them and butchered them.[98] When the seamen failed to return that night, Furneaux was concerned, so next morning sent Burney and Omai with a large party of marines to investigate. After searching all day, just before dusk they came on around 200 Maoris gathered as if for a festivity. When they taunted the approaching boat party, Burney gave the order to open fire. Muskets, musketoons and wall-guns scythed through the packed ranks of Maoris, causing the survivors to run for cover in the trees. Once the beach was clear Burney reconnoitred and found the eyes, hearts, lungs, livers and entrails of their comrades roasting on fires.[99] Reeling with horror and fearing a counter-attack they re-embarked on the launch, first destroying the dozens of canoes drawn up on the beach so that they could not be followed. Burney's party got back to the *Adventure* and gave the news to a stunned Furneaux, who ordered sail hoist. Contrary winds delayed them for a further twenty-four hours, and that night all hands slept fully clothed with their weapons to hand in case of an attack.[100] Finally, on 19 December the *Adventure* cleared from New Zealand. Furneaux preferred the high seas of southern latitudes to the perils of the Maoris.

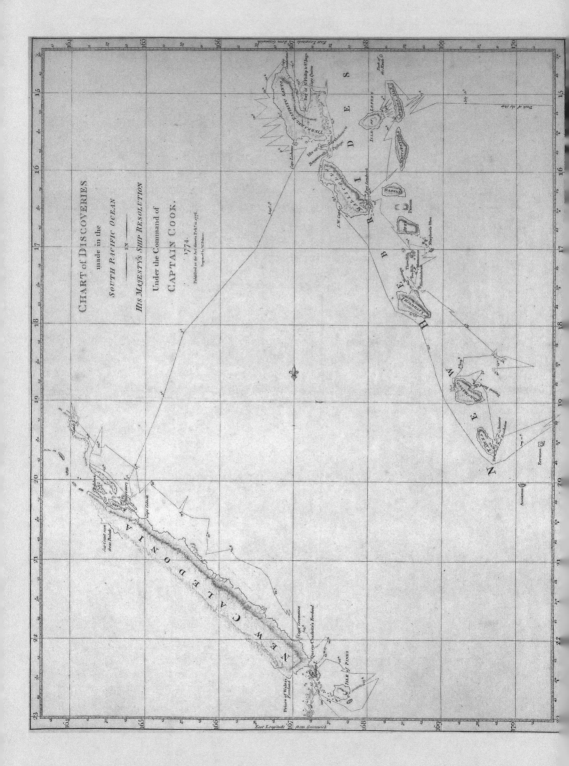

CHART of DISCOVERIES
made in the
SOUTH PACIFIC OCEAN
IN
HIS MAJESTY's SHIP RESOLUTION
Under the Command of
CAPTAIN COOK.
1774.
Published as the Act directs, Feb.ry 1st 1776.
Engraved by W. Whitchurch.

East Longitude from Greenwich

New Caledonia

CHAPTER ELEVEN

Mastering the Pacific

FOR a few days Cook sailed slowly through the strait between North and South Island that now bears his name. He crossed the strait from Cape Palliser to Cape Campbell and back, in the vain eleventh-hour hope that he might still find the *Adventure*, then set a south-easterly course for the Antarctic on 26 November. On his first venture into the Antarctic Ocean he had covered the most southerly areas of the Indian Ocean from Cape Town to Australasia. Now, in Act Three of the drama, he was about to do the same with the most southerly wastes of the Pacific. He claimed that morale was good but this was probably true only in a qualified sense; he himself might have been secretly relieved not to have Furneaux and his turbulent crew along. From the heavy swell Cook inferred that any land to the south of New Zealand must lie well south of latitude 60. On 7 December the voyagers reached longitude 180°, exactly on the other side of the globe from London (now the International Date Line), drank toasts and envied the good fortune of Londoners now abed.[1] Already they had run into the strong gales and squalls which were the accompaniment of any foray into the Southern Ocean; they were continually taking in topsails and mainsails, sometimes lying-to under the mizzen staysail. Five days later they were at longitude 173 and latitude 60. At latitude 62 they encountered their first icebergs, complete with the usual petrels, pintadoes and albatrosses, and at latitude 64 loose ice. Until mid-December they made good progress – 146 nautical miles clocked up in one twenty-four-hour period – but on 15 December they were pulled up short by an extensive field of ice.[2] Here disaster was narrowly avoided. All Cook's officers knew very well from their previous experience that the waters on the seaward side of an iceberg were dangerous. Even so, that evening while Cook was at dinner the officer of the watch made the rash decision to go windward to an iceberg. Caught by the wind, the *Resolution* was in imminent danger of being smashed against the berg. Witnesses said that the horror on every face would have defied the abilities in reproduction of even the greatest artist; Cook himself was convinced they were done for, since a collision with the berg meant certain drowning. Elliott described the sequel: 'We were actually within the back surge of the sea from the island [sc. iceberg] but most providentially for us she went clear, her stern just trailing within the breakers from the island. Certainly never men had a more narrow escape from the jaws of death.'[3]

Profoundly shaken by this brush with doom, Cook hauled away to the north in dark and gloomy weather, then headed north-east and east to clear the pack ice. The *Resolution*'s sails and rigging were hung with icicles. Finding clearer weather on the 20th and thus able to gauge longitude, Cook turned south again and next day crossed the Antarctic Circle for the second time, running through icebergs in thick fog at longitude 143W. The weather was bad, with thick fog and a strong gale of sleet and rain as well as icebergs, but he stayed south of the Antarctic Circle for three days until on Christmas Eve he met the pack ice again[4] – a large field of closely packed and densely impacted floes. By this time the *Resolution* once more looked like a ghost ship, with its rigging like icicles, the sails like boards and the ropes like wires.[5] Beset by gales, sleet and snow yet convinced there was no land south of the ice, Cook might have turned east, but that would have meant leaving a gap of 24 degrees of latitude to the north unexplored – the gap between his present position and his eastward track from New Zealand in July 1773. While he decided what to do next, his men amused themselves by shooting at seals and petrels, of which the giant, Antarctic and mottled species were all around them.[6] At midnight on 24 December the ship's company counted fifty-three icebergs in the vicinity. Cook decided to steer north-east and then north to cover the 'missing' territory. On Christmas Day, fortuitously, the sea was dead calm. According to custom Cook invited his officers and the mates to dinner in the Great Cabin. A riotous dinner ensued, complete with Christmas pudding and large quantities of brandy. More than one of the officers jested that they would die happily among the ice floes provided they could always have a plentiful supply of brandy.[7] Next day brought a necessary return to discipline and vigilance because the ship threaded her way through more than 200 icebergs (one pedant in the crew made a precise count and came up with the number 238); but for the continual daylight and clear weather they could never have kept clear of them. When near the smaller floes Cook ordered boats lowered and the casks replenished with fresh water, using the method they had perfected on the first Antarctic venture.[8]

For the last week of December Cook bore away, at first north-east, then due north. By 2 January 1774 the *Resolution* was at latitude 57, longitude 136, or 560 miles north of her position on Christmas Eve. On this day the 19-year-old midshipman Charles Loggie was given a dozen lashes for getting drunk, drawing a knife and cutting one of the other middies.[9] The below-decks gossip was that Cook had been harsh: everyone knew that Loggie's victim James Maxwell made almost a career out of taunting and needling Loggie, who was otherwise very popular; besides, it was rare for a midshipman to be given the same punishment as a common seaman. Even Elliott, who usually idolised Cook, thought that on this occasion 'he had lost sight of both justice and humanity.'[10] Cook probably acted thus uncharacteristically (at this stage of his career, at least) for two main reasons. He himself was ill, suffering from severe constipation and off his food. Additionally, morale on the ship was starting to plummet. Word had now circulated that the *Resolution* would not be returning to England in 1774, and the wildest rumours were circulating, to the effect that Cook intended to traverse every inch of the barren and storm-tossed Southern Ocean. This seemed confirmed when, as the ship steered east and the men became convinced they were running for Cape Horn, Cook suddenly turned south again on 11 January. Convinced there was no land between his present position and Tahiti, he hauled round and set a course for the south-east.[11] Despite all the provisions loaded on board in Polynesia, the ship was now experiencing food shortages, and Cook had reduced rations so that he could keep to his timetable and not fetch Easter Island until March. Even this short commons was inadequate, for as the stores were opened, more and more of the food was found to be rotten and what remained was tasteless. Matters came to a near-mutinous head on 17 January when the first mate reeled into Cook's cabin, waving a piece of rotten biscuit and asking with heavy irony if the captain could tell him how to fill his belly.[12] Correctly reading this outburst as the tip of a rebellious iceberg, Cook immediately restored full rations. Johann Forster now thoroughly despised Cook as a man who would sacrifice anyone and anything to his ambition and glory-hunting. To show his disgust, he pleaded indisposition and retreated to his cabin on 23 December, not emerging until the end of January. There in the privacy of his journal he ranted and raged against Cook and the madness of this expedition into the Southern Ocean, where the poor food, the mildew and the ubiquitous damp were counterpointed by the pitching and rolling of the ship in never-ending conditions of tempest.[13] His son George, though not quite so censorious, endorsed the officers' complaints that Cook never confided in anyone and always played his cards close to his chest.[14]

There was yet another reason for the mate's insubordination on 17 January. By then weather conditions and sea state alone would have reduced any normal man to terminal despair. For some time the *Resolution* had been running in 'prodigiously high' seas, but on the 16th the ship was hit by a freak wave (unfortunately Cook never recorded exact wave heights). George Forster described it: 'At nine o'clock a huge mountainous wave struck the ship on the beam, and filled the decks with a deluge of water. It poured through the skylight over our heads and extinguished the candle, leaving us for a moment in doubt whether we were not totally overwhelmed and sinking into the abyss.' The giant wave depressed everyone on board; there could be no doubt about the risks they were running: 'A gloomy melancholy air lowered on the brows of our shipmates, and a dreadful silence reigned among us.'[15] The dauntless and implacable Cook pressed on, pursuing a giant, irregular zigzag. Continuing to sail south-east, on 20 January he was at latitude 62 and longitude 116W, puzzled as to why there were no icebergs visible, whereas 600 miles to the east in the same latitude they were surrounded by them. The answer would be provided only after extensive later Antarctic exploration discovered that the incidence of icebergs in south polar waters is greatest in the Atlantic and the western Indian Ocean because of the action of currents and the differential projection of the Antarctic continent northwards.[16] On 26 January he crossed the Antarctic Circle for the third time in longitude 109, and finally sighted a few bergs; there was a false call of 'land ho' from the crow's nest, but it turned out to be a fog bank. On 29 January the *Resolution* was at latitude 70, in open warm water and good weather (January does after all produce the finest weather in the year south of the Antarctic Circle). The sunshine finally tempted the reclusive Johann Forster out from his cabin so that he was on deck to witness Cook's farthest south at latitude 71, longitude 106. On the horizon the men could see a massive ice field, but they were now beginning to be affected by polar mirages: with clouds and icebergs all the same colour, it was impossible to tell by looking at the horizon where the clouds ended and the bergs began.[17]

To have penetrated so far south in a mere sloop was an astonishing achievement and almost beyond the power of historical imagination to recover. To put the exploit in context, one might mention that James Weddell reached latitude 74S in his expedition of 1822–24 in the area now called the Weddell Sea in a longitude where the sea reaches in closer to the South Pole, while James Clark Ross in the *Erebus* and *Terror*, which had been expressly strengthened to force their way through the pack ice, reached 78S on his 1839–43 expedition. The farthest south achieved in Cook's approximate longitude in the entire sailing era was by Charles Wilkes in the *Flying Fish* in 1839, but he got no farther than 70S; in the epoch of steamships the icebreaker *Discovery II* was turned back in January 1931 just short of latitude 70S (at longitude 101).[18] Cook's companions were aware of the magnitude of his feat, and in later years a somewhat absurd contest developed between rival claimants as to who had actually been farthest south on that momentous day; George Vancouver, by then a famous navigator in his own right, alleged that he went to the end of the bowsprit and cried

'*Ne plus ultra*' Anders while, Sparrman claimed that, since his cabin was aftmost when the *Resolution* put about, he was therefore the southernmost person on the ship.[19] All this lay in the future. For the moment Cook reflected on what he had achieved. He was sure the land he had sighted ran all the way to the pole but, with the ice closing in all around him, he was convinced it was folly to push his luck further, for only a madman would try to get in among such an ice field: 'I, whose ambition leads me not only farther than any man has been before me, but as far as I think it possible for man to go, was not sorry at meeting with this interruption, as it in some measure relieved us from the dangers and hardships inseparable with the navigation of the southern polar regions.' He was also sure he would find no land at these latitudes anywhere on either side of Cape Horn.[20] Cook had made the courageous and correct decision, similar to one Ernest Shackleton would make on the Antarctic ice one hundred and thirty-five years later. His prudence was justified as soon as the *Resolution* turned north. Running into a thick fog bank, he wondered about the dire consequences if the fog had descended on the southward journey, for then they would surely have blundered into the pack ice and become stuck fast.[21]

Cook now headed north-east, en route to the eastern Pacific, bemused to see no seabirds wheeling in the sky. To celebrate, the last hog was slaughtered, roasted and distributed to the men while the officers feasted on roast dog. Cook's intention, once out of the polar latitudes, was to look for islands mentioned by the Spanish, especially Quirós, and wheel round almost at South America, possibly at Juan Fernández Island before making a final westward sweep across the South Pacific, trying to follow Quirós's track; Cook rightly rated him as the greatest of the pre-eighteenth-century navigators.[22] First, though, he had to get out of the tempestuous Southern Ocean. There was another terrible storm on 7 February, so violent that his men were unable to cope, and Cook had to order the warrant officers before the mast to ease the pressure on the hard-pressed and freezing seamen aloft.[23] Although discipline had held up well during the weeks of greatest danger, when common peril concentrated minds, once the *Resolution* got into calmer waters – she crossed the track of the *Endeavour* on 17 February and that of Wallis's *Dolphin* on the 19th – the men, relieved of their worst fears and delighted to learn that they would be visiting the Society Islands again, relapsed into their old ways, tempted additionally to devilry by the news that their captain was confined to his cabin with illness. James Maxwell, the midshipman whose provocations had earned Mr Loggie the lash, cut the mainsail while unbending it, was ordered off the quarterdeck and, to universal joy, condemned to work before the mast like a common seaman. There was a more serious episode on 22 February when three men skipped duty, tapped the wine in the hold and drank themselves stupid; Cook ordered twelve lashes for the ringleader and six each for his two minions.[24] All the time the ship was sailing in high seas and a 'prodigious' swell. When Cook had to retire ill to his cabin, he handed over to Robert Palliser Cooper, the quiet, unobtrusive second in command who never seems to feature in any of the contemporary accounts. Cooper managed the *Resolution*, as Cook put it, 'very much to my satisfaction'.

Cook had never been well on the entire second Antarctic trip and was plagued with constipation. He finally took a laxative to ease the condition, but this made him vomit violently. James Patten the surgeon ordered him to bed, but his remedies – ipecacuanha, castor oil and camomile tea – first brought on a twenty-four-hour bout of hiccups and ended by prostrating the captain entirely. Patten then tried opiates, plasters and hot baths. It is unclear from the sources whether Patten ordered Johann Forster to surrender his remaining pet dog, as the only potential source of protein, or if Forster surrendered it willingly.[25] At any rate the dog was killed, and the resultant steaks and meat broth seemed to be decisive in enabling Cook to turn the corner. Although Patten had despaired for Cook's life, in the end the captain made a complete recovery. Patten referred to a 'violent bilious colic', yet all the evidence shows that the illness was altogether more serious than that. The acute stomach pains suggest either scurvy or roundworm, though with Cook's diet it was unlikely to be the former.[26] The consensus view is that it was acute cholecystitis with a complicating internal obstruction, which produces an acute infection of the gall bladder with secondary paralysis of the bowel. Cook's illness recurred later, suggesting an underlying gallstone problem. There had been signs of the malady even before he arrived in Tahiti.[27] The most ingenious recent suggestion is that Cook might have contracted a parasitic infection from eating raw fish; such a condition would be deep-seated and long-lived, having a corrosive and pernicious effect, and might even account for Cook's odd behaviour on his third voyage.[28] Yet Cook was not the only sick man on the *Resolution* as it headed north. Patten himself went down with 'bilious' symptoms very like Cook's; Johann Forster suffered agonising toothache; and his son seemed in the incipient stages of scurvy, with swollen legs, rotting gums, livid blotches on his trunk, and mysterious but excruciating pains. Making landfall had by now become a matter of extreme urgency.[29]

It was to universal satisfaction that land was sighted on 11 March after 103 days at sea and out of sight of land, and with provisions running short. The final days at sea had been on a north-westerly track in pleasant weather. It is not clear whether it was Cook's illness or the parlous state of supplies that led him to abandon his original target of Juan Fernández and make for Easter Island instead, but the famous statues, clearly visible to mariners approaching from the sea, left them in no doubt where they were. The approach and anchorage were difficult, but a safe haven was finally secured on the 14th.[30] This was the third time Europeans had landed on the island, the first being Jacob Roggeveen and the Dutch in 1722, the second the Spanish under Don Felipe Gonzalez in 1770, a few traces of whom were discernible in clothes worn by the locals, especially the unmistakably Castilian hats.[31] The locals seemed remarkably docile, for about a hundred islanders greeted the party that landed by boat peacefully and with not so much as a stick in their hands. The docility was probably explained by folk memories of Roggeveen's visit. With 100 armed men he had barely set foot on shore before his rearguard opened fire and killed a dozen islanders, wounding many more. This was what lay behind Cook's ironical comment: 'They also seemed to know the use of a musket and to stand in much awe of it; but this they probably learnt from Roggeveen who, if we are to believe the authors of that voyage, left them sufficient tokens.'[32] Most of the 15th was spent getting fresh water on board, together with chickens, potatoes, plantains and sugar cane, and it was not until 16 March that a landing party had time to explore the interior and the statues, where they lunched in the shade of the giant Maunga Toata monolith. (Cook himself was still too ill to go inland and stayed on the shore.)[33] Though not hostile, the locals were as expert at thieving as any other Polynesians, though this time there was no shooting. Considering he stayed there just three days, Cook left quite a full account of Easter Island, which was easily explored, being only fifteen miles long and seven wide and shaped like a perfect triangle.[34]

Cook noticed that most of the 600 statues on the island had been toppled, but there his curiosity ended. Typically, he had no interest in the deeper currents of the history, culture and ethnology of the island, and maybe he was wise because everything about this mysterious place is still shrouded in controversy. How was Easter Island settled and from where? The most plausible theory is by one of the heroic transoceanic boat journeys made by early Polynesians, either from the Tuamotus or, more probably, from the Marquesas.[35] When did these journeys take place? Scholars have dated them to AD 400–1700, with most opting for the period 1300–1400. Why were the people living at the very edge of subsistence? Or were they? Cook seemed to have no difficulty getting the fruit and vegetables he needed (meat was another matter) and La Pérouse, when he visited in 1786, thought that a mere three days' work a year was enough to support all the inhabitants of the island.[36] On the other hand there are the modern theories that the Easter Islanders in effect committed suicide by cutting down all their trees, and Cook attested to a barren, desert landscape.[37] Here the most popular interpretation is that some time between 1680 and Cook's arrival there was a violent civil war between the

peoples of the western and eastern ends of the island, and that the previously
dominant 'Long Ears' were overthrown by the 'Short Ears'. The 'Long Ears'
have often been blamed for cutting down all the trees to provide transport
for the gigantic statues of volcanic rock; the statues supposedly represented
deceased 'Long Ears', which was why the statue era had come to an end by
Cook's time. Certainly Easter Island was no paradise before Cook's coming,
with warfare, overpopulation, starvation, infanticide, oppressive taboos,
human sacrifices and slavery forming an index of human idiocy, which the
threat from hurricanes and tsunamis simply compounded. There seems to be
a strong correlation between the destruction of the trees, the era of civil war
and the toppling of the statues. Without wood for canoes the islanders could
not fish, which severely curtailed the food supply, but it may be that the prime
cause of deforestation was not humans' hunger for lumber but the depredations caused by the rats the Polynesians unwittingly brought with them on
their travels; Polynesian rats are particularly fond of palm nuts.[38]

Cook got under sail on 16 March, plied to and fro while the boats made final
foraging expeditions onshore, then cleared from Easter Island on the 18th. He
steered north-west towards the Marquesas and enjoyed fine weather all the
way, though he himself had a relapse of the 'bilious' complaint.[39] This no
doubt accounts for his jaundiced comments on Easter Island which at the time
he had seemed to enjoy: 'No nation will ever contend for the honour (of its
discovery) as there is hardly an island in this sea which affords less conven-
iences for shipping than it does.'[40] This was a rather churlish comment in light
of the fact that the island, on a knife-edge of subsistence, had nonetheless
provided enough roots, bananas and sugar cane to rescue his ailing men from
scurvy. Even more jaundiced was his lack of enthusiasm for the Marquesas,
sighted on 7 April, for these beautiful islands usually sent travellers into
raptures. But he had been in bed with the recurring malady, Forster's dog had
been sacrificed for meat and broth and, in Cook's absence, the crew tested
Cooper's mettle to see how tough he really was. One of the marines was
caught urinating on the lower deck in defiance of Cook's standing orders, so
Cooper ordered him flogged. The lieutenant of marines saw a chance to assert
himself against Cooper and objected to the sentence. A further hearing was
convened and Cook consulted in his sickbed before the punishment of twelve
lashes was confirmed.[41] With dolphins breaching and diving around the ship,
Cook directed the *Resolution* towards the southerly Marquesas islands, which
had been discovered by Mendaña and Quirós in 1595. (The northern and
central Marquesas islands, including Nuku Hiva, by far the largest, lay to the
north of his track and remained undiscovered until they were found by an
American whaler in 1791.) Cook had some difficulty identifying a safe

harbour, but at last found what he was looking for at Vaitahu Bay on Tahuata, a tiny island to the south-west of Hiva Oa. There was another near-disaster as they approached the haven, for a sudden squall sprang up and almost drove them on to the rocks. On the second attempt, however, Cook reached anchorage, still with dolphins and porpoises playing around the ship.[42]

Cook had Mendaña's charts and quickly identified San Pedro (Motane), Dominica (Hiva Oa), Santa Cristina (Tahuata) and Magdalena (Fatu Hiva). It was Mendaña's port of Madre de Dios (Vaitahu Bay) that he was looking for. His reaction to this island group was practical, functional, pragmatic and down-beat. Yet the Marquesas would later become one of the most sought-after desti-nations for celebrities in the Pacific, including Herman Melville, Robert Louis Stevenson, Paul Gauguin, Jack London and Thor Heyerdahl.[43] One of the explanations is that Cook did not visit Fatu Hiva, usually considered the most beautiful of all these islands and made famous by Heyerdahl, or the delightful Nuku Hiva of which Jack London wrote: 'One caught one's breath and felt the pang that is almost hurt, so exquisite was the beauty of it all.'[44] More likely, Cook's lukewarm reaction was a function of the shortage of fresh water on these islands, an intricate effect of the workings of the Humboldt Current. Also, what is beauty to a cushioned traveller can seem to a pioneer explorer Nature at its most forbidding. The forest-cloaked cliffs, which on most of the islands ran sheer to the sea and the eerie volcanic spires, which Stevenson described as like 'the pinnacles of some ornate and monstrous church',[45] would not have appeared so attractive to Cook and his crew, and we should remember that the cult of beauty in Nature had not yet taken its full romantic hold by the 1770s. Finally, Cook probably thought the Marquesas unlucky because a killing occurred before he and his men had even set foot on land. The first afternoon passed peacefully enough, with thirty or forty islanders approaching in a dozen canoes, exchanging fish and breadfruit for nails. But when they swarmed aboard next day the usual thieving began; soon an iron stanchion from a gangway was missing. To discourage further pilfering Cook ordered the marines to fire over the Marquesans' heads, meanwhile trying to cut off from land the thief with the stanchion. Either by accident or design the marines fired low and one man fell dead, at which all the other canoes fled. When the Marquesans returned and tried to steal a buoy, Cook again ordered his men to fire over their heads; the islanders finally got the point and desisted from thieving.[46]

Eventually a proper trade was established, as if nothing had happened. Nails secured them some hogs, but Cook's officers soon ruined the market by breaking his rules about a strict exchange with nails only, and then only for food. The Marquesans soon became bored with nails and petitioned for other trade items. So desperate were Cook's men for pigs that they started exchanging red feathers for swine flesh, and it became clear that for the Marquesans red feathers were like gold dust; soon they would accept no other currency.[47] Despairing of proper revictualling or proper repairs to his ship and finding there was an acute shortage of wood and water, Cook decided to head for the Society Islands as fast as possible. Before he left there was another brush with death when he, Sparrman and the Forsters were in the longboat and were caught out by a high sea; only strenuous rowing, seamanship and a little luck prevented them from being dashed on the rocks.[48] On 12 April he decided to take a close look at the western coast of Hiva Oa, but could find no anchorage so stood away to the south-west. Cook's visit to the Marquesas had been surprisingly inconsequential and incurious: he had not discovered Nuku Hiva, had failed to land on Hiva Oa, and saw Fatu Hiva only from a distance. Anxieties about water, the food supply and his men's health precluded a long exploration. The *Resolution* and its crew had acquired just enough coconuts, plantains and breadfruits to get them through to Tahiti. Nevertheless, some of the observations by Cook and his officers were shrewd and insightful.[49] They noted, that the Marquesas were economically less affluent than the Society Islands, but politically more egalitarian. They conceded that the Marquesans – the men anyway, for few women were seen – were easily the most handsome and good-looking of all Polynesians, but that they were capricious, easily bored and quick to take offence. These impressions were confirmed by later observers of the Marquesas islands.[50] They were also great thieves and would even try to cheat each other while they were bargaining with the Europeans. It was ingrained in oral tradition that the only other whites to visit the islands before Cook (the Spanish with Mendaña) had killed more than 200 of their people, so they were naturally wary of the visitors. The man who made the most impact on them was Hitihiti, who went down in their legends as a great man.[51]

Cook's track now took him once more through the dangerous islands of the Tuamotus, this time the northern ones, some of which had been mentioned but inadequately charted by earlier navigators such as Schouten, Le Maire, Roggeveen and Byron. There were the usual problems with coral reefs, so Cook spent two nights plying under his topsails. A brief landing was made at Takaroa, the so-called Coral Island mentioned by Byron, where Hitihiti successfully bartered for a few dogs and some fish, but when he warned that the local warriors were massing for an attack, Cook put to sea after firing a few cannon shots over the warriors' heads for the sake of credibility; he remembered that Byron had been attacked here. Next the *Resolution* sighted Takapoto and Cook made some excellent lunar observations of longitude to check against the chronometer. After charting four more atolls (Apataki, Toau, Kaukura, Arutua), one of which he called after his friend and patron

Palliser, he found himself once again in clear, open water on the 19th, as was evident from the great swell rolling in from the south.[52]

After completing a seven-month voyage, the *Resolution* was about to begin the fourth act of its epic journey. A long stopover at Tahiti was indicated, not just to repair the ship and lay in adequate victuals, but to give the men time to recover from scurvy and the scientists the leisure to classify specimens or check astronomical observations. Cook, however, told Wales that he intended to stay long enough only to allow the astronomer time to check his instruments; this could be done in Tahiti as its longitude was certain. Hitihiti concluded that he had had enough and would not be proceeding to England; he checked that Cook was prepared to drop him off at Raiatea. His own epic voyage put all previous Polynesian voyagings, even the celebrated journeys of the most famous *arioi*, in the shade. In the Antarctic he had been aghast to find that the sun did not set. He had been in the forefront of all the shore landings, acting as guide, interpreter and expert in cultural hermeneutics. Some of his observations were spot on, as in his summing up of Easter Island: 'Bad land, good people.'[53] Beaglehole (who calls him Odiddy) has this to say: 'Poor delightful Odiddy: it is he among the tempests and icebergs and New Zealand cannibals, not the pretentious Omai, who is the Polynesian hero of the voyage.'[54] Cook anchored in Matavai Bay on 22 April. One of the reasons he had originally decided on a short stay was the much-touted food shortages in Tahiti, but since his last visit the island seemed to have made a miraculous recovery, for there was an abundance of food to trade. He soon discovered the reason. The red feathers he had bought in such quantities at Tongatapu and which had proved such a hit in the Marquesas were an economic talisman. In their lust for the feathers the Tahitians brought out foodstuffs and animals they had preciously hoarded or hidden; from distant Tautira the great Vehiatua sent an embassy with instructions to do what was necessary to bring the plumes back in their dozens.[55] Yet it was not just the financial intricacies of the island that bemused Cook; he had also come back right in the middle of one of Tahiti's periodic bouts of political turbulence. Cook persisted in his fallacious estimate of Tu as a 'king'; it is true that in the long run he would approximate to that status, but in 1774 he was still one of several chiefs jostling for power. Since Cook's last visit the *arii nui* To'ofa had risen to prominence in the northern part of the island.[56] Currently there was a struggle for power on Moorea which Tu wanted to remain aloof from, but he was coming under great pressure from To'ofa and Cook's old friend chief Potatu. Tu, always an exasperating person to deal with, both as regards Europeans and his own countrymen, was on the point of succumbing to the pressure and agreeing to send a fleet against Moorea. He eventually did agree, then changed his mind, frightened of the growing power of To'ofa; the struggle between these two dragged on and was still continuing in 1788 when Bligh and the *Bounty* arrived.[57] At first Cook was not even aware of these undercurrents but waited impatiently for Wales to finish his work. He watched with amusement as Hitihiti was fêted as a great hero by the locals and offered his pick of nubile young women; he was less amused when hordes of similarly desirable females swarmed aboard the ship for more mass orgies.[58] When Potatu arrived with his two wives and a veritable herd of pigs which he promised to trade for the yearned-for red feathers, Cook suddenly rethought his position. It would be folly to sail on and ignore such a cornucopia. A ferocious thunderstorm on the night of the 25th enhanced his prestige; the Tahitians interpreted the bolt that ran down the *Resolution*'s lightning rod as a sign that the god Oro looked with favour on the white men and their treasure trove of feathers.

On 26 April, after deciding on a longer stay, Cook set off to visit Tu at Pare. As they rounded the point they saw a vast armada converging on Tu's village. A fleet of 160 war canoes (doubles) and another 170 smaller canoes (singles), acting as victualling and back-up vessels, were preparing for the assault on Moorea that To'ofa and Potatu were trying to bounce Tu into. Cook did a quick headcount: since there were forty warriors in masks and warpaint in each double canoe, and about eight in each of the smaller boats, he calculated that the armada assembled from just two northern districts must contain more fighting men than Tupaia's estimate of 6–7,000 for the whole island. Even assuming that Tupaia was referring only to the standing army or militia, such numbers indicated a considerable population; it was in fact this event that led Cook to his demographic overestimate mentioned above (see p. 119)[59] At first Cook wondered if such a fleet had been assembled to attack the *Resolution*, but the friendly greetings he received from Tu's uncle Ti'i (also a war chief) soon disabused him of this idea. Ti'i began to lead Cook and his men to Tu's quarters, but suddenly there were sounds of acclamation and a grey-haired man of about 60, still physically vigorous, appeared and was introduced as To'ofa. While Ti'i had hold of Cook's right arm to guide him to Tu, To'ofa grabbed his left arm and tried to pull him towards the war canoes. A farcical scene ensued, with Cook being pulled apart in two different directions in an undignified tug of war.[60] Since neither man would release his hold, Cook cut the Gordian knot by opting to go with To'ofa. But when he refused to board the admiral's canoe, To'ofa, like all Polynesians highly sensitive to real or imagined insults, stormed off. Ti'i then caught up with Cook to tell him that the timorous Tu had reacted to a stressful situation in his usual way and had decamped to the mountains. Ti'i then explained that Tu did not want to join the campaign against Moorea as he did not trust To'ofa and did not think Moorea was his real target; his true objective, he added, was Vehiatua, whom he wanted to attack once he had Tu's levies in the bag. Potatu later appeared to confirm this story, but muddied the waters by suggesting that Amo was his real target.[61]

That afternoon Cook finally met Tu, who was delighted with his guest, since his refusal to go aboard To'ofa's canoe had led to the admiral's loss of face and hence to an increase in his (Tu's) prestige. Next morning Cook paid him another visit and found a chastened To'ofa in conclave with Tu. He invited them both back to the *Resolution* for a lavish lunch. To'ofa was fascinated by all aspects of the *Resolution* while Tu, in unwontedly jovial mood, patronised him, showing him how to eat with a knife and fork and drink wine from a glass. As they grew more and more tipsy, Tu and To'ofa became 'friends' in the way drunkards do in such situations, and they agreed to sail against Moorea. Abandoning his usual caution, Cook offered to sail with them and devastate their enemies (perhaps he too had had too much to drink). At this To'ofa drew back and said they would not need the white man's help; the reason given was that it was still a month to the launch of the expedition and by that time Cook would be gone; the real reason was that To'ofa thought Cook would back Tu when it came to the crunch and might also demand too much booty. In any case Cook soon had second thoughts: musketry had to be kept as the shock weapon of last resort and any overfamiliarity with firearms would increase Tahitian disdain for, and insouciance with, them.[62] Cook soon had more minor matters closer to home to vex him. On 29 April the crew caught a Tahitian trying to steal a water cask. Since this was the kind of theft that could threaten their very survival, Cook ordered the malefactor clapped in irons and then flogged. In vain did local chieftains beg for clemency, on the grounds that in Tahitian culture to steal from a stranger was not a crime but a test of ingenuity and skill. Cook would have none of this special pleading and ordered the maximum possible sentence of twenty-four lashes. The chieftains appealed to Tu, but, not wishing to push Cook in the diretcion of To'ofa, Tu agreed, on condition that the man was not killed. The thief was then stripped and lashed; he bore his punishment with great fortitude.[63]

Tu told his people they should steal from their enemies but not from the Europeans. His relations with Cook were becoming very warm, helped by Cook's tact and diplomacy when theft was not an issue. He asked Tu for permission to cut down trees for wood but promised he would not cut down any fruit-bearing varieties. Tu was so impressed with this that he had the captain's words proclaimed to his people three times.[64] On 7 May Tu visited Cook in his ship and brought his entire family. Yet always the serpent in paradise was the Tahitians' fondness for pilfering and purloining. On the 8th a sentry either fell asleep or quit his post, and a musket was stolen. While the sentry received a dozen lashes for his dereliction of duty, Cook instituted a hue and cry to recover the stolen musket; if Polynesians were allowed to steal firearms with impunity and learned how to use them, the consequences could be disastrous. On hearing the news, Tu, following his usual pattern, decamped to the mountains, but sent Cook word that he would get the musket back; not content with this, Cook followed his custom of taking hostages against the return of the stolen item and then opened fire on Tu's canoes to show he meant business.[65] The Tahitians swore vehemently that the man who had taken the weapon did not even come from Tahiti and had escaped in his canoe to an outlying island, so that it was not in Tu's power to recover it. Cook was sceptical of the story, but the locals offered to accompany him to the unnamed island if he would send an armed force there, for that was the only way those islanders would ever give it back. Cook, suspecting that this was a ruse to inveigle him into island politics – he was certain that when the island was named, it would be Moorea or Tahiti-iti – finally decided to let the entire matter drop and sent word accordingly to Tu.[66] Bizarrely, that very evening the musket was brought in. Had the entire affair been an elaborate plot by Tu and/or To'ofa? Cook suspected Tu was behind it all, for the very next thing that happened was that supplies to the *Resolution* were embargoed on the grounds of what sounded like a very spurious *tapu*. Cook charged Tu with treachery, and to show his anger laid on a demonstration of the power of his cannons which Tu 'viewed seemingly with more pain than pleasure'.[67]

Tu responded a few days later with a demonstration of Tahitian fighting power, allegedly in response to a request from Cook to see how Tu's warriors fought and manoeuvred. The mood swings of the volatile, shifty, subtle, crafty and Machiavellian Tu were a source of amazement to Cook. He wondered if he was doing the right thing in backing him, and worried that To'ofa might win the power struggle.[68] Tu continually blew hot and cold. On the one hand, he lifted the *tapu*, which he had previously declared unbreakable, so that supplies to the *Resolution* resumed. On the other, he intrigued against Cook and colluded with the Irishman Marra, who wanted to desert. The idea was that Marra would dive overboard from the ship as the *Resolution* put to sea from Matavai Bay, and then swim towards the shore where one of Tu's canoes would be waiting to pick him up. But Marra was caught in the act of absconding and brought before Cook who, incredibly, declared that he had a 'good record' and would not be flogged.[69] One wonders what lay behind this curious decision for, so far from having a good record, Marra had already been punished twice (having received eighteen lashes in all) for insolence and would be flogged again before the voyage was over for going absent without official leave; with four punishments marked on his seaman's docket, he was actually the most punished man on both the first two voyages, rivalled only by the marine

Thomas Harford on the final expedition.[70] Moreover, Marra had had the insolence to declare in all seriousness that he was deserting to become the king of
the Society Islands, rather as if he were a forerunner of Kipling's two reprobates in 'The Man Who Would Be King'.[71] A possible reason for the leniency
is that Cook knew that all punishments on board were widely reported around
the islands. If Tu heard that Marra had been punished, he would know that he
had tried to desert and had failed. If no such news was received, he would have
to conclude that Marra did not find his offer attractive enough. Cook may have
reasoned that this was one way to make Tu lose face, even *in absentia*. By now
he was annoyed that he had been cajoled by Tu. He had been ready to sail on
13 May with favourable winds when Tu pleaded with him to postpone his
journey. All that happened during the two days' delay was that Purea, a now
sadly reduced creature, and her ex-husband Amo, had made an inconsequential
visit to the ship and Cook had laid on a firework display.[72]

On the afternoon of 15 May, the *Resolution* anchored in Fare harbour on
Huahine Island. Cook's old friend Ori visited him at once. But just as trading
conditions on Tahiti itself had changed for the better since his last visit, on
Huahine the reverse had happened; the plentiful supplies of hogs were no
more and the people were surly and resentful. Red feathers were not prized
here as they were in Matavai Bay, and the locals had evidently learned how to
drive a hard bargain, since they now demanded an axe per pig. The underlying
reality was that Ori was losing the support of his people and, as his *taio* or
intimate friend, Cook was bracketed with him as an undesirable. What had
aroused popular ire was that Ori had forged an alliance with Puni, chief of the
detested Bora Bora. The consequences for the *Resolution* soon became clear.
When the Forsters and Sparrman went on a botanising expedition, the locals
attacked Sparrman's servant and beat him badly. Even worse, Johann Forster
tried to shoot the assailants, but his musket flashed in the pan, alerting the men
of Huahine that European firearms were not so powerful after all.[73] Next day
Cook stormed into Ori's council to demand retribution. Ori had to explain
that the attack was nothing to do with him and that the culprits had fled to
the mountains, whence he could not immediately dislodge them. Out of his
friendship for Ori, Cook let it go at that, but the return for his restraint was
that the anti-Ori faction escalated its attacks. A young woman who had accompanied the Europeans from Tahiti was seized and stripped, while Clerke
fought with a man who tried to steal his gun. On 20 May three officers out on
a shooting party were set on and stripped of all they possessed.[74] Cook retaliated by seizing the local chieftain's house and its inhabitants against the return
of the stolen goods. Once again Ori lamented that he was heartbroken about
what had happened. Johann Forster wrote sniffily in his diary that none of this

would have happened but for Cook's peaceful policies; a 'shoot to kill' policy would have soon concentrated Polynesian minds.[75]

Next day Ori had the melancholy duty of reporting to Cook that thirteen renegade men of Huahine were responsible for the outrages and were now challenging Cook to come out and fight them. Cook called a council of war, at which it was decided that strong measures were called for. He landed a party of forty-eight heavily armed men and, together with Ori and Hitihiti as guides, marched inland. Soon they were told that the 'bandits' had had second thoughts and had fled to the mountains. Hitihiti meanwhile grew alarmed at the number of men who tagged along with Cook's party whom he suspected of secretly being in the anti-Ori faction; it was also suspicious that Ori himself did not want to go any farther. Eventually Cook saved face by reaching a steep, rocky valley and declaring that the terrain made it impossible to proceed. The 'avengers' returned to the *Resolution*, where Cook gave a display of disciplined, rolling musketry fire.[76] By now the sojourn in Huahine had turned into a dispiriting experience – lots of coconuts and breadfruit but very few hogs, and sustained hostility into the bargain – and Cook was eager to be gone. When he told Ori that he would never see him again, his friend burst into tears. 'Then let your sons come; we will treat them well,' said Ori.[77] It is tempting to see this as an act of cruelty directed at a sentimental man who had failed him, but all the evidence suggests that Cook genuinely did think he would never visit the Society Islands again.[78] On 23 May he sailed away, but because of adverse winds and difficult reefs it took him two days to get to Raiatea, where another *taio*, Oreo, awaited him. Here there were extravagant dances and unbridled sexual licence which delighted the sailors, the whole shot through and informed by the culture of the *arioi*, whose centre Raiatea was as surely as Lesbos was Saphho's. There was the usual spate of thefts, most of them trivial, though the removal of the pinnace's iron tiller was far more serious. Cook went to Oreo to complain, and with his help most of the articles were restored but not, perhaps significantly, the iron tiller. Cook concluded that without Oreo's help in the matter he could do little.[79]

At Raiatea the issue of Hitihiti was finally settled. A great favourite with the crew, affable, genial but neither very intelligent nor very talented – he conspic-uously lacked Tupaia's linguistic skills – Hitihiti had the misfortune to have the Forsters as champions, guides and mentors. On Tahiti he had created a sensa-tion with his traveller's tales, ranging from the bloodthirsty cannibal feasts of the Maoris, which were widely believed, to his narrative of the Antarctic, with its icebergs and midnight sun, which was not. He had had his pick of the local girls and had taken a wife. He could have achieved fame and fortune on Tahiti, and indeed Tu had offered him a high place in his entourage, but the Forsters dissuaded him, saying that he should continue to his homeland in Raiatea. They argued that, once Cook had gone, the jelaous Tahitians would round on him and strip him of all his wealth. Hitihiti, who changed his mind frequently, decided on the way to Raiatea that he would like to continue to England after all, but Cook was by now convinced that he would never be returning to the Society Islands, so how could he ever get back?[80] As for the idea of settling permanently in England, Cook rightly thought it chimerical and was very critical of the fad for taking Polynesians to Europe, as Bougainville, Banks and now Furneaux had all done, so far with disastrous results. Cook thought it irresponsible of the Forsters to hint that Polynesians could make their fortunes in London and thought it more likely that they would be overwhelmed by culture shock. He therefore issued an ordinance that no officers or scientists could take South Sea islanders back to England, whether as pets, mascots or servants. Predictably, Johann Forster railed against this very reasonable stance as an act of autocratic tyranny.[81] Hitihiti's last hurrah was to get wildly drunk on Cook's brandy at a small party hosted for the captain by Hitihiti's brother. When the *Resolution* finally left Raiatea, Hitihiti burst into tears and followed the ship's progress to the horizon with heartbroken melancholy.[82] Cook had been ready to leave on 31 May, but sensational news delayed him for a further three days. Reports reached him that two British ships had anchored at Huahine, one of them captained by Banks, the other by Furneaux. The arrival of the *Adventure* was remotely possible – but *Banks*? Cook sent couriers back to Huahine to learn the truth and attempted to question the man who had originally come in with the news, but he had vanished. Cook called a council of his officers to discuss sailing back to Huahine, but most of them thought the reports a rumour or an elaborate practical joke. Eventually a number of trusted eyewitnesses returned from Huahine to say the whole affair was nonsense.[83] One suspects that a lovesick sailor, still pining for a beloved on Huahine, had set up an elaborate 'sting' to get Cook to sail back there.

Cook cleared from the Society Islands on 4 June and set a south-westerly course, making good progress with easterly winds, intending to investigate the islands reported by Quirós. Next day he passed the atoll Wallis had dubbed Lord Howe's Island, and eleven days later passed Palmerston Island; there had been good weather all the way, always with a large swell from the south in evidence. Land (Niue or, as Cook called it, Savage Island) was sighted on 21 June, and the following day Cook landed to give the Forsters a chance to botanise. The reception by the locals was unusually hostile: they threw stones at the visitors, to which Sparrman and the Forsters responded with musket fire.[84] Cook, often accused of overreaction himself, thought his three scientists unacceptably trigger-happy on this occasion. More islanders rushed out from the woods towards the canoes, and there was more stone-throwing and more musketry in response. Cook ordered his men to cease fire, whereupon the Niueans retreated into the woods and were seen no more.[85] An initial and seemingly gratuitous 'welcome' of outright hostility was unusual in the Pacific islands – usually this was triggered after thefts or some other misunderstanding – and anthropologists have suggested two possible reasons. One is that Cook mistook the Niueans' intentions: they were performing the alarming but friendly ritual of 'challenge' to strangers well known to the Maoris.[86] Defiant gestures with weapons could be explained in this way, but hardly the stone-throwing. The other explanation is that Cook was trying to raise the Union Jack on a sacred site, where the paramount chiefs were traditionally anointed by ritual.[87] Whatever the reason, the belligerence on Niue discouraged botanical expeditions or any further reconnoitring, to the intense frustration of Johann Forster. Once more quoting Virgil, Forster rationalised his anger with the consolation of the classics: 'Thus we left this inhospitable shore with its still more inhospitable inhabitants.'[88]

On 25 June more islands were seen, with reefs and breakers. Cook was off the Otutulu islands, subsidiaries of the Nomuka group, approaching the Tongan archipelago about a degree farther north than the year before. He worked through the maze of islands – by now he was something of a Theseus in being able to thread his way through such labyrinths – and anchored on the 27th off Tasman's Bay. Nomuka had been discovered in 1643 by Tasman, who called it Rotterdam. Here he had stayed for three nights and two days. The inhabitants were friendly but the island had no fresh water and Cook had to take on the brackish variety. The food supply was better, with yams, shaddocks and even some pigs and fowl which were traded for nails and beads; the hunters were able to bag a large number of ducks.[89] Soon enough the thefts began, but when one of the Nomukans stole a gun, for once Cook underreacted, mistakenly eschewing the use of force. At this the locals grew insolent, and thefts and minor assaults became rampant. In the end Cook had to show his muscle: he had muskets fired over the Nomukans' heads and then he landed all his marines with full panoply, telling the locals that they would lay waste the entire island if the musket was not returned; it very soon was. Cook next demanded the return of a stolen adze, whereat the locals complained that he was being 'mean' by making such a fuss over the return of such a 'trivial' item.[90] The classic failure of Europeans and Polynesians to communicate was compounded when an elderly couple offered Cook an extremely comely young girl as his concubine. When Cook tried to make his excuses and leave, the old woman became a raging virago. What kind of man is this, she cried, who would refuse the embraces of a beautiful young woman?[91] Cook could hardly explain that he never consorted with Pacific women as a matter of principle; such 'principle' would have been regarded as madness. He considered taking his 'mistress' on board just to shut the old woman up, but immediately reflected that this would lead to a universal clamour from the men that they be allowed to take women aboard. Cook retired, embarrassed, discomfited, and with loss of face; as Beaglehole remarks archly: 'We see for once the captain driven off a field of battle in utter rout.'[92]

Setting sail on 29 June, still with good weather, Cook passed Tofua, Kao and the islet Vatoa, an outlier of the Fiji group and the nearest Cook ever got to Fiji; had his track been even slightly farther north he would undoubtedly have reached the large islands of Vanua Levu and Viti Levu, providing a distraction that would compensate for not following up on Quirós's discoveries. But Cook was destined to visit neither Fiji nor Samoa. Sailing between them (north of Fiji and south of Samoa), he then swung west, looking for the New Hebrides described by Quirós and Bougainville. Forster chafed at the long stretches at sea: he complained that either Cook would not land at any of the interesting islands they passed or that if the ship did land it was immediately driven off by hostile natives.[93] The voyagers were heading now for Espiritu Santo, but on 17 July their long run of good luck with the weather ran out. A gale now hit them, as described by Cook: 'It blew exceeding hard at times and there went a great sea from the south-east. Besides, several of our sails were split and torn to pieces in the night, particularly a foretop sail which was rendered quite useless as a sail.'[94] On the 18th they stood in for the shores of Maewo, an island slightly to the east of Espiritu Santo. Having the island to windward they then enjoyed a smooth sea while the winds and waves raged on the open ocean. They tacked all day between Maewo and Omba on the 19th, occasionally glimpsing men on the shore with bows and arrows. On the 20th Cook stood over to Pentecost Island. On the 21st the *Resolution* passed the volcanic island of Ambrym and finally made landfall at sunset at Malekula.[95] Cook now intended to chart the entire length of the New Hebrides (modern Vanuatu). The New Hebrides turned out to be formed in the shape of an immense Y, with Maewo, Pentecost and Ambrym on the upper right or eastern arm of the letter, and Makelula and Espiritu Santo on the left or western arm. Cook had entered the eastern group by the top of the eastern arm. From 20 July until the end of August he would sail down inside and out again through the northern part of the 'leg' of the Y on to its eastern side, would then follow the leg to its southern extremity, and finally turn between the eastern islands to come up on the western side and in at the top between the arms again.[96]

On 22 July the *Resolution* was invaded – no other word will do – as hundreds of the locals swam to the ship and swarmed on board. When Cook called a halt and refused to admit any more, those who were barred began shooting poisoned arrows; he responded by firing four-pound shots over the tops of the canoes, whereupon panic ensued and the ship was cleared. Soon the ship's company heard the ominous beating and booming of war drums.[97] Cook and an armed party came cautiously in to land in two boats but found that the 'proofs of toughness' had done their work. Although there were 500 armed men waiting for them on the shore, they parted as the Red Sea for Moses to allow Cook to land, made peaceful signs, and gave no indication of belligerence. Cook's men were struck by the very different physical appearance of these islanders from any they had encountered so far. These had very dark skins and black, frizzled hair, and wore distinctive clothes; not surprisingly, since the inhabitants of Vanuatu are a cross between Polynesians and Melanesians proper. Later research in anthropology and ethnology revealed that the New Hebrideans regarded the Europeans as ghosts or spirits of the departed, with the *Resolution* featuring as the ship of death.[98] Cook conveyed to the men of Makelula that he wanted water, wood and pigs, but trade initially proved difficult as they set no value on nails or iron and wanted only cloth. Cook was struck by the honesty of these people, which was so unlike the Polynesians. There was one minor instance of theft but otherwise it was non-existent. When the *Resolution* was leaving one island in the group, bound for another, Cook's men had often already given their trade goods but the Hebrideans had not completed the exchange. Instead of letting the ship go on its way, delighted to have obtained a 'freebie', as would have been the Polynesian way, these people made strenuous efforts to catch the ship up so that they could hand over their payment goods.[99] In so many ways this land was unlike Polynesia: the coconuts, breadfruit and plantain were of an inferior quality; there were few pigs; and no dogs. The only real novelty was the poison arrows, whose efficacy Cook's surgeon later rather callously tested. He operated on a dog, made a deep incision, inserted poison and sewed up the wound; the dog seemed unaffected, made a full recovery and returned to England.[100]

Despite his moral admiration, Cook was dismayed by the physical ugliness of the Vanuatu people; he and his crew often compared them to monkeys.[101] Yet they seemed friendly, and that was more important than anything else. Far more damage than their poison arrows was caused by two red fish which the midshipman John Elliott caught. When he shared his catch in the officers' mess, the result was a mass outbreak of food poisoning, so acute that all Cook's lieutenants were on the sick list for a week and the dogs and pigs who ate the fish were also extremely ill; a parrot who partook died from the effects.[102] For a week as the ship sailed south, Cook had to use mates and gunners for executive duties on the *Resolution* while the stricken officers recovered. The voyagers passed Paama, Makrum, Montagu Island and Sandwich Island (Efate), pursuing a zigzag route, threading through the many rocks, islets and desolate, uninhabited humps of land, and reached the island of Eromanga on 3 August.[103] At daybreak on the 4th he went ashore in two boats to examine the coastline. At first the locals appeared friendly and invited the visitors to land, but when Cook declined they turned nasty and tried to haul the boats on to the shore. Cook drew a bead on the man who was obviously the chieftain but his musket misfired, which had the unfortunate effect of making the Eromangans think the strangers' weapons were harmless; there followed a fusillade of stones, darts and arrows. Cook ordered the firing of two salvoes, which killed four men and wounded two others, yet even this did not clear the islanders off the beach for a long time; two of his men sustained light wounds from the missiles. When the Eromangans regrouped and reappeared, brandishing two oars they had seized during the scrimmage, Cook ordered a four-pounder fired over their heads.[104] He toyed with the idea of staying longer, but when a northerly breeze sprang up he decided to set his sails and ply out of the bay. He had learned the bitter lesson that Melanesian ideas of hospitality were not the same as Polynesian and that in this part of the world white strangers were regarded as ghosts, in this case specifically spirits of their ancestors.[105]

Next day the voyagers reached Tanna, an island due south of Eromanga, and after much heart-searching Cook decided to try another landing. He sent Cooper ahead with a strong, heavily armed party and they met the usual reception committee of warriors on the beach, but this time there was no opposition and no hostility. Once he had received the all-clear, Cook brought the *Resolution* in close and anchored her in four fathoms of water. Soon an old man came paddling out to the ship bearing coconuts; he introduced himself as a chief named Paowang. But when gifts had been exchanged and the chief returned to the shore, this seemed to be construed as the signal for a free-for-all. Armed warriors surrounded the ship, tried to tear down her ensign, knock the rings off her rudder and steal meat, which was being towed alongside to soften it for cooking. Cook gave the signal to open fire both with muskets and big guns. Since he ordered the shots to be fired over the Tannans' heads, they did not immediately get the intended message, and it was a long time before Cook was able to impress his authority on the contumacious warriors.[106] Cook now moored the ship with four anchors, broadside to the landing place, with his artillery commanding the whole harbour. Next day Paowang reappeared and indicated that there would be no objection to the strangers' obtaining wood and water. Cautiously at first, the men landed and went about their hunting and gathering tasks. When no further incidents occurred over the following days, the tension gradually relaxed; Paowang became a frequent visitor to the ship and seemed generally affable, though volatile and unpredictable. The deep undercurrent on the island seemed to be a state of permanent strife between those on the western side and those on the east: the easterners friendly, the westerners less so.[107] This was why the main expeditionary aim of the landing – ascending the active volcano Mount Yasur – was never fulfilled. The ship's party had seen the pillars of fire and smoke spewing from the cone while they were still at sea and were keen to investigate further, but when they set out to explore, an armed party barred their way; Cook thought it best not to risk a pitched battle over something of consuming interest to the Forsters but not really to the rest of the crew.[108]

Cook has often been criticised for his strong-arm methods in the Pacific, but on Tanna he was a model of enlightenment when compared with his comrades. The armed opposition of the Melanesians, their maddening insistence on *tapu* and superstition – believing him to be the spirit of a returned ancestor the Tannans consistently offered him only tiny morsels of food – and their apparent pedantry over mores and folkways had to be set in context, as he appreciated:

> It was impossible for them to know our real design; we enter their ports without their daring to oppose; we endeavour to land in their country as friends and it is well if this succeeds; we land, nevertheless, and maintain the footing we have got by the superiority of our firearms. Under such circumstances, what opinion are they to form of us? Is it not as reasonable for them to think that we come to invade their country, as to pay them a friendly visit?[109]

Cook tried hard to put his 'liberalism' into practice. When, on 16 August, he wanted to cut down a large tree to make a new tiller and Paowang objected, Cook went to the chief's council and explained to the elders why he needed to fell the tree; they admitted his request was reasonable and agreed to it. He made a point of never touching wood or water without the islanders' express consent. He further conciliated the local elders by inviting them to dine on board; they showed endless curiosity about the *Resolution* itself but were indifferent to its cuisine, particularly shrinking from salt beef and pork.[110] He also made a conscientious effort to understand this new culture and why folkways within island groups, for instance Tanna as compared with Makelula, were so different, to say nothing of the racial mixture. Cook shared George Forster's awe at the Tannans' expertise with clubs and bows and arrows (though not Forster's melodramatic near terror at their skills) and attested that the feats he had seen on Vanuatu made him far less sceptical than previously about the plausibility of the spear-throwing feats in the *Iliad*.[111]

Cook's diplomacy was not shared either by his seamen, who were in surly mood because they could find no women – those on Tanna ran off if they ever sighted a European – or his officers and scientists. Despite his explicit orders, a party of woodcutters responded to stone-throwing on 10 August by opening fire.[112] There were exaggerated rumours that all the Tannans were cannibals – in fact ritual cannibalism was restricted to a small elite – and that they were all bisexual, with pronounced sodomitical tendencies. The latter mistake was caused by the Tannans' inability to make sense of the clothes worn by European servants and the fact that they carried bundles, which only women did in Melanesia.[113] Needless to say, the prime fount of trouble was Johann Forster. Annoyed that his native guide would not agree with his classification of a green pigeon, Forster kicked him and spat in his face in the presence of a number of other islanders. Clerke came over, discovered what was the matter, and reprimanded Forster, who got on his high horse and told Clerke that as a military man he had no authority over civilians. Tempers rose, and in the end both men had drawn their guns.[114] Both appealed to Cook, and Cook upheld Clerke. Forster then demanded to have Cook's opinion in writing, doubtless so that he could show it to King George, which was his usual threat. Cook dug in, stating that Forster had no right to demand anything, and pointing out that his stupid irresponsibility could have precipitated a general attack on the *Resolution* by the locals. Forster once more retired hurt, breathing vengeful fire into his journal, where he stated that no man of education or standing would ever again consent to sail on His Majesty's ships with such uneducated ruffians and that the Royal Navy was a madhouse, whereby in a kind of Swiftian inversion men of learning were commanded and ordered about by morons.[115] The incident increased Forster's unpopularity among the seamen, if that was possible, for Clerke was a great favourite below decks. The officers on board closed ranks around Clerke and ostracised Forster; when a new species of stingray was discovered on the island, the usually calm and rational Cooper cut off its tail and threw it away rather than bring it to the attention of Forster.[116]

Even without Forster to annoy them, the seamen were becoming frustrated and restive. The protracted labour on the tiller went on until 19 August, with no diversions or women to distract the toilers. On the 17th one of the marines was flogged for trading with the locals while on guard duty, which the prickly marines resented as a gratuitous attack by Cook on their *esprit de corps*.[117] They were still in a sour mood when, two days later another marine on sentry-go, William Wedgeborough, picked a fight with some trading locals. He drew a line in the sand, warned them not to cross it and, when they did so, began to pummel them. When one of the Tannans raised his bow and arrow in defiance, Wedgeborough used the excuse to shoot the man dead. A furious Cook, who saw the entire incident, testified that the locals often made the bow and arrow gesture as a face-saver, to show the Europeans they were just as prepared for a fight; he was angry with the sentry whose actions in his eyes had 'not the least cause'.[118] When Cook ordered Wedgeborough clapped in irons, there was uproar from the sailors. Even worse, Cook soon found himself at odds with the rest of his officers. The lieutenant of marines, who was more concerned with the image and prestige of his men than with upholding his captain's orders, haughtily remarked that 'the man was entitled to believe he was not posted there merely to provide a target for arrows'.[119] Cooper weighed in with the argument that Cook's 'lenity' had encouraged the Tannans to become insolent, to the point where all sentries had reached snapping point. Clerke went out on a limb by stating that he had given explicit orders that if a native brandished any kind of weapon, that made retaliatory shooting justifiable homicide. Since Cook had issued standing orders that his men were never to open fire unless they were unambiguously under attack, this intervention by Clerke was a direct challenge to his captain's authority. Cook was in a minority of one.[120] Forster was gleeful that these rebellious Navy men who had humiliated him were now falling out among themselves. Elliott summed up midshipman opinion by saying that whereas Cook was usually the most fair and just man, on this occasion he had lost sight of all justice and humanity.[121] In the end, in the interests of shipboard harmony, Cook did not have Wedgeborough flogged but he kept him in irons for two months, to make the point that he was still the commander. The rift between Cook and his officers later become something of a cause célèbre in a famous disputation between Johann Forster and William Wales.[122]

On the morning of 20 August Cook put to sea, and for the next eleven days he was surveying the rest of the New Hebrides without making landfall. First he headed slightly east, then south, charting the extreme southerly islands in the group, Erronan and Anatom, then he struck almost directly due north past Eromanga, Sandwich Island (23 August) and Malekula, then east through the Bougainville Strait between Malekula and Espiritu Santo, before sailing due north again along the eastern coast of Espiritu Santo, passing Cape Quirós on the 25th and reconnoitring the northern coast on 26–27 August. On the 28th he doubled Cape Cumberland, then turned south and cruised the western coast of Espiritu Santo.[123] Essentially he came up on the western side of the leg of the Y, in at the top between the two arms, then passed right through the western arm, first inside, then outside. His long and meticulous charting of the entire New Hebrides group in the six weeks from 17 July to the end of August was one of his great triumphs of surveying and cartography, perhaps second only to the running survey of New Zealand carried out on the *Endeavour*.[124]

On the last day of August he stood away to the south-west and on 1 September was out of sight of land, making for New Zealand. Once again a Cook decision had stupefied his officers and scientists. They had all regarded it as a certainty that Cook would have to head for Cape Horn and Tierra del Fuego after the New Hebrides, for otherwise he would have a very short Antarctic summer in which to conduct his final sweep in search of the Great Southern Continent.[125] He had not originally intended to return to his 'base' in New Zealand but, some time during the stay at Tanna, had decided that he needed a full shipload of water and food before attempting another foray into the Southern Ocean. It is likely, too, that recent events convinced him that the officers and men needed a period of rest and recreation, a cooling-off period when passions would temper, before the *Resolution* once more tangled with the storm-tossed nightmare of Antarctica.[126] At this stage of his career Cook was still not just a master of surveying and seamanship but also a shrewd reader of human psychology.

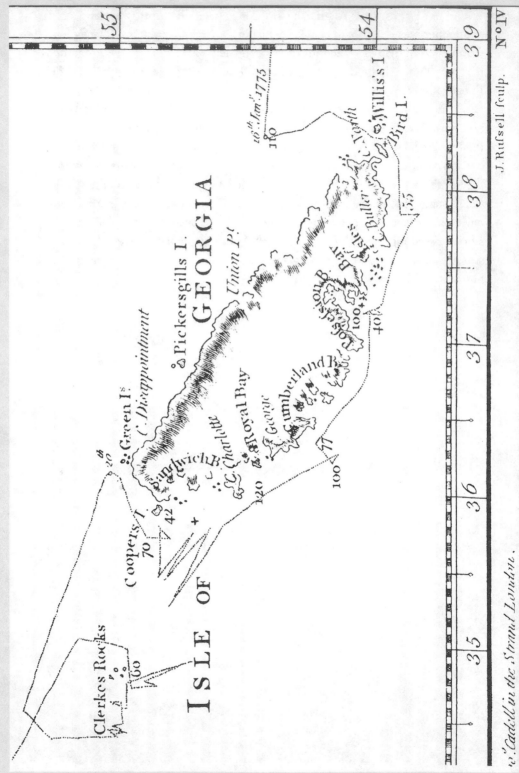

ISLE OF

GEORGIA

Pickersgills I.

Union P.ᵗ

C. Disappointment

Green Iˢ.

Sandwich B.

C. Charlotte

Royal Bay

George

Cumberland B.

Possession B.

Bay of Isles

C. Buller

C. North

Willis's I

Bird I.

16ᵗʰ Jan.ʳ 1775

Coopers I.

Clerkes Rocks

ɯ. Cadell in the Strand London.

CHAPTER TWELVE

Lost Horizon: The Great Southern Continent

Striking south from Vanuatu, after three days Cook reached an unknown and uncharted land to which he gave the name New Caledonia (Noumea). Cook arrived on the north-east corner of Noumea, the fourth largest island in the Pacific, running about 300 miles from south-east to north-west. He remained twenty-seven days in New Caledonia, eight of them at anchor at the northern end of the island and the rest of the time cruising and surveying. The big island was dangerous to shipping, being almost completely surrounded by a coral reef and, towards the south, the coastline disappeared into a confusion of sandy islets, shoals and reefs. On the afternoon of 5 September, Cook and a strong party landed and were given a friendly reception by the locals, full-blooded Melanesians and no longer confusable with Polynesians by any stretch of the imagination. This time the usual phenomenon of islanders swarming over the *Resolution* did not lead to thefts and gunfire. The locals showed a great willingness to trade for beads and nails, but had little to offer the strangers.[1] Much more backward and primitive than Polynesians, they knew nothing of dogs, goats or even hogs, and had never seen a firearm: they were stupefied when Forster brought down a duck with a musket. They lived mainly on roots and fish, since very little of the island 'staples' of plantains, breadfruit and sugar cane were available here. There was no alcohol, but the Melanesians took sustenance by chewing on the bark of a tree which resembled the cinchona of South America. A medium-length stay was dictated by the excellent water found by Pickersgill, whom Cook also used as the head of scouting or reconnoitring parties. By 7 September the visitors were sufficiently relaxed to undertake exploring and botanical expeditions.[2] They identified the local chief of the area, named Tea Puma, and Cook did the usual honours of inviting him and his headmen to dine; they were prepared to eat the yams brought from Tanna but turned their noses up at salt pork and red wine. Dogs were a particular source of amazement to the New Caledonians, so Cook cemented his friendship with

Tea Puma by giving him a pair of breeding dogs, hoping they would not be eaten.[3]

Yet all was not sweetness and light during the sojourn at Noumea. A dark note was struck early during the stay by the death of Simon Monk, the ship's butcher, who fell down the fore hatchway and fractured his skull; he was buried at sea. Then Cook and some of his officers suffered a second case of food poisoning by fish, again through incautiously eating a local variety of puffer fish without inquiring into its qualities. This one was virulent enough to kill a pig and sicken all the dogs that feasted off it.[4] Actually, Cook should have taken warning from the initial gift Tea Puma made him, which was a stinking fish – a present thought appropriate for the ghost of an ancestor who, presumably, was not prey to mortal diseases – but Cook, by all accounts, thought it morally inappropriate to be fastidious about food.[5] Then, on 10 September, he sent Pickersgill and Gilbert out in the cutter to explore the coast, but they botched the operation and, moreover, returned with a damaged cutter which the carpenter had to patch up.[6] There was also more trouble with Johann Forster. The prickly scientist was just sitting down to his midday meal aboard the *Resolution* when Cooper, commanding a landing party, announced that all who wanted to go ashore should immediately muster for embarkation in the boats. Forster took this as deliberate provocation on Cooper's part, forcing him to choose between his dinner and a day's botanising. He stayed on board but complained vociferously to Cook about his second in command's behaviour.[7] By this time there was no sympathy at all for Fortser. His behaviour had so alienated the officers that they had leaked the details of his £4,000 honorarium below decks, where it led to angry uproar and threats to heave the German overboard one dark night. His son George was also fractious. By now having served his apprenticeship many times over in the rites of Venus, he complained that the Melanesian women were mere coquettes and teases, that they promised much but delivered nothing.[8] But Cook had more important things than the Forsters on his mind. By now he had decided not to attempt a complete circum-navigation of New Caledonia. The sea was strewn with shoals; there was no safe anchorage; and it was far better to head south-east where there was a clear sea. It was left to the explorer Bruni d'Entrecasteaux in 1792 to explore the western coast of Noumea.[9]

Cook put to sea again on 13 September and at first explored in a north-westerly direction, but could not be certain whether the land he was seeing was part of Noumea or simply detached islands, and if he moved in closer to investigate he would be at the mercy of wind and reefs. He therefore turned back south-east and ran down along the eastern coast of Noumea. Much that he saw reminded him of Australia, but there was something new, for he formed almost a monomania about a tall tree, which he described as being like a spruce pine but which actually turned out to be the *Araucaria columnaris*, now known as the Cook pine. For ten days he carried out a running survey in the teeth of the most contradictory and varying winds, but at least with clear weather.[10] In attempting to round the southernmost point of Noumea, on 29 September, Cook found himself in a perilous situation, reminiscent of the Barrier Reef four years previously. The wind blowing from the east wafted the *Resolution* dangerously close to a continuous reef. They were surrounded by shoals, a fresh gale was blowing and Cook dared not anchor in case the gale increased and swept them on to the breakers and the reef. The night of 29–30 September was spent in supreme anxiety, the boats once more towing the ship away from the breakers, the *Resolution* herself trying to tack out of danger, and every man hauling on the ropes. Cries of 'Luff!' and 'Breakers ahead' rent the air. It was a supreme test of Cook's seamanship and the disciplined efficiency of his crew. Cook noted: 'Thus we spent the night under the terrible apprehensions of every moment falling on some of the many dangers which surrounded us. Daylight showed that our fears were not ill founded and that we had spent the night in the most eminent danger, having had shoals and breakers continually under our lee at a very little distance from us.'[11] Elliott confirmed this: 'Every way we stood for an hour, the roaring of breakers was heard ... a most anxious and perilous night, at last daylight appeared.' Wales's dry comment was: 'I really think our situation was to be envied by very few except the thief who has got the halter about his neck.'[12] A lesser man would instantly have run for cover to the open sea, but Cook's dogged determination was never so clearly on display (his officers thought it arrant stubbornness). His excuse ran as follows: 'I was now almost tired of a coast I could no longer explore but at the risk of losing the ship and ruining the whole voyage, but I was determined not to leave it till I was satisfied what sort of trees were those which had been the subject of our speculation. With this view we stood to the north in hopes of finding anchorage under some of the isles on which they grow.'[13] The best specimens were found on a smaller island just off the southern tip of Noumea, where the giant trees formed bizarre structures like tall colonnades. Cook was much criticised for sailing into the neck of a funnel and putting himself in another labyrinth of shoals just to look at trees, but the criticism was not open to the Forsters, who had so often lambasted him for *not* stopping to look at natural phenomena. Transfixed by the beauty of Espiritu Santo, they had commented bitterly on Cook's failure to land there.[14]

Nevertheless Cook's hand was forced on 1 October when a heavy gale sprang up. Cook reported: 'We now had a hard gale at south-south-west and a great sea, and had reason to rejoice of having got clear of the shoals before this gale overtook us.'[15] He initially stood away to the south-east and on the same day was out of sight of land. On 2 October he reported a very high sea from the same direction as the wind and by the 3rd the continuing gale had produced a great swell from the south, quashing any lingering idea of returning to New Caledonia. The high seas continued, with a great southerly swell succeeded by an equally awesome undulation from the south-west. The gales continued but the worst was over after three days.[16] On 9 October the seamen managed to harpoon a dolphin, whose flesh was much prized. Cook altered course to the west and, on 10 October, halfway to New Zealand at latitude 29, he discovered an uninhabited island which he named Norfolk Isle. His men landed and brought back a goodly supply of fish and cabbages; the Forsters were delighted with the bird life.[17] Striking south again, Cook enjoyed fine weather for five days but then, at midnight on the 16th, the full fury of the elements hit them once more. A violent storm struck the *Resolution* off the west coast of New Zealand. The wind increased to the point where Cook had to close-reef his topsails and strike the topgallant yards, sailing with only two courses and two close-reefed topsails.

> At midnight we tacked and made a trip to the north till three o'clock next morning, when we bore away for the sound. At nine we hauled round Point Jackson through a sea which looked terrible, occasioned by a rapid tide and a high wind; but as we knew the coast it did not alarm us. At eleven o'clock we anchored before Ship Cove; the strong flurries from off the land not permitting us to get in.[18]

The storm had carried them near Mount Egmont, around Cape Egmont, Cape Stephens and Port Jackson before they found safety. On the 19th Cook warped the ship into the cove, where serious repair work was at once started. Several of the sails had been split in the storm and the main and fore courses were now useless. Cook ordered the topmasts struck and unrigged while a forge was set up to repair the ironwork.[19]

Cook went to look for the bottle in which he had left the message for Furneaux and saw that it was gone. Wales's observations and other obvious traces showed that many trees had been felled in the area. So all in all it was obvious that the *Adventure* had been here.[20] In fact Furneaux was already long in England by this time, having arrived at Spithead on 14 July 1774 after a seven-month voyage from New Zealand via Cape Horn and the Cape of Good Hope. Suspicions as to Furneaux's motives, which could not be voiced in the absence of definite proof, were increased by the absence of any message to Cook suggesting further provisional rendezvous. Cook needed a month in

Ship Cove to do all the repair work on the ship, because the more she was investigated, the more alarming flaws were found. The sails Cook knew about, but he was taken aback to find that the entire hull was in need of caulking. On 24 October the first contact was made with the Maoris, who recognised them and greeted them as long-lost friends. They did not dare to tell Cook the full story about the *Adventure* as they feared the retribution this would bring, but even the snippets Cook picked up about his sister ship made him uneasy. He was pleased to see that the locals had not killed the pigs he left behind, which encouraged him to hope that New Zealand might soon be well stocked with them.[21] The contacts with the Maoris over the following month were inconsequential, but one benefit of the *Resolution*'s stopover was that a new and better entrance into Queen Charlotte Sound, now known as Tory Channel, was found.[22] Cook's leniency also came back to haunt him but it was not his tolerance towards indigenous peoples that was at issue. The incorrigible John Marra, whom Cook had previously and inexplicably pardoned, jumped ship in pursuit of a local woman. Cook was inclined to let him go, quite certain the Maori would kill him as soon as they were gone, but duty and credibility made him get the fellow back; and this time he received a punishment of twelve lashes. Another young able seaman named John Keplin also went absent without leave, intending to go native and live among the Maoris. He changed his mind before he was halfway to his destination, but this time the testy Cook was in no mood for forgiveness or mercy; Keplin also felt the taste of the cat.[23] After completing the repairs to the ship and being assured that Wales had made all necessary longitudinal calculations, Cook bade farewell to his New Zealand 'base' on 20 November, stood out of the sound, raced along the Cook Strait and passed Cape Campbell, heading south-east for Cape Horn.

The passage to Cape Horn was made in record time, with the *Resolution* encountering only mild gales and enjoying a following wind that enabled her to clock up 183 nautical miles in one twenty-four-hour period. Off Tierra del Fuego on 17 December Cook allowed himself a sliver of self-satisfaction: 'I have now done with the Southern Pacific Ocean and flatter myself that no one will think that I have left it unexplored or that more could have been done, in one voyage, towards obtaining that end than has been done in this.'[24] Next he threaded his way through the capes and inlets of Tierra del Fuego, what he called 'coasting', making for Cape Horn. Somewhere along the way William Wedgeborough, the marine who had shot a Tannan and caused the rift between Cook and his officers, fell overboard while drunk and using the heads – only the third and, as it turned out, the final casualty of the voyage on the *Resolution*. On 21 December Cook anchored in a sheltered cove and went out exploring with the botanists. Contact was made with the Fuegians – actually the Alacaluf

people, who had a distinctive language and culture, different from the East
Fuegians or Aush. Small, squat and squarely built, smeared with grease,
stinking, dirty and, to the Europeans, irremediably stupid, they struck Sparrman
as being 'the filthiest, most miserable and pitiable of all the children of men'.[25]
But the abundant food supplies more then compensated for the deficiencies of
the indigenous humans. Apart from excellent wild celery and luscious mussels,
the area teemed with geese and ducks. On Christmas Eve two separate shooting
parties notched up a total of seventy-five bird kills, mainly geese, from which
Christmas fare of roast goose and goose pie was prepared. The Madeira wine
that was left had improved after nearly three years of roving, so when Cook
broached it, everything needed for a merry Christmas was present. 'So that our
friends in England did not, perhaps, celebrate Christmas more cheeerfully than
we did.'[26] Johann Forster thought the liberty Cook allowed his crew to get
roaring drunk was mere licence, and the celebrations more appropriate to a
pagan festival than to the birth of Christ. Even Cook may have thought he had
allowed too much leeway for the following day he sent all the men ashore, out
of reach of liquor, so that they could sober up and work the ship properly.[27]

On 28 December the *Resolution* stood out from 'Christmas Sound' to the
open sea, where they were joined by a pod of whales, spouting, sounding and
breaching around them. At 7.30 that evening they passed the infamous Cape
Horn and entered the South Atlantic. Cook altered course north-east for
the Le Maire Strait, still hoping he could pick up some trace of the *Adventure*.
He landed Pickersgill in the Bay of Good Success and stood off from the
shore, still with whales accompanying them in an armada. When Pickersgill
found nothing of consequence, Cook re-embarked him and made for Staten
Island, off the eastern end of Tierra del Fuego, which they reached on New
Year's Day 1775. Here there occurred a savage massacre, not of native humans
but of hundreds of seals and sea lions that lay basking on the rocks. Seeing the
chance to replenish the larder massively, the seamen ran amok, shooting and
clubbing every mammal in sight. The slaughter continued on 2 January, and
when all murderous passion was spent, hundreds of seals, sea lions and their
pups lay dead on the killing grounds, to say nothing of dozens of penguins,
ducks, geese and shags that the sailors had shot down in the holocaust. The
problem of meat for the rest of the voyage had now been solved, and the seal
blubber was boiled down to provide oil.[28] Cook weighed anchor on 3 January
but, at the beginning of what was effectively the fifth and final act of the three-
year drama, Nature seemed to take its revenge for the slaughter, launching
ferocious gales on the *Resolution* that lasted until 7 January. Buffeted by wind
and waves, with accompanying haze and sleet, the *Resolution* pitched and
rolled while Cook close-reefed the topsails and tried to ride the tempest out.

When the gales blew themselves out, Cook spent a fruitless week searching for the alleged 'Gulf of St Sebastian', confidently marked in these latitudes and longitudes by the egregious Alexander Dalrymple in his Atlantic chart of 1769. Having conclusively established that Dalrymple's land existed only in his over-fecund imagination, by 13 January Cook was ploughing through rough seas in thick fog, accompanied by penguins and snowy petrels.[29]

On the 14th the voyagers saw through a blizzard what seemed at first like a giant iceberg. Gradually they realised it was land, dominated by glaciers, with mountains reaching up to the cloudtops and sheer cliffs of ice plummeting to the shoreline. Beset by squalls, snow and sleet and the buffeting of a 'great sea', Cook finally ran into a full-out storm on the 15th, which forced him to take in topsails and take down the topgallant yards; he stood to the south-west under two courses. At midnight the storm abated and Cook proceeded with the topsails double-reefed. Determined to circumnavigate this new land, which he called South Georgia after his sovereign, he spent eleven days charting it, beginning with the north coast, continually amazed that the island was covered in snow and ice even in summer. The surveying was perilous because of the foggy weather and dangerous rocks, and another great storm enveloped the *Resolution* on 20 January, of which Cook wrote: 'We were certainly very fortunate in getting clear of land before this gale overtook us; it is hard to say what might have been the consequences had it come on while we were still on the north coast.'[30] Finally, on the 24th, after naming many of the bays and rocks after his officers, whether humorously or to placate them is not known, he turned south. All were agreed that South Georgia might just as well have been a giant iceberg for all the comfort it gave to humans. Johann Forster, whose mind often ran to thoughts of draconian punishment for the lower orders and all those 'impertinent' enough to question him, thought it made a perfect prison, a forerunner perhaps of Devil's Island and Alcatraz, and proposed it as the perfect chastisement for 'a captain, some officers and a crew ... convicted of some heinous crimes'.[31] (It does not take a master analyst to imagine who his fantasy victims were.) Cook meanwhile took the ship down to latitude 60, then decided he would go no further without clear signs of land. The first iceberg was sighted on 27 January and soon thereafter what Cook refers to as loose ice – almost certainly the northern edge of the pack ice. On 31 January they came on three rocky islands, which he dubbed the South Sandwich Islands. This was latitude 60 and as far as Cook intended to go. He was by now firmly convinced that the Great Southern Continent was a will-o'-the-wisp, a chimera with no more reality than Swift's Laputa. 'Besides, I was tired of these high southern latitudes where nothing was to be found but ice and thick fogs.'[32]

To universal jubilation among the crew, Cook now turned north and passed Candlemas Island in the northerly Sandwiches on 3 February. His summing up of Antarctica was remarkably shrewd: 'I firmly believe there is a track of land near the pole which is the source of most of the ice that is spread over this vast Southern Ocean. I also think it extends furthest to the north opposite the Southern Atlantic and Indian Oceans because ice was always found by us further to the north in these oceans than anywhere else, which I judge could not be if there was land to the south.'[33] Cook pointed out that ice was found only south of latitude 60 in the Pacific but as far north as latitude 51 in the South Atlantic. If there were no frozen southern continent, the polar ice would presumably lie in the same latitudes in all the southern oceans, but it does not. His shrewdness was matched by his technological prescience, for he predicted that the risks of going so far south to explore a polar continent would mean that it would probably lie undiscovered for ever.[34] Probably on the entire ship only Cook cared for such reflections, as the others, officers and seamen alike, were elated by the northward track of the *Resolution,* which at last suggested they were homeward bound. On 14 February the travellers crossed the meridian of Greenwich in a 'prodigious high sea'. On 15 February Cook altered course to the north-east in a last-ditch attempt to try to find the elusive Cape Circumcision. But conditions were very bad: there was snow and sleet and a continuing great swell from the south. Bouvet de Lozier's errors in longitude meant Cook was never destined to see Cape Circumcision, and after six days he seems to have intuited this himself because on 21 February he altered course to due north. Momentarily he considered going east to find Kerguelen but reasoned that, if it was true that the French had already discovered it, as he was told at Cape Town in 1773, what would be the point of his venture?[35] The continuing huge swell convinced Cook yet again that the Great Southern Continent was a pipe dream if not a hoax, and he held on for Cape Town. He and his comrades were now approaching those latitudes off the South African coast where the winds and currents of the rival Indian and Atlantic Oceans fight each other and pile up monster waves. On 3 March the *Resolution* was hit by the most terrible storm that nearly engulfed her. As he endured the nightmare of very high seas and pyramidal and confused waves of a mountainous kind, Cook recorded the following; 'Very stormy, the wind blew from the south-west and in excessively heavy squalls; at short intervals between the squalls the wind would fall almost to a calm and then come on again with such fury that neither our sails nor riggings could withstand it; several of the sails were split and a middle staysail wholly lost.'[36]

The first two weeks of March turned into something like a battle of wills between Cook and the elements. The high seas never diminished and the only comfort was a temporary respite from the very worst squalls which, however, returned in their howling and screaming fury on 14–15 March.[37] Relief of a kind was afforded by the sighting of two Dutch ships in the distance on 16 March. The subsequent 'gamming' with these vessels produced the true story of the *Adventure* and the news that she had been at Cape Town a good twelve months previously. Finally on 19 March Cook met an English ship very near the Cape (the *True Briton*, homeward bound from China but, unusually, not stopping at the Cape) and learned further details about the sister ship. We can detect a not quite veiled criticism of Furneaux in his cryptic reference to the Maoris: 'I shall make no reflections on this melancholy affair until I hear more about it. I shall only observe, in favour of these people, that I have found them no wickeder than other men.'[38] For once the Forsters agreed with him. In 'emotion recollected in tranquillity' mode they now rated the Maoris above all other Polynesians, their warlike propensities and cannibalism notwithstanding.[39] Cook sent on a brief note for the Admiralty with the *True Briton* and steered for Table Bay, which he entered on 21 March only after enduring another hard gale. Morale was now sky-high and the crew seemed to have forgotten their previous resentment of a 'harsh' captain. Elliott wrote: 'No men could behave better under worse circumstances than they did. The same must be said of the officers, and I will add that there never was such a ship where for so long a period, under such circumstances, more happiness, order and obedience was enjoyed – and yet we had two or three troublesome characters aboard.'[40] In view of Elliott's earlier strictures on his captain, this sounds like more emotion recollected in tranquillity, but the assessment may nonetheless be true. One of the men, Thomas Perry, composed a shanty about the voyage, relating how 'Brave Captain Cook, he was our commander, Has conducted the ship from all eminent danger . . . Thanks be to the Captain he has proved so Good, Amongst all the islands to give us food.'[41]

The five weeks at the Cape were useful, instructive and enjoyable at many different levels. The governor proved remarkably friendly and went out of his way to help Cook though, as at Batavia in 1771, the latter baulked at the high prices charged by Dutch entrepreneurs, shipwrights and sailwrights. The *Resolution* was in dire need of refitting for, after 60,000 nautical miles, with leaking sides, a damaged rudder and most of her sails torn to pieces, she was no longer really seaworthy.[42] Cook had many interesting talks with a variety of sea captains who called at the Cape, most notably with Julien Marie Crozet of the French East Indiaman *Ajax*, with whom he got on famously; the two could often be seen still up late at night, yarning and comparing notes and charts. Crozet had been du Fresne's second in command and had full details of the massacre at the Bay of Islands, Crozet's assumption of command, and his further adventures in the Philippines and Mauritius, as well as Jean François Marie de Surville's voyages, from which Cook learned that there were no reefs between New Caledonia and New South Wales, as he had thought.[43] Less to Cook's taste was a copy of John Hawkesworth's *Voyages* which offended him at a number of levels: it purported to be Cook's first-person narrative and put words into his mouth that he had never spoken; it contained egregious navigational errors; and it falsely claimed that the manuscript had been read to Cook at the Admiralty, that he had made emendations, and had endorsed the finished product.[44] At a mundane administrative level Cook discharged three men at their own request and took on four more for the passage home. Among those departing was Sparrman, who intended to make an expedition into the interior of Africa. The ordinary seamen, in pursuit of drink and women, acted more like characters in an *opéra bouffe*. Elliott reported that when he went riding in the countryside he would often see three tipsy sailors all astride a single horse, swaying uneasily along the road, or even more inebriated specimens sleeping in ditches while the horse they had hired for the day munched grass above them. Elliott was broad-minded enough to remark that this was no great surprise after the many months cooped up on the *Resolution*.[45]

On 27 April Cook quit the Cape in the refurbished *Resolution*. He sailed north in a convoy comprising the English East Indiaman *Dutton* and two foreign vessels, one Spanish, the other Danish. A day out from St Helena the master sent a message to Cook that he was worried about their longitude. Cook, armed with the power of Harrison's chronometer, reassured him and boasted that 'he would run their jibboom on the island if they chose'.[46] The cruise from Cape Town to St Helena took two weeks, but Cook anchored off the island with something of a troubled conscience. The natives of St Helena were very annoyed at Cook's animadversions about them in the published account of the *Endeavour* voyage, and their displeasure had already been conveyed to Cook at the Cape. On landing he went out of his way to win over the locals and was mightily aided by the happy chance that the governor was none other than John Skottowe, son of Thomas Skottowe, his childhood benefactor. Skottowe *fils* fêted Cook and his officers at balls and receptions, while the locals took their revenge on Cook by good-humouredly parking dozens of wheelbarrows outside his lodgings; this was their revenge for Cook's ill-advised comment in the *Endeavour* journal that there were no wheelbarrows on St Helena.[47] The six-day stay on the island that would become famous forty years later for imprisoning Napoleon was highly enjoyable, and it was a good-spirited crew that shoved off on 21 May; Cook himself, relaxed and triumphant, reverted to being the good and beloved captain of the first part of the voyage, before the latter tribulations in the Pacific. He now parted company from the *Dutton*, for the Indiaman wanted to make the fastest possible passage home, while Cook was bound for Ascension Island. Ascension in those days was the centre of a smuggling trade with the American colonists who were at that very moment rising in rebellion against Britain, so on paper it was a place to avoid, but Cook spent an agreeable four days there, laying in turtles for meat; truly in three years the seamen of the *Resolution* must have tasted every variety of flesh.[48] The ship then took a slightly unusual track to the island of Fernando de Noronha (9 June), off the north-eastern coast of Brazil; Cook had seen the island on his way to Rio in 1768 and had always wanted to return to chart it and fix its exact longitude. The final port on the homeward voyage was the island of Faial in the Azores, a routine stopover for wood and water. Although the Azores were well known, Cook took meticulous notes as if this was a new discovery in the Pacific. The *Resolution* left the Azores on 19 July, ten days later she sighted land near Plymouth, and on the 29th anchored at Spithead. Cook had been away three years and eighteen days and had lost only four men.[49]

Cook's second voyage remains the high point of his achievement. To have made three separate forays into the Great Southern Ocean and disproved the existence of a great southern continent would have been an epoch-making feat for any explorer. That Cook on the very same voyage charted most of the major island groups in the South Pacific, accurately establishing their longitudes and thus providing a coherent map of the ocean, in terms of which all previous discoveries made an overarching sense comes close to the incredible. Beaglehole's assessment contains no hyperbole: 'It was a quite astonishing undertaking ... with anyone else the plan would have been preposterous. Cook carried it out precisely.'[50] As Cook said of his Antarctic rovings: 'The risk one runs in exploring a coast in these unknown and icy seas is so very great that I can be bold enough to say that no man will ever venture further than I have done.'[51] In the case of the South Pacific island sweeps, Cook knew that going westward from Easter Island on a different track from any previous navigator all the way to Quirós's Espiritu Santo was wildly ambitious: 'This I own is a great undertaking and perhaps more than I shall be able to perform.'[52] It was a voyage both of original discovery and of synopsis and synthesis. Cook's summary of his exploits, which in the mouth of any other man might sound smug or self-satisfied, was spot-on accurate:

> I had now made the circuit of the Southern Ocean in a high latitude and traversed it in such a manner as to leave not the least room for the possibility of there being a continent, unless near the Pole and out of reach of navigation; by twice visiting the Pacific tropical sea, I had not only settled the

situation of some old discoveries but made there many new ones and left, I conceive, very little more to be done even in that part. Thus I flatter myself that the intention of the voyage has in every respect been fully answered, the southern hemisphere sufficiently explored and a final end put to the searching after a southern continent, which has at times engrossed the attention of some of the maritime powers for near two centuries past and the geographers of all ages.[53]

Cook was the greatest of all seaborne explorers, and his achievements can be closely compared to those of the greatest land-based explorer in history, Henry Morton Stanley. Like Stanley, Cook made three great journeys, the last of them ending badly. Stanley amazed the world by finding David Livingstone in Central Africa in 1871–72, then capped that exploit with a three-year journey of exploration, in which he circumnavigated lakes Tanganyika and Victoria before following the river Congo all the way to the Atlantic Ocean, thus disproving the canards that it was a tributary of the Nile or the Niger. Similarly, Cook won instant fame with his circumnavigation of New Zealand in the *Endeavour* and his exploration of Australia's east coast. He then capped that feat with the stupendous exploit of the *Resolution* voyage of 1772–75. Where Stanley was an administrator and journalist of genius as well as a consummate explorer, Cook complemented his exploring credentials with stunning gifts as seaman and surveyor. As a sailor Cook had the 'green fingers' intuition and sixth sense possessed by only the very greatest humans who brave the ocean. He had an unparalleled eye and, when coming on deck, could often immediately see slackness in a line or rope which the officer of the watch had overlooked.[54] His charts were far superior to Bougainville's, not just in terms of running surveys but also in the areas where both had made landfalls so that a direct comparison is possible, such as Tahiti and Vanuatu.[55] After Cook's work on the second voyage, no one had any excuse for failing to find any island in the South Pacific previously reported, even if Cook had not personally visited it (Pitcairn is an obvious case in point).[56] Of Cook's personal qualities, the one that most impressed observers was his adamantine and almost fanatical perseverance in pursuit of a goal; this astonished people who were by no means uncritical admirers, such as George Forster.[57] Cook's personal gloss on this was in terms of *amour propre*: 'The world will hardly admit of an excuse for a man leaving a coast unexplored he has once discovered.'[58] Yet Cook liked to conceal his raging ambition beneath a carapace of gentle self-deprecation, and in this he showed himself most clearly an Englishman. In the view of some analysts, Cook's humility (whether we construe it as real or bogus) morphed into a tendency to sell himself short; he never, for instance, clearly underlines what a tour de force his complete survey of the New Hebrides was.[59]

Although his record on the second voyage was not perfect, in general in his dealings both with his own crew and with indigenous peoples Cook knew when to act decisively, to order punishment or retaliation, and when to relax and turn a blind eye; this would turn out to be one of the greatest differences between the second and third voyages. He had continued his fruitless campaign against venereal disease, forbidding his men intercourse with local women while knowing full well that human nature would take over and make his ordinances appear Canute-like. Cook always felt a large measure of guilt that he might have introduced sexually transmitted diseases to the 'paradise' of Polynesia, but the Forsters, of all people, came to his rescue by claiming that syphilis was on the islands before Europeans arrived.[60] Amazingly, this debate has still never been cleared up to universal satisfaction. The consensus appears to be that yaws and gonorrhoea were already present before the European advent but that syphilis was introduced by Bougainville.[61] Health issues were salient on the second voyage in another sense since, for the first time, the seemingly iron-constitutioned Cook showed signs of weakness and for a time was gravely ill. What was it that ailed him? The orthodox view is that the constipation and bowel inflammation of which he complained might have allowed colonisation by coliform bacteria which interfere with the absorption of vitamin B complex. The irony is that in his successful fight against scurvy Cook concentrated on greenstuffs, a source of vitamin C, some of which can inhibit vitamin B absorption. As one medical analyst has written: 'It is therefore possible to conclude that Cook fell victim to his known passionate conviction that health at sea has to be found only in the nutrients provided by fresh provisions.'[62] An alternative view is that the incidents with raw, rotting or poisoned fish might be the key to the captain's sickness, that it was a parasitic infection from eating fish that lay at the root of the problem.[63] It is certainly the case that Cook's declining health was far more serious than either he or anyone else realised in 1775, and was to be a crucial factor in the unhappy experiences of 1776–79.

In terms of the everyday practicalities of exploration, it can be said that by the end of the second voyage Cook had perfected his own system. He had three cardinal rules. If a discovery was important, as with the New Hebrides or Noumea, everything must be meticulously committed to paper. If conditions were unfavourable but a key point was at issue, for example the charting of the North Cape of New Zealand in 1769 or searching for the Great Southern Continent in the Antarctic in 1772–75, neither storms, hurricanes, high seas nor thunderbolts should be allowed to deter the explorer. If time were short or adverse weather conditions coincided with the relative unimportance of an objective, one should make the most accurate observations possible, chart what was feasible, and then press on; this maxim was clearly applied to the South Sandwich islands in 1775 and would be the following year to Kerguelen. Cook was above all an empiricist and despised the a priori cosmological conjectures of Dalrymple and his ilk. As he told James Boswell, he made it a rule that he and his officers could not be certain of any information they got on their travels 'except as to objects falling under the observation of sense'.[64] In this respect the facsimile of Harrison's chronometer that he had taken with him had been a triumphant success or, as Cook put it, 'it has exceeded the expectations of its most zealous advocate and being now and then corrected by lunar observations has been our faithful guide through all the vicissitudes of climates'.[65]

The major hurdle Cook had still to overcome – and he never would do so – was communication with the indigenous peoples of the Pacific. To some extent this problem had been solved in the Society Islands, but the writings of the Forsters illustrate the extreme ambivalence with which even these 'good savages' were viewed. As already stated, the Forsters always fluctuated between a retrospective high evaluation of the Tahitians with an on-the-spot revulsion at such phenomena as marital infidelity among the oligarchs, lewdness and prostitution among the lower classes, the cult of the *arioi*, infanticide, and the general climate of laziness and exploitation. Typical eighteenth-century intellectuals, the Forsters were torn between the idealised picture of Polynesia as they would like it to be and the grim reality which they could not avoid – an almost perfect paradigm of Paradise Found and Lost.[66] Yet some of the Forsters' bafflement was shared by bluff, down-to-earth naval officers. The forthcoming behaviour of women on the Society Isles did not necessarily mean what it seemed to, while even obvious visual symbols were misinterpreted because of the general 'failure to communicate'. One obvious example was the display of a white flag. To Europeans this meant a request for truce or safe-conduct, but in Polynesia it was a ritual to appease and control the gods. The white flag was so often seen because the Europeans were fundamentally viewed as malevolent gods with great wealth and powerful weapons who needed to be propitiated.[67] Religion loomed much larger in Polynesian–European dealings than Cook realised. Often the 'treachery' which Cook and his officers perceived occurred simply because the visitors had unwittingly offended against a *tapu*.[68]

Presumably Cook was revolving few of these thoughts in the early days of euphoria immediately after his return. The story of his voyage created a sensation, perhaps particularly the Antarctic sections, and would inspire many artists and writers: Mary Shelley arguably, Coleridge certainly.[69] In contrast to the aftermath of the *Endeavour* voyage, this time the Establishment moved quickly to honour one of its favourite sons. The Earl of Sandwich, prime mover in all things naval, was on a yachting trip in the Channel with his mistress Martha Ray and Joseph Banks. He raced back to London, as Solander informed Banks, and pushed through the necessary paperwork for Cook's promotion and reward. On 9 August Cook was promoted to post captain – the key stage in any naval commander's career as it meant being elevated to admiral in time if the post captain did not die first. On the same day he had an audience with George III at St James's Palace. Originally appointed to the 74-gun HMS *Kent*, Cook was told twenty-four hours later that this had been rescinded and instead he would be given a sinecure at Greenwich Hospital: it involved a pension of £230 p. a., free accommodation, all heating and lighting provided and 1s. 2d. a day dinner money. Cook accepted this position on the understanding that he would still be considered for active service if a suitable opportunity arose.[70] Cook's great triumph and his privileged status seriously vexed some people. Banks made a point of staying away from London until the worst of the initial hoopla surrounding Cook's return was over. Alexander Dalrymple brooded furiously that Cook's discoveries had made nonsense of all his theories, torpedoed all his future prospects, and made his latest volume on the Great Southern Continent virtually unsaleable.[71] Cook returned to the domestic comfort of his house in Mile End, where he very soon impregnated his wife Elizabeth. Only two of his children were alive: the two sons James, 12, and Nathaniel, 11, with James already enrolled at the Naval Academy in Portsmouth and Nathaniel hoping to follow in his footsteps. In May 1776 another son, Hugh, was born. Little is known about Cook's relations with his children or his feelings for them.[72]

Relieved of all financial anxieties for the rest of his life, Cook found it hard to settle to the life of ease of a naval pensioner and soon became restless. He heard that Sandwich was determined to send Omai back to the Society Islands and had appointed Clerke to the command of the *Resolution* for this purpose. One can almost sense the pang in the letter he wrote to his old mentor and patron John Walker in Whitby on 19 August:

The *Resolution* . . . will soon be sent out again, but I shall not command her. My fate drives me from one extreme to another. A few months ago the whole Southern Hemisphere was hardly big enough for me and now I am going to be confined within the limits of Greenwich Hospital, which are far too small for an active mind like mine. I must however confess it is a fine retreat and a pretty income, but whether I can bring myself to like ease and retirement, time will show.[73]

Actually his active mind was taken up for nearly a year in writing up his journals for publication, but the eventual emergence of Cook as author lay at the end of a very long causal line. The *Endeavour* journal had been given over to John Hawkesworth to prepare for publication, with the unhappy results Cook had already witnessed when he perused the finished volume at Cape Town. In a disastrous critical mauling, obloquy was aimed at Hawkesworth from all directions. Horace Walpole, the would-be arbiter of elegance in literary London, remarked scathingly that the book contained only enough interest to fill half a volume and the rest was padding, 'at best an account of the fishermen on the coasts of forty islands'.[74] Dr Johnson said that Hawkesworth was at the mercy of his tedious sources, the banal accounts of voyagers with nothing to say and few discoveries to boast of: 'they have found very little, only one new animal I think'.[75] Hawkesworth, who genuinely fancied himself as a literary giant, was stunned by the tsunami of adverse criticism and antipathy that fell on him, and seems to have been one of the few genuine qualifiers for the clichéd predicate 'died of a broken heart'. He died of a mysterious 'slow fever' in November 1773, not comforted by his book's great commercial success.[76]

Into the vacuum created by Hawkesworth's demise stepped another literary 'chancer' and adventurer, none other than Johann Reinhold Forster, who was now complaining that his fee of £4,000 was not enough for the distinguished services he had performed aboard the *Resolution*. A typical academic, Forster had no street wisdom or even common sense and gradually came to suspect that he had been 'rooked' by the Polynesians and charged prices for curios far above their market value. Noting the German's lack of worldly wisdom, the seamen regularly bought knick-knacks and gewgaws at knock-down prices and then sold them on to Forster at a huge mark-up.[77] Once back in London, Forster realised the extent to which he had been duped and demanded 'compensation' for his own idiocy. Specifically, he wanted to be the new Hawkesworth and write the official account of the voyages of the *Resolution* and *Adventure*, which was likely to make its author a fortune. As barefaced as he was naïve, Forster wrote to Sandwich 'reminding' him that the noble lord had promised him that he would be the author of this work. Sandwich was annoyed at the German's presumption, suspected he had said nothing of the sort, but did not have instant recall of every conversation. By sheer persistence Forster achieved what many bores do: he ground the opposition down by sheer attrition. The Admiralty had already made it clear that this time they wanted Cook to write his own book, to avoid the fiasco of Hawkesworth's infelicities, fabrications and sheer nonsense. Anxious not to receive further effusions from Forster, Sandwich suggested that perhaps the

Herr Doktor and Cook could collaborate, with Cook providing the seafaring narrative and Forster the science.[78] Reasonably enough, the Admiralty then asked Forster for some samples of his writing and, when they received these, informed him that he would have to consent to be edited. The reality was that Sandwich hated the specimen chapter he saw. Forster immediately flew into a rage regarding this 'impertinence' accorded him by his intellectual inferiors; casting about for someone to blame for the fiasco, he hit on Banks, whom he imagined to be jealous of his scientific prowess. Another culprit was Wales, who detested Forster and refused to release his astronomical findings to him.[79] The matter dragged on until June 1776 while Cook continued to plod away at his writing. Finally Sandwich obtained a royal command, against which there was no appeal, that unless Forster submitted to the terms offered, the Admiralty would have nothing more to do with him. The German's pride overcame his greed, and he retired hurt. Sandwich informed Cook that he would be the sole author of the official account. Since Forster had already made over his journal to assist Cook on the understanding that he would be co-author, he was bound by contract not to attempt a rival volume. The slippery Johann got round this by giving his son copies of the material he had provided for Cook, so that George could write a competing account. George Forster was a fast and fluent writer, and his *Voyages* pipped Cook's authorised version to the publishing post by a good six weeks in the spring of 1777.[80]

Forster was not the only person from the second voyage to irritate Cook. There was also Omai, Furneaux's protégé, whom Cook had never liked and considered a lightweight; Tupaia he had disliked while acknowledging his intellect and talents, but Hitihiti remained his favourite of the émigré Polynesians. By the time Cook arrived in London in July 1775, Omai was already a social lion. The *Adventure* had reached England and Omai quickly became the sensation of the hour. Lord Sandwich took a shine to him and he was reintroduced to Banks and Solander and taken up by the Burneys, who were delighted to have second lieutenant James back in the bosom of the family. Fanny Burney found him good-looking with a gift for laughter and graceful manners while James, against all the evidence, described him as very intelligent.[81] Soon Omai was being sought after by society hosts and hostesses, especially when Solander falsely claimed that the young Tahitian was a prince in his own country or, in English terms, a private gentleman of good fortune.[82] His life became a whirligig of dizzying events. He went to the House of Lords to hear the American rebels being denounced, he met Dr Johnson and other luminaries, dined at all the best tables, stayed with Banks and then with Sandwich at his country seat at Hinchinbrooke, where he cooked a Tahitian barbecue for the guests. He took part in a fox hunt, was stung by a wasp, given an electric shock by one of the Duke of Manchester's Franklin-inspired contraptions, went to the Leicester races, and attended a performance of Handel's *Jephtha*.[83] He learned to dance and to skate, was hosted by the Royal Society and Cambridge University, went to the theatre at Sadler's Wells, was painted by three different artists, most notably Sir Joshua Reynolds,[84] and was a frequent guest on Sandwich's yacht which cruised the British coast. All this would have gone to the head of any 'noble savage', even one much more intelligent than Omai. Yet for a while in the eyes of the British elite Omai could do no wrong. A few more thoughtful observers queried his *savoir faire*, as when, given a gun, he slaughtered not just game birds but domestic fowls in a farmyard. And there was his woeful attempt to read and write; after a few exasperating attempts at literacy he gave up, claiming he was 'too busy' with his social life.[85]

But as with all ephemeral crazes, eventually the English Establishment became bored with Omai and his 'cheeky chappy' persona. When introduced to King George, Omai was said to have greeted him with: 'How do, King Tosh!'[86] Banks was the first to drop Omai astern. He had already been criticised for treating him as the pet lion or tiger he had intended Tupaia to be, for spoiling him in every sense and not teaching him any useful skills to take back to the Pacific.[87] When Sandwich invited Banks and Omai to Hinchinbrooke for Christmas, Omai accepted gleefully but Banks sent his excuses, enraging Sandwich who sent him a very cold reply.[88] In the end Omai was essentially pensioned off: he was provided with lodgings close to Banks's house (doubtless this was Sandwich's revenge), given a stipend and a 'minder' in the shape of Mr Andrews, the surgeon from the *Adventure*. Here he learned to play chess and how to ride a horse, attended more plays – and was falsely reported to be about to marry an English girl.[89] This hint at miscegenation tapped into some of the darkest fears entertained about Omai, that underneath the smiling surface there lurked a savage priapism. Martha Ray, Sandwich's mistress, was said to loathe Omai, on the grounds both that she had caught him leering lecherously at her chambermaids and that he was Sandwich's spy, reporting to His Lordship on her secret affair with James Hackman, the man who would eventually murder her in 1779. It must be stressed that although there is circumstantial evidence of a 'dark' Omai (in more senses than one), no worthwhile historical evidence has survived.[90] By the time Cook reached London, educated opinion was shifting strongly towards the proposition that Banks and Sandwich had simply made Omai into a pet monkey, that they had introduced him to privilege and riches that he could never enjoy and thus unsettled him, and that they would callously send him back to the Pacific where he would simply be laughed at and his 'tall tales' of England not believed.[91] It is perhaps significant that when Cook arrived in London, Sandwich, Omai and Martha Ray were off cruising in the yacht. Suppressing his boredom with Omai, Banks used the excuse of his 'duty of care' to avoid taking part in the James Cook festival of August 1775. Instead he took the Polynesian north for another tour of racecourses, holiday spas and shooting parties.[92] Cook was contemptuous. It may at one time have been the thought of being on a ship for an entire year with Omai that initially led him to rule himself out of consideration for any future Pacific voyages.

By January 1776, however, Cook had completely changed his mind. He found retirement stultifying and, like so many adventurers, entrepreneurs, captains of armies or industry, needed constant activity to ward off feelings of pointlessness, depression and, possibly, a consequent early death. The story told by his first biographer was that he, Sandwich and Palliser were having an intimate dinner together in February 1776 to discuss the minute details and fine strategy of the next Pacific expedition when Cook, enraptured by the prospects, suddenly blurted out that he wanted to command.[93] Such a Damascene conversion is unlikely; the reality was that Cook had been unconsciously moving towards such a decision possibly as early as August 1775. His comrades had always secretly wanted him to command, but thought that an explicit request from them would be unreasonable; Cook had already done more than enough for his country and should not be put under such pressure. Nonetheless, once Cook had made the first move, his proposal was accepted with alacrity. The usual protocol of formally requesting command and being accepted, which in normal circumstances would take months, was rushed through in a matter of days.[94] It was taken for granted that the refurbished *Resolution* would once more be battling the Pacific Ocean and Cook had already chosen the sister ship, a 298-ton brig *Diligence*, yet another Whitby-built vessel, eighteen months old and state of the art. Soon renamed the *Discovery*, the brig was converted into a regular ship by having an extra mast added, and was then sheathed and filled as a protection against *Teredo navalis*. Ninety-one feet long and twenty-seven feet broad, the *Discovery* would prove to be faster than the *Resolution* and could claw off a lee shore better. Both vessels were well armed, the *Discovery* with eight four-pounders, eight swivel guns and eight musketoons, the *Resolution* with twelve of each; ominously, though, neither ship was reinforced or given any protection against ice. Clerke, no real friend of Cook's, had originally been assigned the command of the expedition, but it was now decided that he would command the *Discovery*, with the clear understanding that he was as much Cook's subordinate as if he had been first officer on the *Resolution*.[95]

While the preparations for the third voyage went ahead and Cook worked on his book for publication, there were some pleasant social occasions, including a friendship struck up with James Boswell, the friend and biographer of Dr Johnson. On 7 March 1776 Cook was elected a Fellow of the Royal Society: he had twenty-three nominators or proposers, including Banks, Solander and a cluster of the scientific great and good.[96] As a result he was introduced to a wider circle of acquaintances and became something of an inveterate diner-out. On 2 April he met Boswell at a dinner hosted by the president of the Royal Society. Boswell found him a man dedicated to the truth and wedded to fine verbal distinctions: he was 'a plain, sensible man with an uncommon attention to veracity. My metaphor was that he had a balance in his mind for truth as nice as scales for weighing a guinea.'[97] Boswell was fired by his traveller's tales and conceived a mad passion to spend three years in Tahiti and New Zealand. He rushed home to consult Samuel Johnson, but the good doctor was discouraging. His views on seafaring were well known: 'No man will be a sailor who has contrivance enough to get himself into a jail; for being in a ship is being in jail, with the chance of being drowned ... A man in a jail has more room, better food and commonly better company.'[98] This time he was even more forthright in his dashing of his friend's aspirations: 'What could you learn, Sir? What can savages tell, but what they themselves have seen? Of the past, or the invisible, they can tell nothing. The inhabitants of Otaheite [Tahiti] and New Zealand are not in a state of pure nature; for it's plain they broke off from some other people. Had they grown out of the ground, you might have judged of a state of pure nature.'[99] Only temporarily abashed, Boswell met Cook twice more, but the great navigator also dissuaded him, saying that the Pacific was no place for a landsman. The third meeting, at Cook's house in Mile End, was particularly pleasant. The two men drank tea in the garden while a blackbird sang. Boswell recalled: 'It was curious to see Cook, a grave steady man, and his wife, a decent plump Englishwoman, and think that he was preparing to sail round the world.'[100]

Boswell was already well known, but another of Cook's correspondents at this time would achieve fame later, as the only French admiral ever to beat Nelson on points. In August 1775 Captain Latouche-Tréville, a 30-year-old captain in the French navy, wrote to ask Cook's advice on how he could attain fame as a seaborne explorer. Cook wrote back graciously, suggesting he concentrate on the areas he (Cook) had left undone, such as the south coast of Australia, New Guinea and the Solomon Islands; there was further correspondence along the same lines in February 1776.[101] The reason Cook seemed so remarkably generous and unproprietary about the South Pacific was that he felt he had achieved all he wanted to do there, and besides the Admiralty's interest had now shifted overwhelmingly to the North Pacific. Hard on the heels of the mania for the imaginary Southern Continent came an equally frenzied fetish about the Northwest Passage between the Atlantic and the Pacific via the Arctic. This actually did exist – it was finally navigated by Roald Amundsen in 1905 – but the passage as conceived by the Admiralty was a far more dramatic and grandiose affair than the physical and geographical actuality. This was not the first time the Northwest Passage had obsessed British minds, for no less than fifty British voyages to date had had the same objective, beginning with John Cabot in 1497. The late sixteenth and early seventeenth centuries had seen great names such as Frobisher, Davis, Baffin and Hudson occupied on the forlorn quest, yet for a variety of complex geopolitical reasons, the Passage, which had fallen off the Admiralty's radar for a hundred years, again became a subject of consuming interest.[102] One of the main precipitants was Russian activity in the Kamchatka area, and particularly the voyages of Vitus Bering. The potential arrival of Russia as a major player in the affairs of the Americas was deeply worrying to the western European powers, and explains Spain's expansion north from Mexico into California in the 1760s. British interest in the Pacific Northwest was threefold: London wanted to arrest the geopolitical advance of Russia into 'its' sphere of influence in North America; it was attracted by the tales of lucrative opportunities in the fur trade, the profits to be made from seals and sea otters, and the possibility of important new markets; and it hoped to be able to find a short route to the Pacific from the Atlantic so that it could raid or smuggle in the Spanish Empire without having to round Cape Horn.[103]

It is a plausible conjecture that what ultimately made Cook change his mind about going to sea again was not the prospect of taking Omai home – this was very small beer to his mind – but the exciting challenge of the Northwest Passage. From 10 February to 9 July, between the date of his volunteering and having his instructions signed (a mere formality, as by now he virtually wrote his own instructions), a detailed itinerary took shape in Cook's mind and then on Admiralty stationery. He would go straight to the Cape of Good Hope, swing into the Indian Ocean to check on the recent French discoveries and chart Kerguelen, then sail to Tahiti to deliver Omai home. Then he would proceed to the heart of the expedition: a detailed survey of the entire Pacific north-western coast of America as far as Russian waters in Siberia.[104] Sandwich had ambitious and even Promethean plans. While Cook was making his way to the Arctic by this western route, another British expedition would be trying to find the Passage from the Atlantic side, working westwards from Baffin Bay and maybe, on the best-case scenario, even linking up with Cook in a triumphant finale to the assault on the Arctic's great secret. The element of fantasy in the project is clear, for it rested on two questionable, and indeed absurd, foundations: that the Passage would only have to be discovered for it to be navigable; and that they would find an ice-free sea because (according to eighteenth-century orthodoxy), only fresh water freezes.[105] We may suspect the hand of Cook in the appointment of Pickersgill to command the Baffin Bay expedition, but never was the proposition that a good lieutenant is not necessarily a good commander verified more clearly than in this case. Pickersgill set off in the brig *Lyon* in May 1776, ill-prepared, still over-fond of drink, with a weak ship, an inexperienced crew and vague directions. Unable to find his way through the Greenland ice and entirely lacking Cook's doggedness and tenacity, he simply put about and returned to Deptford at the end of October.[106] The Admiralty was furious and soon found a way to cashier him. In January 1777 the *Lyon*'s master brought charges of habitual drunkenness and gross incompetence against Pickersgill; there was a court-martial, the charges were proved, and Pickersgill dismissed from the Navy.[107] His replacement, Lieutenant Walter Young, failed in exactly the same way in his short voyage of March–August 1777 and similarly returned to Deptford, having achieved nothing. Lacking naval commanders who had been trained to deal with Arctic ice, the Lords of the Admiralty simply blamed its captains for inefficiency, but the truth was that they were skimping because of the war with the American colonists and had not provided strong enough ships.[108]

Cook's enthusiasm for Sandwich's dreams about the Northwest Passage is at one level surprising and sits oddly with his usual empiricism. He was particularly impressed with two German writers, one of them Jacob von Stählin of the Academy of Sciences, the other Gerhard Friedrich Müller, official historiographer of the Russian Empire, who wrote exhaustively about the voyages of Bering and other Russians in the seas off Kamchatka.[109] This was out of character. Having been sceptical of the French school of a priori theorists of the Great Southern Continent, he very weirdly went along with the conceptions of German theorists, which proved equally fantastical. Is it fanciful to detect some kind of influence through osmosis of the Teutonic exemplar Johann Reinhold Forster? Whatever the reason, Cook's credulity on this issue would cost him dear. Swept along on a wave of optimism he shelved the question of ends and concentrated on means, specifically the refitting of the *Resolution*. Cook was originally supposed to depart at the end of April 1777, but the inevitable delays put his schedule back three months. *Resolution* was in the dockyard at Deptford from mid-September to mid-March – time enough for a thorough overhaul and refit – but when she was relaunched it turned out that the work had not been properly done and had in fact been so incompetely done that the ship began leaking in the Channel because of the skimped caulking.[110] Some say Cook should have overseen the work more minutely, but this ignored the fact that he had nothing to do officially with the third expedition until 10 February. The real responsibility was Palliser's and he, though Cook's friend, fell down badly on the job and then later reacted angrily when this was pointed out to him. The real villain in the story, however, was the endemic corruption of the dockyards, with pilfering, short measure, payroll padding, sweeteners and rake-offs, and the substitution of cheap and shoddy materials for those which had been charged for at a top-of-the range market rate. As always, profiteering was put before safety and men's lives.[111] Sandwich often appeared at Deptford but never to any purpose and never to examine the work, simply to show off with Omai or use a dockyard visit as an excuse for another bibulous party.

Unaware until he sailed that the *Resolution* was in such bad shape, Cook spent most of his non-writing time between February and July in assembling his crew. The company on the *Resolution* numbered 112 souls and that of the *Discovery* 70. He was pleased to have the 33-year-old Charles Clerke as the captain of *Discovery*, now a veteran both of war service and three circumnavigations. Cook and Clerke did not entirely see eye to eye – Clerke had been disloyal to Cook both in the dispute with Banks in 1772 and over the punishment of the sentry William Wedgeborough on Tanna – but the two men respected each other as seamen and as technicians. Clerke was the perfect complement to Cook, and the two made a good team. There is no sign that Clerke was resentful that he was no longer overall commander of a two-ship expedition, and he was probably secretly glad that the great master of oceanic voyaging was at the helm.[112] Some said he was not decisive enough to command an expedition, but the evidence refutes this. A complex personality, both a strong character and a genial raconteur and humorist, Clerke was the perfect man to have in the wardroom at a dinner party. He had learned a tremendous amount from Cook, but lacked any real ability as a surveyor. The surgeon's mate, David Samwell, a key source for the third voyage, detested him – probably because they were often in competition for the same women – and accused him of being a mere libertine, free with the bottle and always with an eye for pretty women.[113] Among Clerke's evident virtues was over-generosity. He guaranteed the debts of his wastrel brother Sir John Clerke, who promptly decamped to North America, leaving Charles to hold the baby. When it was known that he was shipping out on the *Discovery*, his brother's creditors had Clerke committed to the King's Bench Prison for failing to discharge the debts for which he had stood surety.[114] Third in the pecking order was John Gore, Cook's first lieutenant on the *Resolution*. Another veteran of circumnavigations, he had served on the *Endeavour* voyage but missed the second Pacific epic as he chose to take Banks's shilling and go with him to Iceland instead. Cook was glad to welcome him back since Gore knew his methods, but in truth he was a mediocrity, irritatingly combining luck with timidity. The oldest man on the voyage after Cook (and a handful of aged able seamen), Gore had lost his place in the promotion race to Clerke because of his decision to opt for Banks in the great falling-out of 1772. An old-fashioned sailor and a sentimental romantic, uncertain of himself but stubborn in compensation, Gore was yet another womaniser in an expedition full of philanderers.[115]

In some ways the most interesting officer to sail with Cook on the third voyage, was the second lieutenant James King, the intellectual of the voyage. Aged 23, appointed on the recommendation of Hugh Palliser, King came from a wealthy, well-connected family, was well read, a talented amateur scientist and astronomer and had cerebral interests beyond the ken of most eighteenth-century naval officers, interested as he was in politics and philosophy. A correspondent with Edmund Burke, whom he knew through his family, King had taken a sabbatical from the Royal Navy to study science in Paris and Oxford. Cook put him in charge of the chronometer (a new variant of the invaluable H4 had been issued to the expedition) and King doubled as the *Resolution*'s astronomer. Knowledgeable and erudite on a range of matters and a great observer of geographical features and landmarks, King was widely popular, being charming, sensitive, and reflective.[116] In complete contrast was the third lieutenant, John Williamson, who turned out to be a permanent headache for Cook. An Irishman with severe psychological and personality problems, who had a chip on his shoulder and was forever fighting duels, Williamson was prickly, self-righteous and intolerant; to quote what was later said about Admiral Ernest King, head of the US Navy in World War Two, he was the most even-tempered man conceivable: he was *always* in a rage. He was also a trigger-happy hothead with a perverse genius for 'misunderstanding signals'. Such a man should never have been recruited for a taxing voyage of discovery, and his appointment remains a mystery.[117] Another cross-grained character, later to become notorious as the protagonist of the famous mutiny on the *Bounty*, was William Bligh, the *Resolution*'s master, a 21-year-old Cornishman. In the Royal Navy only since 1770 he had risen in a meteoric and somewhat mysterious fashion. An outstanding seaman and a gifted surveyor, Bligh not surprisingly revered Cook, but for most other people he had secret contempt. Secretly dogmatic, thin-skinned and intolerant, he did not suffer fools gladly but parlayed this into the belief that all his associates and comrades save the captain were fools. For King, whom he described as a pretentious poseur and an intellectual impostor, he reserved the same blind, irrational hatred felt by John Claggart for Billy Budd in Herman Melville's eponymous novella.[118]

On the *Discovery* Clerke had as his first lieutenant James Burney, who had served in North America after his return on the *Adventure* and had then been tipped off by his influential family to return to England if he wanted to sail with Cook on the third voyage; the Burneys meanwhile lobbied hard to secure him this senior berth as second in command to Clerke, with whom he always got on well.[119] The rest of the *Discovery*'s senior personnel are shadowy. Of John Rickman, the second lieutenant, little is known while the master, Thomas Edgar, appears to have been uneducated though careful and capable. The two mates were the American Nathaniel Porlock and Alexander Home, an honest, humorous Scotsman. Notable midshipmen included the future famous explorer and navigator George Vancouver and Edward Riou, later one of Nelson's admirals (he died in action at the battle of Copenhagen in 1801), both on the *Discovery*, and on the *Resolution* James Trevenen, a clever and high-sprited Cornishman.[120] The lieutenant of marines on the *Resolution*, Molesworth Phillips, secured his appointment because of his friendship with the Burneys; Cook regretted the loss of John Edgcumbe, despite his defiance on Tanna, and seems to have accepted Phillips reluctantly. Another Irishman, Phillips at 41 was a failed gentleman-farmer and, because of his position as the wielder of armed force, was predictably destested by the two dark characters Bligh and Williamson.[121] The two ships also boasted six surgeons and their mates. William Patten, a Scot, who was mate on the *Resolution* on the second voyage, was another intellectual, not just a competent physician but a polymath and linguist with an independent mind. Pleasant, generous and very popular, he was naturally drawn to the company of James King. The surgeon's first mate, the Welshman David Samwell, was competent but irreverent, frivolous and another womaniser; he was yet another devoted admirer of Cook.[122] William Ellis, the surgeon's second mate on the *Discovery*, was a Cambridge man and protégé of Banks, an amateur draughtsman and painter. Whatever reservations can be entered against Cook's officers, they were in the main an impressive bunch: twenty of them went on to command ships in their own right.

Of the supernumeraries, William Bayly signed on again as the representative of the Board of Longitude, David Nelson was a gardener from Kew

Gardens and another protégé of Banks, while John Webber, 24, replaced Hodges as the *Resolution*'s artist. Of course there was also Omai, who boarded the ship loaded with regalia and impedimenta: port wine, a globe, some tin soldiers, a hand-organ, a suit of armour, crockery, kitchenware and, to Cook's disgust, a panoply of firearms and bullets; Cook protested at allowing Omai such latitude, fearing that he might literally become a loose cannon, but Sandwich overruled him. There were other fascinating characters on the voyage. Samuel Gibson, the marine whom Cook had flogged on the *Endeavour* voyage, was now his faithful aide and had developed into a talented linguist of Polynesian dialects. Heinrich Zimmermann, an adventurer who had spent much of his time on the waterfront of the Levant, produced an invaluable journal of the voyage. Then there was John Ledyard, another important diarist. An American from Connecticut, Ledyard was Sir Richard Burton *avant la lettre*: he had spent time living among the Iroquois, would later walk across the American continent and through Siberia, and end by perishing while searching for the sources of the Niger.[123] The crew and ordinary seamen remain faceless and shadowy – except in so far as they step forward from time to time to be flogged. Beaglehole's summary: 'ignorant, illiterate, irresponsible, conservative, blockheaded, drunken, lecherous, cruel, sentimental' is harsh but probably accurate.[124] This time the calibre of Cook's crew was lower than on the first two voyages, where he had to an extent been able to pick and choose; now, however, he had to take whatever the press gangs had left over after shanghaiing men for the American war; some commentators feel that this was a factor in the egregiously stressful nature of the third voyage.[125] Certainly none of the sailors thought they were along for a joy ride, and the rate of returnees was, to Cook, disappointingly low. Among the crew of the *Resolution* there were only a dozen men who had sailed with Cook before, and only six such on the *Discovery*. Sixty men who had been signed up for the voyage deserted before the ships left.[126] What there were was plenty of animals, since George III had personally contributed large numbers of goats, sheep, rabbits, pigs, poultry, and even a bull; also two cows with calves, a peacock and a hen, some of these for meat but most to be introduced to Tahiti and New Zealand; in the latter case the pious hope was that the introduction of livestock might make the Maoris stop eating each other.[127] Cook remarked sardonically to Sandwich and Banks about his menagerie: 'Nothing is wanting but a few females of our own species to make the Resolution a complete ark.'[128]

Perhaps the most surprising aspect of the voyage was that Cook took no professional scientists. When James King queried this with the captain, the answer was forthright: 'Curse all scientists and all science into the bargain!'[129]

The impact of Banks and Johann Forster had gone deep; he would make do with King, Bayly, Nelson and William Anderson, a surgeon and an amateur ornithologist, and the bird-painting talents of Ellis. And so, by the end of June 1776, Cook was almost ready to launch out again on the open ocean.

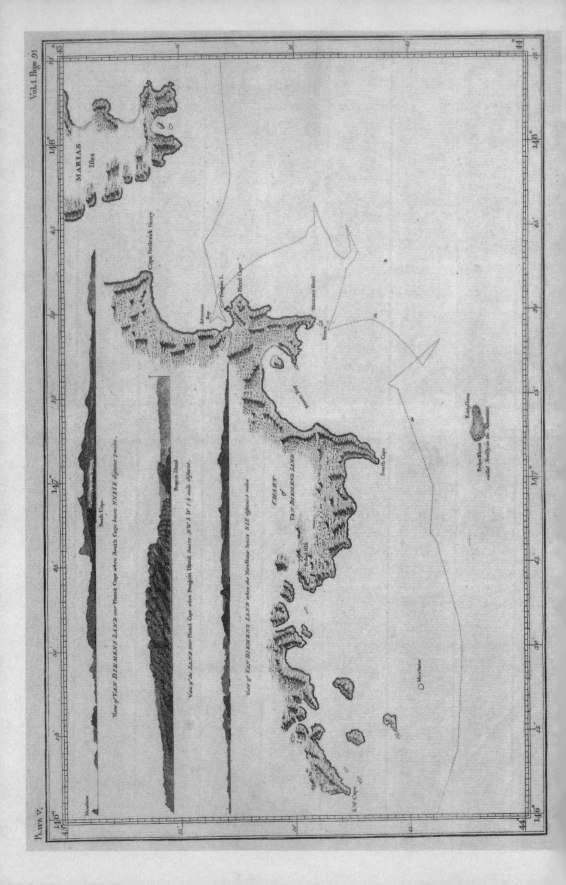

PLATE V.

MARIAS
Islets

Cape Frederick Henry

Penguin I.

Adventure Bay

Fluted Cape

Tasmans Head

Storm Bay

South Cape

CHART
of
VAN DIEMENS LAND

Eddystone

Rocks Blanco
called Southern the Reaumur

Maria Isle

Friars

Fluted Hill

S. W. Cape

South Cape

Penguin Island

South Cape

View of VAN DIEMENS LAND over Fluted Cape when South Cape bears N.N.W E. distant 7 miles.

View of the LAND over Fluted Cape when Penguin Island bears N.W. b. W. 1 & 1/2 mile distant.

View of VAN DIEMENS LAND when the Mewstone bears N.E. distant 6 miles.

Mewstone

CHAPTER THIRTEEN

The Last Voyage

T HE famous dinner party at which Cook definitely accepted command of the the third expedition can be seen in retrospect as the first scene in the first act of an unfolding tragedy. As Beaglehole remarks tersely: 'The dinner party was a great success, a triumph of management. It was a disaster.'[1] It is important to probe Cook's state of mind and his motivations when he set out on the quest for the Northwest Passage. A few days after the dinner Cook wrote to his old friend Captain John Walker in Whitby:

> I expect to be able to sail about the latter end of April . . . I know not what your opinion may be on this step I have taken. It is certain I have quitted an easy retirement for an active and perhaps dangerous voyage. My present disposition is more favourable to the latter than the former, and I embark on as fair a prospect as I can wish. If I am fortunate enough to get safe home, there's no doubt but it will be greatly to my advantage.[2]

Here we have a clear statement that he detested retirement and would rather face danger than idleness. Cook was in that class of great achievers who must have work and reputation, or in his case constant voyages of discovery. 'To my advantage' clearly referred to the long-standing reward of £20,000 offered by the British government to any navigator who would find the Northwest Passage.[3] With such a sum, perhaps roughly equivalent to £1 million in today's money, he could finally become a rich landowner, enter the ranks of the aristocracy and thus surmount the seemingly ineluctable barrier of class. Life was tough even for the most talented meritocrat in the eighteenth century; Cook had already come far but, as an almost chillingly ambitious man, he wanted to break through the ceiling that separated mere achievers from the possessors of vast inherited fortunes. A triumphant third return would almost certainly bring further rewards, in the shape of a huge bounty for his maps and charts, accelerated promotion to admiral, and very probably a knighthood.

Cook could thus simultaneously climb the ladder of honours and that of finance. It is likely that other considerations weighed as well. If Clerke or some other navigator commanded the expedition and found the Passage, would that not eclipse his own achievements to date, so that he would come to seem a mere John the Baptist to a greater Messiah? Cook's psychology was also important. As a 'control freak' he was not suited to life on land, where he was beset by rivals, critics and Admiralty committees. At sea he was the supreme autocrat and dictator whose word was law and whose mere nod could indicate punishment or reprieve.[4]

Deeper than this into Cook's mind we cannot go, for lack of evidence. In his case, more than with almost any other 'great man', the person effectively was the role. As one commentator has put it: 'there were depths; but the soundings are few'.[5] Psychoanalytical investigations of historical figures are always fraught with peril, but in Cook's case they are simply impossible, for we know almost nothing of his childhood and his relations with his parents or with his wife and his own children.[6] A deeply secretive person, as are many great achievers who have risen from lowly origins (again the comparison with H. M. Stanley is instructive), Cook almost never allows the mask of seagoing professional, a kind of navigational machine, to slip; the fact that his wife burned all his personal correspondence completes the cordon sanitaire he managed to throw around his personal life. Of course the fact that one's wife burns all correspondence does not necessarily preclude a biographical approach via depth psychology, as the notable example of the explorer Sir Richard Burton shows, but in Burton's case there was a wealth of published writings available, in which he frequently gave important clues to the workings of his psyche.[7] Cook's writing by contrast was almost entirely about his profession and his career. What can be said quite confidently and without fear of contradiction is that Cook by the time of his third voyage had undergone a personality change. To account for this convincingly, we need hard data not fanciful conjecture, but this is not available.[8] If Cook suffered from intestinal obstruction, roundworm infection and consequent vitamin B deficiency – producing fatigue, constipation, irritability, loss of initiative and depression – or if, as seems probable, he was treated with opiates for sciatica and gradually became dependent on the drug, this could easily explain the marked change noted by everyone who had sailed with him before. To anticipate the narrative for a moment, the old Cook of the second voyage would not have expressed lack of interest when hearing about the Samoan and Fijian islands on Tonga but would have sought them out. Similarly the surveying genius who charted New Zealand would not have become confused in the Bering Sea and identified the same island as three different ones.[9]

Listless and passive as Cook so often was on the third voyage, he clearly suffered from depressive interludes. Many theories can be advanced to explain this, going beyond the explanation of organic physical illness. It is sometimes alleged that he felt peculiarly 'alienated' on his final voyage because this time he had no one to confide in, since the educated men on his ship (such as James King) were much younger and inferior in rank, and may well have been intimidated by his aura, charisma, gravitas or simply the weight of his fame. If objective illness or mood swings caused his integrated ego to fracture, that would explain why he was no longer solely the careful, meticulous technician, obsessed with control and order, but sometimes launched into erratic enterprises, revealing the mentality of a gambler. The mania for precision and mathematical objectivity began to coexist with an equal and opposite penchant for taking chances and defying the odds – exactly the psychological syndrome we observe in the case of Napoleon.[10] Sour, irascible and increasingly autocratic, Cook unhappily collided with a crew more disposed than those of the *Endeavour* or the *Resolution* to question his authority. One can guess at the many sources of stress. As he grows older a man obsessed with control is likely to find the sheer contingency of the world and its stubborn and irreducible nature intolerable, which in turn generates impatience and tantrums, all observed on the *Resolution–Discovery* trip. Unconsciously he may have guessed that the Northwest Passage would turn out to be a chimera and that he was engaged on a fool's errand. He was deeply irritated and indeed angry that he had been sent out with an inadequate flagship and that, because of the incompetence of the authorities at Deptford dockyard, the *Resolution* was never the ship she had been on the second voyage.[11] It is unlikely that he had become bored with navigation but he may have become disillusioned with exploration, and at a number of different levels. The most ingenious suggestion is that the 'fatal impact' of Europeans on Polynesia may have worked the other way and, to use psychoanalytical language, that his unconscious was disturbed by a dangerously contagious and pagan view of happiness he had brought back from the South Seas; to use Jungian terms, his unconscious may have suffered psychic harm as 'compensation' for his conscious refusal to avail himself of the free sexuality on the islands.[12] Finally, and most obviously, Cook was simply too old to command a voyage of exploration. At 48, after six years of virtually non-stop stress conquering the oceans, he had been at sea too long and was exhausted. Normally, 40 was considered an advanced age for a sea captain and those still at sea at this age usually thought themselves hard done by.[13] Beaglehole sums up the situation judiciously: 'We have a man tired, not physically in any observable way, but with that almost imperceptible blunting of the brain that makes him, under a light searching enough, a perceptibly rather different man. His apprehensions as a discoverer were not so constantly fine as they had been; his understanding of other minds was not so ready or sympathetic.'[14]

All this lay in the future in the last week of June 1776 when a seemingly jaunty Cook wrote to his old friend Commodore Wilson at Great Ayton: 'If I am not so fortunate to make my passage home by the North Pole, I hope at least to determine whether it is practicable or not. From what we yet know, the attempt must be hazardous, and must be made with great caution.'[15] The truly interesting thing is that Cook genuinely thought he could sail to the North Pole, and was still fixated on the old orthodoxy that, since seawater did not freeze, the Arctic Ocean must be ice-free.[16] He was obviously preoccupied, doubtless mixing practical concerns with more deep-seated mental revolutions concerning his aims and motives. The motivations of the nation state that sent him out were also being questioned; the time was long gone when Sandwich could brush aside French queries on the purpose of the Cook voyages, as he had done in 1772 by saying that the British government was actuated purely by curiosity about the world.[17] Russia, Spain, France and even the rebellious American colonists were deeply suspicious about the true objectives of the *Resolution–Discovery* venture. The Bourbon powers learned that Russian cooperation in the Bering Strait was being counted on and leapt to the wild deduction that the British were linking up with the Russians in Kamchatka as the prelude to a full-scale invasion of Japan, in self-imposed isolation from the world for the past one hundred and fifty years.[18] Spain was particularly suspicious of Cook and issued empire-wide orders that if he called at any of their ports in the Americas, he was to be arrested.[19] The American colonists were more far-sighted. Convinced that the interests of science were the true goal of the expedition, Benjamin Franklin persuaded his confrères in the American Congress that all possible assitance should be rendered to Cook.[20] After some hesitation, France followed suit: Louis XVI ordered that if French ships encountered Cook they were to leave him alone, as he was engaged in the important task of bringing light to benighted savages.[21]

Early in June the two ships were ordered round to Plymouth for the final 'jump-off', but there were delays, long enough for Sandwich, Palliser and other Admiralty bigwigs to attend a final 'noble dinner' on the *Resolution*. Sandwich told Cook he would be paying Cook's wife Elizabeth an extra pension while he was away so that she would want for nothing material.[22] Since Clerke was still detained in King's Bench prison, it fell to James Burney to take the *Discovery* round to Plymouth, to the intense pride of his family. On 23 June Cook made his final farewells to Elizabeth, who presumably bore the parting with a stoicism that was by now second nature. He picked up Omai in

London at 6 a.m. on the 24th and together they sped to the Nore, arriving in Chatham at 10.30. By now both Sandwich and King George were desperate to see the back of Omai. What had been amusing at first had rapidly become tiresome, especially as Omai was now going in for heavy flirtations with society ladies and irritating the aristocracy with his presumption. His essential clown-like status was well conveyed by Fanny Burney in reporting a social occasion, when all Omai could find to say about whoever was mentioned was that he was 'very *dood* man'.[23] On 25 June Cook sailed the *Resolution* to Plymouth to rendezvous with Burney who had already been there three days. Plans were afoot to help Clerke break out of jail, but these had to be matured. Cook therefore instructed Burney to wait until Clerke made his appearance, presumably with the Bow Street Runners in hot pursuit, and then follow him down to Cape Town. To assist morale, once again two months' wages were paid in advance.[24] In Plymouth he found the town in a hubbub, with press gangs everywhere and ships being fitted out for the American war to convey Hessian mercenaries there. The very first official account of the voyage (in 1784) would point to the irony of Cook trying to explore the north-west coast of North America for Britain at the very moment the American colonists were in revolt against Britain.[25] As a farewell present he was informed that the Royal Society had awarded him its prize medal for his contributions to seamen's health. He cleared for the Cape on 12 July, only to discover almost immediately that the caulking of the *Resolution* had been defective and that the ship was leaking; rain flooded into the officers' cabins and soaked into the storerooms and sailrooms, threatening destruction to everything that was needed for the voyage.[26] A superstitious man, which Cook was not, would have read this as an extremely bad omen.

Cook passed Ushant and by 24 July was off Cape Finisterre. He anchored at Santa Cruz de Tenerife in the Canary Islands on 1 August.[27] Here Cook bought fodder for the animals and provisions for his seamen, including bullocks, pumpkins, onions, potatoes and a huge quantity of wine at a knock-down price. He made some friendly contacts with French and Spanish sea captains who were interested in his chronometer, but most of the others on the *Resolution* did not enjoy the three-day stay on Tenerife. Omai found the Spanish as hostile as the people of Bora Bora would have been to a Raiatean, while Samwell, the Irish surgeon's mate, thought the locals a set of narrow priest-ridden bigots.[28] As they left the Canaries, one of the seamen was given six lashes for neglect of duty. It is unclear whether the poor quality of the sailors or a mistake by one of the officers, Bligh perhaps, or even Cook himself, was responsible for the next worrying incident, when the *Resolution* nearly ran on to the rocks off Bonavista and a violent emergency hard-a-starboard manoeuvre was ordered before the ship narrowly missed the reef.[29] Together, the two incidents might have revealed to the proverbial Martian observer that there was already something very wrong with this third voyage. The bad omens continued after Cook made a brief call at the Cape Verde islands to stock up on provender for the animals. Immediately on leaving these islands they were assailed by heavy rains, which still further exposed the extent to which the *Resolution* was leaking because of the incompetent or corrupt caulking at Deptford.[30] Cook continued making south until he was about at latitude 5N, then swung out with south-east trades in a wide arc towards the coast of Brazil, intending to come in to Cape Town from the west; this was common practice in the sailing ships of the time. Cook, a traditionalist, encouraged the rough horseplay of the Crossing the Line ceremony, which younger captains were increasingly discouraging. Bligh was surprised to find that most men chose to be ducked rather than pay the forfeit of a bottle of rum. Following behind in the *Discovery*, Clerke showed himself to be one of the newer breed of commanders by bribing his men with grog not to perform the ceremony.[31]

Cook put in to Cape Town on 18 October, having shaved twelve days off his previous time from England to the Cape, even though they were in stormy weather most of the time; the crew might have been deficient as seamen but they were evidently good fishermen, to judge from the number of sharks and dolphins hauled aboard once they were in the South Atlantic.[32] Cook was received with a high respect that came close to idolatry, and Samwell was amazed to find that Cook seemed even more famous in South Africa than he was in England.[33] This was Cook's fourth time in Cape Town and Dutch officialdom could not have been more helpful. He set his caulkers, sailmakers and coopers to work on repairing and refitting the *Resolution* while he waited for the arrival of the *Discovery* which was about three weeks behind. The local people, however, treated Cook and his crew with more cynicism than the Dutch bureaucrats. Cook landed all his livestock to graze but some local 'entrepreneurs', coveting the flocks of sheep, deliberately set a large and savage dog among them, which killed a number of sheep and dispersed the rest. Cook protested to the governor and claimed reparation, but this individual at first claimed that the Cape Colony was crime-free. Even when he set his police on the case, they could come up with nothing, so in the end Cook employed a group of low-life 'grasses' and 'narks' to track down the sheep and in this way discovered the villains and recovered his livestock. Thus warned of the temperament and attitude of the proletarian locals, Cook reluctantly herded all his cattle and sheep back into the cramped quarters of the *Resolution*.[34] It was not only the Boers who gave trouble. His men, off the leash on shore leave, committed various offences, including selling some of their winter gear and other necessities of the voyage. No fewer than nine of them felt the lash for this indiscipline. That they were sailing under a new and more intolerant Cook is obvious from one striking statistic. Only just over four months from England, Cook had already meted out a full third of the total lashes he had given as punishment on the entire voyage of 1772–75.[35]

To Cook's immense relief the *Discovery* arrived on 10 November. Clerke had encountered the most sustained spell of stormy weather in his career so far on his way south, being continually mauled by a 'large western sea' on his run to the Cape; his survival was a close-run thing. There was a giant swell from the south, maybe 50–60 feet high, 'so much so as to make our bark plunge exceedingly. I am obliged to keep the reefs in the topsails on that account; it is a most unfortunate swell as it very much impedes our southing and drives us to the eastward.'[36] The same storms and gales tore to pieces the tents Cook had erected on the shore, damaged the astronomical quadrant and battered the *Resolution* as she lay at anchor in Table Bay, but Cook was proud of her as she 'was the only one that rode out the gale without dragging her anchors'.[37] Cook's spirits lifted with Clerke's arrival, and Clerke too seemed suitably cheerful, as is evident from his letter to Banks: 'Here I am hard and fast moored alongside my old friend Captain Cook so that our battles with the Israelites [his creditors and the bailiffs] cannot now have any ill effect upon our intended attack upon the North Pole.'[38] Cook sent his caulkers to work on the *Discovery* and then became involved in a furious altercation with the local bakers. Cook had placed a huge order for bread for the *Discovery*, intending to clear from the Cape at the earliest possible moment after Clerke arrived (this was before he was aware of the extensive storm damage the sister ship had sustained). It now turned out that the bakers had not even started on this order. They claimed a shortage of flour, but the truth was that they had not been willing to start work until the *Discovery* actually arrived; they feared that if Clerke's ship was lost at sea, Cook would simply cancel the order.[39] It turned out that there was time to send out an inland exploring expedition, whose principals were Gore, Omai and the surgeon William Anderson. Meanwhile Cook bought more animals to add to his menagerie: two young bulls, two heifers, two colts, two mares, two rams, several ewes and goats, rabbits and poultry and even some monkeys – all supposedly destined for New Zealand and Tahiti.[40] Here we see further signs of Cook's lack of grip. He should have made allowances for the full implications of his Noah's Ark – not just in terms of the vastly increased need for water and animal fodder and the likelihood that the beasts would not survive in the Antarctic conditions on the way to Kerguelen, but with regard to the vast amount of animal excrement that would be generated and which conflicted with his hitherto fanatical concern with hygiene. The travelling zoo seems just one more piece of evidence pointing to an increasingly erratic personality.

Cook sailed from Cape Town on 30 November, setting a course south-east in search, first, of the Prince Edward and Crozet islands, using the chart Crozet had given him in 1775. He was sailing into some of the stormiest waters in the world and for nearly two weeks the *Resolution* and *Discovery* suffered grievously, pitching and rolling in high seas and mountainous waves. Cook was afraid his seamen might not be up to the severest challenges of these ultra-testing conditions. His particular fear was that a helmsman might panic as a giant wave aft caught up with the ship, causing him to swing round broadside and thus 'broach to', offering the ship as a target and making almost sure she would be engulfed or overwhelmed. Even if the seamen maintained cast-iron discipline, there were still dangers; on 5 December a white squall carried away the mizzen topmast. Cook described his melancholy mood on the pelagic *via crucis* to the south-east:

> We continued our course ... with a very strong gale from the westward, followed by a very high sea which made the ship roll and tumble exceedingly and gave us a great deal of trouble to preserve the cattle we had on board, and notwithstanding all our care several goats, especially the males, died and some sheep, owing in a great measure to the cold which we began now most sensibly to feel.[41]

At last, on 12 December he sighted and sailed between the first of the islands mentioned by Marc-Joseph Marion du Fresne and named them Marion and Prince Edward Island (the two are now called Prince Edward Islands). He then held on to the south-east for Kerguelen, passing the Crozet islands, still confident that he would find the big island discovered by the eponymous French navigator while admitting that the navigation was 'both tedious and dangerous'.[42] That was the bluff Cook's usual understatement when it came to sea states. The high seas and mountainous waves continued, with the sea frequently breaching over the ship.[43] Cook was now in the 'Atlantic convergence', where upwelling cold water from the Antarctic fights with the warmer waters of the Indian Ocean. The result is persistently high winds, routinely generating 40-foot waves; crests of 50 feet are common and those of 60 feet and above by no means rare.

By 21 December a thick fog with nil visibility added to the dangers; the two ships kept in touch only by the frequent firing of their guns. Both Cook and King entered in their logs the concern that if they hove to they would lose valuable time but, if they sailed on through the fog, they might miss Kerguelen altogether. On 24 December Cook, however, found the main island in the Kerguelen group, exactly where he thought it would be. He anchored in what he called Christmas Harbour (Baie de l'Oiseau) and sent out parties to climb hills and reconnoitre. The Kerguelen archipelago consists of over 300 islands and islets between latitude 48'30'–49'45S and longitude 68'40' and 70'30', perhaps only a dozen of any real size or importance, and all of them, like the Prince Edwards and the Crozets, volcanic.[44] The main island (La Grande Terre), 95 miles from east to west and 75 miles north to south, is a mass of rocky, treeless hills, bogs, sounds, inlets and minor bays, with mammal life restricted to seals, especially the elephant variety. It is a paradise for Antarctic birds, boasting thirty species, including the Rockhopper, Macaroni, Gentoo and King penguins, albatrosses, skuas, giant petrels, sheathbills and terns and, because it is the only sizeable land in the southern Indian Ocean, would, after du Fresne's and Cook's visits, become a magnet for polar explorers and whalers.[45] Cook was delighted to send his hunters out on a killing spree that would replenish the larder with penguins, flying birds and seals. He gave his crew furlough on Christmas Day and brought back a bottle with Latin inscriptions written on parchment in its neck, testifying to the French visits to the island in 1772, 1773 and 1774. Since the other side of the parchment was blank, Cook added his own Latin inscription and dated it December 1776. He climbed a hill to get a view of the coast on 28 December and then spent two days on a running survey, passing along the north coast of Grande Terre, then down the west coast and finally halfway back up along the east coast before at last standing away on 30 December, heading for Van Diemen's Land (Tasmania).[46] The bad weather tracked them remorselessly. For a week there was thick fog, which created an impression of unending darkness, then high seas and, on 17 January, a squall so violent that the *Resolution*'s fore-topmast and the main topgallant mast were destroyed. The tangle of rigging prevented them from being swept overboard, and Cook also had a spare topmast, but the devastation and wreckage was such that the crew had to spend an entire day in repairs, and even then the topgallant mast could not be replaced. By now some alien cynics were even questioning Cook's judgement and seamanship. In pursuit of what seemed a quite arbitrary timetable Cook, thought King, had been crowding on too much sail for the prevailing conditions.[47]

Van Diemen's Land (the Tasmanian coast) was sighted on 24 January 1777 and on the evening of the 26th Cook anchored in Adventure Bay, where Tasman had been in 1642 and Furneaux in 1773. On the morning of 27 January Cook sent King in command of two separate parties, one cutting wood, the other grass for the animals; wary of the locals he also sent along a detachment of marines to guard the detail. It was the profusion of poisonous snakes, rather than hostile aborigines, that most concerned the foragers, for on New Zealand and the Pacific Islands such serpents were unknown. Somehow these brave guardians of their comrades managed to smuggle drink on to the boats to take ashore and then got horribly drunk. Five of these men were carried back to the *Resolution* in a stupor and hoisted up the side. All were flogged next day, the ordinary participants with twelve lashes and the 'ringleaders' with eighteen; presumably Cook identified the ringleaders in the time-honoured military way: every fifth man.[48] Cook had originally intended a longer stay in Van Diemen's Land, but this gross breach of discipline upset him and he decided to leave at once. Contrary winds delayed him, so he set the men to fish. Soon there was contact with the aborigines. Nine of the locals, Melanesian in racial type, approached but impressed all the Europeans as being very stupid. Their matter-of-factness about nakedness and physical functions appalled even the veterans of Polynesia. Anderson the surgeon reported that men would play with their penis as if with a bauble and would squat to defecate without any shame or sense of privacy: 'the men never changed their posture on making water and would sometimes not even move their legs out of the way but would suffer the urine to run down upon them'.[49] James Burney confirmed this and he compared their insouciance to the way a dog lifts up its leg to urinate: 'one of these gentlemen will pour forth his streams without any preparatory action or guidance, or even appear sensible of what he is doing; and not in the least interested in whether it trickles down his thighs or sprinkles the person next to him'.[50] The first contact with the aborigines came to an abrupt end when the show-off Omai, always keen to impress his superior *savoir faire* on primitives, fired a gun which made them scatter in panic. Cook was so disillusioned by the impressions he had formed of the locals that he decided he would not after all leave behind the cattle, sheep and goats with which he hoped to turn Van Diemen's Land into a pastoral paradise. He did, however, leave behind a boar and a sow hoping that they would not be killed and eaten and would produce a litter of piglets.[51]

On 29 January the winds still made it impossible to leave, and there was further contact with the aborigines. The seamen took liberties with the indigenous women, examining their genitals with lustful intent, but as soon as it was apparent that they had sexual congress on their minds an aborigine elder gave a signal and the women melted away. This prompted Cook to ponder further the issue of his sailors' sexuality. He realised he could not stop them having intercourse with native women, but was resentful at the way the seamen habitually offered gifts and trinkets in exchange for their sexual favours. It seemed to him that the only possible consequence of such dalliance was to alienate the

local men and make his job more difficult. The unsuccessful overtures the
seamen had made to the aborigine women prompted another reflection: it was
a golden rule in primitive society that if the women were 'easy' the local men
would offer them for prostitution; if this did not happen, it was a waste of time
for the sailors to try to barter for them.[52] At last the winds changed and it
was possible to leave; Cook was anxious to get away and did not bother to
circumnavigate Van Diemen's Land as he took it for granted it was joined to
the mainland. Yet having been delayed by windless days, he was no sooner out
to sea than he was hit by a violent tempest – the kind that is sometimes called
a 'perfect storm' as two different storm fronts collide to produce a hurricane.[53]
When this died away at the end of the first week of February, there was a
further calamity when Clerke signalled from the *Discovery* that one of his
marines had fallen overboard in the night; the man was not seen again.[54] The
only notable event in the crossing of the Tasman Sea thereafter was the fog,
and the conjunction of seeing killer whales (orcas) on the same day as a 'huge
shark', in these waters probably a great white (*Carcharodon carcharias*). Three
days later, on 10 February, the voyagers sighted the coast of New Zealand;
Cook steered for Cape Farewell and on the 12th anchored in Charlotte Sound,
his old New Zealand 'base'. This was his fifth time in New Zealand – the first
had been the circumnavigation in the *Endeavour* in 1769, and the second, third
and fourth stopovers were preludes to exploring the great Southern Ocean on
his second voyage. For romantics this part of the world was always a revelation. Banks had written of the sensuous thrill of the melodious wild music of
the Maoris counterpointing the exquisite beauty of the locale, and this time it
was Thomas Edgar, the *Discovery*'s master who responded in the same way.[55]

Yet for the crew New Zealand and Charlotte Sound had a strong resonance
and a very different and definite meaning: this was where their shipmates on
the *Adventure* had been slaughtered. They expected Cook to extract revenge,
but his very first reaction was to assure the Maoris who came out in canoes
to inspect them that he came in friendship and did not harbour vengeful
thoughts.[56] If this 'liberal' attitude alienated Cook's men, it stupefied the Maoris.
They fully expected that they would have to pay for the killing and eating of the
white men three years earlier, for this was an attack on a chief's *mana*: if he did
not respond, he was nothing, a man of zero credibility. Not for the first or last
time in human affairs, a 'softly softly' approach was read as weakness; restraint,
meant to teach the locals the meaning of civilisation, bred merely contempt.
Cook's peaceable approach seemed wilful perversity, both to his seamen and to
the Maoris. Some of the latter recognised Omai and knew he had been in the
Adventure party, which seemed to make retribution a certainty, yet nothing
happened. Later a chieftain named Kahura, who had led the party that massacred

Furneaux's men, put in an appearance, but Cook did not even try to apprehend him.[57] It was clear to the seamen that Cook favoured 'savages' over them; since the visitors referred to all indigenous people as 'Indians', Cook was what in nineteenth-century American frontier parlance would be called an 'Injun-lover'. In retaliation, at least some of the sailors refused to sleep with the local women who were offered so profusely by the Maori men. In most cases, though, human nature won out and, though with gritted teeth, the seamen still took their pleasure. Cook, who should have been addressing the men's concern about revenge, continued to fuss and fret about intercourse with local women. He admitted he could do nothing about it but dreaded its consequences in all forms, consoling himself with the consensus opinion that 'natives' never attacked while their women were consorting with sailors.[58] Prostitution was not the only form of useful symbiosis, for when Cook set up tents on the shore to enable Bayly and King to start making astronomical observations, the Maoris camped alongside them and generally fetched and carried. Cook spent most of his time either directing grass-cutting parties so that the cattle could be fed or visiting the Maoris *pas*, marvelling at their canoes, and pondering their warlike nature.[59]

The Maoris were astonished at the Noah's Ark Cook disembarked. Although at first Cook posted strong guards to protect the shore parties, once the Maoris bedded down beside his men he gradually relaxed and took the menagerie ashore, partly to distribute horses, cattle, sheep and goats among the locals as part of the 'improving' scheme, and partly to stretch the legs and feathers of those continuing on to the Society Islands. The Maoris appeared not to have seen either horses or horned cattle before.[60] Gradually, too – one is tempted to say inevitably – relations between the locals and the visitors worsened. Some of the sailors took the line that, after the *Adventure* massacre, the Maoris 'owed' them, especially since Cook obviously intended to do nothing about the situation. Meanwhile the Maoris had grown contemptuous of a man who would not reassert his *mana* by taking revenge on the Maoris. They would have had more respect for Cook if he had killed some of them, the strangers seemed of no account, and their confidence grew. Soon they were using the sailors' ploy against them, accepting gifts and refusing to give anything in return.[61] One warrior even boasted openly that he had eaten an *Adventure* man. For Omai, the peaceful reception of Kahura was the last straw. When he first saw him, Omai threatened Kahura with death, but Kahura treated this as an empty threat and, to rub in the humiliation, returned next day with his extended family of twenty souls, virtually laughing in Omai's face. Omai completely lost his temper and in a high rage shouted at Cook: 'There is Kahura. Kill him!' While Kahura went on deck to have his portrait painted by Webber, Omai bearded Cook in the Great Cabin and raged at him. 'Why do you not kill him? You tell me if a man kills another in England he is hanged for it and yet you will not kill him, even though a great many of his own people would like that and it would be very good.'[62] The general derision felt for Cook by his crew found expression on the *Discovery*, where James Burney connived at and encouraged an express act of defiance and contempt for his commander. Edward Riou had acquired a pariah dog from the Maoris, which was deeply unpopular as it liked to bite people. The midshipmen and master's mates staged a mock trial of this dog for cannibalism, convicted it, killed it, then cooked and ate it.[63]

Faced with the dual threat of insubordination from the Maoris and disaffection from his own men, Cook left New Zealand at the earliest possible moment. He cleared from Queen Charlotte Sound on 25 February, taking with him two Maori youths. At the very last moment Te Weherua and Koa, little more than boys, were loaded on, in response to Te Weherua's caprice (and possibly Omai's bad influence), which Cook ought not to have indulged. Once Cook had reached the point of no return on the open ocean, the Maori youths seemed to regret their foolish decision; they wept piteously and continued to do so for days. Eventually, though, they cheered up and became great favourites with the sailors.[64] Cook was behind the impossible schedule drawn up in London which originally envisaged his leaving at the end of April 1776, ready to be on the north-west coast of America by June 1777, but authorities are divided on how much the timetable really mattered to him; he had, after all, been instructed that in the end all was to be at his discretion. At any rate, if speed was his primary concern he should now have headed directly north-east across the Pacific to Tahiti. But Cook estimated that at this time of the year the favourable westerlies would not be with him and therefore that he would have to make northing in a more zigzag manner. For the whole of March he encountered calms and irritating south-easterly breezes, further slowing his progress. Cook complained bitterly in his journal,[65] but things could have been a lot worse; in these latitudes this is the season for cyclones and hurricanes. Whether it was sheer boredom or pent-up resentment about their commander's poor showing in New Zealand, the crew were in mutinous mood. An epidemic of minor thefts ended with a theft of meat from the mess of the *Resolution*. When the men would not surrender the culprits, Cook cut the meat allowance to two-thirds; the seamen responded by refusing to touch even the proferred two-thirds, which Cook considered 'a very mutinous proceeding'.[66] Cook was already being caught between the two fires that would bedevil the entire voyage. On the one hand, he was faced by sailors far more strident, assertive and disaffected than any he had known previously; on the other, forced by circumstances to concede that his 'tolerant' treatment of indigenous people had not worked, he was gradually becoming a hardliner.[67] Whether old age had made him increasingly irritable and short-tempered; whether he regarded the native peoples as ingrates after all he had done for them (at least in his mind); whether he had turned violently against the whole idea of the 'noble savage' and the Rousseauesque view of man as intrinsically good and perfectible, and now regarded humans as sinful and incorrigible; or whether, indeed, he had become the victim of delusions of grandeur and thus regarded any opposition, whether from aboriginals or sailors, as a kind of lèse-majesté; all this must perforce remain at the level of speculation, though it seems there is merit in each of these views.[68]

After a tedious month, on 29 March, Mangaia (one of the Cook islands) was sighted. The reef and pounding surf, as much as the unfriendly locals who came out to meet and challenge them in war canoes, were not inviting, so Cook looked for a more enticing land farther north and found it at Atiu on the 31st, though contrary winds prevented anchorage until 2 April. Again Cook faced high surf, a reef and steep coral rocks. Gore made a tentative sortie in a boat and came back to advise Cook that the best course might be to try to persuade the locals to bring the trade goods the ships needed out to the boats, lying beyond the booming surf. Cook thought this worth a try, so on the 3rd he set out with three boats and Omai as interpreter.[69] Cook was worried that if Gore and his party were attacked, the reef would place an impossible barrier between the ships and the three boats and awaited the outcome nervously. On this occasion Omai finally proved his worth, for his swaggering boastfulness managed to strike just the right note with the islanders. The initial overtures produced a barrage of questions: were the strangers *arioi*, did they come from the Society Islands, were they perhaps envoys of the god Oro?[70] Omai was at first nervous, for to begin with the locals were far from friendly and gave their guests nothing to eat until the evening; when an oven was lit to cook a pig, Omai feared that he himself might be on the menu. Yet gradually he impressed the islanders with the might and power of the newcomers. He told them of the capability of European guns, at which the Atiuans were openly sceptical. Omai then gave a demonstration of firepower by exploding the gunpowder from the cartridges he had brought with him. The crackerjack, pyrotechnical effect of the explosion impressed the locals suitably, especially when Omai added that if the white men were not allowed to come and go at will, they would destroy the whole island.[71] In the resultant calm and friendly atmosphere Omai made the acquaintance of three Society Islanders who had been shipwrecked on Atiu twelve years earlier after being caught in their outrigger in a ferocious storm. Theirs was originally a large fishing party, and they had drifted for weeks in the Pacific before making landfall, by which time only four of them were still alive (one man had subsequently died).[72] A joyful embrace of fellow countrymen set the seal on Omai's most successful day's work yet.

Cook did not get much of what he wanted from Atiu, so the following morning he steered for an uninhabited islet ten miles to the north named Takutea. Here he obtained a quantity of coconuts, scurvy grass and pandanus, which the cattle ate with relish.[73] Next he made for Manuae, which from the previous voyage he also thought uninhabited, but it turned out to be occupied, with the result that canoes came out to meet his ships when they plied there on 6 April. Cook needed a good water supply, but the evident hostility of the new inhabitants made that problematical. These people were aggressive, violent and shameless thieves who tried to steal everything not nailed down, including the oars from the *Discovery*'s cutter and even Bayly's servant. Cook used suffi-cient force to restrain them, but not enough to impress the two young Maoris who, like their elder kinsmen, concluded that Cook lacked *mana*; such were the rewards of restraint in Polynesia.[74] Cook had enough food and fodder to last until the Society Islands but he was seriously short of water. He had taken on 270 tons in New Zealand, but the prodigious thirst of the cattle was the main reason why this was soon reduced to an alarmingly meagre 70 tons. Not wanting to take water by force, he elected to stand away to the Tongan archi-pelago, where the people had been welcoming on the second voyage. The urgency of his position was indicated by the typically Cook throwaway line in his journal: 'As it was necessary to run in the night as well as in the day, I ordered Captain Clerke to keep about a league ahead of the *Resolution*, as his ship could better claw off a lee shore than mine.'[75] Cook was now essentially sailing west, *away* from Tahiti, thus further impairing the precious schedule. The irony was that within the Cook islands he could have found what he needed at either of the rich and fertile islands of Rarotonga and Aitutaki, neither of which, unfortunately, were shown on his charts. With the crew now severely rationed on water (two quarts a day per man), and the water-distilling apparatus proving disappointing, the seamen had to spread the awnings to attempt to catch rain; on 10 April this method proved very effective in a short thunderstorm. The weather seemed to be playing tricks on Cook just when he needed a fine spell, 'with a wind in our teeth whichever way we directed our course'.[76] Yet at last, when both captain and crew were almost in despair, up loomed Palmerston Island.

Here was fresh water and, what was more, plentiful food for man and beast. While the cattle chewed their way through abundant scurvy grass and the green of coconut trees, Cook's foragers gathered nuts, pandanus and palm cabbage for the stock, and fish and seabirds for themselves. Both of these abounded to the point where observers concluded Palmerston must be one of Nature's secret larders. Here for three days the voyagers hunted and fished until the two ships were once again stuffed with edible protein.[77] Refreshed in body and mind, the explorers set out for Nomuka but found the going difficult, encountering thunderstorms, adverse winds, high seas and frequent squalls all the way. It was the night of 24–25 April before they limped past Niue, now called Savage Island after the sad experiences of 1774. Next day the fine weather returned and they could see the glimmer of dolphins swimming alongside them in the dark. On 30 April the two ships reached Nomuka, with Cook approaching a little to the south of his track in June 1774.[78] He and his companions were recognised and the old pattern of trade started up again, with pigs, breadfruit and yams being bartered for hatchets and nails. Cook gave strict orders that no buying of curios was allowed until all food and water stocks on the two ships were wholly replenished, yet in three days he was able to end all rationing and restore everyone to a diet of pork, fruit and roots. Cook stayed a fortnight on Nomuka. The ships worked round to the old anchorage on the northern shore by 2 May. Here the *Discovery* lost its best bower anchor on the sharp rocks and began drifting; on 7 May the small bower anchor got hooked up in the *Resolution*'s cable. It was the evening of the 8th before this small bower was unhooked and all the anchors recovered and secured. Even as the work went on, a Nomukan was caught trying to steal a piece of the *Resolution*'s tackle – specifically, the bolt from the spunyarn winch; he was given a dozen lashes and not released until the ransom of a hog was paid over.[79]

   That particular thief was a minor chief, so the flogging had some effect. The problem was that with the lower orders in Nomuka a flogging made as little impression as it would on a drunken sailor. In exasperation Cook actually sentenced one petty larcenist to sixty lashes – enough to kill a man in the Royal Navy. Yet nothing seemed to work as a deterrent. When Cook appealed for help with the epidemic of thieving to the local chiefs, they replied blandly that Cook should simply kill the thieves; Cook declined, on the somewhat Jesuitical ground that he would not use as a punishment – even the supreme penalty – anything that the locals themselves did not view as punishment. Clerke, vexed with the same problem on the *Discovery*, hit on the idea of shaving the thieves' heads, since a shaven pate was regarded as a great disgrace in local culture. Taking a leaf out of Clerke's book, Cook experimented with the kind of retribution that might be regarded by the locals as a fate worse than death. First he decide to throw all thieves into the sea, and then use them for target practice or get his men to row alongside them and clobber them with oars or transfix them with boathooks. From this he escalated to cutting off their ears.[80] Despite all this, Cook and his men mainly enjoyed extraordinarily good relations with the Nomukans. Their chief Tupoulangi gave up his house so that Cook and Omai could stay in it, the chiefs threw coconuts and stones at their own people if they appeared too demanding or rambunctious towards their guests, the common people hewed wood and drew water for their visitors.[81] The trade in sex was as brisk as ever, with hachets, shirts, nails and red feathers securing the most desirable of the island houris. To his horror Cook found that venereal disease was already rampant, presumably having been introduced on the 1774 visit; in a new version of *la ronde de l'amour* the women of Nomuka transmitted syphilis to comrades of the men who had originally given it to them. But Cook apart, no one seemed especially concerned by the threat from sexually transmitted diseases. Samwell, no mean womaniser himself, who kept a record of his conquests on the islands, thought that Nomuka was paradise on earth, a veritable Elysium.[82]

On 6 May a chief named Finau arrived from Tongatapu. A handsome man of about 35, Finau was presented to Cook by Omai as 'king' of the Tongan islands. Perhaps Omai was trying to put his status in terms that the Europeans would understand or, more likely, he was unaware of all the elite nuances on Tonga and simply wished to have it understood that Finau was a person of importance. Anthropologists have unravelled the tangled skein on the islands and explained that power was really exercised through a troika, containing a sacred chief allegedly descended from the gods (the Tu'i Tonga), his chancellor or prime minister (Tu'i Ha'atakalua) and the wielder of real day-to-day power (the Tu'i Kanokupolo), a kind of committee chairman or chief executive. Cook, who saw things through the Georgian lens of 'kings', at first overrated Finau, thinking him to be the monarch of the isles, then later underrated him because he realised he did not have supreme status. So-called 'kingship' did not work on Tonga, where hierarchies ran horizontally as well as vertically, and where in some contexts a chief could be outranked by someone nominally lower on the pyramid. Actually the deep structure of elite authority was even more complex, as all three Tu'is were outranked by their father's sisters, since sacred status (as opposed to real political power) passed through the female line in Tonga.[83] Finau's arrival certainly made an impression. Tupoulangi deferred to him and bowed his head. When Finau came on board the *Resolution* he laid about him with a stick and drew blood from those of his people foolish enough not to heed his every command. When an officer protested at his brutality, Finau laughed and said that the Tongans expected such a reaction from a Tu'i, for otherwise he would be deemed not to have *mana*.[84] Thereafter Finau dined with Cook every day in the Great Cabin. He was shrewd enough to see that the food supply on Nomuka was becoming exhausted after a fortnight of providing for 200 white men. He did not want the same inroads made on his own island of Vava'u, and suggested that Cook and his ships relocate to Lifuka where he could entertain them properly. Cook therefore weighed anchor on 14 May and threaded a northerly course through reefs and islets, past the volcanic islands of Tofua and Kao, following the guideline of beacons which Finau ordered fired to light their passage. The passage on the lee side of the islands was studded with dangerous reefs, but it was better than being on the explosive windward side where the open Pacific roared in. The voyagers came to anchor on the northern shore of Lifuka on 17 May.[85]

The visitors were greeted by the usual throng and brisk trade began: pigs, fowl, fruit and vegetables for hatchets, knives, cloth and nails. Finau addressed the island elders and then the common people, ordering them not to steal from the Europeans. After Cook had handed over suitable gifts to the island chief and dined him and Finau aboard the *Resolution*, Finau announced a ceremony of welcome for the next day. The following morning a crowd estimated by Cook at 3,000 strong gathered to watch a procession of 100 warriors who stacked masses of yams, plantains, breadfruit, coconuts and sugar cane in two neat piles, topping them off with six hogs and two turtles. Finau explained that one pile was Cook's, the other Omai's.[86] Despite Cook's strictures on Omai's intelligence, the latter had succeeded in making himself the indispensable go-between and now appeared to be Finau's favourite retainer. Another procession then appeared with more fruit and vegetables, and two more hogs and some chickens laid on top. A sensitive soul might have read this as meaning that the islanders had now brought all the food they had, so that the visitors should take it gratefully and depart. Cook, though, never seemed to appreciate the razor-thin margin of subsistence on which Polynesian society operated. He remarked that the food supply 'far exceeded any present I had ever before received from an Indian prince'[87] but seemed to make the unwarranted inference that the Tongans were therefore as rich as maharajahs and nizams. He and his men stayed on to watch boxing and wrestling matches and were appalled to find that some of these bouts were between women. Next morning Cook's officers strolled nonchalantly all over the island. Under the surface the tensions were simmering. It seemed that, even after all the food and produce given them, the strangers would not be departing soon. Then came the real trigger for the subterranean resentments. Tapa, Tupoulangi's deputy, had come to Lifuka with Finau, bringing his son. Now the son took a fancy to one of the *Discovery*'s cats. Caught trying to smuggle the animal off the ship, the boy was clapped in irons. Clerke was especially troubled with an infestation of rats and he needed every last one of his felines to combat them. As he remarked with his trademark irony, the Tongans had managed to take 'all my cats, which were very good ones, and as they did not take the rats with them, of which the ship was full, I felt this proof of their dexterity very severely'.[88] The Tongans were angry that the son of a chief should be punished for such a 'trivial' matter, but Clerke stood firm and let it be known that Tapa's son would not be released until all the stolen cats were returned.

The cat incident and the disinclination of the Europeans to leave convinced the local chiefs that violence against the intruders was the only answer. A conspiracy was hatched; Finau was not the originator but he advised and orchestrated it and without his approval it could not have gone ahead. There would be a great night-time dancing exhibition, illuminated by flambeaux; Cook and his men would be invited and then massacred.[89] Finau pointed out that the coup would be complete only if they could also capture the two ships and that would be very difficult at night; he proposed the killing take place by day, and there would be nothing suspicious about this as Cook had already agreed to attend a day-long exhibition of dances. Finau knew how European firearms worked and he even had a plan to reduce the expected Tongan death toll. He asked Cook if, in return for all the lavish entertainments prepared for him, he would ask his marines to drill in public and fire off their muskets in unison after the first set of dances. Cook, suspecting nothing, agreed.[90] The discharge of the muskets was to be the signal for the Tongans to rise up and kill the 'wizards'. Reinforcements would doubtless arrive and could then be picked off piecemeal until the Europeans were so weak that they would be unable to repel a concerted attack on their ships. If all went well, 200 white bodies would soon be lying bleaching on Lifuka beach. Cook and his men arrived, an exquisite and beguiling 'harlequin dance' was performed, the marines carried out their exercises (albeit in a ramshackle way) and fired off their muskets. Then nothing. What had happened? It seemed that just before the entertainment began the local chiefs had second thoughts and decided to revert to the idea of a night-time attack. When Finau was told this, he flew into a rage at the insolence of these minor chieftains daring to oppose their views to his. He cancelled the entire operation forthwith and stormed off in fury.[91] Any thought the locals might have had of defying Finau and going it alone were dispelled by the performance Cook laid on that night. A display of fireworks and skyrockets accompanied with loud aerial bangs and explosions awed and stunned the Tongans. King reported the psychological ascendancy gained thus:

> Such roaring, jumping and shouting . . . made us perfectly satisfied that we had gained a complete victory in their own minds. Sky and water rockets were what affected them most; the water rocket exercised their inquisitive

faculties, for they could not conceive how fire should burn under water. Omai, who was always very ready to magnify our country, told them they might now see how easy it was for us to destroy not only the earth but the water and the sky; and some of our sailors were seriously persuading their hearers that by means of the sky rocket we had made stars.[92]

The torchlit festivities continued with an unparalleled display of erotic dancing from the Tongans, which in their lubricious intensity aroused lustful thoughts in even the most straitlaced, prudish and puritanical European observers. John Webber sketched furiously, and the evening came to an end with quasi-orgiastic couplings between the sailors and the local beauties, who could be bought for a shirt or an axe.[93] The conspiracy had failed, but the underlying tensions did not go away. Cook continued to be almost breathtakingly naïve in his acceptance at face value of Finau's continued protestations of friendship; doubtless it massaged his ego to think that he was singularly adept at handling 'the natives'.[94] Yet thefts continued apace; Cook complained to Finau but nothing was done. Cook therefore decided on a draconian policy towards all offenders, both the Tongans and his own men. He doled out fifteen lashes to a thieving Tongan while punishing one mariner with twelve strokes for losing a boathook and meting out the same penalty to another for the loss of a ramrod.[95] By now even the rather obtuse Cook was getting the message that he was no longer welcome. Finau asked him to stay on for a few days while he went to his island to fetch some red feathers. Finau's motivation for this is obscure: he might have been planning another coup or he might simply have wished to absent himself from any phoney leave-taking ceremony. Certainly when Cook offered to accompany him to Vava'u, Finau replied with the whopping lie that there was no suitable anchorage there (the harbour at Vava'u was excellent). A more telling pointer to Tongan feelings was the false report spread by the Lifukans that a European ship had made landfall in one of the southern islands; even Cook could see that this was a transparent ruse to get him to move on.[96] Cook accordingly made his way down the coast of Lifuka to its southern neighbour Uoleva, intending to make an inner passage among the islands to Tongatapu. He sent Bligh ahead to reconnoitre, who came back with news that the passage between the islands was studded with shoals, breakers and islets. Cook therefore decided he would have to follow a northward track outside the islands.[97]

While Cook was anchored in a bay off the southern coast of Lifuka, on 27 May, he received what he recorded as a confusing visit from yet another Tongan 'king'. This time the visitor came as close to that title as differential traditions would allow, for this was the Tu'i Tonga himself. Paulaho, as he was called, was a hugely fat man of about 40, deliberately obese to reveal his status

23 The three exploratory forays into the Antarctic Ocean during the second voyage together probably constitute Cook's greatest feat of discovery and navigation. It took until the mid-nineteenth
century for any sailor to surpass his southern most journey and until the twentieth, with steam
technology, before the full gamut of his polar cruising was equalled.

24 Dusky Bay has been well described as 'one of the most remote and wildly magnificent spots in New Zealand'. William Hodges's paintings made it look as forbidding as something from the stories of Edgar Allan Poe. The product of glaciers, the bay's coastline rises up sharply to meet beetling cliffs and is indented with multiple fjords. From the high-water mark to the snowline, thick forests cling to the slope. Islets dotting the deep-water bay are similarly forested.

25 Otoo, better known as Tu, was a supremely crafty politician, the Machiavelli of Tahiti. His policy was to use Cook against rival island chiefs and Cook's was to back him against all rivals. During his son's reign Tahiti was finally united under a single ruler.

26 Tonga or the Friendly Islands, about one-third of the way from New Zealand to Hawaii, comprises 176 islands scattered over 270,000 square miles of ocean. On his three visits Cook explored the entire island system thoroughly, covering 500 miles north to south. He thought the landscape of the islands resembled a very superior country park in England. A particular favourite was Tongatapu (Amsterdam), which he considered a walker's paradise. A curiosity was its chief Otago, who followed him around like a pet dog.

27 Tanna is an island of the modern state of Vanuatu, a complex of Melanesian islands. Cook's title for the islands – New Hebrides – endured until independence in 1980. One of the most southerly isles in the system, Tanna is volcanic and contains Mount Yasur, whose glowing light attracted Cook when he landed in August 1774.

28 It was not only Cook who encountered resistance at Erramanga. In the nineteenth century it had the reputation among missionaries of being the most dangerous island in the Pacific. Cook proved a good prophet when he wrote: 'No one would ever venture to introduce Christianity into Erramanga, because neither fame nor profit could offer the requisite inducement.'

Mr. Omai
presents his Compliments to
Mr. Wag
and Returns him many thanks
for the Favor of his Obliging
Enquiry's.

Hughes Lieut

29 and 30 Foolishly brought back to England by Tobias Furneaux on the *Adventure* during the second voyage, Omai was initially the sensation of London society as the original 'noble savage'. Despite being painted by Sir Joshua Reynolds and granted an audience with George III, Omai became unpopular in part because of his alleged lechery towards society ladies and his putative status as dark ravager – Reynolds's portrait certainly makes him appear a Rudolf Valentino *avant la lettre*. Omai's 'cheeky chappy' persona soon palled, his patrons dumped him, and Cook took him back to the Society Islands on the third voyage, where he met an ignominious early death.

31 The fourth Earl of Sandwich is a controversial figure, with some modern revisionist historians arguing for his status as able and competent director of the Admiralty. A key patron of Cook's, he was more famous in his own time for libertinism and membership of the 'Hell Fire Club'. He was memorably the butt of John Wilkes's famous witticism. Sandwich: 'I am sure, Wilkes, that you will die either of the pox or on the gallows.' Wilkes: 'That depends, my lord, on whether I embrace your mistress or your principles.'

32 John Webber's portrait of Cook shows him apparently in a brown study or deep reverie, emphasising the visionary aspect of the great navigator. There have always been those, both in the eighteenth century and today, who have regarded Cook as a superb technician but a rather cold and inhuman man.

33 Charles Clerke, Cook's deputy on the third voyage, proved to be one of his most able lieutenants and an outstanding seaman. He was a very human figure as heavy drinker, philanderer and raconteur. Optimistic, witty and genial, he made the wardroom light up by his presence. Although he died young, at 38, he achieved a popularity that Cook could never match.

34 William Bligh (1754–1817) accompanied Cook on the third voyage and was one of the most talented of his 'kindergarten'. Like his mentor an outstanding seaman, he seemed fated to provoke mutiny, not just the famous one on the Bounty in 1789, but also in 1797 at Spithead and the Nore, and, most notoriously, in the so-called 'Rum Rebellion' when he was governor of New South Wales. Beaglehole summed him up well: 'He made dogmatic judgements which he felt himself entitled to make; he saw fools about him too easily ... thin-skinned vanity was his curse through life ... [he] never learnt that you do not make friends of men by insulting them.'

35 The night dances in Polynesia were said to be so erotically charged that they aroused lustful thoughts in even the most straitlaced, prudish and puritanical Europeans. The dances often went on for six hours and were followed by mass couplings between the sailors and the local girls.

36 Cook was misled by his friendly reception at Eua and Tongatapu in October 1773 and Nomuka in 1774, which is why he dubbed Tonga the Friendly Isles. Kava-drinking ceremonies were a central component of diplomatic relations, but by Cook's third visit to the islands, in May 1778, the ritual could not ease the simmering tensions.

37 Human sacrifice was said to have been introduced into Polynesia by a high priest named Pa'ao, about whom there is controversy: said to have hailed from Samoa, he is thought by some to be an historical figure, though the best authorities claim him as a pure creation of mythology. Human sacrifice was the greatest tribute one would make to the gods and increased one's power or *mana*. Some say it was a particular feature of Hawaii. Whether human sacrifice was linked to cannibalism is also disputed. Although cannibalism was a Pacific reality, its extent has probably been exaggerated, notably by Robert Louis Stevenson who wrote: 'Cannibalism is traced from end to end in the Pacific, from the Marquesas to New Guinea, from New Zealand to Hawaii.'

38 Red feathers were the supreme currency in Polynesia, an economic talisman, the Pacific's equivalent of gold, with Tonga as the South Africa of the piece. They could produce inflation (sometimes hyperinflation) or economic deflation, depending on the numbers traded. On Hawaii, however, yellow feathers were even more highly prized.

39 Nootka Sound, on the north-western coast of Vancouver Island, is considered one of the most spectacular and beautiful places on earth, but John Webber's watercolours present the melancholy and forbidding appearance which was the abiding impression of Cook and his crew in 1778. The high cliffs, jagged shore, coastal rain forests, cloud-laved valleys, lofty mountain peaks and the 'big sky' of the Pacific Northwest all combined to depress the voyagers.

40 Cook's men were often ordered by their captain to shoot seals, sealions and walruses. A typical holocaust of Antarctic wildlife took place on 2 January 1775 when a landing party slaughtered a great many of these mammals, along with hundreds of penguins, geese, ducks and shags. The irony was that the seamen detested walrus meat, finding it tough, chewy and indigestible, and their refusal to eat it brought on a notable confrontation with Captain Cook.

41 Kealakekua Bay, on the western coast of the 'big island' of Hawaii, was where Cook spent the last month of his life (17 January–14 February 1779). Breathtakingly beautiful, the bay provided excellent anchorage, though the adjacent land was volcanic, with sheer cliffs of lava and black obsidian rock; the whole scene was set off by the looming bulk of Mauna Loa or the Long Mountain.

42 Lono was the Hawaiian god of agriculture, the weather, peace, light and fertility. He had attributes rather like those of God the Father in Christian theology and could incarnate himself in avatars; the high chiefs of Hawaii were thought to be partial manifestations or incarnations of Lono. Because Cook arrived in Hawaii in January 1778 at the time of the annual feast of Lono, he may have been considered such an incarnation.

43 Cook was often regarded by Polynesians as an *atua* – a special kind of almost superhuman being with extraordinary powers. To say that Cook was regarded as a god confuses the issue, for Polynesians did not make a sharp distinction between life and death, mortality and immortality, the human and the divine. The status was also adventitious, for Captain Clerke was expressly offered the status of *atua* by the Hawaiians but declined it, thinking all such honours mumbo-jumbo.

44 No controversy is more heated than that surrounding Cook's tragic death. Was he killed because the Hawaiians considered him an impostor or false god? Or had Cook plunged into a psychotic interlude? Was his murder on the shoreline justifiable homicide? Or was the entire debacle a chapter of accidents, a series of aleatory events that could have turned out otherwise?

45 Almost nothing is known about Cook's wife or their married life. Thirteen years his junior, she survived him by fifty-six years and died aged 93. All her six children predeceased her. After Cook's death she lived in comfort from his property and earnings and a gratuity and generous pension from the Admiralty. The fact that she is a historical 'blank space' has made her an irresistible target for speculation by historical novelists.

– if Cook had known enough about Tongan culture he might have guessed that
the slim-built Finau could not have been the supreme ruler. Paulaho's role
could scarcely be denied, for when Finau returned he too deferred to him – a
hard blow for Omai to take, as he had staked his reputation on identifying the
power in the land, had become friendly with Finau, and now had to endure
this 'interloper'. Cook found him easier to get on with than Finau, doubtless
because the Tu'i Tonga was all pomp and ceremony, and unlike Finau did not
have to make nice political calculations.[98] When Cook was prevented from
setting sail on the 28th by contrary winds, Paulaho 'compensated' him with a
bonnet of red feathers. He seemed to trust Cook much more than Finau ever
did and, when Cook was eventually able to weigh anchor, he left his brother
and six of his retinue behind on the *Resolution*. Fortunately for Cook, he had to
spend only one night with these cuckoos in his cabin, for Paulaho and his court
followed in their canoes and took them back on board; it turned out they had
not been given permission to stay on Cook's ship and Paulaho was angry with
them for their disobedience.[99] Cook intended to call briefly at Nomuka now he
had the protection of the Tu'i Tonga and then proceed to Tongatapu, but the
passage south proved difficult and dangerous, in among reefs and breakers and
beset by sudden squalls. He passed Lofanga but then, on 31 May, went through
yet another of those nerve-shredding experiences in which his career prolifer-
ated. Tacking in a bizarre manner, which makes his track on an oceanic chart
look like the peregrinations of a drunkard, Cook tried to squeeze between the
islets of Kotu and Fotuha'a, but was caught in a severe squall and spent a terri-
fying night tacking in the dark under reefed topsails and foresail.[100] All hands
were on deck all night because of the danger; the *Resolution* had to keep firing
her guns to warn the *Discovery* astern. Cook describes the experience:

I kept the deck till twelve o'clock when I left it to the Master, with such
directions as I thought would keep the ships clear of the dangers that lay
around us; but after making a trip to the north and standing back again to the
south the ship, by a small shift of the wind, fetched farther to windward than
expected; by this means she was very near running plump upon a low sandy
isle surrounded by breakers. It happened very fortunately that the people
had just been turned up to put the ship about and the most of them at their
stations, so that the necessary movements were not only executed with judgment but with alertness and this alone saved the ship . . . Such risks as these
are the inevitable companions of the man who goes on discoveries.[101]

Cook anchored two miles off the uninhabited islet of Kotu and waited
three days for the winds to die down. Paulaho came up with him in his flotilla

of canoes and he and Cook walked Kotu together.[102] On 5 June Cook brought his ships in to Nomuka again for a brief stay. This was the occasion when Finau caught up with Paulaho and evinced his inferior status by being unable to sit at table with the Tu'i Tonga. Paulaho seemed to have no great liking for Finau and told Cook he did not trust him. Perhaps alerted by the supreme ruler to Finau's murderous and mendacious nature, Cook was sceptical when Finau told a long, circumstantial tale, whose upshot was that he was not bringing Cook any provisions since the canoes bearing the goods and their crews had all perished in the recent gales; from looking at Finau's followers' faces Cook could see at once that this was a lie. By now he had come to realise that Finau's main aim was to cut down on the sustenance offered to the visitors in the hopes that they would shortly depart or, at the very least, to keep them away from his beloved Vava'u.[103] Disillusionment with Finau was not the only headache. Many of the crew seemed to be suffering from 'Tonga flu' – a relatively mild virus that produced sore throats and a hacking cough, and on Nomuka the news was bad: all the seeds he had left on the island had been eaten by ants.[104] He stayed no longer on Nomuka this time than he had to. Paulaho went ahead in his canoes to Tongatapu, easily outdistancing the two sloops with his massive rowing power. Finau left behind pilots to guide them to a safe haven, but quite how knowledgeable these 'experts' were must remain problematical (unless Finau had issued secret instructions for sabotage), for as they threaded through the Lahi passage to Tongatapu they nearly ran aground on a coral shoal; both ships grazed the coral slightly but the water was deep so they slid through and came to anchor without damage on 10 June.[105]

Tongatapu, the seat of the Tu'i Tonga, was the largest and richest of all the Tongan islands. The fertility of the island amazed the visitors, as did the warmth of their reception. There were old friends to meet such as Ataongo, Cook's pal from his previous visit and Tupu, Furneaux's 'brother'. There was also the traditional kava-drinking ceremony that Paulaho laid on for them. To the astonishment of the locals Cook unloaded his entire menagerie: pigs, cattle, horses, goats, sheep, turkeys, geese and peacocks.[106] Paulaho next told Cook that the two of them should pay a visit to Tonga's Number Two potentate, the Tu'i Ha'atakalaua, or supreme secular authority, an elderly man named Maealiuaki who in his younger years had done the job Finau was now doing.[107] However, to conform with protocol the Europeans had to strip to the waist, and at this suggestion Cook protested vociferously, pointing out that one did not have to do that even when having an audience with the mighty King George of England. In the end Paulaho said that their naval uniforms would show enough respect for the old man's *mana*. But when they made the trip inland to see Maealiuaki on 12 June, they were told that the old man was ill or unavailable. Cook construed this as a brush-off and stormed off. Whether Maealiuaki had himself been in dudgeon because the strangers would not abase themselves in the prescribed manner and was then talked round by Paulaho, or whether the captain's intemperate behaviour had unbalanced and unsettled the Tu'i Tonga, the upshot was that the previously unapproachable old man next day went himself to Cook's ships for a meeting.[108] This was a great success: Maealiuaki toured the shore camp, inspected the cattle, examined the observatory and, with Paulaho, dined in the Great Cabin. Paulaho developed such a taste for European wine that he made a point of dining aboard the *Resolution* every day she was at the island. Cook and Clerke visited him in his royal residence, while Cook and Omai also made reciprocal visits with Tupu. Cook still relied on Omai for translation but was again starting to lose patience with him. He could never quite make out whether the Society Islander was more or less intelligent than he seemed, and whether Omai misunderstood or mistranslated the Tongans' words or simply kept things from him.[109]

For the first two weeks of the unconscionable one-month stay on Tongatapu Cook maintained good relations with the rulers of Tonga, but this entente was gradually whittled away as Cook began to react more and more harshly to the epidemic of thefts. At some stage during the voyage from New Zealand to Tonga Cook reflected on the ungrateful reaction of the Maoris to his clemency and non-retaliation for Grass Cove, and concluded that he had been gravely mistaken; it was clear that Polynesians reacted only to force and construed restraint as weakness.[110] By the time he reached Tongatapu he had decided that theft warranted the strongest possible retaliation on the offender, short of death. He ordered his sentries not to open fire, or at least not with lethal ammunition, for fear this would spark a general conflagration but instead ordained beating, slashing, ear-cropping, head-shaving and other draconian punishments. As Beaglehole put it: 'He flogged, in ascending dozens, he put in irons, he cropped ears, he slashed with a knife the arms of men he regarded as desperate offenders.'[111] This was certainly, at the pragmatic level, the correct course of action, although it affronted liberal officers such as King. Tongans had scant respect for people who allowed themselves to be put upon with impunity, and the punishments, severe as they were, were a bagatelle alongside some of the local customs, such as human sacrifice.[112] The significance of Cook's change of mind was what it reveals about his changing personality; gone is the 'softly, softly' approach, the benevolent paternalism of the son of the Enlightenment, and in its place is a hawkish, unforgiving hard-liner animated by Old Testament principles of revenge and smiting. Cook had always been short-tempered, but on the third voyage he increasingly exploded in volcanic rages. The midshipman James Trevenen reported that the men used to call Cook's tantrums *heivas*: 'the name of the dances of the Southern Islanders, which bore so great a resemblance to the violent motions and stamp-ings on the deck of Captain Cook in the paroxysms of passion'.[113] James King concurred. According to Edmund Burke, he 'never spoke of him but with respect and regret. But he lamented the roughness of his manners and the violence of his temper.'[114]

Sympathetic observers might say that Cook had plenty to fume and rage about. The Tongans were expert thieves and would steal anything not nailed down and much that was. As Beaglehole wryly remarks: 'They stole from a sentinel set on shore to prevent stealing.'[115] The early thefts – of a pewter basin and a sentry's ramrod – were perhaps no more than irritating, but the thievery soon escalated to a more serious level. An attempt was made on one of the *Discovery*'s anchors – foiled only because it got hooked in a chain-plate and could not be worked free by hand.[116] When a goat was stolen, Cook decided the best way to prevent further purloining of stock was to distribute at once the animals he intended as a parting gift. On 19 June he began distrib-uting the cattle. He delivered a careful lecture on animal husbandry and told the audience that there was no further need for theft because he was giving his prized livestock away free. He then proceeded to apportion the cows according to the rank of the recipients but inevitably, he missed some of the social nuances and left certain individuals aggrieved. Next day he found that a goat and two of the turkeycocks he intended to take on to Tahiti were missing. Incandescent with rage at such 'ingratitude', he seized the three high chiefs of Tonga plus three canoes and their crew and announced that they would be held until the missing animals were returned. The sacrilege in seeing their Tu'i Tonga made prisoner concentrated minds, and the stolen beasts were returned.[117] Cook released the chiefs and Paulaho tried to pour oil on troubled waters by holding a magnificent feast next day, with another extravagant display of dancing. Nonetheless the incident seriously soured relations and caused the chiefs to be wary. When some muskets were stolen on 23 June (perhaps ironically from the two most unpopular officers on the voyage, Bligh and Williamson), the three chiefs, knowing Cook's likely reaction, fled to the hills.[118] From there Paulaho sent an offer of reconciliation to Cook, who was concerned that his men were now coming under sustained attack from stone-throwers and his officers being assaulted while in the countryside. Poulaho offered to provide an escort for any of the scientists or officers proceeding inland. Although Cook accepted this as a gesture of good faith, it did not suit all the Europeans to have Tongans as escorts. Samwell, for instance, spent most of his time on clandestine amatory trysts and needed to be alone. On one of these jaunts he was physically assaulted and responded by opening fire, in defiance of Cook's standing orders. On 28 June a wood-cutting party came under severe and prolonged attack from the islanders, who rained down coconuts on them.[119]

Cook became more hard-line and ferocious, even during the sojourn in Tonga. When he had imprisoned Tapa's son on Lifuka for stealing a cat, the egregious Omai suggested to Cook that he give the culprit one hundred lashes. Cook gave him just one, which even so was taken by the Tongans as a gross insult. By the time he was on Tongatapu, something had snapped and he was prepared to order lashings well above the legal maximum of twelve laid down by Navy regulations.[120] He had by now worked out an effective method of dealing with thievery by chieftains and oligarchs: after they had been flogged, they had to pay an additional penalty in pigs. But he had no deterrent with which to ward off the depredations of the common people, so in desperation turned to the cat-o'-nine-tails. When a dozen lashes did not cut down the incidence of theft, he increased the number to two dozen, then three dozen, then four dozen, eventually going as high as seventy-two lashes. Additionally he cut off men's ears, fired at swimmers in the sea, maimed them with oars and boathooks and ritually cut at least one man on the shoulder.[121] Not only was Cook wildly exceeding the powers granted to him as a Royal Navy captain, he was also alienating the Tongans and shooting himself in the foot, since such extreme penalties bespoke extreme impotence. Even Cook's officers thought his actions constituted 'cruel and unusual punishment' and were self-defeating as well. Where the Tongans at the beginning of the month-long stay in Tongatapu used to be welcoming and hospitable, now they shut the doors of their houses against the visitors, reacted to them sullenly, stopped trading and went out of their way to rob or insult any Europeans they encountered on shore.[122] Passions were rising on both sides. Cook discovered that one of his sentries had seriously wounded a Tongan with a musket ball and set up a board of inquiry to try to discover how his express orders that his men fire only small shot had been flouted. The proceedings ended in farce, because the entire corps of marines closed ranks and swore on a stack of bibles that the Tongan had simply been grazed with small shot.[123]

This came close to mutiny and Cook, sensitive and even paranoid about such manifestations in his crew, struck back hard, ordering multiple lashings for recalcitrant seamen. Undoubtedly, too, he was displacing on to them some of the murderous rage he felt towards the Tongans and which he dared not indulge in openly lest it trigger a bloodbath. He flogged eight of his own men for various offences on Tongatapu, five of them with a dozen lashes each.[124] Alongside Cook's hardening attitude to the Polynesians on the third voyage one can clearly perceive a more brutal response to his men; on the voyage of the *Resolution* and *Discovery* he punished twice as many men (with 736 lashes in total) than he had on the two previous voyages combined.[125] Given that Cook was (literally) lashing out at both seamen and Polynesians in 1777, Omai may be considered lucky to have escaped his wrath. His offences were twofold. In the first place he came to blows with a corporal of marines and, when he appealed to Cook, did not get the satisfaction he required; Cook, indeed, took the line that the affray was Omai's own fault. Then he angered Cook by setting himself up as the official intermediary between the ship's officers, who were complaining about theft, and Paulaho, thus cutting out Cook altogether.[126] Yet Cook took a complaisant attitude to Omai's casual dalliance with a local girl, and in this regard Omai was not the only one to escape the magma of Cook's volcanic wrath on Tongatapu. He drew the line at interfering with his men's sex lives, which were as strenuous here as on all other Pacific islands. Samwell was well to the fore in this regard, but he was far from the only one – hardly surprisingly since the Tongan houris were rated by some of the men as the most lascivious in all the islands.[127] Even the two young Maoris Te Weherua and Koa got into the lubricious action (through Omai's bad influence, Cook thought), as a result of which Te Weherua contracted a sexually transmitted disease (probably yaws). It was the old story. The locals spread yaws among the sailors and they retaliated by infecting their hosts with gonorrhoea and syphilis.[128]

In the (rare) intervals between flogging his own men and the Tongans and making angry moves against the chiefs, Cook (contradictorily) spent most of his time at formal ceremonies with Paulaho, trying to conciliate him. It is surprising that the Tongans, having earlier planned to massacre Cook and the Europeans, did not react with more force to Cook's provocative floggings and maimings, but the answer may be that Paulaho was using Cook in his own power struggle with Finau, who scarcely appears in the accounts of the month-long stay at Tongatapu. Cook's own journals are full of lengthy and somewhat tedious accounts of six-hour-long dances and other rituals, each one seemingly conducted under a different rubric. First, on 17 June, there was a ceremony to ask the gods for a successful yam planting season. This consisted of a theatrical show mimicking yam-planting, the 'presentation' of yams and breadfruit, five hours of daytime dancing and then, in the evening, a long series of night dances.[129] Cook felt that his credibility required an answering ceremony next day, in which his marines were again put through their paces and again failed to impress. Against his own usual practice, Cook allowed his men to fight the locals in wrestling matches. When they were all soundly thrashed, he felt he had to regain the face lost by another display of

European technological superiority, involving fireworks and water-rockets. Then, a few days later, after the chiefs had fled into the hills and Cook had sent Omai after them, there was a propitiation ceremony, which essentially meant another massive presentation of food by the Tongans to their visitors: hogs, turtles, fish, yams and breadfruit, piled into two food mountains each 30 feet high. Paulaho then presented red feathers and the evening closed with night dances.[130] After some further embarrassing incidents, on 25 June, Cook accompanied Paulaho to the ritual centre at Mu'a, visited the sacred burial grounds of the Tu'i Tonga's family and spent the night in his house. All this diplomacy, though cordial enough, and eked out with many a *kava*-drinking ceremony, failed to settle the simmering tensions on the island and the rampant theft.[131] On 1 July Cook announced that he was setting sail, but contrary winds continued to detain him. Paulaho made a formal farewell, the ships moved to a different anchorage ready to sail on the first favourable breeze, and the chapter at Tongatapu seemed closed.[132]

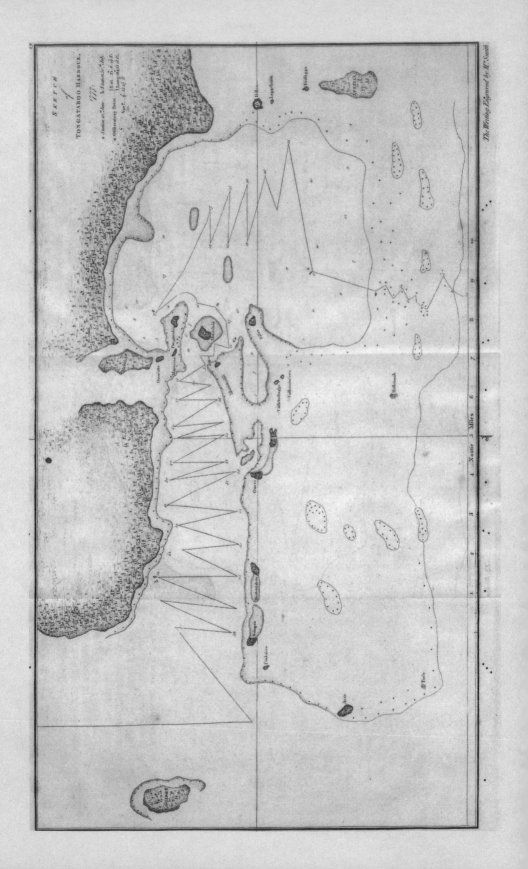

SKETCH
of
TONGATABOO HARBOUR.
1777

CHAPTER FOURTEEN

Tahiti: The Final Phase

IT was not to be. The winds continued to defy Cook. Casting about for something to do, he decided to impress the Tongans with his powers as a magician by predicting the eclipse of the sun he knew would occur on 5 July. Alas for his hopes, the sky that day was cloudy and the eclipse was visible only for moments, so the impact of the 'prophecy' was lost.[1] With the winds still contrary, Cook decided to accept yet another invitation from Paulaho to a ceremonial ritual. This was the *inasi*, or ceremony to inaugurate the planting of the crops and such an Eleusinian mystery of the South Seas that only great chiefs and priests were allowed to be present. At the ceremony Paulaho intended to lift the *tapu* that prevented his son from eating with him. In political terms this meant that he was nominating his son to succeed him.

Once again the Tu'i Tonga was enlisting his impressive visitor as a pawn in his power politics.[2] On 7 July Cook, Clerke and Omai visited the holy of holies at Mu'a, where Paulaho told them that to take part they would have to strip to the waist and let down their hair. Cook was prepared to heed the tonsorial prescription but again refused to strip to the waist, until it became clear that if he did not do so he would be in a virtual limbo, unable to go back to the ships, since the way was barred by hundreds of frenzied warriors, and unable to proceed to the ceremony as that way too was barred, by other club-wielding berserkers who informed them they were in breach of *tapu*. As much to cut through the logjam as anything else, Cook eventually agreed to strip to the waist, and for this he was excoriated by his men, who claimed he had 'gone native'.[3] On the other hand, since Cook did not know how to behave at the ceremony and several times breached *tapu*, the Tongans regarded him as 'bad medicine' and feared that the gods, in their anger, might cause the crops to fail. His defenders claim that Cook's determination to discover the meaning of the ceremony – which seems, from the descriptions, to have been very much variations on the theme of the previous rituals, with dancing, wrestling matches and much involvement of yams – shows 'avid ethnographic curiosity', though it comes across to a modern reader as cultural arrogance and meddling.[4] A veteran missionary on the Tongan isles later commented; 'The wonder is that he was not killed then as the Inaji [sic] was the most sacred ceremony possible and only certain select persons were allowed to be present . . . Only priests were present for a certain part of the ceremony, and being full of fear for their gods, the wonder is, that the Captain escaped being struck, or killed by some of them.'[5]

On 12 July the winds shifted and finally allowed Cook to set sail. He made first for Eua, sailing cautiously through the Piha passage with a gale blowing, anchored in his old position off Eua, met Taione the chief he had known in 1773, and traded for yam and hogs; as if to show his disillusionment with Tongatapu he gave the chief the sheep that Paulaho had seemed not to know what to do with. He climbed the highest point of the island for a panoramic view and expressed great contentment in the beauty of his surroundings.[6] At Taione's urgent request he agreed to stay another couple of days and receive a further supply of fruit. Yet the idyll was abruptly shattered on 16 July when his servant William Collet, together with some of the ship's stewards, was set on by a mob and stripped of his clothes. Cook demanded satisfaction and seized canoes and a hog as ransom. The embarrassed chief instituted a hue and cry, and next morning a shirt and pair of trousers were brought in together with shreds of all the other clothes that had been ripped to pieces. Taione presented a young lad as the chief culprit and ringleader, which Cook construed as an obvious excuse; either the real malefactors were Taione's kinsfolk or he simply could not be bothered to hunt them down. Cook decided to let it go at that and weighed anchor.[7] Just as he was leaving, a message came from Paulaho to say that he should hang on as the Tu'i Tonga was visiting Eua in a few days and would be bringing a goodly supply of hogs. Cook showed his contempt for Paulaho by clearing immediately for the Society islands. His parting words, on 17 July, were: 'Thus we took leave of the Friendly islands and their inhabitants after a stay between two-three months, during which time we lived together in the most cordial friendship; some accidental differences, it's true, now and then happened owing to their great propensity for thieving, but too often encouraged by the negligence of our own people.'[8] As a piece of Panglossian rewriting of history this is hard to beat. And since all the journals and official records show both Tongan thievery and naval flogging at epidemic levels, we are entitled to ask what a judicious summary of Cook's sojourn on Tonga would be and, more importantly, what exactly did he think he was doing there?

There can be no doubt that theft was a far more serious problem than Cook admitted in his 'valedictory' salute to the 'Friendly Islands'. Diary after diary, log after log, journal after journal, they all refer to this as a central problem, especially during the long stay at Tongatapu.[9] It is almost a truism to remark that the longer Cook stayed on a Pacific island, the greater the level of theft, but this was in a sense imbricated in the entire collision of cultures triggered by the great voyages of exploration in the eighteenth century. The core problem was that Europeans exchanged commodities as part of a market economy, whereas for the Polynesians, as for most traditional societies (we see the same thing in Homer's *Odyssey*) the exchange of valuable items answers a different cultural agenda. Polynesians saw precious items not as a means of exchange but as marks and symbols of status; if you came to a foreign shore and were received in friendship you owed your hosts gifts and, in the fullness of time, they might choose to reciprocate with commodities of even greater value. What you did not do was to demand money or its equivalent as an on-the-spot transaction.[10] When the foreigners appeared mean and unforth-coming with their gifts, the Polynesians thought they had a right to help themselves. Moreover, as Johann Forster had noted on the second voyage, theft was a notion that applied only *within* a given society and not to aliens who had no such rights.[11] There was confusion too over customary rights. For a European, hewing wood and drawing water was a non-marketable activity for which no payment should be made, but indigenous peoples did not necessarily see it that way at all. In traditional societies there was always some notion of what Africans called *hongo*: that you had to pay for passage through a tribal territory or for use of its natural assets. There was also the not unimportant point that Polynesians stole from Europeans to acquire their power or *mana*. This was one of the reasons for thefts of navigational equipment, which was of no intrinsic value to Polynesians: they noticed how Europeans guarded their quadrants zealously and concluded that they must be gods.[12] Finally, operating the principles of a market economy when in contact with primitive or traditional societies might have consequences unintended or even undreamed of by Europeans. If you favour one indigenous tribe over another because they offer lower prices, you may unwittingly blunder into serious tribal or clan political struggles. Some say this was the deep cause and core reason for the Grass Cove massacre.[13] We are back with that oldest of clichés: failure to communicate.

As so often, Cook was damned if he did and damned if he did not. If he showed the utmost sensitivity and insight into the Polynesian perspective, the objectives of his own voyage would be jeopardised. If he did not strike back against the thieves, the *Resolution* and *Discovery* would soon be stripped bare.

If he did, he risked endangering his own men by provoking a general indigenous uprising against the Europeans; several observers thought that this was exactly what he had done on Tonga, even without any knowledge of Finau's attempted treachery.[14] On the other hand, any sign of collaboration with the locals, as in the *inasi* ceremony, was construed as 'going native'. In these circumstances it is remarkable that he had anyone to speak up for his attempts to be fair and judicious, and still more remarkable that the chief such spokesman was Samwell.[15] Later commentators would allege that Cook had struck the right balance of strength and restraint in Tonga; this was certainly no island paradise, it was a place characterised by utmost brutality where, in the *inasi* held three months after Cook departed, ten men were killed in ritual human sacrifice. Even King, inclined at first to be a *bien pensant* liberal, finally penetrated the savage reality of everyday life on the Friendly Isles, and remarked that the harmony and peace on the islands did not derive from the gentleness and the sweetness of the tempers or any savage nobility; it was the result of fear, *tapu* and strict social hierarchy.[16] Perhaps most amazing of all was that Cook's reputation continued to be high in Tonga and that when Tongan chiefs heard of his death (in 1793 from the d'Entrecasteaux expedition) they regretted it, despite his known severity, and one chief (Kepa) wept openly.[17] On the other hand, Cook's judgement can certainly be faulted even from a European perspective. Where was the sense or morality in taking the two Maori boys away from New Zealand? The case was unlike that of Omai, for there was no likelihood that a European expedition would ever be able to take them home again. Cook's search for the Northwest Passage would certainly be the swansong even of a navigator who lived as though he were ageless, and it was not certain that any further voyages would be commissioned.[18]

Beyond all this, we have to ask the ultimate question about the Tonga venture: what was Cook doing in the Friendly Islands in the first place?[19] Cook claimed that the winds were against him when he tried to get to Tahiti, so that he had to turn west: in short he expected westerlies and got easterlies. He based his expectations on his experience in June–August 1773 when he sailed north-east from New Zealand to Tahiti, with westerlies most of the way. But a great navigator should have factored in the consideration that he was sailing in different months and that this would bring different winds. It is true that in the Pacific from 40 to 30'S westerlies are regular for seven months of the year; between 30 and 20 there is a belt of variable winds known as the Variables of Capricorn, and then, at 20'S the south-east trade wind takes over. What Cook did not know (but should have done from his previous sweeps across the South Pacific in all seasons) was that from November to March the variables move as far south as New Zealand; indeed they usually bring cyclones and hurricanes in their train, which Cook was lucky to miss.[20] Cook's failure to spot this weather gap, coupled with other errors later on, eventually led his officers to think the unthinkable and conclude that he had lost his touch or even – the ultimate blasphemy – that he had been overrated all along.[21] Cook explained that he had decided to play safe and head for Tonga instead of Tahiti, but that simply removes to another level the criticism of his planning and administration. Given that he was carrying such a menagerie with a colossal thirst for fresh water, should he not have worked out their requirements on a worst-case scenario basis and taken on supplies accordingly before ever he quit New Zealand? There is really no way to avoid the conclusion that the once peerless navigator was no longer the genius of yore. Even if we bracket all this, why did he have to stay so long in Tonga when after a few weeks he had all the supplies and water he needed for the voyage to Tahiti? Moreover, having heard from the Tongans about Fiji, three days' sail from Tongatapu, and about Samoa, two days from Vava'u, why did he not seek them out to explore?[22] Certainly the Cook of the second voyage would have done so. Was Cook simply too old and tired to face further challenges, and, if so, should he have been commanding the *Resolution* and *Discovery*? George Gilbert reported that the Tongans explicitly put it to Cook that he should sail to these islands and chastise their enemies but Cook, hearing that they were mighty warriors and cannibals, declined. The violence he had experienced on Tongatapu was enough without finding new enemies to fight.[23]

The four-week passage to Tahiti was largely uneventful, with favourable winds and serene weather most of the way. Cook was able to reflect that in his extended tour of the Tongan isles he had explored a Pacific locale more meticulously than anywhere else except Tahiti itself and that Anderson's observations there were just as valuable as the much-vaunted work by Banks on the Society Islands.[24] The crew were in good spirits, fortified by the long stopover at Tongatapu and the frenzied lubricious dalliances there; both officers and men continued to remember wistfully the commitment to instant gratification, the casual acceptance of carnality by the local women and the complete absence of sexual jealousy. Interestingly, they thought that although the green-eyed monster was absent, its cousin, envy, was most definitely present, and that this was the real motive for Tongans' habitual theft of European articles.[25] Those who scoff at the 'reductive' notion that human motivation can mainly be traced to sex and money would not have found much comfort on the *Resolution* and *Discovery*, where most of the manifestations of a depraved human nature were present. Another of the sins of the medieval schoolmen, cupidity, was also much in evidence in Tonga and on the voyage to Tahiti, when the entrepreneurs below decks began calculating their possible profits from the exchange of the precious red feathers, the equivalent in Polynesia of gold bullion. Tonga was, as it were, the South Africa of this commodity.[26] Yet these worshippers of the market found that primitive versions of currency speculation could work both ways. In the first place, the Tongans, perceiving the European lust for the feathers, racked the prices up to such extortionate levels that even putative future profits looked risky. Then, on arrival in Tahiti, the sailors found that the supply of these feathers, from visiting European ships and local traders, had produced a counter-inflationary spiral, where the supply easily exceeded demand, prices were driven down, and so the expected profits did not materialise.[27]

The dreamy tenor of the trans-Pacific cruising was shattered when a storm struck the ships on 29 July. Two of Cook's staysails were blown to pieces, but even worse damage was sustained by the *Discovery*. A white squall, erupting within the pre-existing high seas, laid Clerke's vessel on its beam ends, snapped off her main-topmast, and caused other damage. Clerke signalled to Cook his distress and, when the storm subsided, Cook sent him a topsail yard. In his customary matter-of-fact way Cook describes the sequel: 'The next day [1 August] he got up a jury topmast on which he set a mizzen topsail and this enabled him to keep up with the *Resolution*.'[28] Fortunately, the incident did not cause much delay. The next significant development came on 9 August with the discovery of the island of Tubuai (now one of the Iles Australes in French Polynesia), lying to the south-east of Rurutu, which they had reconnoitred on the *Endeavour* voyage. Canoes approached the ships, but there was no easy passage through the reef and anyway Cook saw no point in landing, so altered course to the north to fetch Tahiti. He approached from the south-east and passed the 'signpost' island of Mehetia on 12 August.[29] Contrary winds prevented his anchoring in Vaitepiha Bay until the next morning, but then they were joyfully received. At first there was no hint of island inflation, for when the red feathers were produced by the avid entrepreneurs, to use Cook's words, 'not more feathers than might be got from a tomtit would purchase a hog of 40 to 50 pounds weight'.[30] Their first welcomers told them of significant developments since the last visit. Purea was dead, as was the young Vehiatua whom Cook had met on the second voyage, who had been succeeded by his brother, another Vehiatua, making one each of the same name, all lords of Tahiti-iti, that Cook had encountered. On Tahiti-nui the dour and gloomy Tu, Cook's protégé, was still alive and well. There had been no further significant hostilities or civil wars.[31]

For Cook the truly sensational news was that, since his last visit, the Spanish had tried to establish themselves on the island.[32] It later turned out that Don Domingo de Boenechea, who had been on the island in 1772 and taken away two Tahitian lads to Lima, had returned in 1774–75, brought back his two island adventurers, and landed two Recollect (Franciscan) fathers. Boenechea had then died and been succeeded by Don Tomas Gayangos, who shortly afterwards departed for Lima.[33] The Spanish had made a very favourable impression on the Tahitians. In line with their hidalgo/conquistador culture, the Spanish despised the Anglo-Saxon 'free market' model of commercial intercourse and were extremely generous to the islanders, hoping to establish goodwill; the approach worked, and the Tahitians came to wonder why the English were so niggardly in their trading. The chiefs of Tahiti agreed to accept a permanent Spanish mission in return for the protection of King Charles of Spain, but here the Spanish impact did not work so well, as the two Franciscan fathers left behind turned out to be tremendous cowards, who went about in daily fear of their lives, bitterly regretting the folly that had brought them to the South Seas.[34] Fortunately, perhaps, their 'interpreter and escort', a young marine named Maximo Rodriguez, was a genial extrovert and a huge hit with the Tahitians. Finally, in November 1775, Don Cayetano de Langana de Huarte, commanding a new Spanish expedition, arrived and took home the tremulous fathers.[35] Madrid had decided that there was no point in keeping a permanent mission on Tahiti, as it was not an important objective for any rival European power. Cook found a few traces of the Spanish visit, notably some Iberian hogs and a solitary bull which had mated with the English cows. He also found the missionary's house, complete with a cross on which had been carved the legend CHRISTUS VINCIT CAROLUS III IMPERAT 1774. Cook obliterated this and had inscribed on the reverse side GEORGIUS TERTIUS REX ANNIS 1767, 69, 73, 74 & 77, making it clear that the British had the prior claim.[36]

Noting the profusion of coconut-based alcohol on Tahiti, which Cook thought would make a substitute (the archaism he actually used was 'succedaneum') for grog, he went back on board and assembled all the men on the quarterdeck. He told them of the hardships to come in the cold latitudes of the North Pacific and suggested that they might like to keep their supplies of real alcohol until then, eking out the local beverage meanwhile. In a notable attempt to reach out and conciliate the men with whom he had been on bad terms ever since he cut the meat ration, he put it to them that the choice was entirely theirs: drink all the grog now or save it for the icy waters of the Pacific Northwest. The seamen unanimously fell in with Cook's suggestion.[37] Maybe they had been sobered by the impact of their very success in trading red feathers. The problem was that, now the Tahitians knew these were available, they would not trade for any other goods and turned up their noses at the former currency of nails, beads, trinkets and even axes.[38] Meanwhile the value of the red feathers plummeted in twenty-four hours to one-fifth of the value it had had when Cook made his 'tomtit' remark. The plumes were also the occasion of further irritated journal animadversions by Cook about Omai. When he first arrived, he was pointedly ignored by the Tahitians, even by those who knew him. But when he produced his hoard of red feathers, everything changed and the Tahitians greeted him as a long-lost brother; now everyone wanted to be his friend. Cook noted that the acclaim went to Omai's head and he relapsed into his default mode of boastful loudmouth, particularly delighting in showing off to his sister who came to meet him.[39] Yet the feathers, despite their fluctuating effect elsewhere, did have one beneficial impact. The Tahitians had obviously drunk deeply at the well of anti-British propaganda offered them by the Spanish, especially the taunt that the Anglo-Saxons were mean-minded money-grubbers. Cook decided to override this with a display of fireworks to reinforce the red feathers. This combination worked perfectly: the Tahitians remarked that 'the Lima ships had neither red feathers nor fireworks'.[40]

Cook's ten days on Tahiti-iti were largely spent in meetings and ceremonial encounters with the 13-year-old Vehiatua. The seamen coupled with the local women with the usual gusto; the fact that they possessed the prized red feathers meant that this time even some of the aristocratic ladies were prepared to sleep with them. To an extent the long layover (in all senses) at Tonga had made the sailors blasé: they commented critically that Tongan dances were superior and their warriors more impressive; they did concede, however, that the Tahitian women were of peerless beauty. Piqued by some of the remarks conveyed to them, the Tahitians laid on a super-erotic *heiva*, of a kind that, to use a later idiom, would have made a bishop kick a hole in a stained-glass window. 'A very obscene part performed by ye ladies', as it was cryptically referred to, presumably referred to some kind of troilism or group sex.[41] King, as usual, over-intellectualised things in his journals, contrasting the 'femininity' of Tahitian males with the true masculinity of the Tongan warriors: 'If we wanted a model for an Apollo or a Bacchus we must look for it at Otaheite [sc. Tahiti], and shall find it to perfection, but if for a Hercules or an Ajax at the Friendly Isles.'[42] Meanwhile Omai was continuing to annoy Cook. He persuaded Cook to call on the high priest of the god Oro, but the captain found him 'the greatest jackass' he had ever met in his life.[43] On a subsequent occasion Omai launched into a defence of the priest, of Oro and of his religion, which manifested itself in the following outpouring: 'Ah, Captain Cook. He is a very goog gog! A very good gog, Captain Cook.'[44] Omai then went on with Cook to the meeting with Vehiatua and demonstrated his non-existent talent at diplomacy. He should have been aware of all the undercurrents on the island and of the deadly rivalry that existed between the families of Tu and Vehiatua. Nonetheless, he went to the meeting with Vehiatua in a splendid headdress of yellow and red feathers, which he intended to give to Tu. Cook had advised him to keep it under wraps until they moved round to Matavai Bay but this did not suit the braggart. As was stunningly predictable, Vehiatua took a shine to the 'war-bonnet' and coveted it for himself. The foolish Omai asked the boy to send it on to Tu with his compliments, thereby insulting Vehiatua. The lord of Tahiti-iti, as Cook had warned, simply kept the headdress for himself and sent on a few moulting feathers to Tu, who was of course enraged. By his idiotic trust in the 'honesty and fidelity' of his countrymen, the absurd Omai managed to insult both the powers in the land at one go.[45]

On 23 August Cook set out for his preferred anchorage of Matavai Bay, where he would remain until the end of September. Tu was at Point Venus to meet him, with a large entourage. Omai tried to introduce himself as a person of importance but was contemptuously snubbed; the entire royal family then went on board *Resolution* to dine. Some of Tu's family came round to Omai once they realised how many red feathers he possessed; Cook encouraged this, as he wanted to leave Omai behind under Tu's explicit protection. Yet Omai, as so often, proved his own worst enemy. Instead of humouring the royal family and ingratiating himself with them, he consorted with flatterers, low-lives, vagabonds and wastrels, whose only aim was to fleece him. The chieftains were angry that Omai was flouting social conventions and mores by not giving his feathers to them but to the common people.[46] Omai compounded his stupidity by a long speech in which he praised George III effusively, to Tu's detriment, it was felt; certainly the paranoid Tu felt this. The flavour of Omai's fatuous operation may be caught by this quasi-verbatim report by Lieutenant John Rickman of the *Discovery*:

Omai began by magnifying the grandeur of the Great King; he compared the splendour of his court to the brilliancy of the stars in the firmament; the extent of his dominions by the vast expanse of heaven; the greatness of his power by the thunder that shakes the earth. He said, the Great King of Pretanne had 300,000 warriors every day at his command, clothed like those who now attended the Farees of the ships, and more than double that number of sailors, who traversed the globe from the rising of the sun to his setting . . . He said, the ships of war of Pretanne were furnished with poo-poos [guns] each of which would receive the largest poo-poo which his Majesty had yet seen within it; that some carried 100 or more of these poo-poos, with suitable accommodation for a thousand fighting men, and stowage for all sorts of cordage and war-like stores, besides provisions and water for the men and other animals for 100 or 200 days . . . That in one city only on the banks of a river far removed from the sea, there were more people than were contained in the whole group of islands with which his Majesty [Tu] was acquainted.[47]

The only possible defence of Omai is that Tu and his entourage would have disbelieved even the parts of this effusion which were stark truth.

Cook was too busy at this period meeting all his own acquaintances to have time to babysit Omai. On 24 August he made a courtesy visit to Tu's residence at Pare and took all the poultry with him. To his astonishment he found the Spanish bull grazing in a compound and racked his brains to imagine how Tu could possibly have transported the animal by canoe. Nevertheless, next day he enticed the bull into stud duty by sending his three cows up to Pare; gradually, and gratefully, he was dispossessing himself of his menagerie.[48] Back at Matavai Point he ordered two observatories set up and appointed King as his astronomer. The men were kept busy by the manifold work on the two ships. The *Discovery*'s mainmast was repaired; both ships were caulked; the rigging was overhauled, sails mended, water casks repaired. Rickman complained archly that on a Cook voyage there were no coffee houses or Vauxhall Gardens but added that one was never bored:

> Every nightly assembly in the plantations of this happy isle is furnished by beneficent nature with a more luxuriant feast than all the dainties of the most sumptuous champêtre . . . Ten thousand lamps, combined and ranged in the most advantageous order by the hands of the best artists, appear faint when compared with the brilliant stars of heaven that unite their splendour to illuminate the groves, the lawns, the streams of Oparee. In these Elysian fields, immortality alone is wanting.[49]

On 26 August Cook instituted a kitchen garden, complete with potatoes, melons, pineapples and shaddock trees from the Tonga isles. To his consternation he discovered that the Spanish had introduced the vine but that the locals, picking the grapes before they were ripe and finding them sour, had gone one better than La Fontaine's fox and ripped up the entire vineyard. Cook rescued some cuttings and encouraged Omai to take them and try to set up his own winery.[50] Cook was anxious to find something useful for Omai to do, as the crackpot scapegrace seemed daily to go from bad to worse. Cook had hoped to marry Omai to Tu's younger sister, cementing the wayward scoundrel in kinship bonds with the coming man on the island, but the arrogant Omai turned the girl down on the grounds that she was not pretty enough. To add insult to injury he told Tu, in his own special high and mighty manner, that he would remain on Tahiti only if Tu expelled all his Bora Bora warriors, especially the *arioi*. Not surprisingly, Tu told Cook he had had just about enough of Omai and expressly requested that he depart when Cook departed.[51] The folly of throwing an avuncular mantle around Polynesians seemed reinforced when Hitihiti, who had so often been compared favourably with Omai by Cook and others, reeled into the shore camp drunk, down on his luck and a pale shadow of the firebrand of the second voyage.[52]

On the 27th Cook heard that two Spanish ships had arrived at Vaitepiha Bay with the redoubtable Maximo on board. Convinced by the circumstantial account of the man who brought him the news and who claimed to have been aboard one of the Spanish vessels, Cook mounted his guns and had the decks cleared for action. He sent Williamson on ahead in an improvised gunboat, but he soon returned with word that the tidings were the merest canard.[53] The bringer of the false report jumped overboard and swam to safety before he could be questioned and punished, but it seemed clear the whole affair was a ruse to try to get the ships to leave Matavai Bay; Cook might have remembered that the selfsame trick had been tried on the second voyage, when he was told that both Banks and Furneaux were nearby. It did not take a political genius to work out on a *cui bono* basis that the rumour-mongerer must have been an agent of Vehiatua and the aim to deprive Tu of Cook's support, power and wealth. In some strange way the incident soured the hitherto placid relations with Tu's people; one version was that when Cook mounted his cannons for action, the people of Matavai Bay somehow got it into their heads that they were to be the targets.[54] Whatever the case, suddenly the old pattern of thievery was triggered once more. Next day a barrel, a coat and a hammock were missing from the shore camp while one of the surgeon's mates who went inland was set on and robbed. Bayly woke in the middle of the night in the observatory tent to find an intruder trying to steal the astronomy clock; he was convinced to his dying day that the thief had been none other than Tu himself.[55] Bayly called for help but no one came to his aid; the sentry was either asleep, absent without official leave or simply unwilling to face danger, and none of Bayly's brother officers heard his cries. Cook had the sentry flogged but he felt uneasy in face of the tense and eerie atmosphere in the bay.

Making enquiries, he discovered that Tu was engaged in a running war with Moorea and that Tu's relatives on that island had been attacked; he now thought the rumour of Spanish ships might have been a scheme devised by a Moorean agent.[56]

The war was the continuation of a conflict some of whose manifestations Cook had already witnessed, such as the great fleet of war canoes in 1774. The same 'admiral', To'ofa, was still a hardliner, but his armada had suffered a series of embarrassing failures over the past three years, since the Mooreans simply withdrew into the hills and declined to face Tu at sea, instead tempting his forces to land and be decimated by guerrilla warfare. The latest eruption was yet another attempt to break the stalemate, and Tu once again tried to enlist Cook on his side. Cook came to a grand council meeting on the last day of the month and, in Omai's absence, explained in halting Polynesian that since the Mooreans had done him no harm, he could not in all conscience launch a gratuitous attack on them.[57] To'ofa, who was also absent, sent Tu a message to say that he had already offered human sacrifice and the logical next step was Tu's presence at a *marae* ceremony at Atehuru to call on Oro to help them. Cook asked if he could be present at the ceremony, where there would be human sacrifice, and Tu agreed, still hoping to swing the Europeans over to his side. Cook's party set out in a pinnace, with Anderson, Webber and Omai following in a canoe. They stopped off en route at a small island in the Fa'a'a district where To'ofa and his party met them. To'ofa, less tactful than Tu, virtually demanded that Cook join him and, when he refused, became extremely angry. Cook continued his journey and arrived at the rendezvous early in the afternoon of 1 September. At the promontory of Utuaimahurau on the southern coast of Tahiti four priests waited with Tu for the ceremony to begin; around them was a throng of attendants and drummers, but no women since the ceremony was *tapu* for females.[58] Fortunately for Cook's digestion and general state of mind the human had already been killed and lay trussed to a pole. The custom on such occasions was for an *arii nui*'s killers to earmark a victim from among the lowest untouchable class, preferably a tramp or beachcomber, then club him to death without warning; the barbarism of dragging a live victim to an altar was not practised. Cook deplored human sacrifice and reflected on the ten unfortunates marked down to be killed at the next *inasi* on Tonga and the forty-nine skulls of former victims he had counted on other *marae*, every single one a recent sacrifice.[59]

The ceremony was long and complex, containing prayers and invocations, the production of many allegorical artefacts and the symbolic 'eating' of one of the victim's eyes by Tu, the sacrifice of a dog, the offering of red feathers to Oro and much beating of drums. When the song of a kingfisher was heard in the trees, the Tahitians claimed that this was an avatar of Oro and that the god was well pleased. That did not prevent yet another ceremony on the morning of the 2nd, complete with the sacrifice of a pig and more convoluted feather rituals, and the unveiling of something Cook was not allowed to see but which he construed as the Tahitian equivalent of the Ark of the Covenant. All of this Cook observed meticulously if without very much under-standing.[60] Where the ritual of *inasi* on Tongatapu had struck him as a benign way to confer political legitimacy, the Tahitian ceremony seemed merely barbarous. On the way back to Matavai Bay To'ofa made the mistake of asking Cook what he had thought of the ceremony, and Cook told him and in no uncertain terms. To'ofa was displeased but abstract disgruntlement became outright anger when Omai took a hand. Omai badmouthed To'ofa and told him that in England he would have been hanged for killing the man for human sacrifice; it did not occur to him that, without Cook's protection, he himself would have been hanged or worse for such an expression of lèse-majesté.[61] To'ofa eventually cut Omai short and said he wanted to hear no more on the subject. Cook reflected that To'ofa was probably as contemptuous of European customs as he himself was of those on Tahiti. By now it was clear that one of the reasons Tu and To'ofa's war efforts had been so unsuccessful was that there were at least three factions in his country: the genuine anti-Moorea hawks, an anti-war party and an influential rump of neutrals. This encouraged Cook to discount the glowering looks Tu and To'ofa directed towards him. As Beaglehole remarks with his customary wit: 'Tu was not generally liked. Indeed, it is difficult to find anyone who liked Tu. Cook certainly did not warm to him ... To'ofa seems to have been frequently an angry man.'[62]

One of Tu's problems in prosecuting the war with Moorea was that he had to pull his punches lest To'ofa became too powerful. To'ofa again took his fleet to Moorea, met strong resistance and sent back pleas for reinforcements – which Tu refused, even though Matavai Bay was thronged with his war canoes. Although Cook had effectively put the feuding pair of Tu and To'ofa in their place, he had a fixed policy of backing Tu against any challenges to his 'kingly' authority and felt that, after the recent harsh words, a show of reconciliation was necessary. Another dramatic fireworks display, followed by a dinner pary for the *arii nui* did the trick.[63] Tu took his 'revenge' by holding a second cere-mony of human sacrifice without telling Cook about it; when the captain learned of this, he suggested yet a third ceremony which he could attend, but Tu remarked lamely that he was running out of potential victims for his hired killers. Cook always found Tu sly, secretive, mean and untrustworthy,[64] but he was a political slogger, in the game for the long run, though ironically his political skills deserted him over the next ten years even as his success grew, so that by 1788 Bligh, calling at Tahiti on the ill-fated *Bounty*, was to declare him a busted flush.[65] Cook liked to keep Tu under his eye as much as possible and found the perfect solution to how to do this without giving offence by commissioning his portrait. Webber set to work, and by the end of the stay in Tahiti presented the ruler with a workmanlike painting, about whose quality we can only guess, since it has not survived. Some say Webber's portraiture was not flattering, that Tu disliked it and destroyed it; others that To'ofa or some other leader stole it to deprive Tu of the picture's *mana*.[66] Webber was not normally a 'naturalistic' painter: his scenes of war and barbarism are said to have inspired evangelistic fervour in British missionaries, while in more recent years he has been accused of being Cook's propagandist, presenting an idyllic and false picture of Polynesia.[67] But this may be doing him a disservice. The Europeans who saw the Tu portrait and knew the original sitter testified to its accuracy. Bligh saw it in 1788, as did another voyager, John Watts.[68]

When not keeping Tu under close observation, Cook worried about his menagerie, all of which had now been unloaded. As ever, his fear was that once he had departed, the Tahitians would simply slaughter the stock he had carefully nursed through Pacific storms and horrendously high seas, and that all his care would have been for nothing. He therefore made a point of getting Tu to proclaim throughout his realm that Tute (the Polynesian version of his name) would be returning and would take reprisals for any killings, especially of cattle.[69] Cook was particularly irritated by the dogs the Spaniards had left behind, and when one of these hounds killed a ram, he ordered all dogs approaching his livestock to be shot on sight; the Tahitians heeded this and kept their dogs tethered.[70] The locals were more impressed by another breed of domestic beast for, having observed Omai's incompetence at mounting a steed, they concluded that horses were unrideable. It was therefore a considerable shock to them to see Cook and Clerke riding around the Matavai plain, sometimes at a gallop. Cook thought his centaur-like appearance gave the Tahitians 'a better idea of the greatness of other nations than all the other things put together that had been carried among them'.[71] Yet however awed the locals were, nothing stopped the steady drip-drip of theft, that perpetual bane of Cook's life. He and Clerke experimented with a new method of punishment. Learning of the almost fetishistic attention Tahitians paid to hair and beards, they started shaving off half the beards, hair and eyebrows of the thieves they apprehended, which mortified them as they became an object of ridicule and contempt to their countrymen.[72] None of this seemed to affect the course of everyday relations, for the islanders continued to supply both officers and seamen with a steady stream of luscious girls and young women; when Cook tried to warn them of the dangers of venereal disease, they simply shrugged.[73]

In any case, Cook had irresponsibility closer at home to deal with. Throughout the voyage there had been a continuing feud between the sour-tempered Lieutenant Williamson and Molesworth Phillips, the commander of the marines; they had already fought one duel and their enmity looked like becoming a genuine vendetta. Cook had little time for either of them; although Phillips's personality was more pleasing, he had disappointed Cook twice with a lacklustre public performance by his marines, which had caused the Europeans to lose face, so that when Cook put on his firework display for Tu in early September he did not even ask Phillips and his marines to perform. Basically, Cook took a 'plague on both your houses' attitude to the serial duel-lists and, when they fought yet another duel on Matavai Bay, he did not inter-vene. The pair proved as useless at this as they had been unprofessional as officers; both missed their marks. The seamen had hoped for a Phillips victory for as one of them, William Griffin, said: 'Many persons would have rejoiced if Mr Williamson our third Lieutenant had fell [*sic*], as he was a very bad man and a great tyrant.'[74] Meanwhile Cook had Omai to contend with. The latter made a fool of himself by boasting that he could ride a horse and being contin-ually thrown, and the expertise of Cook and Clerke demolished his self-serving story that the nags were unrideable. Omai was forever puffing himself up, and aped Cook by hosting a lavish dinner on the shoreline.[75] The most grotesque absurdity occurred when Cook began to ponder the possible impli-cations of the Spanish visit and to wonder whether their new-found interest in the Pacific meant they were at war with Britain. Worrying away at the story of the Iberian occupation and the activities of the two Franciscans, Cook tried to reconstruct a chronology, but soon came to realise that the notion of a linear narrative in time, with dates, names and places, was meaningless to the Tahitians and he could therefore get no accurate information about these latter-day conquistadors.[76] In desperation he enlisted Omai to try to find out more details about the Spanish sojourn, but Omai threw a 'hissy fit' of jealousy when he heard that Tahitians had visited Lima.[77]

Cook had stayed longer on Tahiti than he should or would have, had he known what awaited him in North America. By the last week of September he was anxious to be gone, but he had made a cross for his own back by putting his money so squarely on Tu, since the *arii nui* kept inveigling him in the mael-strom of island politics.[78] Word came in that To'ofa's fleet had been surrounded by Chief Mahine's canoes off Moorea but, like medieval kings anxious to avoid the gamble of decisive battle, both sides had sheered away from actual combat. To'ofa was so disillusioned by Tu's failure to back him that he began to consider going over to Mahine, lock, stock and barrel. Even the peaceable factions on Tahiti agreed that Tu had acted in a cowardly manner. Cook was forced to declare to an assembly of chieftains that Tu had his complete backing and that he would use his firepower against those who defied or deserted him.[79] Weakly, Cook then agreed to review that portion of Tu's war fleet that he had not sent against Moorea. Tu invited his visitors to take part in manoeuvres and mock sea fights, and once again Omai saw a chance to hog centre stage. Dressing himself in a suit of armour he had acquired from the Tower of London, he gained further black marks in Tu's eyes by capsizing the *arii nui*'s canoe.[80] The next development was news that To'ofa had signed a humiliating peace with Mahine, so that Tu, as custom dictated, had to go again to Atehuru to carry out the formal peacemaking ritual – yet another esoteric ceremony that Cook attended; this one was also attended by Tu, Mahine's brother and a nervous-looking To'ofa. King, who was close to To'ofa, later told Cook that To'ofa had called down every conceivable exercration on the head of Tu.[81] There was now definitely nothing to detain Cook further, and on 28 September Tu came aboard the *Resolution* to make his farewells. By the usual standards of island stopovers, Cook and his men had enjoyed surprisingly peaceful relations with Tu and his subjects.[82] Cook had even known Tu's kindness at a personal level. As if to compensate him for the well-known fact that the captain never consorted with the island women, on 22 September Tu sent a large bevy of his female relations to the ship to minister to Cook, temporarily stricken with rheumatic pains, very likely a trapped sciatic nerve. The women gave him a quarter-hour head-to-toe massage which made him feel much better, and repeated the treatment next morning and again the following evening.[83] Sadly, despite all Cook's efforts on behalf of his livestock, all the animals he left behind (and their descendants) perished during the dreadful civil wars of 1778–88.[84]

Cook cleared for Moorea on 30 September. Lying nine miles north-west of Tahiti, Moorea is even more beautiful, a wonderland of limpid streams, mountains and hibiscus trees, and, following Burke's essay on 'The Sublime', the eighteenth century was rapidly learning to appreciate grandeur of landscape. Cook's immediate concern was more mundane. Ever since the Tongans had stolen their cats, Cook's two ships had been plagued with rats. By going as close to the shore as he could, and even constructing a 'rat bridge' to enable the rodents to pass easily on to dry land, Cook and Clerke hoped to tempt these pests to leave them; but there were few takers.[85] Here, in the stunning bay of Papetoai, Cook spent the next ten days. The hibiscus made good firewood and the locals set no value on it, so Cook's men loaded all they needed for the run to North America; trees available for felling were virtually non-existent on Tahiti itself.[86] The wood was the reason Cook went to Moorea; there was no compelling reason otherwise, except that Cook had never been there before and, besides, he might just be able to settle the troublesome Omai there. Mahine, the chief of Moorea, was initially fearful that Cook's arrival might herald a second wave of invasion from a peace-breaking Tu – doubtless the Tahitians had already boasted that they had the backing of 'Tute' – but when the visitors made no aggressive moves, he paid Cook a visit. Aged about 40, fat, scarfaced and one-eyed, Mahine disappointed his hosts, who were expecting to find some kind of island Spartacus.[87] It was noteworthy that he was bald with a turban, which some thought might be a pre-emptive move against the Europeans' now notorious habit of shaving heads. Gifts were exchanged, and this had Mahine scratching his head because, applying a Polynesian law of excluded middle, he could not understand how Tu's friend could also be his.[88] After visiting both ships, Mahine mournfully pointed out the devastation caused by To'ofa and his fleet, evident in the gutted houses on the shoreline and the trees which had all been stripped of their fruit.

For nearly a week relations between Cook and the Mooreans were excellent. The trouble began on 6 October and featured, as such incidents so often did, the remaining livestock which Cook had disembarked for grazing. Mahine had asked Cook for two goats as a gift and had been mortified when Cook turned him down. What he could not have by the front door he determined to have by the back. Using the trumped up excuse that one of the sailors had bilked him, a local trader (in reality Mahine's agent) stole a goat and spirited it away to the chief's residence at Paopao. Cook opened negotiations with Mahine, knowing him to be the real culprit, and offered him a vast quantity of red feathers for the return of the goat, but in vain. Just as the short-tempered Cook began to lose patience with Mahine, he was brought to boiling point by the barefaced theft of a second goat, even as he negotiated for the return of the first one.[89] Cook issued the most dire threats of terrible consequences if the goats were not returned. As a result one of the animals was returned. But Cook's blood was now up and he clapped the original thief in irons, put him on bread and water and forbade his kinsfolk to try to bring food to him aboard the ship. Next morning he found Papetoai Bay deserted and learned that Mahine and his people had fled to the far side of the island. His officers urged him to let the matter rest, but Cook was determined that, as he saw it, Mahine should not be allowed to best him; the officers regarded this as further proof that the Cook of the third voyage was deranged and no longer the man they had served under so admiringly in previous years.[90] When Mahine continued to stall, Cook decided on a punitive expedition. On the morning of 9 October he set out with thirty-five heavily armed men. Coming under fire from stones and darts, they marched across the hills to where Mahine was skulking. Finally Cook gave the order to open fire; at least one Moorean was killed. When Cook reached the village of the sub-chief Hamoa and found that the missing goat had still not been surrendered, he informed the villagers that he would not rest and would remain in the mountains for months if need be until Mahine was taken, dead or alive. All Mahine had to do to avert this fate was to return the goat.

When even this provoked no response, Cook ordered his men to lay waste the island. They gutted houses and burned large quantities of war canoes. The prime mover in all these atrocities was Omai who joined in the holocaust with gusto, delighting in putting houses, canoes and crops to the torch.[91] When the men's fury was spent and they returned to the ships for the night, there was the goat sitting forlornly on the beach. Mahine had eventually realised that he was dealing with a fanatic, that if he did not return the animal, the entire island would be a scorched wilderness of devastation. James King wrote disapprovingly of the episode: 'In future they may fear, but never love us.'[92] The irony was that, having refused to join Tu in his campaign against Mahine, Cook had ended up by visiting more damage on him and his island than Tu and To'ofa and their entire armada had been able to manage. Despite his official stance of neutrality in island wars Cook had in effect, albeit for his own reasons, intervened decisively on Tu's side. Once he had got his two goats back, Cook seemed to come to his senses and appeared almost remorseful: 'Thus this troublesome and rather unfortunate affair ended, which could not be more regretted on the part of the natives than it was on mine.'[93] Yet he had made a bad mistake. Not only had he besmirched his reputation in the islands, but he had alienated and disgusted his officers, not a single one of whom supported Cook in the privacy of their journals. From King, Ellis and Samwell the criticism was fair enough, but it went farther than that. Lieutenant Williamson revealed himself as a humbug as well as a despot when he wrote sanctimoniously:

I cannot help thinking the man totally destitute of humanity, that he would not have felt considerably for these poor and, before our arrival, probably happy people, and I must confess this once I obeyed my orders with reluctance. I doubt not but Captain Cook had good reasons for carrying his punishment of these people to so great a length, but what his reasons were are yet a secret.[94]

On 11 October Cook left Moorea for Huahine, one of the Leeward Islands of the Society group, which also comprise Maupiti, Tupia, Taha'a, Bora Bora and Raiatea; actually two islands historically linked by a causeway and surrounded by a coral reef, Huahine was no more than nine miles long and eight miles wide. Omai, following the ships in his canoe, was nearly lost in a sudden squall at night. That morning there was trouble of another sort on the *Resolution* when a stowaway from Moorea was caught stealing. Cook, now almost pathological in his response to theft, had the man shaved and his ears cropped off, then threw him into the sea, leaving him either to swim to shore or be taken by the sharks.[95] On landing at Huahine he soon discovered that there had been many changes since his last visit, and few of them to the good. His old friend Ori had been deposed as regent and in his place a 10-year-old *arii nui* named Teri'itaria had been installed as high chief, with his elderly mother as regent. The problem was that, with the demise of Ori, there was no longer any effective government or law and order on the island, just the 10-year-old, his mother and a bunch of corrupt courtiers.[96] Before he realised the new chief was a mere boy, Cook ordered Omai to smarten himself up and affect some dignity for the coming interview with the island's assembled chieftains. It was Cook's intention to set Omai up in Huahine; he was running out of options, and with Omai alienating the ruling powers wherever he went, he bade fair to become a Flying Dutchman, forever circling the oceans with Cook and unable to find a berth anywhere. Although Omai had by now thrown off his Tahitian claque of low-lives, snivelling sycophants and venal opportunists, he had not lost his talent for boasting. Within hours of the Europeans' arrival, he had spread the rumour that Cook intended to restore him to the island of Raiatea as his personal representative, having first annihilated the warriors of Bora Bora and brought that island to heel. Cook's idea was to stymie Omai by settling him on Huahine, allied now to Bora Bora, so that his bloodthirsty dreams would remain just that.[97]

Omai's interview with Teri'itaria and his chieftains went well. First Omai made offerings of red feathers and joined the priests in saying prayers to Oro. Then gifts were exchanged, and Cook asked the assembled company for permission for his protégé to settle on the island. Omai addressed the assembly, telling them of his adventures in England and stressing that Cook was his patron. Cook knew that Omai's turbulent reputation had gone before him, so he made it a point of understanding with the chieftains that Cook would not use force to restore him in Raiatea and indeed would resist anyone trying to bring this about; it had to be clear to everyone that if Omai were ever to return to Raiatea it could only be with the express consent of Bora

Bora.[98] This was evidently the right note to strike, for one of the chiefs, ingen-
uously and with no irony intended, said that since Cook was the lord of
Huahine he could give Omai whatever he liked. The foolish Omai took heart
at this, thinking he would be granted a palace, but Cook cleverly avoided the
trap and said that both the location of his house and the amount of land he was
to be given were matters the chiefs alone should decide. This arrangement
was agreed and the bargain sealed.[99] Bit by bit Omai started to see what a
fool he had been by his prodigality in Tahiti, that he would now need every
scrap of the wealth he had accumulated, since he was accepted by the island
oligarchs purely and simply as Cook's man and had no other status. He had
siblings and kinfolk on Huahine but they were low-born and had no influence.
Cook feared that as soon as he had gone, Omai would be stripped by the
jealous locals of the little he had, for to the common people, not the *arii*, he
would count as a rich man, yet there was no real mechanism on Huahine for
arresting the envy of the ordinary islanders for one of their own; it was *homo
homini lupus*.[100] Cook therefore suggested to Omai that in return for making
over some of his portable property to them, he should become the client of
two or three powerful chieftains. For once Omai did the sensible thing and
took this advice. Cook backed this up with a declaration that if Omai was
robbed or in any way harmed, he, Tute, would take revenge; the threat seemed
plausible as Cook appeared to have established a pattern of returning every
three years.[101]

While his carpenters and sailors laboured to build Omai's house, Cook
practically disappeared for a week, laid low by some mysterious but not
serious malady.[102] Clerke was more gravely ill with the tuberculosis that seems
to have plagued him ever since his spell in the debtors' prison in London.
Anderson, who was treating him, soon also showed symptoms of consumption and the two men sat down together to discuss their future, which looked
bleak if they had to endure another long stint of polar exploration. They
therefore asked Cook if they could be released from their contracts and left on
Huahine, prepared to take their chances and in hopes that a European ship
would call there in the foreseeable future. Cook, however, was unsympathetic
to their plight, mainly, it is said, because Clerke's papers and accounts were in
a hopeless tangle;[103] with his morbid fear of Admiralty censure Cook may
have felt that he would be blamed on his return for the administrative chaos on
board *Discovery*. Another view is that he was displeased with Clerke for what
he saw as shirking his duty for, Burney relates, the idea that Clerke might
remain behind was originally broached on Tahiti, a decision deferred until
Moorea, then until Huahine, then Raiatea, and so on. This represents a period
of at least three months, during which any conceivable gaps in accounts, ship

logs or other paperwork could easily have been made good.[104] There is another Cook mystery here. Is it possible that the late Cook resembled H. M. Stanley who also refused to believe that anyone but himself could ever be really ill? The suggestion may seem far-fetched, but not more so than Cook's overreaction to the goat theft on Moorea. While he was ill Cook developed something of a mania about cockroach infestation on board the two ships. The omnivorous insects attacked eveything in sight: not just food but curios and artefacts. Cook related that there were two distinct species of cockroach at work, one of which emerged only at night and produced a mass susurration, disturbing to anyone trying to sleep.[105]

Soon he had more immediate things to worry about. On 22 October a precious sextant was stolen. Cook's anger and impatience was fuelled by the chieftains' initial reluctance to take his complaint seriously, as they were preoccupied with a *haiva*. It was detective work by Omai that finally uncovered the culprit. Cook seized the man, took him aboard *Resolution* and confined him. Using Omai as his chief interrogator, Cook grilled the thief in sessions that went on for hours. Ultimately the villain cracked and revealed where he had hidden the sextant.[106] What annoyed Cook was that the thief was a man who had sat in conclave with him at the initial meeting and who seemed to have an entrée to the highest local circles. Learning that he was a Bora Bora man, an habitual criminal whom the local oligarchs appeared reluctant to act against, Cook not only shaved his hair and beard but cut off his ears, then flogged him so severely that 'particles of his skin came away in shreds'.[107] Yet this Bora Boran was evidently a recidivist as well as a fool. On the night of 24–25 October he tried to steal a goat, failed, then threatened to kill Omai once Cook had left. Cook responded by taking him into custody again; the local chiefs seemed glad that someone else was doing their dirty work for them. Incredibly, some time between midnight and 4. a.m. on the night of 29–30 October, the man escaped. Both the sentry and the entire night watch on the quarterdeck were sleeping while on duty, and the alert Bora Bora rogue was able to get the keys from the binnacle drawer and unlock his manacles; he did not stay to try conclusions again but rowed away to Raiatea.[108] Cook was almost apoplectic at the perious breakdown of discipline thus displayed, and unconvinced by the story of a mass sleep-in; he suspected collusion and complicity (his version was later backed by the island's oral tradition). The sentry and the quartermaster were clapped in irons to replace the escapee and were flogged with twelve lashes three days running – the most severe punishment Cook had yet meted out to his men. The mate on watch, William Harvey, was disrated and sent to the *Discovery* as an able seaman, and the midshipman on duty

(Robert Mackay) was sent before the mast.[109] Cook's mood was darkening: in three weeks since reaching Huahine he had ordered no less than 96 lashes to six different men; the marine Thomas Morris, the snoozing sentry, received thirty-six bites of the cat.[110]

Cook was now keen to throw off the dust of Huahine, but first there was the matter of Omai's house to settle. By 26 October it was nearly finished and his movables and portable property were taken ashore. Omai decided that the pots, pans and other kitchen utensils he had so carefully collected in England were superfluous in the Society Islands. He swapped them with the sailors for hatchets and iron tools, which gave him a valuable store of local wealth. On 28 October he gave a firework display to celebrate the completion of his new residence. The house was set in an acre and a half of coastal land, 10 feet high, 24 feet long and 18 feet wide, ingeniously built with very few nails, so that neither he nor others would be tempted to remove them.[111] He assembled a veritable arsenal from his departing comrades: a musket, bayonet and 500 cartridges, musket balls, canisters of powder and a keg of gunpowder, a fowling piece, two pairs of pistols and three cutlasses. There were also his beloved curios from England: a bed, a table, an organ, a globe, a compass, portraits of friends in London, toys, tin soldiers and other knick-knacks. He also possessed a miniature version of Cook's travelling menagerie, for Cook made over to him a horse and mare, a pregnant nanny goat, a boar and two sows, a cow and a calf, some sheep, turkeys, geese, a brace of rabbits, two cats and even a monkey.[112] Some of the sailors had helped the two Maori boys to dig a garden and plant melons, vines, pineapples and shaddocks. To their distress, Koa and Te Weherua, who thought they were going all the way to England with Cook, found that they were being unloaded to be Omai's personal attendants. Koa struggled piteously in the canoe that took him away from the ships for the last time, jumped out of the canoe and swam back after the vessels, but in vain. Te Weherua bore his plight more stoically and simply wept in silence. The two Maori boys were great favourites of the crew, infinitely more popular than the braggart Omai, and the sailors all agreed that Cook's behaviour had been callous, of a piece, perhaps, with his flogging of their shipmates and cruelty to the Bora Bora thief.[113]

The parting from Omai himself was a highly emotional occasion. Despite his many strictures on his character and conduct, Cook had come to have a soft spot for him, particularly valuing his good nature, deference and sense of gratitude.[114] The seamen did not share this high opinion, however, disliking his airs and graces and his blatant instincts of a born sycophant. Omai was a one-trick pony in that his only significance was as a protégé of Cook. He attracted the dislike and envy that ordinary people so often feel for one of their own who has been adventitiously and unjustifiably given a higher station in life than his gifts merit. The officers meanwhile clung to the eighteenth-century view – which Cook battled against all his life – that no matter how much money a man had, if he did not have breeding and the instinctive *gravitas* of the born aristocrat, he was not really of much account.[115] Curiously, the only officer to have a high opinion of Omai was Bligh, who later recorded his opinion that he was much maligned and underrated, and had actually taught the Society Islanders some good and useful things.[116] Williamson, Bligh's brutal confrère, was more ambivalent:

> Omai took his leave of us with manly sorrow, until he came to Captain Cook when with all the eloquence of sincerity he expressed his gratitude and burst into tears. The captain, who was extremely attentive to Omai the whole time of his being on board and [given] the pains he had taken to settle him to his satisfaction in his native country, was much affected by this parting. Omai too late saw his error and often wished himself in England again, saying, his time should be spent in learning what could be useful to him instead of throwing his time away at cards. However sincere Omai might be at this time, I believe had he gone to England again (which was greatly his wish and desire) he would have acted the same part over again, being extremely fond of a gay life and being thought a great man.[117]

The pessimistic prognostications of the Omai watchers were soon borne out. Within four years he was dead of a fever. He acquitted himself well with the help of his firearms when a skirmish was fought with the Bora Bora invaders of Raiatea, and his guns helped secure the victory. Although he was thereafter much respected on Huahine, oral traditions maintain that he lapsed into 'indolence and crime'.[118] After his death his house was gutted and all his possessions removed to Raiatea by his relatives. All his animals died within the four-year space (except for the mare), including the monkey which was said to have been killed after falling from a coconut tree. Deprived of their protector, Te Weherua and Koa languished and died soon afterwards, still pining for their beloved New Zealand.[119]

Cook sailed for Raiatea, second in size only to Tahiti in the Society Islands, on the afternoon of 2 November with an easterly breeze and the following day anchored in Hamanino harbour, though it took him most of the day to warp the ships in. His old friend Oreo, the Bora Boran regent of the island, came to meet him with his family. There was the usual exchange of pigs, fruit and vegetables for red feathers, iron and curios, and the usual process of ship repairs and work in tents in a shore camp. Once again Cook tried unsuccessfuly to get rid of the ships' rats. The high chief of the island, Uru, sent a message that he was too poor to meet Cook as he had no gifts to bring him; the hope was that when the current lord of Raiatea, Bora Bora's chief Puni, died, Uru would come into his own again. Ori too paid a visit, as also did Omai's persecutor on Huahine, who not only taunted the European commanders with his escape from the *Resolution* but pointed a finger at the officer who had helped him escape; it turned out that the sentry had been flogged mercilessly while being innocent of any offence.[120] The initial sensation of the visit was Oreo's allegedly pulchritudinous daughters Poiatura and Tainami, though Webber's portrait of Poiatura does not reveal her as especially beautiful by the standards of the twenty-first century.[121] Morale among the crew was low, as they knew that any day now they would have to bid a sad farewell to their 'wives' and girlfriends; the Raiateans did not help matters by encouraging the malcontented among the sailors to remain among them and set themselves up as lords. The dual prospect of venturing into the unknown seas of the North Pacific and doing so without benefit of female companionship duly had its effect. On 13 November the marine John Harrison absented himself from the shore camp without leave, taking his musket with him. Cook realised he would have to deal fast and effectively with the absconder, for otherwise he would face an epidemic of desertions.[122]

The first search party of marines Cook sent out came back empty-handed. From the fact that Oreo and his family had decamped from Hamanino Bay Cook deduced that the islanders had colluded in the desertion. He therefore circumnavigated the island in two boats, full of heavily armed men. They ran Oreo to earth and threatened to hold him on board ship until the deserter was returned. After a mumbled consultation with his own people, Oreo led Cook to Harrison's hiding place; he appeared to have already 'gone native', for he was naked except for a loincloth and his head was garlanded with flowers. There were two young women with him, one of them a person of property, in the bothy where he was found, and Harrison at once tried the oldest wheeze in the book: the 'woman tempted me' dodge, literally as old as Adam. Cook took him back to the *Resolution*, put him in irons and then gave him twenty-four lashes. Cook used the occasion to address the crew, telling them it was useless to abscond as he would always bring them back; all he had to do was seize the chief and their whereabouts would be divulged.[123] Despite this, a week later on 23 November, the gunner's mate Thomas Shaw and a 16-year-old midshipman named Alexander Mouat jumped ship. Cook was particularly disgusted with Mouat, as he was the son of the Royal Navy captain who had played Clerke to Byron's Cook on his circumnavigations. Cook's search parties combed the island, but these two refugees were determined characters, crazed with desire for the voluptuous and curvaceous island girls; they decamped first to the island of Taha'a, a mile away, and from there they took a boat to Bora Bora.[124] Cook ordered that Oreo and other chiefs again be apprehended pending the return of the two delinquents; meanwhile a sharply worded message was sent to Puni on Bora Bora: return the men or else. The women of the Society Islands were great weepers and wailers, as Harrison's two inamoratae had already demonstrated with a sterling performance on the *Resolution*, but their cacophony was put in the shade when the redoubtable Poiatura and her husband were brought aboard *Discovery*. When news of their capture spread through the island, Raiatea's women lined the shoreline and began lamenting and keening in the manner of an Irish wake.[125]

Oreo was deeply angry about the seizure of his beloved daughter. There seemed no obvious way to break the impasse, for Cook announced publicly that if the deserters were not returned, he would first destroy everything on the island and then take Poiatura and the rest of Oreo's family to England for lifetime exile. Unprepared to take this insult lying down, Oreo worked out a scheme for retaliation. Knowing that Cook and Clerke always always liked to bathe each evening in a limpid and idyllic freshwater stream, he planned an ambush, hoping to turn the tables on the European commanders by holding *them* hostage until his family was returned. However, Oreo in his eagerness to spring the trap, over-egged the pudding by praising the swimming place so extravagantly that Cook became suspicious; meanwhile a girlfriend of one of the sailors tipped him off to what was intended. Just as Oreo was on the point of staging his coup, an armed guard sent from the ships by King arrived.[126] At this Oreo gave up and concluded that the god Oro was not with him; he immediately set out in a canoe for Bora Bora to bring the two men back. The days dragged by and Cook faced an escalating crisis: it seemed as though he would either have to devastate Bora Bora with fire and sword or give up, for the likelihood was that Oreo too had now gone to ground. Suddenly, on 29 November, he returned, bringing the two men with him. Oreo and Puni had collaborated to capture the two recreants at Tubuai.[127] Cook ordered them shackled in irons. Shaw was ordered twenty-four lashes while Mouat was disrated and sent before the mast. After the first dozen lashes, the crew petitioned Cook to reprieve Shaw from a further ordeal; weighing his own credibility against general morale, he agreed. Cook had no time for Shaw, whom he considered full-grown and capable of taking his floggings, but he felt a fatherly concern for young Mouat who had ruined his career by one foolish episode of boyish lust. Nonetheless, he kept both men in irons until the ships were well clear of the Society islands. He told his lieutenants that the two deserters had given him far more trouble than their intrinsic worth.[128] Oreo resumed his friendly relations with Cook as if nothing had happened, and deluged the ships with hogs, plantains and breadfruit. The crew's morale was now at rock bottom at the thought that they would see their beloved Polynesian beauties no more, and there was a further cantata of lamentations from the soon-to-be-deserted women. Additionally, venereal disease was now so rife that Cook and Clerke barely had a credible complement of able-bodied men to man their vessels.[129]

On 7 December Cook sailed for Bora Bora, seriously intending to stay a few days on an island he had never visited. He also wished to recover one of the anchors Bougainville had lost in 1768 and which Puni was reported to have in his possession. After tacking all night off the southern end of Bora Bora, he concluded that the wind and the tides would prevent him from anchoring in Teavanui, the harbour on the western side of the island which was his destination. He therefore decided against mooring the ships and sent his boats in. Puni and a great crowd awaited him. The chief evinced great dignity and statesmanhip by refusing to accept gifts from his visitors until they were satisfied with his offering to them. This was the Bougainville anchor, or what remained of it, really just a hunk of iron. Cook reciprocated with trinkets and, what was more significant, a ewe to mate with a Spanish ram that had somehow reached the island.[130] Then he announced an immediate departure. It is significant that neither Clerke nor Anderson landed. They had continued to lobby Cook with pleas to be left on the Society islands, and Cook had stalled them, never giving a definitive no, perhaps in fear that the possible desertion of his second in command might trigger a general mutiny and that he would face the *Bounty* scenario *avant la lettre*. For Clerke and Anderson Bora Bora represented their last chance for long life, for it was clear to everyone that they would not survive long in polar latitudes.[131] Whether the anchorage at Teavanui really was as problematical as Cook made it out, or whether he was simply determined that Clerke and Anderson should not be allowed to, as he saw it, shirk their duty is unknown. Probably Cook feared the power of example. It made no sense for him to have convulsed Raiatea in pursuit of three low-ranking deserters if he was then going to allow two senior officers to take their leave.[132] That scenario too might conceivably have precipitated a mutiny among men who wanted more than anything to remain in the balmy Elysium of the Society Islands. As the very last woman left the ships, the mood aboard *Resolution* and *Discovery* was sombre, the men preparing once again to face the storms and giant swells of the Pacific. George Gilbert summed it up well: 'We left these islands with the greatest regret imaginable, as supposing all the pleasures of the voyage to be now at an end, having nothing to expect in future but the excess of cold, hunger and every kind of distress and hardship . . . the idea of which rendered us quite dejected.'[133]

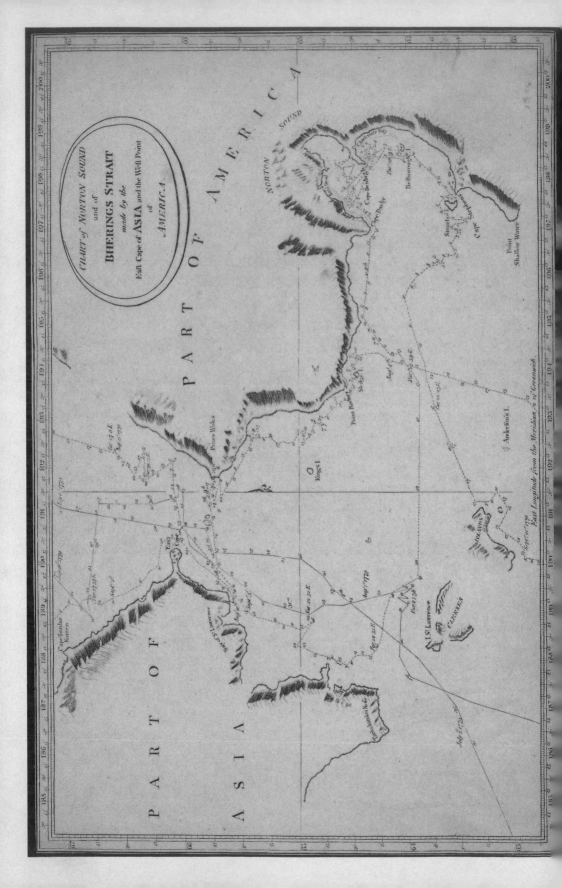

CHART of NORTON SOUND
and of
BHERINGS STRAIT
made by the
Eaſt Cape of ASIA and the Weſt Point
of
AMERICA.

PART OF AMERICA

PART OF ASIA

NORTON SOUND

Clerke's Bay

Cape Prince of Wales

Cape Darby

Bald Head

Besborough I.

Cape Stephens

Point Shallow Water

Stuart's I.

Prince Wales

Sledge I.

Point Rodney

Kings I.

Anderson's I.

Eaſt Cape

Cape Serdze Kamen

Bay of St Lawrence

St Lawrence

CLERKES

Tſchukotskoi Nuſs

Eaſt Longitude from the Meridian of Greenwich

CHAPTER FIFTEEN

Quest for Illusion:
The Northwest Passage

S EVENTEEN months into his journey, Cook was at last headed for the regions supposed to be the real objective of his voyage. On the original schedule he was ten months behind, but on the assumption he would simply write off a year that put him two months ahead. He did not mince words about the weather conditons likely to be expected in a North Pacific winter and had left detailed contingency plans with Clerke for a rendezvous in North America if the *Discovery* was separated from him by storms. Cook knew that it was impossible to steer a direct course to the American coast in the teeth of easterly and north-easterly winds, so his plan was to strike due north until he reached the latitudes where the westerlies wafted the Manila galleon to the coast of northern California. Since the *Discovery* was much faster than *Resolution*, Cook told Clerke to press on ahead during the day, reconnoitre and then link up with the *Resolution* as night fell.[1] Leaving Bora Bora on 7 December the two vessels made good progress due north, crossed the equator on the night of 22–23 December and at dawn on Christmas Eve sighted a large island, ever afterwards to be known as Christmas Island (now also called Kiritimati). Extensive by the usual standards of Pacific atolls (300,000 acres), with a perimeter of ninety miles, Kiritimati contains the greatest land area of any coral atoll in the world. Uninhabited, the island was flat and treeless and provided anchorage on its lee side. A tremendous surf broke along the shore but Bligh, a talented seaman whatever his other defects, went out on a boat expedition and found a double opening in the reef into a shallow lagoon. Knowing that an eclipse of the sun was due on 30 December and soon aware that the fishing was good, Cook decided on an extended Christmas holiday, during which the men would catch the turtles in which the island abounded.[2] He took the ships in, though the passage through the reef was perilous, as James Trevenen reported:

> We had to pull into the lagoon over a very high sea (which, however, never broke) through a narrow passage with which we were little acquainted,

where we could see the bottom the whole way; had any sunken rocks projected higher than the rest, we would have been destroyed, but luckily we never encountered any. On every side of us swam sharks innumerable, and so voracious that they bit our oars and rudder, and I actually struck my hangar into the back of one while he had the rudder in his teeth.[3]

After a typically drunken and riotous Christmas, when they feasted off pork, fish and a double allowance of grog, the sailors were sent inland to reconnoitre, with Cook glad to be able to order shore leave without any fear of sexual promiscuity, venereal disease or desertion. Drought-ridden, Christmas Island was a glorified desert of shrubland and grassland; the only native mammal was the Polynesian rat which had been introduced unwittingly by Polynesian seafarers and would have made short work of any of the black rats that tried to land from Cook's vessels. Nonetheless, there was plenty for amateur ornithologists to enjoy as, though there was only one species native to Kiritimati, the Pacific reed-warbler or *bokikokiko*, there were another thirty-five varieties of seabirds, including the Tuamotu sandpiper which the ailing William Anderson observed closely.[4] The sailors who scattered inland found that turtle-hunting was hard work, for they often had to carry the ubiquitous green turtles two or three miles back to the ships. Two seamen managed the near impossible by getting lost even though, as has been pointed out, the ships' masts would have been visible from almost anywhere on the island. Nevertheless, for twenty-four hours this unfortunate duo came close to perishing; with scorching temperatures in the day and icy cold winds assailing them at night, and with no food and water, they just managed to survive by drinking turtle's blood and were picked up next morning wandering the beach like lost souls in the final extremity. Cook took the incident as further evidence that the calibre of his crew was far inferior to that on the first two voyages, and remarked waspishly that he was only surprised that more of his blundering matelots had not got lost.[5] Cook, aided by Bayly and King, managed to observe the solar eclipse, though Clerke was too ill to do so. After loading more than 200 green turtles on the ships and a huge quantity of fish, Cook left another of his bottles with a message and a dedication of the island to King George. He was in good spirits, for Fate seemed to be with him. They had just got into the lagoon in time because 'During the time we lay here the wind blew constantly a fresh gale . . . but except one or two days we had always a great swell from the northward which broke against the reef in a prodigious surf. We had found this swell before we came to the island.'[6] His only problem was that he had been unable to find supplies of fresh water on the island and henceforth everyone would be on a water ration. Cook cleared from the island at daybreak on 2 January 1778 and almost immediately issued fearnought jackets, on the assumption that the good weather could not long hold. But his luck was in. A week after leaving Christmas Island the sea was so calm that Clerke was able to transfer from the *Discovery* and come to lunch with Cook in the Great Cabin.[7]

Soon the voyagers were once again seeing dozens of turtles in the sea, an infallible guide to the proximity of land. On 18 January, 2,700 miles north of Bora Bora Cook came on a group of islands that were not marked on his charts and that were hitherto completely unknown. That day he sighted Oahu and the next day Kauai, in the north-west of the archipelago of Hawaiian islands which runs from Niihau in the north-west to the big island of Hawaii in the south-east. This was one of the most exciting of all Cook's discoveries and a genuine 'first'. Although he had done the most systematic exploration and charting to date of Easter Island, the Marquesas, the Society Islands, Tonga, and even New Zealand and Australia, he had not been the first European to find these lands. This time he was a genuine trail-blazer, for no European had ever visited these islands before. The secret lay in the chronometer which, guaranteeing a longitudinal fix, enabled him to sail outside the sea lanes established and hallowed by easy winds and currents. Hawaii had lain undiscovered for nearly three centuries of Spanish activity in their 'lake' because it lay far to the north of the outward track of the Manila galleon from Callao and far to the south of its homeward route. Although some Spanish helmets have been discovered on the islands, seducing the unwary into the assertion that the Spanish 'must have' been there, the virtually unanimous consensus of scholars is that they never were.[8] The helmets were probably brought by seafaring Polynesians from islands to the south, or were found on bodies washed ashore in shipwrecks, while the 'impossible' pre-existing presence of iron is explained by its coming ashore on driftwood.

The Hawaiian islands before the coming of Cook were a wholly Polynesian affair. There are two main theories about their settlement, with differential dating. One model proposes an initial settlement from Tahiti *c.* AD 100–300, with a second wave of migrants about a thousand years later from Raiatea and Bora Bora. A more convincing version of the migration pattern postulates a primary sailing from the Marquesas around AD 500–700, with another inflow of immigrants from the Society Islands *c.*1100–1200; this would make better sense of the linguistic and archaeological evidence.[9] In any case, one is again awestruck by the achievements of the early Polynesian navigators. As Cook said in wonderment:

How shall we account for this nation spreading itself so far over this vast ocean? We shall find them from New Zealand to the south to these islands to the north, and from Easter Island to the Hebrides – an extent of sixty degrees of latitude or twelve hundred leagues north and south, and 83 degrees of longitude or sixteen hundred and sixty leagues east and west; how much farther is not known, but we may safely conclude that they extend to the west beyond the Hebrides.[10]

On 19 January Cook was off Kauai, the oldest, greenest and, for some, the most beautiful island in the Hawaiian group, just thirty miles wide and essentially a single great volcano with appendages. Here the cliffs rose in places 3,000 feet vertically from the sea and, at this time of year, a tremendous surf could send waves 50 feet high crashing on to the shore. Any thoughts Cook might have had that this was yet another uninhabited Christmas Island were soon laid to rest as dozens of canoes came surging out to meet the ships. The people spoke a dialect very close to the Tahitian one and were thus immediately intelligible. To Cook's great delight he found that provisions were plentiful and cheap, with taro, coconuts, bananas, breadfruit and fish being offered them, as well as hogs and a very fine variety of sweet potato 'so that we again found ourselves in a land of plenty'.[11] When the Hawaiians clambered aboard, they were more astonished at the ships than any other Polynesians they had met. They seemed almost preternaturally polite and deferential, fearful of giving offence, asking whether they were allowed to sit and where, and whether spitting was allowed on deck. At first they seemed to think that they could help themselves to anything that took their fancy, but when Cook sternly admonished them, they desisted, abashed, and explained that taking gifts from strangers was in their culture a way of showing friendship.[12] Thereafter the Europeans were deeply impressed by the way the people of Kauai abstained from theft, though human nature would stretch only so far. Temptation proved too much for one man, who stole a butcher's cleaver and jumped overboard with it; one of the first things the visitors noted was how expert the Hawaiians were as swimmers.[13] It was difficult to find a secure anchorage, so for the time being the two vessels stood off while boat parties went ashore. Cook himself, together with an armed party and twelve marines, landed at Waimea, at the mouth of the spectacular Waimea Canyon, which Mark Twain, ninety years later, would dub 'the Grand Canyon of the Pacific'. Cook, Webber and Anderson (by now the expedition's best linguist) took a walk up the river valley through taro plantations to view the Hawaiian *heiau*, giant obelisks and pyramids which were the local equivalent of the Tahitian *marae*.[14]

Cook was determined that venereal disease would not be spread on these virgin islands, especially with the epidemic already raging on the *Resolution* and *Discovery*, and issued a set of standing orders to try to achieve this: no women were to be allowed on the ships; no one with yaws, gonorrhoea or syphilis was to be allowed shore leave; no one would be allowed to spend the night ashore. Yet even Cook was doubtful that he could achieve his object; his prescriptions seemed too much like Canute ranged against the sea or the papal bull against the comet.[15] Even the most conscientious commander could not be everywhere, and his officers were just as resentful and rebellious about Cook's anti-sex campaign as the sailors were. To make matters worse, the Hawaiian women seemed promiscuous at levels that eclipsed those encountered hitherto in the South Pacific, and reacted angrily and vociferously to any rebuff or rejection. Moreover, trade had to go on, and seamen and officers had to barter with Hawaiian males; the ingenious local women got round Cook's veto by coming aboard dressed as men. Samwell, particularly, was in his element: not only were sexual favours even easier to obtain than in the Society Islands but, incredibly, the local girls did not seem to want payment.[16] There was yet another impetus towards sexual intercourse. The local priests, initially puzzled about whether their visitors were gods or men, decided on a simple acid test: if their women slept with them and were not consumed by fire, it was a safe assumption that the white men were merely humans.[17] The women needed no urging: on Hawaii sex was the way a woman could break down the rigid social stratification or make contact with the *mana* of the powerful. Hence the absurd later rumour that Cook himself took a Hawaiian 'wife' while he was in the islands; she was named as Lelemaholani, a princess of Kauai.[18] Not only was this strictly against the captain's principles and practice but it is an obvious misreading of purely mythical discourse, whereby women attached themselves to gods or powerful chiefs. Yet, in another demonstration that myth will always triumph over truth in the human imagination, this ludicrous canard was accepted as fact by a powerful anti-Cook lobby, spearheaded by missionaries in the nineteenth century, even though its falsity was palpable: Lelemaholani did exist but she was eight years old at the time of Cook's visit.[19]

Although Cook was not always the most nuanced observer on his island visits, he did notice that on Hawaii the common people paid extreme deference to their chiefs and that, when he himself went ashore, they prostrated themselves on the ground in ritual obeisance or *kapu moe*.[20] Always inclined to be a 'glass half empty man' he now began to worry that the only real beneficiary of his great discovery would be the Spanish, who would surely now move in to make Hawaii a halfway station for the Manila galleon and thence, presumably, colonise the islands.[21] Here Cook was wrong: the great Spanish Empire in the

Americas was already in terminal decay, waiting for the irruption of Napoleon to deal it the *coup de grâce*. The Spanish were tired of the burdens of empire, and the importance of the galleons was diminishing yearly. Kauai was a place that would have entranced the old Cook but, unfortunately for him, on a fortnight's visit to Hawaii he managed to go ashore on just three days only, for problems with the ships occupied him the rest of the time. It was his officers who saw most of the beauties of Kauai, with Clerke striking up a close friendship with the local chief Tamahano.[22] Of course, once Cook's back was turned, relations with the locals became strained and turned to violence, as so often seemed to happen if he was not personally supervising operations.[23] As early as 20 January, just two days into the visit, Williamson, always looking for an excuse for violence, panicked when a large party of locals tried to grapple the oars of the boat in which he was looking for permanent anchorage for the ship; he opened fire and shot a man dead. Fearing the wrath of his captain, he concealed this homicide from him and divulged it only when Cook had already put to sea at the end of the visit.[24] A superstitious man might have read the events on Kauai as 'bad medicine' for, while the voyagers were there, Cook's quartermaster Thomas Roberts died of dropsy and his great admirer, Sergeant Gibson of the marines, got drunk, dropped down comatose on the gangway and was lucky not to be swept overboard, being caught by the 'cowcatcher' Cook had installed on his ship to save drunkards from a salty fate; had the ship been making way at any speed through the water, Gibson would have perished.[25]

For most of the two weeks, Cook was attempting to solve vexatious problems assailing the *Resolution* and *Discovery*. Even while Williamson and others were searching in vain for a secure anchorage, Cook had been forced to move the ships farther out to sea. His run of luck with the weather finally came to an end. There was heavy rain and squalls and a vicious south-east wind which put the vessels on a lee shore, with breakers astern and a very high surf, between 25 and 40 feet, running.[26] After twenty-four hours' anxiety dealing with all this, Cook was further burdened when the wind worked round to the north-east, then east, making it difficult for him to clear the shore. Driven to leeward and with a strong current against him, by 24 January Cook found himself being forced to the west of Kauai and towards Niihau. He tried to stand back towards Kauai to stay in touch with *Discovery* but the winds and currents were so complex that he was unable to make any progress in that direction. Finally on the 29th he found an anchorage on the western side of Niihau.[27] He was now extremely frustrated because, although there was copious fresh water on Kauai, he had been unable to transfer it to the *Resolution* while she battled with the elements. It was therefore necessary to send Gore and a party ashore to get it at Niihau. Gore and his twenty men were not able to locate anything like the aqueous conucopia on Kauai but managed to trade for a large quantity of yams and salt. How much time they spent diligently searching for water is debatable, for as soon as their party was landed, a storm sprang up and heavy surf pounded the shore, making it impossible for Cook to re-embark them.[28] Taking advantage of the absence of their watchful cat, these mice played away in more senses than one. Gore and his seamen coupled frenziedly with the local girls for a good twenty-four hours before Cook was able to get them back on to the *Resolution*. On the way out through the still pounding surf, the scavengers managed to lose most of the salt and yams they had traded for. What upset Cook more than this loss and the absence of water was the certain knowledge that Gore and his men would have spread venereal disease by their liaisons. 'Thus,' he wrote, 'the very thing happened that I had above all others wished to prevent.'[29] He was deluding himself: the damage had already been done on Kauai.

Cook finally lost patience with the Hawaiian islands after he found a sheltered position on the south-east point of Niihau, only to find that, after sunset, his anchor slipped in a heavy swell and the *Resolution* drifted from its mooring. It took a very long time to get in a whole cable, secure the anchor, hoist up the launch alongside and set sail, with the result that next morning found him nine miles adrift of the haven he had had so much trouble finding in the first place. With the prospect of spending at least a day before he could regain the anchorage, Cook signalled the *Discovery* to join him and make way to the north. Clerke asked for confirmation of the signal, since the surf had now gone down and conditions were ideal for a resumption of trade. But Cook had had enough, even though the main purpose of his stay, securing a viable water supply, had not been attained.[30] Despite learning that there were even larger islands to the south-west (Maui and the big island of Hawaii itself), he decided that he had spent enough time in what he had decided to call the Sandwich Islands, after his patron. To an extent this was a repeat of the situation in Tonga, with Maui and Hawaii playing the role of Samoa and Fiji. It was increasingly a characteristic of Cook that he would spend an excessively long time at one stopover, for no good reason that anyone could discover, and then ignore other tempting destinations on the grounds that he was hopelessly behind schedule. In that case, queried the officers, why the long sojourns, as at Tonga and the Society Islands? Now the erratic Cook drove his ships ever northwards over an empty ocean, so barren of life that scarcely a seabird was seen, and no mammals or large fish.[31] Cook held a northward course until almost latitude 45, then turned east to follow the approximate track of the Manila galleon. Once again he had calm weather most of the way and favourable winds: first south-easterlies, then north-easterlies, then south-easterlies again. He kept the men busy with ship repairs: the *Resolution*'s boats had been stove in, and the sails needed attention, but the worst headache was the continuing plague of rats: 'O my poor cats at Anamooka!' Clerke lamented, justifiably. All, especially the invalids, complained of the cold, but Bayly was at least able to comfort himself with a sighting of the aurora borealis.[32] At the beginning of March the first hopeful signs of nearby land were seen in the shape of drifting weed and kelp, and, at last on 6 March, the ocean sprang to life with the appearance of pods of seals and whales. Everyone was confident that the American coast was but a dozen or so leagues away.

During the five-week passage from Niihau to the American coast, Cook and his lieutenants were able to ponder the mass of information they had gained about Hawaii. At one level their observations were impressive, shrewd and praiseworthy in their conscientiousness. Yet as seamen they had a grasp of minute particulars rather than a sociological imagination, and in this respect the lack of a Banks or even of the Forsters was noticeable. King spotted that the Hawaiians were most like the Maori in temperament and were similarly warlike. Their technology was advanced and, in some areas, such as the production of fish-hooks, it excelled anything seen in Europe.[33] The officers were alert, too, to the supreme importance of feathers on Hawaii, but they had received massive hints about this after their experiences in Tonga and the Society Islands. The Hawaiians seemed to have raised feather worship almost to an art form, so that a kind of sumptuary law obtained, with the very greatest chiefs being adorned in spectacularly plumed helmets and coats of fine netting with red and yellow feathers worked on it, while the lesser chieftains had cloaks made of tail feathers only.[34] The hierarchy of feathers, with their numinous associations, hinted at the dangerous conflation of gods and supreme chiefs on Hawaii, something that would have awesome significance for Cook on his next visit to the islands. The red and yellow feathers he received as a gift showed how highly the Hawaiians honoured him, for at the time of his visit Hawaii was inching forward to a full-blooded colour revolution where yellow feathers displaced red ones as the supreme badge of authority; the chief Kamehameha, who would eventually unite all the Sandwich Islands under his rule, would then become the only person to wear an all-yellow cloak.[35] Possession of the high-status feathered cloak was a visble sign that a chief had the support of the all-important priests and artisans, without whose cooperation he could not energise the entire population towards its own ends. Every craft and guild on Hawaii had its own cult and its own priests, and the most important craft was the feather-producing one.[36]

Deeper currents in Hawiian society largely passed the voyagers on the *Resolution* and *Discovery* by, or rather they sometimes saw part of the truth but not all of it. At its most basic level, Hawaiian society was more brittle and explosive than society elsewhere in Polynesia. At least three main elements can be identified: a struggle between what Max Weber would later characterise as the ideal types of the military and the 'clerisy'; a class struggle; and war between the sexes. Whereas elsewhere in Polynesia priests tended to be acolytes of the *arii nui* and rubber-stamp their actions, on Hawaii they competed for power, and the tension between chiefs and priesthood was palpable, with the priests tending to be more pro-European than the secular rulers; the distinctiveness of priestcraft was perhaps why several of the Europeans claimed to find religion easier to understand in Hawaii than elsewhere in the South Seas.[37] Social stratification in Hawaii was more rigid than elsewhere, with social mobility almost nil and the common people more obviously living in fear and subjection. Some of the visitors liked it that way: the American John Ledyard claimed that the strict aristocracy of the Sandwich Islands meant that there was minimal corruption on the islands; there is no point in bribery if rigid social mechanisms choke off unofficial routes to the top or detours to wealth and influence.[38] The gap between the elite and the labouring masses was immense, and one factor in this was the larger population, which provided a much higher number of hewers of wood and drawers of water than in other Pacific islands. Nowhere else could so much labour be forced on the commoners by the oligarchy and nowhere else could there be such an extraction of surplus value. The sociologist Karl Wittfogel famously studied Marx's 'oriental mode of production' and produced a model of what he called 'hydraulic despotism' relating to those societies, as in Egypt, where the peasantry was dragooned in large labour forces to utilise a scarce water supply. Wittfogel confidently included Hawaii in his 'hydraulic' system.[39] One obvious reason for all this was that the elite in Hawaii was tiny and the masses large. Cook estimated the population of Kauai to be about 30,000, which by a rough rule of thumb might mean that the total population of the islands in 1778 was roughly 250,000. The reality is that it was probably four times that.[40]

Finally, and not insignificantly, relations between the sexes were far from satisfactory and this partly explains the enthusiasm with which the local women gave themselves, often without payment, to the lecherous Europeans. Although the sailors and officers concurred in finding the Hawaiian women inferior in beauty to the incomparable Tahitians,[41] their greater availability more than made up for this in their eyes. Yet there was method in the apparent onrush of abandoned females. The only way to break through the rigid social system was for women to have sexual congress with higher-class males, and this included Europeans. The misogyny of Hawaiian culture found expression in a plethora of *tapu* activities, many of them designed to keep women in line. The doctrine of separate spheres and even separate dining places was strictly reinforced, and anyone breaking the rules was severely beaten or worse. Women responded to these restrictions by deliberately breaking the *tapus* once they got aboard European ships, taking special delight in eating food that was forbidden to them on land.[42] Sexual congress with Europeans thus really was a liberating experience for many Hawaiian women. The marginalisation of females was reinforced by an oligarchic cult of homosexuality, which recalls the culture of Ancient Greece. Most eighteenth-century Europeans, and particularly the lower-deck elements, responded with visceral horror to the idea of sodomy or same-sex activity, but for the elite this was an esoteric practice that cemented their feeling of existing apart as a chosen caste.[43] Hawaii, in short, was a combustible society, and if Cook had understood the deep undercurrents on the Sandwich Islands, he might have decided not to return there. He had underrated the Hawaiians at many different levels and, although they were stunned by the demonstration of European firepower on 20 January when the useless Williamson opened fire, they were not as overawed by guns as the Europeans thought.[44] The visitors gained a reputation as men of wealth and iron but, in a sense, they had undermined their own credibility by demonstrating that they had no special gifts after all; like the local elite they dominated through fear and raw power. Cook had arrived in Hawaii with two aims in mind: to avoid the spread of venereal disease, and avoid armed conflict with the locals. Thanks to the pleasure principle and the thoughtlessness of his men, however, he had failed on both counts. It was a bad omen.

At daybreak on 7 March 1778 the American coast was sighted: actually present-day Oregon (in the latitude of the city of Eugene). Cook named the promontory he saw Cape Foulweather, to mark the fury of the elements that now hit him.[45] Ever since leaving Bora Bora he had been expecting the worst from the wind and waves, and now it came. As he turned north along the coast he was continually beset by tempests. The worst storm was one which began at midnight on the 11th when the wind suddenly veered from south-west to north-west, churning up enormous seas and lashings of sleet and snow. Cook reported: 'There was no choice but to stretch to the southward to get clear of the coast. This was done under courses and two close-reefed topsails, being rather more sail than the ships could bear, but it was necessary to carry it to clear the land.'[46] By the morning of the 13th he had been forced back south more than two degrees of latitude. Cook's frustration was threefold: he could not make northing and could not follow the line of the coast, and by the same token he could find nowhere to anchor. More gales followed, once again the voyagers were under courses and close-reefed topsails, assailed by strong westerly and north-westerly winds and a very heavy westerly swell. More storms hit them, but this time from the south so that northward progress was possible. Until almost the end of the month the extreme experience continued: hard gales from the west followed by storms from the south, but at least they were making northing. He passed the Juan de Fuca Strait at night and somewhat arrogantly asserted that as he had not seen it, it did not exist: 'we saw nothing like it, nor is there the least probability that ever any such thing existed'.[47] Cook was now running along the western coast of what is now Vancouver Island and, though he was well out to sea, because the massive island slants north-west to south-east, he saw land again at Nootka Sound on the morning of 29 March. Quickly discovering an inlet, he took the ships in and soon located a cove that would serve as a base while he did ship repairs. On the last day of March he moored the vessels head and stern to the shore, fastened the hawsers to stout pine trees, had the sails unbent and the *Resolution*'s foremast unrigged. The sailors found that the cable had been damaged by catching on jagged rocks at the bottom of the sound; as Cook remarked grimly: 'the hawsers that were carried out to warp the ship into the cove also got foul of rocks'.[48]

Although Nootka Sound is considered one of the most spectacularly beautiful places on earth, to storm-tossed travellers in 1778 it presented mostly a forbidding and melancholy appearance, as Webber's watercolours attest. All around were dense forests of pine, spruce, cedar and hemlock. The high cliffs, jagged shore, coastal rain forests, cloud-laced valleys and the vistas stretching away to peaks some 7,000 feet high thirty miles away but visible through the mist and, perhaps most of all the lowering 'big sky' of the Pacific Northwest, all contributed to depress the voyagers. Hard toil was usually Cook's answer to despondency, so he immediately set his men to work. He set up an observatory, sent out parties to cut wood, and brewed spruce beer, which the seamen initially swore they would never drink but eventually did for lack of an alternative.[49] A forge was set up for repairs to the foremast and the usual caulking that was undertaken on both ships. Now began the trail of disillusionment with the shoddy work in Deptford dockyards that in the end would lead Cook to shock his patrons with a splenetic piece of choice invective. The timbers supporting the fore-topmast were decayed or sprung, but this was remedied in a week. More serious was the discovery that the foremast head itself was defective, the result of inadequate workmanship in England; the mast would have to be removed and repaired on shore. It was also found that the lower standing rigging had rotted, so Cook ordered a new set of main rigging to be fitted, while the remnants of the old were reworked as fore rigging.[50]

Soon he learned that Nootka Sound was far from the perfect anchorage since, though protected from the full might of the sea, it was exposed to the lashing of violent south-easterly gales, a fact evident from the mutilated appearance of the trees. On 8 April a dreadful storm blew through the sound, exposing further criminal incompetence from Deptford. The mizzenmast buckled and proved to be so completely rotten that its head dropped off in the slings. A whole new mast had to be constructed: a tree was felled and dragged to the shore, and the hard-worked carpenters had no sooner finished on the foremast than they had to start on the mizzen. The tree that had been chopped down then proved inadequate, and a further half-day was spent cutting another one down and getting it out of the wood. There was never any end to the work. The new mizzen was no sooner finished (on 21 April) than the carpenters and labourers had to produce a new fore-topmast.[51]

While all this work went on, the Europeans received many visits from the local Nootka people, who would sometimes arrive alongside the ships in as many as a hundred canoes. Accustomed to the beauty of the Polynesians, the visitors were taken aback by the squat, dirty, smelly Indians, dressed in furs and short of stature.[52] Yet they soon overcame their squeamishness when they realised there were vast profits to be made by trade with these people. Unlike in Polynesia, where all forms of big game were unknown, the Nootka people had access to a huge variety of wildlife; among its other distinctions Vancouver Island boasts the largest puma (cougar) populations in the world and the largest concentration of orcas (killer whales). In addition, the Indians could hunt deer, caribou, moose, bear, lynx, wolves, foxes, martens, racoons, wolverines and polecats. The skins of all these animals were valuable, but the most prized possessions were the sea otter pelts.[53] Cook and his officers would have known about the sea otter from the description in Linnaeus's *Systema Naturae* of 1758 which Banks and Solander had brought to their attention. The habitat of the sea otter stretched in a huge north-westerly arc from California to the far Aleutians and Siberia, and at the beginning of the eighteenth century they numbered in hundreds of thousands. The conjuncture of Vitus Bering's 1741 expedition and the 'fur craze' in China led directly to what has been called the 'Great Hunt'. Between 1741 and the international agreement to stop the trade in 1911, the sea otter was hunted almost to extinction, so that by the time of its reprieve only about a thousand were left in the entire world. In the eighteenth century the Russians reduced the sea otter population in the Kamchatka peninsula alone from 25,000 to a mere 750.[54] The eighteenth century was not an era of ecology or animal conservation; the seamen knew nothing of zoology and cared less, but they did know that a single sea otter pelt bought for a handful of beads and trinkets would fetch $300 in the markets of Canton. Not surprisingly, the arrival of the Nootka with their animal furs triggered a burgeoning trade.

At first, though, the locals were understandably nervous. They gazed with astonishment at the ships which they explained in their legends as two giant salmon or a pair of giant seagulls.[55] Other oral traditions portrayed the *Resolution* and *Discovery* as floating islands or aquaria in which were all the different kinds of salmon – humpback, dog, coho, spring – but with magic properties. Other variants included a large bird from the upper air descending to earth to eat humans; the moon coming down from the sky and using a sea serpent as its oceanic canoe; and a fiery island bringing the spirits of their as yet unborn great-great-grandchildren from the other side of the ocean.[56] Once they realised the newcomers had no hostile intent, the Nootka allowed their natural instinct for commerce to prevail. All observers agree that the Nootka were canny traders who even had a primitive understanding of market mechanisms.[57] They drove a hard bargain, sold dear and bought cheap, and did not scruple to cheat. Noting that the strangers valued their animal oil, the Nootka tried to increase their profit margins by mixing the oil with water or even handing over bladders supposedly full of oil but actually empty.[58] As soon as it became clear that the Europeans possessed iron, they would not accept anything else; later during Cook's one-month stay a craze for brass developed and soon they wanted brass above all. The one thing the Nootka would not trade was their women, so the habitually libidinous sailors did not enjoy their usual spell of promiscuity. One or two of the officers, including Williamson, managed to trade for local women, which led the ridiculous Williamson to boast that his personal charms were so great that they had transcended the usual embargo. The truth was that the women rented out were slaves captured from other tribes, not wives, sisters and daughters as in Polynesia. The Europeans insisted on scrubbing them down and removing all the oil, grime and foetor before taking them to bed.[59] Indeed the Nootka attitude to their women was even harsher than on Hawaii. Idle youths made a point of lolling lazily in full view of their toiling sisters and mothers, revolting the natural chivalry of the Europeans, which nevertheless coexisted quite happily with their acceptance of prostitution.

The Nootka skill at trade did not mean that thieving, the bane of the South Seas, was non-existent, for the Nootka appeared to make a clear distinction between goods for trade, subject to market forces, and objects which they claimed the customary right to pilfer.[60] The familiar lamentations about theft were heard. Cook related:

> We soon found that they were as lightfingered as any people we had before
> met with, and were far more dangerous, for with their knives and other

cutting instruments of iron they could cut a hook from a tackle or any other piece of iron from a rope the instant our backs were turned . . . If we missed a thing immediately after it was stolen, we found no difficulty in finding out the thief, as they were ready enough to impeach one another, but the thief generally relinquished his prize with reluctancy and sometimes not without force.[61]

In some ways even more alarming for Cook was the realisation that the Nootka were the first primitive peoples to claim that everything in the land was theirs, including wood and water, and that they intended to fleece the strangers accordingly. As soon as one 'owner' was paid, another would pop up, demanding payment for some right that had not been covered by the initial outlay. As Cook noted sardonically: 'there did not seem to be a single blade of grass that had not a separate owner'. Cook was prepared to barter his way out of trouble, as he did not want war with the locals while his vital ship repairs were being carried out. His men were not so punctilious; a number of grass-cutting parties, finding forage for the sheep and goats Cook still had on board, flatly refused to pay the grasping Indians. The Nootka rationalised this beautifully, saying that if they could not afford to pay, the white men could have the grass as a gift.[62] Also puzzling to the visitors was the endemic factionalism or war of all against all in which the Nootka seemed to specialise; this manifested itself in the idea that the first people to trade with the Europeans should be the only ones allowed to do so ever thereafter. Some of the warlike preparations Cook's men observed were directed not towards them but against would-be interlopers on the valuable trade.[63]

Although he spent a peaceful month in their midst, Cook never liked the Nootka, whom he thought far inferior to the Polynesians in almost every way. His contacts with them were mundane and never acquired a personal quality. His instinct to seek out the most powerful chief and deal with him did not work on Vancouver Island, where there seemed to be no chiefs, merely families living together in loose associations.[64] Used to impressive seafaring craft, he found the Nootka, who knew nothing of sails, backward in this regard, and compared their canoes to a Norway yawl. In some respects, though, the Nootka were ahead of the Polynesians, for their pursuit of big game made them much more skilful hunters: Cook's men were particularly impressed with the hinged harpoons they used for killing whales – weapons with skin bladders attached which slowed down the progress of stricken leviathans trying to evade their tormentors.[65] Partly as a consequence of a life spent tracking big game, and partly because there was almost constant warfare, with one tribe trying to conquer another to secure trading rights, the Nootka were adept at the use of weapons, and especially archery; by contrast, in Polynesia the bow and arrow was used only in sporting contests and never in battle, except in Fiji, which, of course, Cook never visited.[66] From what he learned of their warfare Cook concluded that the Nootka were systematically cowardly and unscrupulous, preferring to take an enemy unawares and catch him while asleep or stage raids without warning. For this reason he always had half an eye cocked for sudden treachery by the Nootka and liked to demonstrate the superiority of his firearms over their bows and arrows, even though the locals were worryingly expert with this weapon.[67] Although Cook downplays his wariness in his journals, many of the other eyewitnesses were adamant that the Nootka had at one time contemplated an attack on the Europeans but drew back once they realised their visitors could not be taken by surprise. Samwell and Gilbert both reported that at one time Cook came close to giving the order to his marines to open fire. The occasion was, as so often, a relatively trivial theft, of a piece of iron.[68]

Later anthropologists revealed that the people Cook met were Mowachaht bands of the Nuu-chah-nulth nation.[69] Certainly Cook treated them better than the later waves of visitors, particularly the American whalers and, when he finally left Nootka Sound they laid on a farewell ceremony, complete with singing and masked theatre. Cook visited their island and had himself rowed all round the sound by his midshipmen while the seamen put the finishing touches to the new masts. Longitude, compass bearings and tides were all tested and examined by the observatory. At last, on 26 April, the ships were ready to go; moorings were cast off, anchors weighed and the boats towed the vessels out of the cove. This time no one could accuse Cook of having delayed too long at a landfall; the ship repairs had occupied a full month. Right to the very end the thieving of the Nootka vexed Cook. Ledyard, acute to any nuance of anti-American feeling in the light of the revolt of the colonies, remembered Cook's dry remark the first time iron was stolen: 'This is an American indeed!'[70] It may be, as has been suggested, that he was already regretting his actions at Moorea, but it is more likely that he agreed with Clerke that it was better to connive at minor theft unless the ships were likely to be in the vicinity for a long time. Cook had not achieved much at the level of exploration in his four weeks in the Sound, but his visit had two significant consequences. In the first place, the reports of the lucrative fur trade and the profits available from transhipment to China triggered a holocaust of the sea otter, which got under way in earnest in the 1780s.[71] Another important result was the revival of Spanish interest in this coast. While trading with the Nootka, Cook's men had noticed that they were offered Spanish artefacts: these came from the *Santiago* commanded by Juan Perez which had called at Nootka Sound (though without landing) in August 1774.[72] By the late 1770s Spain was seriously concerned not only about Cook's incursions into the Pacific but also about his concentration on the western American coast. This was one of the factors in their collaboration with France in 1779 in an ambitious invasion attempt on England.[73] Ten years later it almost took Spain and Britain to war again and probably would have, had not the French Revolution subverted Spain's major ally. Finally, deeply concerned by Anglo-Saxon ventures in the Pacific Northwest, Madrid sent out a major expedition under Alejandro Malaspina, which in a five-year cruise (1789–94) restored some of the glory of Quirós.[74]

It was typical of the intrepidity of Cook as a seaman that he put to sea even though his experienced eye told him that a storm was approaching. Part of his credo was that only the second-rate navigator waited in port for a fair wind instead of standing away and finding one. On this occasion, however, Cook's usual luck deserted him and his actions looked like recklessness, for the two ships had to endure a four-day storm which built into a hurricane. As if the storm itself was not enough, the darkness was so intense that one could not see from one end of the ship to the other, let alone the sister vessel. To avoid the dangers of a lee shore, Cook took the ships farther out to sea. A false alarm that the *Resolution* had sprung a leak forced the ships to heave to for a while, then Cook tried the tactic of running before the wind. When the wind reached Force 12, even Cook conceded that this was too dangerous, and that there was nothing for it but to hunker down grimly and ride out the fury of the elements.[75] The ferocity of the sustained storm meant that the voyagers were out of sight of land for a full six degrees of latitude and made landfall again only at latitude 55, close to the Queen Charlotte and Prince of Wales islands. Cook rightly scouted the idea that there was a strait in this area – it had been reported by the Spanish admiral Bartolome de Fonte in 1708 – but then he had earlier dismissed as mythical the Juan de Fuca strait, which did exist.[76] Slowly he inched further north, noting features of the landscape on the shoreline and giving them names: Cape Edgcumbe (Latitude 57 N), Mount Edgcumbe, Cape Fairweather, Mount Fairweather, Mount St Elias, Cape Suckling. Early May brought the benefit of gentle breezes and calm seas. Trying to make sense of what was essentially a farrago of nonsense from Müller and von Stählin, he became increasingly exasperated, as the geography he saw seemed to bear no relation to their reports.[77] Sailing into the head of the Gulf of Alaska, he reached Cape Hinchinbrook on 12 May. Hitherto the coast had been running in a north-westerly direction but now, in Alaska, it turned west and later slightly south-west. There was a report of a fresh leak on *Resolution* and, with thick fog around them and another storm threatening, Cook needed to get into a safe inlet to investigate and see whether his pumps could deal with the leak.

He managed to find a cove that provided temporary respite from the elements, set the sailors to fish and sent out Gore in a boat to see if he could shoot some eatable birds. Almost immediately Gore was surrounded by about twenty local people in canoes; they did not understand the words of Nootka that Gore was able to pitch at them, and modern anthropologists have not been able to identify them with any certainty – the probability is that they were Inuit, for Cook had reached the no man's land of disputed territory between the Indians to the south and the Eskimos to the north.[78] Finding that his anchorage was not secure enough to allow an investigation of the leak, Cook put to sea again in the teeth of south-east winds blowing at gale force and heavy fog. He was fortunate to find a sheltering inlet (he called it Prince William Sound), but the violence of the squalls was so tremendous that Cook was forced to anchor in thirteen fathoms, not as far into the sound as he wanted. Here the seamen worked on the leak until 17 May, greatly heartened by a change in the weather on the 16th when there was clear visibility and they could see land all round them. Once again Cook had cause to curse the Admiralty and the corruption in the Deptford dockyards. During the over-hauling of the *Resolution*, when the sheathing was taken off, it was discovered that some of her seams had hardly any caulking at all.[79] While this work went on, Cook sent Gore out to explore the arms of the inlet but he returned with discouraging news about any potential north-west passage. Cook decided that the search for the passage was futile, situated where he was, and, the wind having dropped, he ventured out into the Gulf of Alaska once more.[80] After leaving Prince William Sound he steered south-west, now off the south-eastern coast of the Kenai peninsula, past a promontory at latitude 59N 207E that he named Cape Elizabeth after the princess's birthday that day (21 May). Driven back by a gale, by the 23rd he was more confused than ever, with capes, islands and snow-capped mountains all around him, Stahlin's and Müller's charts inaccurate and with minimal guidance from the accounts of the voyages of Bering and Aleksai Chirikov.[81]

At last the contrary winds ceased, and on 25 May Cook steered into a very large inlet between two landmarks he called Cape Douglas and Mount St Augustine. At first the travellers thought this might be the longed-for Northwest Passage but 'Cook Inlet' turned out to be another false friend. Cook had his suspicions from the appearance of the mountains on all sides that this would be merely another part of the American coastline but allowed his scepticism to be overruled by the enthusiasm of his officers, especially Gore, who urged that he would surely find the Passage if he would only persevere;[82] it is not being cynical to suggest that the lure of the £20,000 reward weighed more with them than sober probability. After finding an anchorage (unoriginally dubbed Anchor Point), though not without losing a hawser and a kedge anchor irrecoverably in deep water through a freak accident, Cook then spent ten days futilely exploring the inlet, not even desisting when the water turned fresh on 31 May.[83] Cook sent Bligh ahead on an advance reconnaissance trip (which discovered that the inlet turned east and branched into two rivers), met some more Inuit, then in a mood of high irritation called off the search, annoyed that he had wasted more time. He was just one day short of establishing that the huge inlet was a mere cul-de-sac and could not be the Passage. To justify the diversion, which ran contrary to Admiralty instructions not to explore rivers and inlets unless there was a strong probability of finding the Passage, Cook claimed it was a moral certainty that one of the two branches would lead into the sea at Hudson's Bay.[84] Sixteen years later, when his midshipman George Vancouver returned as a great navigator and explored the inlet thoroughly, he was critical of his former captain. He should, Vancouver thought, have 'dedicated one more day to its further examination' which 'would have spared the theoretical navigators who have followed him in their closets, the task of ingeniously ascribing to this arm of the ocean a channel, through which a north-west passage, existing according to their doctrines, might ultimately be discovered'.[85] Despite his pious rationalisations, Cook was in a sour mood, and perhaps this contributed to the near-disaster on the passage back down 'River Turnagain' (the malapropism by which Cook described the inlet). The *Resolution* struck a large sandbank, ran aground and had to be floated off on the flood tide.[86] Again Vancouver was critical, both of the shoddy seamanship of the helmsman and of the lack of proper reconnoitring of the highly dangerous sandbanks.[87] Such was the voyage in what later came to be known as Cape Inlet.

On 6 June Cook once more emerged on to the open sea. He avoided the obvious passage through the Shelikof Strait, doubtless fearing that it would be yet another dead end like the Cook Inlet, and sailed to the east and south of the massive Kodiak Island, sailing three days in constant mist and drizzling rain to the Trinity islands. Soon he was off Chirikof Island, to the accompaniment of a 'prodigious' swell, a thick fog and a strong gale which damaged several sails.[88] He was now seriously concerned that he was being carried ever more southwards, which made him doubt that any route to Baffin Land or Hudson's Bay could exist. Bitter at the Russian fantasies that kept him pursuing a will-o'-the-wisp, he found himself being driven in diametrically the opposite direction from his Admiralty instructions, being carried south-west along the huge sweeping arm of the Gulf of Alaska. There was almost continual dense fog, heavy rain and snow so that glimpses of land were rare, and, when he could descry it, all he could make out was snow-capped mountains plunging dramatically down to a craggy, cruel and inhospitable shore. For days he and his officers could not see the sun so could not take sightings. Morale plummeted as the voyagers blundered through a labyrinth of shoals, rocks and islets without ever being able to work out exactly where they were.[89] They were in fact sailing along a coastline that modern sailors are told to avoid, as much for the 100-foot freak waves which suddenly appear from nowhere as for the danger from shoals and sandbars. The next landmark was the Shumagin islands, something of an animal paradise, for the voyagers were surrounded by flocks of both land and seabirds, wheeling in the air and mewing, while around them seals and whales breached and gambolled. The sailors dodged the dangerous breakers of the Sandman Reefs (which, again, even modern shipping is told never to venture into) and fished for halibut under the icy shadow of the smoking Shishaldin volcano.[90] Everyone agreed that in the treacherous conditions they had had almost supernatural good luck, dodging perilous rocks, breakers and fog banks. It had been three weeks of tedious navigation, along rocky shores and past cliffs where it was impossible to tell island from mainland, where snow ran down to the beach and almost into the sea and the weather was consistently foul: mist, drizzling rain, fog, then rain, then drizzle, then fog again, almost ad infinitum.[91] It was 24 June and Cook had now reached the island of Unimak, separated from the American continent by the narrowest of straits. Although he did not know it, he had arrived at the north-eastern end of the 1,000-mile-long string of the Aleutian islands, stretching across the North Pacific for 25 degrees of longitude from the tip of Alaska to the Kamchatka peninsula. He also did not know that sea conditions in the Aleutians are among the worst in the world.[92]

From 24 to 26 June, Cook was at both his perigee and apogee. Those who had long believed Cook had lost his touch might have felt vindicated when he unaccountably missed the Unimak Pass at the south of the island – a ten-mile-wide strait that led directly into the Bering Sea and the only way north, Cook's supposed objective. Next day Cook seemed almost to have flipped over in a bipolar seizure, for he ordered the ship to run with the wind in virtually nil visibility. Suddenly the sound of breakers was heard on the larboard bow and the lead found the water depth dropping alarmingly. Cook brought the ship to with her head to the north, and gave the same orders to the *Discovery*. When the fog lifted, it turned out that the ships had been heading straight for the shore and would have been wrecked but for the sound of the breakers. Cook noted in his journal: 'There were several breakers about them [*sc.* rocks] and yet providence had conducted us through these rocks where I should not have ventured on a clear day, and to such an anchoring place that I could not have chosen a better.'[93] Clerke summed up the situation with a dry

irony: 'Very nice pilotage, considering our perfect ignorance of our situation.'[94] Cook stayed where he was for twenty-four hours until the fog lifted.
Then there was another perilous passage between islands when the *Resolution*
virtually skied through to clear water on a flood tide; following in her wake,
Discovery got into difficulties, was caught in the ebb and twirled round with the
sea breaking over her decks until by great good luck she was shot clear of the
race. With no wind at all now, Cook was obliged to anchor the vessels, then
had the boats tow them into a bay on Sedanka Island, off the north-east coast
of the large island of Unalaska. On the way they saw indigenous peoples
towing in whales they had killed.[95] Cook then worked his way between
Unalaska and Unalga Island to a secure harbour at Samgunuda, aka English
Bay. Here they learned a lot about the Russians from the Inuit, to supplement
the intelligence they had gleaned a week earlier from some Aleuts from Unga
Island, and were delighted to find that the Inuit seemed to have no interest in
thieving.[96] There was plentiful water and within twenty-four hours Cook had
all his casks replenished. Yet he was delayed there for three days by thick fog
and contrary winds. King climbed a mountain and narrowly missed falling
into an icy crevasse. The irrepressible womaniser Samwell managed to sleep
with some Inuit women by bartering tobacco for their favours. Most of the
crew had no such libidinous luck; large numbers were already stricken by
gonorrhoea, but Cook was relaxed in his attitude, since he reasoned that venereal disease already had a grip on the Americas, so precautionary action was
futile; this had also been his policy among the Nootka.[97]

On 2 July the ships finally left Unalaska Island and emerged into the Bering
Sea, where Cook steered north-east past Amak Island to skirt the far side of the
Alaskan peninsula, making east by north in heavy fog. It was easy to replenish
food supplies, for the most maladroit fisherman could not fail to haul in a
mammoth catch in seas that were a veritable cod bank.[98] Cutting across Bristol
Bay, Cook sent Williamson in a boat to land briefly on the west coast of Alaska
to take possession of the territory in King George's name; this was at Cape
Newenham on 16 July. Forty to fifty miles north of Cape Newenham the ships
became snarled up in the fearsome shoals of Kuskokwim Bay, parallel banks of
sand, stones and mud flats, some of them dry at low water and stretching far
out of sight of land. Cook anchored to consider his options, but the *Resolution*'s
cable parted from her anchor. Having already lost one anchor, Cook was determined not to repeat the feat, and once again he was lucky. A diver sent down in
icy temperatures found it very quickly, almost miraculously. After reconnoitring the intricate pattern of shoals with boat parties, Cook chose not to risk
a possible narrow channel to the north. He decided to retrace his course to the
south and then swing out to the open sea to avoid the shoal-strewn coast. Even

this was more easily said than done. The ships had to proceed gingerly and cautiously, preceded by three boats continually taking soundings; on one occasion they narrowly missed a shoal in a depth of just five feet of water. Five days were consumed in this ticklish, circumspect process, and the travellers were lucky to enjoy fine weather all the way back.[99] Once at Cape Newenham Cook set a semicircular course out into the Bering Sea, initially steering south and south-west to make sure he would avoid any shoals. By 28 July they were in the middle of the Bering Sea, beginning to make northing again. The absurdity of the maps they had been working from became clear when they took their bearings that day in clear sunshine; according to Müller they should have been in the middle of a land mass and according to von Stählin they should have been plumb centre of an archipelago. Contrary winds, constant drizzle and, most of all, thick fog impeded their progress, and contact between the *Resolution* and *Discovery* was difficult: 'at times the ships were in a constant noise of guns, drums and bells to keep in touch'.[100]

On 29 July the voyagers sighted St Matthew Island, about halfway between the Aleutians and the Bering Strait. Two days later William Anderson, who had been ailing since the Society Islands, died suddenly. Cook, who usually recorded death on ships coldly and unemotionally, was deeply affected and shaken: 'He was a sensible young man, an agreeable companion, well skilled in his profession and had acquired much knowledge in other sciences that, had it pleased God to spare his life, might have been useful in the course of the voyage.'[101] By the normal buttoned-up Cook standards that was the most eulogistic of panegyrics and was a unique journal-based obituary, accorded to no other shipmate. Clerke added a eulogy of his own, which concluded: 'If we except our commander, he is the greatest public loss the voyage could have sustained.'[102] In his honour Cook named the huge island that bars the entrance to the Bering Strait Anderson Island; unfortunately for Anderson's memory, it had already been discovered, claimed and given the name of St Lawrence Island by Bering fifty years before. On 4 August the fog cleared sufficiently for Cook to sight land and take bearings. He was at latitude 64°30 at Sledge Island, just off the Alaskan coast and near the modern town of Nome. The brief landing he made there was the most northerly point of North America where he set foot. Slowly and cautiously he edged north-west in thick drizzle but calm seas until on 9 August he anchored off Cape Prince of Wales, the easternmost point of the Seward peninsula and at the eastern tip of the Bering Strait, where the channel narrows before emerging into the Chukchi Sea; at latitude 65°37, he was just south of the Arctic Circle.[103] On land they saw a fox and, what would have delighted Anderson the amateur ornithologist, a skein of American golden plovers, birds famous for their migratory flights from the coast of Alaska to Hawaii, the Marquesas and the Tuamotus. On the 10th the ships crossed the Bering Strait west to east and were soon off the shores of eastern Siberia. On the way over they were hit by a ferocious storm. In the strait the winds and currents worked against each other and piled up enormous waves, which frequently broke over the ship. After grimly hanging on through this very nasty experience, Cook anchored in Lawrence Bay on the Chukotski peninsula on 10 August.[104]

Immediately they were confronted (for welcomed would not be the word) by a large group of local Mongoloid people known as the Chukchi. These were the 'fishing Chukchi' of the coast as opposed to the 'reindeer Chukchi' of the interior, a tough, fierce and warlike nation who had seen off both Russians and Inuit intruders. When Cook and a landing party stepped on to the shore and moved towards them, the Chukchi retreated slowly and raised their spears, with a rearguard at their back ready to loose off arrows. Cook, as his journal entries reveal, was in no mood to soft-pedal with primitive peoples and at first the signals seemed ominous, as if the Chukchi were about to pay for all the frustrations Cook had experienced in Polynesia.[105] Yet the crisis passed: somehow (he does not explain fully) he induced them to trade for bead and knives but it was tobacco they were chiefly interested in. Even while bartering the Chukchi remained wary, their weapons always within reach; they had had bad experiences with the Russians and thought their visitors were either a fresh set of Russians or their allies. Cook meanwhile gradually softened in his attitude once he noticed that their weapons, clothes and artefacts all showed them to be a much more advanced people than the American Indians and Inuits he had encountered so far; they were more handsome, well-proportioned and had long faces where the Nootka and others had been short and squat. In the few hours Cook spent ashore he conquered the Chukchi reservations and misgivings sufficiently that they allowed him to visit their village. The stopover was never intended to be a long one and, as soon as the wind veered to the south, Cook stood out of the bay and steered north-east, aiming for the gap between the two capes (on the Siberian and Alaskan sides), the Chukchi Sea and the Arctic Circle.[106] By 13 August he was through the Bering Strait, still heading north-east. His track for the next three weeks would be triangular: to latitude 70N and beyond, almost to Point Barrow, the northernmost tip of Alaska, then across the Chukchi Sea, and finally down the eastern coast of Siberia. The first leg of the triangle duplicated Bering's effort in 1728 when he sailed north from Kamchatka and through the strait that thereafter bore his name, though he did not sight Alaska.[107]

King testified that the crew was in high spirits as the drive towards the 'ice free' Arctic Ocean commenced. Yet after a week's sailing their hopes began to fade. On 17 August they passed the 70N latitude mark and the sun and moon were seen together in the sky. Around noon there was a sudden brightness in the sky, of a kind with which Cook was familiar from his Antarctic rovings. It was the phenomenon known as 'ice blink'. An hour later he saw a huge field of ice, with solid walls ten to twelve feet high looming out of the water, impenetrable and stretching as far as the eye could see, but quite typical of the ice barrier north of the Bering Strait. There would be no sailing to the North Pole. On 18 August Cook reached his farthest north at 70'44.[108] He then stood south for about eighteen miles and came to the penultimate cape in Alaska before Point Barrow, now known as Icy Cape after Cook's experiences. Here, driven by a west wind, they were in serious danger from shoals, in shallow water, on an icy lee shore and with the ice closing in on them. 'Our situation was now more and more critical' was Cook's typically laconic and understated journal entry.[109] Whether by luck, consummate seamanship or a mixture of both, the *Resolution* managed to lead her sister ship out of danger to the south-west by the only stretch of open sea; this was the third disaster in three weeks they had narrowly avoided. Turning west into open water, Cook left behind the solid ice of the glaciers and found instead numerous ice floes on the sea. On 19 August he took advantage of this and ordered his men to kill the walruses that basked on the floes, so that they would have fresh meat.[110] There followed a bloody massacre of the prodigious herds of the basking beasts, which also yielded valuable oil from their blubber. The foolish walruses watched the approach of the hunters with unconcern until the first shot was fired, whereupon there was mass panic. Yet the killing was no simple turkey-shoot. Cook's marksmen had to be deadly accurate, for any walrus that made it into the water was never recovered by the seamen, even if it was mortally wounded. Heartened by the day's work, Cook evinced an unconscionable stubbornness, still unwilling to concede totally that he had been beaten by the ice. He spent 20 August tacking in thick fog and, finding deeper water, tried to thread his way through loose ice. Only when he heard the surge and thunder of the sea on the main ice pack did he finally give up and set a westward course to Siberia, though even on the passage there he would sometimes divert defiantly into the loose ice as if he were a Prometheus defying the harsh laws of Nature.[111]

On 29 August the voyagers reached Cape Schmidt on the Siberian coast. Once Cook turned south and began running along the eastern shores of Siberia, the crew, surly and semi-mutinous ever since the first joust with the ice, partly recovered its equanimity; on Cook's voyages a rise in morale could always be correlated with the captain's turning away from the polar regions. In his journals Cook pondered and to an extent fumed about his defeat by the ice. Why had the scientists been wrong about the freezing of the salt sea? Why had he not been able to get farther north, when he knew that previous explorers and even Greenland whalers had reached 80N? There was Henry Hudson in 1607, there was Constantine John Phipps as recently as 1773, though both of these had been in the environs of Spitzbergen.[112] Cook did not reflect that he had been lucky on two counts: if he had arrived in these latitudes in June instead of August, he would have found the Bering Strait icebound and probably much of the Bering Sea, too. Conversely, in a warmer August than that of 1778 he might have been tempted up a lane of clear sea north of Icy Cape and then been trapped when the ice closed up again. It was an unfortunate aspect of Cook's personality that he tended to attribute all his remarkably good luck to his own peerless seamanship and all his bad luck, in paranoid fashion, to a malign Fate. Trying to salve his extreme disappointment, he began an extensive running survey of the Siberian (and later Alaskan) coastline.[113] His observations led him to a deep admiration for Bering and a corresponding increase in contempt for von Stählin. After a week he was through the Bering Strait again and back on the American coast. He sighted Sledge Island on 6 September, anchored off Cape Darby on the 8th and next day nearly came to grief again in another set of shoals; to escape from these Cook had to tack into the wind in another bravura demonstration of seamanship. As part of a meticulous examination of Norton Sound, he sent several parties ashore while he lay at anchor off Cape Denbigh. One of these was a shooting party, but the others were more unusual, for the sailors had not been put to berry-picking before. They returned with groaning vats of raspberries, redcurrants, blackcurrants, whortleberries and Alpine partridge berries.[114]

Next Cook set a south-westerly course, once more cruising past St Matthew Island. As he saw it, there was no point in heading down the Alaskan coast, for that would soon bring him to the terrible shoal labyrinth of Kuskokwim Bay. Prudence, predictability and the preference for the known over the unknown all pointed to another stopover at Unalaska. The passage down through the Bering Sea was unpleasant. On 25 September the most tremendous storm, with an enormous swell and very high seas came upon them; the pounding was so terrific that the *Resolution* sprang another leak and every man on board had to bail for his life.[115] Eventually the storm moderated to a gale but the high seas and ferocious winds did not abate until 2 October, when Cook finally sighted Unalaska and brought the ships back to their old anchorage. There was serious work to do on the leak, which turned out to be in the starboard futtock; had it been below the waterline, the probability is that all aboard the *Resolution* would have perished. Cook also ordered an overhaul of the pumps, so that they would work more efficiently. Once again he was angered to discover shoddy Deptford workmanship; this time when the carpenters examined the sheathing many of the seams were found to be open.[116] One advantage of Unalaska while all this work went on was that it provided abundant fresh water and easy fishing for beginners; the men went out in boats in the morning and returned in the evening with bumper catches of halibut and salmon – one halibut weighed 254 pounds. There were also half a dozen types of berry growing in profusion, as well as spruce beer, which was served instead of grog on alternate days. Cook tried to conserve meat supplies for another long cruise in the Pacific by trying to get the men to eat the walrus meat which they still had in profusion, and ordered all rations except biscuit stopped. The men protested loudly: they found walrus flesh tough, chewy and indigestible. Cook lost his temper and branded them as mutineers; harsh words were spoken and Cook made it plain that as far as he was concerned the sailors could eat walrus meat or starve. The men revived their pejorative nickname for Cook – Tute – which they had taken over from the Polynesians and which was supposed to connote his harsh and capricious nature.[117] The consequence was a hunger strike. Soon the men were almost on their knees and incapable of work. Reluctantly Cook was forced to abandon his hard line; his officers meanwhile were disillusioned by his willingness to jettison cajolery in favour of brute force. King thought the subtle thing to do was to issue a ration of half salt meat and half walrus, since salt meat not being a particular delicacy, the seamen would soon come round to what they disparagingly called 'sea horse'.[118]

The three-week layover at Unalaska saw prolonged contact with the Aleut people of the 1,000-mile-long chain of islands. Cook found them the most peaceful and inoffensive people he had ever encountered, though two things should be borne in mind: they were not warlike and were to the Chukchi warriors as the Hopi were to the Apaches in New Mexico; moreover, they had felt the lash, or firepower, of the Russians already. The normally upbeat Beaglehole is dyspeptic in his approach to Cook and the Aleuts: he claims that all the extant journals provide 'an account of a primitive society under the first impact of commercial exploitation that is rare in the records of exploration, and not found elsewhere in the records of Cook's own voyages', adding bitterly that 'there was ample opportunity to add to the stock of venereal disease on board'.[119] The promiscuous Samwell luxuriated in the fact that the Aleut men did not have 'the least objections to our lying with their wives', cynically overlooking the fact that the tradition of sexual hospitality was rife among the Inuit and the Aleuts.[120] Cook was fascinated by the Aleuts and used his leisure during the three-week stopover to compile an amateur sociology of the primitive peoples of North America, accurately observing, for instance, that the linguistic similarities of the Aleuts and the Inuit, and even the Greenland Eskimos, meant they must come from a common stock.[121] In attempting to assess the Aleuts Cook was largely out of his depth; he needed the insights of a Banks, a Johann Forster or even the recently deceased Anderson, but his assessment of them was warm, positive and appreciative. He was soon to receive decisive proof of the intelligence of the locals, for on 8 October one of them brought a present of a rye loaf, attached to which was a message in a script the Europeans guessed to be Russian. It turned out that there were Russian fur traders living on the other side of the island, so Cook decided to contact them and reciprocate the gift with bottles of rum, wine and porter. The dauntless American John Ledyard, now corporal of marines on the *Resolution*, volunteered to go in search of the Russians. Two days later he returned in triumph with a trio of fur traders.[122]

The three Russians proved to be affable, intelligent and bibulous but the language barrier made communication between them and Cook impossible at any but the most basic level. Fortunately they were able to tell Cook that on the island there was an even more important Russian, sometimes referred to in the journals as 'the governor', though in reality he was a factor for a Russian fur company. This man, Gerasim Grigoryevich Izmailov, came on 14 October and, though speaking no language but Russian, was able to find better ways to communicate with Cook than his compatriots had earlier.[123] Grigoryevich was histrionically scornful about the von Stählin and Müller maps Cook laid before him, and made it understood that their so-called discoveries were chimerical; Cook's critics say he should have realised this early on and not spent so much time trying to align their myths with reality.[124] Cook enjoyed his contact with Grigoryevich and spent an enjoyable week with him. The officers shared his pleasure: in this wilderness, Russian fur traders rated as high society. Cook's officers made frequent trips to the Russian base at Egoochac, where the hard-swilling fur traders tended to drink them under the table. Before he departed Grigoryevich gave Cook letters of introduction to the governor of Kamchatka and the commandant at Petropavlovsk.[125] The idea of going into winter quarters at Petropavlovsk in Kamchatka had many attractions and was tempting but Cook feared the impact of months of inactivity on his hedonistic crew. Cook composed a letter to the Admiralty, setting out his intentions for 1779. After wintering on Hawaii, he would return to the north, explore the Kamchatka coast and then make a final attempt to find the elusive Northwest Passage. Grigoryevich told him that a Russian sloop was soon to set out for Europe and that its captain would take the letter. The captain Jacob Ivanovich was supposed to meet Cook on 22 October, but failed to appear. The impatient Cook tried to get to sea that day, but just as he was setting sail, the wind turned against him and he had to return to harbour. In that interval of serendipity between 22 and 26 October, when Cook finally did manage to stand away from Unalaska, Ivanovich arrived and was handed the precious letter.[126] Now it was time to make the voyage to Hawaii, and everyone hoped that the weather would be as gloriously favourable as it had been on the trip north. Nobody could have foreseen that Cook and his ships were about to enter an oceanic hell.

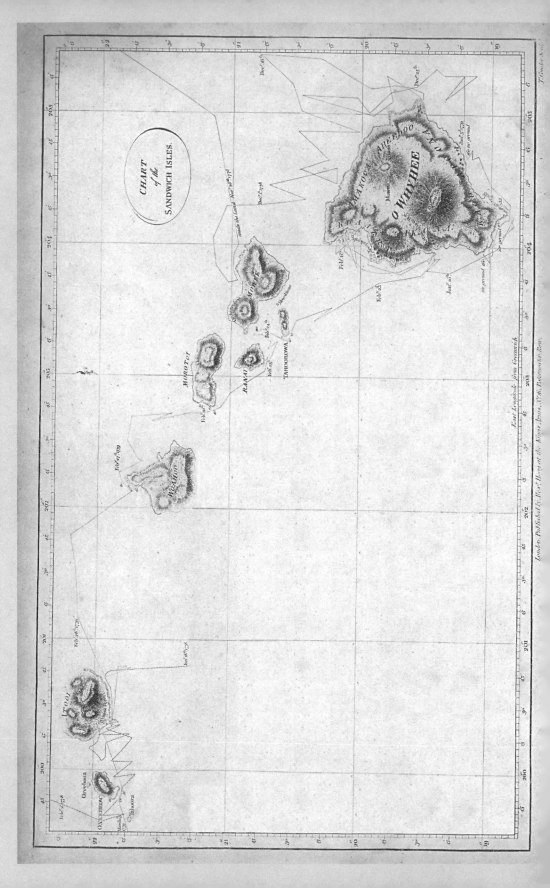

CHART
of the
SANDWICH ISLES.

—◆—

CHAPTER SIXTEEN

Hawaiian Nightmare

TWENTY-FOUR hours out from Unalaska, Cook spent an unhappy fiftieth birthday. He may have been having doubts about his own abilities for it was noticeable eccentricity that he had failed to chart his landmarks with the panache of yore. The Cook of the second voyage would never have made the blunder he made when at the southern end of Norton Sound and off the mouth of the Yukon – identifying as three islands (Clerke's Island, Anderson Island and St Lawrence Island) what turned out to be one and the same.[1] If his mastery of surveying had slipped a notch, the easy rapport he had had with his crew on the first two voyages was also no more, with the men sullen and semi-mutinous and Cook ever more angry and semi-paranoid about their disobedience. He exhibited much bipolar behaviour in the northern latitudes. James Trevenen related that the man who went out on boat trips with his officers to explore inlets was a very different animal from the tyrant on the bridge of the *Resolution*: 'he would sometimes relax from his almost constant severity of disposition and now and then to converse familiarly with us. But it was only for a time; as soon as on board the ship he became again the despot.'[2] Most of all, the real objectives of the third voyage seemed to be slipping from his grasp. He had signed on for a third joust with the Pacific in hopes of even greater fame, a knighthood and riches, unable to resist the challenge of finding the Northwest Passage. He had paranoid feelings not just about the crew but about the Admiralty too. As the example of Omai showed, the British elite were great ones for taking up men as temporary heroes, only to grow bored with them. Might not the same fate await him? Might it not be said that he had not only failed to find the Northwest Passage but claimed it did not exist? Would that not tempt the anti-Cook faction of Dalrymple and others to revive the controversy about the Great Southern Continent and assert that Cook was an ultra-sceptic, that he never found what he was sent to look for, and merely substituted his own glory-hunting voyages of discovery in the Pacific? Come to think of it, was not the whole project of the transit of Venus also a signal failure? Cook knew that the Admiralty was uneven in its interest in the Pacific[3] and feared his halo would slip. In fact he had no reason whatever to reproach himself. His voyage around Alaska and through the Bering Strait was a stupendous feat of exploration, underrated in part because the Russians themselves showed so little interest in the area. He had accurately charted virtually the entire coast of Alaska and convincingly shown how the north-west American coastline related to Siberia and the Aleutians.[4] As it later transpired, he had done much more. Having awoken the Spanish from their dogmatic slumbers by his venture on Vancouver Island, he now roused the Russian bear by sailing in waters where only Russians had been before. Despite some scepticism from scholars who say that St Petersburg responded to stimuli only from its own fur traders, and that Cook had a certain vogue and *succès d'estime* in Romanov court circles but nothing else, ample evidence exists to show that Cook's voyage once again focused Russian attention on their own far eastern maritime frontier.[5]

Besides, not all Cook's officers felt alienated from him. Though critical, Gilbert thought that the 'providential escape from instant destruction' on the night of 25–26 June (see above p. 355) had in some sense to be laid at Cook's door, for he was either the most brilliant seaman imaginable or one beloved by the gods and therefore worth treasuring.[6] Trevenen, despite his many strictures, thought Cook a genuine phenomenon:

> He who once revolves in his mind the immense extent of the coast that Captain Cook has in this voyage surveyed, the earliness of the season when he began it, and the advanced state of it when he left off, the badness of the provisions which had already been three years from England, the intricacies of the coast, the inlets, rocks and shoals that would make, when well known, the boldest pilot tremble to venture on it, the length of time which its crew remained in and bore with the consequent fatigue of such uncommon and accumulated circumstances of distress, passed among rocks and fields of ice in thick fogs, with the entire privation of fresh meat and such necessary comforts as alone can render men capable of undergoing extreme hardships, with the allowed hazard of navigating among ice, must wonder at and admire [his] boldness of daring and skill in executing projects big with every danger.[7]

It was as well that so many officers felt such confidence, for little more than a day out from Unalaska the Pacific hurled all its fury at the *Resolution* and *Discovery*. First there were four days of non-stop hard gales, with the wind boxing the compass, accompanied by rain, hail and snow, and sometimes all three falling together. In the early hours of 28 October a fearful squall killed a seaman and injured others on the *Discovery* while collapsing the ship's main tack. Cook had originally set a course west but, faced with mountainous seas, turned east on the 30th and ran through the Unimak Strait to the east of Unalaska Island. If he thought he had thereby escaped the elements he was mistaken, for the gales followed him and built up by 2 November into the most violent storm; King said these were the worst seas he had seen on the entire voyage. With a frighteningly high swell running, the two ships hove to for the night, both captains in a state of something like desperation. Fortunately, the storm abated by morning, and Cook and Clerke could take stock of the damage. The *Discovery* had lost its foresail, the fore-staysail had been blown to pieces and the reefed topsail had been impaired.[8]

The ships limped haltingly south, with the daily rate of progress becoming slower and slower. It was calm enough on 7 November for Cook to visit Clerke on the *Discovery*, but the disoriented and distressed seabird that flew round and round the ships seemed a fitting symbol for their state of mind. It was not long before another severe gale hit the voyagers, this time meting out most damage to the *Resolution* and ripping apart the main-topsail that had only just been repaired. Bit by bit the ships crept south, until by 25 November Cook estimated that he was once again in the latitude of the Hawaiian islands but about four degrees of longitude to the east; essentially he would now approach the south-westerly islands in the group from the east. Next morning there was the island of Maui in all its glory, for many the jewel of the entire Hawaiian group, dominated by the extinct volcano of Haleakala at 10,000 feet.[9] Cook began running west along the north coast of the island. Canoes started to leave the land to come out the three miles or so to meet them, but before they reached the ships Cook issued his standing orders for the Hawaiian isles. Private trade by the seamen was forbidden, no firearms of any kind were to be taken ashore unless as part of an armed party personally commanded by the captain, and no women were to be allowed on board; Cook explained patiently that this was to prevent venereal disease.[10] However, when the canoes reached them, it became obvious that this was another case of stables and horses; the bloated and inflamed organs they exhibited and about which they complained piteously to the ship's surgeons showed that the disease was already rampant on the island. At the same time, and in apparent contradiction to this, the Hawaiian women who came out in the canoes to hire themselves out to the sailors reacted at first indignantly and later became splenetic with rage when it was explained to them that they were banned. A perfunctory exchange of roots and pigs for nails and iron was all that was possible on this first encounter. Cook made no attempt to land but came close to the shore during the day and then stood off at night. So passed 26–27 November. On the second night he noticed that the current was carrying him to windward, so he decided, literally, to go with the flow. He would ply to windward, get round to the east side of the island and thus have a lee shore, preparatory to finding an anchorage.[11]

The Hawaiians followed them respectfully about a mile astern of the ships, trading with an honesty that led Cook to contrast the 'virtuous merchants' of Maui with the rank thieves of Tahiti.[12] Soon Kahekili, high chief of Maui, came alongside the *Discovery* in his large double canoe and asked to come aboard. Clerke welcomed him to the Great Cabin and loaded him with presents; Kahekili reciprocated with a pig and a surprise offering. When a black cat fell overboard in shark-infested waters, the sailors expected to see it no more, but the men of Maui picked it up and returned it to the ship, giving it to Kahekili to present triumphantly to Clerke; he was rewarded for this with the particular gift of a hatchet.[13] Whether there was genuine inter-island rivalry or whether it was coincidence was uncertain at first, but the sequel was a visit to the *Resolution* by Kalani'opu'u, high chief of Hawaii, the big island. Sixty years old, with a wondrous feather cloak and a helmet of black and yellow feathers, Kalani'opu'u was a legendary warrior in the islands; his one blemish was over-fondness for kava. When he climbed back into his canoe after a couple of hours, he left four 'ambassadors' aboard the *Resolution*, one of whom was the young Kamehameha, who would later rule over the united islands of Hawaii and be perhaps the most famous figure in the islands' history.[14] The envoys explained the situation. Ever since Cook had arrived on Kauai in early 1778, the fame of this demigod and his two great 'seabirds' had spread across the islands (along with venereal disease), and Kalani'opu'u, then engaged in a titanic struggle for mastery with Kahekili, wanted to make sure the chief of Maui had not enlisted these mighty strangers on his side. On 1 December, still in search of a harbour (or so he said), Cook decided to abandon Maui and try his luck on the 'big island' instead. Canoes continued to follow them. Cook's seamen, who loathed sharks and took great delight in catching them and hauling them aboard, were amazed both at the proficiency of the Hawaiians as swimmers and by the fact that they swam around large and dangerous sharks with unconcern.[15]

Having been battered by storms on the way down from Unalaska, the seamen found that the nightmare continued. For nearly seven weeks Cook cruised around the big island of Hawaii in almost continual gales and high seas; he confided to his journal that these were the worst seas he had ever seen in tropical latitudes: 'I have nowhere within the tropics met with so high a sea as we have had since we have been about these islands; it has never been once down, though it frequently shifts three or four points or more.'[16] The obvious question arises: why did he not make landfall? His apologists say that after his experiences at Kauai and Niihau at the beginning of the year, he had no wish to anchor again in another open bay, with a huge surf booming on shore. This makes no sense, for if true it would have prevented him from ever landing. Besides, the evidence does not show Cook conscientiously searching for a safe anchorage. A day-to-day examination of the track of the *Resolution* shows her remaining off the north coast of the island of Hawaii for weeks, constantly zigzagging away to the north, coming in close to the shoreline, then zigzagging away north once again.[17] So why did Cook not make landfall? The idea that he did not want to spread venereal disease does not work, since on his first day off Maui he had seen that it had already spread. If he was not going to find a harbour, why had he come to Hawaii in the first place? Would he not have been better off in Kamchatka? The suspicion arises that there had already been a calamitous breakdown in relations between captain and crew, maybe over issues that did not even find their way into the various journals, and that Cook was punishing them and showing them who really ruled the roost. If so, he was playing a dangerous game, pushing his men to breaking point, and tempting them to mutiny; certainly Cook's actions in the seven weeks off Maui and Hawaii were even more provocative than the behaviour by Bligh that led to the *Bounty* mutiny ten years later. The alternative explanation is that Cook himself had already cracked and scarcely knew what he was doing or why. His actions fulfilled the classic definition of fanaticism by Santayana: redoubling one's efforts after losing sight of one's aim.[18]

Buffeted by high seas and breaking waves, sailing in a Dantesque diabolical circle and led by a captain who seemed to have taken leave of his senses, the seamen and officers could have been forgiven for thinking, to use Fletcher Christian's famous later phrase, that they were in hell. The sensation of being in a chaotic world was reinforced by the clashes between captain and crew which, on a strict reckoning of causality, should have happened *before* Cook's demonstration of absolute power, not after. Cook came close in to shore again on 6 December to trade and obtained enough pork, fruit and roots to last for another five days at sea.[19] Next he returned to his obsession with beer made from sugar cane, insisting that his men drink it even though they loathed it; his motive was to conserve grog for the next season of Arctic exploration. For the seamen this was the last straw. They had not been allowed to land to obtain provisions and were still on the half-rations Cook had ordered in Unalaska after the conflict over the walrus meat; they had not been permitted to have female companionship; they were constantly storm-tossed on a cruel ocean; and now Cook was ordering them to drink this vile decoction. Cook was now perceived as an insane glory-hunter, obsessed with his reputation and, as John Ledyard said, 'wholly influenced by motives of interest, to which he was evidently sacrificing not only the ships, but the health and happiness of the brave men, who were weaving the laurel that was hereafter to adorn his brows'.[20] On 7 December the men drafted a letter protesting against the continued half-rations and the sugar-cane beer. When he received it, Cook exploded with anger against his 'mutinous, turbulent crew' and ordered the issuing of grog to be stopped forthwith. Calling all hands on deck, he addressed them coldly and told them they had a choice: either drink the sugar-cane beer on alternate days and get a supply of grog, or drink none of it and get no grog at all. As for the victuals, Cook ordered the restoration of full rations, lamely claiming to have 'forgotten' that his ordinance was still in force. He gave the men twenty-four hours to accept his beverage proposals. When they continued defiant, Cook replied in kind and had the brandy cask stowed in the hold. As a concession he told the seamen that he was relaxing his proscription on women, but by this time they were so far out to sea that no canoes accompanied them, and hence no Polynesian beauties.[21]

Cook evidently meant the offer of women to be a formal olive branch, an offer that could never be 'cashed' and meanwhile he saved face by refusing to back down on the grog issue. Yet soon he had to come close to shore to obtain more victuals and, even in the continuing rough seas, there were enough hardy female souls prepared to row out in canoes and swarm aboard.[22] Momentarily quietened by the joys of sex, the seamen subsided for a time, while Cook displaced the anger he felt towards his men on to the Admiralty and the corrupt contractors at Deptford. It must be stressed that Cook's ire about the poor state of his ships was entirely rational. Even as the decks pitched and heaved under the tremendous swell, the luckless sailors were forever knotting and splicing ropes, sewing canvas, bending and unbending sails. Everyone had expected a decent period on land in which to make necessary repairs, and now both ships were in a bad state, with vital parts and equipment giving way before the pitiless heaving and roaring of the ocean and the sickening pitching, rolling and corkscrewing of the battered ships.[23] In continuing gales and storms all the deficiencies and botchings of corrupt entrepreneurs in naval dockyards were thrown into dreadful relief, with cordage and canvas clearly substandard, bolt-ropes for the sails of insufficient strength, standing rigging, running rigging and sails of inferior quality, condemned brace blocks having been fitted and, in some ways worst of all, a rotting food supply in stores which the contractors clearly knew would not last even half the journey when they cynically 'supplied' the ship. Finally sickened by the corruption and murderous treachery of the provisioners and the providers of ships' parts,

Cook launched an eloquent attack on the competence of the Navy Board, intended for the eyes of his old friend and patron Hugh Palliser, Comptroller of the Navy, the man ultimately responsible for everything that came out of the naval dockyards.[24] Here was strong proof that Cook had finally snapped. A careful man who had made a career out of deference to his social superiors, Cook was now indicting the British Establishment for incompetence. Everyone knows that, be the accusations never so true and one hundred per cent accurate, the British elite will never tolerate such criticism, which is inevitably 'spun' as proof that the critic is 'unsound', unreliable, treacherous and should never have been given the position in the first place. Almost certainly the truth was that Palliser, instead of doing his duty conscientiously, had been lunched and dined over-liberally by the contractors; there is nothing new under the sun. Yet Palliser, when he read Cook's accusations, reacted in the way typical of the elite: he conceded that some of the equipment given Cook might have been 'accidentally' deficient, but he denied with the emphatic passion born of a guilty conscience that abuse, mismanagement or corruption had entered into the case.[25]

Meanwhile the oceanic nightmare continued. The big island of Hawaii has a triangular shape, and the sharp acute angle formed when the coast running south-east abruptly turns back south-west results in the formidable Cape Kumukahi. On the evening of 18 December Cook attempted to double it, but at 1 a.m. on the morning of the 19th the wind fell and the *Rosolution* was suddenly at the mercy of a giant north-easterly swell carrying her fast towards the land, in rainy darkness with flashes of lightning and peals of thunder. When daylight came the surge and thunder of the surf told him that land was not more than a mile and a half away. Once again Cook was almost supernaturally lucky: at the last minute a breeze sprang up and he was able to swing the *Resolution* away, but not before a heart-stopping moment when the ship's ropes gave way.[26] The escape joined the list of close shaves Cook had experienced; some commentators feel it was the closest he ever came to disaster. Certainly the price of salvation was that both the main-topsail and topgallant sails were split in two. Fortunately, the *Discovery* had been labouring some way in Cook's wake and so escaped the danger. Cook always believed that after a moment of supreme peril one should return to the fray lest one's nerve fail for ever; he made another attempt to double the cape later that day and failed again. He continued to ply, hoping for that shift of the wind that would carry him round the promontory, still trading occasionally in goods and local women when the seas abated long enough (if briefly) for such commerce to take place.[27] On 23 December, once more in the dark hours before dawn, the wind again died away and left him at the mercy of a heavy swell driving towards land. This was not so severe a crisis as that of four days earlier, for there were enough gusts of wind to make the ship manoeuvrable, and he was still some seven miles from the shore. Cook stubbornly plugged away at the task of rounding the cape but on 24 December a terrible storm once again struck him; this time the *Discovery* lost touch with the *Resolution* and Cook did not see her again for thirteen days, in which time the storm blew with undiminished ferocity, piling up huge waves, some of them 70–80 feet high. The one advantage was that the ferocious blow finally allowed Cook to get windward of Kumukahi and he began to sail south-west.[28]

It is hardly surprising that the non-stop stress, coupled with the conflict with the captain over grog, sex and landing rights, should have driven the men close to mutiny. Any hint of defiance on the sugar-cane issue was especially harshly punished, as when one of the *Resolution*'s sailors was given twelve lashes for emptying away a cask of the despised liquor, even though it had clearly gone sour.[29] The nickname Tute and the old references to *heivas* were revived and openly mouthed around the ship, almost certainly in the hearing of officers secretly disaffected themselves, while Trevenen took it upon himself to compose doggerel highly derogatory to the captain. Also whispered below deck was the canard that whereas Cook had turned into a Judge Jeffreys of the high seas no one had ever seen him show a similar harshness towards the Polynesians, who by contrast were virtually allowed to get away with murder.[30] On Christmas Eve Cook announced a double issue of food and grog for the next day but it was the universal opinion that Christmas 1778 was the worst anyone aboard could remember; not only were they plunging up and down in the troughs and crests of the huge Pacific swell but they contrasted the present with the happy Yuletides spent on Kerguelen two years before and Christmas Island just one year ago. Cook did not even deign to make a journal entry for that day, but we learn from Samwell that the *Resolution* was not a happy ship. Finding that their girlfriends were unwilling to make love through being almost permanently seasick in the continuing storm, the seamen improvised their own entertainment which turned into a gigantic donnybrook; one of the Hawaiian 'envoys' still on board went in fear of his life in the ensuing mayhem. Samwell describes the fight:

> Being Christmas Day it was kept by the people according to ancient usage from time immemorial. At night there was a general battle among them between decks and the poor Indian [*sic*] was hemmed in with the thickest of them; one of the gentlemen, seeing him, with great difficulty got him out. The poor fellow was in the utmost terror and apprehension though no one had offered to touch him; as it is natural to suppose, such a scene of uproar

and confusion must strike him, and he no doubt looked upon them all, as a parcel of madmen and was glad to escape from their fury.[31]

It would be just too neat and coincidental if the luckless Hawaiian turned out to be Kamehameha, the future lord of the isles, but the sources do not allow us to reach this tempting conclusion.

The high seas continued, though there was a marginal improvement – gales rather than storms – once they got round Kumukahi. Cook stood away to the east well to sea before coming back close to land off the Kau desert, about halfway along the south-western coast of Hawaii, still hoping that Clerke would be able to join him and therefore deliberately slowing his own progress. Eventually, by the year's end he concluded that Clerke had opted to sail anti-clockwise around the island and would probably link up with him on the west coast. The New Year came in with a hard rain,[32] and it was not until 5 January that Cook rounded the southernmost point of the island – the cape known as Ka Lae – and started slowly working up the west coast. Now at last there was respite from the persistent winds, huge swells and high seas that had followed them all the way from Maui and, to complete the upturn in fortunes, on the 6th the *Discovery* joined them. Clerke had shown himself a brilliant seaman. He had not opted to go to leeward, as Cook had thought; for five days he cruised around the area where they had been separated in the storm, then had gone even farther east into the ocean than Cook had to get round Kumukahi, and, two days behind the *Resolution* on the south-westerly run from Kumukahi to Ka Lae, had finally caught up with the sister ship. Clerke begged Cook to land and encouraged him to call a meeting of senior officers to explain why he had stayed so long at sea. Cook argued that he had to make their supplies of iron last, that if he landed immediately the men would waste it all on paying for women and they would end up short of food. At the same time, occasional trade with the locals for food from canoes, instead of bulk purchase on land, meant that fruit and vegetables would not rot, so there would be no wastage.[33] Finally, he had been made aware of the impact on local subsistence economies of demands for food for more than 200 men. Given that they could not return to Unalaska until next season, Cook had therefore to limit the time he spent on shore. None of this was really convincing when set against the dangers of high seas and shipwreck, to say nothing of possible mutiny. The logic of Cook's arguments pointed inescapably to the conclusion that he should have spent the winter in Kamchatka. There was clearly some other factor at play which Cook either did not want to divulge or which, if it was an unconscious actuating factor, he was unaware of. Whatever Cook's original motives for staying at sea, even he admitted that the time had now come to make landfall. Both ships were in a desperate state of disrepair, the

Resolution had sprung another leak, while the *Discovery* was so riddled with leaks that Clerke dared not wash down her decks.[34] Although Cook was fairly well provisioned with emergency rations, because the trading had ceased in the gales and storms both vessels were by now acutely short of fresh water. The problem was that they could now find no suitable anchorages and, on the rare occasions that the intrepid Bligh, Cook's appointed troubleshooter, found plausible stopping places, they turned out to be waterless, or the water was brackish. It took eleven days from Cook's reunion with Clerke and the decision to make landfall to the discovery of a suitable haven. Progress up the coast was also agonisingly slow; adverse winds and currents at one point drove the ships back almost the whole way to Ka Lae.[35]

At last, on 15 January, there were some glimmers of hope. The sun came out, the canoes sortied from the coast in sympathy, and on the 16th Bligh finally found what they were looking for: good anchorage, fresh water, friendly people. On the morning of 17 January Cook anchored 400 yards from the shore in Kealakekua Bay. This bay, the best anchorage on the western side of the island, protected from all storms except the infrequent south-westerly ones, was, like so many locations on the Hawaiian islands, breathtakingly beautiful. In the background loomed the volcanic bulk of Mauna Loa (Long Mountain) and the bay was 'bracketed' by black obsidian rock long since spewed out by Mauna Loa. The cliff rising from the bay was a sheer 1,000-foot wall of lava, topped with *pili* grass, half a mile wide, and plunging so sharply to the water that there was no real shoreline; the cliff itself was a geologist's delight, separated as it was into multi-layered bands of black, blue-grey, rust and chocolate strata, pitted with lava tubes. The bay was not large: the distance from Cook Point in the north to Palemano Point in the south was little more than a mile. In the north-western corner of the bay was the royal residence of Kaawaloa and, only 300 yards away was the great sacrificial centre or *heiau* of Hikiau, hard by the modern village of Napoopoo.[36] The *Resolution* anchored near Kaawaloa while the *Discovery* came to rest farther inside the bay close to the *heiau*. In the limpid tranquillity of the bay the sailors could peer 100 feet down into the water. Cook scarcely had time to take any of this in, as his arrival created a sensation among the locals. About 10,000 people in no less than 1,500 canoes came out to meet them. Cook wrote in amazement: 'I have nowhere in this sea seen such a number of people assembled at one place. Besides those in the canoes all the shore of the bay was covered with people and hundreds were swimming about the ships like shoals of fish.'[37] Ledyard added his impressions:

> The beach, the surrounding rocks, the tops of houses, the branches of trees and the adjacent hills were all covered, and the shouts of joy and admiration

proceeding from the sonorous voices of the men confused with the shriller exclamations of the women dancing and clapping their hands, the overset-ting of canoes, cries of the children, goods on float, and hogs that were brought to market squealing formed one of the most tumultuous and the most curious prospects that can be imagined.[38]

The festival atmosphere continued. Women swarmed aboard the two ships and began coupling avidly with the sex-starved sailors, under decks or some-times in plain view; observers described the scenes as Babylonian in their pagan joy of copulation. One female, said to be the most beautiful Polynesian girl anyone had ever seen, gazed at herself in a mirror and provoked sympa-thetic laughter when she exclaimed over her own pulchritude.[39] The few seamen who remained on duty to unbend the sails and strike yards and topmasts found themselves unable to work the ropes because of the throng of Hawaiians who had clambered up the rigging; to make any progress they had to throw the intruders into the sea, which was accepted with hilarity as a great game. Those thrown overboard happily swam alongside the vessels, some-times for as long as five hours, inexhaustible, once again displaying that amazing prowess in swimming that had already astonished the Europeans.[40] The weight of extra humans on the _Discovery_ was so great that she heeled over and might have capsized had not two important chiefs arrived and ordered their people off, personally hurling into the sea any who did not obey the orders with sufficient rapidity. The two chiefs were called Kanina and Palea, the latter a significant personality who was the male lover of Kalani'opu'u. He introduced a small, wizened and emaciated priest named Koa'a, an ugly red-eyed creature showing the serious physical effects of habitual overindulgence in kava. Koa'a treated Cook with reverence, wrapped a length of red bark-cloth around his shoulders and gave him gifts of pigs, coconuts, fruit and root vegetables.[41] Cook invited the trio of Kanina, Palea and Koa'a to lunch (dinner in the eighteenth century) in the Great Cabin, then set out with them in the afternoon, taking King and an unarmed party, on an escorted trip to the _heiau_ of Hikiau, a more elaborate structure than the Tahitian _marae_. The 'temple' was made of stone, 40 yards long, 20 yards wide and 14 feet high, with a flat top adorned by the skulls of enemy warriors from Maui. On the way to the _heiau_ heralds called out that 'Erono' or 'Orono' was coming. As Cook passed, all the locals except the priests prostrated themselves before him.[42]

The ceremony on the 17th, which Beaglehole rightly describes as 'long and rather tiresome', consisted of a series of prayers and chants, hog sacrifices and the offering of a large piece of red cloth to a semicircle of images, culminating in Koa'a's prostrating himself in front of the central image which, though only

three feet tall and thus half the height of the others, was clearly the most important one. The crux of the ceremony was that Koa'a also required Cook to prostrate himself before the image, which he did. To round things off, the visitors
were offered kava and putrid hog. Cook gagged on this and could not swallow
a morsel, even when Koa'a chewed it for him to 'tenderise' it. All the way back
to the ships Cook was again acclaimed with cries of 'Erono' or 'Orono'.[43] The
captain had evidently been recognised as an *atua* or semi-divine being; this is
not the same as the European conception of God, for high chiefs were also *atuas*
by virtue of their *mana*. In other words, Polynesian cosmology did not draw a
hard and fast distinction between this world and the next, mortality and immortality, immanence and transcendence, the natural and the supernatural, and thus
the Judaeo-Christian connotation of God, and probably the Islamic and Hindu
ones as well, offered no guidance to exactly what the status was that had been
conferred on Cook that day.[44] One function of an *atua* was to be able to declare
objects and locations *tapu* and to be exempt from the prescriptions of normal
tapus. This was extremely useful to Cook. With the cooperation of Palea and
Koa'a, he was able to have a walled-off field near the *heiau* declared *tapu*, so
that he could erect the tents of his shore party and set up an observatory
without fear of theft.[45] James King was in charge of the observatory and
Molesworth Phillips of the party of marines who stood guard, but there was
nothing for them to do. Nothing could induce the ordinary people to breach
tapu. Since it was impossible to taboo the ships, as that would have stopped all
trade, Cook persuaded Palea to do a daily clearout each morning of the women
who had spent the night on board in the arms of their seagoing beloveds; had
they remained on board during the day, the normal work of the vessel –
cleaning, caulking, overhauling, repairing – could not have been done. There
was nothing Cook could do about the alarming daily 'inventory shrinkage' of
iron and nails. So many nails were removed from the bodywork of the ship by
the sailors – to pay for their nightly fornication – that it is a wonder the two
ships did not simply collapse. The Hawaiians joined in this pilferage with gusto,
even devising special tools like claw hammers with which they could prise away
the treasured nails from the ship's sheathing and elsewhere.[46]

   The cries of 'Erono' or 'Orono' by the locals was the dialect version of Lono,
the god of light, peace and fertility. Since Cook had been acclaimed as Lono, it
is important to establish exactly what that meant, for it may have had a crucial
significance in the unfolding of events over the following month. Elsewhere in
Polynesia, Cook, his officers and his scientists had all tended, mistakenly, to
think that religion was unimportant, or that it had once been important but no
longer was.[47] On Hawaii, though, it was obvious that religion was important –
the sheer size of the priesthood indicated that – and the ceremonies even had a

certain vague resemblance to European rituals.[48] The original Polynesian mythology, found in its purest form on the Society Islands, envisaged four main gods: Ta'aroa, the god of the sea, Tnane, god of the forests, Tu, god of war, and Ro'o, god of agriculture and the weather. In time, the notion of a supreme deity, Oro (originally the son of Ta'aroa), evolved, and Oro became a kind of Polynesian Zeus.[49] On the Hawaiian islands the Oro cult never took hold and the four original deities, albeit with the slightly altered names Kanaloa, Kane, Ku and Lono), held sway. One of these, Lono, was the god of peace, light and fertility, roughly the equivalent of the Tahitian Ro'o. Lono had attributes rather like God the Father in Christian theology: that is to say, he had different manifestations and could incarnate himself in avatars, not very different from the doctrines of the Trinity and Incarnation in mainstream Christianity, which some observers thought was the best makeshift analogy for Hawaiian religion.[50] Many legendary figures in Hawaiian history were thought to be incarnations of Lono or, as they were usually termed, Lono-i-ka-makahiki, following the analogy of God the Son. *Atuas* were generally held to be avatars of Lono, and most high chiefs were regarded as *atuas*; this was not primarily a theological point but it reinforced political legitimacy, just as concepts such as the divine right of kings or papal infallibility did in Europe. When Cook first appeared at Kauai in early 1778 and the people prostrated themselves, they were making it clear that they regarded him as an *atua* in this sense; which is very different from the bald statement, sometimes advanced without qualification, that the Hawaiians regarded Cook as a god.[51]

When Cook arrived off Kauai in January 1778, his advent coincided with the annual 'feast' of Lono, lasting four months roughly from mid-September to mid-January. All the signs were there: the appearance of the Pleiades, the wondrous seabird in which Cook/Lono travelled, the powerful sticks that thundered. Cook's very regime of sexual abstinence helped, for the priests (as mentioned) had devised sexual intercourse as the acid test of whether the travellers were gods or men. The fact that his followers were men did not preclude Cook's being an avatar of Lono; the only thing that raised doubts was the venereal disease the strangers left in their wake – hardly something a god such as Lono would visit on them – and the killing of a man, which seemed more redolent of Ku, the god of war.[52] Nevertheless, on balance, Cook's earlier visit seemed to fit the Lono matrix. The sailors told the Hawaiians that they had come from Tahiti, and in the traditional myth of Lono he had sailed away from Hawaii to Kahiki (Tahiti) after striking his wife in a fit of jealousy, promising that he would return some day.[53] Now, on the second visit, there were even stronger circumstantial pointers. Once again he had arrived in the Makahiki season, when warfare was forbidden, hard work banned, games and sports held, censuses held and taxes collected. Lono's symbol was a long staff bearing a banner of *tapa* attached to a crosspiece and thus very like the yard of a ship's mast. Traditionally, when Lono came there would be terrible storms, and these had duly manifested themselves during the terrible seven weeks from late November to 17 January. The legend also said that when Lono returned, he would sail slowly round the big island of Hawaii and come to haven at Kealakekua Bay – exactly what Cook had done.[54] Cook's reception and the veneration shown to him at the induction ceremony at the *heiau*, the *kapu moe*, the sacred obeisance made only to an *atua*, was a special *tapu*, applied only to semi-divine beings. And, after all, if Cook was not being recognised as an avatar of Lono at the *heiau* ceremony, what was its point or purpose? It was quite evident that he was not being given the secular authority of a high chief of the islands. All in all, there is no reason to doubt Clerke's assertion to the Admiralty that Cook was greeted as a being more than human;[55] to say that the Hawaiians regarded him as a god is to indulge in unnecessary semantic confusion. One pointer that Cook was not regarded as a god in a European or mainstream theistic sense comes from Hawaiian attitudes to Clerke. At first they treated him also as an *atua* but Clerke, who despised such attitudes as mumbo-jumbo and disapproved of Cook's playing along with it, expressly requested Palea and Kanina to get their people to desist from treating him with reverence, which they did.[56]

Cook as avatar of Lono also had a political dimension, and this was very complex. When it is asserted that Cook either was or was not regarded as a god by the Hawaiians, one has reluctantly to wheel out the oldest weapon in the armoury of linguistic philosophy: which Hawaiians? All of them? The masses? The elite? The clerisy? As already mentioned, there was a struggle in Hawaii *within* the elite, between priests and chiefs and between the elite at the top of a narrowly tapering pyramid and the vast mass of people at the bottom. To what extent the priesthood really believed in Cook as Lono is debatable – probably some did and some did not – but they could all see the political advantages of playing along with the powerful stranger. A further complication was that the priests of Ku had different aims and aspirations from the priests of Lono.[57] Furthermore, in terms of class conflict the cult of Lono was associated with the political interests of the common people and that of Ku with those of the elite. Mythology said that the priests of Lono were descended from the aboriginal inhabitants of the island who had been defeated by a later wave of immigrants, who in turn provided descendants who kept alive the cult of Ku. The four months of the Makahiki therefore represented in some ways an extended carnival of the Lord of Misrule. All associated with Ku had to keep a low profile and even to some extent remain under house arrest during this period. As has been well said: 'It was as though, in old England, a season when the Saxons had to withdraw and defer to the gods of the Celts.'[58] Cook as Lono had dangers for the elite, for it seemed to associate the strangers with their powerful weapons with the masses and, potentially, with revolution. One of the interesting aspects of the recondite ceremony at the *heiau* that Cook attended, and of which he was totally unaware, was that the captain exchanged names with the absent Kalani'opu'u and thus shared his *mana*; this was 'compensation' so that Cook was also aligned with the elite and shared almost a blood-brotherhood with the high chief. Since avatars of Lono and *atuas* were thought to share family connections in a mystic, non-biological kinship, this made perfect sense.[59]

Yet another dimension to the politics of Lono was later provided by Kamehameha, shrewd, far-sighted and Machiavellian. In January–February 1779 Kamahamema distanced himself from Cook and formed close bonds with Clerke, precisely because Clerke had disavowed Lono status and was thus a useful ally for the devotees of Ku, who represented elite interests. Those close to Cook noticed this arm's-length policy by the young Hawaiian chief and resented it. King particularly disliked Kamehameha while Samwell thought he had a 'clownish, blackguard appearance'.[60] Kamahameha, with the patience of a chess player or a watchmaker, was playing a long game. To use the language of political science, he had spotted how a ruler of Hawaii could be truly 'hegemonic', appealing to people across the barriers of caste and strata and building a trans-class basis for his future power. The trick was to fuse the actual power of the Ku faction with the symbolic power of the Lono devotees, and one obvious way to do this was to use the legend of Cook as Lono. With Lono/Cook standing for peace and Ku for war, a synoptic vision of a unified Hawaiian society could be constructed. The marriage of symbolic and actual, dignified and efficient, political and theological, power and mystical obfuscation could be achieved by a chief clever enough to employ political camouflage.[61] From an early stage Kamehameha had spotted that the key to dominance in the Hawaiian islands was the technological edge Cook's weapons provided. Supremacy in warfare had hitherto been impossible, for no island chief had the technical superiority firearms would provide and the ability to wage a short but utterly successful military campaign. Long periods of armed warfare with primitive weapons simply foundered on the brute fact that Hawaii lived close to subsistence level. Fields and crops had to be planted, so wars always had to be suspended before a decisive encounter could be fought.[62] The weapons introduced by Cook, and, more especially, those who came after him to Hawaii, enabled Kamehameha to carry out his grand design, all the time appropriating the Cook-as-Lono myth as an overarching ideology of island unification; twenty years later only Kauai still held out against him.[63]

Unaware of all these nuances and complexities Cook and his men for a week basked in an unwonted atmosphere of daily cooperation and no thieving except for the nails. Palea proved invaluable, for he broke up fights among the Hawaiians vying for the Europeans' attention and punished any major thefts. When one man stole a large butcher's cleaver, he chased him in a canoe and recovered it. If his compatriots got out of hand or proved rambunctious, Palea would pelt them with stones. Once, just after he had repeated a stern admonition about not stealing, he caught a man blatantly defying him by making off with a forbidden item from the *Discovery*; he was so angry that he dragged him underwater and drowned him.[64] It is perhaps significant of Kamehameha's concentration on Clerke rather than Cook that Palea based himself on board the *Discovery*. Palea was the agent of Kalani'opu'u, whose chief counsellor was Kamehameha; the less important Kanina did the same job aboard the *Resolution*. Both men were quite obviously intelligence agents, asking King and the other officers endless questions, not just about the working of the ships and their armaments but also about the population of England, its number of soldiers and the nature of European warfare.[65] On 19 January both men left the ships to receive further orders from Kalani'opu'u, who had used the enforced layoff during Makahiki to carry his wars over to Maui, though without success. There were further rituals involving pig sacrifice and red cloth to enhance Cook's status and, whenever he went ashore, a priest preceded him calling out the name of Lono, obliging the people to prostrate themselves.[66] When Palea returned two days later, the emphasis on Clerke rather than Cook was even more pronounced. To Clerke's visible embarrassment, Palea gave him the privileged red cloth and pigs treatment. Evidently Kalani'opu'u and Kamahemeha had decided to escalate their policy of playing Clerke off against Cook, perhaps to identify Clerke as a Ku man rather than a Lono figure. What this portended became clear on 24 January when it was suddenly announced that Kalani'opu'u would be arriving shortly at the bay and that the festival of Makahiki was over. The immediate consequence was that the whole of Kealakekua Bay was placed under *tapu*.[67]

The pleasant tenor of the past week was shattered. Because of the *tapu* there were no further deliveries of vegetables and, more seriously from the sailors' point of view, all the Hawaiian women left the ships, abandoning their lovers to celibacy. As always, many of the men tried to get ashore to meet up with their sweethearts outside the tabooed area. To make matters worse, one of them had been expressly banned from sexual intercourse because he had gonorrhoea; his flight constituted a double disobedience. Cook brought the reprobates back and gave twelve lashes to three men found absent without official leave; the man with the venereal disease was given twenty-four.[68] Cook was certainly becoming harsher in his attitude to punishment but he was dispassionate, unbiased and equitable in his draconian severity. Hawaiians and crew alike got the same punishment, the effect of which was to enhance Cook's reputation among the islanders as 'Lono the just'. Another man he had to punish was a gunner who hit Palea when he drove off some renegade Hawaiians trying to breach the *tapu*.[69] It was the evening of the 25th before Kalani'opu'u finally put in an appearance. Cook had been told that 'the chief of chiefs' was coming and expected someone he had never met before. To his surprise he found that Kalani'opu'u was the chief he had met off Maui two months before, the same tall, 60-year-old, red-eyed kava addict he had found so unprepossessing the first time round; the confusion may have arisen because Cook heard the man's name the first time round as Terreeoboo.[70] Kalani'opu'u explained that Makahiki was now over, and that the cult of Ku would take over. There was an exchange of gifts followed by dinner in the Great Cabin with the high chief and his family. Next day there was a tour of the observatory, after which the chief cemented the entente by taking off his feathered cloak and helmet and putting them on Cook, symbolising that they were now brothers. Shortly afterwards the *tapu* was lifted. There were further ceremonial gift exchanges over the next few days and Kalani'opu'u had his son stay overnight on the *Resolution* to demonstrate that the youth now had a second father.[71]

After the lifting of the *tapu*, the Europeans again enjoyed a halcyon period, watching boxing and wrestling matches (mindful of their bruising experiences on Tonga, they declined all exhortations to take part), trying unsuccessfully to ascend Mauna Loa, playing draughts and generally being treated hospitably by the locals, who fed them as they went on hikes and rambles and volunteered to carry lumber back to the ships when the woodcutters had felled trees.[72] Once Cook was confident he had all the provisions he needed for the return to Unalaska, he relaxed his former trade restrictions. Samwell was amazed to see young children playing fearlessly in the waves as giant rollers roared into the bay, and provided the first known description of surfing: 'We saw with astonishment young boys and girls about nine or ten years of age playing amid such tempestuous waves that the hardiest of our seamen would have trembled to face, as to be involved in them among the rocks, on which they broke with a tremendous noise, they could look upon as no other than certain death.'[73] In the two weeks since landing on 17 January the visitors learned a vast amount about Hawaiian culture and folkways. Samwell was stupefied by Kalani'opu'u's bisexuality. His wife had no objection to the many concubines he had around him, and in addition there were the *aikane* or male lovers, plus attendants whose job it was to masturbate the ruler if he felt too lazy to indulge in full intercourse. Samwell was bemused by homosexuality: 'This, however strange it may appear, is fact, as we learnt from frequent enquiries about this curious custom, and it is an office that is esteemed honourable among them and they have frequently asked us on seeing a handsome young fellow if he was not an Ikany [*sic*] to some of us.'[74] The differential attitudes of the European observers to 'same-sex vice' was fascinating. Clerke was disgusted, referring to 'this infernal practice', and King thought it perverse in the sense that Hawaiian oligarchs seemed to reserve their keenest feelings for other men instead of women, rather as the Ancient Greeks had done. Ledyard took a detached view, but reported violent prejudice against 'queer' sexuality from the below-decks squad.[75] All agreed that homosexuality was used as a means of restraining and harnessing women, and it seemed connected with what to the Europeans was the oddest thing about Hawaii: the apparent absence of marriage. The elite took the same cynical, pragmatic, functional view of wedlock that was common among the eighteenth-century oligarchs in England, but it seemed unknown in the lower classes. The amateur sociologists among the European diarists wondered how society could operate without the social cement of marriage.[76]

As January merged with February cracks started to appear on an apparently tranquil surface. Samwell was disturbed to find that the seamen, far from requiting the kindness and hospitality of the locals, treated them with contempt and routine brutality; on one occasion one of Cook's stewards seriously wounded a Hawaiian man simply because he did not move out of the way fast enough; imagine the uproar, Samwell added, if the roles had been reversed.[77] Cook's woodcutters displayed gross insensitivity by cutting down the fence around the *heiau* at Haiku. King, in charge of the detail, claimed that permission had been given by the priests, but this is flatly contradicted in an eyewitness account by Ledyard.[78] Bit by bit the visitors were making themselves more unwelcome. In a curious way the death on 1 February of a popular able seaman, William Watman, diminished Cook's prestige, since it seemed that this avatar of Lono was powerless to prevent the passing of his own men.[79] On his deathbed Watman had asked to be buried on the *heiau*. The priest Keli'ikea, who had assisted Koa'a at Cook's 'Lono' ceremony there on the 17th, agreed. He and his priests performed an elaborate ceremony of burial while Cook's marines formed a guard of honour and a fifer played a funeral march. Samwell claimed that Cook set up a board at the foot of one of the images in the *heiau* which read HIC JACET GULIELMUS WATMAN, though some historians claim that the epitaph was a product of his own imagination.[80] When Kalani'opu'u heard about the ceremony, he was angry and thought the priests had stepped outside their bounds. By now he was coming to think that the presence of Cook on the island simply strengthened the hand of the priest-hood in their perennial power struggle with the chiefs and oligarchs. More pragmatically, he was becoming concerned about the impact on fragile food supplies of an extended visit by 200 voracious sailors. It is not surprising that on 2 February he asked Cook pointedly when he was planning to leave the island.[81] Cook said it would be very soon, at which the chief looked pleased. To speed his visitors on their way, he called on his followers to make a generous farewell present of food, clothes and feathers.

By the time the ships were ready to leave on 4 February, the atmosphere had soured noticeably. Whether it was because of the ending of Makahiki, which meant that their inherent belligerence no longer had to be restrained, or simply because of the many insults they had hitherto endured from the seamen, the Hawaiian labourers, thus far compliant, turned nasty. When asked to haul the rudder across the bay, they did so but mimicked the sailors and jeered at them. The taunts turned to fisticuffs, the fistic encounters to stone-throwing, and soon there was a general melee.[82] Clerke, the target of Kalani'opu's special regard, ruined the entente by claiming that the *Discovery*'s jolly boat was missing, accusing the Hawaiians of theft and seizing a number of canoes against the boat's return. Palea intervened and tried to calm matters but Clerke treated him brusquely, regarding him as the official face of the malefactors. After a series of interviews with likely culprits Palea returned and told Clerke that he could swear on his honour no Hawaiians had taken the boat. Clerke was unconvinced and swore at him angrily, only to become redfaced a few moments later as he admitted that the jolly boat had been found under the bows of a ship; the carpenter's mate had used the craft, then stowed it in an unusual place without telling anyone.[83] A dignified but angry Palea went away to report the incident to Kalani'opu'u. Clerke's fall from grace in Hawaiian eyes was doubtless the genesis of an extraordinary request the high chief next made to Cook: that King be allowed to stay on as Cook's ambassador (here we surely detect the hand of Kamehameha). Cook replied that he could not allow 'his son' (which was how the Hawaiians imagined King's relationship to Cook) to stay behind as he was needed for the great voyage north but that, on his (Cook's) return to Hawaii next year, he would probably grant the request. Here Cook was being disingenuous: he had no intention of returning to Hawaii after his quest for the Northwest Passage.[84] Cook then stowed all the produce brought to him by Kalani'opu'u and signed off with a massive firework display.

On the morning of 4 February the *Resolution* and *Discovery* stood out of the bay and headed north towards Maui, where Cook intended to investigate the western side of the island. He would then top up his water casks on Kauai before heading north to Unalaska. The ships were full of local women, who had decided to stay with their lovers until the last moment, confident they could get back home from Maui or even from Kauai. It was almost impossible, it seemed, for Cook to sail between any islands in Polynesia without having a local celebrity of some kind on board, and this time the 'guest' was Koa'a who had unexpectedly announced he wanted to visit Britain and was thus renaming himself 'Britanee'. Koa'a had evidently never ventured far from shore, for the giant swells the ships encountered in the Alenuihaha Channel between Hawaii and Maui terrified him; he made secret plans to jump ship at the earliest opportunity. This channel had the reputation of being one of the roughest passages in the Pacific, and it lived up to its reputation. The gales which had dogged Cook all around the Hawaiian islands struck again, first squalls, then a hard gale, finally a full storm on 6 February. Thrown around their bunks like eggs in a tin, the seamen had little time or enthusiasm for sexual intercourse with their violently seasick girlfriends.[85] Having ridden this out with difficulty, yet still managing to pick up some storm-tossed local fishermen who would have been doomed otherwise, Cook hove to off the coast of Maui and sent Bligh ashore in a cutter to look for water; Koa'a went with him, landed, and was seen no more.[86] Meanwhile on 8 February Cook's men investigated the storm damage and what they found alarmed them. Once again the shoddy workmanship of Deptford returned like a spectre to haunt them. The base of the foremast on the *Resolution* had shifted off the plate holding it to the hull because it was badly rotten. With the foremast sprung, Cook needed to make landfall for extensive repairs. On the 'devil you know' principle he elected to return to Kealakekua Bay. King had serious misgivings. He had seen signs of increasing hostility in their last few days on the big island, with familiarity and the long stopover starting to breed contempt, and he had seen the nasty gleam in Kalani'opu'u's eyes when Cook turned down his request for a residence by King. It seemed to the perceptive lieutenant that there was a latent hostility on the island that was only just contained by the authority of the autocratic chiefs; if they ever changed their attitude to the Europeans, this would mean serious trouble.[87]

The return passage to Kealakekua Bay was made dejectedly through more gales, one of which came close to wrecking the ships off Keahole Point, the westernmost tip of Hawaii island. On the evening of 10 February they were off the bay again in fading light, so Cook decided to wait until morning before moving into anchorage. The ships were immediately spotted, and visitors came out to meet them. Priests climbed aboard the *Resolution* while the *Discovery* was dignified by the visit of no less a personage than Kamehameha, who brought his retinue with him and stayed the night on board ship, closeted with one of his male lovers. Next morning Cook resumed his former anchorage. The priests gave them permission to set up a shore camp and observatory once more, though the officers thought it ominous that, in contrast to their previous arrival, there was no one to greet them on the beach. Ledyard wrote: 'Our return to this bay was as disagreeable to us as it was to the inhabitants, for we were reciprocally tired of each other. They had been oppressed and were weary of our prostituted alliance, and we were aggrieved by the consideration of wanting the provisions and refreshments of the country.'[88] The absence of people on the shoreline was explained by a *tapu* recently ordained by Kalani'opu'u. Although most of the officers were depressed and apprehensive, the irrepressible Samwell struck an optimistic note, garnished by a tag from Virgil which he might almost have appropriated from the *Aeneid*-loving Johann Forster: 'It is three years today [10 February] since the two ships were put in commission . . . though we have still a long prospect before us and an arduous undertaking in hand, yet when we consider that the man who is to lead us through it we all agree that "*Nil desperandum Teucro Duce et Auspice Teucro.*" '[89] In retrospect, never has such a Panglossian sentiment seemed less appropriate, as Lono's next four days would prove.

SKETCH
of
KARAKAKOOA BAY.

Lat 19.28 N. Lon. 204.0 E.

N. The dotted Line shews the Extent of the Foul ground

CHAPTER SEVENTEEN

Tragedy on Kealakekua Beach

FROM 11 to 13 February Cook's men worked hard to unstep the *Resolution*'s foremast, carry it ashore and set it up ready for the carpenters and sailmakers. Cook asked the local priests if they could pronounce a *tapu* on an area on the shore where the observatory and sailmakers' house would be built; they obliged willingly. Yet on the morning of the 12th Kalani'opu'u arrived, evidently angry. He berated the priests for granting the *tapu* at Cook's request, then stormed on board the ships, bent on confrontation. He was on the *Resolution* in the morning and the *Discovery* in the afternoon, questioning, querying, probing. Gone was all the earlier affability. Testily he asked Cook why he had returned despite his solemn promise not to. Had he not been simply trifling with the people of Hawaii? 'He had amused them with lies that when he went away he took his farewell of him and said he did not know he should ever come again.'[1] Actually, though this was probably an accurate summary of Cook's intentions, the chief was putting words into his mouth; when he had asked for King as a resident envoy, Cook had said that was a possibility for 1780. Cook told him his mast was broken and that he needed to return to repair it. Kalani'opu'u seemed unable to grasp that a ship could move only with sails and for that it needed a mast; presumably his point was that an avatar of Lono should not be dependent on the banal laws of mechanics and physics. He kept repeating 'What brought you back?', unable to form any 'notion of our distress or what was the matter with our mast'.[2] It was plain from the chief's body language that he suspected Cook of duplicity and of evil intentions towards him. The easy compliance of the priests annoyed him, for this seemed yet another notch in the ratcheting increase of their power under Cook's aegis. Beyond that, for 'Lono' to appear in the season of Ku could mean only that the white men intended to ally themselves with the common people in bloody revolution against the elite. The ultimate horror was that Cook might be intending to stay on Hawaii permanently. From that moment Kalani'opu'u decided on a campaign of harassment against his unwelcome visitors. Yet to lull them into complacency, he lifted the *tapu*. For a few joyful hours, as canoes once again thronged the harbour with hogs and fruit to sell, it seemed as though the good old days of January had returned.[3]

The 13th of February revealed the reality. Not only were the Hawaiians acting in a high-handed way, asking sky-high prices for their goods, but they were belligerent and haughty. Even worse, an epidemic of thievery began, the worst the Europeans had experienced in all their time in Polynesia. As Beaglehole puts it: 'The propensity to mischief was also strong, as if the return had released some instinct in the people that had hitherto been pent up, something like the devilry that had made the Tongans, after a while, their awe surmounted, throw stones at working parties and laugh among the bushes.'[4] Among the many thefts that day was a concerted effort to steal the armourer's tongs from the *Discovery*, which became a fetish for the thieves. One man caught trying to steal them was tied to the main shrouds and flogged with forty lashes, a would-be exemplary punishment that seemed to produce no effect at all.[5] The tension that day was palpable, and the next serious incident was an assault on a water-gathering party. A large party of Hawaiians started throwing stones down a slope on to seamen drawing water from a well, and then rolled larger rocks down the hill. When this was reported to Cook, he ordered that the marines should in future fire ball instead of shot; the aim was deadly fire, designed to kill or maim their tormentors.[6] That afternoon around five o'clock Palea came to visit the *Discovery*. While he was aboard, there was another attempt on the tongs, this time successful. A Hawaiian seized them while the watch was distracted and leapt into the sea, where an accomplice was waiting in a canoe. By the time Clerke realised what was happening and ordered his men to open fire, the canoe was out of range. Clerke ordered his master Thomas Edgar to give chase in the cutter. Edgar chose the first three men to hand, one of whom was George Vancouver, but in his rush to give chase neglected to take any firearms. Palea told Clerke not to worry as he could get the tongs back, but Clerke suspected that his apparently generous offer masked the fact that Palea was himself the mastermind behind the theft. Palea's real motive was to make sure he was not held on board the *Discovery* on suspicion. Reckoning that there was nothing to lose, Clerke let him go on his way.[7]

Meanwhile Cook was ashore with King, supervising the mast repairs. Hearing gunfire, they ran to the water's edge to see what the matter was. Seeing a canoe heading pell-mell for the shore, Cook, along with King and two other men, started running along the strand to try to intercept the canoe; their other men were told to follow along the shoreline in the pinnace. The thieves beat Cook's land-based party to the shore, landed in a sandy cove, and made off inland. Cook and his two men gave chase but were given the runaround by local 'guides' and soon gave up. Next Edgar, approaching the cove in the cutter, saw another canoe approaching, which handed over not just the tongs but a chisel, and a stolen water cask no one had yet realised was missing. Edgar was the wrong man for this job. A hard-drinking firebrand, who spent most of his time arguing violently with Clerke,[8] he may even have been selected by his captain for this task simply to put him in his place. If so, it was a serious error of judgement. The foolish Edgar should have been glad to retrieve the stolen items and called it a day but, possibly envious of the many assignments Cook had given to Bligh, his opposite number on the *Resolution*, he decided this was his big chance. Determined to make a name for himself, he confiscated the canoe.[9] At this moment Palea arrived as if by magic and told Edgar that the canoe was his property and it could not be removed; this was a virtual admission that he was the brains behind the theft. Edgar insisted that he had to take the canoe, but Palea seized it and for a few moments the two men were engaged in an unseemly tug-of-war. By this time a crowd of Hawaiians had gathered. When one of the men from the pinnace struck Palea on the head, the crowd started throwing stones. This was serious, for these 'stones' were one-pound lumps of lava that could inflict very grave injuries. Edgar, Vancouver and the men in the pinnace were forced to back off. So alarmed indeed were the pinnace men that they swam to the shelter of some rocks, where they were picked up by the cutter. The unfortunate Edgar could not go with them as he could not swim, and dutifully Vancouver stayed by his side. While Vancouver tried to climb into the pinnace, Edgar, knee deep in water, struggled towards some rocks, hoping to get out of range of the flying missiles. A burly Hawaiian got hold of a broken oar and tried to bash Edgar with it; Vancouver jumped out of the pinnace to ward off the blow and was hit instead.[10] Another Hawaiian then smashed a surfboard over Edgar's head. Palea ordered his men to stop. Like the sorcerer's apprentice transfixed by the returning magus, they did so. Palea then told Edgar and Vancouver that if they valued their lives, they should take the pinnace and be gone.[11]

By this time the pinnace was too badly smashed to row, and besides there were no oars. Palea left, promising to return with some. Immediately on his departure the stone-throwing began again. Edgar made another of his foolish decisions, this time plunging into the hostile crowd, in pursuit of Cook, or so he said. Vancouver, taking the more sensible decision to stay put until Palea returned, had to weather the storm. The Hawaiians attacked again, knocked him over and ransacked the boat. Soon a struggling Edgar was brought back, the captive of a trio of Hawaiians. Suddenly Palea reappeared, with two broken oars in his hands. Again he exhorted the two Europeans to leave if they valued their lives, urging them to do the best with the broken oars. Edgar and Vancouver signalled to the cutter, which had been lying out of range of the stones, the cutter came in under a flag of truce, took them aboard and departed for the *Discovery*, towing the shattered pinnace behind them.[12] On the way back they put in to shore and reported to Cook, who was now in Kakooa village, having abandoned the quest for the thieves. Edgar made his report and received an angry response from the captain, who was furious with him for the loss of face his folly had caused. It was not enough that he had physically attacked the one chief who seemed cooperative. Yes, Palea might be duplicitous and manipulative but he had at least returned the stolen goods. Rather pointlessly – since Edgar had already told him all there was to tell – Cook ordered King to return with the *Discovery* men to that ship overnight and re-interview Edgar prior to making a detailed report. The incident was very serious, since the hawks among the Hawaiians would now think they had the upper hand in the struggle with the *haoles*. As a preliminary measure Cook ordered all islanders cleared from the ships, including the seamen's 'wives' and girlfriends.[13] Calling his officers together, Cook explained that credibility dictated that they make a vigorous response to the latest aggression, or the locals would simply escalate their violence: 'In going on board, the captain expressed his sorrow, that the behaviour of the Indians would at last oblige him to use force; for that they must not, he said, imagine they have gained an advantage over us.'[14] Edgar had botched what should have been a simple recovery mission, but Palea must be faulted too: his deviousness called for nice calculations, factoring in the unexpected, which he had not made. In the heat of the moment he had forgotten where his best two-faced interests lay.[15]

King was in command of the watch on the *Discovery* that night and gave explicit orders to the sentries to open fire on any intruders. Some Hawaiians did approach around midnight and were fired on. The thieves then decided to go for the ship's big cutter, which was moored to one of the anchor buoys and sunk below the water level to protect it from the fierce daytime heat; this was easy work for those so expert in driving wooden objects through the surf. They silently cut the moorings and took the boat away; it was quickly broken up for its iron and never recovered.[16] This was a most serious loss, by far the worst Cook had sustained in all his Pacific rovings. Each ship had two cutters, a large and a small, and without the large cutter the Northwest Passage quest would have to be abandoned, for in polar regions it was dangerous folly to venture into the ice without the cutters as guides.

There can be little doubt that the mastermind behind this theft was, once again, Palea, and that he targeted the *Discovery* rather than the *Resolution* because he knew Clerke was a laxer disciplinarian than Cook and was therefore likely to have set a less vigilant guard, and also because it was Edgar from the *Discovery* who had struck him. Yet Palea's motives are mysterious and perhaps even contradictory, as his ambivalent behaviour over the tongs had already demonstrated. One possibility is that Kalani'opu'u's inner council was already riven with factionalism between 'doves' led by Kamehameha who wanted to take a 'softly softly' approach to the white men, and 'hawks' led by Palea, hoping to influence the high chief to adopt aggressive measures.[17] The loss of the cutter was probably discovered at first light (around 6.15 a.m.). Clerke immediately reported the theft to Cook, and the two men consulted on how to react. Cook's first idea was to seize all canoes in Kealakekua Bay so as to stifle economic life on the island; such sanctions would surely bring Kalani'opu'u and his chieftains to heel and secure the return of the launch. The first thing to do was to blockade the bay, so that no canoes could exit or enter. Cook sent boats off to the southern and northern points of the bay and ordered his men to load ball and shoot to kill at any canoeists trying to evade the blockade.[18]

Clerke rowed back to the *Discovery*, issued the necessary orders, and the launch and small cutter, commanded by Lieutenant John Rickman, were sent to the south point. He returned to inform Cook of the dispositions, but in the meantime Cook had gone. Earlier King had arrived on the *Resolution* to make his report on the affray the evening before involving Edgar, but Cook informed him brusquely that all that was now irrelevant; the Hawaiians had escalated affairs by stealing the cutter, which gave Cook no option but to use main force.[19] King noticed Cook loading his double-barrelled pistol with a determined look on his face and noticed that the marines were loading with ball. Cook sent him back to the observatory with orders to be on his guard in case of a surprise attack and to let none of his men wander from the compound. Cook then set off with three boats, with himself in a small pinnace, the others being the small cutter and the large launch from the *Resolution*. Without telling either Clerke or King, Cook had secretly decided to arrest Kalani'opu'u and hold him hostage against the return of the stolen cutter. Since Clerke was ill, Cook decided to make the arrest himself.[20] He was in a hurry, as he was worried that the high chief and his entourage would withdraw from the coastline at the least sign of trouble and skulk in the steep hillsides around the village of Kowrowa, which lay at the bottom of a cliff. Cook knew that the geography of Kealakekua Bay was tricky: it was not even possible to walk between the two villages of Kakoa and Kowrowa at high tide, and he wanted to save his men the strenuous business of sweating up almost vertical cliffs and hills. He sent the cutter under William Lanyon, the master's mate, to cruise off the north-west corner of the bay, within signalling distance. He himself landed together with Molesworth Phillips, lieutenant of marines, and nine marines (including his trusty Sergeant Gibson), leaving the pinnace under Henry Roberts, the other master's mate, to wait a few yards offshore so as not to ground, and gave the same instructions to Lieutenant Williamson in the launch. Altogether Cook's party comprised about thirty-five armed men: himself, Phillips and the marines in the landing party; Roberts and ten other men; Williamson and about a dozen more in the launch.[21]

When he returned to the *Resolution*, Clerke learned that Cook intended to pay a visit to Kalani'opu'u, to pressurise him into returning the cutter, it was said. He had no idea that Cook intended anything so dangerous as to arrest the high chief. Either Cook changed his mind soon after speaking to Clerke or, more probably, given his secretive nature, he did not tell Clerke of his true intentions. The new intention was clearly signalled when Cook ordered Molesworth Phillips to join his party, since Phillips was originally on guard duty at the northern end of the bay. As Cook rowed past him, he called on him to leave his station and follow him. Cook was now engaged on a desperate and dangerous venture which he had not thought through properly. One strand in the confidence with which he set out was his conviction that the Hawaiians had a mortal terror of his firepower. Certainly they had seemed impressed on 17 January when, surrounded by more than 1,000 canoes, he opened up with his booming cannons.[22] What he failed to realise was that at that stage the islanders were bowing down to Lono, not European technology. All Polynesians were aware by this time that European guns were not infallible: they could miss, misfire and needed to be reloaded after each shot.[23] If Cook wanted to apprehend the high chief of the island, he needed to take at least double his total numbers on the shoreline up into Kalani'opu'u's village; as it was, he proceeded with ten men when he should have taken at least six times that number. Beyond this, his ideas were seriously flawed, since he should not have been implementing an armed blockade at sea and an arrest on land at the same time. A moment's thought would have shown that these two operations were in conflict with each other. Even as he rowed across the bay, what happened should have demonstrated to him that he was, as it were, shooting himself in the foot. The blockading boats opened up on canoes trying to run the blockade, and the booming sound of gunfire, echoing and ricocheting off the high cliffs, made an amplified cacophony that should have scared off any jittery chief. If Kalani'opu'u made off into the interior, the blockade would be pointless, as there would be no one to put pressure on.[24] Again, the sixty men he needed to effect the arrest were not available, simply because they were busy tightening the cordon around the bay; if, on the other hand, he recalled all his boats to concentrate on the arrest, Kalani'opu'u would have time to get away. Yet thinking all this through would have required calm and patience – exactly the traits the short-fused Cook did not possess. By definition a man who wants quick results is not a careful planner.[25]

At all events, Cook landed near Kowrowa, full of confidence that he needed only to shoot two or three Hawaiians for the others to clear a path to their chief and let Cook carry him off like a common criminal. It is difficult to know which is more deplorable: the pathological secrecy with which Cook carried out his design or the staggering extent to which he had not thought things through on a what-if, multiple case scenario. Some have asserted that the lack of scientists or savants on the third voyage meant that Cook had no one of proven intellect to rely on, and that this in the end brought about his downfall.[26] The secretiveness was, of course, one of the reasons the blockade and the landing had to be conducted simultaneously, with disastrous results. The village of Kowrowa was no more than a hundred yards from Cook's landing place and, if Kalani'opu'u could be found quickly, Cook seemed to have deployed his men well. Only twenty yards away from the shore, riding at oars, was the pinnace under Roberts. Close to him was the launch commanded by Williamson and, covering him, was the other launch under Lanyon. Protecting them, about three-quarters of a mile out in the bay was the *Resolution* and, two hundred yards to the south of her, the *Discovery*, nominally under Clerke but, since Clerke had retired ill to his cabin, temporarily under Burney. Somewhere between the *Resolution* and the southern shore was Cook's best fighting man, one he should have had at his side, William Bligh, who had just run down a blockade-running canoe.[27] Much depended on the attitude of the locals and at first, as Cook entered the village of Kowrowa, he was received deferentially as Lono. Suspicions were soon aroused when the red-coated marines spread out in a house to house search; why had Lono come with armed men this time when he had never done so before? And what had all that gunfire been about? As they proceeded through the village, Ledyard noticed an ominous hostility, of a kind he had never encountered before. Instead of joviality and friendliness there was morose surliness and peevishness.[28]

Cook's men uncovered the chief's sons, and Cook questioned them about their father's whereabouts. Ingenuous and lamb-like, they led him to Kalani'opu'u's hut, which was indistinguishable from the other dwellings.

The sons disappeared inside to tell the old man that 'Lono' wanted to see him. When he did not appear instantly, the impatient Cook sent Williamson inside to roust him out. This was provocative both as a breach of protocol and as showing implicit contempt for the locals' religion, since the Hawaiians believed that if a chief was roused from slumber, his spirit might wander away before he was properly awake; the boundaries between sleep and waking were strictly observed in Hawaiian culture, as they believed that to be woken from a deep sleep could trigger instant death.[29] Kalani'opu'u was indeed drowsy – maybe he had had his useful quota of kava the night before – but he responded with alacrity; or so said Phillips. Other accounts say that he was unhappy and resentful – a more likely scenario if Phillips shook him out of a sleep so deep that, as he later said, he had not heard the gunfire. The chief emerged into the daylight to face aggressive cross-questioning by Cook. As they talked, Cook became more and more convinced that the old man knew nothing about the theft.[30] This would be entirely plausible if the thesis of a pre-emptive coup led by Palea and his fellow hardliners is correct; working independently, Palea would be trying to engineer a confrontation between the chief and Cook. At this juncture a simple polite request for Kalani'opu'u to visit him on board the *Resolution* might have done the trick, ended the crisis and seen all resolved peacefully. Yet Cook's blood was up and, though finding the high chief personally innocent, he was still convinced he had to teach the locals a lesson, to show he could not be trifled with. Even faced with Cook's aggressive behaviour, the chief accepted Cook's request that he accompany him to the ships. His two young sons, popular regulars on board the vessels, ran joyfully ahead, quickly covered the short distance to the landing place, and swam out to the pinnace where they were received in the usual friendly way.[31]

One of Kalani'opu'u's favourite wives now appeared and tearfully begged him not to accompany Cook. Whether the meeting was fortuitous or (more likely) something she was put up to by the Palea faction, the immediate result was to galvanise an already sullen crowd into active opposition to the white men. As if on cue, two of Kalani'opu'u's associate chiefs came forward and added their voices to the wife's pleas. All three men sat down on the ground, arguing loudly and gesticulating wildly, with the high chief looking dejected and depressed, more and more like a cipher or a rag doll caught between two lots of contenders. The fact that the high chief was seated was 'in itself a shocking posture for a great chief surrounded by his warriors'.[32] As the hostile crowd around the Europeans swelled in size, Cook kept dragging at the chief's sleeve, insisting he should accompany him; the two associate chiefs equally vehemently declared that he should not. This was the point where a wise man would have cut his losses and concluded that he was on a forlorn quest. Yet the demon in Cook made him persist. As Cook again began to lose patience and to show signs of wanting to force Kalani'opu'u to accompany him, the two chiefs seized on this as proof of what they were saying, that the *haoles* meant their beloved ruler no good. As the minutes ticked by, Phillips grew increasingly apprehensive about the size of the mob around them and asked permission to back off and form up at the water's edge in defensive formation. Cook, now like an Ahab and consumed by monomania, seemed unaware that there was a throng around him, and persisted in trying to drag the dejected high chief with him.[33] Almost absent-mindedly he gave the nod to Phillips. He formed the marines up on the shoreline, now several paces behind Cook and Gibson. Meanwhile the two chiefs had told Kalani'opu'u bluntly that Cook intended to kill him. Cook angrily denied this and, according to Phillips, told him that only bloodshed would now get the old man on to the *Resolution*. Controversy has always attended this remark – if indeed it was ever uttered. Did it mean that Cook was finally admitting failure? Or, more sinisterly, did it mean that Cook intended to kill to get what he wanted? The second option contained two glaring flaws: in the middle of such a hostile crowd it was impracticable and, if attempted, would conclusively prove the truth of what the associate chiefs were saying.[34]

At some stage during these confused proceedings in the village, word came in that a canoe had been fired upon in the bay and the important chief Kalimu killed. Whether, as some scholars say, these tidings were received round about the time Williamson was shaking Kalani'opu'u awake and that this was itself the cause of the initial hostility noticed by Ledyard, or whether, in *deus ex machina* fashion the news arrived just at the critical moment of the tug-of-war between Cook and the two minor chiefs, it was certainly a contributing factor to the local fury at the waterside. The lethal shots on Kalimu came from a boat commanded by Rickman but, in the manner of good melodrama, it seemed too good a trick to miss not to bring Bligh into the frame, working back from his *Bounty* notoriety. Without any foundation it has been asserted that Bligh shot Kalimu and that therefore Bligh indirectly caused Cook's death.[35] What is more likely is that the Hawaiians interpreted the death of their chief as definite proof that 'Lono' intended to wage a general war on Kalani'opu'u. This would have been the revolution that the high chief and his counsellors so dreaded. It follows that, whatever the exact chronology of the news of Kalimu's death, it was an important factor in the rapidly escalating hostility.[36] By this time the tension on the beach had moved up a notch, for genuine warriors, protected by thick war mats, had begun to arrive. Now if ever was the time to cut and run. Yet Cook, confident in the superiority of European firepower, persisted. One of the newcomers, holding a spear in one hand and a stone in the other, made menacing gestures at Cook. Cook shouted at him to back off, but the warrior remained defiant. Out of the crowd came a missile – either a stone or a breadfruit – which struck Cook in the face.[37] He then fired at his original tormentor with his double-barrelled pistol, but the bullet failed to penetrate the war mat. This was the worst possible outcome, since the crowd concluded that the firearms were ineffective. They began to rain stones down on the marines, and one man tried to stab Phillips. Cook fired the second barrel and this time killed a man; the sources cannot agree whether this man or someone else was his original target. There was another hailstorm of stones and an answering fusillade from the marines. So far from cracking, as Cook predicted, the Hawaiians took the salvo unflinchingly although several of them dropped dead, then hurled themselves on the marines when they paused to reload.[38]

Faced with this surge, the marines panicked, dropped their weapons and rushed into the water. Those who could swim struck out seawards, but those who could not were left to the mercy of the baying crowd, and among these non-swimmers was Cook himself. Phillips, attacked by what appeared to be a chieftain, clubbed him with the butt end of his musket. He then managed to reload but was knocked to the ground and stabbed. As his assailant prepared to deliver the *coup de grâce*, Phillips shot him dead. Able to swim though badly weakened both by the stab wound and a nasty strike on his head by a stone, he staggered into the water and headed for the pinnace. Corporal Thomas was stabbed to death in the stomach, Private Hinks appeared to be hacked to pieces in a frenzy by his assailants, Private Fatchett was seen to fall with a grievous wound to the head, while Private Jackson, a veteran of campaigns in Germany, took a mortal thrust from a spear just under his eye.[39] Roberts in the pinnace moved in to support Cook, and his men got off another fusillade but it was difficult to reload in a moving boat and attempts to do so nearly capsized the pinnace. Trying to steady the boat, all the while assailed by a hail of stones, the pinnace men were unable to get off another volley. Cook, now in desperate straits, signalled to Williamson to come in and pick him up. Williamson, finally revealed in his true colours, stayed offshore and attempted neither to rescue Cook nor to pick up any of the swimming marines; his main concern was to remove himself out of range of the flying missiles. Lanyon's men did manage to come close enough to fire a volley, but by then it was too little, too late.[40] Having fired his two shots, with no other weapon and unable to swim, Cook had no chance at all. As he was waving vainly to Williamson to come in, with his back to the crowd, a Hawaiian warrior struck him in the back with a heavy club. As Cook sank to his knees, another man stabbed him in the neck. Cook fell forward into the water, and the Hawaiians fell on him like wolves. Some held his head under water while others stabbed him repeatedly. Having finished their gruesome business, the warriors hauled the lifeless body out of the water. From initial altercation with the associate chiefs to the final chapter, the whole affair lasted no more than ten minutes. It was just after 8 a.m.[41] So died the greatest navigator of the ages.

Cook's death prompts a number of questions, some of immediate practicality, others of deeper import. Why did the marines turn in such a dismal and craven performance? The warning signs had already been there in the form of their lacklustre drill displays, so bad that Cook had actually cancelled one of them in embarrassment. It was sheer folly for them to fire all their muskets simultaneously, leaving themselves without a reserve. Here the blame must be laid at Cook's door, for Phillips had always advocated the more conventional, and intelligent, procedure of having one group fire while another reloaded. Cook overruled this tactic, on the ground that he wanted a massive display of concentrated firepower. The outcome was as Phillips had warned it would be.[42] Yet this does not acquit the marines of cowardice. As Bligh pointed out with his characteristic forthrightness, why did the marines not then fix bayonets and disperse the attackers with a resolute charge, which he was convinced would have been successful?[43] Yet the worst cowardice came from Williamson. Not only did he leave Cook to his fate but he did not even try to recover his body and that of the four dead marines afterwards, to save them from being ritually dismembered. His absurd excuse that Cook's waving from the shore meant he should move farther out, not farther in, convinced nobody. Had he come in, the firepower from his launch would have made a considerable difference and might have saved his captain. Clerke, disgusted by Williamson's conduct, held an inquiry to establish his culpability, but the mates changed their initial story, reluctant to support the marines against one of their own officers.[44] These inquiry papers were not found among Clerke's effects after his death, and the probability is that Williamson got hold of them and then destroyed them; he had ample opportunity to do so. Yet another duel was later fought (at Cape Horn) between Williamson and Phillips but, both being hopeless shots, once again no one was hurt.[45] There was apparently no limit to Williamson's Machiavellianism. While in Kamchatka on the return journey he established a mason's lodge and bribed all the material witnesses to his conduct in Kealakekua Bay with prodigious quantities of brandy to become masons; thereafter his 'brothers' could not testify against his cowardice at a court-martial in England.[46] Unjustifiably promoted to post captain, the dreadful Williamson finally came to grief at the battle of Camperdown in 1797 when he failed to press the attack against the Dutch with enough vigour. Tried for cowardice before a court-martial, he was found guilty and dismissed from the service; Nelson said he should have been shot.

As for the deeper causality of Cook's death, this has always been controversial. More than half a dozen competing theories can be identified, each purporting to provide *the* key to the tragedy. Perhaps the most basic of these is the proposition that Cook was old and tired when he embarked on his third voyage, no longer the man he used to be, increasingly cross-grained and short-fused and no longer up to the combined stresses of his Admiralty orders, dealings with hostile or recalcitrant Polynesians and the perils of the Pacific. The events on Kealakekua beach on 14 February were, then, an accident waiting to happen.[47] This theory in turn bifurcates into the view that Cook was out of his depth from the moment he left England to the more nuanced one that his 'breakdown' was progressive, that the worst manifestations of his derangement occurred after he left Unalaska for the second time and were most noticeable during the crazy, stormy voyage around Maui and Hawaii island from late November 1778 to 17 January 1779; certainly when Clerke linked up with him on 7 January, he reported him looking more gaunt and iller than he had ever seen him before.[48] Put simply, this radical version of the breakdown theory is that Cook went mad during the seven-week storms around Hawaii, which was why he embraced his identification as Lono with such avidity. Is the whole Lono topos the key to the story? What one might call the 'Kipling' scenario postulates that the Hawaiians killed Cook once they discovered he was not Lono but a mere human – which Cook had proved to them by returning out of season when he was not supposed to.[49] It will be remembered that in Kipling's 'The Man Who Would Be King' Daniel Dravot is killed because he pretended to be a god but was revealed as a human. In glaring contrast to this is the 'Conrad' scenario, the view that the Hawaiians never thought Cook was Lono, but that his own self-identication with the god was a Jungian process whereby the civilised consciousness is overwhelmed by a savage unconscious. This is not so far-fetched as it might sound. On Stanley's Emin Pasha expedition of 1886–90, his associate Jameson degenerated to the point where he ended up sketching a murder and subsequent cannibal feast with perfect equanimity. Kurtz's 'Exterminate all the brutes . . . the horror, the horror' in Conrad's *Heart of Darkness* is the *locus classicus*, but this is by no means a merely fictional phenomenon. One Cook scholar has hypothesised that Cook's journals, which end abruptly on 17 January, did survive but that they showed him plummeting into darkness in the Kurtz manner and were therefore suppressed.[50]

Most of the theories are pitched at a more mundane level. Some see Cook's death as the final result of a clash between irresistible force and immovable object, damned if he did and damned if he did not. Trying to break out of the trap whereby his men perceived him as weak because of his hitherto liberal and lenient attitude to Polynesians' insolence, while the Polynesians took his civilised restraint for weakness, Cook abruptly changed tack, lashed out at his men, who became mutinous, and, when he lashed out at the Polynesians, he was finally killed. Here is one such assessment: 'It was a cross-cultural combination of forces that killed him.'[51] Still others bring in notions of the tragic hero, either Shakespearean with a fatal flaw or, in the manner of Greek tragedy, beset by hamartia, hubris and nemesis.[52] There are many different testimonies to Cook's pride, arrogance and vanity. One view is that, having greatly enjoyed the adulation as Lono until 4 February, when he returned he was so angry to find a different reception that he wanted to teach the locals a lesson.[53] The professional soldiers – and on this even Williamson and Phillips concurred – thought that Cook's notion of a careful escalation of violence was mistaken; at the very first sign of trouble, possibly as early as January, Cook should have gone in for a policy of 'massive retaliation'.[54] Yet Cook, with his overweening confidence that he alone knew how to handle Polynesians, ignored all advice. Clerke thought that wounded vanity had a lot to do with Cook's fatal decision to shoot the warrior with his pistol; this was 'over the top', for Cook's life was not being threatened. The entire expedition to arrest Kalani'opu'u filled Clerke with distaste; to him it smacked far too much of the infamous seizures of Montezuma by Cortés and Atahualpa by Pizarro – exploits fitted only for thugs.[55] However, Clerke saw no overarching pattern or matrix of inevitability about Cook's death. To him it was pure contingency: one aleatory event succeeding another, each of which might easily have turned out differently.[56] This approach brings us to what one might call the 'radical empirical' end of the theories about Cook's death, embracing those who think that there was no deep pattern, structure or under-lying meaning to the events in Kealakekua Bay, that it was all mere chance. Cook's strongest supporters, who claim that he uncharacteristically 'snapped' on 14 February, always asserted that he had simply had an off day, like Napoleon at Waterloo.[57]

Yet another school of thought holds that neither the 'deep structure' thesis involving Cook as Lono nor pure contingency can adequately explain the events on Kealakekua Bay, that a middle-range explanation has to be sought that combines an analysis of the motives of the actors on both sides. The argument about whether the Hawaiians regarded Cook as an incarnation of Lono has been bitter and hard-fought.[58] Yet we cannot even be sure whether or not Cook regarded himself as Lono. Was he playing a dangerous game of cynically colluding with 'native superstition' for his own ends? Or had he indeed gone mad during the seven weeks sailing round Hawaii in never-ending storms and consoled himself with the ultimate delusion of grandeur? Meanwhile, what of Hawaiian attitudes? Can we be really certain that their hostile and gloomy reaction when Cook returned was entirely to do with the Lono cult? Certainly Kamehameha, for one, seems to have been remarkably clearheaded and lacking in superstition, and it is probable that his greatest fear was that Cook returned because he had had second thoughts and decided to turn the Hawaiian islands into a colony for King George. Maybe the first step was going to be the assassination of Kalani'opu'u once he was on board the *Resolution*.[59] The permutations and combinations of 'failure to communicate', cultural misunderstandings, Cook's possible dementia and the stock of aleatory and adventitious circumstances arising from Cook's highly charged attempt to arrest Kalani'opu'u throw up dozens of possible scenarios, even if we leave the Lono business entirely out of the reckoning.[60] Those who delight in the combination of long causal chains may even like to consider that the ultimate cause of the tragedy on the big island on 14 February was the British class system. It was the results of the corruption in the Deptford dock-yard that forced Cook to return to Hawaii, thus precipitating the fatal final events. Without the rigid aristocratic ethos of Georgian England it might have been possible for Cook to press Palliser harder so as to ensure that all the sheathing and mastwork was done properly. Again, Cook's chilling ambition might well have been satisfied in a more egalitarian and meritocratic society without pushing himself to the limit, but in eighteenth-century England, in order to secure the fortune and social status he so yearned for, Cook had to make a third Pacific voyage when he was too old and tired to do so efficaciously.

When the dreadful news was brought to Clerke, on whom the command of the expedition now devolved, he acted quickly to safeguard his most vital assets: the mast which was being repaired at Kikiau under King's supervision but with just half a dozen marines as guards, and the indispensable chronometer in the observatory. He sent Bligh and a strong party of his men to advise King to wind up the observatory at once but to try to finish all the work on the mast that could not be completed on the ships. Bligh, together with King's marines, dug in at the *morai* and repelled a fierce attack. Reinforcements were rushed over and soon the well-entrenched defenders numbered sixty. After repelling further attacks, King and Bligh received word that they should transfer to the ship, where the carpenters could finish the work on the mast in safety. By 11.30 a.m. everyone and everything was aboard the two ships.[61] The atmosphere was extremely despondent, as Gilbert related the sequel to the news that Cook was dead:

A general silence ensued throughout the ship for the space of nearly half an hour: it appearing to us like a dream that we could not reconcile ourselves to for some time. Grief was visible in every countenance: some expressing it by tears and others by a kind of gloomy dejection, more easy to be conceived than described, for as all our hopes centred in him, our loss became irreparable and the sense of it was so deeply impressed upon our minds as not to be forgot.[62]

By midday Clerke was able to collect his thoughts. At first he was inclined to yield to the clamour of the lower deck for a revenge landing, but on mature reflection decided against it. While not endorsing Mark Twain's later verdict that Cook's death was 'justifiable homicide',[63] he and most of the officers agreed that Cook had been ill-advised to try to arrest Kalani'opu'u and that the Hawaiians had at least the ghost of a case. Even though there was a strong party in favour of retaliation, of which Bligh was certainly one, Clerke would not be swayed.[64] Clerke was confident that he could win anything in the nature of a pitched battle, but he respected the Hawaiians as tough opponents and realised there would be casualties on his side which he could ill afford. Clerke had much more of a sense than Cook of how different Hawaii was from the rest of Polynesia. It was more populous; its warriors more formidable; its political system more attuned to a heroic resistance against European firearms. Cook had been misled by the ease with which he had been able to intervene decisively in the politics of Tahiti and Tonga, and extrapolated that to the situation on Hawaii. But, as King knew, here on the big island of Hawaii there was no low-level civil war between a Tu and a Vehiatua that he could energise. Clerke therefore opted for diplomacy.[65]

His first objective was to secure the return of Cook's body. This was going to be difficult for, despite losing thirty men dead (seventeen in the affray on the beach, the rest in the assault on King and Bligh's forces), the Hawaiians regarded themselves as the victorious party. In the late afternoon of the 14th King and Burney and a strong party approached the shore in two boats under a flag of truce and demanded the return of the bodies of their fallen. The priests seemed pleased to see them, and soon Koa'a put in an appearance: he swam out to the boats and parleyed with a distrustful King. Clearly Koa'a hoped that reconciliation with the whites would restore his prestige, which had taken a battering when Lono came back.[66] Koa'a promised them that the body of Cook would be given back soon and returned to shore to tell the people that the *haoles* were their friends again. Initially belligerent and in war mats, the Hawaiians on the beach noticeably relaxed when they saw the white flag and heard Koa'a's report.[67] While the boats were off Kaawaloa, some of the chiefs called out to King that he should come ashore but King, fearing he would be murdered, declined. Finally, a senior representative from Kalani'opu'u arrived to say that Cook's body had been taken upcountry and would be returned next day. Only Burney heard something of the truth when he was told that the captain's corpse had already been cut up. Evidently the Hawaiians had not yet decided what their final stance towards the Europeans would be. The volatile state of affairs was highlighted when King and party started to row back to the ships. Young Hawaiian males jeered at them and 'mooned' at them with bare backsides. To add to the insult, a man appeared in Cook's jacket and trousers, while others brandished weapons taken from him and the dead marines.[68] The two ships' companies then spent a tense night, watching the many fires and beacons on the hillside and listening to the loud and persistent ululations. Rumours spread that their dead comrades were now being sacrificed to savage gods, but the truth was that they were being incinerated in Hawaiian crematoria, as burnt offerings to the god of war.[69]

The Hawaiian elite for their part were considering their next move. The hardliners and hotheads advocated an attack on the European ships, but Kamehameha counselled against this, and his wisdom carried the day. Even if the attack was completely successful – unlikely, he thought – and even if every last man was massacred, that would not be the end of the story. Cook's very fanaticism had alerted him to the perseverance and obduracy of Europeans; the last thing he wanted was a powerful war fleet of *haoles* in Hawaiian waters. It was no use arguing, as the hotheads did, that no one would live to tell the tale; such stories always got out. Clerke had made a mental connection between the attempted arrest of Kalani'opu'u and Cortés's seizure of Montezuma. Kamehameha, though he knew nothing of Cortés's alliance with the Tlaxcalans – the decisive factor in compassing the destruction of the Aztecs – was able to work out that the very first thing European avengers would do was form an alliance with Kalani'opu'u's enemies on Maui. For all these reasons he vehemently opposed any hostile move against the *Resolution* and *Discovery*.[70] In so doing, he had to oppose his close friend Kekuhaupi'o, one of the chiefs who had warned Kalani'opu'u not to go aboard the *Resolution* with Cook.[71] Vancouver, among the most intelligent of Cook's complement, claimed to be a great admirer of Kamehameha's methods. Many years later he outwitted the great Hawaiian chiefs by using his own methods on him: when Kamehameha, in his lust for guns and ammunition, placed a *tapu* on all trade for victuals except in exchange for arms and bullets, Vancouver countered by saying that George III had put a *tapu* on these.[72] Undoubtedly Kamehameha displayed great statesmanship on this occasion but there were

other, religious, factors at play. After Cook's death the high chief retired to a
cave in the mountains, accessible only by rope ladders, down which basic
food was supplied, and remained in seclusion. The reason was simple.
According to the Polynesian belief in mystical kinship between *atuas*, it
followed that when Cook/Lono was killed in Kealakekua Bay, in a sense
Kalani'opu'u had also been killed.[73] Yet the high chief's plight was even worse.
Cook's death did not impugn his status as Lono, for it was known that he eter-
nally came again. His death on the beach no more implied his final disappearance than the crucifixion of Jesus Christ meant that he could not rise again on
the third day. Yet a high chief, even an *atua* of the sacred blood, would not be
expected to come again unless he was a man of truly heroic mould – which
Kalani'opu'u was not.[74]

While the desperately ill Clerke awaited developments, he rearranged the
command structure on the two ships. He himself transferred to the *Resolution*
as commander and appointed John Gore as captain of the *Discovery*. Some
interpret Clerke's promotion of Williamson to second lieutenant as a coded
message: he realised Williamson had acted in a craven way on Kealakekua Bay
but was making it known that he held Cook to blame for what had happened.
In any case, his attention was soon on the more immediate matter of Cook's
remains. The two middlemen who negotiated their return and an eventual
peace were the priests Koa'a and Keli'ikea. By now Koa'a was a hate figure to
the seamen, for the chiefs, as part of their continuing battle with the priests,
had spread the rumour that Koa'a had been the prime mover in the killing of
Cook – which is very unlikely, since the priesthood derived much of its prestige from Cook as Lono.[75] Koa'a visited both ships on the 15th on a peace
mission, but it was the less hated Keli'ikea who was nearly shot, fired on by a
sentry when he called out to request an audience with Lieutenant King.
Keli'ikea brought a piece of flesh from Cook's thigh. He explained that Cook's
body had been dismembered and parts of it burnt, but that the bones had been
distributed among the most important chiefs because of the *mana* they
possessed. He was appalled at the suggestion that the Hawaiians had eaten
Cook and insisted vehemently that his people were not cannibals.[76] The
seamen were sickened and revolted. Roberts reported: 'It is impossible to
express the feelings that every officer and seaman suffered on this occasion, a
sight so horribly shocking; distraction and madness was in every mind, and
revenge the result of all.'[77] Keli'ikea pretended that he was the Europeans'
special friend, accused Koa'a of treachery to their cause and said that his own
friendly overtures to the Europeans would be regarded as treachery by the
hardliners. Next morning the flesh from Cook's thigh was buried in the ocean,

and the seamen went to Clerke and asked to be allowed to go on a revenge raid. Clerke told them to be patient for twenty-four hours while he warped the *Resolution* closer in to cover them with his big guns.[78]

Next morning came the revenge party. Curiously this was not directed at Kaawaloa, the village where the hostile crowd that killed Cook had gathered, but at Keli'ikea's settlement at Kealakekua. What lay behind the change of plan is unknown, but perhaps it is explicable because both Clerke and his trusted deputy King were ill that day. As a watering party set out for the settlement, a crowd gathered on the beach. Clerke, true to his word had come close in, so the big guns opened up. The landing party then came under a fusillade of stones, to which they responded with a volley. For a short time they were embarrassed by a solitary Hawaiian hero who kept throwing stones even though riddled with musket balls before he finally fell down dead.[79] Enraged by this 'insolence', the seamen went on the rampage, gutting houses, shooting those who emerged from the burning huts, and decapitating two of the corpses and sticking them on poles. The seamen were now no better than their savage adversaries. When a party of Hawaiians approached under a flag of truce, they too were fired on. A parley was eventually arranged and the newcomers turned out to be Keli'ikea and his priests, the only real friends the Europeans had on the island.[80] To their consternation, they found their houses burned and their temple destroyed. Keli'ikea's lamentations were so piteous, especially when he saw the severed heads, that to pacify him the leader of the watering party invited him back to the *Resolution*. There he got a mixed reception: King, whose friendship he relied on, expressed regret for the attack on the village but warned him that if he did not bring Cook's body next time he came to the ships he would be executed. To placate King the priest left and sent over canoes full of provisions. Later in the day he sent a message to him that he could not bring Cook's body as all the bones had been distributed among the chiefs. That evening a personal envoy from Kalani'opu'u arrived with a message from the chief. He conveyed Kalani'opu'u's sorrow that his friend Cook had been killed and said he wanted to make peace with the Europeans. This time Clerke lent a hand, dealing chief to chief as it were, and sent back a reply that peace would be ratified once they had Cook's body.[81]

The stalemate continued until 20 February, when two canoes arrived to inform Clerke that a formal handing over of Cook's remains would take place on the beach later that day. Finally, with both sides under white flags, Hiapo, the personal envoy of the high chief with whom Clerke had been dealing, approached. After a formal peace offering of fourteen hogs and a red baize cloak edged with green cloth. Hiapo handed him a large bundle draped in a black feather cloak. Clerke thanked the envoy and returned to the *Resolution*, where the bundle was opened in the Great Cabin. The amazed witnesses found some bones with burnt flesh attached, including the captain's thighs and legs, both arms, his skull and scalp with one ear attached and his right hand, recognisable from the old Newfoundland scar when the powder horn had disfigured the hand. Also in the package was Cook's hanger, the barrels from his musket and a few other curios.[82] The following morning Hiapo came again, this time bringing Cook's jawbone and feet, as well as his shoes. It only now remained to auction off Cook's effects and commit his remains to the deep. On the evening of 21 February the formal burial service took place. The flags were at half mast, bells were tolled and a ten-gun salute fired. Clerke pronounced the funeral oration before the catafalque slid off the *Resolution* into the ocean.[83] Trade resumed, as did intercourse with the women and a partial reconciliation was effected. Throughout his week-long steward-ship on Hawaii, Clerke, though ill, had performed magnificently. He lacked Cook's toughness and could not control or discipline the seamen as the great navigator could – the disgraceful exhibition in Keli'ikea's village proved that – but he was a better diplomat and negotiator. As Beaglehole rightly commented:

His perceptiveness was matched by his tact and his firmness, and made him the master of a situation that could easily have gone from disaster to disaster. His men would have turned the bay into a shambles; the Hawaiians might have put the ships into such a state of siege as to cancel the rest of the voyage. Vengeance on a grand scale would certainly have been both difficult and inept.[84]

Cook's death transformed his reputation both in Hawaii and with his own men – surely a choice irony, given that it was poor relations with both that contributed to the captain's sad end. Although the chiefs had surrendered Cook's long bones, the smaller ones were kept as talismanic mementoes. As the years went on, the memory of Cook's provocative behaviour at Kealakekua Bay on the morning of 14 February 1779 faded, to be replaced by a glorious legend.[85] Kamehameha concluded from his experiences with Cook that European methods and alliances with the white man were the way forward, and so eventually became the ruler of all the Hawaiian islands, even though his critics say he jettisoned everything that was valuable in the old culture in favour of modernisation and ties with the West.[86] It seems beyond question that Cook as Lono was taken seriously many years after his demise. The later run of bad luck on the islands – volcanic explosions, venereal disease, constant warfare – was even thought to be Cook's revenge, to the point where Europeans were later asked how they could appease his angry shade.[87] On board the *Resolution* and *Discovery* Cook's rehabilitation proceeded with miraculous speed. There was no more talk of 'Tute', the despotic captain. The men now remembered his leadership, his peerless skill as a navigator, his exemplary chastity, his abstemiousness, virtual teetotalism, fairness and love of equality, his tolerance and the absence of forced Christianity on his ships. They remembered how he had tried to stave off scurvy with his sometimes pedantic dietary requirements, and the way he insisted on hygiene and cleanliness.[88] Zimmermann defended him against the oft-made charge that he favoured Polynesians over his own men by saying that he simply expected higher standards from them and treated them as equals, albeit of lower rank, whereas his attitude to the islanders was paternalistic:

> He was very strict and hot tempered, so much so that the slightest insubor-dination of an officer or sailor upset him completely. He was unyielding where the ship's rules and punishment inflicted for breaches of the same were concerned . . . Perhaps no sea officer has ever had such supreme authority over the officers serving under him as he, so that not one of them dared to contradict him. He would often sit at the table with his officers without saying a word, and was always very reserved. In small matters he was more strict with the crew than the officers, but at times was very affable.[89]

On 22 February, with the mast finally repaired, Clerke stood away from Kealakekua Bay, slowly made his way in the teeth of contrary winds past Maui and Oahu and anchored in Waimea Bay on Kauai on 1 March. Perhaps the dramatic news from the big island had made its way north-west, for the people were surly and hostile, and Clerke had to open fire on them. After a week Clerke crossed to Niihau to take on more supplies, still battered by heavy weather. Finally the ships headed west on 15 March, turning north at longitude 180 to make for Kamchatka. On this leg of the voyage Clerke was amazed at the vast numbers of sharks that followed them.[90] On 11 April the two vessels crossed the track of the Manila galleon, but there were no new discoveries of islands, only the remorseless pounding of gales which caused sails to split, rigging to give way and both ships to leak. The temperature plummeted alarmingly the farther north they went, and on 19 April was below freezing, a fall of a full 53 degrees since the beginning of the month. Snow and ice festooned the ships and the men began to lament their folly in having bartered all their warm clothes for sexual favours on the islands. It was fortunate indeed that the fearnought jackets had been stowed in the hold; these were now produced. Land was sighted on 23 April, but the continuing gales and thick fog prevented them from making landfall.[91] For a few days the ships lost sight of each other, then on 29 April the *Resolution* found its way into Avacha Bay and the village of Petropavlovsk, where the *Discovery* joined her on 1 May. Clerke made contact with the Russian governor of Kamchatka, Major Magnus von Behm, who furnished the British with all the supplies they needed and refused payment. Behm was delighted that, because Cook's contacts with the Chukchi people had been so friendly, and the the Chukchi took them for Russians, this fierce tribe had now indicated that it was prepared to accept vassal status under the Russians. After a long layover for rest and ship repairs, Clerke took his two ships to sea again in mid-June.[92]

They ran along the Kamchatka coast to the familiar St Lawrence Island, passed through the Bering Strait on 6 July, but soon found themselves amid thick drift ice. Three weeks of utter frustration followed, with the voyagers blocked by ice at every turn. Clerke drove the ships on to latitude 70, a few miles short of Cook's farthest north, and on 19 July the seamen shot and killed two polar bears for meat – which was found more palatable than walrus. It was soon clear to the ailing Clerke that he was on a fool's errand, since there was no gap in the ice that would allow him to penetrate farther north nor any sign of the fabled Northwest Passage. After surviving some narrow squeaks with the ice, and with the *Discovery* now sporting a serious leak, Clerke formally abandoned the quest on 27 July.[93] The ships passed back through the Bering Strait and then turned west along the coast of Kamchatka. Having used up his last ounce of energy on the futile quest, the rapidly declining Clerke wrote his final letters and journal entries on 10 August, handed over command to King on the 15th and died a week later.[94] He was just 38. He had never recovered from the tuberculosis he contracted in prison before escaping to command the *Discovery*, and Cook's refusal to leave him in the warmth of the Society Islands had been a virtual death sentence. Although Samwell tried to damn him with faint praise, and sometimes worse, he was a superb seaman, and a loyal, though not unquestioning, second in command to Cook and had always striven to carry out his captain's orders, no matter how difficult or controversial; the contrast with Tobias Furneaux could scarcely be more stark.[95] Gore now became the commander of the expedition and transferred to the *Resolution*, bringing with him Burney and Rickman as the senior lieutenants.

King took over the *Discovery*, with Williamson and Lanyon under him.
Seven more weeks were spent on the Kamchatka peninsula, mainly at
Petropavlovsk, while the ships underwent major repairs. Governor Behm had
been replaced but his successor, although initially suspicious, proved accommodating enough. The officers of *Resolution* and *Discovery* amused themselves
with bear hunts, duck-shooting excursions and even dances with Russian
women.[96]

Gore took his men to sea again on 10 October. The ships ran south-west
from Kamchatka past Sakhalin Island to Japan where Gore at first toyed with
the idea of doing a complete New Zealand-style survey and chart. Yet 1779
had been a year of storms, and the worst was yet to come. Any thoughts of a
Japanese venture were stifled when they ran into a typhoon off the Japanese
coast that nearly overwhelmed them; all they saw of Nippon was a few
Japanese fishing vessels floundering in the giant waves. The lashing from
storms and high seas accompanied them all the way from Japan to China: 'a
continual gale of wind, with very severe squalls, thunder, lightning and rain
and an extraordinarily high sea . . . the sea running very high, we shipped one,
which struck us with great violence, carrying away the weather gunwale rail,
with some of the stanchions overboard, and filled between decks, knee deep in
water, our fore hatchings at this time not being closed.'[97] The voyagers limped
into Macao on 4 December, where two men deserted and got clean away. Gore
was astonished to learn that the war with the American colonists, which Cook
and all his officers had considered a storm in a teacup, likely to last no longer
than the Jacobite Rising of 1745, was still raging fiercely. This was the moment
when the seamen who had held on to the furs acquired at Nootka Sound made
their fortunes. There was a delay in getting supplies from the British
merchants at Canton until they were completely certain the Admiralty would
pay them but, at last, on 13 January 1780, Gore was able to put to sea again.[98]
Progress to the Cape of Good Hope via Sumatra, the Sunda Strait and the
Indian Ocean was slow, not helped by another ferocious mid-ocean storm
when they were two weeks out from Macao. Although Gore had wanted to
bypass Cape Town and make his next landfall at St Helena, the winds forced
him into Simonstown on 12 April. Setting out again on 9 May, the two ships
again laboured against contrary winds and did not reach the western
approaches of the Channel until 9 August. That was as far as they could
progress: shut out from the Channel by a persistent easterly, Gore took his
ships first to the west of Ireland, looking for anchorage, was still baffled by the
winds and finally forced to settle for a berth, the first since the Cape, at
Stromness in the Orkney Islands (22 August). Gore lacked the seamanship of
Cook or Clerke and refused to stir from here until the winds were highly

favourable, to the near-mutinous fury of the crew, who were itching to get ashore to their pay and their women. During this time Cook's favourite, Sergeant Samuel Gibson, died. At last the lacklustre Gore put to sea, and anchored in the Thames on 4 October. It was a dismal homecoming by dejected sailors, still lamenting the tragic loss of the seaman's seaman.[99]

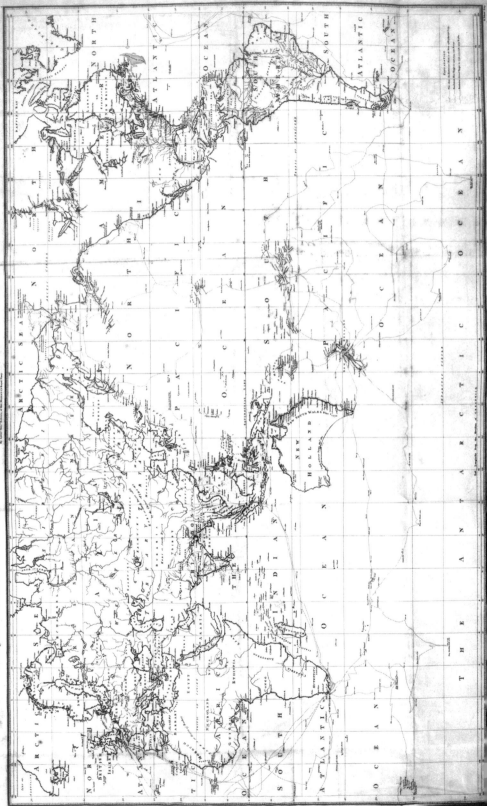

A GENERAL CHART:

Exhibiting the DISCOVERIES made by Capt.ⁿ JAMES COOK in this and his two preceeding VOYAGES, with the TRACKS of the SHIPS under his Command.

Conclusion

W ITHOUT question James Cook was one of the sublimest explorers and
discoverers in the entire history of the world. I have often compared
him to H. M. Stanley, the greatest overland explorer, for both were men who
were highly talented technicians, chillingly ambitious, ruthless and, at the limit,
not prepared to shrink from violence to secure their ends; both too were men
who seemed to have sublimated libido in the lust for glory. Cook returned at
the end of the *Endeavour* voyage with what one scholar has called 'an explorer's
vocation as intense as any the Pacific had seen since the days of Quirós'.[1] At his
peak, roughly until the end of the second voyage, he evinced an almost superhuman indefatigability. If baulked in a major objective, he would immediately
switch gears and pursue a minor one with the same tenacious avidity.
Procrastination and irresolution were not in his nature when he was in his
prime. As with Stanley, life to him was action, and repose and relaxation a kind
of death. His achievements certainly cannot be belittled, even by his many
detractors. On his voyages he added Hawaii, New Caledonia and the New
Hebrides to the map and to the corpus of knowledge. He effectively refuted the
notion that there existed a great southern continent and established the outer
limits of Antarctica, adding to his polar laurels by exploring the Bering Sea and
the southerly limits of the Arctic Ocean. An incomparably brilliant surveyor,
he circumnavigated New Zealand and published a map of the two islands
which is staggering in its accuracy. By charting the eastern coast of Australia he
established himself in popular lore as the discoverer of that continent. He
covered every single degree of longitude and 140 of the 180 degrees of latitude. By the time of his death he had sailed more than 200,000 miles – the
equivalent of circling the equator eight times or travelling to the moon.

Great as he was as an explorer, there are those who say he was even greater
as a navigator and seaman, in roughly the same proportions as the highly
talented individual differs from the true genius.[2] It is hard to disagree with this
assessment. Certainly Cook seems to have been that exceptional individual,

rare even among sea captains, who had no fear of the sea and was confident he could deal with the very worst the oceans could throw at him. The only caveat is that Cook was always lucky, and never encountered the most extreme sea conditions.[3] This is not to say that he was not often faced by fearsome terrors of wind, wave and current.[4] His quality was demonstrated by his remarkable versatility, born both of the variety of ships he served on or commanded and the breadth and depth of his experience. As Beaglehole has noted: 'The captain of an East Indiaman, the master of a line-of-battle ship who would face an Atlantic storm with equanimity, might be little at ease in the midst of the Tuamotu archipelago.'[5] Cook's consummate seamanship meant that he knew what to do even in the most extreme and unexpected circumstances. By analogy one might compare him to an aviator who could take in his stride the failure of an engine in extreme turbulence, landing a plane in massive wind shear or losing speedometer readings during a tropical storm in cumulo-nimbus clouds. The cynic might say that even to keep his vessels at sea for voyages lasting three years was a major feat, given the incompetence and corruption in the naval dockyard. Of Cook's peerless qualities as master and commander there can be no serious doubt. The twentieth century's master navigator Alan Villiers had this to say about him: 'I may well be the last person on earth who has sailed a ship like Cook's round the world with the power of the free wind, taking and using what comes. And so I may see perhaps a little more clearly than most just how great and infinitely admirable were the achievements of Captain Cook.'[6]

Cook's impact on European opinion and his fellow explorers was enormous. Whatever Palliser may have thought when he finally read Cook's animadversions on corruption in His Majesty's Dockyards, the Admiralty always entertained the highest regard for their star navigator. The decision to colonise Australia was one consequence of this for, as Glyn Williams has said, 'It is doubtful whether the First Fleet would have been sent 14,000 miles to Botany Bay in 1788 on the report of a single brief visit to the spot eighteen years earlier, had it not been Cook who had made the visit.'[7] Cook's 'nursery' of budding seamen also produced some famous apprentices. He can hardly be to blame for the character deficiencies of William Bligh, who so disastrously precipitated the mutiny on the Bounty in 1789, but he can claim credit for having turned out a master seaman, whose 3,600 miles open-boat voyage from mid-Pacific to Timor in April–June of that year remains one of the great sagas of survival. Even more talented was his trainee George Vancouver, whose Hawaiian and British Columbian ventures in the 1790s are sometimes claimed to be even more important than Cook's.[8] Cook's voyages also roused the French, Spanish and Russians from their dogmatic slumbers and triggered in the 1780s, as an immediate response to his explorations, the epic voyages of the second-greatest navigator of the Pacific, Jean-François de Galaup de La Pérouse, a particular favourite of the ill-starred Louis XVI but a man of superlative talents withal. La Pérouse explicitly paid tribute to Cook when he set out from France in 1785 in his own apologia:

> Although this voyager, famous for all time, has greatly increased our geographical knowledge; although the globe he travelled through in every direction where seas of ice did not halt his progress, is known well enough for us to be sure that no continent exists where Europeans have not landed; we still lack a full knowledge of the Earth, and particularly of the North-West Coast of America, of the coast of Asia which faces it, and of islands that must be scattered in the seas separating these two continents. The position of several islands shown to lie in the southern ocean between Africa and America, whose existence is known only from reports made by navigators who discovered them, has not yet even been determined; and in eastern seas several areas are still only roughly sketched out.[9]

La Pérouse, then, expressly set out to complete Cook's work and to don his mantle. After leaving France in 1785 he rounded Cape Horn and put in at Concepción, Chile, before crossing to Easter Island and then setting a course to the Hawaiian islands. From Maui he made for Alaska (reached in June 1786), but already it was clear that he did not possess that vital Napoleonic attribute Cook always had until the end: luck. A boat accident drowned twenty-one of his men.[10] La Pérouse then ran down the Pacific coast of America as far as Monterey before making a Magellan-like crossing of the Pacific to China, passing to the north of the Hawaiian islands. Next came his comprehensive charting of the so-called Tartary Coast – his most important achievement in pure exploration. After stopovers in Macao and Manila, he turned north past Formosa (Taiwan) and into the Strait of Korea. Then his track lay through the East China Sea and the Sea of Japan, whence he sighted Japan itself, and on to the Gulf of Tartary; he was now happy, as he was in seas Cook had never explored.[11] After numerous meetings with Tartar peoples, he explored Sakhalin, went through the La Pérouse Strait between Sakhalin and Hokkaido, ran along the west of the Kuril islands into the Sea of Okhotsk, and finally reached the Kamchatka peninsula. It was now 1788, and meanwhile news of the First Fleet expedition to Botany Bay had reached Paris. In Kamchatka La Pérouse received orders from Louis XVI, routed across Russia, that he should abandon the rest of his projected itinerary (Guam–Tahiti–Solomon Islands – New Zealand) and instead investigate what the British were doing at Botany Bay. Accordingly he struck south-east across the Pacific and through Micronesia to northern Polynesia. Once again misfortune followed him, for eleven of his men were massacred at a landfall in Samoa.[12] By this time La Pérouse had adopted a hard-line attitude to islanders similar to that of the Cook of the third voyage. Not only did he find their thieving intolerable but he had been led to a scathing denunciation of the 'noble savage' or Rousseau's 'man in the State of Nature.' As far as the State of Nature was concerned, Hobbes, not Rousseau, was right: far from being a noble savage, pre-social man was 'savage, deceitful and malicious' and man in the State of Nature more malevolent than the wolves of the tundra or the tigers of the forest.[13] Curiously, La Pérouse's extreme pessimism, like Cook's, prefigured ultimate disaster. From Samoa, La Pérouse headed to Botany Bay for a brief visit, then stood away north-east, calling at New Caledonia and the Santa Cruz islands. Off Vanikoro he was overwhelmed by a hurricane more ferocious than anything Cook had ever encountered. His ship was wrecked, and all trace of his expedition vanished for more than forty years.

If Cook's impact on his fellow explorers and successors was highly beneficial, that on the indigenous peoples of Polynesia was less so. This is probably the most controversial aspect of Cook in historiography. The idea that in the fifty years from the 1760s traditional Polynesian society was utterly destroyed, and that Cook was the prime mover in this process, was popularised in the 1960s as the 'fatal impact' thesis.[14] Actually, this seemingly novel idea was simply the updating of very old criticism of the 'Pacific craze' of the 1760s and its consequences; the basic proposition was first adumbrated by the acidulous Horace Walpole.[15] Cook himself thought that the encounter with Polynesians was probably a net loss for Polynesia, and the idea was taken up by many Enlightenment thinkers, disillusioned with eighteenth-century 'globalism' (Voltaire fits into this category); it was often explicitly stated that it would have been better for Tahiti, usually the epicentre of such investigations, not to have been visited by Europeans.[16] William Bligh thought that Tahitians had been corrupted by contact with Europeans, to the extent that they had even picked up the sailors' filthy and obscene language.[17] Yet some critics think the term 'impact' too blunt an instrument for historical analysis. Once we distinguish between the direct, short-term impact of an individual explorer and the longer-term consequences of his penetration of a traditional society, all kinds of conceptual difficulties arise. The impact of an African or Pacific explorer on indigenous cultures and groupings is bound to be different from the impact, say, of the United States on Native American society, simply because the power an explorer could deploy was limited; both Africans and Polynesians perceived explorers as secondary actors, to be used in the wars of one tribe against another (or, in the Pacific, one island against another), but not as a primary threat.

The notion of a fatal impact has in turn been subjected to highly critical analysis. Devotees of 'postcolonialism' assert that the very idea is patronising to the developing countries, as it insinuates the idea of helpless 'natives' bowing down before the might of European culture and technology. Others assert that there can be no general 'fatal impact' for Polynesia as a whole, since the experience of different island groups was so vastly different. While the thesis might stand up in the case of the luckless Marquesas islands, which really did suffer in the stereotypical or 'ideal type' model of a fatal impact,[18] other societies remained relatively untouched. Tonga, for example, untouched by the Anglo-German conflict so important in Samoa and elsewhere, stayed largely independent. In this connection, and if Cook is to be indicted under the 'fatal impact' rubric, it is worth pointing out that Cook spent prolonged periods in Tonga on both the second and third voyages. Finally, there is a school of thought that stresses the 'organic' congruence and symbiosis of European and Polynesian society. The esoterica of religious ceremonies aside, at the basic level Europeans and Polynesians understood each other well enough; the only thing that seriously puzzled the islanders was that the strangers had no women with them.[19] Cynics who say that there was nothing in ancient Polynesian society worth preserving are answered by others who say that the corrupt eighteenth-century English society of the Bloody Code or the moribund *Ancien Régime* of France were scarcely beacons of civilisation either. As one critic has written: 'the key . . . is continuity through superficial change, not disruption through a fatal impact'.[20]

Whatever the merits of the notion of a fatal impact, the subsequent unhappy fate of indigenous societies has gravely vitiated Cook's reputation. By a far from rigorous logic, the fact that Cook was prepared to use force in the Pacific has implied in some minds that he can be blamed for *all* subsequent misfortunes suffered by Polynesia. Once again, as in the case of the fatal impact, the germ of this idea can be traced to Cook's own lifetime. William Cowper initially praised Cook as a shining contrast to Cortés, then changed his mind once he realised that Cook had encouraged the Hawaiians to treat him as a god.[21] One modern critic has gone so far as to say that in every Pacific land from the American Northwest to Australia, aboriginal peoples are still recovering from the unpleasant consequences of his actions.[22] Scholars are now virtually unanimous that the European voyagers introduced venereal disease into Polynesia, and the paradigm case was that of Cook in Hawaii; on his first visit in 1778 syphilis was unknown on the islands but when he returned nearly a year later it was rampant.[23] Yet Cook himself struggled heroically to avoid this outcome, only to be defeated by simple human nature. His critics will not allow him this obvious escape route and continue to lay all the subsequent ills of Polynesia at Cook's personal door. Few things have plummeted more disastrously than Cook's reputation. In the Victorian era he was the classic Boy's Own hero, saint and martyr, bringing light to benighted savages, perceived as a larger-than-life figure from the long eighteenth century who died, like Wolfe and Nelson, while fighting for empire.[24] Certainly for the first half of the nineteenth century all voyagers and navigators who called at the Pacific islands brought back honorific mentions and glowing testimonials to the legendary Captain Cook.[25] As the twentieth century merged into the twenty-first his reputation could scarcely be lower. Allegedly, racist, imperialist, man of violence and spreader of venereal disease, he is the object of almost universal execration in all societies that have lived through colonialism.[26] Anglophobic American missionaries in Hawaii started this ball rolling in the nineteenth century, anti-imperialists of the postcolonial era after 1945 took it up with avidity, and the process shows no signs of slowing.[27]

If Cook's reputation has shrunk from the onslaughts of critics (some more howling and foaming-mouthed than others) and developing countries propagandists determined to stop their ears against any nuanced or dispassionate critique of Cook, viewing him merely as an 'evil white man', cynical killer and imperialist agent, academics have sometimes seemed to swim towards the dismembered hero like sharks, determined to finish him off. With certain scholars there is a contempt and hatred of biography *tout court*, and a determination to downgrade all individuals and dissolve them into a soup of structures, cultures and 'spaces'. To this end there is much talk of hypostatic spaces and cultures of exploration.[28] The other approach to cutting Cook down to size is to stress that all his expeditions were collaborative ventures, involving back-up from scientists, botanists, the Admiralty, the Royal Society and other patrons, to say nothing of his officers and crew. The old approach was to stress that by taking naturalists and botanists on his voyages, Cook paved the way for such momentous experiments as Darwin's on the voyage of the *Beagle*. Cook's academic critics ingeniously turn this argument on its head, and underline the notion of collaboration. In philosophical terms, therefore, 'Cook' is a phenomenological construct and, in Hegelian terms, he is simply the locus for a number of different impulses and forces. Though obvious and even banal, the point is well taken, for biography should never be the equivalent of French *auteur* film theory, with the hero as 'director' and all other collaborators – producer, scriptwriter, composer, actors, etc., etc. – considered as mere adjuncts. On the other hand, the danger of the revisionist approach is that the baby will be thrown out with the bathwater and no human subject left who was a great navigator and surveyor. Finally, academic critics are prone to join forces with the postcolonial agitators and view Cook as a 'prodromos' for imperialism and its active promoter.[29]

Unquestionably Cook in some sense symbolised a world transformed by Enlightenment thought, the Industrial Revolution and the consequent quantum-jump in technology. Those who like to emphasise the collaborative nature of his voyages sometimes attempt a grand-slam unified theory, uniting the notion of imperialism with the new tools and techniques Cook had at his disposal. The aids for navigation (such as the chronometer), his own methods of mapping and surveying, the collecting and classifying systems of Banks and the Forsters, and even the textual and visual representation of his voyages thus become culturally 'hegemonic' tools.[30] Farther than this the evidence will not stretch. The relationship of Cook to nineteenth-century imperialism is that of unintended consequences, and it is absurd, anachronistic and unhistorical to make Cook responsible for all the later ills of the Pacific. In some quarters one can even discern a desire to have it both ways. While Cook is diminished, shrunk and cut down to size by an emphasis on his collaborators he, contradictorily, is still held to be personally responsible for the later plight of the Nootka, the Maoris, or the Australian aborigines. The idea is sometimes entertained, one does not know how seriously, that it would have been better if Europeans had never gone to the Pacific and if Polynesian society had remained unchanged. Apart from the romantic view of Polynesia thus insinuated – which a study of the societies of the South Seas will not bear out, disfigured as they were by human sacrifice, infanticide, cannibalism and intrasociety exploitation and extraction of surplus value of an extreme kind – is it really the case that Polynesians would have been better off without the advent of Europe? Even in the impassioned arena of American slavery, voices have arisen within the US black community to suggest that the descendants of slaves have fared better in the USA than they would have done under the benighted regimes of West Africa. The wisest, if not the last, word in this debate should be left with Marx, who summed up the essential ambiguity of the general situation. While deploring the exploitation of the British Empire in India, he pointed out that its beneficial consequence was the destruction of another form of subjection and degradation, that of the individual Hindu to Hanuman the monkey and Sabbala the cow.[31]

In terms of the global imperialism of the nineteenth century Cook was a mere dot, as insignificant as the *Endeavour* when contrasted to the total area of the Pacific. To make him in any way responsible for the exploitation and atrocities of the post-Napoleonic period comes close to the post hoc fallacy. No single historical actor can be held responsible for later developments that can perhaps be traced to him/her by an elaborate causal chain, unless that person is a truly *conscious* agent. Cook could not have been such an agent for the later imperialism for neither he nor anyone else in the eighteenth century understood its later global logic; this would take the genius of Marx to explicate. The relationship between European explorers of Africa and imperialism is tenuous but at least some of them, H. M. Stanley, for example, would have understood something of the implications of their expeditions. Although Stanley cannot be held responsible for the later enormities of King Leopold and his Congo fief, he cannot be entirely acquitted of responsibility, since he knew Leopold well; if he did not understand where his ambitions tended, he must have been stupid, which he was not; but if he did understand and did nothing – which was the case – he can be held *indirectly* culpable. It is difficult to see how Cook can be similarly indicted on this score. The great Cook scholar Glyn Williams has suggested that the issue of an explorer's responsibility for the long-term consequences of his actions is not straightforward, because Cook explicitly claimed territories in the name of the British Empire.[32] This, I submit, is to confuse two senses of imperialism: on the one hand, the relatively simple and even naïve one which underlay the struggle between Britain and France for global political dominance in the eighteenth century; and the later, much more serious and sinister octopus-like embrace of the world by international capitalism.[33] When the aboriginal spokesmen of Australia, New Zealand, Hawaii or Vancouver Island denounce the malign impact of Cook, it is really the consequences of the latter, not the former, they are deploring. Yet with the latter Cook has nothing significant to do. Cook was certainly no paragon, yet justice must be done. At the same time we should perhaps be grateful to his critics that he can no longer be considered, in the words of one of his contemporary admirers, as 'the most moderate, humane and gentle circumnavigator that ever went upon discoveries'.[34]

Appendix

I T has been stated on several occasions that Cook satisfied Napoleon's prerequisite for a marshal: he was lucky. Modern oceanography enables us to see this very clearly, for Cook never encountered the worst monsters of the deep, the 100-foot-plus waves whose very existence was doubted until the last two decades. On the old 'linear' model of wave formation, the highest wave could be no greater than 45 feet from crest to trough, for thereafter it would implode from its own stature. The loss of so many merchant vessels every year (about one a week worldwide, according to the Lloyd's Register) used to be set down generically to 'rough seas' – an actuarial fact built into the calculations of insurance companies. Only after 1995 did scientifically unimpeachable data emerge which not only proved the existence of these monster waves but, more alarmingly, indicated that they were a reasonably common phenomenon; the latest satellite radar research shows about ten of them roaming the world's oceans at any one time. The scientific validation of these giants, variously referred to as 'rogue waves', 'freak waves' and even 'freaque waves', enabled maritime historians to reinterpret many of the unexplained disasters of the past and to verify accounts previously thought far-fetched, possibly the products of the delusional minds of 'old salts' who had spent too many years before the mast. The amazing thing about the scientific arrogance of the past was that it was confidently asserted that all these reports of giant waves at sea 'must have been' false as they did not accord with the then prevailing oceanographic models.

Huge waves of the 100-foot-plus variety are basically of three kinds. Tsunamis can attain huge heights as they crash on to land (the Krakatoa wave of 1883 was 130 feet high) but are harmless to mariners on the open sea, where they are seen as passing ripples. Massive waves generated by severe and long-lived storms are a second kind of hazard. The height of waves in typhoons, hurricanes and cyclonic storms is determined by a threefold causality: the strength of the wind, how long it has been blowing, and the 'fetch' of the sea or the extent of open ocean uninterrupted by land. For example, in the barren wastes of the eastern Pacific, where the ocean enjoys 6,000 miles of 'fetch' a 100 m.p.h. wind blowing continuously for a week would be bound to churn up a monster. Yet even these waves are basically pyramidal and are therefore in theory survivable, as the USS *Ramapo* proved in 1933. When the ship was hit by a severe hurricane, the officers were able to take unimpeachable measurements of the following sea, and recorded a wave of 112 feet in their wake. It is the third kind of giant wave that is the most fearsome. For reasons that are not yet understood, a vertical wall of water, 70–100 feet high, can sometimes appear, seemingly from nowhere, preceded by a deep trough known to mariners as a 'hole in the ocean'. Against such an apparition even the most modern liner has scanty defences. It can now be confidently asserted that the unexplained loss of so many merchant ships can be attributed to this cause. Notable incidents of ships encountering these wave monsters include the *Glamorgan* in the North Atlantic on 15 February 1883, the *Daniel Steinman* south of Halifax, Nova Scotia on 3 April 1884, the yacht *Mignonette* off the coast of West Africa on 19 May 1884 and the *Peconic* off the coast of Georgia on 27 August 1905. In the twentieth century famous ship tragedies involving the loss of vessel and all on board included the liner *Waratah* between Durban and Cape Town on 29 July 1909, the *Cretan Star* in the Indian Ocean in 1976 and the *Derbyshire*, lost in a typhoon off the coast of Japan on 9 September 1980. The most notorious loss was that of the 'unsinkable' state-of-the-art German supertanker *München*, which disappeared in the North Atlantic on 7 December 1978.

Even ocean liners are at serious risk from the 100-foot wave preceded by the 'hole in the ocean'. In 1966 the Italian *Michelangelo* reported a 'near miss' after a collision with a wave that the best experts assert was within the 60–70-foot range. Most sensationally, all three 'Queens' of the Cunard Line have had close encounters with the monsters of the ocean. In 1943 in the North Atlantic the *Queen Elizabeth* ploughed into a trough and was then hit by two massive waves in succession; the windows on the bridge, 85 feet above sea level, were smashed and shattered. In December 1942 there occurred an event that nearly produced the greatest tragedy in all maritime history and could conceivably have altered the course of the war. The *Queen Mary*, carrying 15,000 troops from the USA to Europe, fell into a trough off the north coast of Scotland, was hit by a wave estimated as 75–80 feet, rolled at an angle of 45 degrees and came within a few feet of capsizing. Had she done so, the loss of life would have been by far the greatest fatality at sea, ten times that of the *Titanic*. For the Allies to lose 15,000 fighting men at the very time they had just won the victory of Alamein in North Africa and stood poised to win at Stalingrad might have undone all the effects of these victories, sent morale into a tailspin and given new heart to Hitler and the Nazis. Yet the ocean had not yet finished with the Queens. In September 1995 the *QE2* was hit by a 95-foot wave in the North Atlantic, described by her captain as like watching the white cliffs of Dover advancing towards him. As if to underline the danger of the Atlantic, in February–March 2001 two liners in quick succession came close to disaster in the South Atlantic after being hit by giant waves of 90–100 feet. Experts considered that both the *Bremen* and *Caledonian Star* were lucky to survive.

Cook, then, was very lucky that in all his oceanic rovings he never met the ultimate peril. It is thought that Columbus did, or almost so. On his third voyage, on 4 August 1498, his ships encountered a huge wave, higher than the vessels' masts, which seemed to lift the explorer's fleet up as if with a giant hand and then drop it again into an enormous trough. The description makes it sound as if the ships hit the reverse slope, as it were, of the dreaded 'hole in the ocean'. Nothing like this was ever reported on any of the Cook voyages and the inference that the captain was above all lucky is strengthened by the fate of his French rival and most distinguished successor La Pérouse, for the cyclonic storm that destroyed him in 1788 must have been one of exceptional ferocity. Historians often scoff at the notion of a 'Protestant wind' yet it is a historical fact, observable in many sea battles from 1588 to 1759, that the elements consistently favoured the British defending the homeland and punished would-be foreign invaders. It is perhaps not too far-fetched to say that Britons have always enjoyed the luck of the draw in their encounters with the ocean. Chauvinists would doubtless say that Cook's greatest slice of luck was that he was born a Yorkshireman.

Notes

ABBREVIATIONS

Adm.   Admiralty records, National Archives (formerly PRO)
Banks Journal   A. M. Lysaght, ed., *The Journal of Joseph Banks in the Endeavour* (Guildford 1980)
BL   British Library
EV   J. C. Beaglehole, ed., *The Journals of Captain James Cook On His Voyages of Discovery*, Vol 1: *The Voyage of the Endeavour, 1768–1771* (Cambridge 1968)
RAV   J. C. Beaglehole, ed., *The Journals of Captain James Cook On His Voyages of Discovery*, Vol 2: *The Voyage of the Resolution and Adventure, 1772–1775* (Cambridge 1969)
RDV   J. C. Beaglehole, ed., *The Journals of Captain James Cook On His Voyages of Discovery*, Vol 3 (two parts): *The Voyage of the Resolution and Discovery, 1776–1780*, 2 vols (Cambridge 1967)

The place of publication is London unless otherwise stated.

CHAPTER 1: A YORKSHIRE APPRENTICESHIP

1. For a full analysis of this idea see Frank McLynn, *Hearts of Darkness: The European Exploration of Africa* (1992)
2. For this see Daniel Szechi, *1715: The Great Jacobite Rebellion* (New Haven, 2006)
3. John Walker Ord, *The History and Antiquities of Cleveland* (1846) p. 547
4. J. C. Beaglehole, *The Life of Captain Cook* (1972) pp. 3, 455
5. See, for example, Walter Besant, *Captain Cook* (1894) p. 5
6. Much more judicious is Beaglehole's summing up: 'What combination of factors in the mingled blood of a Lowland Scots labourer and a Yorkshire village woman went to produce that remarkable career we may ask without useful answer' (*Life*, p. 3)
7. Tony Horwitz, *Into the Blue: Boldly Going where Captain Cook has Gone Before* (2002) p. 291
8. John Tuke, *A General View of the Agriculture of the North Riding of Yorkshire* (1794)
9. John Graves, *The History of Cleveland* (Carlisle 1808) p. 197; cf. also E. Baines, *Yorkshire Past and Present* 2 vols (1870); *Victoria County History of York: North Riding* 2 vols (1923)
10. See J. C. Beaglehole, 'Some problems of Cook's biographer', *Mariner's Mirror* 55, 4 (1969) pp. 365–81
11. Vanessa Collingridge, *Captain Cook: The Life, Death and Legacy of History's Greatest Explorer* (2002) p. 21
12. Graves, *History of Cleveland* p. 456; D. O'Sullivan, *Great Ayton: A History of the Village* (Great Ayton 1996); Clifford Thornton, *Captain Cook in Cleveland* (Middlesbrough 1978) p. 23; R. R. Hastings, *Essays in North Riding History, 1780–1850* (Northallerton 1981)
13. Robert Tate Gaskin, *The Old Seaport of Whitby* (1909) p. 383
14. For a full explanation of all this see Frank McLynn 'Newcastle and the Jacobite Rising of 1745', *Journal of Local Studies* 2 (1982) pp. 95–105
15. Richard Hough, *Captain James Cook: A Biography* (1994) p. 5

16. Beaglehole, *Life* p. 5; cf. also J. Howard, *Staithes: Chapters from the History of a Seafaring Town* (Scarborough 2000); Thornton, *Captain Cook in Cleveland*, p. 23

17. Richard C. Allen, ' "Remember me to my good friend Captain Walker": James Cook and the North Yorkshire Quakers', in G. Williams, ed., *Captain Cook: Explorations and Reassessments* (Woodbridge, Suffolk 2004) pp. 21–36

18. The entire subject is a muddle. Beaglehole appeared to establish the truth of the matter in *Life* p. 6. But the Grape Lane faction continues strong, as in Allen, ' "Remember me" ' p. 22. For the latest thinking, favouring Grape Lane over Haggersgate, see John Gascoigne, *Captain Cook* (2007) pp. 223–24

19. Julia Hunt, *From Whitby to Wapping: The Story of the Early Years of Captain James Cook* (1991) pp. 3–14

20. George Young, *A History of Whitby and Streonshalh Abbey* 2 vols (Whitby 1871) ii. pp. 514–18, 850–52

21. Thomas and Cordelia Stamp, *James Cook: Maritime Scientist* (Whitby 1976) p. xi; Allen, ' "Remember me" ' p. 29; Horwitz, *Into the Blue* p. 308; Thornton, *Captain Cook in Cleveland*

22. Horwitz, *Into the Blue* p. 297

23. Daniel Defoe, *A Tour through the Whole Island of Great Britain* (1722) Letter 9; S. K. Jones, 'A maritime history of the port of Whitby 1700–1914', Ph.D. thesis, University of London (1982)

24. Edward J. Cashin, *The King's Ranger: Thomas Brown and the American Revolution on the Southern Frontier* (Athens, GA 1989)

25. Alan Villiers, *Captain Cook: The Seaman's Seaman* (1967) pp. 10–12, 88–90, 238–40

26. Rosalin Barker, 'Cook's nursery: Whitby's eighteenth century merchant fleet', in Williams, *Explorations and Reassessments* pp. 7–20

27. Michael W. Flinn, *The History of the British Coal Industry, Vol. 2, 1700–1830: The Industrial Revolution* (Oxford 1984) p. 171

28. Raymond Turner, 'The English coal industry in the 17th and 18th centuries', *American Historical Review* 27 (1921) pp. 1–23

29. See *Diary of a Tour in 1732 through Parts of England, Wales, Ireland and Scotland made by John Loveday of Caversham* (Roxburghe Club 107 1890) p. 172

30. Flinn, *History* pp. 215–20

31. Turner, 'English Coal Industry', pp. 9–12, 19; Walter Scott Dunn, *The New Imperial Economy: The British Army and the American Frontier 1767–1768* (2001) p. 22

32. W. J. Hausman, 'Size and profitability of English colliers in the eighteenth century', *Business History Review* 51 (1977) pp. 460–73 thinks profits were around the 12 per cent mark, but Simon Ville, 'Size and profitability of English colliers in the eighteenth Century: a reappraisal', *Business History Review* 58 (1984) pp. 103–20 thinks this a considerable underestimate. See also Ralph Davis, 'Earnings of capital in the English shipping industry, 1670–1730', *Journal of Economic History* 17 (1957) pp. 409–25; Ralph Davis, *The Rise of the English Shipping Industry in the 17th and 18th Centuries* (1962); R. B. Westerfield, *Middlemen in English Business, particularly between 1660 and 1760* (New Haven 1915); Julian Hoppit, *Risk and Failure in English Business 1700–1800* (Cambridge 1987); James D. Tracy, ed., *The Political Economy of Merchant Empires: State Power and World Trade, 1350–1750* (Cambridge 1991)

33. Henry Taylor, *Memoirs* (1811) p. 71; Flinn, *History* p. 180

34. Taylor, *Memoirs* p. 2; Flinn, *History* p. 172

35. Taylor, *Memoirs* p. 6

36. Ibid. pp. 4–5

37. Philip L. Woodworth, 'The meteorological data of William Hutchinson and a Liverpool air pressure time series spanning 1768–1999', *International Journal of Climatology* 26 (2006) pp. 1713–26; Woodworth, *A Study of the Changes in High Water Levels and Tides at Liverpool during the Past 230 Years with some Historical Background* (Birkenhead 1999)

38. Julian P. Boyd, ed., *The Papers of Thomas Jefferson* (1958) iv. p. 249

39. Villiers, *Captain Cook* pp. 10–12, 238–40

40. See Barry Cunliffe, *The Extraordinary Voyage of Pytheas the Greek* (2002); C. F. C. Hawkes, *Pytheas: Europe and the Greek Explorers* (Oxford 1977)

41. Hubert Lamb, *Historic Storms of the North Sea, British Isles and Northwest Europe* (Cambridge 1991); D. N. Bresch et al. eds, *Storm over Europe: An Underestimated Risk* (Zurich 2000)

42. Edward Bryant, *Natural Hazards* (Cambridge 2004) pp. 60–62
43. Flinn, *History* pp. 173–74
44. Ibid. p. 174
45. Taylor, *Memoirs* pp. 27–30
46. Ibid. pp. 23–26, 87
47. Ibid. pp. 31–32, 71, 73
48. Ibid. p. 58
49. Ibid. p. 161.
50. Hausman, 'Size and profitability', p. 464
51. Arthur Kitson, *Captain James Cook, The Circumnavigator* (1907) pp. 11–12
52. Beaglehole, *Life* pp. 11–12
53. Taylor, *Memoirs* p. 32
54. William Hutchinson, *A Treatise On Practical Seamanship* (1787) p. 129
55. Andrew Kippis, *The Life of Captain James Cook* (1788) p. 4
56. O. H. K. Spate, *Paradise Found and Lost* (1988) p. 133; Collingridge, *Captain Cook* pp. 43–44
57. Beaglehole, *Life* p. 17
58. Hough, *Captain James Cook* p. 10
59. Tony Barrow, *The Whaling Trade of North-East England* (Sunderland 2001) p. 15
60. Ibid. *passim*; cf. Alan Whitworth, ed., *Aspects of the Yorkshire Coasts* (Barnsley 1999)
61. Beaglehole, *Life* p. 15
62. N. A. M. Rodger, *The Wooden World: An Anatomy of the Georgian Navy* (1986) pp. 116–18
63. Ibid. p. 265
64. N. A. M. Rodger, *The Insatiable Earl: A Life of John Montagu, Fourth Earl of Sandwich 1718–1792* (1993) p. 173
65. H. Zimmermann, *Account of the Third Voyage of Captain Cook 1776–1780*, trans. U. Tewsley (Wellington 1926) p. 41
66. Gascoigne, *Captain Cook* pp. 151–55
67. D. Baugh, 'The Eighteenth-century Navy as a national institution 1690–1815', in J. R. Hill, ed., *The Oxford Illustrated History of the Royal Navy* (Oxford 1995) p. 157; John Brewer, *The Sinews of Power, War, Money and the English State 1688–1783* (1989) p. 40
68. F. W. Howay, ed., *Zimmermann's Captain Cook* (Toronto 1929) pp. 98–100; Beaglehole, *Life* p. 697

CHAPTER 2: THE SEVEN YEARS WAR

1. Muster book, Adm. 36/5533
2. Hamer log, Adm. 51/292
3. Bissett log, Adm. 52/578
4. Hamer log, 29 September 1755, Adm. 51/292
5. R. M. Hunt, *The Life of Sir Hugh Palliser* (1844)
6. John Charnock, *Biographia Navalis*, V. (1795) pp. 483–96
7. Peter D. Jeans, *Seafaring Lore and Legend: A Maritime Miscellany of Myth, Superstition, Fable and Fact* (2004) p. 121
8. Palliser to Clevland, 27 November 1755, Adm. 1/2292
9. Arthur Kitson, *Captain James Cook, The Circumnavigator* (1907) p. 20
10. Palliser to Clevland, 13 April 1756, Adm. 1/2293; cf. Palliser log Adm. 51/292
11. Palliser to Clevland, 3, 4 June 1756, Adm. 1/2993
12. Palliser to Clevland, 12 June 1756, Adm. 1/2993
13. Palliser to Clevland, 6, 18 July, 2 August 1756, Adm. 1/2993
14. Kitson, *Captain James Cook* p. 22
15. Palliser log, 17 December 1756, Adm. 51/292
16. Palliser to Clevland, 6, 13 January, 17 April 1757, Adm. 1/2294; Palliser log, 30 May 1757, Adm. 51/292
17. Andrew Kippis, *The Life of Captain James Cook* (1788) pp. 4–5
18. N. A. M. Rodger, *The Wooden World: An Anatomy of the Georgian Navy* (1986) p. 264
19. Ibid. p. 20
20. Log of the *Solebay*, 30 July–7 September 1757, Adm. 52/1033

21. Kitson, *Captain James Cook* p. 29
22. Simcoe to Clevland, April–June 1757, Adm. 1/2471
23. For events in North America to the end of 1757 see Fred Anderson, *Crucible of War: The Seven Years War and the Fate of Empire in British North America 1754–1766* (New York 2000) pp. 86–207
24. George F. G. Stanley, *New France: The Last Phase 1744–1760* (Toronto 1968) pp. 165–94
25. Stanley M. Pargellis, *Lord Loudoun in North America* (New Haven 1968) pp. 356–58; Anderson, *Crucible* pp. 235–36; R. Middleton, *The Bells of Victory: The Pitt-Newcastle Ministry and the Conduct of the Seven Years War 1757–1762* (Cambridge 1985) pp. 51–54
26. Jean Elizabeth Lunn, 'Agriculture and war in Canada, 1740–1760', *Canadian Historical Review* 16 (1935) pp. 130–32
27. Stanley, *New France* pp. 196–200
28. Anderson, *Crucible* p. 259
29. Rex Whitworth, *Field-Marshal Lord Ligonier* (Oxford 1958) pp. 236–42
30. F. G. Halfpenny, ed., *Dictionary of Canadian Biography*, 13 vols (Toronto 1994) iii. pp. 70–71
31. Simcoe's log, Adm. 51/686
32. J. C. Beaglehole, *The Life of Captain Cook* (1972) p. 31
33. Stephen Brumwell, *Paths of Glory: The Life and Death of General James Wolfe* (2006) p. 144
34. Beaglehole, *Life* pp. 31–32
35. There is exhaustive detail on all this in J. S. McLennan, *Louisbourg from its Foundation to its Fall, 1713–1758* (Sydney 1969)
36. J. Clarence Webster, ed., *The Journal of Jeffrey Amherst: Recording the Military Career of General Amherst in America from 1758 to 1763* (Toronto 1931) pp. 50–51
37. Lawrence Henry Gipson, *The Great War for Empire: The Victorious Years 1758–1760* (New York 1967) pp. 198–201; Christopher Moore, *Louisbourg Portraits: Life in an Eighteenth-Century Garrison Town* (Toronto 1982) pp. 209–15
38. J. Mackay Hitsman and C. C. J. Bond, 'The assault Landing at Louisbourg, 1758', *Canadian Historical Review* 35 (1954) pp. 314–330
39. Brumwell, *Paths of Glory*, pp. 150
40. Gipson, *Great War* pp. 202–07; McLennan, *Louisbourg* pp. 267–68
41. Anderson, *Crucible* pp. 254–56
42. Beaglehole, *Life* p. 32
43. McLennan, *Louisbourg* p. 284
44. Hugh Carrington, *Life of Captain Cook* (1939) p. 22
45. Brumwell, *Paths of Glory* pp. 158–60
46. Samuel Holland to John Graves Simcoe, 11 January in Willis Chipman, 'The life and times of Major Samuel Holland, Surveyor-General 1764–1801', *Ontario Historical Society Papers and Records* 21 (1924) pp. 13–24
47. Cook log, 27 July 1758, Adm. 52/978
48. Charnock, *Biographia Navalis* V. p. 259. Simcoe (1710–49) was the father of the more famous John Graves Simcoe, the first Lieutenant-General of Upper Canada and an important figure in early Canadian history. See Mary Beacock Fryer and Christopher Dracoff, *John Graves Simcoe, 1752–1806: A Biography* (Toronto 1998)
49. For these campaigns see Anderson, *Crucible* pp. 240–49, 259–85
50. A. McNairn, *Behold the Hero: General Wolfe and the Arts in the Eighteenth Century* (Liverpool 1997) p. 31. Stephen Brumwell's attempts to defend Wolfe on this score are to my mind unconvincing (Brumwell, *Paths of Glory* pp. 167–68)
51. Brumwell, *Paths of Glory* pp. 168–70
52. Beaglehole, *Life* p. 34
53. Willis Chipman, 'Samuel Holland', pp. 18–19
54. Beaglehole, *Life* pp. 37–39
55. Thomas Raddall, *Halifax: Warden of the North* (Garden City, NJ 1965)
56. Cook's log, 11 December 1758, 6, 11 January, 13, 19 February 1759, Adm. 51/686; 52/978
57. Markus Eder, *Crime and Punishment in the Royal Navy of the Seven Years War: 1755–1763* (Ashgate, Aldershot 2002) pp. 24–25
58. Rodger, *Wooden World* pp. 205–9, 216–20
59. Ibid. pp. 220–28

60. Eder, *Crime* pp. 18–31
61. A. N. Gilbert, 'Buggery and the British Navy 1700–1861', *Journal of Social History* 10 (1976) pp. 72–98
62. Peter Aughton, *Endeavour: The Story of Captain Cook's First Great Epic Voyage* (Moreton, Gloucestershire 1999) pp. 63, 93–97; Vanessa Collingridge, *Captain Cook: The Life, Death and Legacy of History's Greatest Explorer* (2002) pp. 137–38, 363
63. Julia Rae, *Captain James Cook Endeavours* (1997) p. 44
64. Anne Salmond, 'Tute: the impact of Polynesia on Captain Cook', in G. Williams, ed., *Captain Cook: Explorations and Reassessments* (Woodridge, Suffolk 2004) pp. 77–93 (at p. 84)
65. Brumwell, *Paths of Glory* p. 198
66. Victor Suthren, *To Go Upon Discovery: James Cook and Canada, from 1758 to 1769* (Toronto 2000) pp. 61–63
67. R. Baldwin, 'The charts and surveys of James Cook', in David Cordingly, ed., *Captain James Cook, Navigator: The Achievements of Captain James Cook as a Seaman, Navigator and Surveyor* (Sydney 1988) p. 90
68. EV p. cxi.
69. Rodger, *Wooden World* p. 62
70. Brumwell, *Paths of Glory* pp. 187–88
71. Jonathan R. Dull, *The French Navy and the Seven Years War* (Lincoln, NE 2005) p. 143
72. See Frank McLynn, *1759: The Year Britain Became Master of the World* (2004)
73. William H. Whiteley, 'Saunders, Sir Charles', in F. G. Halperin, ed., *Dictionary of Canadian Biography* 13 vols (1994) iv. pp. 698–702; Edward Salmon, *Life of Admiral Sir Charles Saunders, K.B.* (1914)
74. Charnock, *Biographia Navalis* V. pp. 167–70
75. Kitson, *Captain Cook* p. 38
76. Log, 17 May 1759, Adm. 52/978
77. Charnock, *Biographia Navalis* VI. (1798) p. 286
78. Anderson, *Crucible* pp. 346–49
79. See McLynn, *1759* pp. 50–53
80. Some say the British also had invaluable information given them by Captain Robert Stobo, who had recently escaped from Quebec after being a prisoner of war there for four years. See Robert C. Alberts, *The Most Extraordinary Adventures of Major Robert Stobo* (Boston 1965)
81. C. P. Stacey, *Quebec 1759: The Siege and the Battle* (Donald Graves, ed., with new material) (Toronto 2002) pp. 47–54
82. Cook's log, 10 June 1759, Adm. 52/978
83. Cook's log, 25 June 1759, Adm. 52/978
84. John Knox, *An Historical Journal of the Campaigns in North America for the Years 1757, 1758, 1759 and 1760* (1769) i. pp. 290–91
85. Ibid. i. pp. 379–81
86. Brumwell, *Paths of Glory* p. 209
87. Cook's log, Adm. 52/978
88. Stacey, *Quebec* p. 74
89. It is interesting to compare the pro- and anti-Wolfe accounts of this battle, respectively in Brumwell, *Paths of Glory* pp. 220–25 and Anderson, *Crucible* pp. 348–49
90. There is considerable disagreement among experts on this story. Some say the ship's master almost cut off was Bissett of the *Eagle* and that the anecdote was later attached to Cook as the man with the household name (See Kitson, *Captain Cook* p. 45; Carrington, *Life of Captain Cook* p. 28.) I am content to leave the last word to Beaglehole who says: 'There is nothing inherently implausible about the story' (*Life* p. 47)
91. For these victories see Anderson, *Crucible* pp. 325–43
92. Once more see the contrasting views in Brumwell, *Paths of Glory* pp. 262–63 and Anderson, *Crucible* pp. 351–52
93. Donald Olson et al., 'Perfect tide, ideal moon: an unappreciated aspect of Wolfe's generalship at Queec, 1759', *William and Mary Quarterly* 59, 4 (2002) pp. 959–74 (at p. 973)
94. Whitelock log, 11, 12 September 1759, Adm. 51/686; Cook log, 13 September 1759, Adm. 52/978

95. Cook log, 19 September 1759, Adm. 52/978
96. Whitelock log, 23 September 1759, Adm. 51/686; Cleander log, Adm. 52/978
97. Charnock, *Biographia Navalis* VI. pp. 345–46
98. Saunders to Clevland, 22 April 1760, Adm. 1/482

CHAPTER 3: CHARTING NEWFOUNDLAND

1. Willis Chipman, 'The Life and times of Samuel Holland, Surveyor-General 1764–1801', *Ontario Historical Society Paper and Records* 21 (1924) pp. 21–24
2. Adams log, 24–25 April 1760, Adm. 51/3925; Colville to Clevland, 10 April 1761, Adm. 1/482
3. David Reynolds, *America: Empire of Liberty: A New History* (2009) pp. 52–53. This is, of course, simplistic. The crucial year was 1759, for the naval victories of Lagos and Quiberon that year destroyed French naval power and meant that New France, unable to be supplied from France, was thereafter living on borrowed time.
4. For the 1760 campaign see Fred Anderson, *Crucible of War: The Seven Years War and the Fate of Empire in British North America, 1754–1776* (New York 2000) pp. 387–409
5. For Bateman see John Charnock, *Biographia Navalis*, IV. (1798) pp. 386–87
6. Colville journal, 19 January 1761, Adm. 50/22
7. J. C. Beaglehole, *The Life of Captain Cook* (1972), p. 55
8. These surveys are conveniently collected in Victor Suthren, *To Go Upon Discovery: James Cook and Canada, from 1758 to 1779* (Toronto 2000) pp. 109–17
9. Max Savelle, *The Origins of American Diplomacy: The International History of Anglo-America 1492–1783* (New York 1967) p. 475; James K. Hiller, 'The Newfoundland fisheries issue in Anglo-French treaties 1713–1904', *Journal of Imperial and Commonwealth History* 24, 1 (1996) pp. 1–23
10. Jean-François Brière, 'L'État et le commerce de la morne de Terre Neuve en France au 18e siècle', *Revue d'histoire de l'Amérique française* 36 (1982) pp. 323–38 and, at greater length Jean-François Brière, *La Pêche française en Amérique du Nord au XVIIIe siècle* (Newfoundland 1990)
11. Colvill to Clevland, 2, 24 July, 17 August 1762, Adm. 1/482
12. Olaf Janzen, 'The French raid upon the Newfoundland fishery in 1762 – A study in the nature and limits of eighteenth-century sea power', in William B. Cogar, ed., *Naval History: The Seventh Symposium of the US Naval Academy* (Washington DC 1988) pp. 35–54
13. Cook log, 19 September 1762, Adm. 52/959
14. For his long and interesting life see G. N. D. Evans, *Uncommon Obdurate: The Several Public Careers of J. F. W. DesBarres* (Toronto 1969)
15. Stephen B. MacPhee, 'DesBarres and his contemporaries as mapmakers', *Nova Scotia Historical Review* 5, 2 (1985) pp. 15–23 (at p. 18). This number of the *NSHR* contains a number of articles on DesBarres which shed light on his difficult personality and turbulent private life.
16. Andrew David, 'James Cook's 1762 survey of St John's Harbour and adjacent parts of Newfoundland', *Terrae Incognitae* 30 (1998) pp. 63–71
17. Colville to Clevland, 25 October 1762, Adm. 1/482
18. Cook's log, 11 November 1762, Adm. 52/959
19. Arthur Kitson, *Captain James Cook, The Circumnavigator* (1907) p. 59
20. Colville to Clevland, 30 December 1762, Adm. 1/482
21. Hugh Carrington, *Life of Captain Cook* (1939) pp. 33–34
22. Vanessa Collingridge, *Captain Cook: The Life Death and Legacy of History's Greatest Explorer* (2002) p. 73 says 'probably he had known Miss Batts and her family for more than a decade', though how she knows this is not clear.
23. Beaglehole, *Life* pp. 61–62
24. The enigmatic Mrs Cook has always fascinated students of Cook. All that can be known for certain about her is summed up in Beaglehole, *Life* pp. 689–95. All her six children predeceased her. After her husband's death she was given a pension of £300 a year (a tidy sum in those days) by the Admiralty and was left most of Cook's property and accumulated wages; she was also (a little later) paid a gratuity of £500. She moved from the marital home in Mile End to Clapham where she lived in great comfort. She died in 1835 aged 93, seventy-two years after marrying Cook and fifty-six years after his death. Unfortunately for the biographer there is no evidence of any

kind for Cook's marriage. 'Were there either unhappiness or infidelity, neither fact would have been recorded' (Nicholas Thomas, *Discoveries: The Voyages of Captain Cook*, 2003, p. 141). This has not prevented authors from writing about Mrs Cook, often lapsing into historical novel mode when documentary evidence fails. See S. Sinclair, *Elizabeth Cook: The Captain's Wife 1741–1835* (Sydney 1995); Marele Day, *Mrs Cook: The Real and Imagined Life of the Captain's Wife* (2002).

25. James K. Hiller, 'Utrecht revisited: the origins of French fishing rights in Newfoundland waters', *Newfoundland Studies* 7, 1 (1991) pp. 23–39. See also F. F. Thompson, *The French Shore Problem in Newfoundland: An Imperial Study* (Toronto 1961); Brière, *La Pêche française*

26. Keith Matthews, 'A History of the West of England – Newfoundland Fishery', D. Phil thesis, University of Oxford, 1968; Keith Matthews, *Lectures on the History of Newfoundland 1500–1830* (St John's, Newfoundland 1973)

27. Matthews, 'A history' pp. 181, 335–41; John Mannion, *Irish Settlements in Eastern Canada* (Toronto 1973)

28. Matthews, 'A history', *passim*.

29. Olaf Uwe Janzen, 'The illicit trade in English cod into Spain, 1739–1748', *International Journal of Maritime History* 8, 1 (1996) pp. 1–22

30. Graves to Clevland, 2 January 1763, Adm. 1/1836

31. Kitson, *Captain Cook* pp. 63–64

32. Graves to Stephens, 5, 12, 15 April 1763, Adm. 1/1836

33. For example, instead of granting Cook 'supply' to buy the instruments he needed, the Admiralty insisted that Cook buy them from his own pocket, submit receipts and then obtain reimbursement. The entire saga of bumbledom appears in the correspondence between Graves and Stephens (Admiralty to Graves, 19 April, Stephens to Cook 19 April 1763, Adm. 2/90; Graves to Stephens, 21, 29 April 1763, Adm. 1/1836; Admiralty to Graves, 3 May 1763, Adm. 1/90)

34. Whatever happened, Test's career was not harmed, for he rose to be chief draughtsman at the Tower in 1801 (R. A. Skelton, *James Cook, Surveyor of Newfoundland* (San Francisco 1965) p. 11

35. W. H. Whiteley, 'James Cook and British policy in the Newfoundland fisheries, 1763–67', *Canadian Historical Review* 54 (1973) pp. 245–72 (at p. 247)

36. R. A. Skelton, Captain James Cook as a hydrographer', *Mariner's Mirror* 40 (1954) pp. 92–119

37. Adm. 36/6901

38. Jean-Yves Ribault, 'La Population des îles St Pierre et Miquelon de 1763 à 1793', *Revue française d'histoire d'outre-mer* 53 (1966) pp. 5–66; cf. also Jean-Yves Ribault, 'La Pêche et la commerce et la morne aux îles St Pierre et Miquelon de 1763 à 1793', *Congrès National des Sociétés Savantes. Actes du 91e Congrès à Rennes 1966* (Paris 1969) i. pp. 251–92

39. Admiralty to Graves, 2 May 1763, Adm. 2/90

40. Douglas to Stephens, 3 May 1764; Douglas, log of the *Tweed*, Adm. 51/1016. For d'Anjac see Carrington, *Life of Captain Cook* p. 37

41. Victor Suthren, *To Go Upon Discovery: James Cook and Canada, from 1758 to 1769* (Toronto 2000) p. 133

42. Beaglehole, *Life* p. 74

43. Andrew Kippis, *The Life of Captain James Cook* (1788) p. 517

44. Beaglehole, *Life* p. 76

45. Cook to Palliser, 7 March 1764, Adm. 1/2300

46. Palliser to Stephens, 4 April 1764, Adm. 1/2300; Stephens to Palliser, 13 April 1764, Adm. 2/724

47. Log of the *Grenville*, 14 June–14 July 1764, Adm. 52/1263

48. Log of the *Grenville*, 4 July–4 August, Adm. 52/1263

49. J. M. Murray, ed., *The Newfoundland Journal of Aaron Thomas, Able Seaman in H.M.S. Boston* (1968) p. 189

50. Log of the *Grenville*, 6 August 1764, Adm. 52/1263

51. Colin Podmore, *The Moravian Church in England 1728–1760* (Oxford 1998)

52. W. H. Whiteley, 'The establishment of the Moravian mission in Labrador and British policy, 1763–83', *Canadian Historical Review* 45, 1 (1964) pp. 29–50

53. George Cartwright, *A Journal of Transactions and Events during a Residence of nearly Sixteen Years on the Coast of Labrador* 3 vols (1792) pp. 301–13; Marcel Mauss in collaboration with Henri Beuchat, trans. with a new Foreward by James J. Fox, *Seasonal Variations of the Eskimo: A Study in Social Morphology* (2004) p. 23

54. Log of the *Grenville*, 19–20 August 1764, Adm. 52/1263
55. Log of the *Grenville*, 26 August–17 October 1764, Adm. 52/1263
56. Cook to Stephens, 13 December 1764; Stephens to Cook, 18 December 1764, Adm. 2/725
57. Palliser to Stephens, 6 March 1765, Adm. 1/2300; Stephens to Cook, 5 April 1765, Adm. 2/725
58. Log of the *Grenville*, 22 April–31 May 1765, Adm. 52/1263
59. Olaf Janzen, 'The Royal Navy and the interdiction of aboriginal migration to Newfoundland, 1763–1766', *International Journal of Naval History* 7, 2 (2008)
60. For further details see Leslie F. S. Upton, *Micmacs and Colonists: Indian–White Relations in the Maritimes, 1713–1867* (Vancouver 1979)
61. Ribault, 'La Population' p. 35
62. Log of the *Grenville*, 2 June–12 September 1765, Adm. 2/1263
63. Log of the *Grenville*, 10 October–17 December 1765, Adm. 2/1263
64. Palliser to Stephens, 14 December 1765, Adm. 1/2300; Palliser to Stephens, 3 February 1766, Adm. 1/470; Kitson, *Captain Cook* pp. 79–80
65. Stephens to Cook, 17 March 1766, Adm. 2/726
66. Log of the *Grenville*, 20 April–2 July 1766, Adm. 2/1263
67. Kitson, *Captain Cook* pp. 76–77
68. Beaglehole, *Life* pp. 87–90
69. Log of the *Grenville*, 5 August–5 November 1766, Adm. 2/1263
70. Stephens to Cook, 27 November 1766, Adm. 2/726
71. For Cook's multifaceted brilliance, see Peter Whitfield, *The Charting of the Oceans: Ten Centuries of Maritime Maps* (1996) p. 10; John Noble Wilford, *The Mapmakers* (New York 2000) p. 243
72. Stephens to Cook, 24 March 1767, Adm. 2/727
73. Palliser to Stephens, 7 April 1764, Adm. 1/2300; Stephens to Palliser, 7 April 1764, Adm. 2/74; Palliser to Stephens, 2 December 1766, Adm. 1/2300
74. Beaglehole, *Life* p. 91
75. Log of the *Grenville*, 8 April–15 May 1767, Adm. 2/1263
76. See Stephen A. Davis, *Mi'kmaq: Peoples of the Maritimes* (1998); Harold E. L. Prins, *The Mi'kmaq: Resistance, Accommodation and Cultural Survival* (1996)
77. Log of the *Grenville*, 16 May–1 July 1767, Adm. 2/1263
78. Log of the *Grenville*, 9 July–23 October, Adm. 2/1263
79. Stephens to Cook, 12, 13 November 1767, Adm. 2/727 (answering Cook's letters)
80. Stephens to Cook, 11 April 1768, Adm. 2/727
81. Palliser to Stephens, 30 November 1767, Adm. 1/2300
82. See R. A. Skelton and R. V. Tooley, *The Marine Surveys of James Cook in North America 1758–1768, Particularly the Survey of Newfoundland* (1967) pp. 7–8, 14–17
83. Beaglehole, *Life* p. 85
84. Vice-Admiral Sir Archibald Day, *The Admiralty Hydrographic Service 1795–1919* (1967)
85. William H. Whiteley, *James Cook in Newfoundland 1762–1767* (Newfoundland Historical Society, 1975)
86. Frederick W. Rowe, *A History of Newfoundland and Labrador* (Toronto 1980) p. 187. See also C. Grant Head, *Eighteenth Century Newfoundland: A Geographer's Perspective* (Carleton, Canada 1976); Don Downer, *Turbulent Tides: A Social History of Sandy Point* (Newfoundland 1997); Jerry Bannister, *The Rule of the Admirals: Law, Custom and Naval Government in Newfoundland 1699–1832* (Toronto 2003)

CHAPTER 4: THE CHALLENGE OF THE PACIFIC

1. EV pp. cxii–cxiii
2. J. C. Beaglehole, *The Life of Captain Cook* (1972) p. 153
3. See the routine correspondence in Adm. 3/76
4. Glyndwr Williams, 'The Endeavour voyage: a coincidence of motives', in Margarette Lincoln, ed., *Science and Exploration in the Pacific: European Voyages to the Southern Oceans in the Eighteenth Century* (Woodbridge, Suffolk 1998) pp. 3–18
5. H. B. Carter, *Sir Joseph Banks: 1743–1820* (1988) p. 76

6. Mary Terrall, *The Man Who Flattened the Earth: Maupertuis and the Sciences in the Enlightenment* (Chicago 2002); Robert Whitaker, *The Mapmaker's Wife: A True Tale of Love, Murder and Survival in the Amazon* (New York 2004)

7. For a broad survey see Jonathan Shectman, *Groundbreaking Scientific Experiments: Innovations and Discoveries of the Eighteenth Century* (Burnham, Buckinghamshire 2003); cf. G. N. Clark, *Science and Social Welfare in the Age of Newton* (1949)

8. J. Bronowski and B. Mazlish, *The Western Intellectual Tradition: From Leonardo to Hegel* (1963) p. 54

9. William Sheehan and John Westfall, *The Transits of Venus* (New York 2004); Eli Maor, *Venus in Transit* (Princeton 2002)

10. Peter Aughton, *The Transit of Venus: The Brief, Brilliant Life of Jeremiah Horrocks, Father of British Astronomy* (2004) p. 112

11. Ibid. p. 180

12. See Henry Woolf, *The Transits of Venus: A Study of Eighteenth Century Science* (Princeton 1959) which, however, is more about 1761 than 1769

13. Sir Henry Lyons, *The Royal Society 1660–1940: A History of its Administration under its Charters* (Cambridge 1944) *passim*

14. See the Navy's positive response in Admiralty to Morton, 15 August 1766, Adm. 2/540. See also E. N. da C. Andrade, *A Brief History of the Royal Society* (1960) pp. 1–28

15. The reasons suggested by Vanessa Collingridge, *Captain Cook: The Life, Death and Legacy of History's Greatest Explorer* (2002) pp. 102–03 seem far-fetched and implausible.

16. C. Jack-Hinton, 'Alexander Dalrymple and the rediscovery of the Islands of Solomon', *Mariner's Mirror* 50, 2 (1964) pp. 93–114

17. For his career in general see Howard T. Fry, *Alexander Dalrymple (1737–1808) and the Expansion of British Trade* (1970)

18. H. Tregonning, 'Alexander Dalrymple: the man whom Cook replaced', *Australian Quarterly* 13, 3 (1951) pp. 54–63

19. See Alfred Friendly, *Beaufort of the Admiralty: The Life of Sir Francis Beaufort* (1977); Scott Huler, *Defining the Wind: The Beaufort Scale and How a 19th Century Admiral Turned Science into Poetry* (New York 2004)

20. Alan H. Cook, *Edmond Halley: Charting the Heavens and the Seas* (Oxford 1998)

21. Quoted in Beaglehole, *Life* p. 125

22. For Hawke see R. F. Mackay, *Admiral Hawke* (1965); Andrew Kippis, *The Life of Captain James Cook* (1788) p. 16

23. The most recent study of Dalrymple is a Ph.D. dissertation accepted by the University of St Andrew's, 1992 (Andrew S. Cook, ' "An author voluminous and vast." Alexander Dalrymple (1737–1808), hydrographer to the East India Company and to the Admiralty as publisher')

24. Admiralty minutes, 25 May 1768, Adm. 3/76

25. Andrew S. Cook, 'Cook and the Royal Society', in G. Williams, ed., *Captain Cook: Explorations and Reassessments* (Woodbridge, Suffolk 2004) pp. 37–55

26. I. Kaye, 'Captain James Cook and the Royal Society', *Notes and Records of the Royal Society of London* 24, 1 (1969) pp. 7–18

27. Beaglehole, *Life* p. 126

28. R. T. Gould, *Captain Cook* (1935) p. 36

29. The classic study of Magellan is Visconde de Laguna, *Fernão de Magalhãis* (Lisbon 1938)

30. For the details see Antonio Pigafetta, *The Voyage of Magellan: The Journal of Antonio Pigafetta* ed. and trans. N. J. Paige (Englewood Cliffs, NJ 1969); Antonio Pigafetta, *Magellan's Voyage: A Narrative Account of the First Circumnavigation* ed. and trans. R. A. Skelton (New Haven 1969)

31. E. Roditi, *Magellan of the Pacific* (1972)

32. O. H. K. Spate, *The Spanish Lake* (1979) pp. 90–105

33. A. Sharp, *The Discovery of the Pacific Islands* (Oxford 1960) pp. 24–26

34. EV p. lxviii

35. W. L. Schurz, *The Manila Galleon* (New York 1939) pp. 216–43

36. Spate, *Spanish Lake* p. 105

37. Sharp, *Discovery of the Pacific Islands* pp. 13–42, 86–88

38. C. Jack-Hinton, *The Search for the Islands of Solomon 1567–1838* (Oxford 1969) pp. 13–26

39. Alvaro de Mendaña, *The Discovery of the Solomon Islands by Alvaro de Mendaña in 1568* eds and trans. by Lord Amherst of Hackney and Barry Thomson (Hakluyt Society, 2nd Series 6–7, 1901) i. pp. 70–105

40. Jack-Hinton, *Search* pp. 35–79

41. Pedro Fernandes de Quirós, *The Voyages of Pedro Fernandez de Quirós* ed. and trans. Sir Clements Markham (Hakluyt Society, 2nd series 14–15, 1904)

42. Fray Martin de Munilla *La Austrialia del Espiritu Santo* ed. and trans. Cel sus Kelly (Hakluyt Society, 2nd series 126–27, Cambridge 1966)

43. Jack-Hinton, *Search* pp. 129–32

44. For Quirós's complex career see John Toohey, *Quirós* (Sydney 2002); M. Estensen, *Terra Australis Incognita: The Spanish Quest for the Mysterious Great South Land* (Oxford 2006)

45. Jack-Hinton, *Search* pp. 133–83

46. H. N. Stevens, ed., *New Light on the Discovery of Australia: As Revealed by the Journal of Captain Don Diego de Prado y Tovar* (Hakluyt Society, 2nd series 64, Cambridge 1930) pp. 123–25

47. Kelly, *La Austrialia* i. pp. 88–96

48. K. G. McIntyre, *The Secret Discovery of Australia: Portuguese Ventures 200 years before Cook* (1977) pp. 320–23

49. For Drake's famous circumnavigation see H. R. Wagner, *Sir Francis Drake's Voyage Around the World: Its Aims and Achievements* (Whitefish, MT 2006); K. R. Andrews, 'The aims of Drake's expedition of 1577–80', *American Historical Review* 73, 3 (1968) pp. 724–41

50. This is the theme of *Monopolists and Freebooters* by O. H. K. Spate (1983)

51. J. E. Heeres, ed., *Abel Janszoon Tasman's Journal* (Los Angeles 1965); A. Sharp, *The Voyages of Abel Janszoon Tasman* (1968)

52. EV p. lxviii

53. Jacob Roggeveen, *The Journal of Jacob Roggeveen* ed. and trans. A. Sharp (Oxford 1970)

54. Spate, *Monopolists and Freebooters* p. 131

55. For Dampier see C. Wilkinson, *Dampier* (1929); Diana and Michael Preston, *A Pirate of Exquisite Mind: Explorer, Naturalist and Buccaneer: The Life of William Dampier* (2004)

56. For Dampier's influence on Defoe and Swift see W. H. Bonner, *Captain William Dampier: Buccaneer-Author* (Palo Alto, CA 1934).

57. For Anson see G. Williams, *Documents relating to Anson's Voyage round the World 1740–1744* (Navy Records Society 109, 1967) and Williams's biography of Anson, *The Prize of All the Oceans* (1999)

58. Alan Frost, 'Shaking off the Spanish yoke: British schemes to revolutionise America, 1739–1807', in Lincoln, ed., *Science and Exploration* pp. 19–37

59. O. H. K. Spate, *Paradise Found and Lost* (1988) p. 77. For Bering see R. H. Fisher, *Bering's Voyages: Whither and Why* (Seattle 1977)

60. Spate, ' "South Sea" to "Pacific Ocean": a note on nomenclature', *Journal of Pacific History* 12 (1977) pp. 205–11

61. Alexander von Humboldt, *Cosmos* (1864) ii. p. 649

62. Glyn Williams, *Voyages of Delusion: The Search for the Northwest Passage in the Age of Reason* (2002) pp. 273–75. For Cowley see Spate, *Monopolists and Freebooters* pp. 145–47

63. R. F. Gallagher, ed., *Byron's Journal of his Circumnavigation 1764–1766* (Cambridge 1964)

64. EV pp. lxxxvi–vii

65. Adm. 2/1332 pp. 145–52

66. Hugh Carrington, ed., *The Discovery of Tahiti: The Journal of George Robertson* (1948) p. 135

67. A vast amount has, predictably, been written on this subject, but the most balanced account is probably Douglas Oliver, *Polynesia in Early Historic Times* (2002)

68. Helen Wallis, ed., *Carteret's Voyage round the World 1766–1769* (Cambridge 1965)

69. EV p. xcvii

70. For a general survey see John Dunmore, *Vision and Realities: France in the Pacific 1695–1995* (Waikanae 1997). For a more detailed study of Surville and Kerguelen see John Dunmore, *French Exploration in the Pacific: Volume One: The Eighteenth Century* (Oxford 1965) especially pp. 144–65 (on Surville) and pp. 196–249 (on Kerguelen)

71. Alan Carey Taylor, *Le Président de Brosses et l'Australie* (Paris 1937)

72. See Bougainville's instructions in Archives de la Marine, Archives Nationales, Paris, B2/382 ff. 483–95. Also Bibliothèque Nationale. Nouv. acq. français 9, 407

73. See J. E. Martin-Allaric, *Bougainville navigateur et les découvertes de son temps* (Paris 1964); E. Taillemitte, ed., *Bougainville et ses compagnons autour du monde 1766–1769* 2 vols (Paris 1977)

74. John Robson, 'A comparison of the charts produced during the Pacific voyages of Louis-Antoine de Bougainville and James Cook', in G. Williams, *Captain Cook: Explorations and Reassessments* (Woodbridge, Suffolk 2004) pp. 137–60

75. For full details see John Dunmore, ed., *The Pacific Journal of Louis-Antoine de Bougainville 1767–1768* (2002)

76. Louis-Antoine de Bougainville, *Voyage autour du monde* (Paris 1771) pp. 183–84

77. EV p. lxvi

78. See Charles de Brosses, *Histoire des navigations aux Terres Australes* (Paris 1756); Alexander Dalrymple, *An Account of the Discoveries made in the South Pacifick Ocean* (1767)

79. EV p. lxxviii; Beaglehole, *Life* p. 121

80. Kippis, *Life of Captain Cook* p. 184

81. Alan Villiers, *Captain Cook. The Seaman's Seaman* (1967) pp. 95–97

82. C. Knight, 'HMS Bark Endeavour', *Mariner's Mirror* 19 (1933) pp. 292–302

83. Adm. 2/237

84. A. P. McGowan, 'Captain Cook's Ships', *Mariner's Mirror* 65 (1979) pp. 109–18. *Endeavour*, even more than Cook's more famous ship *Resolution*, has attracted a number of full-length studies, as, for example, Antonia MacArthur, *His Majesty's Bark Endeavour: The Story of the Ship and her People* (1997). Possibly the best and most complete account of every aspect of the ship is Ray Parkin, *HM Bark Endeavour: Her Place in Australian History* (Melbourne 1997). See also Karl-Heinz Marquardt, *Captain Cook's Endeavour* (1995)

85. Frank McLynn, *Crime and Punishment in Eighteenth Century England* (1989) pp. 227–29

86. Spate, *Paradise* pp. 62–63

87. EV p. cxxx

88. EV p. cxxxv

89. EV p. cxxix.

90. Nicolas Thomas, *Discoveries: The Voyages of Captain Cook* (2003) p. 30 claims he was forty-nine but does not give a source.

91. Spate, *Paradise* pp. 77–78

92. The standard biography is H. B. Carter, *Sir Joseph Banks: 1743–1820* (1988). See also Patrick O'Brian, *Joseph Banks: A Life* (1987); John Gascoigne, *Joseph Banks and the English Enlightenment: Useful Knowledge and Polite Culture* (Cambridge 1994)

93. Averil M. Lysaght, *Joseph Banks in Newfoundland and Labrador, 1766* (Berkeley 1971)

94. Tony Horwitz, *Into the Blue: Boldly Going Where Captain Cook has Gone Before* (2002) p. 24

95. Patricia Fara, *Sex, Botany and Empire: The Story of Carl Linnaeus and Joseph Banks* (New York 2004). For Solander see Edward Duyker, *Nature's Argonaut: Daniel Solander 1733–1782* (Carleton, Victoria 1998)

96. Sir James E. Smith, *A Selection of the Correspondence of Linnaeus to other Naturalists from the Original Manuscripts* (1821), i. p. 230

97. Banks, Journal i. p. 12

98. Spate, *Paradise* p. 191; cf. also Felipe Fernandez-Armesto, *Pathfinders* (2006) pp. 294–98

99. James Lind, *A Treatise of the Scurvy* (1753); Beaglehole, *Life* pp. 135–36. See also Kenneth J. Carpenter, *A History of Scurvy and Vitamin C* (Cambridge 1986)

100. N. Broc, *La Géographie des philosophes* (Paris 1974) pp. 37–43

101. J. B. Hewson, *A History of the Practice of Navigation* (Glasgow 1963) pp. 79–84

102. W. E. May, *A History of Marine Navigation* (Henley 1973) pp. 53–77; cf. E. G. R. Taylor, *Navigation in the Days of Captain Cook* (Greenwich 1974)

103. The whole story is well told in the best-selling book by Dava Sobel, *Longitude: The True Story of a Lone Genius who Solved the Greatest Scientific Problem of his Time* (1995)

104. D. House, *Greenwich Time and the Discovery of Longitude* (Oxford 1980) pp. 1–80

105. C. H. Cotter, *A History of Nautical Astronomy* (1968) pp. 195–205

106. E. G. Forbes, *The Birth of Navigational Science: Tobias Meyer* (Greenwich 1974) pp. 12–14; Taylor, *Navigation in the Days of Captain Cook* pp. 3–7

107. E. G. R. Taylor, *The Haven Finding Art* (1965) pp. 245–63
108. In addition to Sobel, *Longitude* see H. Quill, *John Harrison: The Man Who Found Longitude* (1966); William J. H. Andrews, ed., *The Quest for Longitude* (Harvard 1996)
109. Hewson, *A History of the Practice of Navigation* pp. 223–51
110. May, *A History of Marine Navigation* pp. 156–71
111. Carter, *Sir Joseph Banks* p. 75
112. See Alan Frost, *The Precarious Life of James Mario Matra* (Melbourne 1995). Magra later changed his name to Matra.
113. O'Brian, *Joseph Banks* p. 65
114. Douglas W. Freshfield, *Life of Horace Bénédict de Saussure* (1920) p. 32

CHAPTER 5: FIRST CONTACTS WITH TAHITI

1. R. A. Skelton and R. V. Tooley, *The Marine Surveys of James Cook in North America 1758–1768, particularly the survey of Newfoundland* (1967) pp. 8–9
2. EV pp. cclxxx–cclxxii; Bernard Smith, *European Vision and the South Pacific: A Study in the History of Art and Ideas* (1969) p. 14
3. For the Articles of War see N. A. M. Rodger, *The Wooden World: The Anatomy of the Georgian Navy* (1986) pp. 221–22 and, in far greater detail N. A. M. Rodger, *Articles of War: The Statutes Which Governed our Fighting Navies, 1661, 1749 and 1886* (Hampshire 1982)
4. Banks Journal i. p. 3
5. J. C. Beaglehole, *The Life of Captain Cook* (1972) p. 154
6. O. H. K. Spate, *Paradise Found and Lost* (1988) p. 168. See also John Collins, 'The Bark Endeavour and Life Aboard Her', in J.V.S. Megaw, ed., *Employ'd as a Discoverer* (Sydney 1971) pp. 41–54
7. Beaglehole, *Life* p. 154
8. Tony Horwitz, *Into the Blue: Boldly Going Where Captain Cook has Gone Before* (2002)
9. Rodger, *Wooden World* p. 39
10. H. G. Thursfield, ed., *Five Naval Journals 1789–1817* (1951) p. 245
11. Roy and Lesley Adkins, *Jack Tar: Life in Nelson's Navy* (2008) pp. 306–7
12. R. V. Hamilton and J. K. Laughton, ed., *Recollections of James Anthony Gardner* (1906) p. 220
13. Rodger, *Wooden World* pp. 20–24
14. Adkins and Lesley Adkins, *Jack Tar* pp. 29–31
15. EV pp. 5–7
16. George Forster, *A Voyage round the World* (1777), i. p. x; William Wales, *Remarks on Mr. Forster's Account of Captain Cook's Last Voyage Round the World in the Years 1772, 1773, 1774 and 1775* (1778) pp. 11–12
17. EV p. 8
18. EV p. 9
19. Banks Journal pp. i. 13–33
20. For these early days see Greene Journal, Adm. 51/4545/151 and Forwood Journal, Adm. 51/4545/133
21. Banks Journal i. pp. 38, 50
22. EV p. 16
23. Banks Journal i. pp. 56–60
24. EV p. 17; Banks Journal i. p. 63
25. The official correspondence covering the entire period 13 November–7 December 1768 is at EV pp. 486–89
26. EV pp. 23–26
27. EV p. 25
28. See Marcus Cheke, *Dictator of Portugal: A Life of the Marques of Pombal 1699–1782* (1969); Kenneth Maxwell, *Pombal: Paradox of the Enlightenment* (Cambridge 1995)
29. EV p. cxl
30. EV p. 27
31. Banks Journal i. pp. 79–131 (esp pp. 83–92, 113)
32. Ibid. i. pp. 134–35

33. Ibid. i. pp. 132–44; EV p. 39

34. Banks Journal i. p. 163

35. EV p. 44. The people Cook encountered were the Haush or Selkinam (see Nicholas Thomas, *Discoveries: The Voyages of Captain Cook* (2003) pp. 48–61). For visual evidence see Rudger Joppien and Bernard Smith, *The Art of Captain Cook's Voyages* (1985) i. pp. 88–92. A famous later visit by the *Beagle* is in Robert Fitzroy, *Narrative of the Surveying Voyages of HMS Ships Adventure and Beagle* (4 vols 1939). The modern anthropological 'take' on these peoples is Anne Mackay Chapman, *The Selkinam of Tierra del Fuego* (Cambridge 1982)

36. EV p. 46

37. Ibid.

38. For the mountainous seas around Cape Horn on the Anson voyage see G. Williams, *The Prize of All the Oceans: Anson's Voyage Around the World* (1999) pp. 46–47, 50–54

39. EV p. 49

40. Banks Journal i. pp. 179–80; EV p. 62

41. EV p. 60; Banks Journal i. pp. 179–83

42. Banks Journal i. p. 186

43. EV p. 66

44. EV p. 67; Banks Journal i. pp. 196–98

45. EV pp. 66–74

46. EV p. 84

47. EV pp. 520–21, 553; Banks Journal i. pp. 230–31

48. Oliver Warner, ed., *An Account of the Discovery of Tahiti from the Journal of George Robertson, Master of HMS Dolphin* (1955) pp. 24–32

49. Ibid. p. 43; William Ellis, *Polynesian Researches* 4 vols (1859) i. p. 302

50. For traditional Tahitian peace offerings see Ellis, *Researches* i. pp. 318–20. For the shark worship see Teuira Henry, *Ancient Tahiti* (Honolulu 1928) pp. 192, 389–90, 403–4, 414

51. Anne Salmond, *The Trial of the Cannibal Dog: The Remarkable Story of Captain Cook's Encounters in the South Seas* (2003) p. 49

52. Howard Smith, 'The introduction of venereal disease into Tahiti: A re-examination', *Journal of Pacific History* 10 (1975) pp. 38–47; James Watt, 'Medical aspects and consequences of Cook's voyages', in Robin Fisher and Hugh Johnston, eds, *Captain Cook and His Times* (Canberra 1979) pp. 150–51

53. Ellis, *Researches* ii. p. 66

54. Henry, *Ancient Tahiti* p. 227; Ellis, *Researches* i. p. 331

55. BL, Add. MSS. 42,714 f. 30; H. Zimmermann, *Account of the Third Voyage of Captain Cook 1776–1780* trans. U. Tewsley (Wellington 1926) p. 41. For a more protracted study of sexual abstinence see Lee Wallace, 'Too darn hot: sexual contact in the Sandwich Islands on Cook's third voyage', in Jonathan Lamb, Vanessa Smith, et al., eds, *Exploration and Change: A South Seas Anthology* (Chicago 2001) eds, *Exploration and Exchange* pp. 232–42; Bridget Orr, 'Southern Passions mix with northern art: miscegenation and the *Endeavour* voyage', ibid. pp. 212–31

56. Sydney Parkinson, *A Journal of a Voyage to the South Seas in HMS the Endeavour* (1784) p. 13

57. EV pp. 78–79

58. Banks Journal i. pp. 206–24

59. Neil Rennie, 'The Point Venus "scene"', in Margarette Lincoln, ed., *Science and Exploration* pp. 135–46; Wayne Orchison, 'From the South Seas to the sun: the astronomy of Cook's voyages', ibid. pp. 55–72

60. Parkinson, *Journal* p. 15; EV pp. 79–80, 552–53

61. EV pp. 551–52

62. William Bligh, *The Log of the Bounty* (1937) ii. p. 62; EV pp. 553–54

63. EV p. 84; Banks Journal i. p. 238

64. EV pp. 84–85, 554–56

65. EV p. 85

66. Douglas Oliver, *Ancient Tahitian Society* 3 vols (1874) iii. pp. 1198–203

67. EV p. clxxii; see also J. A. Moerenhaut, *Voyage aux îles du Grand Ocean* 2 vols (Paris 1837), ii. pp. 407–8

68. EV p. clxxiii–iv

69. Oliver, *Ancient Tahitian Society* iii. pp. 1249–53; C. Newbury, *Tahiti Nui. Change and Survival in French Polynesia 1767–1945* (Honolulu 1980) pp. 7–20
70. EV pp. 85–86
71. Ibid.
72. Banks's own account quoted in John Gascoigne, *Captain Cook* (2007) p. 185
73. Banks's relations with women can be found at Banks, Journal i. pp. 248–49, 266–67. Since his handwriting is often hard to read, I have also consulted Beaglehole, ed., *The Endeavour Journal of Joseph Banks 1768–1771* (Sydney 1962) i. pp. 254–55, 279, 292 and the 1980 version at pp. 256–58, 272–73. See also Salmond, *Cannibal Dog* pp. 72, 454–55; C. Roderick, 'Sir Joseph Banks, Queen Oberea and the satirists', in W. Veit, ed., *Captain James Cook: Image and Impact: South Seas Discoveries and the World of Letters* 2 vols (Melbourne 1972) ii. pp. 67–89
74. EV pp. 89–92
75. EV pp. 85–86
76. Banks Journal i. pp. 239–40
77. EV pp. 91–96
78. Parkinson, *Journal* pp. 20–21
79. Ibid. p. 31; Banks Journal i. pp. 256–57
80. Beaglehole, *Life* p. 181
81. EV pp. 98, 559–60
82. EV pp. 93–94, 557
83. R. T. Gould, *Captain Cook* (1935) pp. 59–60. But some say Cook's observations were truly significant. See Richard Woolley, 'The significance of the transit of Venus', in G. Badger, ed., *Captain Cook: Seaman and Scientist* (Canberra 1970) pp. 118–35; W. H. Robertson, 'The *Endeavour* voyage and the observation of the transit of Venus', in Megaw, ed., *Employ'd as a Discoverer* pp. 109–16; C. E. Herdendorf, 'Captain Cook and the transit of Mercury and Venus', *Journal of Pacific History* 21 (1986) pp. 49–55; J. Waldersee, '*Sic transit*: Cook's observations in Tahiti', *Journal of the Royal Australian Historical Society* 55 (1969) pp. 113–23; Orchiston, 'From the South Seas to the sun', Neil Nennie, 'The Point Venus scheme', in Lincoln, ed., *Science and Exploration* pp. 135–46.
84. Beaglehole, *Life* p. 184
85. EV p. 98; Salmond, *Cannibal Dog* p. 433
86. EV pp. 102, 560; Banks Journal i. p. 273. On the rumours of mutiny see EV pp. cxlvi–vii
87. Parkinson, *Journal* p. 32
88. EV pp. 100–1
89. Banks Journal i. p. 269
90. EV pp. 100–1
91. EV p. 101
92. Banks Journal i. pp. 274–75
93. EV pp. 109–14, 531–34. For details on Vehiatua see Oliver, *Ancient Tahitian Society* iii. pp. 1174–75
94. Banks Journal i. pp. 285–87
95. Ibid. p. 284
96. R. A. Skelton, 'Captain James Cook as a hydrographer', *Mariner's Mirror* 40 (1954) pp. 94–99; John Noble Wilford, *The Mapmakers* (2000) pp. 235–43
97. John Robson, 'A comparison of the charts produced during the Pacific voyages of Louis Antoine de Bougainville and James Cook', in G. Williams, ed., *Captain Cook: Explorations and Reassessments* (Woodbridge, Suffolk 2004) pp. 137–60 (at p. 146)
98. Banks Journal i. pp. 290–95
99. Ibid. p. 294
100. EV pp. 114–15, 562–63
101. EV p. 116
102. Henry, *Ancient Tahiti* p. 253; Oliver, *Ancient Tahitian Society* iii. pp. 1199–202; Anders Sparrman, *A Voyage round the world with Captain James Cook in H.M.S. Resolution*, trans. Huldine Bearnish and Averil Mackenzie-Grieve (1953) p. 63
103. Banks Journal i. pp. 299–301
104. For Tupaia and his place in Tahitian politics see Henry, *Ancient Tahiti* p. 18; Anne Salmond, 'Tute: the impact of Polynesia on Captain Cook', in Williams, ed., *Explorations and Reassessments* pp. 77–93 (at pp. 82–83). Above all there is G. Williams, 'Tupaia: Polynesian warrior, navigator, high

priest and artist', in Felicity Nussbaum, ed., *The Global Eighteenth Century* (Baltimore 2003) pp. 38–51.

105. Parkinson, *Journal* p. 73
106. For Ori see Oliver, *Ancient Tahitian Society* iii. pp. 1211–12
107. EV pp. 143–51
108. Banks Journal i. pp. 316–23; James Magra, *A Journal of a Voyage Round the World in HMS Ship Endeavour* (1771) pp. 61–65; Banks Journal i. pp. 341, 428
109. Ibid. i. p. 324

CHAPTER 6: THE ISLE OF CYTHERA

1. Sydney Parkinson, *A Journal of a Voyage to the South Seas in HMS Endeavour* (1784) pp. 16–24. See in general D. J. Carr, ed., *Sydney Parkinson: Artist of Cook's Endeavour Voyage* (Auckland 1983) and R. Joppien and B. Smith, *The Art of Captain Cook's Voyages* 3 vols (1988)
2. EV pp. 118–40
3. Nicolas Thomas, *Discoveries: The Voyages of Captain Cook* (2003) pp. 81–82
4. For Cook's estimate see EV p. clxxv. Beaglehole thinks the correct figure is 40–50,000 (EV p. clxxvii) but M. Stahlins opts for a Cook-like 180,000 (Stahlins, *Social Stratification in Polynesia* Seattle 1958, pp. 164–65 while Douglas Oliver proposes the suspiciously exact figure of 36,366 (Oliver, *Ancient Tahitian Society* 3 vols, Canberra 1974, i. pp. 26–34). Clearly there is no agreement on populations in Polynesia before the coming of the European explorers. Even circumstantial evidence is ambiguous. The widely practised infanticide would argue for the lower estimate but the dire food shortages, of which Cook was unaware until his final days in Tahiti on the third voyage, points rather to the high figure.
5. Patrick Kirch and Roger Green, *Hawaii, Ancestral Polynesia: An Essay in Historical Anthropology* (Cambridge 2001)
6. W. Ellis, *Polynesian Researches* (1831) iii. p. 77; Teuira Henry, *Ancient Tahiti* (Honolulu 1928) pp. 206–7
7. James Magra, *A Journal of a Voyage round the World in HMS Ship Endeavour* (1771) p. 48
8. Anders Sparrman, *A Voyage Round the World with Captain James Cook in H.M.S. Rosolution* trans. Huldine Bearnish and Averil Mackenzie-Grieve (1953) p. 126; John Marra, *The Journal of the Resolution's Voyage in 1772, 1773, 1774 and 1775* (1975) p. 227
9. For Tupaia's rituals see Ellis *Researches* i. pp. 95–96; ii. pp. 336–37; Henry, *Ancient Tahiti* p. 177
10. EV p. 134; RAV p. 410; George Forster, *A Voyage Round the World* ed. N. Thomas and O. Berghof, 2 vols (Honolulu 2000) i. p. 199
11. BL, Add. MSS 38, 530 f. 52; B. Hooper, ed., *With Captain James Cook in the Antarctic and Pacific: the Journal of James Burney, 2nd Lieutenant of the Adventure on Cook's Second Voyage, 1772–1773* (Canberra 1975) p. 69
12. As the main sources for Tahitian social structure I have used Henry, *Ancient Tahiti*; E. G. Craighill Hardy, *History and Culture in the Society Islands* (Honolulu 1930); and R. W. Williamson, *Social and Political Systems of Central Polynesia* 3 vols (Cambridge 1924)
13. Williamson, *Social and Political Systems* i. pp. 356–404; iii. pp. 137–50. For *tapu* see also Williamson, *Religion and Social Organisation in Central Polynesia* (1937) pp. 130–47
14. Williamson, *Social and Political Systems* iii. pp. 229–319
15. R. Firth, 'The analysis of *Maua*: an empirical approach', in T. G. Harding and B. J. Wallace, *Cultures of the Pacific* (New York 1970) pp. 316–33; Oliver, *Ancient Tahitian Society* i. pp. 68–69, 139
16. R. Bowden, '*Tapu* and *Maua*: ritual authority and political power', *Journal of Pacific History* 14 (1979) pp. 50–62; R. M. Keesing, 'Rethinking *Maua*', *Journal of Anthropological Research* 40 (1984) pp. 137–56
17. Most scholars now accept cannibalism as a proven historical fact. W. Arens, *The Man-eating Myth: Anthropology and Anthropophagy* (New York 1979) made a notable attempt to debunk the 'myth' of cannibalism but his work suffers from an iadequate knowledge of world history, especially as relating to New Zealand, Fiji and the Congo.
18. For the *raatira* as a subject of consuming interest to contemporary anthropologists see Vittori Lanteman, *La grande festa: vita rituale e sistemi di produzione nelle societa sudizionali* (Bari 2004) pp. 204–06; H. J. M. Claessen and Peter Skalnik, *The Early State* (1978) p. 458

19. Frederick O'Brien, *Mystic Isles of the South Seas* (1921) p. 355
20. Williamson, *Social and Political Systems* iii. p. 141
21. H. J. M. Claesssen and Piet van de Velde, eds, *Early State Economics* (1991) pp. 293–302
22. Marra, *Journal* pp. 45–46; E. Taillemitte, ed., *Bougainville et ses compagnons autour du monde 1766–1769* 2 vols (Paris 1977) i. p. 321
23. Taillemitte, *Bougainville* pp. 170, 173; R. E. Gallagher, *Byron's Journal of his Circumnavigation 1764–1766* (Hakluyt Society 122, Cambridge, 1964) pp. 98–101; W. H. Pearson, 'The reception of European voyagers on Polynesian islands 1568–1797', *Journal de la Société des Océanistes* 26 (1970) pp. 12–54
24. O. H. K. Spate, *Paradise Found and Lost* (1988) p. 220
25. Oliver, *Ancient Tahitian Society* ii. pp. 938–44; Ellis, *Researches* i. pp. 311–18; E. de Bovis, *Tahitian Society before the Arrival of the Europeans* (1855) trans. R. D. Craig (Honolulu 1980) p. 47
26. The classic modern work on the *arioi* is Wilhelm Emil Muhlmann, *Arioi und Mamaia: Eine ethnologische, religionssoziologische und historische: Studie uber polynesische Kuttbunde* (Wiesbaden 1955)
27. Oliver, *Ancient Tahitian Society*
28. For confirmation of this view see George Forster, *Voyage* ii. p. 54; J. R. Forster, *Observations Made during a Voyage Round the World* (1778) pp. 392–93; William Wales, *Remarks on Mr Forster's Account of Captain Cook's Last Voyage Round the World in the Years 1772, 1773, 1774 and 1775* (1778) pp. 51–53; Owen Rutter, ed., *The Journal of James Morrison* (1935) pp. 235–37
29. Williamson, *Social and Political Systems, passim*
30. See Beaglehole's remarks at EV p. clxxxvi
31. This is made clear in all the popular books about Cook. See Vanessa Collingridge, *Captain Cook: The Life, Death and Legacy of History's Greatest Explorer* (2002) pp. 137–38, 363; Peter Ayrton, *Endeavour* (Moreton, Glos. 1999) pp. 63, 93–97
32. EV pp. 98–99, 556; Banks Journal i. pp. 365–67, 413–14. For a wider discussion of sex on Tahiti see H. Carrington, ed., *The Discovery of Tahiti* (Hakluyt Society, 2nd series 98, Cambridge 1948) pp. 166–67, 180, 184, 196–200. Cf. also Taillemitte, *Bougainville* ii. pp. 384–87. When Cook fastened the blame on Bougainville there was a storm of protest from across the Channel, and a genuine Franco-British fracas developed. For further discussions see B.G. Corney, ed., *The Quest and Occupation of Tahiti* 2 vols (1919) ii. p. 288; William Bligh, *The Log of the Bounty* (1937) ii. p. 60; J. Forster, *Observations* pp. 489–91. There is a good summary in S. M. Lambert, *A Doctor in Paradise* (1942) pp. 30–32
33. See especially Robin Fisher and Hugh Johnston, eds, *Captain Cook and his Times* (1979) pp. 149–54; Linda Evi Mezians, *The Secret Malady: Venereal Disease in Eighteenth Century Britain and France* (Kentucky 1996)
34. The vast subject of eighteenth-century Europe's response to reports of sexuality in the Pacific is covered in Alan Bewell, 'Constructed places, constructed peoples: charting the improvement of the female body in the Pacific', *Eighteenth Century Life* 18 (1994) pp. 37–54; Bridget Orr, 'Southern passions mix with northern art. Miscegenation and the *Endeavour* voyage', *Eighteenth Century Life* 18 (1994) pp. 21–41. See also Michael Sturma, *South Seas Maidens: Western Fantasy and Sexual Politics in the South Pacific* (Westport, CT 2002); Pamela Cheek, *Sexual Antipodes, Enlightenment, Globalisation and the Placing of Sex* (Stanford, CA 2003); Deryck Scarr, *A History of the Pacific Islands: Passages through Tropical Time* (2001); Margarette Lincoln, *Science and Exploration in the Pacific* (2001); Daniel O'Quinn, *Staging Governance: Theatrical Imperialism in London 1770–1800* (2005). The entire subject of the 'noble savage' is comprehensively dealt with in Ter Ellingson, *The Myth of the Noble Savage* (Berkeley 2001). It was Dryden in *The Conquest of Granada* (1672) who first used the term 'noble savage'. Oskar Spate is one of many who have pointed out that the myth of the 'noble savage' has nothing to do with Jean-Jacques Rousseau (Spate, *Paradise* pp. 245–46). Beaglehole characterises both the 'noble savage' and the idea of the Pacific as a utopia as 'nonsense on stilts' (EV p. clxxiii)
35. Parkinson, *Journal* pp. 25–26
36. E. Duyker, *Nature's Argonaut: Daniel Solander, 1733–1782* (Melbourne 1998) p. 140
37. For the latest investigation of this subject see Evelyn Lord, *The Hell-Fire Clubs* (2008)
38. Jack K. Dowling, 'Bougainville and Cook', in Walter Veit, ed., *Captain James Cook: Image and Impact: South Seas Discoveries and the World of Letters* (Melbourne 1972) pp. 25–42

Chapter 7: Peril in Australasia

1. Banks Journal i. p. 325; EV pp. 155–57
2. Banks Journal ii. pp. 1–2
3. EV pp. 158–59; Banks Journal ii. pp. 3–4
4. For the 1769 comet see Horace Walpole to Madame du Deffand, 7 September 1769 in W. S. Lewis, ed., *Yale Edition of the Horace Walpole Correspondence* (1974) vii. p. 311
5. EV pp. 161–62; Banks Journal ii. p. 5
6. Sydney Parkinson, *A Journal of a Voyage to the South Seas in HMS the Endeavour* (1784) p. 82
7. Banks Journal ii. pp. 6–14; EV p. 166
8. Parkinson, *Journal* pp. 85–86
9. Tony Horwitz, *Into the Blue: Boldly Going Where Captain Cook has Gone Before* (2002) p. 104
10. O. H. K. Spate, *Paradise Found and Lost* (1988) pp. 16–17
11. EV pp. 169, 565–68
12. EV pp. 170–72
13. EV pp. 534–37
14. EV p. 171
15. Banks Journal ii. p. 26
16. J. C. Beaglehole, *The Life of Captain Cook* (1972) p. 200
17. These issues are dealt with at length by John White, *The Ancient History of the Maori* (Wellington 1887) and Anne Salmond, *Two Worlds: First Meetings between Maori and Europeans 1642–1772* (Auckland 1991) esp. pp. 87–298
18. EV pp. 173–78, 571–80. For Maori confirmation of the dead (but they say only two) see A. G. Baynall and G. C. Petersen, *William Colenso* (Wellington 1948) p. 462
19. Parkinson, *Journal* p. 97; Joel Samuel Polack, *New Zealand: Being a Narrative of Travel and Adventures* (1838) ii. pp. 120–36
20. Michael King, *A History of New Zealand* (2003) pp. 103–06
21. EV p. 442
22. Banks Journal ii. pp. 65–84
23. EV p. 196
24. White, *Ancient History* pp. 121–30
25. EV pp. 197–200
26. EV pp. 189–92
27. White, *Ancient History* pp. 121–28; Salmond, *Two Worlds* pp. 176, 216, 395
28. EV pp. 202–13
29. Banks Journal ii. pp. 84–96
30. EV pp. 214–15; Banks Journal ii. pp. 96–108
31. EV pp. 216–19
32. EV p. 223
33. For Surville see J. Dunmore, ed. and trans., *The Expedition of the St Jean Baptiste to the Pacific* (1981). For the fight with the Maoris see Salmond, *Two Worlds* pp. 299–356
34. Beaglehole, *Life* p. 212
35. Banks Journal ii. p. 113
36. Ibid.; EV p. 227
37. EV p. 228
38. Banks Journal ii. pp. 120–40
39. EV pp. 236–42; Banks Journal ii. pp. 136–37; Parkinson, *Journal* p. 119; James Magra, *A Journal of a Voyage round the World in HMS ship Endeavour* (1771) pp. 95–96
40. Charles and Neil Begg, *Captain Cook and New Zealand* (Wellington 1969) pp. 62–65
41. EV p. cclxxxiii
42. Banks Journal ii. pp. 145–51
43. EV p. 258
44. Banks Journal ii. pp. 151–52
45. EV pp. 256–63
46. Abel Janszoon, *Tasman and the Discovery of New Zealand* (Wellington 1942) p. 45
47. EV p. 265

48. EV pp. 266–71; Banks Journal ii. pp. 153–60
49. EV pp. 272–73
50. EV p. cxlix. For one aghast at Cook's talents see H. Ling Roth, *Crozet's Voyage to Tasmania* (1891) p. 22. Lt Hohn Crozet was second in command of Marc-Joseph Marion du Fresne's *Mascarin*, which was on the New Zealand coast in 1772.
51. Flinders, *Voyage to Terra Australis* (1814) i. p. cxix
52. Banks Journal ii. p. 213; EV pp. 273–94
53. EV pp. 293–94
54. Banks Journal ii. p. 231. For Banks's plants see R. C. Carolin, 'The natural history of the *Endeavour* expedition', in J. V. S. Megaw, *Employ'd as a Discoverer* (Sydney 1971) pp. 94–108
55. Banks Journal ii. p. 236
56. Beaglehole, *Life* p. 227
57. EV pp. 296–303
58. EV pp. 304–6
59. Parkinson, *Journal* p. 134. This was the scene famously (and mistakenly) portrayed as two men facing the invaders with swords (Bernard Smith and Rudger Joppien, *The Art of Captain Cook's Voyages: the Art of the Endeavour*, 1985, p. 45)
60. Banks Journal ii. pp. 244–60
61. EV pp. 306–9
62. See the volumes edited by A. W. Reid, *Captain Cook in Australia* (Wellington 1969); *Captain Cook in New Zealand* (Wellington 1969)
63. For Cook's exploration of this coast see Ida Lee, *Early Exploration in Australia* (1925) pp. 516–34
64. Banks Journal ii. pp. 267–71
65. Parkinson, *Journal* p. 138
66. EV pp. 323–24
67. EV p. 324
68. Parkinson, *Journal* p. 207
69. Flinders, *Voyage* ii. pp. 19, 24–25, 40–41, 54–55
70. Banks Journal ii. pp. 275–81
71. EV pp. 336–43
72. David Hopley, G. Scott and Kevin E. Parnell, eds, *The Geomorphology of the Great Barrier Reef: Development, Diversity and Change* (Cambridge 2007); James and Margarita Bowen, *The Great Barrier Reef: History, Science, Heritage* (Cambridge 2002); Dorothy Hill, 'The Great Barrier Reef', in G. M. Badger, ed., *Captain Cook, Navigator and Scientist* (Canberra 1970) pp. 70–86
73. EV pp. 343–46
74. Banks Journal ii. p. 287
75. Ibid. ii. p. 289
76. Parkinson, *Journal* p. 142
77. Banks Journal ii. p. 292
78. EV p. 347
79. EV pp. 348–49
80. EV p. 347
81. EV pp. 350–56. The time at the Endeavour river was the first time on this voyage that proper observations of kangaroos were made. Yet everything about Cook and this marsupial invites controversy. One view is that the very name is a version of aboriginal answer when asked what the beast was; on this view, 'kangaroo' meant 'I do not understand' (Nicolas Thomas, *Discoveries: The Voyages of Captain Cook* (2003) pp. 122–24). See also Markman Ellis, 'Tales of wonder: constructions of the kangaroo in late eighteenth-century scientific discourse', in Margarette Lincoln, ed., *Science and Exploration in the Pacific: European Voyages to the Southern Ocean in the Eighteenth Century* (Woodbridge 1998) pp. 163–82. See also John B. Haviland, 'A last look at Cook's guugu Yimidhirr wordlist', *Oceania* 44 (1974) pp. 216–32; Dennis J. Carr, 'The identity of Captain Cook's kangaroo', in D. J. Carr, ed., *Sydney Parkinson: Artist of Cook's Endeavour* (Auckland 1983) pp. 242–49
82. Banks Journal, ii. pp. 282, 299–332. See also David Turnbull, 'Cook and Tupaia, a tale of carto-graphic *méconnaisance*?' in Lincoln, *Science and Exploration* pp. 117–31

83. EV pp. 359–62
84. Perhaps surprisingly, a lot has been written on Cook's fleeting contacts with the aborigines. See J. V. S. Megaw, 'Cook and the aborigines', in Megaw, *Employ'd* pp. 55–63; D. Rose, 'The saga of Captain Cook. Morality in aboriginal and European law', *Australian Aboriginal Studies* 2 (1984) pp. 24–39; R. Rose and T. Swain, eds, *Aboriginal Australian Christian Missions* (Canberra 1988) pp. 355–60. Stuart Murray, 'Notwithstanding our signs to the contrary: textuality and authority at the endeavour river, June to August 1771', in Williams, ed., *Explorations and Reassessments* pp. 59–76 seems *parvum in multo* and is not helped by being a year out in his dates. Thomas, *Discoveries* pp. 119–30 has established that Cook made contact with two distinct racial groups, the Eora people around Botany Bay and the Dyirmadi and Mungurru at the Endeavour river. There is a wealth of material on these peoples in D. J. Mulvaney and J. Peter White, eds, *Australians to 1788* (Sydney 1988); Melinda Hinkson, *Aboriginal Sydney* (Canberra 2001); W. E. Roth, *The Queensland Aborigines* (Victoria Park 1984); Tulo Gordon and John B. Haviland, *Milbi: Aboriginal Tales from Queensland's Endeavour River* (Canberra 1980). All this academic energy is in contrast to the relative lack of interest in the aborigines shown by Cook and his men, whose concerns tended to be functional. Banks, for instance, was appalled that the aboriginals would not trade and contrasted them in this regard to all the other 'primitive' peoples they had met so far (H.B. Carter, *Sir Joseph Banks 1743–1820* (1988) p. 97)
85. Banks Journal ii. p. 332
86. EV pp. 362–70
87. Banks Journal pp. 339–40
88. EV pp. 372–73
89. Banks Journal ii. pp. 342–47. In my mimeographed copy of Banks's autograph journal the pagination goes seriously awry at p. 300 and unaccountably returns to p. 200. I will therefore refer to both the proper page and the improper pagination in the manuscript.
90. EV pp. 378–79
91. This is the longer version quoted by Beaglehole, *Life* p. 246 from his researches in the Mitchell Library. The account in Cook's journals is pithier: 'And now, such is the vicissitude of life, we thought ourselves happy in having regained a situation which but two days before it was the utmost object of our hope to quit.' (EV p. 380)
92. Banks Journal ii. p. 349 (249); EV p. 381
93. Beaglehole, *Life* p. 247
94. EV pp. 381–85
95. EV pp. 389–403
96. EV pp. 404–10
97. EV pp. 380, 546–47
98. EV p. 380
99. Beaglehole, *Life* p. 246
100. There is a considerable literature on HMS *Pandora* which sheds important light on navigation in the Great Barrier Reef: Rif Winfield, *British Warships in the Age of Sail 1714–1792* (2007); Peter Gesner, *HMS Pandora, an Archaeological Perspective* (Brisbane 2000); Christiane Conway, ed. *Letters from the Isle of Man: The Bounty Correspondence of Nessy and Peter Heywood* (2005), to say nothing of the many books on the *Bounty* mutineers in general.
101. EV p. clvi
102. Ibid.
103. Horwitz, *Into the Blue* p. 201

CHAPTER 8: HOMEWARD BOUND

1. Banks Journal, ii. pp. 320–27
2. Ibid. ii. p. 371
3. EV pp. 418–21
4. Banks Journal ii. pp. 339–41
5. Ibid. ii. pp. 344, 383–86; EV pp. 421–25. It is typical of Cook that he gave high marks to Savu and its inhabitants because 'fornication and adultery is hardly known among them' (EV p. 424)
6. Banks Journal ii. pp. 390–92; EV p. 428

7. EV pp. 429–31; James Magra, *A Journal of a Voyage round the World in HMS ship Endeavour* (1771) pp. 93–94
8. Banks Journal ii. pp. 43–443
9. EV pp. ccxviii–xxli, 499–501
10. EV pp. 433–43
11. Jan Lucassen, 'A multinational and its labour force: the Dutch East India Company, 1595–1795', *International Labor and Working Class History* 66 (2004) pp. 12–39
12. Kerry Ward, *Networks of Empire* (Cambridge 2009); Bob Moore and Henk F. K. van Nierop, *Colonial Empires Compared: Britain and the Netherlands 1750–1850* (2002)
13. Leonard Blusse, *Strange Company: Chinese Settlers, Mestizo Women and the Dutch in VOC Batavia* (Dordnecht 1998) pp. 128–31; see also Blusse and Chen Menkong, eds, *The Archives of the Kong Koan of Batavia* (Leiden 2003)
14. Jean Gelman Taylor, *The Social World of Batavia: Europeans and Eurasians in Dutch Asia* (1983) p. 88; J. de Vries and A. van der Woude, *The First Modern Economy. Success, Failure and Perseverance of the Dutch Economy, 1500–1815* (Cambridge 1997) pp. 449–55; M. C. Richlefs, *A History of Modern Indonesia since c. 300* (1991) pp. 28–29; Milton E. Osborne, *South East Asia: An Introductory Survey* (2005) p. 52
15. Sydney Parkinson, *A Journal of a Voyage to the South Seas in HMS the Endeavour* (1784) p. 182
16. John Marra, *The Journal of the Resolution's Voyage in 1772, 1773, 1774 and 1775* (1975) p. 219
17. Nicholas Thomas and Oliver Berghof, eds, *George Forster's A Voyage Round the World* 2 vols (Honolulu 2000) i. p. 389
18. G. Williams, 'Tupaia. Polynesian warrior, navigator, high priest and artist', in Felicity Nussbaum, ed., *The Global Eighteenth Century* (Johns Hopkins University Press 2003) pp. 38–51 (esp. pp. 42–49)
19. Banks Journal ii. pp. 420–25
20. EV pp. 442–43; J. C. Beaglehole, *The Life of Captain Cook* (1972) p. 263
21. Beaglehole, *Life* pp. 247, 261–62
22. Banks Journal ii. pp. 512–30
23. For the list of deaths see EV pp. 448, 450, 452, 458
24. EV p. 451
25. Tony Horwitz, *Into the Blue: Boldly Going Where Captain Cook has Gone Before* (2002) p. 208
26. EV pp. 453–54
27. EV pp. 455–46; Banks Journal ii. pp. 538–41
28. Banks's useful observations on Cape Town are at Banks Journal ii. pp. 542–73
29. EV pp. 460–61; Beaglehole, *Life* pp. 266–67
30. EV pp. 468–69; Banks Journal ii. pp. 578–95
31. Banks Journal ii. p. 592
32. EV p. 471
33. Banks Journal ii. p. 603
34. EV pp. 504–5
35. EV pp. cxii–iii
36. EV p. clxv
37. For good general surveys see K. J. Carpenter, *The History of Scurvy and Vitamin C* (Cambridge 1986); Francis Cuppage, *James Cook and the Conquest of Scurvy* (Westport, CT 1994); Sir James Watt, 'Medical aspects and consequences of Cook's voyages', in R. Risher and H. Johnston, eds, *Captain Cook and his Times* (Canberra 1979) pp. 129–57 (esp. pp. 143–45). Cook's own utterances on scurvy are in J. Keevil, *Medicine and the Navy 1714–1815* (1961) pp. 31, 316. The harsh criticisms of Cook and the consequences in the Americas are in O. H. K. Spate, *Paradise Found and Lost* (1988) p. 195
38. Anne Salmond, *The Trial of the Cannibal Dog: The Remarkable Story of Captain Cook's Encounters in the South Seas* (2003) pp. 433–34
39. Stephens to Cook, 20 September 1771, Adm. 2/731
40. Quoted in Salmond, *Cannibal Dog* pp. 57, 118
41. Parkinson, *Journal* p. 15
42. Ibid. p. 69
43. Quoted in Salmond, *Cannibal Dog* p. 149

44. Arthur Kitson, *Captain James Cook, The Circumnavigator* (1907) pp. 211–12
45. Beaglehole, *Life* p. 274
46. Much has been written about the *Endeavour*. See C. Night, 'H. M. Bark *Endeavour*', *Mariner's Mirror* 19 (1933) pp. 292–302; K. H. Marquardt, *Captain Cook's Endeavour* (1995); Ray Parkin, *HM Bark Endeavour* (2003)
47. *General Evening Post*, 3 April 1772
48. Johnson to Banks, 27 February 1772, in James Boswell, *The Life of Dr Johnson* (1830) p. 199
49. *London Evening Post*, 13 July 1771
50. Ibid., 23 July 1771
51. *London Chronicle*, 6–8 August 1771
52. Ibid., 27–29 August 1771
53. For this story see Andrew Kippis, *The Life of Captain James Cook* (1788) p. 182
54. For the myth and reality of the Monks of Medmenham see Evelyn Lord, *The Hell-Fire Clubs* (2008)
55. Stephens to Cook, 2 August 1771, Adm. 2/731
56. EV pp. 637–38
57. EV p. 505
58. For the *Scorpion* see RAV pp. 898–99
59. *London Evening Post*, 30 August 1771
60. Beaglehole, *Life* pp. 277–79
61. *London Chronicle*, 24–27 August 1771
62. Patricia Fara, *Sex, Botany and Empire* (2003) pp. 1–2; Richard Connaughton, *Omai: The Prince Who Never Was* (2007) p. 63
63. For this see Betsy Corner and Christopher C. Booth, *Charms of Friendship: Selected Letters of Dr John Fothergill of London 1735–1780* (Harvard 1971) p. 457; Karen Harvey, ed., *The Kiss in History* (Manchester 2005) chapter 5
64. There was clearly something ill-starred about this rush to publication. Stanfield Parkinson died insane in 1776 while Hawkesworth died suddenly in 1773, after an adverse critical reception of his volume (see John L. Abbott, *John Hawkesworth: Eighteenth-century Man of Letters*, Madison, WI 1982)
65. A. R. Ellis, ed., *The Early Diary of Frances Burney 1768–1778* 2 vols (1889), i. pp. 133–34; P. A, Scholes, *The Great Dr Burney, his Travels, his Works, his Family and his Friends* 2 vols (1948), i. pp. 194–96
66. Ellis, ed., *Early Diary of Frances Burney* pp. 138–39
67. Frances Burney, *Memoirs of Dr Burney* (1832) i. pp. 270–71
68. J. E. Smith, *A Selection of the Correspondence of Linnaeus and Other Naturalists* 2 vols (1821), i. pp. 259–60, 263–66, 275
69. Beaglehole, *Life* p. 279
70. See Cook's extended remarks in BL, Add. MSS 27,889
71. RAV p. xxv
72. See, for example, Cook to Stephens, 14 December 1771; Stephens to Cook, 17 December 1771, Adm. 2/731
73. George Young, *The Life and Voyages of Captain Cook* (1836) p. 121; Robert Tate Gaskin, *The Old Seaport of Whitby* (1909) p. 391
74. See R. T. Gould, *John Harrison and his Timekeepers* (Greenwich 1935) p. xxxix and, more generally. Derek House and Beresford Hutchinson, *The Clocks and Watches of Captain Cook 1769–1969* (1969)
75. Beaglehole, *Life* pp. 291–92
76. Salmond, *Cannibal Dog* pp. 169–70
77. RAV p. 4
78. James Boswell, *A Life of Samuel Johnson* (New York 1992) p. 410
79. BL, Add. MSS 27,888 f. 5
80. Beaglehole, *Life* pp. 293–94
81. BL, Add. MSS 27,888 f. 4
82. RAV pp. 929–31
83. 'Memoirs of the Early Life of John Elliott', BL, Add. MSS. 42,714 ff. 10–11
84. H. B. Carter, *Sir Joseph Banks 1743–1820* (1988) p. 76

85. RAV pp. 704–07
86. Richard Hough, *Captain James Cook* (1994) p. 188; *London Magazine,* June–July 1772
87. *London Chronicle,* 9–11 June 1772
88. Salmond, *Cannibal Dog* p. 172
89. BL, Add. MSS. 27,888 f. 5
90. Admiralty minutes, 27, 29 November 1772, Adm. 3/79
91. 'Cook we should like to hear talk of course, but Clerke would be more indiscreet, he would laugh more.' (Beaglehole's judgment at RAV p. xxxv)
92. RAV pp. 936–37
93. Robert McNab, ed., *Historical Records of New Zealand* (Wellington 1914) ii. pp. 95–96
94. 'There is something desperately serious about Pickersgill, as about so many of his fellow-romantics, something, in the end, of pathos. There are good intentions, never realised, the something beyond his grasp, whether because of lack of training or lack of mental stamina one does not know. When he amuses us, it is not of set purpose. A less striking figure than Clerke, he is a more complex one, less on good terms with the world; where Clerke writes down a jest, Pickersgill explains a grievance.' (Beaglehole, *Life* p. 298)
95. See Rupert Furneaux, *Tobias Furneaux* (1960)
96. RAV pp. 11–12
97. Christine Holmes, ed., *Captain Cook's Second Voyage: The Journal of Lieutenants Elliott & Pickersgill* (1984) pp. xxx–xxxi.
98. BL, Add. MSS 42,714 f. 13
99. Spate, *Paradise* pp. 198–99
100. Ibid. p. 198
101. For George Forster see B. Smith and R. Joppien, *The Art of Captain Cook's Voyages* (Melbourne 1985) ii. pp. 23–24; Walter Veit, 'Intellectual tradition and Pacific discoveries – the function of quotation in George Forster's "Voyage Round the World" ', in Walter Veit, ed., *Captain James Cook: Image and Impact: South Seas Discoveries and the World of Letters* (Melbourne 1979) pp. 95–117. For Johann Forster see M. E. Hoare, *The Tactless Philosopher: Johann Reinhold Forster 1729–98* (Melbourne 1976). Among the Forsters' admirers are the following: G. Williams, ' "Enlarging the Sphere of Human Contemplation": the exploration of the Pacific', in P. J. Marshall and G. Williams, eds, *The Great Map of Mankind* (1982) pp. 258–98 (especially pp. 276–83); G. Williams, 'Seamen and philosophers in the South Seas in the age of Captain Cook', *Mariner's Mirror* 65 (1979) pp. 2–22; C. Glacken, *Traces on the Rhodian Shore: Nature and Culture in Western Thought* (Berkeley 1967) pp. 610–19, 702–95; M. E. Hoare, ed., *The Resolution Journal of Johann Reinhold Forster 1772–1775* (Hakluyt Society, 2nd series 152–55, 1982); George L. Bodi, 'George Forster: the "Pacific expert" of eighteenth-century Germany', *Historical Studies* 32 (1969) pp. 345–63; M. E. Hoare, 'The legacy of J. R. Forster to European science and letters', in Veit, ed., *Captain James Cook* ii. pp. 64–75. For the Forsters' influence on modern geography see B. Smith, *European Vision and the South Pacific* (Sydney 1985) p. 55; R. Hartshorne, *The Nature of Geography* (Lancaster, PA 1949) p. 42; D. R. Stoddart, *On Geography and its History* (Oxford 1986) pp. 33–35
102. Salmond, *Cannibal Dog* pp. 172, 466
103. BL, Add. MSS. 42,714 ff. 40–41
104. For the entire sequence of events July 1771–July 1772 in detail see RAV pp. 874–945

CHAPTER 9: ANTARCTICA

1. G. E. Mainwaring, *My Friend the Admiral* (1931) p. 13
2. BL, Add. MSS 42,714 ff. 11–12; J. R. Forster, *Observations Made during a Voyage Round the World* (1778) i. p. 8
3. RAV p. 21
4. RAV p. ccxxxii
5. RAV pp. 21, 685; John Elliott and Richard Pickersgill, *Captain Cook's Second Voyage: The Journals of Lieutenants Elliott and Pickersgill* ed., Christine Holmes (1984) pp. 11–12
6. Forster, *Observations* i. p. 41; *Journals of Lieutenants Elliott and Pickersgill* pp. 11–12. Forster thought the incident showed Cook's essential cruelty, but William Wales, *Remarks on Mr.*

Forster's Account of Captain Cook's Last Voyage Round the World in the Years 1772, 1773, 1774 and 1775 (1778) p. 20 said that Cook was right, since he concentrated on the health of his men rather than on a sentimental attachment to monkeys.

7. RAV p. 32; Forster, *Observations* i. p. 43. Anne Salmond, *The Trial of the Cannibal Dog: The Remarkable Story of Captain Cook's Encounters in the South Sea* (2003) confirms the shark attack but J. C. Beaglehole, *The Life of Captain Cook* (1894) p. 307 says merely that the man fell overboard and did not resurface.

8. The whole process is described in John William Norie, *A Complete Epitome of Practical Navigation and Nautical Astronomy* (1900) p. 124

9. RAV p. 36; Forster, *Observations* i. p. 49

10. Salmond, *Cannibal Dog* p. 434

11. RAV pp. 33–34, 37, 39

12. RAV pp. 39, 46

13. Forster, *Observations* i. p. 51; RAV pp. 40–45

14. Adm. 1/1610

15. BL, Add. MSS. 27,890 f. 2

16. Beaglehole, *Life* pp. 301–02

17. RAV p. 688; Beaglehole, *Life* p. 310

18. Forster, *Observations* i. p. 68

19. John Callander, *Terra Australis Cognita* (1768) iii. pp. 641–44. See also A. Rainaud, *Le Continent d'Austral: hypothèses et découvertes* (Paris 1894) iii. pp. 407–10

20. O. H. K. Spate, *Paradise Found and Lost* (1988) p. 70. There is an almost identical formulation in R. T. Gould, *Captain Cook* (1935) p. 111. For Bouvet Island see W. E. LeMasurier and J. W. Thompson, eds, *Volcanoes of the Antarctic Plate and Southern Ocean* (1990) p. 512. For Bouvet himself see O. H. K. Spate, 'Between Tasman and Cook: Bouvet's place in the history of exploration', in J. Andrews, *Frontiers and Men* (Melbourne 1966) pp. 174–86

21. William James Mills, *Exploring Polar Frontiers: A Historical Encyclopedia* (2003) p. 346

22. Roland Huntford, *Shackleton* (1985) p. 560

23. RAV pp. 52–54

24. Forster, *Observations* i. pp. 89–90

25. RAV pp. 55–56

26. RAV pp. 56–58

27. Forster, *Observations* i. pp. 99–100. Franklin's findings were published in *Experiments and Observations on Electricity* (1751), which by this time had gone through six editions.

28. RAV pp. 60–61

29. RAV pp. 62–63

30. RAV p. lxi

31. Adm. 55/108

32. Anders Sparrman, *A Voyage round the World with Captain James Cook in H.M.S. Resolution*, trans. Huldine Bearnish and Averil Mackenzie-Grieve (1953) pp. 12–16

33. RAV p. 69

34. RAV pp. 71–72

35. Forster, *Observations* i. pp. 76–102 worked out that the theory was false, that the seas did freeze and produce pack ice.

36. RAV pp. 72–75

37. RAV pp. 77–80

38. RAV pp. 82–86

39. RAV pp. 87–88

40. RAV p. 89

41. RAV pp. 90–92

42. Furneaux's account (RAV pp. 730–45) gives no hint that he deliberately went missing, but then he would hardly admit to desertion.

43. RAV pp. 93–94

44. Arthur Kitson, *Captain James Cook, the Circumnavigator* (1907) p. 251

45. Salmond, *Cannibal Dog* p. 434

46. RAV p. 962
47. RAV p. 97
48. RAV p. 98
49. RAV p. 99
50. RAV p. 100
51. RAV p. 102
52. RAV pp. 102–5
53. RAV pp. 105–8
54. Beaglehole, *Life* p. 323
55. RAV p. lxvi
56. RAV p. 106
57. See the detailed description in A. Charles Begg and Neil C. Begg, *Dusky Bay* (Christchurch 1966)
58. Sparrman, *Voyage* p. 43
59. George Forster, *A Voyage around the World*, ed. N. Thomas and O. Berghof, 2 vols (Honolulu 2000), i. pp. 105–06
60. Johann Reinhold Forster, *The Resolution Journal 1772–1775*, ed. M. Hoare, 4 vols (1982) ii. pp. 233, 251
61. Salmond, *Cannibal Dog* p. 181
62. Forster, *Observations* i. pp. 137–38; cf. also Elliott in BL, Add. MSS 42,714 ff. 16–17
63. RAV p. 116
64. RAV pp. 118–19
65. Forster, *Observations* i. pp. 181–85
66. There is a huge amount of material on Dusky Bay in the sources: BL, Add. MSS 27,889 f. 75; BL, Add. MSS 31,360, 15,500. See aso RAV pp. 131–38 and 776–87 (Wales's account)
67. RAV p. 131
68. RAV pp. 140–43
69. For Marion du Fresne see Edward Duyker, *An Officer of the Blue: Marc-Joseph Marion du Fresne* (Melbourne 1994) and Duyker, ed., *The Discovery of Tasmania* (Hobart 1992)
70. A. E. Orchard, *A History of Systematic Botany in Australia* (1999)
71. RAV p. 736
72. BL, Add. MSS 27,890 ff. 6–10
73. RAV pp. 152–57, 740–45
74. RAV p. 145
75. RAV p. 148
76. RAV p. 155
77. RAV p. lxix
78. RAV p. 173
79. RAV pp. 174–75
80. He remarks: 'There is a naive oddity about these bursts of sentimental nonsense from Cook. Had the captain been too much exposed to the oratory of J. R. Forster?' (Beaglehole, *Life* p. 335
81. Sparrman, *Voyage* p. 57
82. RAV p. 169
83. RAV pp. 170–71
84. BL, Add. MSS. 27,890 f. 8; RAV pp. 135, 170
85. RAV p. xlvi
86. RAV pp. 174, 579–80
87. Beaglehole, *Life* p. 336
88. RAV p. 173
89. RAV p. 170
90. Sparrman, *Voyage* p. 56
91. *Journals of Lieutenants Elliott and Pickersgill* p. 18
92. RAV p. 790
93. Anne Salmond, *Two Worlds: First Meetings between Maori and Europeans 1642–1772* (Auckland 1991)
94. M.E. Hoare, ed., *The Resolution Journal of Johann Reinhold Forster 1772–1775* (Hakluyt Society, 2nd Series 152–55, 1982) ii. p. 261

95. RAV p. 172
96. G. Forster, *Voyage around the World* i. pp. 127–28
97. G. Williams, 'Tupaia. Polynesian Warrior, Navigator, High Priest and Artist,' in Felicity Nussbaum, ed., *The Global Eighteenth Century* (John Hopkins 2003) pp. 50–51

Chapter 10: Tongans and Maoris

1. Anders Sparrman, *A Voyage round the World with Captain James Cook in H.M.S. Resolution* trans. Huldine Bearnish and Averil Mackenzie-Grieve (1953) p. 57; RAV p. 791
2. For events in July and August see RAV pp. 180–86. Clerke's logs for the period are at RAV pp. 737–55
3. RAV p. 729
4. RAV pp. 187–89
5. BL, Add. MSS. 27,890 f. 146.
6. Some of the problems encountered by R.L. Stevenson in the Tuamotus are described in Frank McLynn, *Robert Louis Stevenson* (1993) pp. 326–28
7. RAV pp. 197–99
8. Sparrman, *Voyage* pp. 51–52
9. RAV pp. 199–201
10. Anne Salmond, *The Trial of the Cannibal Dog: The Remarkable Story of Captain Cook's Encounters in the South Seas* (2003) p. 193
11. RAV pp. 204–5, 767–75. For Reti see Douglas Oliver, *Ancient Tahitian Society* 3 vols (1874) iii. pp. 1176–77
12. RAV p. 201.
13. John Marra, *The Journal of the Resolution's Voyage in 1772, 1773, 1774 and 1775* (1975) p. 45
14. George Forster, *A Voyage round the World* eds N. Thomas and O. Berghof (1777) i. p. 150
15. M. E. Hoare, ed., *The Resolution Journal of Johann Reinhold Forster 1772–1775* (Hakluyt Society, 2nd Series 152–55, 1982) ii. pp. 187, 336
16. RAV p. 205
17. RAV pp. 796–97
18. John Elliott and Richard Pickersgill, *Captain Cook's Second Voyage: The Journals of Lieutenants Elliott and Pickersgill* ed. Christine Holmes (1984) p. 31
19. Oliver, *Ancient Tahitian Society* iii. pp. 1225–32
20. Ibid. iii. pp. 1249–53
21. William Bligh, *The Log of the Bounty* (1937) ii. p. 28; cf. also BL, Add. MSS 38,530 f. 35
22. Oliver, *Ancient Tahitian Society* iii. pp. 1256–90
23. B. G. Corney, *The Quest and Occupation of Tahiti by Emissaries of Spain during the Years 1772–1776* (1919), i. pp. 226–308. Spain was inspired not by Cook's voyages but by Bougainville's (ibid. i. pp. 5–6)
24. For the details about Tu and his biography, see Oliver, *Ancient Tahitian Society* iii. pp. 1179–86
25. Hoare, ed., *Resolution Journal* ii. pp. 303–4
26. RAV p. 207
27. G. Forster, *Voyage* i. pp. 333–35
28. RAV pp. 208–9
29. Salmond, *Cannibal Dog* p. 434
30. RAV pp. 209–10
31. RAV pp. 770–75
32. RAV p. 211
33. RAV p. 801
34. RAV pp. 216–17
35. Oliver, *Ancient Tahitian Society* iii. pp. 1211–13
36. Sparrman, *Voyage* p. 93; RAV pp. 218–19
37. RAV pp. 220–21
38. E. H. McCormick, *Omai: Pacific Envoy* (Oxford 1977) pp. 182–83. The correct form of Omai's name is Mai. The 'O' was an honorific form of address used by great chiefs, which Mai, a social climber, self-assigned. But since his confidence trick was so successful, and the portraits by

Reynolds and others bear the legend 'Omai', I have thought it more convenient to retain the conventional (albeit ignorant) eighteenth-century appellation.

39. RAV pp. 221–22
40. G. Forster, *Voyage* i. pp. 458–59
41. RAV pp. 223–24
42. McCormick, *Omai*
43. G. Forster, *Voyage*, i. p. 228
44. *Journals of Lieutenants Elliott and Pickersgill*, p. 20. For the Bora Bora tattoos see Sparrman, *Voyage* p. 82
45. Hoare, ed., *Resolution Journal* ii. p. 355
46. William Wales, *Remarks on Mr Forster's Account of Captain Cook's Last Voyage Round the World in the Years 1772, 1773, 1774 and 1775* (1778) pp. 97–98; George Forster, *Reply to Mr Wales's Remarks* (1778) pp. 36–38
47. Hoare, ed., *Resolution Journal* ii. p. 365; RAV p. 225
48. See the detailed narrative of these events in Salmond, *Cannibal Dog* pp. 210–11
49. Ibid. p. 211
50. RAV pp. 226–27
51. RAV pp. 226, 228–29
52. Holmes, ed., *Journals* p. 19; RAV pp. 230, 236
53. RAV pp. 236–39, 796–97
54. Marra, *Journal* p. 43
55. RAV p. 220
56. RAV pp. 231, 234–35
57. For the ambivalence of the Forsters see J. R. Forster, *Observations Made during a Voyage Round the World* (1778) pp. 161–86, 582–86 and George Forster, *Voyage* i. pp. 295–97, 391–93; ii. pp. 85–101
58. J. Forster, *Observations* pp. 69–101 (on ice) and pp. 148–51 (on atolls)
59. J. Forster, *Observations* pp. 389–92
60. G. Forster, *Voyage* ii. pp. 190–91, 207
61. J. Forster, *Observations* pp. 286–300
62. Ibid. pp. 301–7, 333–34
63. G. Forster, *Voyage* i. pp. 364–68
64. See, for example, a comparison of the remarks of Johann (*Observations* p. 306) with those of George (*Voyage* i. pp. 302–03)
65. RAV p. 239
66. RAV p. 268
67. For the stay in Tonga see RAV pp. 243–71
68. RAV pp. 249–50
69. RAV p. 252. On Cook's likening Tongatapu to an English country park, Beaglehole remarks waspishly: 'Is there, after all his experience of wild and craggy lands, a lingering trace of the farm boy in Cook?' (J. C. Beaglehole, *The Life of Captain Cook* (1894) p. 353)
70. RAV pp. 254–56
71. Ibid.
72. Elizabeth Bott, *Tongan Society at the Time of Captain Cook's Visits* (Wellington 1982); John Martin, ed., *Tonga Islands: William Mariner's Account* (Tonga 1991); Elizabeth Bott, 'Power and rank in the kingdom of Tonga', *Journal of the Polynesian Society* 90 (1981) pp. 10–11; Adrienne Kaeppler, 'Rank in Tonga', *Ethnology* 10 (1971) pp. 174–93
73. RAV p. 271
74. J. Forster, *Observations* pp. 390–92; *Journals of Lieutenants Elliott and Pickersgill* p. 31
75. G. Forster, *Voyage* i. p. 249. For further Forster animadversions on sex and sexuality in the Pacific, see Hoare, ed., *Resolution Journal* iii. pp. 390–91. See also G. Forster, *Voyage* i. pp. 264–66, 277, 383–86, 400; ii. pp. 54–55, 107–13, 137–38, 129–35, 151–52, 469–70; J. Forster, *Observations* pp. 350–52, 365, 409–14. For sex on the *Bounty* voyage see O. Rutter, ed., *The Journal of James Morrison* (1935) pp. 225–38. Oliver has some interesting remarks on the subject, including the observation that whereas nails and cloth were the usual currency in island prostitution, on Tahiti red feathers were the preferred medium of exchange (Oliver, *Ancient Tahitian Society* i. pp. 354–57; ii. pp. 838–41)

76. RAV p. 813
77. For Forster's (inconsequential) quote, see Hoare, ed., *Resolution Journal* iii. p. 405. For the theft of literature, see Salmond, *Cannibal Dog* pp. 186, 218
78. Hoare, ed., *Resolution Journal* iii. p. 406
79. RAV p. 279
80. RAV p. 281
81. G. Forster, *Voyage* i. p. 488
82. RAV p. 283
83. RAV pp. 284–85
84. G. Forster, *Voyage* i. p. 271; RAV p. 287
85. RAV pp. 287–91, 815–20
86. For the protracted debate on Maori cannibalism and its alleged difference from Tahitian and other Polynesian practices, see RAV pp. 292–94, 819; G. Forster, *Voyage* i. pp. 503–4, 518–23; George Forster, *Voyage* ed. Thomas & Berghof i. pp. 280–81; J. Forster, *Observations* pp. 325–35
87. RAV p. 292
88. BL, Add. MSS 42,714 f. 22
89. O. H. K. Spate, *Paradise Found and Lost* (1988) pp. 223–24
90. Supporting evidence for these remarks can be found in Hoare, ed., *Resolution Journal* ii. pp. 354–55; iii. pp. 515, 517–20; iv. pp. 586, 590, 611–13 and G. Forster, *Voyage* i. pp. 513, 535–36; ii. pp. 10–11, 124–26, 254–58, 349–53, 425–28
91. RAV p. 292
92. RAV p. 297
93. RAV pp. 297–99
94. Rupert Furneaux, *Tobias Furneaux* (1960) pp. 91–94
95. It is only fair to say that the leading authorities give Furneaux the benefit of the doubt. Beaglehole acknowledges the suspicion but defends Furneaux from the charge of cowardice/desertion by pointing out that he sailed as far as 61S and rounded the Horn before going to the Cape of Good Hope (RAV p. xxxi). Anne Salmond says that Furneaux was 'bitterly disappointed' not to find the *Resolution* waiting for him (*Cannibal Dog* p. 226)
96. For details see Salmond, *Cannibal Dog* p. 223
97. Furneaux, *Tobias Furneaux* pp. 145–47
98. B. Cooper, ed., *The Private Journal of James Burney* (Canberra 1975) pp. 95–99. For a full reconstruction see D. W. Orchiston and L. C. Horrocks, 'Contact and conflict: the Rowe massacre', *Historical Studies* 19 (1975) pp. 519–38 (esp. pp. 536–37)
99. Adm. 51/4523
100. Adm. 51/4521; Marra, *Journal* p. 96. The entire saga of Cook's turbulent relations with the Maoris on the second voyage is covered in detail in Anne Salmond, *Between Worlds: Early Exchanges between Maori and Europeans 1773–1815* (Auckland 1997) pp. 36–170.

CHAPTER 11: MASTERING THE PACIFIC

1. RAV p. 302
2. RAV pp. 303–4
3. George Forster, *A Voyage round the World* eds N. Thomas and O. Bergholf, 2 vols (Honolulu 2000) (1777) i. p. 531
4. BL, Add. MSS 42,714 ff. 24–26
5. RAV pp. 305–8
6. RAV p. 309
7. Anders Sparrman, *A Voyage round the World with Captain James Cook in H.M.S. Resolution* trans. Huldine Bearnish and Averil Mackenzie-Grieve (1953) p. 111; G. Forster, *Voyage* i. p. 535
8. RAV pp. 310–11
9. Anne Salmond, *The Trial of the Cannibal Dog: The Remarkable Story of Captain Cook's Encounters in the South Seas* (2003) pp. 233, 434
10. John Elliott and Richard Pickersgill, *Captain Cook's Second Voyage: The Journals of Lieutenants Elliott and Pickersgill* ed. Christine Holmes (1984) p. 43

11. BL, Add. MSS 42,714 f. 24
12. RAV p. 317
13. M. E. Hoare, ed., *The Resolution Journal of Johann Reinhold Forster 1772–1775* (Hakluyt Society, 2nd Series 152–55, 1982) iii. pp. 438, 444
14. G. Forster, *Voyage* i. p. 540
15. Ibid. i. pp. 540–43
16. RAV pp. 319, lix
17. RAV pp. 319–21
18. For Weddell see James Weddell, *A Voyage towards the South Pole: Performed in the Years 1822–1824* (1825). For James Clark Ross see Alan Gurney, *Below the Convergence: Voyages towards Antarctica 1699–1839* (1997) p. 112–20; For Wilkes see Wilkes, *A Narrative of a Voyage round the World* (1849), i. p. 154. See also Nathaniel Philbrick, *Sea of Glory: America's Voyage of Discovery: The US Exploring Expedition 1838–1842* (2003). For *Discovery II* see Roland Huntford, *Shackleton* (1985) p. 34 and Lincoln P. Paine, *Ships of Discovery and Exploration* (Boston 2000) p. 43
19. Sparrman, *Voyage* p. 112; Vancouver in *The Naval Chronicle* 1 (1799) p. 125
20. RAV p. 322
21. Ibid.
22. RAV p. 326
23. RAV p. 328
24. Salmond, *Cannibal Dog* p. 434
25. RAV p. 333. For the cause of Cook's illness see G. Forster, *Voyage* i. pp. 181, 538, 543
26. Sir James Watt, 'Medical Aspects and Consequences of Cook's Voyages', in Robin Fisher and Hugh Johnston, eds, *Captain Cook and his Times* (Canberra 1979) pp. 129–57
27. W. R. Thrower, 'Contributions to medicine of Captain James Cook FRN, RN', *Lancet* 241 (1951) p. 218
28. James Watt, E. J. Freeman and W. F. Bynum, eds, *Starving Sailors: The Influence of Nutrition upon Naval and Maritime History* (Greenwich 1981) pp. 51–72
29. G. Forster, *Voyage* i. p. 298. For Forster's scurvy see ibid. i. p. 550
30. RAV pp. 336–39
31. For full details see Andrew Sharp, ed., *The Journal of Jacob Roggeveen* (Oxford 1970); B. G. Corney, ed., *The Voyage of Captain Don Felipe González . . . to Easter Island* (Cambridge 1908)
32. RAV pp. 340–42
33. G. Forster, *Voyage* i. p. 591
34. For the accounts by Cook and his officers see RAV pp. 339–43, 758–60, 820–28
35. Thomas S. Barthel, *The Eighth Land: The Polynesian Settlement of Easter Island* (1978)
36. See the work by A. Matraux, especially *Ethnology of Easter Island* (Honolulu 1940) and *Easter Island: A Stone Age Civilization of the Pacific* (1967); cf. also *Voyage de La Pérouse autour du monde* (Paris 1797)
37. Jared Diamond, *Collapse: How Societies Choose to Fail or Succeed* (2005) pp. 107–12
38. For the very different views on these issues see especially the outstanding synthesis by John Flenley and Paul Bahn, *The Enigmas of Easter Island* (New York 2003). For older views, many of them discredited by recent research, see Thor Heyerdahl, *Aku Aku* (1958) and O. H. K. Spate, *Paradise Found and Lost* (1988) pp. 18–23
39. G. Forster, *Voyage* ii. pp. 1–3
40. RAV p. xc
41. Sparrman, *Voyage* p. 118; Salmond, *Cannibal Dog* pp. 239–40, 434
42. RAV pp. 363–64
43. Melville's *Typee: A Peep at Polynesian Life* is set on Nuku Hiva, where he jumped ship in 1842. Gauguin made the long, fertile Atuoa valley on Hiva Oa famous with his paintings. Thor Heyerdahl spent eighteen months on Fatu Hiva in 1938–39 (Heyerdahl, *Fatu Hiva: Back to Nature*, 1974). Robert Louis Stevenson visited Nuku Hiva and Hiva Oa in 1888, while Jack London arrived in the Marquesas in 1907 on his famous cruise on the *Snark*. For a general survey of the earliest European contacts see Greg Dening, *Islands and Beaches: Discourses on a Silent Land: Marquesas 1774–1880* (Honolulu 1980)
44. For London's 1907 visit see Jack London, *The Cruise of the Snark* (1915) pp. 93–159

45. For Stevenson's visit see *In the South Seas* (Tusitala edition of the Works of Robert Louis Stevenson, 35 vols, 1924, xx. pp. 55–119)

46. RAV pp. 365, 761, 828

47. Sparrman, *Voyage* p. 119

48. RAV pp. 366–69

49. RAV pp. 369–71, 762, 829–34

50. See Frank McLynn, *Robert Louis Stevenson: A Biography* (1993) pp. 319–25

51. Dening, *Islands and Beaches* p. 102

52. RAV pp. 376–80

53. G. Forster, *Voyage* i. p. 324

54. RAV p. lxiii

55. J. C. Beaglehole, *The Life of Captain Cook* (1894) p. 380

56. For To'ofa see R. W. Williamson, *Social and Political Systems of Central Polynesia* 3 vols (Cambridge 1924) pp. 197–200; Teuira Henry, *Ancient Tahiti* (Honolulu 1928) p. 73; John Davies, *History of the Tahitian Mission* ed. C. W. Newbury (Cambridge 1961) pp. xxxv, xxxvii, 102–03

57. Douglas Oliver, *Ancient Tahitian Society* 3 vols (1874) iii. pp. 1192–93, 1197

58. G. Forster, *Voyage* i. p. 351

59. RAV pp. 384–85

60. RAV p. 385

61. Oliver, *Ancient Tahitian Society* iii. pp. 1237–55

62. RAV p. 398

63. John Marra, *The Journal of the Resolution's Voyage in 1772, 1773, 1774 and 1775* (1975) pp. 180–83

64. RAV p. 392

65. RAV pp. 393–94

66. RAV p. 395

67. RAV p. 397

68. RAV pp. 404–6

69. RAV p. 403

70. Salmond, *Cannibal Dog* pp. 434–37

71. Marra, *Journal* p. 236

72. Cook's vacillations and indecisiveness can be charted on an almost daily basis throughout the three-week stay (RAV pp. 382–406)

73. RAV p. 412

74. RAV pp. 413–15

75. Hoare, ed. *Resolution Journal* iii. p. 517

76. RAV pp. 416–18, 841–42

77. RAV p. xciii

78. RAV p. xci

79. RAV p. 421

80. RAV p. 400

81. Hoare, ed., *Resolution Journal* iii. p. 509

82. RAV p. 845

83. RAV pp. 424–27

84. Sparrman, *Voyage* p. 129

85. RAV pp. 434–38

86. Edwin M. Loeb, *The History and Traditions of Niue* (Honolulu 1926) p. 30; S. McLachlan, 'Savage island or savage history: an interpretation of early European contacts with Niue', *Pacific Studies* 6 (1982) pp. 26–51

87. Salmond, *Cannibal Dog* pp. 259, 473

88. Hoare, ed., *Resolution Journal* iii. p. 538

89. RAV pp. 440–41

90. RAV pp. 442–43, 762–63

91. RAV p. 444

92. Beaglehole, *Life* p. 390

93. Hoare, ed. *Resolution Journal* iii. pp. 550–52

94. RAV p. 457

95. RAV pp. 457–58
96. RAV pp. 458–60; Beaglehole, *Life* p. 395
97. RAV p. 461
98. See Ron Adams, *In the Land of Strangers: A Century of Human Conflict on Tanna 1774–1874* (Canberra 1984) pp. 25–26. See also Evelyn Cheesman, *Camping Adventures on Cannibal Islands* (1949); Edward Schlieffelin and Robert Crittenden, eds, *Like People You See in a Dream: First Contact in Six Papuan Societies* (Stanford 1991)
99. RAV pp. 462–68
100. RAV p. 468. For the poisoned arrows see C. H. Coddrington, *The Melanesians* (Oxford 1891) pp. 306–13
101. *Journals of Lieutenants Elliott and Pickersgill* p. 34; G. Forster, *Voyage* ii. pp. 480–81
102. Hoare, ed., *Resolution Journal* iv. p. 570; G. Forster, *Voyage* ii. pp. 237–38; BL, Add. MSS. 42,714 f. 33; RAV pp. 469–70
103. RAV pp. 471–77
104. RAV pp. 477–79
105. For the Eromangan oral history version of this encounter see Cheesman, *Camping* pp. 146–49; H. A. Robertson, *Eromanga, the Martyr Isle* (1903) pp. 14–19
106. RAV pp. 480–86
107. For the full esoteric details of the civil war on Tanna see Jean Guiart, *Un Siècle et demi de contacts culturels à Tann, Nouvelles-Hebrides* (Paris 1956) pp. 11–14, 90–92
108. RAV pp. 486, 490
109. RAV p. 493
110. RAV pp. 495–98
111. RAV pp. 503–8, 849–63; G. Forster, *Voyage* ii. pp. 278–80
112. RAV p. 490
113. RAV pp. 859–60
114. Hoare, ed., *Resolution Journal* iv. p. 605
115. Ibid. iv. pp. 606–07
116. Salmond, *Cannibal Dog* p. 275
117. Ibid. p. 435
118. RAV p. 499
119. Sparrman, *Voyage* p. 151
120. G. Forster, *Voyage* ii. pp. 350–53
121. BL, Add. MSS. 42,714 ff. 32–33, Holmes, ed., *Journals* p. 34
122. William Wales, *Remarks on Mr. Forster's Account of Captain Cook's Last Voyage Round the World in the Years 1772, 1773, 1774 and 1775* (1778) pp. 83–88
123. RAV pp. 508–19
124. For full details see RAV pp. 520–26
125. Wales, *Remarks* p. 89; G. Forster, *Voyage* ii. p. 376; RAV p. 856
126. RAV p. 520

CHAPTER 12: LOST HORIZON: THE GREAT SOUTHERN CONTINENT

1. RAV pp. 527–29
2. RAV pp. 530–32
3. Important light is shed on Cook's visit to this part of Noumea in Douglas Bronwen, 'A contact history of the Balad people of New Caledonia', *Journal of Polynesian Society* 79 (1990) pp. 180–200
4. RAV p. 535
5. For the fish and the ghosts see Douglas Bronwen, 'Discourses on death in a Melanesian world', in Donna Mernicks, ed., *Dangerous Liaisons* (Melbourne 1994) p. 362. For Cook's attitude to food see J. C. Beaglehole, *The Life of Captain Cook* (1972) p. 413
6. RAV pp. 536–37
7. M. E. Hoare, ed., *The Resolution Journal of Johann Reinhold Forster 1772–1775* (Hakluyt Society, 2nd Series 152–53 1982) iv. p. 647
8. George Forster, *A Voyage round the World* (1777) ii. pp. 383–84, 402–3

9. There is a huge literature on D'Entrecasteaux. See Edward Duyker and Maryse Duyker, eds, *Bruny d'Entrecasteaux: Voyage to Australia and the Pacific 1791–1793* (Melbourne 2001); F. B. Horner, *Looking for La Pérouse: D'Entrecasteaux in Australia and the South Pacific 1792–93* (Victoria 1995); Ian F. McLaren, *La Pérouse in the Pacific* (Melbourne 1993)
10. RAV pp. 546–55, 763–64, 863–67
11. RAV p. 556
12. BL, Add. MSS. 42,714 f. 34; RAV p. 868
13. RAV p. 557
14. G. Forster, *Voyage* ii. p. 376
15. RAV p. 561
16. RAV pp. 563–64
17. Hoare, ed., *Resolution Journal* iv. p. 670; G. Forster, *Voyage* ii. p. 600; RAV pp. 565–66, 868–69
18. RAV p. 569
19. RAV p. 570
20. RAV pp. 572–73
21. RAV p. 573
22. RAV pp. 573–82
23. John Elliott and Richard Pickersgill, *Captain Cook's Second Voyage: Journals of Lieutenants John Elliott and Richard Pickersgill* ed. Christine Holmes (1980) p. 36; RAV p. 576
24. RAV p. 587
25. Anders Sparrman, *A Voyage round the World with Captain James Cook in H.M.S. Resolution* trans. Huldine Bearnish and Averil Mackenzie-Grieve (1953) pp. 192–93
26. RAV p. 598
27. Hoare, ed., *Resolution Journal* iv. p. 697
28. RAV pp. 605–6, 764–66
29. RAV pp. 617–18
30. RAV pp. 619–26
31. Hoare, ed., *Resolution Journal* iv. p. 713
32. RAV pp. ciii, 627–28
33. RAV p. 637
34. Ibid.
35. RAV pp. 643–47
36. RAV p. 648
37. RAV pp. 649–51
38. RAV p. 653
39. J. R. Forster, *Observations Made during a Voyage Round the World* (1778) pp. 318–32; G. Forster, *Voyage* i. p. 240; ii. p. 478
40. *Journals of Lieutenants Elliott and Pickersgill* p. 44
41. RAV pp. 870–71
42. RAV pp. 654–55
43. For Crozet and Surville see John Dunmore, *French Explorers in the Pacific* (Oxford 1965), especially pp. 135–45; Colin Jack-Hinton, *The Search for the Islands of Solomon 1567–1838* (Oxford 1969) pp. 261–66
44. Beaglehole, *Life* pp. 439–40; John Gascoigne, *Captain Cook* (2007) p. 202. There is an extended discussion of Hawkesworth's errors, solecisms and follies in Nicholas Thomas, *Discoveries: The Voyages of Captain Cook* (2003) pp. 152–59
45. *Journals of Lieutenants Elliott and Pickersgill* p. 44
46. Ibid. p. 45; BL, Add. MSS. 42,714 f. 41
47. RAV pp. 660–68
48. RAV p. 668
49. RAV pp. 669–82
50. RAV p. lxxxviii
51. RAV p. 637
52. RAV p. lxxxviii
53. RAV p. 643

54. G. Williams, 'Reassessing Cook', in G. Williams, ed., *Captain Cook: Explorations and Reassessments* (Woodbridge, Suffolk 2004) p. 232
55. Williams, ed., *Explorations and Reassessments* pp. 153–58. Cf. in general Andrew Davis, ed., *The Charts and Coastal Voyages of Captain Cook's Voyages* 3 vols (1997)
56. Simon Betron and Andrew Robinson, *The Shape of the World* (1991) p. 131
57. Michael E. Hoare, 'Cook the discoverer: an essay by George Forster, 1778', *Records of the Australian Academy of Science* 1 (1969) pp. 7–16
58. R. A. Skelton, 'Cook as hydrographer', *Mariner's Mirror* 40 (1954) p. 92
59. As Beaglehole has remarked: 'He never, in explaining his own shortcomings, lost a faint touch of naivety' (RAV p. xcvi)
60. Hoare, ed., *Resolution Journal* ii. pp. 306–9; J. Forster, *Observations* pp. 492–94; G. Forster, *Voyage* i. pp. 237–40, 369–70
61. Howard M. Smith, 'The introduction of venereal disease into Tahiti: a re-examination', *Journal of Pacific History* 10, 1 (1975) pp. 38–45
62. James Watt, 'Medical aspects and consequences of Captain Cook's voyages', in R. Fisher and H. Johnston, eds, *Captain Cook and his Times* (Canberra 1979) pp. 128–57.
63. James Watt, 'Medical Aspects and Consequences of Cook's Voyage' in Robin Fisher and Hugh Johnston, eds, *Captain Cook and his Times* (Canberra 1979) pp. 129–57
64. James Boswell, *The Journals of James Boswell 1760–1795* (1991) pp. 306–7
65. RAV p. 692. As Beaglehole remarks: 'The voyage was the vindication of that great genius John Harrison' (RAV p. xxxix)
66. J. Forster, *Observations* pp. 293–94, 247–52, 357–58, 411–17, 582–86; Hoare, ed., *Resolution Journal*, iii. pp. 390, 515–17; G. Forster, *Voyage* i. pp. 391–93, 295–97; ii. pp. 110–13
67. Hoare, ed., *Resolution Journal* i. pp. 260–62; G. Forster, *Voyage* i. pp. 167–68
68. See R. Adams, *In the Land of Strangers: A Century of European Contacts with Tanna 1774–1874* (Canberra 1984) p. 14; H. E. Maude, *Of Islands and Men: Studies in Pacific History* (Melbourne 1968) p. 343; Tom Dutton, ' "Successful intercourse was had with the natives": aspects of European methods in the Pacific', in Donald C. Laycock and Werner Winter, eds, *A World of Language* (Canberra 1987) pp. 152–71
69. Bernard Smith, 'Coleridge's Ancient Mariner and Cook's second voyage', *Journal of the Warburg and Courtauld Institutes* 19 (1956) pp. 117–54
70. RAV p. 958
71. His *A Collection of Voyages* appeared just a month before Cook returned
72. Beaglehole, *Life* p. 455
73. RAV p. 960
74. H. B. Carter, *Sir Joseph Banks 1743–1820* (1988) p. 120
75. James Boswell, *The Life of Samuel Johnson* (1991) pp. 476–77
76. Beaglehole, *Life* pp. 457–59. Beaglehole clearly dislikes the idea that career disappointments can finish a man off. 'It may be too much to say, as was commonly said at the time, that he died of chagrin. There are other wasting diseases of which a man may die.' He does, however, acknowledge that 'the nervous strain was acute' (ibid. p. 459)
77. Kitson, *Captain Cook* p. 232
78. Beaglehole, *Life* pp. 461–62, 465
79. Hoare, ed., *Resolution Journal* i. p. 71
80. Beaglehole, *Life* pp. 467–70
81. Fanny Burney, *Early Diary* (1913) i. p. 334; cf. also Lars E. Troide, ed., *The Early Journal and Letters of Fanny Burney* (Oxford 1990) ii. pp. 41, 59–63; Beverley Hooper, ed., *The Private Journal of James Burney* (Canberra 1975) pp. 70–72
82. RAV pp. 949–51
83. Eric McCormick, *Omai: Pacific Envoy* (Auckland 1977) pp. 94–114, 124–25, 169–73. See also Michael Alexander, *Omai: Noble Savage* (1977) and R. M. Connaughton, *Omai: The Prince Who Never Was* (2005)
84. McCormick, *Omai* pp. 182–83
85. Edward Lascelles, *Granville Sharp* (1928) pp. 108–11
86. McCormick, *Omai op. cit.*
87. Ibid. p. 129

88. Ibid. p. 132

89. *London Chronicle*, 20–22 April 1775

90. For Martha Ray see John Brewer, *A Sentimental Murder: Love and Madness in the Eighteenth Century* (2004); Martin Levy, *Love and Madness: The Murder of Martha Ray, Mistress of the 4th Earl of Sandwich* (2004). The allegedly lecherous Omai is the central figure in the 1930s novel by Constance Wright, *The Chaste Mistress*, which has been much criticised for racism

91. Troide, ed., *Early Journal and Letters of Fanny Burney* pp. 91–92

92. McCormick, *Omai*

93. Andrew Kippis, *The Life of Captain James Cook* (1788) pp. 324–25

94. RDV pp. 1486–88

95. Beaglehole, *Life* pp. 494–95. See also J. J. Colledge and Ben Warlow, *The Ships of the Royal Navy* (2006); Rif Winfield, *British Warships in the Age of Sail 1714–1792* (2007)

96. Andrew S. Cook, 'Cook and the Royal Society', in Wiliams, ed., *Explorations and Reassessments* pp. 37–55 (at p. 52)

97. C. Ryskamp and F. A. Pottle, eds, *Boswell: The Ominous Years 1774–1776* (1963) p. 308

98. James Boswell, *The Life of Samuel Johnson* J. W. Cropker ed., (1832); pp. 367–68

99. Ryskamp and Pottle, eds, *Boswell: The Ominous Years* pp. 659–60

100. Ibid. p. 309

101. RAV pp. 695–96, 700–3. For the French admiral's later career see Rémi Monaque, *La touche-Tréville 1745–1804: l'amiral qui défiait Nelson* (Paris 2000). At Boulogne between 4–15 August 1801 Latouche-Treville decisively repelled the attack by Nelson on the French invasion flotilla. On every conceivable index – numbers of men killed and wounded, ships and materiel lost, mission aborted – the Frenchman was the easy winner on points.

102. For an outstanding survey of all the issues involved see G. Williams, *Voyages of Delusion: The Search for the Northwest Passage in the Age of Reason* (2002)

103. Ibid. pp. 299–300; H. T. Fry, 'The commercial ambitions behind Captain Cook's last voyage', *New Zealand Journal of History* 7 (1973) pp. 186–91

104. See the instructions at RDV pp. ccxx–xiv

105. Beaglehole, *Life* p. 475

106. Adm. 2/101; Adm. 51/540

107. Adm. 1/5308

108. Williams, *Voyages of Delusion* pp. 305–06

109. Beaglehole, *Life* pp. 475–90 and Williams, *Voyages of Delusion* pp. 258–63, 290–93 deal with these writers at some length. See also Williams, 'Myth and reality: James Cook and the theoretical geography of North-West America', in Fisher and Johnston, eds, *Captain Cook and his Times* pp. 59–80

110. Beaglehole, *Life* pp. 493–94

111. The best study of corruption in the dockyards is in R. J. B. Knight, 'The Royal Dockyards in England at the time of the American War of Independence', Ph.D. thesis, University of London, 1972. None of the published sources is as rich on this topic though there are pointers in James Haas, *A Management Odyssey. The Royal Dockyards 1714–1914* (1994) and Daniel Baugh, *British Naval Administration in the Age of Walpole* (Princeton 1965). For conditions at Deptford dockyard see Peter Linebaugh, *The London Hanged: Crime and Civil Society in the Eighteenth Century* (2003) p. 374; see also David Cordingly, 'HM Dockyards at Deptford', in David Cordingly, ed., *Captain James Cook: Navigator* (1988) pp. 45–53

112. RDV pp. lxxii–lxxv

113. RDV pp. 1271–72. Beaglehole accuses Samwell of 'an excess of moral cant' (RDV p. lxxv)

114. Troide, ed., *Early Journals and Letters of Fanny Burney* ii. p. 206

115. RDV pp. lxxv–lxxvi, 1512

116. RDV pp. lxxvi–lxxvii

117. RDV pp. lxxix–lxxx

118. RDV p. lxxix. There are, of course, many biographies of Bligh, for example, George Mackaness, *The Life of Vice Admiral William Bligh* (1931); Gavin Kennedy, *Captain Bligh: The Man and his Mutinies* (1989)

119. *Burney Early Diary* i. p. 321; ii. p. 38

120. James Trevenen, *A Memoir of James Trevenen 1760–1790* eds C. Lloyd and R.C. Anderson (1959)

121. RDV p. lxxiii
122. William Davies, 'David Samwell', *Transactions of the Honourable Society of Cymmrodorion* (1928) pp. 70–133
123. For Ledyard see Edward Gray, *The Making of John Ledyard* (New Haven, CT 2007); Bill Gifford, *Ledyard: In Search of the First American Explorer* (New York 2007); James Zug, *American Traveler: The Life and Adventures of John Ledyard, the Man Who Dreamed of Walking the World* (New York 2005); Michael Oren, *Power, Faith and Fantasy: The United States in the Middle East: 1776 to the present* (New York 2007)
124. RDV p. lxxxix
125. O. H. K. Spate, *Paradise Found and Lost* (1988) p. 194
126. Beaglehole, *Life* p. 503
127. Adm. 55/117
128. RDV pp. 1520–21
129. Beaglehole, *Life* p. 502

CHAPTER 13: THE LAST VOYAGE

1. RDV p. xxxi
2. RDV p. 1488
3. Glyn Williams, *Voyages of Delusion: The Search for the Northwest Passage in the Age of Reason* (2002) p. 138
4. There are good discussions of Cook's motives in Beaglehole, RDV pp. ccxx–ccxv and Vanessa Collingridge, *Captain Cook: The Life, Death and Legacy of History's Greatest Explorer* (2002) pp. 332–33
5. O. H. K. Spate, *Paradise Found and Lost* (1988) p. 135
6. Gananath Obeyereseke, *The Apotheosis of Captain Cook: European Mythmaking in the Pacific* (Princeton 1992) p. 11. On the very different and quite separate issue of the structural relationship of psychoanalysis to colonialism see R. Khanna, *Dark Continents: Psychoanalysis and Colonialism* (Durham, NC 2003)
7. For the most recent psychoanalytical investigation of Burton see Ben Grant, *Postcolonialism, Psychoanalysis and Burton* (2008)
8. There is a regrettable tendency in some modern writers to try to get round this obstacle by simply inventing a version of the subject's state of mind. In Cook's case this has been done (unconvincingly) by Martin Dugard in his *Farther Than Any Man: The Rise and Fall of Captain James Cook* (2001)
9. See below pp. 355–57
10. This case is developed in detail in Frank McLynn, *Napoleon: A Biography* (1997), esp. pp. 285–91
11. J. C. Beaglehole, *The Life of Captain Cook* (1972) pp. lxix, 493–94
12. For disillusionment with exploration see Bernard Smith, *Imagining the Pacific: In the Wake of the Cook Voyages* (New Haven, CT 1992) p. 80–81, 199–202. For the reverse 'fatal impact' see Andrew Martin, 'Dangerous liaisons in the South Pacific. Surfing the revolution: the fatal impact of the Pacific in Europe', *Eighteenth-Century Studies* 41 (2008) pp. 141–47. Martin's starting point is the famous statement in Freud's *Civilisation and its Discontents* (1930) that the three great causes of unhappiness in the modern age were religion, psychoanalysis itself and the consequences of the eighteenth-century exploration of the Pacific.
13. R. Barker, 'Cook's Nursery', in G. Williams, *Captain Cook: Explorations and Reassessments* p. 20
14. RDV p. cliv
15. George Young, *The Life and Voyages of Captain James Cook:* (1836) pp. 304–5
16. John K. Wright, 'The open Polar Sea', *Geographical Review* 43 (1953) pp. 338–65. Cf. Beaglehole: 'The ice-free Arctic sea was a notion that had more in common with the Southern Continent: a logical deduction from premises not quite wilfully asserted, accepted rather with a determination to believe – that the ocean cannot freeze, for example, that oceanic ice is therefore a river product' (RDV pp. ccxxiii)
17. Spate, *Paradise* p. 81
18. G. Lefevre-Pontalis, 'Un Projet de conquête au Japon par l'Angleterre et la Russie en 1776', *Annales de l'Ecole Libre des Sciences Politiques* 5 (1889) pp. 533–57. The Polish adventurer

Benyowski was probably responsible for this canard. See G. V. Blue, 'Rumor of an Anglo-Russian raid upon Japan, 1776', *Pacific Historical Review* 8, 1939, pp. 453–63; J. E. Martin-Allaric, *Bougainville navigateur et les découvertes de son temps* (Paris 1964) ii. pp. 1448–51

19. Charles E. Chapman, *The Founding of Spanish California* (New York 1916) pp. 376–80
20. RDV p. 1535
21. Archives de la Marine, Archives Nationales, Paris, B4/313
22. RDV p. 3
23. Lars E. Troide, ed., *Early Journals and Letters of Fanny Burney* (Oxford 1990) pp. 193–97
24. RDV p. 7. For Clerke's escape see ibid. pp. 1513–14
25. John Douglas, *A Voyage to the Pacific Ocean* 3 vols (1784) i. p. 9
26. RDV p. 8
27. RDV pp. 8–9, 723–29
28. RDV pp. 729–34, 1515
29. RDV pp. 736–37
30. RDV pp. 15, 739–53
31. RDV pp. 15, 17
32. RDV p. 741
33. RDV p. 1515
34. RDV pp. 19–23, 754–59
35. Anne Salmond, *The Trial of the Cannibal Dog: The Remarkable Story of Captain Cook's Encounters in the South Seas* (2003) p. 435
36. RDV p. xcii
37. RDV p. 18
38. RDV p. 1518
39. RDV p. 19
40. RDV p. 1520
41. RDV pp. 24, 760–61
42. RDV pp. xciv, 762–63
43. RDV p. 26
44. See W. E. LeMasurier and J. W. Thompson, eds, *Volcanoes of the Antarctic Plates and Southern Ocean* (1990)
45. William James Mills, *Exploring Polar Frontiers: A Historical Encyclopedia* (2003) pp. 345–46
46. RDV pp. 29–48, 766–76, 990
47. RDV pp. 48–49, 777–82, 991–94
48. Salmond, *Cannibal Dog* p. 310
49. RDV p. 787
50. RDV p. 54
51. RDV pp. 51–53. Beaglehole commented acidly: 'The geography of Tasmania owes nothing to Cook' (RDV p. xcvi)
52. RDV pp. 55–57, 782–94
53. RDV p. 58
54. RDV pp. 795–97
55. RDV p. 59
56. Samwell's reaction to all this is at RDV pp. 994–1000
57. For the entire sequence of events in New Zealand see RDV pp. 58–75, 797–818
58. RDV pp. 61–62. For some interesting reflections on the increase in Maori prostitution over the five visits see Nicholas Thomas, *Discoveries: The Voyages of Captain Cook* (2003) pp. xxiv, xxvi, 184–85, 299–300
59. Cook and his scientists always took a detailed interest in the war canoes of Poynesian indigenous peoples. For a detailed analysis see John Gascoigne, *Captain Cook* (2007) pp. 64–72
60. RDV p. 995
61. Robert McNab, *Historical Records of New Zealand* (1914), ii. pp. 198–99
62. RDV p. 68. For the Webber portrait of Kahura see Thomas, *Discoveries* pp. 303–06
63. George Home, *Memoirs of an Aristocrat* (1838) pp. 271–73; Salmond, *Cannibal Dog* pp. 316–17 and pp. 1–9. The Burney family felt strongly that the Grass Cove massacre was an outrage that should be avenged. See Fanny Burney, *The Early Diary of Fanny Burney* (1913) ii. p. 283

64. Beaglehole, *Life* pp. 523, 526
65. RDV pp. 76–77
66. RDV p. 77
67. RDV pp. 69, 71
68. Smith, *Imagining the Pacific* p. 207
69. RDV pp. 79–83, 825–30, 1003–8
70. On Cook's reception in what are now the Cook Islands there is a wealth of anthropological material. See John Williams, *A Narrative of Missionary Enterprises in the South Sea Islands* (1838) esp. pp. 57, 104; William Wyatt, *Historical Sketches of Savage Life in Polynesia* (Wellington 1880); Tauira Henry, *Ancient Tahiti* (Honolulu 1928) pp. 126–28; Hank Driessen, 'Outriggerless canoes and glorious beings', *Journal of Pacific History* 17 (1982) pp. 3–28
71. RDV pp. 84–87, 833–41
72. The loss of life seems normal and typical. Janet Davidson, *The Prehistory of New Zealand* (Auckland 1984) p. 89 estimates that in 2,000 years of Polynesian voyaging more than 500,000 souls were lost at sea.
73. RDV pp. 88, 843–44
74. Adm. 51/4528/45; RDV pp. 845–48, 1005–10
75. RDV p. 91
76. RDV p. 92
77. RDV pp. 92–93, 849–57, 1011
78. RDV pp. 96–97, 859–61
79. RDV pp. 101, 865
80. RDV pp. 101, 133, 862–68, 1013–23
81. Anne Salmond, *Between Worlds: Early Exchanges between Maori and Europeans 1773–1815* (Auckland 1997) p. 377
82. RDV p. 1014. For Samwell's detailed accounts of his sexual conquests see RDV pp. 987, 1030–31, 1044, 1054–55, 1085, 1093–96, 1143–45, 1181–82, 1295
83. Elizabeth Bott, *Tongan Society at the Time of Captain Cook's Visits* (Wellington 1982) pp. 89–164; E. W. Gifford, *Tongan Society* (Honolulu 1929)
84. For other examples of such routine brutality on Tonga see John Martin, ed., *Tonga Islands. William Mariner's Account* (Tonga 1991) pp. 62–63
85. RDV pp. 102–5, 869–72
86. RDV pp. 873–78
87. RDV pp. 105–6
88. RDV p. 1310. Beaglehole notes that Clerke never got his cats back and concludes archly: 'the rats of the *Discovery* rioted without opposition' (RDV p. cvii)
89. John Martin, *An Account of the Natives of the Tonga Islands . . . from the Extensive Communications of Mr William Mariner* (Edinburgh 1827) i. pp. 116–20; ii. pp. 71–72; cf. also Martin, ed., *Tonga Islands* pp. 279–80
90. RAV p. 109
91. Martin, *An Account* p. 72
92. RDV pp. 1361–62
93. RDV pp. 110, 113
94. Thomas, *Discoveries* pp. 317–19
95. RDV p. 111
96. RDV p. 112
97. RDV p. 115
98. RDV pp. 115–17, 881
99. There is a conflict of authorities here. I follow Salmond, *Cannibal Dog* p. 334 but Beaglehole (*Life* p. 538) says Cook's passengers were not dropped until he reached Kotu
100. RDV p. 883
101. RDV p. 119
102. RDV p. 884
103. For a lengthy analysis of Finau see Thomas, *Discoveries* pp. 316–25
104. RDV pp. 120, 885–86
105. RDV p. 122

106. RDV p. 1024
107. Bott, *Tongan Society* pp. 28, 50
108. RDV pp. 887–90
109. RDV p. 123
110. See esp. RDV p. 71
111. RDV p. cvi
112. Salmond, *Cannibal Dog* p. 338
113. C. Lloyd and R. C. Anderson, eds, *A Memoir of James Trevenen 1760–1790* (1959) p. 21
114. P. J. Marshall and John Woods, eds, *The Correspondence of Edmund Burke Vol. 7 1792–August 1794* (Cambridge 1968) p. 589
115. RDV p. cvi
116. RDV p. 132
117. RDV pp. 134–35, 1028–29
118. RDV pp. 1362–63
119. RDV p. 909
120. For this see N. A. M. Rodger, *The Wooden World: An Anatomy of the Georgian Navy* (1986) p. 220
121. George Gilbert, *Captain Cook's Final Voyage: The Journal of Midshipman George Gilbert*, ed. Christine Holmes (Horsham 1982) pp. 3–4
122. See, for example, Burney's testimony in Adm. 51/4528/45 ff. 203–04
123. RDV p. 142
124. Salmond, *Cannibal Dog* p. 436
125. Salmond, 'Tute', in Williams, ed., *Explorations and Reassessments* p. 87
126. RDV pp. 137, 1032
127. RDV p. 1042
128. S. M. Lambert, *A Doctor in Paradise* (New York 1941) pp. 30–32
129. For this and other Tongan ceremonies see Arne Terminow, 'Captain Cook and the roots of precedence in Tonga', *History and Archaeology* 12 (2001) pp. 289–314; Phyllis Herder, 'Gender, rank and power in eighteenth-century Tonga', *Journal of Pacific History* 22 (1987) pp. 195–208
130. RDV pp. 132–34. For the ceremony see also Martin, ed., *Tonga Islands* pp. 94–96
131. For the complex oscillation between the different ceremonies and the outbreak of thefts see RDV pp. 1023–48
132. RDV p. 145

CHAPTER 14: TAHITI: THE FINAL PHASE

1. RDV p. 913
2. John Martin, ed., *Tonga Islands. William Mariner's Account* (Tonga 1991) pp. 94–96
3. RDV p. 151; Adm. 55/117 f. 64; H. Zimmermann, *Account of the Third Voyage of Captain Cook 1776–1780*, trans. U. Tewsley (Wellington 1926) p. 20
4. For detailed descriptions on the *inasi* ceremony see RDV pp. 147–55, 915–17, 1049; Martin, ed., *Tonga Islands* pp. 147, 289, 342–46; John Martin, *An Account of the Natives of the Tonga Islands . . . from the extensive communications of Mr. William Mariner* (Edinburgh 1827) ii. pp. 168–73; N. Rutherford, ed., *Friendly Islands: A History of Tonga* (Melbourne 1977) p. 76. For a defence of Cook's 'intrusiveness' see Nicholas Thomas, *Discoveries: The Voyages of Captain Cook* (2003) p. 329. The whole of this section of Thomas's book (pp. 325–30) sheds further interesting light on the *inasi* ceremony. Beaglehole claims that *inasi* was a generic term and that the ceremony witnessed by Cook may have been a 'one off'. He also praises Cook's description as an unpretentious classic of anthropological observation (J. C. Beaglehole, *The Life of Captain Cook* (1972) pp. 543, 554)
5. John Thomas, a missionary who worked in Tonga in 1825–59, quoted in Anne Salmond, *The Trial of the Cannibal Dog: The Remarkable Story of Captain Cook's Encounters in the South Seas* (2003) p. 348
6. RDV pp. 157–58
7. RDV pp. 158–59, 960–65

8. RDV p. 160

9. See RDV pp. 920–60 (esp p. 929), 1340–43

10. I. Goldman, *Ancient Polynesian Society* (Chicago 1970) pp. 478, 509

11. M. E. Hoare, ed., *The Resolution Journal of Johann Reinhold Forster 1772–1775* (Hakluyt Society, 2nd Series 152–55, 1982) iii. p. 401

12. A. Howard and R. Berkley, eds, *Development in Polynesian Ethnology* (Honolulu 1989) p. 259; A. Kenaven, *Museums, Anthropology and Imperial Exchange* (Cambridge 2005) p. 33

13. I. Barber, 'Early contact ethnography and understanding: an evaluation of the cook expeditionary account of the Grass Cove massacre', in A. Calder, J. Lamb and B. Orr, eds, *Voyages and Beaches: Pacific Encounters 1769–1840* (Honolulu 1999) pp. 17–42

14. J. K. Munford, ed., *John Ledyard's Journal of Captain Cook's Last Voyage* (Corvalis, OR 1963) pp. 37–41

15. RDV p. 1044

16. RDV p. 174

17. J. J. H. Labillardière, *Account of a Voyage in Search of La Pérouse* (1802) ii. pp. 149–50, 181–82. For the d'Entrecasteaux expedition see Edward and Maryse Duyker, *Bruny d'Entrecasteaux's Voyage to Australia and the Pacific 1791–1793* (Melbourne 2001); Edward Duyker, *Citizen Labillardière* (Melbourne 2003); F. B. Horner, *Looking for La Pérouse: d'Entrecasteaux in Australia and the South Pacific 1792–1793* (Victoria 1995)

18. RDV p. xcviii

19. The question is posed sharply in Richard Hough, *Captain James Cook* (1994) pp. 299–300

20. RDV pp. xcix–c

21. See the criticism from officers on the *Discovery* in John Rickman, *Journal of Captain Cook's Last Voyage to the Pacific Ocean* (1781) pp. 78–81, 96, 147 and from those on the *Resolution* in RDV pp. 736–37, 823–24, 849, 858

22. O. H. K. Spate, *Paradise Found and Lost* (1988) p. 137

23. George Gilbert, *Captain Cook's Final Voyage: The Journal of Midshipman George Gilbert* ed. Christine Holmes (Horsham 1982) p. 35; W. Bayly, *The Original Astronomic Observations made in the Course of a Voyage to the North Pacific Ocean* (1782) p. 107. However, it is worth mentioning that Nicholas Thomas believes that Cook's lack of interest in Samo and Fiji was entirely rational and desribes the whole issue as 'a non problem' (Nicholas Thomas, *Discoveries: The Voyages of Captain Cook* (2003) pp. 332–33)

24. RDV p. cii

25. RDV pp. 929, 945–46, 1361–68

26. George Forster, *A Voyage round the World* eds N. Thomas and O. Berghof, 2 vols (Honolulu 2000) i. p. 353

27. For a valuable discussion of the whole red feathers phenomenon see John Gascoigne, *Captain Cook* (2007) pp. 94–95

28. RDV pp. 183–84

29. RDV pp. 185, 966–71, 1051–53

30. RDV p. 187

31. RDV pp. 975–79

32. RDV pp. 1053–55, 1370–72

33. B. G. Corney, *The Quest and Occupation of Tahiti by Emissaries of Spain during the Years 1772–1776* (1919) ii. pp. 103–316

34. 'On what criterion Fathers Jeronimo Clota and Narciso Gonzalez were selected for the misison it is impossible to discuss, but one suspects that it was on the time-honoured principle that those two were the two whom their superiors could most gladly spare. The pair did nothing whatever towards conversion of the lost souls around them; in fact they rarely stirred outside their house. To be fair, they may have feared less for their lives than lest they suffer the fate of Diderot's chaplain, who fell into earthly sin. The fact remains that the result of their missionary presence was *minus* two converts (since the previous ones relapsed)' (Spate, *Paradise* p. 1250)

35. Corney, *Quest* ii. pp. 319–75

36. RDV p. 188

37. RDV p. 189
38. RDV pp. 187–88
39. Ibid.
40. RDV p. 1372
41. For sex on Tahiti see especially Gascoigne, *Captain Cook* pp. 193–95
42. RDV p. 1373
43. For the god Oro see Robert D. Craig, 'Oro,' in *Dictionary of Polynesian Mythology* (1989) pp. 193–94
44. RDV p. 1066
45. For this incident see also Michael Alexander, *Omai: Noble Savage* (1977) pp. 182–83; Richard Connaughton, *Omai: The Prince Who Never Was* (2005) pp. 224–25
46. RDV p. 192
47. Rickman, *Journal* pp. 131–33
48. RDV pp. 192–95, 1374–75
49. Rickman, *Journal* pp. 139–40
50. RDV pp. 195–98
51. The entire Omai saga can be followed at RDV pp. cx, 193, 1368–70, 1372
52. RDV pp. 1058–59
53. Beaglehole, *Life* p. 552
54. RDV pp. 1058–65
55. Salmond, *Cannibal Dog* pp. 357–58.
56. For a summary of the war and its issues see Beaglehole, *Life* pp. 553–55
57. RDV p. 198
58. According to J. C. Beaglehole, ed., *The Endeavour Journal of Joseph Banks 1768–1771* 2 vols (Sydney 1962) ii. p. 383; women had their own *marae* on Tahiti.
59. RDV pp. 201–2
60. For the accounts by Cook and Anderson see RDV pp. 199–204, 978–84. For the analyses and comments by modern anthropologists see Roger and Kaye Green, 'Religious structures. *marae* of the Windward Society Islands: the significance of certain historical records', *New Zealand Journal of History* 2 (1968) pp. 66–89; Salmond, *Cannibal Dog* pp. 359–61; Thomas, *Discoveries* pp. 338–41
61. Thomas, *Discoveries* p. 341
62. J. C. Beaglehole, *Cook and the Russians: An Addendum to the Hakluyt Society Edition of the Voyages of the Resolution and Discovery 1776–1780* (1973) pp. 552, 554
63. RDV pp. 206–9
64. RDV p. 219
65. William Bligh, *The Log of the Bounty* (1937) i. p. 401
66. Polynesians paid special attention to the head, face and eyes of their chiefs as the outward manifestations of the soul, so they read particular significance into portraiture (Owen Rutter, ed., *The Journal of James Morrison*, (1955) p. 117)
67. Respectively, Thomas, *Discoveries* p. 343 and Bernard Smith, *Imagining the Pacific: In the Wake of the Cook Voyages* (New Haven, CT 1992) p. 206
68. Bligh, *Log of the Bounty* i. pp. 372–73; Arthur Philip, *Voyage to Botany Bay* (1789) pp. 233–34
69. RDV p. 1066
70. RDV pp. 207, 1376–77
71. RDV p. 209. Cook's remark was echoed in almost identical words by King (RDV p. 1376)
72. RDV p. 210
73. Ibid.
74. Ibid.
75. RDV pp. 209, 1375
76. RDV pp. 222–23
77. RDV p. 224
78. Holmes, ed., *Journal of Gilbert* p. 47
79. RDV p. 214
80. This was 'over the top' behaviour. For the norm see Gascoigne, *Captain Cook* pp. 110–12
81. RDV pp. 1377–81; Salmond, *Cannibal Dog* p. 365

82. RDV p. 1055
83. RDV p. 214
84. Bligh, *Log of the Bounty* i. pp. 378–79
85. RDV p. 226
86. RDV p. 232
87. RDV p. 227
88. RDV p. 1382
89. William Ellis, *An Authentic Narrative of a Voyage Performed by Captain Cook and Captain Clerke 1776–80* 2 vols (1782) i. p. 146
90. Holmes, ed., *Journal of Gilbert* pp. 46–47
91. RDV pp. 228–31
92. RDV p. 1383
93. RDV pp. 231–32
94. Adm. 55/117
95. RDV p. 233
96. RDV pp. 1068–69
97. Beaglehole, *Life* pp. 560–61
98. Bayly's account in Adm. 51/117 f. 9
99. RDV pp. 234–36
100. Burney in Adm. 51/4528
101. Salmond, *Cannibal Dog* p. 372
102. Rickman, *Journal* pp. 162–63
103. James Burney, *A Chronological History of North-eastern Voyages of Discovery* (1819) p. 233
104. Beaglehole, *Life* pp. 568–69
105. RDV p. 235
106. RDV pp. 236–37
107. F. W. Honay, ed., *Zinnemann's Captain Cook* (Toronto 1929) p. 58. This is a translation of the account originally published at Mannheim in 1781 by Heinrich Zinnemann under the title *Reise um die Welt mit Capitan Cook*
108. RDV pp. 1070–71
109. Rickman, *Journal op. cit.* p. 167
110. Salmond, *Cannibal Dog* p. 436
111. RDV pp. 183–84
112. RDV pp. 237–39
113. RDV pp. 1072–73, 1386–88
114. RDV pp. 240–41
115. Rickman, *Journal* p. 166
116. Bligh, *Log of the Bounty* i. pp. 393, 417
117. RDV p. 240
118. William Ellis, *Polynesian Researches* (1829) ii. pp. 91–95
119. Bligh, *Log of the Bounty* ii. p. 83; Rutter, ed., *Journal of James Morrison* p. 112
120. RDV pp. 1072–74
121. Thomas, *Discoveries* pp. 351–52
122. Ellis, *An Authentic Narrative* i. p. 154
123. RDV p. 244
124. BL, Add. MSS 37,528 f. 77; Adm. 55/117 f. 76
125. RDV pp. 1074–76, 1318
126. RDV pp. 248–49, 1077
127. RDV pp. 250–51, 1077–78, 1388–91
128. Adm. 55/117 f. 76; RDV p. 251
129. RDV p. 1078
130. Beaglehole, *Life* pp. 569–70
131. Burney, *Chronological History* pp. 233–34
132. RDV p. 245
133. RDV p. 256

Chapter 15: Quest for Illusion: The Northwest Passage

1. RDV p. 256
2. RDV pp. 257, 1345–47
3. James Trevenen, *A Memoir of James Trevenen*, eds C. Lloyd and R. C. Anderson (1959)
4. For details on Christmas Island see Kenneth P. Emory, *Archaeology and the Pacific Equatorial Islands* (Honolulu 1934) pp. 17–24; Peter Buck, *Vikings of the Sunrise* (1938)
5. RDV p. 260
6. RDV pp. 262–63
7. RDV pp. 1079–80
8. J. F. G. Stokes, 'Hawaii's discovery by Spaniards: theories traced and refuted', *Papers of the Hawaiian Historical Society* 20 (1939) pp. 128–34; E. E. Dahlgren, *Were the Hawaiian Islands Visited by the Spaniards before their Discovery by Captain Cook in 1778?* (Stockholm 1916). For a dissenting view see B. Andersson, *The Life and Voyages of Captain George Vancouver* (Toronto 1960) pp. 128–34. For the idea that Japanese junks might have reached Hawaii see W. E. Braden, 'On the probability of pre-1778 Japanese drifts to Hawaii', *Hawaiian Journal of History* 10 (1976) pp. 75–89
9. Kenneth P. Emory 'East Polynesian relationships', *Journal of the Polynesian Society* 72 (1963) pp. 78–100
10. RDV p. 279. See also Brian Durcans, 'Ancient Pacific voyaging: Cook's views and the development of interpretation', in T. C. Mitchell, ed., *Captain Cook and the South Pacific* (1979) pp. 137–66. Cf. Ben Finney, 'James Cook and the European discovery of Polynesia', in Robin Fisher and Hugh Johnston, eds, *From Maps to Metaphor: The Pacific World of George Vancouver* (Vancouver 1993) and K. R. Howe, 'The intellectual discovery and exploration of Polynesia', ibid. pp. 245–62
11. RDV p. 263
12. Adm 55/116 f. 39; Holmes, ed., *Journal of Gilbert* p. 62
13. RDV pp. 272, 1322–23
14. RDV pp. 270–76
15. BL, Add. MSS. 35,728 f. 86; W. Bayly, *The Original Astronomic Observations made in the course of a voyage to the North Pacific Ocean* (1782) p. 165; Adm. 55/21; RDV pp. 265–66
16. RDV p. 1084. W. Ellis, *An Authentic Narrative of a Voyage Performed by Captain Cook and Captain Clerke 1776–80* 2 vols (1782) ii. p. 153
17. Samuel Kamakau, *Ruling Chiefs of Hawaii* (Honolulu 1992) pp. 92–95; Abraham Fornander, *An Account of the Polynesian Race* (1969) ii. pp. 168–69
18. The *fons et origo* of this nonsense was Sheldon Dibble, *History of the Sandwich Islands* (1843)
19. For the myth see S. M. Kamakau, *Ka Po'E Kahiko: The People of Old* (Honolulu 1962); James J. James, *History of the Hawaiian or Sandwich Islands* (Boston 1843). For the explanations and refutations see A. Taylor, *Sesquicentennial Celebration of Captain Cook's Discovery of Hawaii 1778–1928* (Honolulu 1929) p. 66; Glyn Williams, *The Death of Captain Cook* (2008) pp. 143–50. On this whole issue – mistaking myth for historical fact – the wise words of Greg Dening are worth pondering: 'myth and common sense answer different questions' (Greg Dening, *Mr Bligh's Bad Language: Passions, Power and Theatre on the Bounty* (Cambridge 1992) p. 209–40)
20. Adm. 55/116 f. 124; RDV pp. 269, 277
21. RDV pp. 285–86
22. RDV pp. 1500–3 p. 158
23. John Rickman, *Journal of Captain Cook's Last Voyage* (1781) *op. cit.* p. 83
24. There is an extended treatment and analysis of this incident in Nicholas Thomas, *Discoveries: The Voyages of Captain Cook* (2003) pp. 359–61
25. J. C. Beaglehole, *The Life of Captain Cook* (1972) pp. 576–77
26. RDV p. 1085
27. RDV pp. 1391–93
28. RDV pp. 1347–50
29. RDV p. 276
30. Beaglehole, *Life* p. 577
31. RDV pp. 1086–88
32. RDV p. 288
33. RDV pp. 483, 1186; John Gascoigne, *Captain Cook* (2007) p. 74

34. RDV pp. 1179, 1392
35. V. Valeri, *Kingship and Sacrifice: Ritual and Society in Ancient Hawaii* (Chicago 1985) p. 153
36. A. Kaepler, 'Aspects of Polynesian aesthetic tradition', in P. Gathercole et al., eds, *The Art of the Pacific Islands* (Washington 1979) pp. 71–100 (at pp. 81–82); I. Goldman, *Ancient Polynesian Society* (Chicago 1970) p. 552
37. Adm. 55/121 f. 118; RDV p. 620; M. Sahlins, *Islands of History* (Chicago 1985) p. 125
38. J. Munford, ed., *John Ledyard's Journal of Captain Cook's Last Voyage* (Corvallis, OR 1963) pp. 130–31; see also BL, Add. MSS. 38,530 ff. 127–28
39. Karl Wittfogel, *Oriental Despotism* (Yale 1957) pp. 240–46
40. See the estimates in O. A. Bushnell, *The Gifts of Civilization: Germs and Genocide in Hawaii* (Honolulu 1993) and Tom Dye, 'Population trends in Hawaii before 1778', *Hawaiian Journal of History* 28 (1994) pp. 1–20; Andrew F. Bushnell, 'The horror reconsidered: an evaluation of the historical evidence for population decline in Hawaii, 1778–1803', *Pacific Studies* 16 (1993) pp. 115–61
41. RDV pp. 1393–94
42. RDV pp. 624, 1181; I. Goldman, *Ancient Polynesian Society* (Chicago 1970) pp. 215, 538–39; Valeri, *Kingship* p. 85
43. Mumford, ed., *Ledyard Journal* pp. 132–33; RDV pp. 1171–72, 1184
44. RDV pp. 267, 490, 1083, 1158, 1348
45. RDV p. 289
46. RDV p. 292
47. RDV p. 294
48. RDV pp. 294–95
49. RDV p. 479
50. RDV p. 300
51. Beaglehole, *Life* pp. 583–84
52. For lengthy descriptions of the Nootka peoples, their houses, food, customs etc. see RDV pp. 303–30, 1083–103, 1350–51, 1393–414. See also Daniel Clayton, 'Captain Cook's command of knowledge and space: chronicles from Nootka Sound', in G. Williams, ed., *Captain Cook. Explorations and Reassessments* (Woodbridge, Suffolk 2004) pp. 110–33; J. C. H. King, 'The Nootka of Vancouver Island', in Hugh Cobbe, ed., *Cook's Voyages and the Peoples of the Pacific* (1979) pp. 89–108
53. RDV p. 296
54. Alvin and Virginia Silverstein, *The Sea Otter* (Brookfield, CT 1995) pp. 35–38; James R. Gibson, *Otter Skins, Boston Ships and China Goods: The Maritime Fur Trade of the Northwest Coast, 1785–1841* (Montreal 1992)
55. RDV pp. 304, 308, 1088–89, 1350, 1394; B. Gough, 'Nootka Sound in James Cook's Pacific world', in Barbara Efrat and W. J. Langlois, eds, *Nutka: Captain Cook and the Spanish Explorers on the Coast* (1978; Volume 7 of *Sound Heritage*) p. 13; D. Clayton, *Islands of Truth: The Imperial Fashioning of Vancouver Island* (Vancouver 2006) pp. 23–25; King, 'The Nootka of Vancouver Island', p. 107
56. B. Efrat and W. Langlois, 'The contact period as recorded by Indian oral tradition', in Efrat and Langlois, eds, *Nutka* pp. 54–62; Daniel Clayton, 'Chronicles from Nootka Sound', in Williams, ed., *Explorations and Reassessments* pp. 110–24; F. W. Honay and E. O. S. Scholefield, *British Columbia: From the Earliest Times to the Present* 4 vols (Vancouver 1914), i. pp. 81–83
57. RDV pp. 296–97, 301, 303, 312
58. RDV p. 302
59. Adm. 55/117 f. 100; Ellis, *An Authentic Narrative* i. p. 216
60. RDV p. 1091; R. Fisher, 'Cook and the Nootka', in R. Fisher and H. Johnston, *Captain James Cook and his Times* (Canberra 1979) p. 88
61. RDV pp. 297–98
62. RDV p. 1401; D. Connor and L. Miller, *Master Mariner: Captain James Cook and the Peoples of the Pacific* (Edinburgh 1978) p. 93
63. R. Inglis and J. Haggarty, 'Cook to Hewitt: three decades of change in Nootka Sound', in B. Trigg et al., eds, *Le Castor Fait Tout: Selected Papers of the Fifth North American Fur Trade Conference* (Montreal 1987) pp. 196–97. For the different Nootka tribes see Philip Ducker, *The Northern and Central Nootkan Tribes* (Washington, DC 1951)

64. BL, Add. MSS. 38,530 f. 68
65. RDV pp. 316, 1102, 1325
66. BL, Add. MSS. 38,530 f. 67; RDV p. 1312
67. BL, Add. MSS 37,528 f. 91
68. George Gilbert, *Captain Cook's Final Voyage: The Journal of Midshipman George Gilbert* ed. Christine Holmes (Horsham, 1982) p. 70; Adm. 51/4529 ff. 78–89; RDV pp. 1092–93, 1397. Cf. also the account at Adm. 5/4529
69. Thomas, *Discoveries* pp. 361–62
70. Mumford, ed., *Ledyard Journal* p. 72
71. J. S. Matthews, *Early Vancouver: Narratives of Pioneers of Vancouver, British Columbia* 2 vols (Vancouver 1933) ii. pp. 130–31; Derick Petherick, *The Nootka Connection: Europe and the Northwest Coast 1790–1795* (Vancouver 1980) pp. 7–13; Clayton, *Islands of Truth*
72. Jose Mariano Mozino, *Noticias de Nutka: An Account of Nootka Sound in 1792* ed. and trans. Iris H. Wilson Engstrand (Seattle 1970) pp. 66–67
73. A. Temple Paterson, *The Other Armada* (Manchester 1960)
74. H. R. Wagner, *Cartography of the Northwest Coast of America in the Year 1800* (Berkeley 1937) i. pp. 183–85; Dolores Higueras, 'The Malaspina expedition (1789–1794): a venture of the Spanish Enlightenment', in Carlos Martinez Shaw, *Spanish Pacific from Magellan to Malaspina* (Madrid 1988) pp. 158–62; Robin Inglis, *Spain and the North Pacific Coast: Essays in Recognition of the Bicentennial of the Malaspina Expedition 1791–1792* (Vancouver 1992). Andrew David, Felipe Fernandez-Armesto, Carlos Nori and G. Williams, eds, *The Malaspina Expedition 1789–1794: Journal of the Voyage of Alejandro Malaspina* (2001); Donald C. Cutter, *Malaspina and Galliano. Spanish Voyages to the North-west Coast 1791 and 1792* (Vancouver 1991)
75. RDV pp. 307, 333–34
76. RDV p. 335
77. RDV pp. 338–41
78. For Vancouver's later voyage in these waters see George Vancouver, *A Voyage of Discovery* (1798) iii. pp. 261–65
79. RDV pp. 342–53
80. RDV pp. 1107–13, 1414–21
81. RDV pp. 358–59
82. RDV p. 1116
83. RDV pp. 1115–17, 1421–24
84. RDV pp. 361–68
85. Vancouver, *Voyage* iii. p. 125
86. RDV pp. 369–70
87. Vancouver, *Voyage* iii. p. 120
88. RDV pp. 374–79. For Chirikov Island see Vancouver, *Voyage* iii. p. 87
89. RDV pp. 380–83, 1118–20
90. RDV pp. 384–85
91. BL, Add. MSS. 37,528 f. 173; Holmes, ed., *Journal of Gilbert* p. 52
92. For a modern confirmation of this see Tony Horwitz, *Into the Blue: Boldly Going Where Captain Cook has Gone Before* (2002) pp. 333–74
93. RDV pp. 388–89
94. RDV p. 389
95. RDV p. 390
96. BL, Add. MSS. 37,528 f. 174
97. RDV pp. 391–94, 1121–25, 1351–59, 1424–28
98. RDV p. 395
99. RDV pp. 399–403, 1429
100. RDV p. cxxx
101. RDV p. 406
102. RDV pp. 1429–30
103. RDV pp. 407–9, 1430–31
104. RDV pp. 409–11

105. RDV p. 411
106. RDV pp. 411–14.
107. For Bering's voyages (which the Russians failed to follow up) see Frank A. Golder, ed., *Bering's Voyages* (New York 1925); Raymond H. Fisher, *Bering's Voyages: Whither and Why* (Seattle 1977); O. W. Frost, ed., *Bering and Chirikov, The American Voyages and their Impact* (Anchorage 1992). The Russian fur trade, indirectly triggered by Bering's voyages, was an entrepreneurial activity entirely distinct from government policy in St Petersburg. For this see Glynn Barrett, *Russia in Pacific Waters, 1725–1825* (1981); J. M. Gibson, *Feeding the Russian Fur Trade: Provisionment of the Okhotsk Seaboard and the Kamchatka Peninsula 1639–1856* (Madison 1969)
108. RDV pp. 417–20
109. RDV p. 418
110. RDV pp. 419–22, 1453–54
111. Beaglehole, *Life* pp. 620–21
112. Ibid. pp. 622–23
113. RDV pp. 428–44
114. Ellis, *An Authentic Narrative* ii. p. 18
115. RDV p. 446
116. RDV p. 227
117. Lloyd and Anderson, eds, *Memoir of Trevenen* pp. 27–28
118. RDV pp. 1453–54
119. RDV pp. cxxxvii
120. RDV pp. 1142, 1182
121. Thomas, *Discoveries* pp. 375–76
122. Mumford, ed., *Ledyard Journal* pp. 91–100
123. RDV pp. 450–53
124. G. Williams, 'Myth and reality. Cook and the theoretical geography of Northwest America', in Fisher and Johnston, *Captain Cook and his Times* pp. 58–80, esp. pp. 69–79
125. RDV pp. 449–57, 700–7, 1240–60, 1272–82
126. RDV pp. 1137–49, 1441–55

CHAPTER 16: HAWAIIAN NIGHTMARE

1. RDV p. cxxxvi
2. James Trevenen, *A Memoir of James Trevenen 1760–1790* eds, C. Lloyd and R. C. Anderson (1959) p. 20
3. G. Williams, 'To make discoveries of countries hitherto unknown. The Admiralty and Pacific exploration in the eighteenth century', in Alan Frost and James Samson, eds, *Pacific Empires. Essays in Honour of Glyndwr Williams* (Melbourne 1999) pp. 13–31
4. J. C. Beaglehole, *The Life of Captain Cook* (1972) pp. 634–35
5. James R. Gibson, 'The significance of Cook's third voyage to Russian tenure in the North Pacific', *Pacific Studies* 1 (1978) pp. 119–46; Gibson, 'A notable absence: the lateness and lameness of Russian discovery and exploration in the North Pacific, 1639–1803', in Robin Fisher and Hugh Johnston, eds, *From Maps to Metaphors: The Pacific World of George Vancouver* (Vancouver 1993) pp. 85–103; Y. M. Svet and S. G. Fedorova, 'Captain Cook and the Russians', *Pacific Studies* 1 (1978) pp. 1–19; J. C. Beaglehole, *Cook and the Russians: An Addendum to the Hakluyt Society Edition of the Voyages of the Resolution and Discovery 1776–1780* (1973). The sceptical viewpoint is put in Simon Werrett, 'Russian responses to the voyages of Captain Cook', in G. Williams, ed., *Captain Cook Explorations and Reassessments* (Woodbridge, Suffolk 2004) pp. 179–97; Terence Armstrong, 'Cook's reputation in Russia', in R. Fisher and H. Johnston, *Captain Cook and his Times* (Canberra 1979) pp. 121–286.
6. George Gilbert, *Captain Cook's Final Voyage: The Journal of Midshipman George Gilbert*, ed. Christine Holmes (Horsham 1982) p. 83
7. Lloyd and Anderson, *Memoir of Trevenen* pp. 26–27
8. RDV p. 472

9. RDV pp. 473–74

10. RDV pp. 1534–35

11. RDV p. 1151

12. RDV p. 483

13. RDV p. 474

14. Samuel Kamakau, *Ruling Chiefs of Hawaii* (Honolulu 1992) pp. 34–104

15. These sharks were almost certainly the tiger shark (*Galeocerdo cuvier*). All other man-eating species seem ruled out, since the great white and mako prefer the more temperate waters of Australia, New Zealand, South Africa and North America, while the blue and white-tip are pelagic (open ocean) predators.

16. RDV p. cxl

17. Beaglehole, *Life* pp. 640–41

18. Sadly, the various scholarly studies of Cook, and even those relating to his death, pass over the seven crazed weeks he spent at sea cruising around Hawaii virtually without comment, though the entire incident is crucial to an understanding of Cook's state of mind.

19. RDV p. 478

20. J. K. Munford, ed., *John Ledyard's Journal of Captain Cook's Last Voyage* (Corvalis, Oregon 1963) p. 102

21. RDV pp. 479–80

22. RDV pp. 1152–54

23. Douglas, *A Voyage to the Pacific Ocean* 3 vols (1784) ii. p. 538

24. RDV pp. 481–82

25. BL Egerton MSS. 2189 f. 71

26. RDV p. 481

27. Beaglehole, *Life* pp. 643, 645

28. RDV pp. 1154–56

29. Anne Salmond, *The Trial of the Cannibal Dog: The Remarkable Story of Captain Cook's Encounters in the South Seas* (2003) p. 437

30. Lloyd and Anderson, eds, *Memoir of Trevenen* pp. 21, 27–28; RDV pp. 1348–49

31. RDV p. 1155

32. RDV p. 485

33. RDV pp. 503–4

34. RDV pp. 486–89

35. RDV pp. 1156–58

36. RDV p. 1158

37. RDV pp. 490–91

38. Munford, ed., *Ledyard Journal* p. 103

39. William Ellis, *An Authentic Narrative of a Voyage Performed by Captain Cook and Captain Clerke* 2 vols (1782) ii. p. 85. The detail about the girl and the mirror is at RDV p. 1158

40. Holmes, ed., *Journal of Gilbert* p. 102

41. RDV pp. 490–91

42. RDV p. 504

43. RDV pp. 505–6

44. M. E. Hoare, ed., *The Resolution Journal of Johann Reinhold Forster 1772–1775* (Hakluyt Society, 2nd Series 152–55, 1982) iii. p. 393; James Magra, *A Journal of a Voyage round the World in HMS Ship Endeavour* (1771) pp. 48–49; cf. also Adm. 55/ f. 73

45. For the significance of the ceremony Cook had undergone and the privileges it conferred on him see A. Biersach, *Clio in Oceania: Towards an Historical Anthropology* (Washington, DC 1991) pp. 133–37; V. Valeri, *Kingship and Sacrifice: Ritual and Society in Ancient Hawaii* (Chicago 1985) pp. 191–339

46. RDV pp. 490–91

47. J. C. Beaglehole, ed., *The Endeavour Journal of Joseph Banks 1768–1771* 2 vols (Sydney 1962), i. p. 277; ii. p. 34; Magra, *Journal* p. 48

48. Mumford, ed., *Ledyard Journal* p. 58

49. Robert D. Craig, *Dictionary of Polynesian Mythology* (1989) pp. 193–94

50. Anders Sparrman, *A Voyage round the World with Captain James Cook in H.M.S. Resolution*, trans. Huldine Bearnish and Averil Mackenzie-Grieve (1953) p. 126; Munford, ed., *Ledyard Journal* p. 95

51. For the complexities of all this see Martha Beckwith, *Hawaiian Mythology* (Yale 1940); David Malo, *Hawaiian Antiquities* (1951) esp. pp. 141–59

52. Abraham Fornander, *An Account of the Polynesian Race, its Origins and Migrations and the Earliest History of the Hawaiian People to the Times of Kamehameha I* 3 vols (1878), ii. pp. 168–69; A. Taylor, ed., *Sesquicentennial Celebration of Captain Cook's Discovery of Hawaii 1778–1928* (Honolulu 1929) pp. 66–67

53. There is a huge literature on Hawaiian mythology and, *en passant*, Cook's relationship to the Lono myth. See, for example, Ross Cordy, *Exalted Sits the Chief: The Ancient History of Hawaii Island* (Honolulu 2000) especially pp. 225–39; Samuel Kamakau, *Ruling Chiefs of Hawaii* (Honolulu 1992) pp. 47–63, 92–103; Martha Beckwith, ed., *The Kumulipo: A Hawaiian Creation Chart* (Honolulu 1951) pp. 20–21; Dorothy Kahananui, ed. and trans., *Ka Moolelo Hawaii* (Honolulu 1984) pp. 171–73; Laura Fish Judd, *Honolulu: Sketches of Life in the Hawaiian Islands from 1828 to 1861* (Chicago 1966) pp. 64–65

54. Judd, *Honolulu*

55. RDV pp. 621, 1535–36

56. RDV pp. 596–97; cf. also Munford, ed., *Ledyard Journal* pp. 102–7

57. For a consideration of all these points see Gavan Daws, *Shoal of Time: A History of the Hawaiian Islands* (Honolulu 1968) pp. 11–27; M. Sahlins, *Historical Metaphors and Historical Realities: Structure in the Early History of the Sandwich Islands Kingdom* (Ann Arbor, MI 1981) pp. 11–24; M. R. de Brossard, *Moana, Ocean Cruel: Les dieux meurent à la grande mer du sud* (Paris 1966) pp. 289–319; J. Friedman, 'Captain Cook, culture and the world system', *Journal of Pacific History* 20 (1985) pp. 191–201

58. Nicholas Thomas, *Discoveries: The Voyages of Captain Cook* (2003) p. 382

59. Salmond, *Cannibal Dog* p. 403

60. RDV pp. 512–13, 545, 1190

61. Williams, ed., *Explorations and Reassessments* pp. 100–6 (esp. pp. 100–6)

62. Ralph Huyhendall, *The Hawaiian Kingdom, 1778–1854* (Honolulu 1953) i. p. 22

63. W. Kaye Lamb, *The Voyage of George Vancouver, 1791–1795* (1984) iii. p. 816 For a general survey of Kamehameha see Stephen L. Desha, *Kamehameha and his Warrior Kekuhaupio* (Honolulu 2000) pp. 76–82; Mary Kawena Pukui, ed. and trans., *Ka Po'e Kahiko* (Honolulu 1991) pp. 4–5

64. It is typical of the sceptical approach used by Nicholas Thomas that he says, cautiously, that Palea '*seemed* [italics mine] to strangle [him] underwater' (*Discoveries* p. 386)

65. James Cook and James King, *A Voyage to the Pacific Ocean* 2 vols (Dublin 1784) ii. p. 131

66. RDV p. 1162

67. Mumford, ed., *Ledyard Journal* p. 111

68. Salmond, *Cannibal Dog* p. 437

69. John Rickman, *Journal of Captain Cook's Last Voyage* (1781) pp. 300–1

70. Cook has often been criticised for having versions of Polynesian names so unlike those in modern orthography. Beaglehole defends him on the grounds that Hawaiian 'received pronunciation' changed dramatically *c.*1750–1800 and that the captain actually had a rather good ear (Beaglehole, *Life* p. 653)

71. RDV pp. 513, 1184

72. RDV p. 1173

73. RDV p. 1164

74. RDV pp. 1171–72

75. Munford, ed., *Ledyard Journal* pp. 132–33; RDV pp. 596, 1184. See also R. Morris, '*Aikane*: accounts of Hawaiian same-sex relations in the journals of Captain Cook's third voyage', *Journal of Homosexuality* 19 (1990) pp. 21–54; L. Wallace, *Sexual Encounters, Pacific Texts, Modern Sexualities* (Ithaca, NY 2003)

76. Munford, ed., *Ledyard Journal* p. 132; RDV p. 596. See also M. Sahlins, *Islands of History* (Chicago 1985) p. 23; P. Kirch, *The Evolution of the Polynesian Chiefdoms* (Cambridge 1984) p. 254

77. RDV p. 1171

78. See the interesting discussion of this point in Gavin Kennedy, *The Death of Captain Cook* (1978) pp. 26–27

79. H. Zimmermann, *Account of the Third Voyage of Captain Cook 1776–1780* (Wellington 1926) p. 37

80. RDV pp. 516–17; Beaglehole, *Life* p. 656

81. RDV p. 517

82. Munford, ed., *Ledyard Journal* pp. 135–39

83. Ibid. pp. 137–39

84. RDV p. 519

85. RDV pp. 525–26

86. RDV p. 1189–90

87. RDV pp. 525–27

88. Munford, ed., *Ledyard Journal* p. 141

89. 'There is nothing to despair about with Teucer as our leader and Teucer as our protector.' RDV p. 1191

CHAPTER 17: TRAGEDY ON KEALAKEKUA BEACH

1. Quoted in Anne Salmond, *The Trial of the Cannibal Dog: The Remarkable Story of Captain Cook's Encounters in the South Seas* (2003) p. 409

2. Marshall Sahlins, *How 'Natives' Think: About Captain Cook, For Example* (1995) pp. 80–81

3. RDV p. 528

4. RDV pp. cxlvii, 529–31

5. RDV p. 1191

6. RDV p. 529

7. RDV p. 1192

8. Gavin Kennedy, *The Death of Captain Cook* (1978) p. 14

9. Ibid. p. 33

10. RDV p. 1360

11. Ibid. See also the more lengthy Edgar report at Adm. 55/24

12. Kennedy, *Death*

13. RDV pp. 530–33

14. RDV p. cxlviii

15. As he seems to have realised a little later (RDV p. 1193)

16. RDV pp. 533, 549

17. For the complexities of Kamehameha's political position in 1778–79, his attitude to Cook, and his appropriation of the Lono legend, see the very different views advanced by Marshall Sahlins, 'Captain Cook in Hawaii', *Journal of the Polynesian Society* 98 (1989) pp. 371–425; and Steven Bergendorff, Uta Hasage and Peter Henriques, 'Mythopoesis and history: on the interpretation of the Makahiki', *Journal of the Polynesian Society* 97 (1988) pp. 391–408

18. RDV p. 1195

19. RDV p. 549

20. James Burney, *A Chronological History of Northeastern Voyages of Discovery* (1819) p. 260

21. Kennedy, *Death* pp. 40–41

22. RDV pp. 490, 1158. For Cook's overt statement that 'Indians' could not abide the report of a single musket see ibid. pp. 549–50, 1194

23. G. E. Mainwaring, *My Friend the Admiral* (1931) p. 133

24. Kennedy, *Death* pp. 48–51

25. J. C. Beaglehole, *The Life of Captain Cook* (1972) pp. 667–69

26. U. Tewsley, ed., *Zimmerman's Account of the Third Voyage of Captain Cook* (Auckland 1926) p. 42

27. Kennedy, *Death* pp. 56–57

28. J. K. Munford, ed., *John Ledyard's Journal of Captain Cook's Last Voyage* (Corvalis, Oregon 1963) p. 145; Ross Cordy, *Exalted Sits the Chief* (2000) pp. 300–4

29. Salmond, *Cannibal Dog* p. 412

30. F. W. Honay, ed., *Zimmerman's Captain Cook* (Toronto 1929) p. 92

31. The two sons have been identified in Charles Ahlo and Jerry Walker, eds, *Kamehameha's Children Today* (Honolulu 2000) p. 26

32. O. H. K. Spate, *Paradise Found and Lost* (1988) p. 143
33. Andrew Kippis, *The Life of Captain James Cook* (1788) p. 374; R. F. Kuykendahl, *The Hawaiian Kingdom 1778–1854: Foundation and Transformation* (Hawaii 1938) i. pp. 18–19
34. Kennedy, *Death* pp. 65–66
35. Richard Hough, *Captain Bligh and Mr Christian: The Men and the Mutiny* (1972) p. 35. For the view that the news of Kalimu's death came in about an hour before the confrontation on the beach see Kippis, *Life of Captain Cook* pp. 373–74
36. William Ellis, *Polynesian Researches* (1842) pp. 131–32
37. Kippis, *Life of Captain Cook* pp. 375–76
38. RDV pp. 535–38
39. Apart from all the other sources in RDV one should mention R. T. Gould, 'Some unpublished accounts of Cook's death', *Mariner's Mirror* 14 (1928) pp. 301–19 and James K. Munford, 'Did John Ledyard witness Cook's death?' *Pacific Northwest Quarterly* 54 (1963) pp. 75–78
40. RDV pp. 550–58, 1196–202
41. R. T. Gould, 'Bligh's notes on Cook's last voyage', *Mariner's Mirror* 14 (1928) pp. 371–85
42. RDV p. 1197; A. Home, *Memoirs of an Aristocrat* (1838) p. 303
43. Gould, 'Bligh's notes' p. 380
44. Kennedy, *Death* pp. 85–86
45. Beaglehole, *Life* p. 685
46. Home, *Memoirs of an Aristocrat* p. 305. Scott Ashley, 'How navigators think: the death of Captain Cook revisited', *Past and Present* 194 (2007) pp. 107–37 unwisely (to my mind) tries to defend Williamson's action in ignoring Cook's wave. In his forensic, tendentious tone Ashley reminds me of Robert Graves's equally unconvincing defence of William Palmer, the Rugeley poisoner, in *They Hanged My Saintly Billy* (1957). Ashley provides us with this gem: 'What that gesture signified we do not know; as Clifford Geertz reminds us, a wink of the eye or a wave of the hand can mean many different things.' Williamson's guilt is reinforced in Kerry Howe, 'The death of Captain Cook: exercises in explanation', *Eighteenth Century Life* (1994) pp. 198–211 (esp. pp. 199–203)
47. This is what one might call the Beaglehole theory. Nicholas Thomas (*Discoveries: The Voyages of Captain Cook* (2003) p. 442) has contested it on the grounds that (1) Cook's diminishing empathy for his men dates from the middle of the *second*, not the third, voyage; (2) Until 14 February 1779 fewer Polynesians were killed on the third than on the first and second expeditions
48. Richard Hough, *Captain James Cook* (1994) p. 333
49. Sahlins, *How 'Natives' Think* pp. 78–84
50. Gananath Obeyesekere, *The Apotheosis of Captain Cook* (Princeton 1992) pp. 11–12, 216
51. Salmond, *Cannibal Dog* p. 416
52. BL, Add. MSS. 37,327 ff. 24–25; Adm. 55/121 f. 16
53. Honay, ed., *Zimmerman's Captain Cook* pp. 100–01
54. RDV pp. 1348–49
55. RDV pp. 538–39. For others who endorsed the idea of Cook as vain, arrogant and suffering from hubris see Mumford, ed., *Ledyard Journal* pp. 102, 144
56. RDV p. 594; cf. also J. Cook and J. King, *A Voyage to the Pacific Ocean* 2 vols (Dublin 1784) p. 60
57. James Burney, *A Chronological History of North-Eastern Voyages of Discovery* (1819) pp. 263–66; David Samwell, *A Narrative of the Death of Captain Cook* (1786) pp. 9–10
58. Gavan Daws, *Shoal of Time: A History of the Hawaiian Islands* (Honolulu 1968) pp. 1–29 For the famous Sahlins/Obeyesekere controversy (which I believe Sahlins wins on points) see Rod Edmond, *Representing the South Pacific: Colonial Discourse from Cook to Gauguin* (Cambridge 1997) pp. 23–62
59. BL, Add. MSS 38,530 f. 99; RDV p. 1218
60. See the very different views in Howe, 'The death of Captain Cook' pp. 198–211
61. Kennedy, *Death* pp. 87–90
62. George Gilbert, *Captain Cook's Final Voyage: The Journal of Midshipman George Gilbert*, ed. Christine Holmes (Horsham, 1982) pp. 107–8
63. Mark Twain, *Roughing It* (1872) Chapter 71
64. Gould, 'Bligh's notes'
65. RDV p. 540

66. M. R. de Brossard, *Moana: Ocean Cruel: Les dieux meurent à la grande mer du Sud* (Paris 1966) pp. 308–10, 317, 327–28
67. RDV pp. 540–41
68. RDV pp. 1203–7
69. Meredith Filia, 'Rituals of sacrifice in early post-European contact with Tonga and Tahiti,' *Journal of Pacific History* 34 (1999) pp. 5–22
70. RDV pp. 566–67
71. Samuel Kamakau, *The Ruling Chiefs of Hawaii* (Honolulu 1992) p. 102
72. W. Kaye Lamb, ed., *Vancouver's Voyage of Discovery to the North Pacific Ocean* (Hakluyt Society, 2nd Series 163–66, 1984) ii. p. 470; iii. p. 800
73. Sahlins, *How 'Natives' Think* pp. 96, 147
74. William Ellis, *Narrative of a Tour through Hawaii* (1827) p. 120. For the belief that Cook would come again see Sahlins, *How 'Natives' Think* p. 96; John Gascoigne, *Captain Cook* (2007) pp. 217–19
75. Abraham Fornander, *An Account of the Polynesian Race, its origins and migrations and the earliest history of the Hawaiian people to the times of Kamehameha I* 3 vols (1878) ii. pp. 174, 183
76. RDV p. 542
77. Ibid.
78. RDV pp. 1207–9
79. RDV p. 1212
80. RDV p. 545
81. RDV pp. 1209–15. For the Hawaiian horror at the decapitation see Christopher Lloyd and R. C. Anderson, *A Memoir of James Trevenen 1760–1790* (1959) p. 24. For the *mana* conferred by Cook's bones see Gascoigne, *Captain Cook* p. 214
82. RDV pp. 1215–17
83. RDV pp. 546–48, 1217
84. Beaglehole, *Life* p. 673
85. Ellis, *Narrative of a Tour through Hawaii* pp. 52, 103–6, 115–22; Ellis, *Researches* p. 137
86. Pauline Nawahineokala, 'Some thoughts on Native Hawiian attitudes towards Captain Cook', in G. Williams, ed., *Captain Cook: Explorations and Reassessments* (Woodbridge 2004) pp. 94–109 (at p. 107)
87. F. W. Honay, ed., *The Journal of Captain James Colnett aboard the Argonaut* (Toronto 1940) p. 220
88. J. Cook and J. King, *A Voyage to the Pacific Ocean* 2 vols (Dublin 1784) pp. 48–49
89. Honay, ed., *Zimmerman's Captain Cook* pp. 98–102
90. RDV pp. 635, 1218–35
91. RDV pp. 638–44, 1235–39
92. RDV pp. 646–74, 1240–57
93. RDV pp. 689–97, 1257–70
94. RDV pp. 1542–44
95. RDV pp. 703, 1271–72
96. RDV pp. 1273–80
97. RDV p. 711
98. RDV pp. 713, 1283–89
99. Beaglehole, *Life* pp. 685–86

CONCLUSION

1. Felipe Fernandez-Armesto, *Pathfinders: A Global History of Exploration* (Oxford 2006) p. 299
2. This is the argument, ably carried out and with a wealth of technical illustration, in Alan John Villiers, *Captain Cook: The Seaman's Seaman* (1967)
3. See Appendix
4. There are two very good examples of such conditions in Nicholas Thomas, *Discoveries: The Voyages of Captain Cook* (2003) pp. xviii, 44
5. J. C. Beaglehole, *The Life of Captain Cook* (1972) p. 699
6. Villiers, *Captain Cook: The Seaman's Seaman* Preface. See especially Villiers's crossing from Cook Strait to Tahiti in 1936 (ibid. pp. 175–76)

7. Williams, 'Reassessing Cook', in G. Williams, ed., *Captain Cook: Explorations and Reassessments* (Woodbridge, Suffolk 2004) p. 232

8. For Vancouver see B. Anderson, *The Life and Times of Captain George Vancouver: Surveyor of the Sea* (Seattle 1966); G. Vancouver, *A Voyage of Discovery to the North Pacific Ocean and around the World* (1798); cf. also W. Kaye Lamb's Hakluyt Society edition of the same (2nd series Cambridge, 1984)

9. J. Dunmore, *Journal of La Pérouse* (1994), i. p. cxi. La Pérouse's motivations occupy much of the introduction to this edition (i. pp. xvii–ccxl), which also includes Louis XVI's amazingly detailed instructions (ibid. i. pp. cx–cl). See also Catherine Gaziello, *L'Expedition de La Pérouse 1785–1788: réplique française aux voyages de Cook* (Paris 1984)

10. Robin Inglis, 'La Pérouse 1786: a French naval visit to Alaska', in Stephen Haycox, James Barnett and Caedmon Liburd, eds, *Enlightenment and Exploration in the North Pacific, 1741–1805* (Seattle 1997) pp. 49–64

11. Dunmore, *Journal of La Pérouse* ii. p. 276

12. Ibid. ii. p. 446

13. Ibid. i. pp. 68–69, 133; ii. p. 394; Robin Inglis, 'Successors and rivals to Cook: the French and the Spaniards', in Williams, ed., *Explorations and Reassessments* pp. 161–78 (at p. 170)

14. Alan Moorehead, *The Fatal Impact: An Account of the Invasion of the South Pacific 1767–1840* (1966)

15. W. S. Lewis, ed., *The Yale Edition of Horace Walpole's Correspondence* (New Haven 1974) ii. p. 225

16. James Dunbar, *Essays on the History of Mankind in Rude and Cultivated Ages* (1780) pp. 356–57

17. I. Lee, *Captain Bligh's Second Voyage to to the South Seas* (Melbourne 1929) pp. 74–87; Douglas Oliver, *Ancient Tahitian Society* 3 vols (1874) iii. pp. 1284–86; C. Newbury, *Tahiti Nui: Change and Survival in French Polynesia 1767–1943* (Honolulu 1980) p. 14

18. Greg Dening, *Beach Crossings: Voyaging across Times, Cultures and Self* (Carleton, Victoria 2004)

19. This is a vast subject. Some pointers are available in I. C. Campbell, 'Polynesian perceptions of Europeans in the eighteenth and nineteenth centuries', *Pacific Studies* 5 (1982) pp. 64–80; W. H. Pearson, 'European intimidation and the myth of Tahiti', *Journal of Pacific History* 4 (1969) pp. 199–218; Pearson, 'The reception of European voyagers on Polynesian islands, 1568–1797', *Journal de la Société des Océanistes* 26 (1970) pp. 12–54. See also C. Ralston, *Grass Huts and Warehouses: Pacific Beach Communities in the Nineteenth Century* (Canberra 1977) pp. 1–8

20. O. H. K. Spate, *Paradise Found and Lost* (1988) p. 211

21. Rod Edmond, *Representing the South Pacific: Colonial Discourse from Cook to Gauguin* (Cambridge 1997) pp. 27–28

22. David Mackay, 'Exploring the Pacific. Exploring James Cook', in Alan Frost and Jane Samson, eds, *Pacific Empires: Essays in Honour of Glyndwr Williams* (Melbourne 1999)

23. David Samwell, *A Narrative of the Death of Captain James Cook* (1986) pp. 30–34

24. See in particular Bernard Smith, 'Cook's posthumous reputation', in R. Fisher and H. Johnston, eds, *Captain Cook and his Times* (Canberra 1979) pp. 159–61; Edmond, *Representing the South Pacific* pp. 26–27; William Scott, 'Cook, France and the savages', in Paul Dukes, ed., *Frontiers of European Culture* (Lampeter 1996)

25. Nathaniel Portlock, *A Voyage round the World but more particularly to the North-West Coast of America* (1789) pp. 61, 309; John Meares, *Voyages from China to the North-West Coast of America* (1790) pp. 4–10, 13–15, 343–44; Robert Galois, ed., *A Voyage to the North West Side of America: The Journals of James Colnett, 1786–89* (Vancouver 2004) pp. 188, 192, 388–89; Tim Flannery, ed., *Life and Adventures of John Nicol 1776–1801* (Melbourne 1997) p. 83; George Little, *Life on the Ocean Wave* (Boston 1846) pp. 131–32; Pauline King Joerger, ed., *Robert Dampier. To the Sandwich Islands in HMS Blonde* (Honolulu 1971) pp. 65–67, 70; A. L. Korn, *The Victorian Visitors* (Honolulu 1958) p. 65; James Morrison, *The Journal of James Morrison, Boatswain's Mate of the Bounty* (1935) p. 85; George Hamilton, *A Voyage round the World in HM Frigate Pandora* (Sydney 1998) pp. 57–59

26. The astonishing amount of vituperation Cook attracts even today is evident in Tony Horwitz, *Into the Blue: Boldly Going Where Captain Cook has Gone Before* (2002)

27. See G. Williams, *The Death of Captain Cook: A Hero Made and Unmade* (2008) pp. 142–64

28. Edmond, *Representing the South Pacific*; Felix Driver, *Geography Militant: Cultures of Exploration and Empires* (Oxford 2000); Nicholas Jardine, James Secord and Emma Spary, eds, *Cultures of Natural History* (Cambridge 1996); David Philip Miller and Peter Hans Veit, eds, *Visions of Empire: Voyages, Botany and the Representation of Nature* (Cambridge 1996); Bernard

Smith, *Imagining the Pacific: In the Wake of the Cook Voyages* (New Haven 1992); Nicholas Thomas and Diane Losch, eds, *Double Visions: Art Histories and Colonial Histories in the Pacific* (Cambridge 1999); David N. Livingstone and Charles W. J. Withers, eds, *Geography and Enlightenment* (Chicago 1999)

29. Vincent T. Harlow, *The Founding of the Second British Empire, 1763–1793* 2 vols (1953); Bernard Smith, *European Vision and the South Pacific 1768–1850: A Study in the History of Art and Ideas* (Oxford 1960); Patrick Brantlinger, *Fictions of the State: Culture and Credit in Britain 1694–1994* (Ithaca, NY 1996)

30. See John Gascoigne, *Science in the Service of Empire: Joseph Banks, the British State and the Uses of Science in the Age of Revolution* (Cambridge 1998); Gascoigne, 'Motives for European exploration of the Pacific in the Age of Enlightenment', *Pacific Science* 54 (2000) pp. 227–43; G. Williams, 'The Pacific: exploration and exploitation', in P. J. Marshall, ed., *The Oxford History of the British Empire: Volume 2: The Eighteenth Century* (Oxford 1998) pp. 552–75

31. Leszek Kolakowski, *Main Currents of Marxism* (2005) p. 285

32. Williams, *The Death of Captain Cook* pp. 174–75

33. See the discussions in Norman Etherington, *Theories of Imperialism: War, Conquest and Capital* (1984)

34. Charlotte Barrett, ed., *Diary and Letters of Madame d'Arblay 1778–1781* (1904) i. p. 318

Index

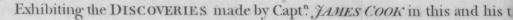